P9-CQQ-273

THE THEORY
AND
PRACTICE OF
GROUP
PSYCHOTHERAPY

THE THEORY

AND

PRACTICE OF

GROUP

PSYCHOTHERAPY

SECOND EDITION

IRVIN D. YALOM

Basic Books, Inc., Publishers

NEW YORK

To my mother,

RUTH YALOM

and to the memory of my father,

BENJAMIN YALOM

Library of Congress Cataloging in Publication Data

Yalom, Irvin D   1931–
  The theory and practice of group psychotherapy.

  Includes bibliographical references and index.
  1. Group psychotherapy. I. Title.
RC488.Y3 1975   616.8'915   75-7637
ISBN 0-465-08446-X

CONTENTS

ACKNOWLEDGMENTS
TO THE FIRST EDITION

Many have helped me in the preparation of this book. Drs. C. Peter Rosenbaum, Jerome Frank, and Morris Parloff have reviewed the entire manuscript and provided invaluable encouragement and substantive assistance. Several colleagues have read critically sections of the manuscript. These include Drs. Morton Lieberman, Herbert Leiderman, David Hamburg, Peggy Golde, Rudolf Moos, Daniel Miller, Leonard Solomon, and a large number of Stanford psychiatric residents.

My wife, Marilyn, offered moral support, as well as considerable advice on stylistic matters.

My secretary at Stanford, Mrs. Nancy Phillips, did a superlative job. She has struggled with the manuscript from the earliest fragmented scribblings to the final draft.

Stanford University and the Tavistock Clinic were extraordinarily cooperative and generous to me during the two years of preparation of this book.

To all, my thanks. Most of all, however, I am indebted to my teachers: Drs. John Whitehorn, Jerome Frank, and David Hamburg. All three have offered me invaluable guidance, stimulation, and support; they have contributed significantly to my substantive education, and they have become models for me of professional excellence and personal integrity.

PREFACE

Though I didn't know it at the time, I began this revision almost immediately after I finished writing the first edition. Like a retired milk horse who, unable to comprehend his freedom, continues to make his appointed daily rounds, I continued to make copious notes after every group meeting I led or supervised. For six years, the notes of two thousand meetings inexorably invaded and encroached upon my life space until finally they buried desks and tables, glutted drawers and seeped out of file cabinets. A revised edition seemed my only possible defense.

The first edition of *The Theory and Practice of Group Psychotherapy* has been widely read, more widely than I had dared hope. Moreover, on innumerable occasions, the readers have provided me with information about the strengths and weaknesses of the book; this revision is my effort to be responsive to their feedback. I have also learned the identity of my readers and the use they have made of the book. Such information provided me with many specific guidelines while working on this revision; it produced an entirely different set from that present when I, more privately, more blindly, wrote the first edition knowing that I was tossing it out to an audience unknown. It is abundantly evident now that my readers are clinicians and that they range widely in experience from senior therapists to young novitiates. I have, accordingly, added material and made textual alterations to make the book more clinically relevant. One unrealistic, now relinquished, goal of the first edition was that it should be not only a clinical guide but a technical manual for the group researcher. Though I continue to cite relevant research, to build conceptually upon it (provided it is rigorous and credible), and to describe the methodology of any work heavily cited, I shall not in this volume discourse upon research method or strategy per se.

These changes—new observations and alterations to increase the relevance of the book for its readers—along with the inclusion of much new clinical illustrative material and considerable stylistic modification—all result in an extensive revision; few pages of the first edition remain entirely unchanged. There are several major additions which warrant mention here. To the presentation, in the first four chapters, of the ten mechanisms of change, or curative factors, I have added an eleventh: "Existential Factors." Chapter 4 discusses, at length, this widely employed, rarely recognized factor in the therapeutic process. Chapters 5 and 6 have been revised more heavily than any other part of the text. Chapter 5 (The Tasks and Techniques of the Therapist) describes how the group therapist creates a therapeutic culture and shapes an appropriate set of norms, or unwritten rules of behavior. The therapist's tasks in the here-and-now are discussed in depth. They involve both here-and-now activation (plunging the group into its own experience) and here-and-now process illumination (clarifying the nature and meaning of the emotional experience.) There is in Chapter 5 an expanded discussion of the recognition of process, including a section on the differentiation of the patient's primary task in therapy from his secondary gratification in the group. Process commentary is described in detail: the general strategy, the framing of interpretations so as to increase the patient's receptivity, and the pathways whereby process commentary effects change.

Chapter 6 explicates the role of the therapist; the discussion is constructed around two fundamental issues: transference and transparency. Chapters 7 through 10 contain, as does the entire text, much new clinical illustrative material. Marathon groups, the addition of new members, and the developmental stages are discussed in greater length. Chapter 11 includes a lengthy clinical vignette which not only documents the complications of subgrouping but also illustrates many therapeutic principles presented elsewhere in the text. The management of termination (of both the successful and unsuccessful patient) is dealt with in depth. To the discussion, in Chapter 12, on problem patients I have added sections on the narcissistic patient and the boring patient. Chapter 13 on specialized techniques includes more extensive discussion of co-therapy, structured exercises, gestalt techniques, video taping, and describes the use of the written summary as an aid to patient participation. Chapter 14 on encounter groups has been updated. Throughout the text, when appropriate, I cite the results of a recent research project on the process and outcome of encounter groups * which was a lengthy collaborative venture involving Morton Lieberman, Matthew Miles, and myself. In Chapter 14 the method, basic results, and implications of this research are discussed. Chapter 15 is devoted entirely to training and discusses some basic components of a training program: supervision, participation in an experiential group, observation of senior clinicians, and a personal therapeutic experience.

This edition was largely written during a six month sabbatical at Oxford University where the hospitality of the faculty in the Department of Psychiatry, the constant encouragement and editorial assistance of my wife, Marilyn, and the six months of leaden sky and incessant rain, all provided optimal writing conditions. The patience and helpfulness of my secretary, Maxine Harris, never flagged. As before, I am grateful to the many Stanford Residents who critically reviewed parts of the text.

---

* *Encounter Groups: First Facts*, M. A. Lieberman, I. D. Yalom, M. B. Miles, Basic Books, Inc., New York, 1973.

PREFACE TO
THE FIRST EDITION

Half of this book was written in London, the other half in California. The practice of group therapy is so different in the two settings that in the former I felt like a radical and in the latter an arch conservative. Even a cursory examination of the field of group therapy reveals great diversity in practice. The term "group therapy" is an oversimplification; one should speak instead of the group therapies. Alcoholics Anonymous is group therapy, and so is a group for pregnant women in a prenatal clinic, a group of schizophrenics in a chronic hospital ward, a group of parolees at a probation officer's office, or a group of relatively well-functioning individuals with neurotic or characterologic disorders meeting in an outpatient clinic or a psychotherapist's private office.

The current picture is complicated still further by the emergence of a large variety of new groups; a recent survey [1] of representative groups run in the Northern California Bay area discloses a bewildering array of approaches: psychoanalytic groups, psychodrama groups, crisis groups, Synanon, Recovery, Inc., Alcoholics Anonymous, marital couples groups, marathon encounter groups, family therapy groups, traditional T-groups, personal growth T-groups, nude therapy groups, multi-media groups, nonverbal sensory awareness groups, transactional analysis groups, and Gestalt therapy groups. Many of these are designated as therapy groups; others straddle the blurred boundary between personal growth and therapy (see Chapter 14 for a discussion of this issue).

With so much apparent diversity and flux in the field, it was with considerable hesitation that I ventured to write a book which might

have relevance to all the group therapies. My first strategy was simpli-
fication; I attempted to introduce order by separating "front" [2] from
"core" in each of the group therapies. The "front" consists of the
trappings, the form, the techniques, the specialized language, and the
aura surrounding each of the schools of therapy; the core consists of
those aspects of the experience which are intrinsic to the therapeutic
process—that is, the bare-boned mechanisms of change. Disregard the
"front," consider only the actual method of effecting change in the patient, and one will find that these methods are limited in number and
remarkably similar across groups. Therapy groups which appear totally different in form may rely on identical mechanisms of change. I
have, perhaps too expansively, referred to these mechanisms of
change as "curative factors," ten of which are identified and discussed
in this book.

By classifying groups according to their curative factors rather than
to their "front," the array of group therapies seems less variegated and
more ordered. It is my contention that groups with similar goals use
similar curative factors. The goals of group therapy, which depend on
the set of the leader and the composition of the group, may vary from
support, suppression, and inspiration (Alcoholics Anonymous, Recovery, Inc.) to the maintenance of reality testing and prevention of ward
friction (groups on chronic psychiatric wards), to the restoration of
functioning and the reinstitution of old defenses (groups on acute,
rapid-turnover psychiatric wards), to the building of new defenses and
a change in coping style and characterologic structure (groups of patients with neurotic and characterologic problems).

Consider, for example, the ambitious goal of characterologic
change. Therapy groups which effect this change rely heavily on the
curative factors of cohesiveness and interpersonal learning (Chapters
2 and 3). Regardless of whether the group leader espouses Freudian,
neo-Freudian, Rogerian, Adlerian, or eclectic viewpoints and techniques, the actual mechanism of change in the patient in groups with
these goals is the same. (Member interaction plays such a crucial role
in group therapy with the goal of character change that throughout this
book I have referred to intensive group therapy as "interactional
group therapy.")

Although the curative factors are the primary agents of change, the
"front" of the group is by no means expendable. Each therapist, depending upon his professional training and his personal style, will
master a system of therapy which enhances the operation of the curative factors. Often the enthusiasm and dedication of the therapist to a
particular style of therapy is itself a critical aid in the initial stages of

therapy; the patient's faith and positive expectations are heightened, he is more prone to value the group, to attend more regularly, and to participate more actively. Without question the "front" has its value; the danger comes in not distinguishing "front" from core. If the "front" is considered to be the agent of change, then the curative factors may be neglected, as the "front" becomes more elaborate and revered. Occasionally this has resulted in an elaborate façade which, like Gaudi's Sagrada Familia in Barcelona, has no interior.

This book approaches the field of group therapy through these curative factors. The first four chapters describe the derivation and operation of the curative factors: Chapter 1 discusses the minor curative factors (minor from the perspective of intensive interactional group therapy with ambitious goals); Chapters 2 and 3 discuss the major factors, group cohesiveness and interpersonal learning; while Chapter 4 discusses the comparative importance and the interdependence of the curative factors. The next nine chapters are an inductive sequence describing a system of therapy based on these curative factors: Chapters 5 and 6 consider basic principles regarding the therapist's role and technique; while Chapters 7 through 13 present a chronological view of the therapy group, emphasizing group phenomena and therapist techniques relevant to each stage. Chapter 14 describes the rapidly expanding world of the T-group or encounter group, with special attention to the relationship between these groups and therapy groups. (Some readers whose primary background is in human relations training may prefer to read Chapter 14 first.) The final chapter presents an overview of the dual goals of this book: (1) to provide a guide for the training of group therapists and (2) to describe the scientific basis of group therapy.

The dual research-clinical orientation of this book reflects, of course, my own interests and values. I have over the past few years become increasingly conscious that the field urgently needs a dual humanistic-scientific foundation if it is to deal effectively with the mounting human stresses created by a machine-oriented scientific technology. In preparation of this book I have often, while searching through library stacks, browsed through ancient psychiatric texts. It is unsettling to realize that the devotees of therapy through venesection, cold-water immersion, starvation, purgation, and trephining were obviously men of high intelligence, dedication, and integrity. The same may be said of the last generation of therapists who advocated hydrotherapy, leucotomy, insulin coma, and carbogen inhalation. Their texts are as well written, their optimism as unbridled, and their reported results as impressive as those of practitioners of the most modern current techniques.

Many other fields have left us far behind because they have applied the principles of the scientific method in research. Without methodological refinement it is quite obvious that the workers of today who are enthusiastic about current treatment modes—analytic therapy, Gestalt therapy, marathon groups, conjoint family therapy, etc.—are tragically similar to the hydrotherapists of yesterday. Without utilization of scientific method to test basic principles and relative treatment efficacies, the field remains unstable and at the mercy of passing current fashions. Throughout this book I have therefore attempted to cite the hard relevant research data where it exists and to call attention to areas in which research seems especially necessary and feasible. Some areas (for example, group composition) have been heavily (though not definitively) studied, while others (for example, "working through" or countertransference) have been virtually untouched by research. Naturally the relevant chapters reflect this distribution of research emphasis: some chapters may appear, to clinicians, rarefied and irrelevant, while other chapters may appear, to research-minded colleagues, to lack rigor.

It would be unrealistic to expect research to effect a rapid major change in the practice of psychotherapy. Therapists faced with suffering patients have obviously been unable to wait for science. Complex systems of therapy have been constructed which will change slowly and only in the face of very substantial evidence. Beyond this there is yet another consideration: unlike the physical sciences, many aspects of psychotherapy defy quantification. Psychotherapy is both art and science. Research findings will ultimately guide the broad brush strokes of therapy, but the human encounter will always be a deeply personal, nonmeasurable experience.

The field of group therapy has become ideologically cosmopolitan. Readers of this text will probably stem from many disciplines: psychiatry, psychology, social work, nursing, the ministry, corrections, education, and organizational behavior. Furthermore, the ideological differences within any of these disciplines may be greater than between disciplines. This book reflects my own eclectic ideological background beginning with a grounding in Freudian psychoanalytic theory and technique which was, over the years, complemented by a series of other influences: neo-Freudian theorists (especially Sullivan and Horney), brief-therapy approaches including behavior and somatic therapy, in-patient therapeutic community groups, conjoint family therapy with a period of valuable collaboration with the late Don Jackson, social psychology and small-group dynamics, and sensitivity group work and affiliation with the National Training Laboratories. Throughout I have been influenced by such rigorous behavioral scientists as Jerome Frank, David Hamburg, and Morris Parloff. My group work has spanned all these ideological phases and has, I think, drawn on all of them to produce the system presented in this book. The method of therapy I describe is not original and is to a large extent already used by the majority of American group therapists. This book attempts to suggest a scientific basis for the method and to offer a systematization so as to facilitate the training of students. Although my group work has been in many settings, this book chiefly emphasizes out-patient group therapy, which has the ambitious goal of characterologic change for its members. It is my hope, however, that the broad principles of theory and technique presented herein will have general value for all group therapists.

IRVIN D. YALOM

December, 1969

REFERENCES

1. M. Lieberman, P. Golde, and I. Yalom, unpublished data, 1969.
2. E. Goffman, *The Presentation of Self in Everyday Life* (Garden City, New York: Doubleday Anchor Books, 1959).

THE THEORY
AND
PRACTICE OF
GROUP
PSYCHOTHERAPY

1

THE CURATIVE
FACTORS IN
GROUP THERAPY

❧

How does group therapy help patients? If we can answer this seemingly naive question with some measure of precision and certainty, we shall have at our disposal a central organizing principle by which to approach the most vexing and controversial problems of psychotherapy. Once identified, the crucial aspects of the change process will constitute a rational basis upon which the therapist may base his tactics and strategy.

I suggest that therapeutic change is an enormously complex process and that it occurs through an intricate interplay of various guided human experiences, which I shall refer to as "curative factors." There is considerable advantage in approaching the complex through the simple, the total phenomenon through its basic component processes, and, accordingly, I shall begin by describing and discussing these elemental factors.

From my viewpoint, natural lines of cleavage divide the curative factors into eleven primary categories:

1. Instillation of hope
2. Universality
3. Imparting of information
4. Altruism
5. The corrective recapitulation of the primary family group
6. Development of socializing techniques
7. Imitative behavior
8. Interpersonal learning

9. Group cohesiveness
10. Catharsis
11. Existential factors

The rest of this chapter will discuss the first seven factors. I consider "interpersonal learning" and "group cohesiveness" so important and complex that they are treated separately in the next two chapters. "Existential factors" are discussed in Chapter 4, where they are best understood in the context of other material presented at that time. "Catharsis" is intricately interwoven with other curative factors and will also be discussed in Chapter 4. Keep in mind that, though I discuss these factors singly, the discriminations are arbitrary and, to a large extent, the factors are interdependent: they neither occur nor function separately.

Moreover, these factors may represent different parts of the change process; some refer to actual mechanisms of change, whereas others may be more accurately described as conditions for change. Though the individual curative factors operate in every type of therapy group, their interplay can vary widely from group to group; factors which are minor or implicit in one group approach may be major or explicit in another. Furthermore, patients in the same group may be benefited by widely differing clusters of curative factors. At its core, therapy is a deeply human experience, and, consequently, there are an infinite number of pathways through the therapeutic process. (All of these issues are discussed more fully in Chapter 4.)

The inventory of curative factors I propose issues from my clinical experience, from the experience of other therapists, from the views of the successfully treated group patient, and from relevant systematic research. None of these sources of conviction is beyond doubt, however; neither group members nor group leaders are entirely objective, and our research methodology is both crude and often inapplicable.

From the group therapists we obtain a variegated and internally inconsistent inventory of curative factors (see Chapter 4). Therapists are by no means disinterested or unbiased observers. They have invested considerable time and energy in mastering a certain therapeutic approach, and their answers will be largely determined by their particular school of conviction. Even among therapists who share the same ideology and speak the same language, there may be no consensus as to why patients improve. In some recent research on encounter groups, my colleagues and I [1] learned that many successful group leaders attributed their success to factors which were quite irrelevant to the therapy process; for example, the "hot seat" technique, or nonverbal exercises, or the direct impact of their own person (see Chapter

14). But that does not surprise us; the history of psychotherapy abounds with healers who were effective, but not for the reasons they supposed. At other times we therapists throw up our hands in bewilderment. Who has not had a patient who made vast improvement for reasons entirely obscure to us?

From the group therapy patients at the end of a course of treatment we can obtain data concerning those therapeutic factors which they consider as most and least helpful; or, during the course of therapy, they can supply evaluations of the significant aspects of each group meeting. For these purposes an interview or a variety of data-collecting approaches may be employed. Yet we know the patients' evaluations will be subjective. Will they not, perhaps, focus primarily on superficial factors and neglect some profound healing forces which may be beyond their awareness? Will their responses not be influenced by a variety of factors difficult to control? For example, their views may be distorted by the nature of their relationship to the therapist or to the group. (One team of researchers demonstrated that when patients were interviewed four years after the conclusion of therapy, they were far more apt to comment on unhelpful or harmful aspects of their group experience than when interviewed immediately at termination.) [2]

The search for commonly shared curative factors is made even more difficult by the fact that the patient's experience in the group is very personalized; research has demonstrated the extent to which different group patients perceive and experience the same event in different ways.[3,4] Any given experience may be important or helpful to some members and inconsequential or even harmful to others.

Despite these limitations, patient reports are a rich and relatively untapped source of information. After all, it is *their* experience, theirs alone, and the further we move from the patient's experience, the more inferential are our conclusions. To be sure, there are aspects of the process of change which operate outside the awareness of the patient, but it does not follow that we should disregard what they *do* say. It is my experience that the richness and the accuracy of the patient's report is largely determined by the mode of inquiry. The more the questioner can enter into the experiential world of the patient, the more lucid and meaningful does the report of the therapy experience become. To the degree that he is able to bracket his bias, the therapist becomes the ideal questioner: he is trusted and, more than anyone else, understands the inner world of the patient.

In addition to the therapist's views and patients' reports there is yet a third important method of determining the curative factors: the systematic research approach. The most common research strategy is to correlate a series of in-therapy variables with ultimate patient outcome in therapy. By discovering which variables are significantly related to successful outcome, one can establish a reasonable base from which to begin to delineate the curative factors. However, the research approach is not beyond reproach. There are many inherent problems: the measurement of outcome is itself a methodological morass and the selection and measurement of the in-therapy variables are equally problematic (generally the accuracy of the measurement is directly proportional to the triviality of the variable).

I have used all these methods to derive the curative factors discussed in this book. I do not present these factors as definitive; rather, they are offered as provisional guidelines which may be tested and perhaps expanded by other clinical researchers. For my part, I am satisfied that they derive from the best available evidence and constitute the basis of an effective approach to therapy.

Instillation of Hope

The instillation and maintenance of hope is crucial in all of the psychotherapies; not only is hope required to keep the patient in therapy so that other curative factors may take effect, but faith in a treatment mode can in itself be therapeutically effective. Several research inquiries have demonstrated that a high pre-therapy expectation of help is significantly correlated with positive therapy outcome.[5] Consider also the massive data documenting the efficacy of faith healing and placebo treatment, therapies entirely mediated through hope and conviction.

Therapy groups invariably contain individuals who are at different points along a coping-collapse continuum. Patients have continual contact with group members who have improved in the group. They also often encounter patients who have had problems very similar to their own and have coped with them more effectively. Hadden,[6] in his description of group therapy with homosexuals, argues that there should be, for this very reason, patients in the group at varying stages of improvement. I have often heard patients remark at the end of their therapy how important it was for them to have observed the improvement of others. Group therapists should by no means be above exploiting this factor by periodically calling attention to the improvement that members have made. Therapy group members themselves often proffer spontaneous testimonials when new, unconvinced members enter the group.

No less important is that the therapist believe in himself and in the efficacy of his group. It is my conviction that I am able to help every patient who commits himself to therapy and remains with the group for at least six months. In my first meetings with each patient, I share this conviction with him and attempt to imbue him with my optimism.

Some of the other group therapies place heavy emphasis on the instillation of hope. A major part of the Recovery, Inc., and Alcoholics Anonymous meetings is dedicated to testimonials. Recovery, Inc. members give accounts of potentially stressful incidents in which they avoided tension by the application of Recovery, Inc., methods. Successful Alcoholics Anonymous members tell their stories of downfall and salvation at each meeting. One of the great strengths of Alcoholics Anonymous is the fact that the leaders are all ex-alcoholics—living inspirations to the others. Synanon, also, mobilizes hope in the patient by using recovered drug addicts as group leaders. The members develop a strong conviction that they can be understood only by someone who has trod the same path as they and who has found the way back.

Universality

Many patients enter therapy with the disquieting thought that they are unique in their wretchedness, that they alone have certain frightening or unacceptable problems, thoughts, impulses, and fantasies. There is a core of truth in this, since many patients have had an unusual constellation of life stresses and are commonly flooded by material which is usually unconscious. Their sense of uniqueness is often heightened by their social isolation; because of interpersonal difficulties, opportunities for frank and candid consensual validation in an intimate relationship are often not available to patients. In the therapy group, especially in the early stages, the disconfirmation of their feelings of uniqueness is a powerful source of relief. After hearing other members disclose concerns similar to their own, patients report feeling more in touch with the world and describe the process as a "welcome to the human race" experience. Simply put, the phenomenon finds expression in the cliché, "We're all in the same boat," or perhaps more cynically, "Misery loves company."

There is no human deed or thought which is fully outside the experience of others. I have heard group members reveal such acts as incest, burglary, embezzlement, murder, attempted suicide, and fantasies of an even more desperate nature; invariably I have observed other group members reach out and embrace these very acts as within the realm of their own possibilities. Long ago Freud noted that the staunchest taboos (against patricide and incest) were constructed precisely because these very impulses are part of man's deepest nature.

Nor is this form of aid limited to group therapy. Universality plays a role in individual therapy also, although in that format less of an opportunity for consensual validation exists. Once I reviewed with a patient his 600 hour experience in individual analysis with another therapist. When I inquired about his recollection of the most significant event in his therapy, he recalled an incident in which he was profoundly distressed about his feelings toward his mother. Despite strong concurrent positive sentiments, he was beset with death wishes for her so that he might inherit a very sizable estate. His analyst, at one point, commented simply "That seems to be the way we're built." The statement offered considerable relief and furthermore enabled him to explore his ambivalence in great depth.

Despite the complexity of human problems, certain common denominators are clearly evident, and the members of a therapy group are not long in perceiving their similarities. An example is illustrative: for many years I have asked members * of T-groups (see Chapter 14) to engage in a "top secret" task. The group members are asked to write, anonymously, on a slip of paper their top secret—the one thing they would be most disinclined to share with the group.† The secrets prove to be startlingly similar, with a couple of major themes predominating. The most common secret is a deep conviction of basic inadequacy—a feeling that if others really knew him, they would discover his incompetence and see through his intellectual bluff. Next in frequency is a deep sense of interpersonal alienation. Individuals re-

* Nonpatients—primarily medical students, psychiatric residents, nurses, psychiatric technicians, and Peace Corps volunteers. This exercise was first suggested to me by Gerald Goodman, Ph.D.

† There are several methods of employing this data in the work of the group. One technique which has proved effective is to collect the anonymous secrets and redistribute them to the members, each one receiving another's secret. Each member is then asked to read the secret aloud and to reveal how he would feel if he had such a secret. This usually proves to be a valuable demonstration of universality, empathy, and the ability of others to understand.

port that they do not or cannot really care for or love another person. The third most frequent category is some variety of sexual secret, often a dread of homosexual inclinations. These chief concerns, in nonpatients, are qualitatively the same in individuals seeking professional help, who become labeled as patients. Almost invariably, patients experience deep concern about their sense of worth and their sense of interpersonal relatedness.

Universality, like the other curative factors, cannot be appreciated separately. As patients perceive their similarity to others and share their deepest concerns, they benefit further from the accompanying catharsis and from the ultimate acceptance (see Chapter 3, "Group Cohesiveness") by the other members.

Imparting of Information

Under this general rubric I include the didactic instruction about mental health, mental illness, and general psychodynamics given by the therapists, as well as advice, suggestions, or direct guidance about life problems offered either by the therapist or other patients. Generally, when therapists or patients retrospectively examine their experience in interactional group therapy, they do not highly value this curative mode.

Most patients, at the conclusion of successful interactional group therapy, have learned a great deal about psychic functioning, the meaning of symptoms, interpersonal and group dynamics, and the process of psychotherapy. However, the educational process is a very implicit one; most group therapists do not offer explicit didactic instruction in interactional group therapy. There are, however, some group therapy approaches in which formal instruction is an important part of the program. For example, Maxwell Jones,[7] in his early work with large groups, devoted three hours a week to lectures which instructed patients about the structure and function of the central nervous system and the relevance of this material to psychiatric symptoms and disability. Klapman [8] developed a form of didactic group therapy for outpatients in which he used formal lectures and textbook assignments. Marsh [9] also organized groups of patients into classes and created a classroom atmosphere by means of lectures, homework, and grading procedures.

Recovery, Inc., is basically organized along didactic lines.[10] This self-help organization was founded in 1937 by the late Abraham Low, M.D., and by 1974 had 1,030 operating groups with a regular attendance of over twelve thousand individuals. The membership is completely voluntary and consists of individuals complaining of any type of psychological problem. The leaders spring from the membership, and though there is no formal professionl guidance, the conduct of the meetings has been highly structured by Dr. Low—parts of his textbook *Mental Health Through Will Training* [11] are read aloud and discussed at every meeting. Psychological illness is explained on the basis of a few simple principles which are memorized by the members: e.g., the neurotic symptom is distressing but not dangerous; tension intensifies and sustains the symptom and should be avoided; the use of free will is the solution to the nervous patient's dilemmas, etc.

Malamud and Machover [12] report an exciting, innovative approach organized on a didactic base. They organized "workshops in self-understanding" consisting of approximately twenty patients drawn from a psychiatric clinic waiting list. The workshop's goal was to prepare patients for group psychotherapy and consisted of fifteen two-hour sessions which were carefully planned to clarify important reasons for psychological dysfunction as well as methods of self-exploration. The technique was not only successful in preparing patients for further treatment, but proved to be an effective therapy modality; at the conclusion of the workshop, many patients felt sufficiently improved so that no further treatment was required.

Groups in prenatal clinics for primiparous mothers [13] and groups in Peace Corps training centers [14] also use considerable didactic instruction. The new mothers are informed of the physiological basis of the physical and psychological changes they are undergoing, the actual mechanics of labor and delivery are clarified, and an attempt is made to dissipate irrational fears and beliefs by an appeal to reason. Peace Corps training groups often used an "anticipatory guidance" approach in which the stresses and conflicts likely to be encountered in the new culture were predicted and discussed. In my work with the Peace Corps, I found it useful to include a staff member from the country to which the trainees were going. He was able, through didactic means, to describe the culture realistically and disconfirm many of the groundless fears of the trainees.

My colleagues and I have used an analogous type of anticipatory guidance for psychiatric patients about to enter a new culture—the psychotherapy group.[15] By predicting patients' fears, by providing them with a cognitive structure, we helped them to cope more effectively with the initial "culture shock." (This procedure is described in detail in Chapter 9.)

Didactic instruction has thus been employed in a variety of fashions in group therapy: to transfer information, to structure the group, to explain the process of illness. Often it functions as the initial binding force in the group until other curative factors become operative. In part, however, explanation and clarification function as effective curative agents in their own right. Man has always abhorred uncertainty and through the ages has sought to order his universe by providing explanations, primarily religious or scientific. The explanation of a phenomenon is the first step toward control of the phenomenon. If a volcanic eruption is caused by a displeased volcanic god, then there are methods of pleasing and eventually controlling the god. Frieda Fromm-Reichman [16] underscores the role of uncertainty in the production of anxiety. She points out that the individual's awareness that he is not his own helmsman, that his perceptions and behavior are controlled by irrational forces, is in itself an important source of anxiety. Jerome Frank,[17] in a study of Americans' reactions to an unfamiliar South Pacific disease (Schistosomiasis), demonstrates that secondary anxiety stemming from uncertainty often creates more havoc than the primary disease. Similarly with psychiatric patients: fear and anxiety which stem from uncertainty of the source, meaning, and seriousness of psychiatric symptoms may so compound the total dysphoria that effective exploration becomes vastly more difficult. Thus, didactic instruction, through its provision of structure and explanation, has intrinsic value and deserves a place in our repertoire of therapeutic instruments. (See Chapter 5 for a more complete discussion of this issue.)

Unlike explicit didactic instruction from the therapist, direct advice from the members occurs without exception in every therapy group. In dynamic interactional therapy groups, it is invariably part of the early life of the group and occurs with such regularity that it can be used to estimate the age of the group. If I observe or hear a tape of a group in which the patients with some regularity say "I think you ought to. . ." or "What you should do is. . ." or "Why don't you. . . ," then I can be reasonably certain that the group is either a young group or that it is an older group facing some difficulty which has either impeded its development or effected a temporary regression. Despite the fact that advice-giving is common in early interactional group therapy, I can recall few instances in which a specific suggestion concerning some problem was of any direct benefit to any patient. Indirectly, however, it serves a purpose; the process of advice-giving rather than the content of advice may be beneficial, since it implies and conveys a mutual interest and caring. In other words, it is not the advice given that is important, but the fact that advice was given.

Advice-giving or advice-seeking behavior is often an important clue to the elucidation of interpersonal pathology. The patient who, for example, continuously pulls advice and suggestions from others only to reject it ultimately and frustrate others is well known to group therapists as "the help-rejecting complainer" [18] or the "yes . . . but" [19] patient (see Chapter 12). Other patients may bid for attention and nurturance by asking for suggestions about a problem which is either insoluble or which has already been solved. Others soak up advice with an unquenchable thirst yet never reciprocate to others equally needy. Some group members are so intent on preserving a high status role in the group or a facade of cool self-sufficiency that they never ask directly for help; some are effusive in their gratitude; others never acknowledge the gift, but take it home, like a bone, to gnaw on privately.

Other types of groups, noninteractionally focused, make explicit and effective use of direct suggestions and guidance. For example, discharge groups (preparing patients for discharge from a hospital), Recovery, Inc., and Alcoholics Anonymous all proffer considerable direct advice. Discharge groups may discuss the events of a patient's trial home visit and offer suggestions for alternative behavior. Alcoholics Anonymous makes use of guidance and slogans; for example, patients are asked to remain abstinent for only the next twenty-four hours, one day at a time. Recovery, Inc., teaches members how to "spot symptoms," how to "erase and retrace," "rehearse and reverse," how to apply willpower effectively.

Altruism

There is an old Hasidic story of the Rabbi who had a conversation with the Lord about Heaven and Hell. "I will show you Hell," said the Lord and led the Rabbi into a room in the middle of which was a very big, round table. The people sitting at it were famished and desperate. In the middle of the table there was a large pot of stew, enough and more for everyone. The smell of the stew was delicious and made the Rabbi's mouth water. The people round the table were holding spoons with very long handles. Each one found that it was just possible to reach the pot to take a spoonful of the stew, but because the handle of his spoon was longer than a man's arm, he could not get the food back into his mouth. The Rabbi saw that their suffering was terrible. "Now I will show you Heaven," said the Lord, and they went into another room, exactly the same as the first. There was the same big, round table and the same pot of stew. The people, as before, were equipped with the same long-handled spoons—but here they were well nourished and plump, laughing and talking. At first the Rabbi could not understand. "It is simple, but it requires a certain skill," said the Lord. "You see, they have learned to feed each other."

In therapy groups, too, patients receive through giving, not only as part of the reciprocal giving-receiving sequence but also from the intrinsic act of giving. Psychiatric patients beginning therapy are demoralized and possess a deep sense of having nothing of value to offer others. They have long considered themselves as burdens, and it is a refreshing, self-esteem–boosting experience to find that they can be of importance to others.

And, of course, patients are enormously helpful to one another in the group therapeutic process. They offer support, reassurance, suggestions, insight, and share similar problems with one another. Not infrequently patients will listen and absorb observations from another member far more readily than from the group therapist. To many, the therapist retains his identity as the paid professional, but the other members can be counted upon for spontaneous and truthful reactions and feedback. When patients look back over the course of therapy, they invariably credit other members as having been important in their improvement; if not for deliberate support and advice, then at least for having been there and permitting the patient to learn about himself from their relationship.

Nor has this curative factor been unused in other psychotherapeutic systems. In primitive cultures, for example, the patient is often given the task of preparing a feast or performing some type of service for the community.[20] Altruism plays an important part in the healing process at Catholic shrines such as at Lourdes, where the sick pray not only for themselves but for one another. Warden Duffy is reputed to have claimed that the best way to help a man is to let him help you. People need to feel they are needed. I have known ex-alcoholics who have continued their AA contacts for years after they achieved complete sobriety; one worker said he had told the story of his downfall and subsequent reclamation at least a thousand times.

This source of help is not appreciated at first. Quite the contrary.

Many patients resist the suggestion of group therapy with the question, "How can the blind lead the blind?" Or they ask, "What can I possibly get from others as confused as I? We'll end up pulling one another down." Exploration of this sentiment usually reveals that the patient is really saying, "What do I have to offer anyone?" Such resistance to entering the group is best worked through from the direction of the patient's critical self-evaluation.

There is another, more subtle, benefit inherent in the altruistic act. So many patients are immersed in a morbid self-absorption, which takes the form of obsessive introspection or a teeth-gritting effort to "actualize" oneself. But self-actualization or meaning in life can never be attained via a deliberate, self-conscious pursuit. I agree with Frankl [21] that these qualities ensue but cannot be successfully pursued; that they are always derivative phenomena which appear on our peripheral landscape when we have transcended ourselves, when we have forgotten ourselves in an absorption in someone (or something) outside of ourselves. The therapy group, implicitly, teaches its members that lesson and provides a new counter-solipsistic perspective.

The Corrective Recapitulation
of the Primary Family Group

Without exception, patients enter group therapy with the history of a highly unsatisfactory experience in their first and most important group—their primary family. The group resembles a family in many aspects, and many groups are led by a male-female cotherapy team in a deliberate effort to simulate the parental configuration more closely. Depending upon their assumptive world (shaped to a large degree by their early family experience), members interact with leaders and members as they may have once interacted with parents and siblings. There are an infinite variety of patterns: they may be helplessly dependent upon the leaders, whom they imbue with unrealistic knowledge and power; they may defy the leaders at every step because they regard them as individuals who block their autonomous growth or strip them of their individuality; they may attempt to split the cotherapists and to incite disagreements or rivalry between the two; they may compete bitterly with other members in their efforts to accumulate units of attention and caring from the therapists; they may search for allies among the others in an effort to topple the therapists; they may forgo their own interests in a seemingly selfless effort to appease or provide for other members.

Obviously, the same principle operates in individual therapy. The difference, however, is that the group provides a vastly greater number and array of recapitulative possibilities. In one of my groups a patient who had been silently pouting for a couple of meetings bemoaned the fact that she was not in one-to-one therapy. The group could not satisfy her needs and she found herself unable to speak in the meeting, whereas she knew she could speak freely of herself in a private conversation with the therapist or with any one of the members. When pressed, the patient disclosed her anger that, in a recent meeting, another member had been welcomed so warmly upon returning from a vacation. She, too, had recently returned from a vacation, but without a correspondingly warm reception from the group. Furthermore, another patient was praised for offering an important interpretation to a member, whereas she made a very similar statement weeks ago which went unnoticed. For some time, too, she had noticed her growing resentment at sharing the group time; she was impatient while waiting for the floor and angry when attention was shifted away from her. All of these experiences obviously had a long history and were deeply rooted in her early relationships with her siblings. Together, they did not constitute a valid criticism for the group therapeutic mode; quite to the contrary, the group format was particularly valuable for her since it provided the opportunity for her envy and her cravings for attention to surface. In individual therapy these particular conflicts emerge very belatedly, if at all; the therapist is always there, the patient is expected to take all the time, there is no one with whom he must share the therapist or the therapy hour.

What is important, though, is not only that early familial conflicts are recapitulated but that they are relived correctively. Growth inhibiting relationships must not be permitted to freeze into the rigid, impenetrable system that characterizes many family structures. Instead, behavior stereotypes must be constantly challenged, and ground rules of reality testing, exploration of relationships, and testing out of new behaviors constantly encouraged. For many patients, then, working out problems with therapists and other members is also working through unfinished business from long ago. (How explicit the working in the past need be is a complex and controversial issue, which we shall address in Chapter 5.)

Development of Socializing Techniques

Social learning—the development of basic social skills—is a curative factor which operates in all therapy groups, although the nature of the skills taught and the explicitness of the process varies greatly depending upon the type of group therapy. In some groups, for example, groups preparing long-term hospitalized patients for discharge or adolescent groups, there may be an explicit emphasis on the development of social skills. Role playing may be employed in which patients learn to approach prospective employers for a job or in which adolescent boys learn to invite a girl to a dance. In dynamic group therapy with ground rules encouraging open feedback, patients may obtain considerable information about maladaptive social behavior. They may, for example, learn about their disconcerting tendency to avoid looking at the person with whom they are conversing; or they learn about others' impressions of their haughty, regal attitude or a variety of other social habits which, unbeknownst to them, have been undermining their social relationships. For individuals lacking intimate relationships, the group often represents the first opportunity for accurate interpersonal feedback. One patient, for example, who obsessively included endless, minute, irrelevant details in his social conversation realized this for the first time in therapy group. For years he had been aware only that others either avoided or curtailed their social contacts with him. Obviously, therapy involves far more than the simple recognition and deliberate alteration of social behavior, but, as we shall show in Chapter 3, these gains are more than fringe benefits and are often exceedingly instrumental in the initial phases of therapeutic change.

One frequently notes that the senior members of the therapy group have acquired some highly sophisticated social skills. They are attuned to process (see Chapter 5), they have learned how to be helpfully responsive to others, they have acquired methods of conflict resolution, they are less prone to judgmentalism and more capable of experiencing and expressing accurate empathy. These skills cannot but help to serve them well in future social interactions.

Imitative Behavior

Pipe-smoking therapists often beget pipe-smoking patients. Patients during psychotherapy may sit, walk, talk, and even think like their therapists. In groups the imitative process is more diffuse, as patients may model themselves upon aspects of the other group members as well as of the therapist. The importance of imitative behavior in the therapeutic process is difficult to gauge, but recent social psychological research suggests that we may have underestimated its importance. Bandura,[22,23] who has long claimed that social learning cannot be adequately explained on the basis of direct reinforcement, has experimentally demonstrated that imitation is an effective therapeutic force. For example, he has successfully treated a large number of individuals with snake phobias by asking them to observe their therapist handle a snake. In group therapy it is not uncommon for a patient to benefit by observing the therapy of another patient with a similar problem constellation—a phenomenon generally referred to as "vicarious" or "spectator" therapy.[24] Even if specific imitative behavior is short-lived, it may function to help the individual "unfreeze" by experimenting with new behavior. In fact, it is not uncommon for patients throughout therapy to try on, as it were, bits and pieces of other people and then relinquish them as ill-fitting. This process may have solid therapeutic impact; finding out what we are not is progress toward finding out what we are.

REFERENCES

1. M. A. Lieberman, I. Yalom, and M. Miles, *Encounter Groups: First Facts* (New York: Basic Books, 1973).
2. H. Feifel and J. Eells, "Patients and Therapists Assess the Same Psychotherapy," *J. Consult. Psychol.*, 27: 310–318, 1963.
3. F. Taylor, *The Analysis of Therapeutic Groups* (London: Oxford University Press, 1961).
4. B. Berzon and R. Farson, "The Therapeutic Event in Group Psychotherapy: A Study of Subjective Reports by Group Members," *J. Indiv. Psychol.*, 19: 204–212, 1963.
5. A. P. Goldstein, *Therapist Patient Expectancies in Psychotherapy* (New York: Pergamon Press, 1962).
6. S. Hadden, "Treatment of Male Homosexuals in Groups," *Int. J. Group Psychother.*, 16: 13–22, 1966.

7. M. Jones, "Group Treatment with Particular Reference to Group Projection Methods," *Am. J. Psychiat.*, *101:* 292–299, 1944.
8. J. W. Klapman, "The Case for Didactic Group Psychotherapy," *Dis. Nerv. Sys.*, *11:* 35–41, 1950.
9. L. C. Marsh, "Group Therapy and the Psychiatric Clinic," *J. Nerv. Ment. Dis.*, *82:* 381–390, 1935.
10. H. Wechsler, "The Self-Help Organization in the Mental Health Field: Recovery, Inc.—A Case Study," *J. Nerv. Ment. Dis.*, *130:* 297–314, 1960.
11. A. A. Low, *Mental Health Through Will Training* (Boston: Christopher Publishing House, 1950).
12. D. I. Malamud and S. Machover, *Toward Self-Understanding: Group Techniques in Self-Confrontation* (Springfield, Ill.: Charles C. Thomas, 1965).
13. C. W. F. Burnett, *A Textbook of Obstetrical Nursing* (Oxford: Blackwell Scientific Publications, 1964), pp. 88–92.
14. G. Caplan, *Principles of Preventive Psychiatry* (New York: Basic Books, 1964).
15. I. D. Yalom, P. S. Houts, G. Newell, and K. H. Rand, "Preparation of Patients for Group Therapy: A Controlled Study," *Arch. Gen. Psychiat.*, *17:* 416–427, 1967.
16. F. Fromm-Reichman, *Principles of Intensive Psychotherapy* (Chicago: University of Chicago Press, 1950).
17. J. Frank, "Emotional Reactions of American Soldiers to an Unfamiliar Disease," *Am. J. Psychiat.*, *102:* 631–640, 1946.
18. F. Frank *et al.*, "Behavioral Patterns in Early Meetings of Therapy Groups," *Am. J. Psychiat.*, *108:* 771–778, 1952.
19. E. Berne, *Games People Play* (New York: Grove Press, 1964).
20. J. Frank, *Persuasion and Healing, A Comparative Study of Psychotherapy* (New York: Schocken Books, 1963).
21. V. Frankl, *The Will to Meaning* (Cleveland: World Publishing Press, 1969).
22. A. Bandura, E. B. Blanchard, and B. Ritter, "The Relative Efficacy of Desensitization and Modeling Approaches for Inducing Behavioral, Affective, and Attitudinal Changes," *J. Personal. Soc. Psychol.*, in press.
23. A. Bandura, D. Ross, and S. Ross, "Vicarious Reinforcements and Imitative Learning," *J. Abnorm. Soc. Psychol.*, *67:* 601–607, 1963.
24. J. L. Moreno, "Psychodramatic Shock Therapy," *Sociometry*, *2:* 1–30, 1939.

2

INTERPERSONAL

LEARNING

Interpersonal learning, as I define it, is a broad and complex curative factor representing the group therapy analogue of such individual therapy curative factors as insight, working through the transference, the corrective emotional experience, as well as processes unique to the group setting. To define the concept of interpersonal learning and to describe the mechanism whereby it mediates therapeutic change in the individual, I shall first need to discuss three other concepts:

1. The importance of interpersonal relationships
2. The corrective emotional experience
3. The group as a social microcosm

The Importance of Interpersonal Relationships

As we study human society we find that, regardless of the magnification we employ, interpersonal relations play a crucial role. Whether we scan man's broad evolutionary history or scrutinize the development of the single individual, we are at all times obliged to consider man in the matrix of his interpersonal relationships. As Hamburg [1] has pointed out, there is convincing data from the study of primitive human cultures and nonhuman primates that man has always lived in groups which have been characterized by intense and persistent inter-member relationships. Man's interpersonal behavior has been clearly adaptive in an evolutionary sense; without intense, positive, reciprocal interpersonal bonds, both individual and species survival would not have been possible. Bowlby,[2] from his studies of the early mother-child relationship, concludes also that attachment behavior is built into us. If the mother and infant are separated, both experience marked anxiety concomitant with their search for the lost object. If the separation is prolonged, the consequences will be proportionately profound. Goldschmidt,[3] on the basis of an exhaustive review of the ethnographic evidence, states:

> Man is by nature committed to social existence, and is therefore inevitably involved in the dilemma between serving his own interests and recognizing those of the group to which he belongs. Insofar as this dilemma can be resolved it is resolved by the fact that man's self-interest can best be served through his commitment to his fellows. . . . Need for positive affect means that each person craves response from his human environment. It may be viewed as a hunger, not unlike that for food, but more generalized. Under varying conditions it may be expressed as a desire for contact, for recognition and acceptance, for approval, for esteem, or for mastery. . . . As we examine human behavior, we find that persons not only universally live in social systems, which is to say they are drawn together, but also universally act in such ways as to attain the approval of their fellow men.

Similarly, eighty years ago, William James said, "We are not only gregarious animals liking to be in sight of our fellows, but we have an innate propensity to get ourselves noticed, and noticed favorably, by our kind. No more fiendish punishment could be devised, were such a thing physically possible, than that one should be turned loose in society and remain absolutely unnoticed by all the members thereof." [4]

Although all modern schools of psychiatric thought are interpersonally based, none is as explicit and systematic as Harry Stack Sullivan's interpersonal theory of psychiatry. Sullivan's formulations are exceedingly helpful for understanding the group therapeutic process. A comprehensive discussion of his interpersonal theory of psychiatry is obviously beyond the scope of this book, and the reader is referred to Sullivan's works [5,6] or, because of Sullivan's often obscure language, to a lucid review of his contributions.[7] However, mention of a few key concepts is in order. Sullivan contends that the personality is almost entirely the product of interaction with other significant human beings. Man's need to be closely related to others is as basic as any biological need and, considering the prolonged period of helpless infancy, equally necessary to survival. As he develops, the child, in his quest for security, tends to stress those traits and aspects of himself which meet with approval and will squelch or deny those aspects which meet with disapproval. Eventually, the individual develops a concept of himself (self-dynamism) which is based on these perceived appraisals of significant others.

The self may be said to be made up of reflected appraisals. If these were chiefly derogatory, as in the case of an unwanted child who was never loved, of a child who has fallen into the hands of foster parents who have no real interest in him as a child; as I say, if the self-dynamism is made up of experience which is chiefly derogatory, it will facilitate hostile, disparaging appraisals of other people and it will entertain disparaging and hostile appraisals of itself.[8]

Sullivan used the term "parataxic distortions" to describe the individual's proclivity to distort his perceptions of others. A parataxic distortion occurs in an interpersonal situation when one person relates to another not on the basis of the realistic attributes of the other, but wholly or chiefly on the basis of a personification existing chiefly in his fantasy. Parataxic distortion is similar to the concept of transference but broader in scope. It refers not only to the therapeutic but to all interpersonal relationships. It includes not only the simple transferring of attitudes from real life figures but also the distortion of interpersonal reality in response to intrapersonal needs.*

Interpersonal distortions tend to be self-perpetuating. An individual may, through selective inattention, distort his perceptions of another so that an individual with a derogatory, debased self-image may incorrectly perceive another to be a harsh, rejecting figure. Moreover, the process compounds itself because he may gradually develop mannerisms and behavioral traits, for example, servility, defensive antagonism, or scorn, which eventually will cause others to relate to him as he expected. The term "self-fulfilling prophecy" has been applied to this phenomenon.

Parataxic distortions, in Sullivan's view, are modifiable primarily through consensual validation, through comparing one's interpersonal evaluations with those of others. This brings us to Sullivan's view of the therapeutic process. "Psychiatry is the study of processes that involve or go on between people." [9] Mental disorder, psychiatric symptomatology in all of its varied manifestations, is translated into interpersonal terms and treated accordingly. "Mental disorder as a term refers to interpersonal processes either inadequate to the situation in which the persons are integrated, or excessively complex because of illusionary persons also integrated into the situations. It implies sometimes a greater ineffectiveness of the behavior by which the person is

* Although their origins differ, transference and parataxic distortions may be considered operationally identical. Many therapists today use the term "transference" to refer to all interpersonal distortions rather than confining its use to the patient-therapist relationship (see Chapter 6).

conceived to be pursuing the satisfactions that he requires." [10] Accordingly, psychiatric treatment should be directed toward the correction of interpersonal distortions, thus enabling the individual to lead a more abundant life, to participate collaboratively with others, to obtain interpersonal satisfactions in the context of realistic, mutually satisfying interpersonal relationships. "One achieves mental health to the extent that one becomes aware of one's interpersonal relationships." [11] Psychiatric cure is the "expanding of the self to such final effect that the patient as known to himself is much the same person as the patient behaving to others." [12]

Thus therapy is broadly interpersonal, both in its goals and in its means. Group therapy patients, somewhere between the third and sixth month of therapy, often undergo a shift in their therapeutic goals.[13] Their initial goal, relief of suffering, is modified and eventually replaced by new goals, usually interpersonal in nature. Thus goals changed from wanting relief from anxiety or depression to wanting to learn to communicate with others, to be more trusting and honest with others, to learn to love. One of the early tasks of the therapist is to facilitate this translation of symptoms into interpersonal constructs. Chapter 9 describes a systematic preparation of the new group therapy patient which focuses quite explicitly upon this task.

Sullivan's statement of the overall process and goals of therapy is clearly consistent with those of interactional group therapy. However, the emphasis on the patient's understanding of the past, of the genetic development of those maladaptive interpersonal stances, may be less crucial in group therapy than in the individual setting where Sullivan worked (see Chapter 5).

Sullivan's professional fate has been similar to that of many another innovator. The conservative community responded to his ideas at first by ignoring them, then by attacking them, and finally by so assimilating them that their innovative nature is forgotten. The theory of interpersonal relationships is presently so much an integral part of the fabric of psychiatric thought that it scarcely needs underscoring. Empirical documentation of the critical nature of man's social needs is voluminous. Consider, for example, the studies of bereavement in which surviving spouses have been shown to suffer increased incidence of physical illness,[14] mental illness,[15] and a greater mortality rate.[16]

People need people—for initial and continued survival, for socialization, for the pursuit of satisfaction. No one transcends his need for human contact, neither the dying, the outcast, nor the mighty.

I recently led a group of patients, all of whom had some advanced form of cancer. I was repeatedly struck by the realization that, in the face of death, our dread is not so much that of nonbeing, nor of nothingness, as it is that of the accompanying utter loneliness. The dying patient's concerns are often chiefly interpersonal ones. He is distressed at being abandoned, even shunned, by the world of the living. One patient, for example, had planned to give a large evening social function and learned that very morning that her cancer, heretofore believed contained, had metastasized. She kept the information secret and gave the party, all the while dwelling on the horrible thought that the pain from her disease would be so unbearable that she would become less human and, finally, unacceptable to others.

I agree with Kübler-Ross [17] that the question is not whether or not to tell the patient but how to tell the patient of his condition openly and honestly; the patient is always informed covertly that he is dying by the demeanor of the living, by their shrinking away.

Their dying often separates them from those to whom they are closest. They protect or cheer their friends by an airy facade. They avoid morbid talk to such an extent that a wide gulf is created between them and the "living." Physicians often keep patients with far advanced cancer at a considerable psychological distance, probably in an effort to deal with dread of their own death, their sense of guilt, limitation, and futility. There is, after all, nothing more they can do. Yet from the patients' standpoint this is the time when they need the physician the most—not for his technical aid but for his sheer presence.

Nowhere have I seen the terrifying loneliness of the dying person more poignantly portrayed than in Bergman's film *Cries and Whispers*, where the spirit of a recently dead woman pleads for a living person to stay with her. What is needed is contact, to be able to touch others, to voice concerns openly, to be reminded that they are not only "apart from" but also "a part of."

The outcast, the individual often thought to be so inured to rejection that his interpersonal needs have become heavily calloused, he too has compelling social needs. A recent experience in a prison provided me with a forceful reminder of the ubiquitous nature of this human need.

An untrained psychiatric technician requested consultation with his therapy group composed of twelve inmates. The members of the group were all hardened recidivists, whose offenses ranged from aggressive sexual violation of a minor to murder. The group, he complained, was sluggish and persisted in focusing on extraneous extragroup material. I agreed to observe his group and suggested that first he obtain some sociometric information by asking each member privately to rank order everyone in their group for "general popularity." (I had hoped that the discussion of this task would induce the group to turn its attention upon itself.) Although we had planned to discuss these results before the next group session, unexpected circumstances precluded our pre-session consultation. During the next group meeting the therapist, enthusiastic but still unsophisticated and insensitive to interpersonal needs, decided that he would simply read out the results of the popularity poll. The group began the meeting in a somewhat agitated manner and, clearly frightened and threatened, soon made it very explicit that they did not wish to know the results of the poll. Several members spoke so vehemently of the possible devastation at learning that they might appear at the bottom of the list that the therapist quickly and permanently abandoned his plan of reading aloud the list. I suggested an alternative plan: each member was asked to indicate whose vote he cared about most in the group and explain his choice. This, also, was too threatening, and only one-third of the members ventured a choice. Nevertheless, the group shifted to an interactional level and developed a degree of tension, involvement, and exhilaration previously unknown. These human beings had received the ultimate message of rejection from society at large; they were imprisoned, segregated, and explicitly labeled as outcasts. To the casual observer these people, of all people, seemed calloused, hardened, and indifferent to the subtleties of interpersonal approval and disapproval; yet they cared, and cared very deeply.

The need for acceptance and intercourse with others is no different among those at the opposing pole of human fortunes—those who occupy the ultimate realms of power, renown, or wealth. I once worked for three years with an enormously wealthy patient. The major issues revolved about the wedge money created between herself and others. Did anyone value her for herself rather than her money? Was she continually being exploited by others? To whom could she complain of the burdens of a twenty million dollar fortune? If she kept her identity or her wealth a secret from others, she felt like a fraud. How could she possibly give others appropriate gifts without their feeling disappointed or awed. There is no need to belabor the point; the loneliness of the very great is common knowledge. (These experiences are, incidentally, not irrelevant to the group therapist. Chapter 6 will discuss the loneliness inherent in the role of group leader.)

Every group therapist has, I am sure, encountered patients who profess an indifference to or detachment from the group. "I don't care what they say or think or feel about me. They're nothing to me. I have

no respect for the other members." Or words to that effect. My experience has been that if I can keep such patients in the group long
enough, another aspect inevitably surfaces. They are concerned at a
very deep level about the group. They may dream about the group,
feel great anxiety before meetings, feel too shaken after meetings to
drive home or to sleep that night. One patient who maintained her indifferent posture for many months was once invited to ask the group
her secret question, the one question she would like most of all to
place before the group. To everyone's astonishment, her question
was, "How can you put up with me?" People do not long feel indifferent toward others in a group. Patients do not quit the therapy group
because of boredom. Believe scorn, contempt, fear, discouragement,
shame, panic, hatred—believe any of these, but never believe
indifference!

In summary, then, we have reviewed some aspects of personality
development, mature functioning psychopathology, and psychiatric
treatment from the point of view of interpersonal theory. Many of the
issues that we have raised have a vital bearing on the curative process
in group therapy: the concept that mental illness emanates from disturbed interpersonal relationships, the role of consensual validation
in the modification of interpersonal distortions, the definition of the
therapeutic process as an adaptive modification of interpersonal relationships, and the enduring nature and potency of man's social needs.

The Corrective Emotional Experience

In 1946 Franz Alexander, when describing the mechanism of psychoanalytic cure, introduced the concept of the "corrective emotional experience." The basic principle of treatment, he stated, is "to expose
the patient, under more favorable circumstances, to emotional situations which he could not handle in the past. The patient, in order to be
helped, must undergo a corrective emotional experience suitable to
repair the traumatic influence of previous experience." [18] Alexander
underscores the importance of an emotional experience; intellectual
insight alone is insufficient. Furthermore, the essence of the curative
mechanism is the accompanying reality testing. The patient, while af-
fectively interacting with the analyst in a distorted fashion because of
transference (or parataxic distortion), gradually becomes aware of the
fact that "these reactions are not suited to the analyst's reactions, not

only because he (the analyst) is objective, but also because he is what he is, a person in his own right. They are not suited to the situation between patient and therapist, and they are equally unsuited to the patient's current interpersonal relationships in his daily life." [19]

These basic principles of therapy—the importance of the emotional experience in therapy, and the patient's discovery of the inappropriateness of his interpersonal reactions through reality testing—are equally crucial to the group therapeutic experience. In fact, the group setting offers far more opportunities for the generation of corrective emotional experiences; in the individual setting the corrective emotional experience, valuable as it is, may be hard to come by because of the insularity and unreality of the patient-therapist relationship. In fact, Alexander suggested that the analyst may have to be an actor and to play a role in order to create the desired emotional atmosphere.[20] Frank and Ascher [21] described two corrective emotional experiences in group therapy which significantly altered the course of therapy for the involved patients. In each of these incidents the appearance of the critical incident was facilitated by three therapeutic processes: support, affect stimulation, and reality testing. Patients must obtain enough support from the group so that they are willing to express themselves honestly and to work through the incident afterwards. The group offers considerable stimulation for the activation of noxious attitudes: "competition for the doctor, struggles for status, differences in background and outlook among patients, transference reactions to other group members, etc." [21] Furthermore, the group, because of ground rules of honesty of expression, offers ample opportunity for consensual validation.

In a recent study [13] of twenty successful group therapy patients, I asked each whether he could recall some single critical incident in therapy which seemed to be a turning point for him, or which was the most helpful single event in therapy for him. Although the single critical incident is not synonymous with "curative factor," clearly the two are not unrelated and much may be learned from an examination of single important events. Of the twenty patients, only two were unable to recall a critical incident; the other eighteen recalled a total of twenty-nine such incidents. Almost invariably, the incident involved some other group member, rarely the therapist, and was highly emotionally laden.

The most common type of incident reported, as well as the two described by Frank and Ascher, involved the patient's suddenly expressing strong feelings of anger or hatred toward another member. In each instance communication was maintained, the storm was weathered, and the patient experienced a sense of liberation from inner restraints as well as an enhanced ability to explore his interpersonal relationships more deeply.

The common characteristics of these critical incidents were:

1. The patient expressed strong negative affect.
2. This expression was a unique or novel experience for him.
3. The feared and fantasied catastrophe did not occur; no one left or died, the roof did not collapse.
4. Reality testing ensued in which the patient realized either that the affect he expressed was inappropriate in intensity or direction or that his prior avoidance of affect expression was irrational; he may or may not have gained some knowledge of the source of the distortion or the prior avoidance.
5. The patient was enabled to interact more freely and to explore his interpersonal relationships more deeply.

The second most common type of critical incident also involved strong affect, but, in these instances, positive affect. For example, a schizoid patient ran after and comforted a distressed patient who had bolted out of the group room; later he spoke of how profoundly he was affected by learning that he could care for and help someone else. Others similarly spoke of discovering their "aliveness" or of feeling "in touch with" themselves. These incidents had in common the following characteristics:

1. The patient expressed strong positive affect, which was unusual for him.
2. The feared fantasied catastrophe did not occur; he was not rejected, derided, engulfed, nor were others damaged by his display of caring.
3. The patient discovered a previously unknown part of himself, which enabled him to relate to others in a new dimension.

The third most common category of critical incident was quite similar to the second. Patients recalled an incident, usually involving self-disclosure, which plunged them into greater involvement with the group. For example, a previously withdrawn reticent patient who had missed a couple of meetings disclosed to the group how desperately he wanted to hear the group say that they had missed him during his absence. Others, too, in one fashion or another openly asked the group for help.

To summarize, the corrective emotional experience in group therapy may have several components:

1. A strong expression of emotion which is interpersonally directed and which represents a risk taking on the part of the patient
2. A group supportive enough to permit this risk taking

3. Reality testing which allows the patient to examine the incident with the aid of consensual validation from the other members
4. A recognition of the inappropriateness of certain interpersonal feelings and behavior or of the inappropriateness of certain avoided interpersonal behaviors
5. The ultimate facilitation of the individual's ability to interact with others more deeply and honestly

This dual nature of the therapeutic process is of elemental significance and we shall return to it again and again in this text. Therapy is *an emotional and a corrective* experience. We must experience something strongly, *but we must also,* through our faculty of reason, understand the implications of that emotional experience. This formulation has direct relevance to the concept of the "here-and-now"—a key concept of group therapy which shall be discussed in depth in Chapter 5. For the present, I shall state only the basic premise: to the degree that the therapy group focuses on the here-and-now, it increases in power and effectiveness. But a focus on the "here-and-now" (on what is happening in this room in the immediate present) is a dual-pronged focus: the group members experience one another with as much spontaneity and honesty as possible and *they also reflect upon that experience.* The self-reflective loop is crucial if the experience is to become a therapeutic one. As we shall see in our discussion of the therapist's task (Chapter 5), most groups have little difficulty in entering the emotional stream of the here-and-now; it is the therapist's job to keep directing the group toward the self-reflective aspect of that process.

The mistaken assumption that a strong emotional experience is, in itself, a sufficient force for change is seductive as well as venerable. Modern dynamic psychotherapy was conceived in that very error, as Freud and Breuer in their 1895 book on hysteria [22] described their method of cathartic treatment. They were convinced that hysteria was caused by a traumatic event to which the individual never fully responded emotionally. Since illness was caused by strangulated affect, treatment thus consisted of giving a voice to the stillborn emotion. It was not long before Freud recognized that emotional expression, though necessary, was not a sufficient condition for change. Freud's discarded ideas, tossed away carelessly, have been the seed for many of today's extreme cultish psychotherapeutic movements. In the mid-1970s, for example, the Viennese *fin de siècle* cathartic treatment lives on with the primal scream, bioenergetics, structural integration, and with many of the least thoughtful of gestalt therapy practitioners and encounter group leaders.

My colleagues and I [23] recently conducted an intensive investigation of the process and outcome of many of the ultramodern encounter techniques (see Chapter 14 for a full description of this research), and our findings provide much support for the dual emotional-intellectual components of the psychotherapeutic process.

We explored, in a number of ways, the relationship between each member's experience in the group and his outcome. For example, we asked each member to reflect, retrospectively, on those aspects of his group experience which he deemed most pertinent to his change. We also asked him during the course of the group (at the end of each meeting) to describe the event of that meeting which had the most significance for him personally. When we correlated the type of event with outcome, we obtained surprising results which disconfirmed many of the current stereotypes about the prime ingredients of the successful encounter group experience. Although emotional experiences (expression and experiencing of strong affect, self-disclosure, giving and receiving feedback) were considered extremely important, they did not differentiate between successful and unsuccessful group members. In other words, the members who were unchanged or even had a destructive experience were as apt as successful members to value highly the emotional incidents of the group.

What types of experiences did differentiate the successful from the unsuccessful members? There was very clear evidence that a cognitive component was essential; the successful members either acquired information or personal insight. That these findings occurred in groups led by leaders who did not attach much importance to the intellectual component speaks strongly for their being part of the core, and not the facade, of the change process.

The Group as a Social Microcosm

A freely interactive group, with few structural restrictions, will, in time, develop into a social microcosm of the participant members. I mean by this that, given enough time, every patient will begin to be himself, to interact with the group members as he interacts with others in his social sphere, to create in the group the same interpersonal universe which he has always inhabited. In other words, patients will begin to display their maladaptive interpersonal behavior in the group; there is no need for them to describe their pathology— they will sooner or later act it out before the group's eyes.

This concept is of paramount importance in group therapy and constitutes a keystone upon which our entire approach to group therapy rests. It is widely accepted by clinicians, although each therapist's perception and interpretation of group events and his descriptive language are determined by his school of conviction. Freudians may see patients manifesting their oral, sadistic, or masochistic needs in their relationship to other members; correctional workers may see "conning," exploitative behavior; certain social psychologists may see manifold bids for dominance, affection, or inclusion; students of Karen Horney [24] may see the detached, resigned person putting his energies into acting noncommittal and indifferent, or the arrogant-vindictive person struggling to prove himself right by proving others wrong; Adlerians may speak more of compensatory behavior and are very prone to observe ordinal position behavior (youngest sister, older brother, etc.).

The important point is that, regardless of the type of conceptual spectacles worn by the therapist-observer, each member's interpersonal style will eventually appear in his transactions in the group. Some life styles have greater inherent possibilities for interpersonal friction and will manifest themselves in the group more rapidly than others. Individuals who are, for example, angry, vindictive, harshly judgmental, self-effacing, or grandly coquettish will generate considerable interpersonal static early in the group. Their maladaptive social patterns will seem clear far earlier than those of individuals equally or more severely troubled who may, for example, subtly exploit others or achieve intimacy to a point but then, in panic, disengage themselves. The initial business of a group usually consists of dealing with the member whose pathology is most interpersonally blatant. Some interpersonal styles become crystal clear from a single transaction, others from a single group meeting, while others require months of observation to understand. The development of the ability to identify and put to therapeutic advantage maladaptive interpersonal behavior as seen in the social microcosm of the small group is one of the chief tasks of a training program for group psychotherapists. Some clinical examples may make these principles more graphic.

The Grand Dame

Mrs. Cape, a twenty-seven-year-old musician, sought therapy primarily because of severe marital discord of several years' standing. She had had considerable, unrewarding, individual and hypnotic uncovering therapy. Her husband, she reported, was an alcoholic who was reluctant to engage her socially, intellectually, or sexually. Now the group could have, as some groups do, investigated her marriage interminably. They might have taken a complete history of the courtship, of the evolution of the discord, of her husband's pathology, of her reasons for marrying him, of her role in the conflict; they may have given advice for new behaviors, trial or permanent separations—but all would have been in vain. This approach not only disregards the unique potential of therapy groups but is also based on the highly questionable premise that the patient's account of the marriage is even reasonably accurate. Groups which function in this manner not only fail to help the particular protagonist but also suffer demoralization as the group becomes aware of its impotence.

As one attended to Mrs. Cape's group behavior, several interesting patterns unfolded. First, her grand entrance, always five or ten minutes late. Bedecked in flamboyant, ever different garb, she swept in, sometimes throwing kisses, and immediately began talking, oblivious of the possibility that some other member may have been in the midst of a sentence, or indeed in the midst of a word. Here was narcissism in the raw! Her world view was so solipsistic that she did not consider that life might have been going on in the group before her arrival.

After a very few group meetings, Mrs. Cape began to give gifts in the group: to an obese female member, a copy of a Mayo diet; to a female with strabismus, the name of a good ophthalmologist; to a male homosexual patient, a subscription to *Field and Stream* magazine (to masculinize him); to a twenty-four-year-old virginal male, an introduction to a divorcee friend of hers. Gradually it became apparent that the gifts were not duty free. For example, she intruded in the relationship between the male member and her divorcee friend by serving gratuitously as a third-party go-between. In so doing she exerted considerable control over both individuals.

Her efforts to dominate soon colored all of her interactions in the group. The therapist became a challenge to her and various efforts to control him unfolded. The therapist, by chance, saw her sister in consultation and referred her to a competent therapist, a clinical psychologist. In the group Mrs. Cape congratulated him for his "brilliant tactic" of sending her sister to a psychologist; he "must have divined her deep-seated aversion for physicians." Similarly, on another occasion, the therapist made a comment to her and she responded, "How perceptive you were to have noticed my hands trembling." Now in fact, the therapist had not divined her sister's alleged aversion for physicians, he had simply referred her to the best therapist he knew; nor had he noted her hands trembling. The trap was set: if he silently accepted her tribute, then he and Mrs. Cape became unhappy accomplices; on the other hand, if he admitted that he had not been sensitive to either the trembling of the hands or to the sister's aversion, then in a sense he has also been bested. In such situations, the therapist does well to concentrate instead on the process and to comment about the nature and the meaning of the entrapment. (We shall have a great deal more to say about relevant therapist technique in Chapter 5.)

She vied with the therapist in many other ways. Intuitive and intellectually gifted, she became the group expert on dream and fantasy interpretation. On one occasion she saw the therapist between group sessions to ask whether she could take a book out of the medical library under his name. On one level the request was a reasonable one: the book (on music therapy) was related to her profession; furthermore she, as a layman, was not permitted the use of the library. However, in the context of the group process the request was a complex one in which she was testing limits, and which, if granted, would have meant to her and the rest of the group that she did occupy a "special place" vis-à-vis the therapist and the other members. The therapist clarified these considerations to her and suggested further discussion in the next session. Following this perceived rebuttal, however, she called the three male members at home and, after swearing them to secrecy, arranged to see them, and engaged in sexual relations with two. She failed with the third, a homosexual, only after a strenuous attempt.

The following meeting was a horrific one. It was extraordinarily tense, unproductive, and demonstrated the axiom (to be discussed later) that if something important in the group is being actively avoided, then nothing else of import is talked about either. Two days later Mrs. Cape, overcome with anxiety and guilt, asked to see the therapist and made a full "confession." It was agreed that the whole matter should be discussed in the next group meeting. This meeting was opened by Mrs. Cape, who said, "This is confession day! Go ahead Charles!" and then later, "Your turn, Louis." The men performed as she bade them and later in the meeting received from her a critical evaluation of their sexual performance! Later in the course of the group Mrs. Cape accidentally let her estranged husband know of this event and soon he sent threatening messages to the men in the group, who then decided they could no longer trust Mrs. Cape and she was thereupon voted out of the group—the only occasion I have known of this. (She was continued in therapy with another group.) The saga does not end here, but perhaps we have gone far enough to illustrate the concept of the group as social microcosm.

To summarize, Mrs. Cape clearly displayed her interpersonal pathology in the group context. Her narcissism, her need for adulation, her need to control, her sadistic relationship with men—the entire tragic behavioral scroll—unfolded. Finally she began to receive crucial feedback as the men, for example, talked of their deep humiliation and anger at having to "jump through a hoop" for her and at having received "grades" for their sexual performance. They began to reflect that "No wonder your husband avoids you!" "Who wants to sleep with his mother?" etc. The female patients and the therapist also shared their feelings about the tremendously destructive course of her behavior—destructive for the group as well as herself. Most important of all she had to deal with this fact: she had started in the group with a number of troubled individuals who were anxious to help each other and whom she grew to like and respect; yet, in the course of one year, she had so poisoned her environment that, against her conscious wishes, she became a pariah, an outcast from a group of potentially intimate friends. It was the facing and working through of these issues in subsequent therapy that, in part, enabled her to change and to employ much of her considerable potential constructively in her future relationships and endeavors.

The Timid Homosexual

Mr. Flagge, a twenty-eight-year-old clerk, sought therapy because he felt that his life had "come to a grinding halt," had become constricted and stagnant; he repetitively became embroiled in "sick" unsatisfactory homosexual relationships; he was being exploited at work but was too timid to assert himself there and too anxious and unsure of himself to seek work elsewhere. His sexual expression was exclusively homosexual and he expressed no desire to change his orientation.

In the group his participation soon took on a characteristic pattern. He engaged animatedly in the sexual discussions and disclosed his intimate sexual life quite freely; however, he often became a nonparticipant for long intervals. Mr. Flagge never addressed a question to another patient nor, indeed did he appear to share in any of the joys or travails or interests of the other members; only when sex was mentioned did Mr. Flagge stir, illuminated as though his master switch had just been thrown, rousing him from his arid world. The group became aware of this after living with Mr. Flagge in the sessions for many weeks, and one day a member told him, "You're a homosexual first and a human being second." Other members agreed and in various fashions confronted Mr. Flagge with the banal, restricted life space he had created for himself. In his friends, his conversations, his feeling life, his range of interests, he had isolated himself from all but a narrow band of human experience.

One day in the group a member made a disparaging remark about a friend of Mr. Flagge's with whom he had seen him walking during the week; he continued to make some very insulting remarks about "queers" in general. Mr. Flagge flushed but did not comment and the incident was forgotten as the group became involved in another pressing issue. However, Mr. Flagge missed the next meeting and in the following session reported that for the first time in months he found himself extraordinarily sexually driven and had been relentlessly cruising gay bars, parks, Turkish baths, and public lavatories since his last group meeting. Furthermore, he described to the group, in great detail, the type of "sick" sex in which he had been engaging, including such perversions as copraphagia and bizarre sado-masochistic practices. Although the group was a mature, sophisticated one, this was more than they could take and they responded with aversion and withdrawal from him. When we analyzed the process of these events, the pattern seemed clear. Mr. Flagge, instead of expressing his great anger to the other member—the appropriate target—had reacted in a characteristic fashion. He had plunged himself into a cycle of activity that he personally experienced as degrading; furthermore, he castigated himself still more by behaving in the group in such a way as to invite rejection and scorn. This insight was a profound one for Mr. Flagge and it was of paramount relevance to his presenting problem: his inability to assert himself, to demand, to avoid being exploited. He appeared so fearful of expressing anger that he sought safety symbolically by self-degradation. Who will fear or harm the man at the bottom of the heap? Mr. Flagge eventually faced his anger in the group, directed it toward the proper target, and survived. The incident was a crucial one for him and the eventual carryover to the outside world was considerable. Mr. Flagge's major interpersonal difficulties, therefore, were manifested in his relationships with the group members. His limited involvement, his overevaluation of the sexual basis of relatedness, his fear of assertiveness, and his maladaptive manner of dealing with his anger by turning it upon himself all unfolded in the group and were available for analysis and change.

Men Who Could Not Feel

Mr. Steele sought therapy for a single, sharply delineated problem: "I want to be able to feel sexually stimulated by a woman." Intrigued by this conundrum, the group searched for the answer. They investigated his early life, sexual habits, fantasies, and finally, baffled, turned away. As life in the group continued, Mr. Steele, a regular attender, seemed peculiarly impassive. He spoke in a monotone and seemed entirely insensitive to others' pain. On one occasion, for example, a member in great distress announced in sobs that she was illegitimately pregnant and was planning to have a criminal abortion. During her account she also mentioned incidentally that she had had a bad marijuana trip. Mr. Steele, seemingly unmoved by her tears, persisted in questioning her intellectually about marijuana effects and was puzzled when the group turned on him because of his insensitivity. So many similar incidents occurred that the group came to expect no emotions from him. When he was directly queried about his feelings, he responded as if he had been addressed in a foreign language. After some months the group formulated a new answer to his oft-repeated question, "Why can't I have sexual feelings toward a woman?" They asked him to consider instead why he couldn't *have any kinds of feeling* toward man or woman.

Changes in his behavior occurred very gradually and were mediated via an investigation of his autonomic expressions of affect. The group wondered about his frequent facial flushing; he described his gastric tightness during emotionally laden episodes in the group. On one occasion a very volatile girl in the group called him a "god-damned faggot" and said that she couldn't relate to a "psychologically deaf and dead" individual and threatened to leave the group. Mr. Steele again remained impassive, stating that he wasn't going to "get down to her level." However, the next week he told the group that after the meeting he had gone home and cried like a baby. When he looked back at the course of his therapy, this seemed to be a turning point, and gradually he was able to feel and express sorrow, fear, and anger with others. His role within the group changed from that of a tolerated mascot to that of an accepted compeer.

In another group Ed, a forty-seven-year-old engineer, sought therapy because of loneliness and his inability to find a suitable mate. He had no male friends and unsatisfying short-lived relationships with women whom he did not respect and who invariably rejected him. Ed had good social skills, a lively sense of humor, and was initially highly valued by other members. However, as time went on and as members deepened their relationship with one another, Ed was left behind until his experience in the group resembled closely his social life outside the group. The most obvious aspect of Ed's behavior was his limited offensive approach to women. His gaze was primarily directed toward their breasts or crotch; his attention was in a voyeuristic fashion directed toward their sexual life; his suggested solutions were typically simplistic and sexual in nature. The men in the group were considered unwelcome competitors and he ignored them; for months he did not initiate a single transaction with a man.

He could not appreciate attachments and for the most part considered people interchangeable. For example, one woman described her obsessive fantasy whenever her boyfriend was late that he would be killed in an automobile accident. His response was to assure her that she was young and attractive and would have little trouble finding another man of at least equal quality. He was always puzzled that the members were troubled by the temporary absence of one of the cotherapists or, later, at the impending permanent departure of a therapist. Doubtless there was, even among the students, a therapist of equal competence. (In fact, he had seen in the hall a bra-less female psychologist, whom he would welcome as the therapist.)

He put it most succinctly when he described his M.D.R. (minimum daily requirement) for affection; in time it became clear to the group that the identity of the M.D.R. supplier was less relevant than the dependability and regularity of flow.

Thus, the first phase of the group therapeutic process evolved: Ed's typical interpersonal behavior was displayed in the group. He did not relate to others but used others as equipment, as objects to supply his life needs. Soon he had recreated in the group his habitual, lonely, interpersonal universe: he became extremely isolated in the group, the men reciprocated his total indifference, the women were not stimulated by the prospect of serving as his M.D.R. Those whom he especially craved were repulsed by his narrowly sexualized attentions.

The Person and His Group Environment: Dynamic Interaction

There is a rich and subtle interplay between the group member and his group environment. He at once shapes and responds to his social microcosm. The more each member spontaneously interacts, the more varied will be the environment and the greater the likelihood that problematic issues will, for each member, be touched upon.

For example, Andrew, a young borderline patient, entered the group because of a disabling depression and a subjective state of disintegration. His symptoms were intensified by a threatened breakup of the small commune in which he lived. Andrew regularly experienced great anxiety when he was left alone. He had long been sensitized to the breakup of nuclear units; for years he had felt it was his task to keep his explosive family together. He had long nurtured a fantasy that his wedding would result in a reunion and permanent reconciliation of the various factions among his relations.

In the group, Andrew, sometimes for weeks on end, would work smoothly and comfortably on important but minor conflict areas. Periodically, certain events in the group would fan his major concerns into full anxious conflagration. Often Andrew became very upset when members were absent. At the end of therapy, looking back, he recalled feeling so stunned at the absence of anyone that he frequently found himself unable to participate for the entire session. When a member thought about termination, Andrew was similarly concerned and could be counted upon to exert maximal pressure upon the member to continue in the group regardless of the best interests of the member. When members subgrouped and arranged contacts outside of the group meeting, Andrew became anxious at the threat to the integrity of the group. He longed for sameness and safety but, in fact, it was the very appearance of unsettling vicissitudes which made it possible for his major conflict areas to become exposed and to enter the stream of the therapeutic work.

Not only does the small group provide a social microcosm in which the maladaptive behavior of the members is clearly displayed but also it becomes a laboratory in which one can, often with great clarity, understand the dynamics of the behavior. The therapist sees not only the behavior but also the events which trigger the behavior and, sometimes, more important, the responses of others.

Leonard entered the group with a major problem of procrastination. Procrastination was considered both a problem and an explanation. It "explained" his failures both professionally and socially; it "explained" his discouragement, depression, and alcoholism. And yet it was an explanation which obscured meaningful explanation. In the group we became well acquainted with Leonard's procrastination. It served as his supreme mode of resistance when all other resistance had failed. When members worked hard with Leonard and when it appeared that part of his neurotic character was about to be uprooted, Leonard found ways to delay the group work. "I don't want to be upset by the group today. This new job is make or break for me. I'm just hanging on by my fingernails. Don't rock the boat. After the last meeting I had my first drink in months," etc. The variations were many but the theme was consistent.

One day Leonard announced a major step, one for which he had long labored; he had quit his job and obtained a new one as a teacher. Only one step remained—getting a teaching certificate, a matter of filling out an application requiring approximately two hours' labor. And yet he could not do it! He delayed until the time had practically expired and with only one day remaining informed the group about the deadline and lamented the cruelty of his personal demon—procrastination. Everyone in the group, including the therapists, experienced a strong desire to sit Leonard down, possibly even in one's lap, place a pen between his fingers, and guide his hand along the application form. And one patient, the most mothering member of the group, did exactly that: she took him home, fed him, and school-marmed him through the application form.

As we began to review what had happened, we could now see his procrastination for what it was: a plaintive, anachronistic plea for a lost mother. Many things fell into place: Leonard's depressions (another type of plea for love, an even more desperate one), his alcoholism, and compulsive overeating.

The major point, I believe, is sufficiently clear: if the group is so conducted that the members can behave in an unguarded, unself-conscious manner, they will, most vividly, present their pathology to the group. Furthermore, in the in vivo drama of the group meeting, the trained observer has a unique opportunity to understand the dynamics of the patient's behavior.

Recognition of Behavioral Patterns in the Social Microcosm

Note that in the incident involving Leonard, the vital clue was the emotional response of the members and leaders to Leonard. These emotional responses are valid and indispensable data: they should not be overlooked or underestimated. When the therapist or the other group members feel angry toward a patient, or exploited, or sucked dry, or steamrolled, or intimidated, or bored, or tearful, or any of the infinite number of ways one person can feel toward another, that is data, it is a bit of the truth about the other person, and it should be taken very seriously. If the feelings elicited in others are highly discordant with the feelings that the patient would like to engender in others, or if the feelings aroused, though desired, are, as in the example of Leonard, obviously growth-inhibitory, then therein lies an important part of the patient's problem, and it is to this phenomenon that the therapist should direct his attention.

There are many complications inherent in this thesis. The most obvious one is that a strong emotional response is often due not to pathology in the subject but to pathology in the respondent. If, for example, John, a self-confident, assertive male evokes strong feelings of intense envy or bitter resentment or homosexual panic in Edward, one can hardly conclude that the response is reflective of John's pathology. And so the therapist looks for confirmatory evidence, for the reactions of other members, for repetitive patterns over a period of time, and, significantly, the therapist examines his own emotional responses.

By no means, though, are the responses of patients, even those who are highly disturbed, to be disregarded. First, these responses still contain valid information for the subject: there is always a core of reality in even the most exaggerated irrational response. Furthermore, the disturbed patient may be a valuable, accurate source of feedback at other times (no individual is highly conflicted in *every* area). Lastly, an idiosyncratic response contains much information about the respondent. This latter point is an important one leading to a basic axiom for the group therapist: in a general sense everyone in the group is exposed to the same stimuli; therefore, differential responses among the group members must be explained on the basis of the individual meaning of these stimuli for each person. For example, everyone in the group may be exposed to the same person, a controlling monopolistic individual. The members, according to their character structure, respond very differently to this person, ranging from obsequious acquiescence, to impotent fury, to effective confrontation. Or again, consider certain structural aspects of the group meeting: members have markedly differing responses to sharing the group or the therapist's attention, or to disclosing themselves, or to helping others. Nowhere is this more clearly seen than in the transference phenomenon, in the responses to the therapist; the same therapist will be experienced as warm, cold, rejecting, or accepting by different members. Understanding the basis of these varying responses always leads to rich material for the therapeutic process.

Not infrequently the concept of the social microcosm is challenged by patients. They may claim that, though they do behave in a certain manner in this group, it is atypical behavior for them, not at all representative of their normal behavior. Or that this group is an unusual one which persists in perceiving him bizarrely. Or even that group therapy is not real; it is an artificial, contrived experience which distorts rather than reflects his real behavior. To the neophyte therapist these arguments may seem formidable, even persuasive, but they are in fact truth-distorting. In one sense the group *is* "artificial": members do not choose their friends from the group, they are not central to one another; they do not live, work, or eat together; they meet together in a professional's office for ninety minutes once or twice a week; the end of their relationship is built into the social contract at the very beginning.

When faced with these considerations, I often think of Earl and Marguerite, two patients in a group long ago. Earl had been a member of a group for four months when Marguerite was introduced. They both blushed to see one another in the group room since, by chance, they had only a month previously gone on a Sierra Club camping trip and been "intimate" together. Neither wanted to be in the group with the other. To Earl, Marguerite was a foolish, empty girl, a "mindless piece of ass," as he was to put it later in the group. To Marguerite, Earl was a dull nonentity, someone whose penis she had once used as a means of retaliation against her husband. They worked together in the group once a week for about a year. During that time they came to know one another intimately in the full sense of the word; they shared their deepest feelings, they weathered some fierce, vicious battles, they helped each other through suicidal depressions, and, on more than one occasion, they wept for each other. Which was the "real" world and which the artificial?

Paradoxically, the group can be far more "real" than the world out there. There are no social, prestige, or sexual games in the group; members go through some vital life experiences together; the reality-distorting facades are doffed as members become as honest as possible with one another. How many times have I heard group members say, "This is the first time I have ever told this to anyone." These are not strangers but quite the contrary; these are individuals far more likely to know one another deeply and fully. Psychological reality is not equivalent to physical reality. Psychologically, they spend infinitely more time together than the one or two meetings a week in which their physical beings occupy the same professionally sponsored room.

Overview

Let us now return to the primary task of this chapter: to define and describe the curative factor "interpersonal learning." All the necessary premises have been posited and described in our discussion of:

1. The importance of interpersonal relationships
2. The corrective emotional experience
3. The group as a social microcosm

If these principles are organized into a logical sequence, the mechanism of interpersonal learning as a curative factor becomes more evident.

1. The study of human behavior is the study of interpersonal relationships. Psychiatric symptomatology has both its origins and its contemporary expression in disturbed interpersonal relationships.
2. The psychotherapy group, provided its development is unhampered by

severe structural restrictions, evolves into a social microcosm, a miniaturized representation of each patient's social universe.

3. The group members, through consensual validation and self-observation, become aware of significant aspects of their interpersonal behavior:
   their strengths, their limitations, their parataxic distortions, and their
   maladaptive behavior which elicits unwanted responses from others.
   The patient in the past often has had a series of disastrous group experiences in which he has been rejected and consequently has gradually internalized a derogatory self-image. He has failed to learn from these experiences because the other members, sensing his general insecurity
   and abiding by the rules of etiquette governing normal social interaction,
   have not communicated to him the reasons for his rejection. He has
   never learned to discriminate between objectionable aspects of his behavior and a picture of himself as totally objectionable. The therapy
   group with its encouragement of accurate feedback makes such a discrimination possible.

4. A regular interpersonal sequence occurs:
   a. the member displays his behavior;
   b. through feedback and self-observation, he:
      (1) appreciates the nature of his behavior;
      (2) appreciates the impact of his behavior upon:
          (a) the feelings of others;
          (b) the opinions that others have of him;
          (c) the opinion he has of himself.

5. Once the patient is fully aware of this sequence, he also becomes aware
   of the fact that he is responsible for it; he is the author of his interpersonal world.

6. When he is fully and deeply aware of his responsibility for his interpersonal world, he may then begin to grapple with the corollary of this discovery: since he created his world, it is only he who can and must alter it.

7. The depth and meaningfulness of this awareness is directly proportional
   to the amount of affect associated with the sequence. The more real and
   the more emotionally laden the experience, the more potent is the impact; the more objectified and intellectualized the experience, the less
   effective the learning.

8. As a result of this awareness, the patient may gradually change or may
   more abruptly risk new types of behavior and expression. The likelihood
   that change will occur is a function of:
   a. the patient's motivation for change; the amount of personal discom-
      fort and dissatisfaction with current modes of behavior;
   b. the patient's involvement in the group, his need for acceptance by
      the group, his respect and appreciation of the other members;
   c. the rigidity of the patient's character structure and interpersonal
      style.

9. The change in behavior may generate a new cycle of interpersonal learning via self-observation and feedback from other members. Furthermore,
   the patient appreciates that some feared calamity which had hitherto
   prevented such behavior was irrational; his new behavior did not result

in such calamities as death, destruction, abandonment, derision, or engulfment.

10. The social microcosm concept is a bi-directional one; not only does outside behavior become manifest in the group, but behavior learned in the group is eventually carried over into the patient's social environment and alterations appear in his interpersonal behavior outside the group.

11. Gradually an *adaptive spiral* is set into motion, at first inside and then outside the group. As the patient's interpersonal distortions diminish, his ability to form rewarding relationships is enhanced. Social anxiety decreases, self-esteem rises, there is less need to conceal himself; others respond positively to this behavior and show more approval and acceptance to the patient, which further increases self-esteem and enhances further change. Eventually the adaptive spiral achieves such autonomy and efficacy that professional therapy is no longer necessary.

Each of these steps requires specific facilitation by the therapist. Different sets of therapist behaviors are needed: offering specific feedback, encouraging self-observation, clarifying the concept of responsibility, encouraging risk-taking, disconfirming fantasied calamitous consequences, reenforcement of transfer of learning, etc. Each of these tasks and techniques will be fully discussed in Chapter 5.

Before concluding the examination of interpersonal learning as a mediator of change, I wish to call attention to two concepts which deserve further discussion. "Transference" and "Insight" play too central a role in most formulations of the therapeutic process to be passed over lightly. I rely heavily on both of these concepts in my therapeutic work and do not mean to slight them. What I have done in this chapter is to embed them both into the mechanism of interpersonal learning.

Transference is a specific form of interpersonal perceptual distortion. In individual psychotherapy, the recognition and the working through of this distortion is of paramount importance. In group therapy, working through interpersonal distortions is, as we have seen, of no less importance; however, the range and variety of distortions is considerably greater. Working through distortion in his relationship to the therapist now becomes only one of a series of distortions to be examined by the patient.

For many patients, perhaps for the majority, it is the most important relationship to work through since the therapist is the living personification of all parental images, of teachers, of authority, of established tradition. But for most patients there is more that needs to be done. Patients can explore their competitive strivings toward their peers, their conflicts in the areas of assertion, of intimacy, of sexuality, of giving, of greed, of envy. The meager research [25,26,27] which does address this issue underscores the importance which many members place on working through relationships with other members rather than with the leader. We shall have a great deal more to say on this issue in Chapter 6.

"Insight" defies precise description; it is not a unitary concept. I prefer to employ it in its most general sense, encompassing clarification, explanation, and derepression. Insight occurs when the individual discovers something important about himself—about either his behavior, motivational system, fantasy life, or his unconscious.

In the group therapeutic process, patients may obtain "insight" on at least four different levels:

1. Patients may gain a more objective perspective on their interpersonal behavior. They may for the first time learn how they are seen by other people—how they manifest themselves interpersonally. Are they tense, warm, aloof, seductive, bitter, etc.?

2. Patients may gain some understanding into *what* they are doing to and with other people. Unlike what occurs on the first level, they learn more than how their disparate bits of behavior are seen by others; they learn instead about their dealings with others over a longer time span. Are they exploiting others, rejecting others, courting constant admiration from others, seducing and then withdrawing from others, relentlessly competing with others? Are they so needy of acceptance and love that their effacing behavior elicits the opposite response from others? What do they want from the therapist? From the other men or women in the group?

3. A third level of insight might be termed "motivational insight." Patients may learn *why* they do what they do to and with other people. Aloof, detached patients may begin to learn what they fear so much about intimacy. Competitive, vindictive, controlling patients may learn about their needs to be taken care of, to be nurtured. Seductive-rejecting individuals may learn more about their hostility and their dread of its consequences. A common form of insight is the discovery that one behaves in certain ways because of a belief that were he to behave differently, some catastrophe would occur: he would be humiliated, scorned, destroyed, abandoned, engulfed, rejected, or perhaps would himself become murderous or uncontrollable.

4. A fourth level of insight, "genetic insight," attempts to help patients understand how they got to be the way they are. Through an exploration of his developmental history, the patient understands the genesis of present patterns of behavior. The theoretical framework and the language in which the genetic explanation is couched are, of course, largely dependent on the therapist's school of conviction.

These four levels have been listed in the order of their implied degree of inference. An unfortunate and longstanding conceptual error has resulted, in part, from the tendency to equate a "superficial-

deep" sequence with this "degree of inference" sequence. Furthermore, "deep" has become equated with "profound" or "good" and
"superficial" equated with "bad," "obvious," and "inconsequential."
Many have come to believe that the more profound the therapist, the
deeper the interpretation (from a genetic perspective) and the more
complete the treatment; there is, however, not a shred of evidence to
support this contention. In fact, there is considerable question even
about the validity of our most revered assumptions about the relationship between types of early experience and adult behavior and
character structure.[28,29,30]

A fuller discussion of causality would take us too far afield from "Interpersonal Learning," but we shall return in depth to the issue in
Chapter 5. For now it is sufficient to emphasize that what is important
is that insight occur—insight in its generic, not its genetic, sense.
There is, in my view, little question that intellectual understanding is
one of the lubricants which facilitates the movement of the machinery
of change. In group therapy the "superficial-deep" (behavioral-
genetic; low inference-high inference) continuum by no means coin-
cides with a "least curative-most curative" continuum. In terms of
degree of occurrence and usefulness to the patient, there is a sharp
downward gradient between level three ("motivational") and level
four ("genetic") interpretations. Furthermore, all therapists have encountered the patient who has obtained a high degree of genetic insight based on some accepted child developmental theory, be it Freudian, Kleinian, Sullivanian, etc., and yet has made no therapeutic
progress. On the other hand, it is commonplace for significant clinical
change to occur in the absence of genetic insight; nor is there a demonstrated relationship between the acquisition of genetic insight and
the persistence of the change. It seems that in group therapy we need
to disengage the term "deep" or "profound" from temporal considerations: something that is deeply felt or has deep meaning and deep
significance for the patient may, or as is usually the case, may not be
related to the understanding of the early genesis of behavior.

REFERENCES

1. D. A. Hamburg, "Emotions in Perspective of Human Evolution," in P. Knapp,
    (ed.), *Expressions of the Emotions of Man* (New York: International Universities
    Press, 1963).

2. J. Bowlby, "The Nature of the Child's Tie to His Mother," *Int. J. Psychoanal.*, 39: 1–23, 1958.
3. W. Goldschmidt, as quoted by D. A. Hamburg, *op. cit.*, p. 308.
4. W. James, *The Principles of Psychology*, Vol. 1 (New York: Henry Holt, 1890), p. 293.
5. H. S. Sullivan, *The Interpersonal Theory of Psychiatry* (New York: W. W. Norton, 1953).
6. H. S. Sullivan, *Conceptions of Modern Psychiatry* (New York: W. W. Norton, 1940).
7. P. Mullahy, *The Contributions of Harry Stack Sullivan* (New York: Hermitage House, 1952).
8. *Ibid.*, p. 22.
9. *Ibid.*, p. 10.
10. H. S. Sullivan, "Psychiatry: Introduction to the Study of Interpersonal Relations," *Psychiatry*, 1: 121–134, 1938.
11. Sullivan, *Conceptions of Modern Psychiatry*, p. 207.
12. *Ibid.*, p. 237.
13. I. D. Yalom, J. Tinklenberg, and M. Gilula, "Curative Factors in Group Therapy." Unpublished study.
14. C. M. Parkes, "Effects of Bereavement on Physical and Mental Health—a Study of the Medical Records of Widows," *Brit. Med. J.*, 2: 274–279, 1964.
15. C. M. Parkes, "Recent Bereavement as a Cause of Mental Illness," *Brit. J. Psychiat.*, 110: 198–204, 1964.
16. A. S. Kraus and A. M. Lilienfeld, "Some Epidemiological Aspects of the High Mortality Rate in the Young Widowed Group," *J. Chron. Dis.*, 10: 207, 1959.
17. E. Kubler-Ross, *On Death and Dying* (New York: The Macmillan Company, 1969).
18. F. Alexander and T. French, *Psychoanalytic Therapy: Principles and Applications* (New York: Ronald Press, 1946).
19. F. Alexander, "Unexplored Areas in Psychoanalytic Theory and Treatment," in G. Daniels (ed.), *New Perspectives in Psychoanalysis Sandor Rado Lectures 1957–1963* (New York: Grune & Stratton, 1965), p. 75.
20. *Ibid.*, pp. 79–80.
21. J. Frank and E. Ascher, "The Corrective Emotional Experience in Group Therapy," *Am. J. Psychiat.*, 108: 126–131, 1951.
22. J. Breuer and S. Freud, *Studies On Hysteria* (London: The Hogarth Press Limited, 1955).
23. M. A. Lieberman, I. Yalom, and M. Miles, *Encounter Group: First Facts* (New York: Basic Books, 1973).
24. B. B. Wassel, *Group Analysis* (New York: Citadel Press, 1966).
25. B. Berzon, C. Pious, and R. Farson, "The Therapeutic Event in Group Psychotherapy: A Study of Subjective Reports by Group Members," *J. Indiv. Psychol.* 19: 204–212, 1963.
26. G. Talland and D. Clark, "Evaluation of Topics in Therapy Group Discussions," *J. Clin. Psychol.*, 10: 131–137, 1954.
27. J. Frank, "Some Values of Conflict in Therapeutic Groups," *Group Psychother.*, 8: 142–151, 1955.
28. L. W. Hoffman and M. Hoffman (eds.), *Review of Child Development Research*, Vol. 1 (New York: Russell Sage Foundation, 1964).
29. L. W. Hoffman and M. Hoffman (eds.), *Review of Child Development Research*, Vol. 2 (New York: Russell Sage Foundation, 1966).
30. P. Chodoff, "A Critique of the Freudian Theory of Infantile Sexuality," *Am. J. Psychiat.*, 123: 507–518, 1966.

3

GROUP
COHESIVENESS

❧

Beginning with the hypothesis that cohesiveness in group therapy is the analogue of "relationship" in individual therapy, this chapter deals with the available evidence for group cohesiveness as a curative factor and the various pathways through which group cohesiveness exerts a therapeutic influence.

For decades there has been strong clinical sentiment that successful individual therapy depends on the nature of the therapist-patient relationship; until recently, however, research confirmation has been lacking. In fact, Eysenck and others [1,2] have long maintained that the overall efficacy of psychotherapy has not been proven since their data indicate no measurable difference in outcome between treated and untreated patients. Hence, they saw little point in determining critical variables in so-called successful therapy.

In the past few years Bergin [3] and Truax and Carkhuff [2] have marshaled evidence that "patients receiving psychotherapy show significantly greater *variability* in personality change indices at the conclusion of psychotherapy than do the no-treatment controls. . . . In other words, treatment may be for better or for worse." [4] Some psychotherapists help their patients, whereas others may, in fact, do harm. If one, however, averages the effective and ineffective therapist recovery rates, only two-thirds of the patients will have been helped—the same figure cited by Eysenck for neurotics receiving no treatment.

Truax and Carkhuff pursued this finding by searching for the critical differences between effective and noneffective therapists.[5] In a series of rigorously controlled studies, they found that the successful therapist establishes a relationship with his patients which offers them "high levels of accurate empathy, non-possessive warmth and genuineness." [6] Others have demonstrated that patients who are liked or consider themselves liked by their therapist are more likely to improve in therapy.[7,8]

Furthermore, it has been long established that the quality of the relationship is independent of the individual therapist's school of conviction. Fiedler,[9,10] in a series of studies, states that expert clinicians from different schools (Adlerian, Freudian, nondirective) resemble one another (and differ from nonexperts in their own school) in their conception of the ideal therapeutic relation and in the nature of the relationship they themselves establish with their patients.

Thus, effective therapists generate a specific type of therapeutic relationship with their patients. Furthermore, patients attribute their improvement to the nature of this relationship.[11,12] The evidence supportive of the critical role of the relationship in individual therapy outcome is now so considerable that it compels us to ask whether "relationship" plays an equally critical role in group therapy. *It is obvious that the group therapy analogue of the patient-therapist relationship is a broader concept, encompassing the patient's relationship to his group therapist, to the other group members, and to the group as a whole.* At the risk of courting semantic confusion, I shall refer to all these factors within the term "group cohesiveness."

Definition of Cohesiveness

Cohesiveness is a widely researched, poorly understood, basic property of groups. Several hundred research articles exploring cohesiveness have been written, many with widely varying definitions. In general, however, there is agreement that groups differ from one another in the amount of "groupness" present. Those with a greater sense of solidarity or "we-ness" value the group more highly and will defend it against internal and external threats; voluntary attendance, participation, mutual help, defense of the group standards are all greater than in groups with less esprit de corps. There are many methods of measuring cohesiveness, and a precise definition depends upon the method employed. In this book cohesiveness is broadly defined as "the resultant of all the forces acting on all the members to remain in the group," [13] or more simply "the attractiveness of a group for its members." [14] There is also a difference between total group cohesiveness and individual member cohesiveness (or, more strictly, the indivudal's attraction to the group). The two, of course, are interdependent, and group cohesiveness is often computed by summing the indivudal members' level of attraction to the group; nevertheless, we must keep in mind that group members are differentially attracted to their group. At times we shall be referring to the therapy-facilitating effects of cohesiveness on the total group, while at other times we shall refer to the effects of an individual member's attraction to the group on his own process of therapy.

Before leaving the matter of definitions, it is well to remember that "group cohesiveness" is not per se a curative factor but instead a necessary precondition for effective therapy. When, in individual therapy, we say that "it is the relationship that heals," we do *not* mean that love or loving acceptance is enough; we mean that an ideal therapist-patient relationship creates conditions in which the necessary self-disclosure, intra- and interpersonal testing and exploration may unfold. In group therapy, similarly, group cohesiveness enhances the development of other important phenomena. Cohesiveness is not, for example, synonymous with intermember acceptance and understanding, but is interdependent with these factors. Cohesiveness is both a determinant and effect of intermember acceptance: the members of a highly cohesive therapy group will respond to one another in this manner more frequently than will the members of a non-cohesive group; groups with members who show high mutual understanding and acceptance are, by definition, cohesive.

Cohesiveness as a Therapeutic Factor in Group Psychotherapy

Although we have discussed the curative factors separately, they are, to a great degree, interdependent. Catharsis and universality, for example, are part processes. It is not the sheer process of ventilation that is important, it is not only the discovery of others' problems similar to our own and the ensuing disconfirmation of our wretched uniqueness that is important; it is the affective sharing of one's inner world and *then* the acceptance by others that seems of paramount importance. To be accepted by others brings into question the patient's belief that he is basically repugnant, unacceptable, or unlovable. Provided he adheres to the group's procedural norms, the group will accept an individual regardless of his past life, transgressions, or perceived failings in his social universe. Deviant life styles, history of prostitution, sexual perversion, heinous criminal offenses all can be accepted by the therapy group, provided norms of acceptance are established early in the group.

Very frequently psychiatric patients have had few opportunities for affective sharing and acceptance. The decreased opportunities stem from the fact that, because of disturbed interpersonal skills, they have had fewer intimate relationships. Furthermore, their conviction of the abhorrence of their impulses and fantasies has made interpersonal sharing even more difficult. I have known many isolated patients for whom the group represented their only deeply human contact. After only a few sessions, they have a deeper sense of being "at home" in the group than anywhere else. They may remember the sense of belonging and the basic acceptance years afterward, when most other recollections of the group have faded from memory. As one successful patient looking back over two and a half years of therapy put it, "The most important thing in it was just having a group there, people that I could always talk to, that wouldn't walk out on me. There was so much caring and hating and loving in the group and I was a part of it. I'm better now and have my own life, but it's sad to think that the group's not there anymore."

Some patients describe the group as a haven from the stress of life, a source of strength for them. One reason that American prisoners did poorly during the Korean conflict was that they were not permitted this source of stability. Chinese captors disrupted cohesive group formation by methodically removing emergent group leaders. The Turks, on the other hand, maintained their morale and group structure. Leadership among them was determined solely on the basis of military rank and seniority; as soon as one leader was removed, his role was filled automatically by the most senior remaining individual.

Patients may internalize the group. "It's as though the group is sitting on my shoulder, watching me. I'm forever asking, 'What would the group say about this or that?' " Often therapeutic changes persist and are consolidated because the members are disinclined to let the group down.[14]

Group membership, acceptance, and approval are of the utmost importance in the development of the individual. The importance of belonging to childhood peer groups, adolescent cliques, fraternities, the proper social "in" group can hardly be overestimated. There seems to be nothing of greater importance for the adolescent, for example, than to be included and accepted in some social group, and nothing more devastating than exclusion. Consider in the United

States the "blackball" suicides following exclusion from fraternities, or in the West Indies the bone-pointing voodoo deaths, the latter mediated by total exclusion from the community, which regards the outcast as dead from the time the voodoo spell is cast. Most psychiatric patients have an impoverished group history; never before have they been a valuable, integral, participating member of a group. For these patients, the sheer successful negotiation of a group experience may in itself be curative.

We rely on others not only for approval and acceptance but also for continual validation of our important value systems. *When Prophecy Fails* [15] is a study of a religious cult which had predicted the end of the world. When the doomsday passed without incident, the cult reacted, not with a crisis of doubt, but by increasing its proselytizing efforts; doubt in the belief system of the group apparently required a greater degree of interpersonal validation.

Thus, in a number of ways, members of a therapy group come to mean a great deal to one another. The therapy group, at first perceived as an artificial group which doesn't count, may in fact come to count very much. I have known groups to experience together severe depressions, psychoses, marriage, divorce, abortions, suicide, career shifts, sharing of innermost thoughts, and incest (sexual activity among the group members). I have seen a group mourn the death of one of its members and another group physically carry one of its members to the hospital. Relationships are often cemented by moving or hazardous adventures. How many relationships in life share such a panoply of vital experiences?

Evidence

Research evidence for the importance of group cohesiveness in the therapeutic process is rudimentary compared to the research documenting the importance of "relationship" in individual psychotherapy. Nevertheless, there are a few relevant studies in the group therapy and in the experiential group literature. (See Chapter 14 for a discussion of experiential ["encounter"] groups and for the justification of applying research on these groups to the group therapeutic process.)

Dickoff and Lakin,[16] in a study of former group psychotherapy patients, find that, from the patients' point of view, group cohesiveness is of major therapeutic value.* They transcribed and categorized patients' explanations of the curative factors in their group experience. The investigators found that "more than half of the former patients indicated that the primary mode of help in group therapy is through mutual support." Patients who rejected the group more frequently complained of not having experienced meaningful social contact with the other members. Those patients who perceived their group as cohesive attended more sessions, experienced more social contact with other members, and judged the group as having offered a therapeutic mode. Those patients who either reported themselves improved or expressed regret at having to leave the group prematurely were significantly more prone to have:

1. Felt accepted by the other members
2. Perceived similarity of some kind among group patients
3. Made specific references to particular individuals when queried about their group experience

The authors conclude that group cohesiveness is in itself of therapeutic value and is essential for perpetuation of the group.

Kapp *et al.*[17] arrive at similar conclusions after a study of forty-seven patients who had been in twelve different psychotherapy groups for a mean duration of thirteen months. They administered a questionnaire designed to measure self-perceived personality change and the individual's assessment of the degree of cohesiveness among the members of the group. The findings indicate that self-perceived personality change correlates significantly with both the members' feelings of involvement in the group and with their assessment of total group cohesiveness. The authors conclude that perceived group unity (cohesiveness) may be an important factor in promoting personality change.†

My colleagues and I conducted two studies which attest to the importance of cohesiveness in the group therapeutic process. In one project (Yalom, Tinklenberg, Gilula),[18] twenty successful group ther-

---

* Twenty-eight patients who had been in either clinic or private outpatient groups were studied. The chief limitation of this exploratory inquiry is that the group therapy experience was of exceptionally brief duration (mean number of meetings attended = 11).

† These findings are tentative. The instruments to measure change were not, as recognized by the authors, standardized for reliability or validity. Furthermore, when personality change and group cohesiveness are tested simultaneously by a self-administered questionnaire, we cannot control for the possibility that patients who are attracted to their groups will be inclined to support their stance by reporting or perceiving themselves as improved. Cognitive dissonance theory teaches us that when an individual has made a decision, he will misperceive, deny, and distort data which would discredit that decision.

apy patients were studied, and the relative importance of all the curative factors described in this book were assessed. This project will be reported in detail in the next chapter. For the present, it is sufficient to state that patients retrospectively considered cohesiveness to be of considerable import.

Yalom, Houts, Zimerberg, and Rand [19] examined at the end of a year all the patients (N = 40) who had started therapy in five outpatient groups. The degree of improvement in symptoms, functioning, and relationships was assessed both in a psychiatric interview by a team of raters and by a self-assessment scale. Outcome was then correlated with a host of variables which had been measured in the first three months of therapy. Positive outcome in therapy correlated with only two predictor variables—"group cohesiveness" * and "general popularity." † That is, patients who were most attracted to the group (high cohesiveness) and who were rated as more popular by the other group members at the sixth week and the twelfth week had a better therapy outcome at the fiftieth week. The popularity finding, which in this study correlated more positively with outcome than did cohesiveness, is, as we shall discuss shortly, quite relevant to group cohesiveness and sheds light upon the mechanism through which group cohesiveness mediates change.

Two highly relevant experiential group studies merit discussion. A rigorously designed study by Clark and Culbert [20] demonstrates a significant relationship between the quality of intermember relationships and outcome in a T-group of eleven subjects who met twice

---

* Cohesiveness was measured by a post-group questionnaire filled out by each patient at the seventh and at the twelfth meetings, consisting of eleven questions (each answered on a five-point defined scale):
1. How often do you think your group should meet?
2. How well do you like the group you are in?
3. If most of the members of your group decided to dissolve the group by leaving, would you like an opportunity to dissuade them?
4. Do you feel that working with the group you are in will enable you to attain most of your goals in therapy?
5. If you could replace members of your group with other "ideal group members," how many would you exchange (exclusive of group therapists)?
6. To what degree do you feel that you are included by the group in the group's activities?
7. How do you feel about your participation in, and contribution to, the group work?
8. What do you feel about the length of the group meeting?
9. How do you feel about the group therapist(s)?
10. Are you ashamed of being in group therapy?
11. Compared to other therapy groups, how well would you imagine your group works together?

† Popularity was measured sociometrically: each member, at the sixth and twelfth meetings, was asked to rank order all the group members for general popularity.

a week for a total of sixty-four hours. They correlated outcome * for the group members with intermember relationships.† Their results demonstrated that the members who entered into the most two-person mutually therapeutic relationships showed the most improvement during the course of the group. Furthermore, the perceived relationship with the group leader was unrelated to the extent of change. The authors conclude that the quality of the member-member relationship is a prime determinant of individual change in the group experience.

A large study of 210 subjects in eighteen encounter groups, encompassing ten ideological schools (gestalt, Transactional Analysis, N.T.L. "T" groups, Synanon, personal growth, Esalon, psychoanalytic, marathon, psychodrama, encounter tape) was conducted by Lieberman, Yalom and Miles.[23] (See Chapter 14 for a detailed discussion of this project.) Cohesiveness was assessed in three ways:

1. A critical incident questionnaire. Each member was asked, after each meeting, to describe the most significant event of that meeting. All events pertaining to group attraction, communion, belongingness, etc., were tabulated.
2. A cohesiveness questionnaire, quite similar to the one described in the Yalom, Houts, *et al.* study,[19] was administered early and late during the course of the group.
3. A "curative factor" questionnaire including a cohesiveness dimension was administered at the end of the group.

The results indicated that attraction to the group is indeed a strong determinant of outcome. All of the methods demonstrated a positive correlation between cohesiveness and outcome. If an individual experienced little sense of belongingness or attraction to the group, even when measured early in the course of the sessions, there was little hope that he would benefit from the group and, in fact, a high likelihood that he would have a negative outcome. Furthermore, the *groups* with the higher overall levels of cohesiveness had a significantly higher total outcome than those with low cohesiveness.

---

* Outcome was measured by a well-validated rating scale designed by Walker, Rablen, and Rogers [21] to measure change in the individual's ability to relate to others, to construe his experience, to approach his affective life, and to confront and cope with his chief problem areas. Samples of each member's speech were independently rated on this scale by trained naïve judges from taped excerpts early and late in the course of the group.

† Intermember relationships were measured by the Barrett-Lennard Relationship Inventory,[22] which provided a measure of how each member viewed each other member (and the therapist) in terms of "unconditional, positive regard, empathic understanding, and congruence."

Summary of Foregoing

We have cited evidence that patients in group therapy consider group cohesiveness to be a prime mode of help in their therapy experience. There is tentative evidence that self-perceived positive therapy outcome is related to individual attraction to the group. Individuals with positive outcome have had more mutually satisfying intermember relationships. Positive patient outcome is correlated with individual attraction to the group and also to group popularity, a variable related to group support and acceptance. Highly cohesive groups have an overall higher outcome. Although further controlled research is needed, these findings taken together do support the contention that group cohesiveness is an important determinant of positive therapeutic outcome.

There is, in addition to this direct evidence, considerable indirect evidence stemming from research with other types of groups. A plethora of studies demonstrates that in laboratory task groups, increased group cohesiveness produces many results which may be considered as intervening therapy outcome factors. For example, group cohesiveness results in better group attendance, greater participation of members, greater influenceability of the members, and many other effects. We shall consider these findings in detail shortly, as we attempt to determine the mechanism through which cohesiveness fosters therapeutic change.

Mechanism of Action

INTRODUCTION

For the remainder of this chapter we shall discuss the various ways in which cohesiveness produces change in group patients. How do group acceptance, group support, intermember trust and acceptance help troubled individuals? Surely there is more to it than simple support or acceptance; therapists learn very early in their careers that love is not enough, that therapy does not consist of merely furnishing affective supplies for the patient. Although the quality of the relationship is crucial, therapy consists of more than relating warmly and honestly to the patient. The relationship creates favorable conditions for other processes to be set into motion. What other processes? And how are they important? In this discussion we shall approach this question from many different perspectives, all or some of which may be valid for any given patient.

Perhaps no one has thought more deeply about the therapeutic relationship than Carl Rogers. Let us start our investigation by examining his views about the mode of action of the therapeutic relationship in individual therapy. In his most systematic description of the process of therapy,[24] Rogers states that when the conditions of an ideal therapist-patient relationship exist, a characteristic process is set into motion:

The patient is increasingly free in expressing his feelings.
He begins to test reality and to become more discriminatory in his feelings and perceptions of his environment, his self, other persons, and his experiences.
He increasingly becomes aware of the incongruity between his experiences and his concept of self.
He also becomes aware of feelings which have been previously denied or distorted in awareness.
His concept of self, which now includes previously distorted or denied aspects, becomes more congruent with his experience.
He becomes increasingly able to experience, without threat, the therapist's unconditional positive regard and to feel an unconditional positive self-regard.
He increasingly experiences himself as the focus of evaluation of the nature and worth of an object or experience.
He reacts to experience less in terms of his perception of others' evaluation of him and more in terms of its effectiveness in enhancing his own development.

Central to Rogers' views is his formulation of an "actualizing tendency," an inherent tendency of the organism to expand and to develop itself. The therapist in individual and in group therapy functions as a facilitator and must help create conditions favorable for self-expansion. The first task of the individual is self-exploration; he must begin to consider feelings and experiences previously denied awareness. This task is a ubiquitous stage in dynamic psychotherapy. Horney,[25] for example, emphasizes the individual's need for self-knowledge and self-realization, stating that the task of the therapist is to remove obstacles in the path of these autonomous processes. There is some experimental evidence that good rapport in individual therapy and cohesiveness in group therapy enable the individual to gain greater self-awareness. For example, Truax,[26] studying forty-five hospitalized patients in three heterogeneous groups, demonstrated that patients in cohesive groups will be significantly more inclined to engage in deep and extensive self-exploration (measured by the Rogers-Rablen scale [21]).

Over the last few years Rogers has become increasingly interested in the group experience as a therapeutic medium; and although his views of the important growth-potentiating factors in groups are similar to his views of those in the individual relationship, he has commented upon additional powerful factors inherent in the group setting. He underscores, for example, that member-member acceptance and understanding may carry with it a greater power and meaning than acceptance by a therapist. Other group members, after all, don't have to care, don't have to understand, they're not paid for it, it's not their "job." [27] This peer acceptance occurs regularly in childhood but not for many of our patients, who find validation by other group members a vital experience. In the affluence of modern American society, we have moved up the hierarchy of needs [28] from survival needs to emotional ones. Modern man, steeped in abundance, turns to the question, "With whom can I be personal?" With the breakup of the extended nuclear family and the isolation of contemporary life, the problem becomes a considerable one. The intimacy developed in a group may be seen as a counterforce in a culture "which appears to be bent upon dehumanizing the individual and dehumanizing our human relationships." [29] The deeply felt human experience in the group may be of great value to the patient, Rogers believes; even if there is no visible carryover, no external change in behavior, the patient may still experience a more human, richer part of himself and have this as an internal reference point.

Group members' acceptance of one another, though crucial in the group therapeutic process, may be quite slow to develop. Acceptance by others and self-acceptance are mutually dependent; not only is self-acceptance basically dependent on acceptance by others, but acceptance of others is fully possible only after the individual can accept himself. The members of a therapy group may experience considerable self-contempt and a deep contempt for others. A manifestation of this may be seen in the patient's initial refusal to join "a group of nuts" or his reluctance to become closely involved in the group for fear of being sucked into a maelstrom of misery. The importance of self-acceptance for the acceptance of others has been demonstrated in research by Rubin,[30] who studied fifty individuals before and after an intensive live-in two-week T-group laboratory and found that an increase in self-acceptance was significantly correlated with increased

acceptance of others. These results are consonant with Fromm's statement many years ago that only after one is able to love himself is he
able to love others. I would add, however, that only after he has once
been loved will he be able to love himself.

Although we have not yet used the term, we have begun to discuss
"self-esteem," a core concept in any approach to personality change.
Hamburg [31] has stated that all individuals seeking assistance from a
mental health professional have in common two paramount problems:
(1) a difficulty in establishing and maintaining meaningful interpersonal relationships and (2) a difficulty in maintaining a sense of personal worth (self-esteem). It is difficult to discuss these two interdependent areas as separate entities, but, since we have in the
preceding chapter dwelled more heavily on the establishment of interpersonal relationships, we shall now concentrate on self-esteem.

In a scholarly review and analysis of identity and esteem, from
which this discussion draws heavily, Miller [32] underscores the interdependence between self-esteem (the individual's evaluation of his
identity) and public esteem (the group's evaluation of the worth of
that aspect of his identity germane to that particular group). Self-
esteem refers to the individual's conception of what he is really like,
what he is really worth, and is indissolubly linked to his experiences
in social relationships. Recall Sullivan's statement, "The self may be
said to be made up of reflected appraisals." [33] The individual regards
and values himself as he, during his personal development, believed
others to have regarded and valued him. Depending upon the congruence of the individual's life experiences, he internalizes certain
relationships and learns to evaluate himself with a measure of independence, but to a greater or lesser degree he is always concerned
and influenced by his public esteem—the evaluation given him by the
groups to which he belongs.

How influenced the individual is by his public esteem in the group
and how inclined he is to use the group's frame of reference depends
on several factors: the importance of the group for him, the frequency
and specificity of the group's communications to him about his public
esteem, and the salience to him of the traits in question. (Presumably,
in therapy groups, the salience is very great indeed, since the traits in
question are close to his core identity.) In other words, the more the
group matters to him, the more he subscribes to the group values, the
more he will be inclined to agree with the group judgment.[34]

The self-esteem–public esteem system is thus closely related to the
concept of group cohesiveness. We have said that the degree of a
group's influence on self-esteem is a function of its cohesiveness. The

more attracted an individual is to the group, the more he respects the judgment of the group, the more he will attend to and take very seriously any discrepancy between his public esteem and his self-esteem. A discrepancy between the two will place the individual in a state of dissonance and he will initiate activity to remove the dissonance.

If this discrepancy veers to the *negative* side—if the group evaluates him less highly than he evaluates himself—how can he resolve the discrepancy? One recourse is to misperceive, deny, or distort the group's evaluation of his public esteem. In a therapy group, this development generates a vicious circle. His public esteem is low because of his nonparticipation in the group task, and any increase in communicational problems and defensiveness will only beget further devaluation of public esteem. Eventually, the group's communication to him will break through unless he uses near-psychotic mechanisms to distort reality.

Another more common method of dealing with the discrepancy is to devalue the group. He may rationalize, for example, that the group is an artificial one or one composed of highly disturbed individuals, and compare it unfavorably with some anchor group (for example, a social or an occupational group) which might evaluate him differently. This sequence, characteristic of the group history of "group deviants" described in Chapter 7, usually results in termination of membership.

A final and therapeutic method of resolving the discrepancy is for the individual to attempt to raise his public esteem by changing those traits and attitudes which have been criticized by the group. This method of resolution is more likely if the individual is highly attracted to the group and if the discrepancy between the low public esteem and higher self-esteem is not too great. Is this final approach—the use of group pressure to change individual behavior or attitudes—a form of conditioning? Is it not mechanical, neglecting deeper levels of integration, and thus destined for transience? Indeed, group therapy does employ conditioning principles; in fact, psychotherapy is, in all its variants, basically a form of learning. Even the most nondirective approach invokes operant conditioning techniques which are not, however, consciously employed by the therapist.[35] Patients learn through explicit statements or through more subtle implications what their therapists desire of them. However, these comments in no way imply a more superficial approach to behavior change or less enduring results, nor do they imply a dehumanization of the therapy process. Aversive or operant conditioning of behavior and attitudes is, in my opinion, neither feasible nor effective when approached as an isolated technique.* In fact, as I have repeatedly stressed, all the curative factors are intricately interdependent and must be appreciated as part of a complex spiraling process. Behavior and attitudinal change, regardless of origin, begets other changes. The group changes its evaluation of the patient, he feels more satisfied with himself in the group and with the group itself, and the adaptive spiral described in the previous chapter is initiated.

Far more common, in the properly guided therapy group, is a discrepancy in the opposite direction: the group evaluates the individual more highly than he evaluates himself. Once again the patient, in a state of dissonance, will attempt to resolve the discrepancy. In some groups he might seek to lower his public esteem by revealing inadequacies. However, in therapy groups, this behavior has the opposite effect of raising public esteem still more, since disclosure of inadequacies is a cherished group norm and further enhances acceptance by the group. Instead, the individual may begin to reexamine and reevaluate his low level of self-esteem. An illustrative clinical vignette may flesh out this bare-boned formulation.

Mrs. Ende, a thirty-four-year-old housewife with an emotionally impoverished background, sought therapy because of anxiety and guilt stemming from a series of extramarital affairs. Clinically, her self-esteem was exceedingly low; she was self-derogatory about her physical appearance and about her functioning as a mother and a wife. She had received some solace from her religious affiliation, though she had never considered herself good enough to socialize with the "church people" in her community. She had married a man whom she considered repugnant but nonetheless a good man and certainly good enough for her. Only in her sexual affairs, and particularly in an arrangement in which she had sexual relationships with several men at once, did she seem to come alive. Only here did she feel attractive, desirable, and able to give something of herself which seemed of value to others. However, this behavior clashed with her religious convictions and resulted in considerable anxiety and self-derogation.

Viewing the group as a social microcosm, the therapist soon noted characteristic trends in her group behavior. She related to the other members around sexual issues, and for many hours the group struggled with all the exciting ramifications of her sexual dilemma. At all other times in the group, however, she disengaged and offered nothing. She related to the group as to her social environment. She could not associate with the good church people and, in fact, felt she had nothing to offer save her genitals.

---

* Although lasting patient improvement is often reported following a removal, by behavioral therapy techniques, of some disabling complaint, closer inspection of the process inevitably reveals that important interpersonal relationships have been affected. Either the therapist-patient relationship has been more meaningful than the therapist realized or some important changes, initiated by the symptomatic relief, have occurred in the patient's social relationships which have served to reinforce and maintain the patient's improvement.

Her course of therapy consisted, in large part, of the gradual reexamination and eventual disconfirmation of her belief that she had nothing of value to offer others. As she began to respond to others, to offer warmth and support, to exchange problems and feelings, she found herself increasingly valued by other members. The public esteem–self-esteem discrepancy eventually widened to the point that upward shifts in her self-esteem levels resulted. Her behavior changed to such a point that meaningful nonsexual relationships in and out of the group were possible, and these in turn further enhanced self-esteem, thereby generating an adaptive spiral.

SELF-ESTEEM, PUBLIC ESTEEM, AND GROUP COHESIVENESS—EVIDENCE

Group therapy research has not specifically investigated the relationship between public esteem and shifts in self-esteem.* However, there are some interesting data on group popularity—a variable closely synonymous with public esteem. In the study [19] of forty group therapy patients previously described, we demonstrated that patients "elected" by the other members as most popular at the sixth and twelfth weeks of therapy had significantly better therapy outcomes than the other group members at the end of one year. Thus, it seems that patients who have high public esteem early in the course of the group are destined to have a better therapy outcome.

To understand this phenomenon, the investigators studied the determinants of popularity. What factors seemed responsible for the attainment of popularity in therapy groups? Three variables, which did not themselves correlate with outcome, correlated significantly with popularity, namely:

1. Previous self-disclosure.†
2. Interpersonal compatibility.‡ Individuals who had (perhaps fortuitously) those interpersonal needs which happen to blend well with those of the other group members become popular in the group.

* Lundgren and Miller [36] reported a relevant study on nonpatients in a Bethel T-group (see Chapter 14). They found that self-esteem decreased when public esteem (measured by sociometrics) decreased. They also discovered that the more a member underestimated his public esteem, the more acceptable he was to the other members; in other words, the ability to face one's deficiencies or even to judge oneself a little harshly increased one's public esteem. Humility, within limits, is far more adaptable than arrogance.

† Before beginning therapy the patients completed a questionnaire (a modified Jourard self-disclosure questionnaire) [37] which indicated that individuals who had previously disclosed much of themselves (relevant to the other group members) to close friends or to groups of individuals were destined to become popular in their groups. In a recent study, Hurley [38] demonstrated, in a ten-week counseling group, that popularity was correlated with self-disclosure *in* the group as well as prior to group therapy.

‡ Measured by the FIRO-B questionnaire (see Chapter 8).

3. Other sociometric measures; group members who were highly chosen as leisure companions or work committee colleagues became popular in the group.

A clinical study of the most popular and least popular members revealed that members, in their selection of popular patients, placed a premium on youth, education, intelligence, and the ability to introspect. The popular patients all assumed leadership in their groups, helping to fill the leadership vacuum which occurred early in the group when the therapist declined to assume the traditional leader role.

The most unpopular patients in our sample were markedly rigid, moralistic, nonintrospective, and least involved in the group task. Four were blatantly deviant in their groups and quickly became group isolates. They responded to this defensively, attacking the group and thereby ensuring their exclusion. Others who were more schizoid appeared frightened of the group process and remained on the periphery, never entering the interactional wave length of the group.

The Lieberman, Yalom, and Miles encounter group study [23] corroborated these conclusions. They found from a study of sociometric data (asking members to rank order one another on several variables) that members who were most influential were also those who engaged in behavior closely in harmony with encounter group values (risk-taking, spontaneity, openness, self-disclosure, expressivity, group facilitation and support). Furthermore, these members had a significantly higher outcome.

To summarize these findings, members attain a position of popularity and influence in groups by dint of active participation, self-disclosure, self-exploration, emotional expression, and leadership behavior. In short, we may say that they gain approval (and ultimately improve) in the group by participating maximally in the group task.

What is the task of a therapy group? Most therapy groups come to value:

1. Acceptance of the patient role
2. Self-disclosure
3. Honesty about feelings toward oneself and other members
4. Nondefensiveness
5. Interest in and acceptance of others
6. Support of the group
7. Personal improvement

Adherence to these behaviors is rewarded by the group. As Homans [39] has demonstrated, the member who abides most closely to the group norms is the member who is considered by the rest of the group as the most popular and the most influential.*

It is important to note that not only is the individual who adheres to the group norms rewarded by increased public esteem, but he also reaps other dividends. The behaviors required by the group norms will serve him in good stead in his relationships outside of the group. In other words, the social skills the individual uses in the group to attain popularity are reinforced by the popularity he achieves, and these very same skills are likely to help him deal more effectively with his interpersonal problems outside the group. Thus, increased popularity in the group acts therapeutically in two ways: by influencing self-esteem and by reinforcing adaptive social skills.

GROUP COHESIVENESS AND GROUP ATTENDANCE

Continuation in the group is obviously a necessary, though not sufficient, prerequisite for successful treatment. Several studies indicate that interactional group therapy is long-term therapy and that patients who terminate early in the course of therapy receive little benefit.[19,42,43,44] Over fifty patients who dropped out of therapy groups within the first twelve meetings reported that they did so because of some stress encountered in the group. They were neither satisfied with their therapy experience nor improved; indeed, many of Nash's [45] patients felt worse. Patients remaining in the group for at least several months, however, had a very high likelihood (85 percent in one study) [19] of profiting from therapy.

The greater the patient's attraction to the group, the more inclined he will be to continue membership in therapy groups [46] as well as in laboratory and task groups.[47,48] For example, Sagi et al.[47] found a significant correlation between attendance and group cohesiveness in twenty-three college student organizations. Yalom and Rand [44] studied cohesiveness among forty members of five therapy groups and found that the least cohesive members terminated within the first twelve meetings. In another study Yalom et al.[19] found that the members with the highest cohesiveness scores at the sixth and at the

* Bales,[40] in his research with leaderless discussion and task groups, has found that two leaders arise in the group: a "task executive" leader and a "social-emotional" leader. Only rarely are these two roles filled by the same person, "the great man." In therapy groups, however, when the therapist is omitted from the sociometric selection, the patients usually select the same person to fill these roles.[41]

twelfth meetings attended significantly more meetings during the year.

The Lieberman, Yalom, and Miles encounter group study [23] discovered a high correlation between low cohesiveness and eventual dropping out from the group. The dropouts did not have a sense of belongingness and most often dropped out because they felt rejected or attacked by the group.

The relationship between cohesiveness and maintenance of membership has implications for the total group as well. Not only do the least cohesive members terminate membership and fail to benefit from therapy, but noncohesive groups with a high patient turnover prove to be less therapeutic for the remaining members as well.

Stability of membership is a necessary condition for effective group therapy. Most therapy groups go through an early phase of instability, as some members drop out and replacements are added. Following this, the groups often enter into a long, stable phase in which much of the solid work of therapy occurs. Some groups seem to enter this phase of stability early, while others never achieve it. Dropouts at times beget other dropouts, some patients terminating soon after the departure of a key member. In a group therapy follow-up study,[18] patients often spontaneously underscored the importance of membership stability.* A study carried out in an inpatient facility for sexual offenders treated by group therapy indicated also that the overriding critical factor in successful outcome is a stable therapist-group relationship.[49]

GROUP COHESIVENESS AND THE
EXPRESSION OF HOSTILITY

It would be a mistake to equate cohesiveness with comfort. Although cohesive groups may show greater acceptance, intimacy, and

---

* What are the implications of these observations about membership stability for groups which cannot avoid considerable member turnover; for example, inpatient groups on a busy psychiatric admission ward? Must we conclude that such groups cannot be effective? I would suggest that the therapist must first recognize the inflexible conditions of his clinical setting and on the basis of these conditions formulate appropriate goals for the group. Obviously, a group which has new members entering and old members leaving every week cannot be conducted in the same fashion as long-term stable groups; moreover, the goals of the group experience must be altered. If the therapist hopes for important characterologic shifts in such a setting, he cannot avoid discouragement and eventual therapeutic pessimism.

What can be accomplished in a group in which every meeting must be considered as an entity rather than as an incomplete part of a process which unfolds over many understanding, there is evidence that they also permit greater development and expression of hostility and conflict.

Unless hostility is openly expressed, persistent and impenetrable hostile attitudes may develop which will hamper effective interpersonal learning. Hostility which is unexpressed simply smolders within only to seep out in many indirect ways, none of which facilitates the group therapeutic process. It is not easy to continue communicating honestly with someone you dislike. The temptation to avoid the other and to break off communication is very great, and yet when channels of communication are closed, so too are any hopes for conflict resolution, for personal growth and attitude change. As Frank [50] reminds us, this is as true on a national, megagroup level as on a dyadic level. Consider the experimental evidence offered by Sherif in his famed Robbers' Cave experiment.[51]

A camp of eleven-year-old well-adjusted boys was divided at the outset into two groups which were placed in competition with each other in a series of hotly contested events. Soon each group developed a high degree of cohesiveness and internal organization as well as a deep sense of hostility toward the other group. Any meaningful communication between the two groups became impossible. If, for example, they were placed in physical proximity in the dining hall, the group boundaries remained impermeable and the members merely exchanged taunts, insults, and spitballs.*

In the therapy process, communication must not be ruptured; the adversaries must continue to work together in a meaningful way, to take responsibility for their statements, and be willing to go beyond name calling. This is, of course, a major difference between therapy groups and social groups, in which conflicts often result in the permanent rupture of relationships. Patients' descriptions of the critical in-

months? There are many appropriate and realistic goals. Patients may share problems and concerns, thus alleviating their loneliness and sense of unique unworthiness. They may be taught social skills. They may learn simply that there is help to be obtained through talking and thus be better prepared and motivated to pursue psychotherapy after discharge. It is important, even if the patient's group experience consists of only a couple of meetings, that he encounter a group atmosphere of trust, mutuality, and support; otherwise, even the most limited goals cannot be attained.

* The communications block between the members of the two groups was finally relieved only by instilling a degree of cohesion and allegiance in a single large group. Some superordinate goals were created which disrupted the small group boundaries and forced the boys to work together in a single large group. For example, a truck carrying food for an overnight hike was stalled in a ditch and could be rescued only by cooperative efforts of all the boys; a highly desirable movie could be rented only by the pooled contributions of the entire camp; the water supply was cut off and similarly could be restored only by the cooperative efforts of all campers. What is needed for the resolution of terrestrial hostility, then, is an urgently felt worldwide crisis that only meganational cooperation could avert: e.g., a world pollution crisis, oxygen depletion, or, best of all, a Martian invasion.

cident in therapy (see Chapter 2) often involve an episode in which they expressed strong negative affect. However, in each instance they were able to weather the storm, to continue relating (often in a more gratifying manner) to the other member.

Underlying these events is the condition of cohesiveness. The group and the members must mean enough to each other so that they will be willing to bear the discomfort of working through the conflict. Cohesive groups are, in a sense, like families with much internecine warfare but nonetheless a powerful sense of loyalty.

Once the conditions are such that conflict can be constructively dealt with in the group, therapy is enhanced in many ways. We have already mentioned the importance of catharsis, of risk-taking, of gradually exploring previously avoided or unknown parts of oneself and recognizing that the anticipated dreaded catastrophe is chimerical. It is also important for many patients to have the experience of being aggressed against. In the struggle, as Frank [52] suggests, each may become better acquainted with the reasons for his position and learn to withstand pressure from another. The conflict may enhance self-disclosure, as each tends to reveal more and more of himself to clarify his position. As members are able to go beyond the mere statement of position, as they begin to understand the other's experiential world, past and present, and view the other's position from his frame of reference, they may begin to understand that the other's point of view may be as appropriate for him as their own is for themselves. The coming to grips with, working through, and eventual resolution of extreme dislike or hatred of another person is an experience of great therapeutic power.

A clinical illustration demonstrates many of these points. Susan, a forty-six-year-old proper school principal, and Jean, a twenty-one-year-old high school dropout, became locked into a vicious struggle. Susan despised Jean because of her libertine life style and what she imagined to be sloth and promiscuity. Jean was enraged by Susan's judgmentalism, her sanctimoniousness, her inveterate spinsterhood, her closed posture to the world. Fortunately, both were deeply committed members of the group. (Fortuitous circumstances played a part here. Jean had been a core member of the group for a year and then married and went abroad for three months. Just at that time Susan entered the group and during Jean's absence became heavily involved in the group.)

Both had had considerable past difficulty in expressing and dealing with anger. Over a four-month period of time they interacted heavily, at times in pitched battles (for example, when Susan erupted sanctimoniously upon learning that Jean was obtaining illegal food stamps and when Jean learned of Susan's virginity and ventured the opinion that Susan was a curious mid-Victorian relic). Much good group work was done; they learned a great deal about each other and eventually realized the cruelty of their mutual judgmentalism. Finally, they could both understand how much each meant for the other on both a personal and symbolic level. Jean desperately wanted Susan's approval; Susan deeply envied Jean for the freedom she had never permitted herself. In the working-through process, both fully experienced their rage; they encountered and then accepted previously unknown parts of themselves; they ultimately developed an empathetic understanding and then an acceptance of one another. Neither could possibly have tolerated the extreme discomfort of the conflict were it not for the strong cohesion which, despite the pain, bound them to the group.

Not only are cohesive groups more able to express intermember hostility, but there is evidence that they are also more able to express hostility toward the leader.* Regardless of the personal style or skill of the group leader, the therapy group will nonetheless come, often within the first dozen meetings, to experience some degree of hostility and resentment toward him. (See Chapter 10 for a full discussion of this issue.) He does not fulfill their fantasied expectations, he does not care enough, he does not direct enough, he does not offer immediate relief. If the group does not express these feelings openly, several harmful consequences may ensue. They may attack a convenient scapegoat, either another group member or some institution like "psychiatry" or "doctors"; they may suppress the anger only to experience a creeping irritation within themselves or the group; they may, in short, begin to establish norms discouraging open expression of resentment. On the other hand, it is clearly helpful to the group if they are able to express their hostility and then observe that no irreparable calamity has occurred. It is obviously better for the therapist to face this attack than some scapegoated member who will be far less able to

* A study by Pepitone and Reichling [53] offers experimental confirmation. Paid college student volunteers were divided into thirteen high and thirteen low cohesion laboratory task groups. Cohesion was created in the usual experimental manner: members of high cohesive groups were told before their first meeting that their group had been composed of individuals who had been carefully matched from psychological questionnaires to ensure maximum compatibility. The members of low cohesive groups were given the opposite treatment and were told the matching was unsuccessful and that they would probably not get along well together. The groups, while waiting for the experiment to begin, were systematically insulted by a member of the research staff. After he had left, the members of the high cohesive groups were significantly more able to express open and intense hostility about the authority figure. Wright [54] obtained similar findings in research on nursery school groups.

withstand and to understand it. Moreover, the process is a self-reinforcing one; a concerted effective attack on the leader which is handled in a non-defensive, non-retaliatory fashion serves to increase
cohesiveness still further. For example: One group in its eighth meeting spent much of the session on nonpersonal subjects such as poli-
tics, hypnosis, vacations, etc. Since some members were obviously
uninvolved, the therapist questioned what the group was doing. He
noted that one patient said she was bored, and he wondered why the
group was dealing with boring issues. An onslaught on the therapist
ensued; it was the first time the group had attacked him. Everyone as-
serted that he had been intensely interested in the discussion; they
wondered what the therapist's function was anyway; he was accused
of giving them all the same "line" before they entered therapy; and finally he was informed that the group was having a good controversial
discussion before he "butted in and changed the subject."

The group, as part of ongoing research, filled out questionnaires
after each meeting. Of great import was the fact that the members
rated the meeting, along several parameters, as the best they had ever
had.

GROUP COHESIVENESS AND OTHER
THERAPY—RELEVANT VARIABLES

Research has demonstrated in laboratory groups and dyads that
group cohesiveness has many other important consequences.[55,56]
Many of these have obvious relevance to the group therapeutic process; for example, it has been shown that the members of a cohesive
group, in contrast to the members of a noncohesive group, will: *

1. Try harder to influence other group members [57]
2. Be more influenceable by the other members [58]
3. Be more willing to listen to others [59] and are more accepting of others [60]
4. Experience greater security and relief from tension in the group [61]
5. Participate more readily in meetings [60,62]

  * These findings stem from experimentally composed groups and situations. To illustrate the methodology used in these studies, consider an experiment by Schachter,[57]
who organized groups of paid volunteers to discuss a social problem—the correctional
treatment of a juvenile delinquent with a long history of recidivism who is currently
awaiting sentence. In the manner described previously, several groups of low and high
cohesiveness were formed, and paid confederates were introduced into each group who
deliberately assumed an extreme position on the topic under discussion. The content of
the discussion, sociometric data, and other post-group questionnaires were than analyzed to determine, for example, the intensity of the efforts of the group to influence the
deviant and the degree of rejection of the deviant.

6. Protect the group norms and, for example, exert more pressure on individuals deviating from the norms [57,63]
7. Be less susceptible to disruption as a group when a member terminates membership [56]

Summary

By definition, cohesiveness refers to the attraction that members have for their group and for the other members. Members of cohesive groups are more accepting of one another, more supportive, more inclined to form meaningful relationships in the group. Cohesiveness seems to be a significant factor in successful group therapy outcome. In conditions of acceptance and understanding, patients will be more inclined to express and explore themselves, to become aware of and integrate hitherto unacceptable aspects of self, and to relate more deeply to others. Self-esteem is greatly influenced by the patient's role in a cohesive group. Social behavior demanded of highly cohesive members is heavily reinforced by the group and is eventually socially adaptive to the individual both in and out of the group. In addition, highly cohesive groups are more stable groups with better attendance and less turnover. Evidence was presented to indicate that this stability is vital to successful therapy: early termination precludes benefit for the involved patient and impedes the progress of the rest of the group as well. Cohesiveness favors the constructive expression of hostility in the group—an expression which may facilitate successful therapy in several ways.

What we have yet to consider are the determinants of cohesiveness. What are the sources of high and low cohesiveness? What does the therapist do to facilitate the development of a highly cohesive group? These important issues will be discussed in the chapters dealing with the group therapist's tasks and techniques.

REFERENCES

1. H. J. Eysenck, "The Effects of Psychotherapy," in H. J. Eysenck (ed.), *Handbook of Abnormal Psychology* (New York: Basic Books, 1961).
2. C. B. Truax and R. R. Carkhuff, *Toward Effective Counseling and Psychotherapy: Training and Practice* (Chicago: Aldine Publishing Co., 1967), pp. 6–14.

3. A. E. Bergin, "The Effects of Psychotherapy: Negative Results Revisited," *J. Counsel. Psychol., 10:* 244–250, 1963.
4. Truax and Carkhuff, *op. cit.*, p. 19.
5. *Ibid.*, p. 25.
6. *Ibid.*, pp. 82–143.
7. J. Seeman, "Counselor Judgments of Therapeutic Process and Outcome," in C. Rogers and R. Dymond (eds.), *Psychotherapy and Personality Change* (Chicago: University of Chicago Press, 1954).
8. M. B. Parloff, "Therapist-Patient Relationships and Outcome of Psychotherapy," *J. Consult. Psychol., 25:* 29–38, 1961.
9. F. Fiedler, "Factor Analyses of Psychoanalytic, Non-Directive and Adlerian Therapeutic Relationships," *J. Consult. Psychol., 15:* 32–38, 1951.
10. F. Fiedler, "A Comparison of Therapeutic Relationships in Psychoanalytic, Non-Directive and Adlerian Therapy," *J. Consult. Psychol., 14:* 436–445, 1950.
11. H. Strupp, R. E. Fox, and K. Lessler, *Patients View Their Psychotherapy* (Baltimore: The Johns Hopkins Press, 1969).
12. H. Feifel and J. Eells, "Patients and Therapists Assess the Same Psychotherapy," *J. Consult. Psychol., 27:* 310–318, 1963.
13. D. Cartwright and A. Zander (eds.), *Group Dynamics: Research and Theory* (Evanston, Ill.: Row, Peterson, 1962), p. 74.
14. J. D. Frank, "Some Determinants, Manifestations and Effects of Cohesion in Therapy Groups," *Int. J. Group Psychother., 7:* 53–62, 1957.
15. L. Festinger, H. W. Riecker, and S. Schachter, *When Prophecy Fails* (Minneapolis: University of Minnesota Press, 1956).
16. H. Dickoff and M. Lakin, "Patients' Views of Group Psychotherapy: Retrospections and Interpretations," *Int. J. Group Psychother., 13:* 61–73, 1963.
17. F. T. Kapp *et al.*, "Group Participation and Self-Perceived Personality Change," *J. Nerv. Ment. Dis., 139:* 255–265, 1964.
18. I. D. Yalom, J. Tinklenberg, and M. Gilula, "Curative Factors in Group Therapy." Unpublished study.
19. I. D. Yalom, P. S. Houts, S. M. Zimerberg, and K. H. Rand, "Prediction of Improvement in Group Therapy," *Arch. Gen. Psychiat., 17:* 159–168, 1967.
20. J. B. Clark and S. A. Culbert, "Mutually Therapeutic Perception and Self-Awareness in a T-Group," *J. Appl. Behav. Sci., 1:* 180–194, 1965.
21. A. M. Walker, R. A. Rablen, and C. Rogers, "Development of a Scale to Measure Process Changes in Psychotherapy," *J. Clin. Psychol., 16:* 79–85, 1960.
22. G. T. Barrett-Lennard, "Dimensions of Therapist Response as Causal Factors in Therapeutic Change," *Psychol. Monogr., 76:* No. 43, 1962.
23. M. A. Lieberman, I. Yalom, and M. Miles, *Encounter Groups: First Facts* (New York: Basic Books, 1973).
24. C. Rogers, "A Theory of Therapy, Personality and Interpersonal Relationships," in S. Koch (ed.), *Psychology: A Study of a Science, Vol. 3* (New York: McGraw-Hill, 1959), pp. 184–256.
25. K. Horney, *Neurosis and Human Growth* (New York: W. W. Norton, 1950), p. 15.
26. C. Truax, "The Process of Group Therapy: Relationships between Hypothesized Therapeutic Conditions and Intrapersonal Exploration," *Psychol. Monogr., 75:* No. 5111, 1961.
27. C. Rogers, personal communication, April 1967.
28. A. H. Maslow, *The Farther Reaches of Human Nature* (New York: Viking Press, 1972).
29. C. Rogers, "The Process of the Basic Encounter Group," unpublished mimeograph, Western Behavioral Science Institute, La Jolla, California, 1966.
30. I. Rubin, "The Reduction of Prejudice Through Laboratory Training," *J. Appl. Behav. Sci., 3:* 29–50, 1967.
31. D. A. Hamburg, personal communication, 1965.
32. D. Miller, "The Study of Social Relationships: Situation, Identity, and Social Interaction," in Koch, *op. cit.*, pp. 639–737.
33. H. S. Sullivan, *Conceptions of Modern Psychiatry* (London: Tavistock, 1955), p. 22.
34. Miller, *op. cit.*, p. 696.

35. E. J. Murray, "A Content Analysis for Study in Psychotherapy," *Psychol. Monogr.*, *70:* No. 13, 1956.
36. D. Lundgren and D. Miller, "Identity and Behavioral Change in Training Groups," *Human Relations Training News*, *9*, Spring 1965.
37. S. Jourard, "Self-Disclosure Patterns in British and American College Females," *J. Soc. Psychol.*, *54:* 315–320, 1961.
38. S. Hurley, "Self-Disclosure in Small Counseling Groups," unpublished doctoral thesis, Michigan State University, 1967.
39. G. C. Homans, *The Human Group* (New York: Harcourt, Brace, 1950).
40. R. F. Bales, "The Equilibrium Problem in Small Groups," in A. Hare, E. Borgatta, and R. F. Bales (eds.), *Small Groups: Studies in Social Interaction* (New York; Knopf, 1962), pp. 424–456.
41. I. D. Yalom and P. S. Houts, unpublished data.
42. I. D. Yalom, "A Study of Group Therapy Dropouts," *Arch. Gen. Psychiat.*, *14:* 393–414, 1966.
43. G. Bach, *Intensive Group Therapy* (New York: Ronald Press, 1954).
44. A. E. Bergin and S. Garfield (eds.), *Handbook of Psychotherapy and Behavior Change* (New York: John Wiley and Sons, 1971).
45. E. Nash, J. Frank, L. Gliedman, S. Imber, and A. Stone, "Some Factors Related to Patients Remaining in Group Psychotherapy," *Int. J. Group Psychother.*, *7:* 264–275, 1957.
46. I. D. Yalom and K. Rand, "Compatibility and Cohesiveness in Therapy Groups," *Arch. Gen. Psychiat.*, *13:* 267–276, 1966.
47. P. C. Sagi, D. W. Olmstead, and F. Atalsek, "Predicting Maintenance of Membership in Small Groups," *J. Abnorm. Soc. Psychol.*, *51:* 308–311, 1955.
48. L. Libo, *Measuring Group Cohesiveness* (monograph; Ann Arbor, Mich.: Institute for Social Research, 1953).
49. S. W. Morgan, personal communication, 1967.
50. J. Frank, *Sanity and Survival: Psychological Aspects of War and Peace* (New York: Vintage Books, 1968), p. 125.
51. M. Sherif, O. J. Harvey, E. J. White, W. R. Hood, and C. W. Sherif, *Intergroup Conflict and Cooperation: The Robbers' Cave Experiment* (Norman, Okla.: University of Oklahoma Book Exchange, 1961).
52. J. Frank, "Some Values of Conflict in Therapeutic Groups," *Group Psychother.*, *8:* 142–151, 1955.
53. A. Pepitone and G. Reichling, "Group Cohesiveness and the Expression of Hostility," *Human Relations*, *8:* 327–337, 1955.
54. M. E. Wright, "The Influence of Frustration Upon the Social Relations of Young Children," *Character and Personality*, *12:* 111–122, 1943.
55. D. Cartwright and A. Zander, "Group Cohesiveness: Introduction," in *Group Dynamics: Research and Theory*, pp. 69–74.
56. A. Goldstein, K. Heller, and L. Sechrest, *Psychotherapy and the Psychology of Behavior Change* (New York: John Wiley and Sons, 1966).
57. S. Schachter, "Deviation, Rejection and Communication," *J. Abnorm. Soc. Psychol.*, *46:* 190–207, 1951.
58. Cartwright and Zander, *op. cit.*, p. 89.
59. K. Back, "Influence Through Social Communication," *J. Abnorm. Soc. Psychol.*, *46:* 398–405, 1951.
60. G. Rasmussen and A. Zander, "Group Membership and Self-Evaluation," *Human Relations*, *7:* 239–251, 1954.
61. S. Seashore, *Group Cohesiveness in the Industrial Work Group* (monograph; Ann Arbor, Mich.: Institute for Social Research, 1954).
62. Goldstein *et al.*, *op. cit.*, p. 329.
63. A. Zander and A. Havelin, "Social Comparison and Intergroup Attraction," cited in Cartwright and Zander, *Group Dynamics: Research and Theory*, p. 94.

4

CURATIVE FACTORS— OVERVIEW

❧

The inquiry into the curative factors in group therapy began with the rationale that the delineation of these factors would lead to the development of systematic guidelines for the tactics and strategy of the therapist. The compendium of curative factors presented in Chapter 1 is, I believe, a comprehensive one but yet not in a form which has great clinical applicability. For one thing, the factors have, for the sake of clarity, been considered as separate entities when in fact they are intricately interdependent. I have taken the therapy process apart to examine it and am now obliged to put it back together again.

One question this chapter will consider is: How do the curative factors operate when they are viewed not separately but as part of a dynamic process? A second issue to be considered is the comparative potency of the curative factors. Obviously, not all are of equal value. However, an absolute rank ordering of curative factors is not possible. Many contingencies must be considered. The importance of various curative factors depends upon the type of group therapy practiced. Some are important at one stage of the group, whereas others predominate at another. Even within the same group, different patients benefit from different curative factors. Some factors are not mechanisms for change as much as they are conditions for change; for example, Chapter 1 describes how instillation of hope may serve largely to prevent early discouragement and to keep patients in the group until other, more potent forces for change come into play.

Our efforts to evaluate and integrate the curative factors will, to some extent, always remain conjectural. There is little truly definitive research demonstrating the efficacy of any of the curative factors and even less research bearing on the question of the comparative value or the interrelation of these factors. Nor may we ever expect to attain a high degree of certainty. I do not speak from a position of investigative nihilism but instead argue that the nature of our data is so highly subjective that, to a large degree, it makes scientific methodology inapplicable. What we must do is to learn to live effectively with uncertainty, to consider the best available evidence from research and from intelligent clinical observation, and to evolve a reasoned therapy which offers the great flexibility needed to cope with an infinite range of human problems.

Comparative Value of the Curative Factors— The Therapist's View

Many group therapists have published their opinions about group therapeutic curative factors. A review of this vast literature reveals the range of curative factors but little about their comparative value. Moreover, it is possible that the various schools of conviction are not equally represented in print; the Rogerian school, for example, because of its academic roots and large number of Ph.D. dissertations and ancillary studies, commands a disproportionately large share of the literature.

Corsini and Rosenberg,[1] in a widely cited report, abstracted the curative factors from three hundred pre-1955 group therapy articles; 175 factors were clustered into nine major categories, which show considerable overlap with the factors I have described. Their categories and my analogous categories are:

1. Acceptance (analogous to "group cohesiveness")
2. Universalization ("universality")
3. Reality testing (includes elements of "recapitulation of the primary family" and "interpersonal learning")
4. Altruism
5. Transference (includes elements of "interpersonal learning," "group cohesiveness," and "imitative behavior")
6. Spectator therapy ("imitative behavior")
7. Interaction (includes elements of "interpersonal learning" and "cohesiveness")
8. Intellectualization (includes elements of "imparting of information")
9. Ventilation ("catharsis")

The considerable overlap between the two sets of curative factors increases confidence in the exhaustiveness of the factors posited in this book.

One pertinent issue that must be raised here is the question of whether or not the curative factors (and relevant leader behavior) deemed important by the therapists actually occur in the group; it is possible that the therapist's belief system may show little correlation with his actual behavior. There are some interesting studies that highlight this issue.

Fiedler's study,[2] described in Chapter 3, indicates that experts, regardless of their schools of conviction, closely resemble one another in the nature of their relationship with patients. Heine,[3] who studied the patients of therapists from different schools (psychoanalytic, Adlerian, non-directive), found that the successfully treated patients attributed their improvement to similar factors, regardless of the particular discipline of the therapist. Truax and Carkhuff's work,[4] discussed in Chapter 3, brings further evidence to support the conclusion that effective therapists operate similarly in that they establish a warm, accepting, understanding relationship with their patients. Strupp, Fox, and Lessler,[5] in a comprehensive study of 166 patients in individual therapy, reached a similar conclusion: successful patients underscore the fact that their therapists were attentive, warm, respectful, and, above all, "human."

In their research on encounter groups, Lieberman, Yalom, and Miles [6] (see Chapter 14) studied leaders from ten different ideological schools. They closely observed the actual behavior of the leader and learned that the ideological school (what leaders believed, what they said they did) bore little relation to their actual behavior. For example, two Transactional Analysis leaders resembled each other no more closely than they resembled any of the other sixteen leaders in the study. The researchers devised a new classification of leader style based on actual behavior and found that these new clusters of leader styles correlated with outcome; there were patterns of leader behavior (for example, extensive provision of support and cognitive structuring) which were unrelated to ideological schools and were highly conducive to successful outcome.

These studies suggest, then, that successful therapists closely resemble one another in several areas highly relevant to successful outcome and that the proclaimed differences between schools may be more apparent than real.

Two other studies approach this topic from another perspective and compare the views of the successfully treated patient and his therapis about the factors responsible for his successful outcome. Feifel and Eells [7] studied seventy-three patients and their twenty-eight psychoanalytically oriented therapists. They found that, although the patients attributed their successful therapy to relationship factors, their therapists gave precedence to technical skills and techniques. Blaine and McArthur [8] did a detailed retrospective study of the psychoanalytically oriented treatment of two patients. The patients and their therapists were interviewed and queried about the factors regarded as therapeutic turning points: significant insights, derepression, etc. There were startling differences between the patients and the therapist. Major differences occurred in the weighting of unconscious factors which were made conscious and the correlation between childhood experiences and present symptoms; the therapist placed great importance on these factors, whereas the patients "denied that this sort of thing had occurred in therapy." The patients valued the personal elements of the relationship, the encounter with a new, accepting type of authority figure, and their changed self-image and perception of other people. A turning point in the treatment of one of the patients starkly illustrates the differences. In the midst of treatment the patient had an acute anxiety attack and demanded and was granted an emergency interview with the therapist. Both therapist and patient regarded the incident as a critical one: the therapist, because he thought that during the emergency session there had been a derepression of memories of early incestuous sex play and a subsequent freeing up and working through of oedipal material; the patient, on the other hand, considered the content of the emergency session unimportant and instead valued the meeting because of the relationship implications—the fact that the therapist would see him in the middle of the night conveyed a caring and concern that was of the utmost importance.

A similar discrepancy between the patient's and therapist's view of therapy is to be found in a book (*Every Day Gets a Little Closer*, Basic Books, 1974) which I co-authored with a patient (Ginny Elkin). Throughout the course of treatment she and I wrote independent, impressionistic summaries of each meeting, each remembering and valuing different aspects of our work together: I, the intellectual, interpretive conquests, and she the soft, personal exchange.

These studies, then, demonstrate that although effective therapists of different disciplines may disagree cognitively about the curative processes in therapy, they resemble one another operationally. Furthermore, therapists and their patients may have different views about the responsible curative factors in their therapy. Although many of these findings stem from individual psychotherapy research, it is highly likely that they have equal pertinence to group therapy. It is important to note that in the studies so far considered there is a common conceptual thread running through the patients' views about therapy. They consistently emphasize the importance of the relationship and the personal, human qualities of their therapists. Let us now look at the few studies dealing with the assessment by group psychotherapy patients of the curative factors in the therapy process.

Comparative Value of the Curative Factors— the Patient's View

I shall cite four studies which bear on this issue: two examining the views of patients in short-term therapy, one studying members of encounter groups, and one studying patients after long-term successful group therapy.

Berzon *et al.*[9] studied eighteen members of two outpatient, time-limited therapy groups which met for fifteen sessions. After each meeting the patients filled out a questionnaire in which they described the incident which they considered the most personally important. Two hundred and seventy-nine incidents were obtained and then sorted by three judges into nine categories, which were, in order of frequency:

1. Increased awareness of emotional dynamics—a broad category in which the subject "was helped to acquire new knowledge about himself, his strength and weakness, his pattern of interpersonal relating, his motivations, etc."
2. Recognizing similarity to others
3. Feeling positive regard, acceptance, sympathy for others
4. Seeing self as seen by others
5. Expressing self congruently, articulately, or assertively in the group
6. Witnessing honesty, courage, openness, or expressions of emotionality in others
7. Feeling responded to by others
8. Feeling warmth and closeness generally in the group
9. Ventilating emotions

The authors noted that the main curative mechanisms were reported to reside in the interaction between group members; few of the reports involved the therapists. Interpersonal feedback enabled the patients to restructure their self-image and to validate the universality of problems.

Dickoff and Lakin [10] studied twenty-eight former members of two outpatient groups run by one psychiatrist. The patients attended an average of eleven group sessions. In a semistructured interview the patients' retrospective views about the curative factors in group therapy were discussed. Responses were taped, transcribed, and sorted by two judges into categories constructed a priori as they emerged from the data:

1. Support (reduction of isolation, universality, sharing problems, learning to express oneself)
2. Suppression (including catharsis)
3. Tools for action (understanding problems, insight of interpersonal and intrapersonal nature)

The results demonstrated that social support was experienced by the patients as the chief therapeutic mode. From the patients' point of view, group cohesiveness was seen as not only necessary for perpetuation of the group but in itself of great therapeutic value. The "tools for action" category was considered by far the least important by the patients; however, there was a significant correlation between high verbal I.Q. and the selection of this category.

The encounter group study by Lieberman, Yalom, and Miles [6] investigated the members' views of the mechanisms of change in two different ways: (1) the most significant incident of the session (collected at the end of each session) and (2) a mechanism of change questionnaire completed at the end of the group. The study is a large one and the data very complex; we shall summarize the major conclusions.

Data from the significant incident questionnaire indicated that though experiencing and expressing feelings is a commonly cited significant incident, it did not seem to be related to successful outcome (those members who had poorer outcomes were as likely as high changers to consider this a significant event). This is not to say that these experiences are unrelated to learning; it means only that, in themselves, they are not sufficient. It seemed that emotional experiencing and expression were necessary to the group, that the group would be dismal in their absence, but that they were not enough. Something else is needed. The same may be said for self-disclosure and spectatorism (learning through watching others); both, in themselves, were unrelated to outcome, but when combined with *some type of cognitive learning* they were clearly related to successful outcome.

In fact, a pervasive, and surprising, finding was the overall importance of some form of cognition (insight, accumulation of information about oneself, etc.) in the process of change. What is surprising is that encounter groups are commonly thought to eschew "head trips"; yet no matter how the data was approached, cognition was clearly seen to be an essential cog in the gears of change.

The data from the mechanism of learning questionnaire led to similar conclusions. These are the fourteen items in the questionnaire listed in order of frequency cited by the members with positive outcome. (However, only those items with an asterisk were chosen significantly more often by the members with successful outcome than by the members who were unchanged by the group experience.)

1.	Feedback (I learned about my impact on others.)
2,3,4 (tie)	Universality
	* Received advice or suggestions
	* Understanding—discovering previously unknown parts of self
5.	* Cohesiveness
6,7,8,9 (tie)	* Recapitulation of family experience
	* Getting insight into the causes of my hang-ups
	Catharsis
	Altruism
10.	Experimenting with new forms of behavior
11.	Imitative behavior
12.	Revealing embarrassing things about myself and still being accepted
13.	Existential
14.	* Instillation of Hope

These data will be discussed later. For now it is sufficient to note that though feedback, universality, and catharsis were commonly chosen, they were also commonly selected by those who did *not* have successful outcomes. Hence, we could conclude that they represent necessary but not sufficient conditions for change. Other items such as "insight," received advice, cohesiveness, and recapitulation of family experience seemed to be robust mechanisms of change.

We must exercise some caution in evaluating the findings of these three studies. The Berzon and the Dickoff and Lakin studies deal with only the early stages of group therapy (less than fifteen meetings), whereas the Lieberman, Yalom, and Miles project studied encounter groups (of nonpatients) lasting a total of thirty hours. When, however, the findings are considered with those of the next study, then we do arrive at a position of considerable internal consistency.

Yalom, Tinklenberg, and Gilula [11] studied the curative factors in twenty successful long-term group therapy patients. This study will be described in greater detail than the others since I have not reported it elsewhere and because I draw upon it considerably in this book. This is in keeping with the general plan of calling to the reader's attention the nature of the data from which important conclusions are derived.

The investigators asked a number of group therapists who were leading groups of middle-socioeconomic-class outpatients with neurotic or characterologic problems for their most successful patients * who had recently terminated or were about to terminate group therapy. The subjects were required to have been in therapy a minimum of eight months. The range of duration of therapy was eight months to twenty-two months; the mean duration was sixteen months. All nominated subjects (N = 20) completed a curative factor Q-sort and were interviewed by the three investigators.

CURATIVE FACTORS—Q-SORT

Twelve categories of curative factors were constructed from the sources outlined throughout this book,† and five items describing each category were written, making a total of sixty items, which are listed in Table 1. Each item was typed on a 3 x 5 card; the patient was given the stack of randomized cards and asked to place a specified number of cards into seven piles labeled in the following manner:

1. Most helpful to me in the group (2 cards)
2. Extremely helpful (6 cards)
3. Very helpful (12 cards)
4. Helpful (20 cards)

* There were four checks to ensure that our sample was a successfully treated one: (1) the therapists' evaluation, (2) length of treatment (previous research [12] in the same clinic demonstrated that group patients who remained in therapy for that length of time had an extremely high rate of improvement), (3) the investigators' independent interview ratings of improvement along a thirteen-point scale in four areas—symptoms, functioning, interpersonal relationships, and self-concept, and (4) the patients' self-rating along the same scale.

† The list of sixty curative factor items passed through several versions and was circulated among many senior group therapists for suggestions, additions, or deletions. Some of the items are nearly identical, but it was convenient methodologically to have the same number of items representing each category. The twelve categories are: altruism; group cohesiveness; universality; interpersonal learning, "input"; interpersonal learning, "output"; guidance; catharsis; identification; family reenactment; self-understanding; instillation of hope; existential factors. They are not quite identical to those described in this book; we attempted, unsuccessfully, to divide interpersonal learning into two parts—input and output. One category, "self-understanding," was included to permit examination of the importance of derepression and genetic insight.

5. Barely helpful (12 cards)
6. Less helpful (6 cards
7. Least helpful to me in the group (2 cards) *

TABLE 1
Curative Factors

Rank Order

1. Altruism	1.	Helping others has given me more self-respect.	40 T (tie)
	2.	Putting others' needs ahead of mine.	52 T
	3.	Forgetting myself and thinking of helping others.	37 T
	4.	Giving part of myself to others.	17
	5.	Helping others and being important in their lives.	33 T
2. Group Cohesiveness	6.	Belonging to and being accepted by a group.	16
	7.	Continued close contact with other people.	20 T
	8.	Revealing embarrassing things about myself and still being accepted by the group.	11 T
	9.	Feeling alone no longer.	37 T
	10.	Belonging to a group of people who understood and accepted me.	20 T
3. Universality	11.	Learning I'm not the only one with my type of problem; "We're all in the same boat."	45 T
	12.	Seeing that I was just as well off as others.	25 T
	13.	Learning that others have some of the same "bad" thoughts and feelings I do.	40 T
	14.	Learning that others had parents and backgrounds as unhappy or mixed up as mine.	31 T
	15.	Learning that I'm not very different from other people gave me a "welcome to the human race" feeling.	33 T

* The number in each pile thus approaches a normal distribution curve and facilitates statistical assessment. For further information about the Q-sort technique, see J. Block, *The Q-Sort Method in Personality Assessment and Psychiatric Research.*[13]

Rank Order

4. Interpersonal Learning, "Input"	16.	The group's teaching me about the type of impression I make on others.	5 T
	17.	Learning how I come across to others.	8
	18.	Other members honestly telling me what they think of me.	3
	19.	Group members pointing out some of my habits or mannerisms that annoy other people.	18 T
	20.	Learning that I sometimes confuse people by not saying what I really think.	13 T

5. Interpersonal Learning, "Output"	21.	Improving my skills in getting along with people.	25 T
	22.	Feeling more trustful of groups and of other people.	10
	23.	Learning about the way I related to the other group members.	13 T
	24.	The group's giving me an opportunity to learn to approach others.	27 T
	25.	Working out my difficulties with one particular member in the group.	33 T

6. Guidance	26.	The doctor's suggesting or advising something for me to do.	27 T
	27.	Group members suggesting or advising something for me to do.	55
	28.	Group members telling me what to do.	56
	29.	Someone in the group giving definite suggestions about a life problem.	48 T
	30.	Group members advising me to behave differently with an important person in my life.	52 T

7. Catharsis	31.	Getting things off my chest.	31 T
	32.	Expressing negative and/or positive feelings toward another member.	5 T
	33.	Expressing negative and/or positive feelings toward the group leader.	18 T
	34.	Learning how to express my feelings.	4
	35.	Being able to say what was bothering me instead of holding it in.	2

Rank Order

8. Identification

36. Trying to be like someone in the group who was better adjusted than I.   58
37. Seeing that others could reveal embarrassing things and take other risks and benefit from it helped me to do the same.   8
38. Adopting mannerisms or the style of another group member.   59
39. Admiring and behaving like my therapist.   57
40. Finding someone in the group I could pattern myself after.   60

9. Family Reenactment

41. Being in the group was, in a sense, like reliving and understanding my life in the family in which I grew up.   51
42. Being in the group somehow helped me to understand old hang-ups that I had in the past with my parents, brothers, sisters, or other important people.   30
43. Being in the group was, in a sense, like being in a family, only this time a more accepting and understanding family.   44
44. Being in the group somehow helped me to understand how I grew up in my family.   45 T
45. The group was something like my family—some members or the therapists being like my parents and others being like my relatives. Through the group experience I understand my past relationships with my parents and relatives (brothers, sisters, etc.).   48 T

10. Self-Understanding

46. Learning that I have likes or dislikes for a person for reasons which may have little to do with the person and more to do with my hang-ups or experiences with other people in my past.   15
47. Learning why I think and feel the way I do (i.e., learning some of the causes and sources of my problems).   11 T
48. Discovering and accepting previously unknown or unacceptable parts of myself.   1

Rank Order

10. Self-
    Understanding
    (continued)

49. Learning that I react to some people or situations unrealistically (with feelings that somehow belong to earlier periods in my life).   20 T

50. Learning that how I feel and behave today is related to my childhood and development (there are reasons in my early life why I am as I am).   50

11. Instillation
    of Hope

51. Seeing others getting better was inspiring to me.   42 T

52. Knowing others had solved problems similar to mine.   37 T

53. Seeing that others had solved problems similar to mine.   33 T

54. Seeing that other group members improved encouraged me.   27 T

55. Knowing that the group had helped others with problems like mine encouraged me.   45 T

12. Existential
    Factors

56. Recognizing that life is at times unfair and unjust.   54

57. Recognizing that ultimately there is no escape from some of life's pain and from death.   42 T

58. Recognizing that no matter how close I get to other people, I must still face life alone.   23 T

59. Facing the basic issues of my life and death, and thus living my life more honestly and being less caught up in trivialities.   23 T

60. Learning that I must take ultimate responsibility for the way I live my life no matter how much guidance and support I get from others.   5 T

INTERVIEW

Following the Q-sort, which took approximately thirty to forty-five minutes, each patient was interviewed for an hour by the three investigators. Their reasons for their choice of the most and least helpful items were reviewed and a series of other areas relevant to curative factors was discussed (e.g., other, nonprofessional therapeutic influences in their lives, critical events in therapy, goal changes, timing of improvement, curative factors in their own words).

RESULTS

A sixty-item, seven-pile Q-sort for twenty subjects makes for complex data. Perhaps the clearest way to consider the results is a simple rank ordering of the sixty items.* Turn again to the list of sixty items (Table 1). The number after each item represents its rank order. Thus, item 48 ("discovering and accepting previously unknown or unacceptable parts of myself") was considered the most important curative factor by the consensus of patients; item 38 ("adopting mannerisms or the style of another group member") the least important, and so on. ("T" represents a tie.)

The ten items deemed most helpful to the patients were (in the order of importance):

48. Discovering and accepting previously unknown or unacceptable parts of myself.
35. Being able to say what was bothering me instead of holding it in.
18. Other members honestly telling me what they think of me.
34. Learning how to express my feelings.
16. The group's teaching me about the type of impression I make on others.
32. Expressing negative and/or positive feelings toward another member.
60. Learning that I must take ultimate responsibility for the way I live my life no matter how much guidance and support I get from others.
17. Learning how I come across to others.
37. Seeing that others could reveal embarrassing things and take other risks and benefit from it helped me to do the same.
22. Feeling more trustful of groups and of other people.

Note that seven of the first eight items represent some form of catharsis or of "insight." I again use "insight" in the broadest sense; the items, for the most part, reflect the first level of insight (gaining an objective perspective of one's interpersonal behavior) described in Chapter 2. This remarkable finding lends considerable weight to the principle, described in Chapter 2, that therapy is a dual process consisting of emotional experience and reflection upon that experience. More about this later.

If we turn our attention away from the individual items and onto the

* Arrived at by ranking the sum of the 20 pile placements for each item.

twelve general categories,* we see that they rank in order of importance.†

1. Interpersonal input
2. Catharsis
3. Cohesiveness
4. Self-understanding
5. Interpersonal output
6. Existential factors
7. Universality
8. Instillation of hope
9. Altruism
10. Family reenactment
11. Guidance
12. Identification

Rather than discuss this study further, I shall instead incorporate these findings in a broader discussion of questions posited at the beginning of this chapter; viz., the interrlationships of the curative factors and their comparative potency.

CATHARSIS

Catharsis has always assumed an important role in the therapeutic process, though the rationale behind its use has varied considerably. For centuries patients have been purged to cleanse themselves of excessive bile, evil spirits, and infectious toxins. Since Breuer and Freud's 1895 treatise on the treatment of hysteria, many therapists have attempted to help patients rid themselves of suppressed, choked affect. What Freud and subsequently all dynamic psychotherapists (except, as we have discussed, certain revivalist cults such as primal screamers) have learned is that catharsis is not enough. After all, we have emotional experiences, sometimes very intense ones, all our lives without ensuing change.

The data support that conclusion. The Lieberman, Yalom, and Miles study and the Berzon study starkly illustrate the limitations of catharsis per se. Those members whose critical experiences consisted

---

* The twelve categories are used only for our analysis and interpretation. The patients, of course, were unaware of these categories and dealt only with the sixty randomized items. The rank of each category was obtained by summing the mean rank of the five items (as rated by twenty patients).

† In considering these results, we must keep in mind that the subject's task was a forced sort, which means that the least chosen items are not necessarily unimportant but are, instead, less important relative to the others.

only of strong emotional expressions were not destined for a positive outcome; in fact, there was a slightly better chance that they would have a negative growth experience. In the group therapy curative factor study, the more heavily chosen items in the catharsis set conveyed a sense of something further than the sheer act of ventilation: "*Being able to* say what was bothering me" or "*Learning how to* express my feeling" convey a sense of liberation, of acquiring skills for the future. "Expressing feelings toward another member" indicates the role of catharsis in the ongoing interpersonal process. The item (#31) conveying a pure sense of ventilation was an underchosen one. Interviews with the patients investigating the reasons for their selection of items confirmed this view. Catharsis is part of an interpersonal process; no one ever claimed enduring benefit from ventilating feelings in an empty closet. Furthermore, as we discussed in Chapter 3, the strong expression of emotion enhances the development of cohesiveness; members who express strong feelings toward one another and work honestly with these feelings will develop close mutual bonds.

In summary, then, the open expression of affect is without question vital to the group therapeutic process; in its absence a group would degenerate into a sterile academic exercise. Yet it is only a part process and must be complemented by other factors.

One last point. The intensity of emotional expression is highly relativistic and must be appreciated not from the leader's perspective but from the perspective of each member's experiential world. A seemingly muted expression of emotion may, for a highly constricted individual, represent an event of considerable intensity.

EXISTENTIAL FACTORS

The category labeled "Existential Factors" was almost an afterthought. We first constructed the Q-sort instrument with eleven major factors. It appeared neat and precise but incomplete. Something was missing. Important sentiments expressed by both patients and therapists had not been represented, and we dutifully constructed a factor consisting of these five items:

1. Recognizing that life is as times unfair and unjust
2. Recognizing that ultimately there is no escape from some of life's pain and from death
3. Recognizing that no matter how close I get to other people, I still face life alone

4. Facing the basic issues of my life and death, and thus living my life more honestly and being less caught up in trivialities
5. Learning that I must take ultimate responsibility for the way I live my life no matter how much guidance and support I get from others

Several issues are represented in this cluster: responsibility, basic isolation, contingency, the recognition of our mortality and the ensuing consequences for the conduct of our life, the thrownness or capriciousness of existence. What to label this category? We finally settled, with much hesitation, on "Existential Factors." I didn't care for the word "existential"—it had become embedded in its own mystique; it meant something to everyone yet nothing precise to anyone.

Despite the desultory origin of this category, it was clear that the "existential" items struck some very responsive chords in the patients, and many cited some of these five statements as having been crucially important to them. In fact, the entire category of "Existential Factors" was ranked highly by the patients, ahead of such greatly valued modes of change as universality, altruism, recapitulation of the primary family experience, guidance, identification, and instillation of hope. One of the items—"Learning that I must take ultimate responsibility for the way I live my life no matter how much guidance and support I get from others"—was very highly ranked by the patients, and its mean score ranked it fifth of the entire sixty items! It is important to listen to our data; obviously, the existential factors in therapy deserve far more consideration than they generally receive.

It is more than happenstance that the "Existential Factors" category was included almost as afterthought and yet proved to be so very important to patients. Existential factors play an important but generally unrecognized role in psychotherapy. It is only when therapists look deeply at their techniques and at their basic view of man that they discover, usually to their surprise, that they are existentially oriented. Most dynamically oriented therapists who use analytically oriented technique inwardly eschew or at best inattend to much of the fundamental, mechanistic analytic theory. Classical psychoanalytic theory is based quite explicitly on a specific, highly materialistic view of man's nature.

It is not possible to understand Freud fully without considering his allegiance to the Helmholtz School, an ideological school which dominated Western European medical and basic research in the latter part of the nineteenth century. The basic Helmholtzian doctrine was simply stated:

No other forces than the common physical-chemical ones are active within the organism; that, in those cases which cannot at the time be explained by these

forces one has either to find the specific way or form of their action by means
of the physical-mathematical method, or to assume new forces equal in dignity to the chemical-physical forces inherent in matter, reducible to the force
of attraction and repulsion.[14]

Freud never swerved from his adherence to this postulate and to its
implications about man's nature; many of his more cumbersome, more
relentless formulations (for example, the dual instinct theory, the
theory of libidinal energy conservation and transformation) were the
result of his unceasing attempts to fit man and man's behavior to
Helmholtzian rules. This doctrine posits that man is precisely the sum
of his parts; it is deterministic, antivitalistic and materialistic in that it
attempts to explain the higher by the lower. *The Helmholtzian mani-
festo constitutes a negative definition of the existential approach.* If
you feel restricted by its definition of you, if you feel that there's
something missing, that the doctrine has no place for some of the central features that made us human—i.e., purpose, responsibility,
sentience, will, values, courage—then to that degree you are an
existentialist.

This is not the place for a thorough treatise on the ideological development of the existential approach in psychotherapy. I have written
on this elsewhere and refer interested readers to that publication.[15]
For now, it is perhaps sufficient to note that modern existential therapy represents an application of two merged philosophical traditions.
The first is substantive—Lebens-philosophie (the philosophy of life,
or Philosophical Anthropology) and the second is methodological—phenomenology—a more recent tradition, fathered by Ed-
mund Husserl, which argued that the proper realm of the study of man
was consciousness itself. Understanding thus takes place from within,
by bracketing the natural world and attending instead to the inner experience which is the author of the natural world.

The existential therapeutic approach, with its emphasis on choice,
freedom, responsibility, meaning in life, contingency, has until recently been far more acceptable to the European therapeutic community than to the American one. The European philosophic tradition,
the geographic and ethnic confinement, the greater familiarity with
limits, war, death, and uncertain existence all favored the spread of
the existential influence. The American Zeitgeist of expansiveness,
optimism, limitless horizons, and pragmatism embraced instead the
Scientific Positivism profferred by a mechanistic Freudian metaphys-
ics or a hyper-rational, empirical behaviorism (strange bedfellows).

Recently, however, a major development in American psychotherapy has been the emergence of what has come to be known as the

"third force" in American psychology (third after Freudian Psycho-analysis and Watsonian Behaviorism). This force has often been la-beled "Humanistic Psychology," and its influence upon modern ther-apeutic practice has been enormous. Note, however, that there has been an Americanization as well as an importation of the European existential tradition. The frame is European but the accent is unmis-takeably New Worldish. The European focus is on the tragic dimen-sions of existence, on limits, on facing and taking into oneself the anxi-ety of uncertainty and non-being. The humanistic psychologists, on the other hand, speak less of limits and contingency than of human po-tentiality, less of acceptance than of awareness, less of anxiety than of peak experiences and oceanic oneness, less of life meaning than of self-realization, less of apartness and basic isolation than of I-Thou and encounter.

Of course, when one has a basic doctrine with a number of postu-lates and the accent of each postulate is systematically altered in a specific direction, there is significant risk of mutation of the original doctrine. To some extent this has occurred, and some humanistic psy-chologists have lost touch with their existential roots and espouse a narrow, simplistic goal of "self-actualization" with an associated set of quick actualizing techniques. This is a most unfortunate develop-ment; it is most important to keep in mind that the existential ap-proach in therapy is not a set of technical procedures but basically an attitude toward man, his concerns, and his change.

The items in the Q-sort that struck meaningful chords in patients related to their arriving at certain important but painful truths about their existence. They realized that there were limits to the guidance and support they could receive from others and that the ultimate re-sponsibility for the conduct of their lives was theirs alone. They learned also that though they could be close to others, there was none-theless a point beyond which no one could accompany them: there is a basic aloneness to existence which must be faced and cannot be avoided. Many patients learned to face their limitations and their mor-tality with greater candor and courage. Coming to terms with one's own death in a deeply authentic fashion permits one to cast the trou-blesome concerns of everyday life in a different perspective. It per-mits one to trivialize life's trivia.

The course of therapy of Gail, a patient who at the end of treatment selected the existential Q-sort items as having been instrumental in her improvement, illustrates many of these points. Gail was a twenty-five-year-old perennial student who complained of depression, loneliness, purposelessness, and se-vere gastric distress for which no organic cause could be found. In her initial session she lamented repetitively, "I don't know what's going on!" I could not discover what precisely she meant by this and since it was embedded in a lengthy litany of self-accusations, I soon forgot it. However, in the group, too, she did not understand what happened to her: she could not understand why others were so uninterested in her, why she developed a conversion paralysis, why she entered sexually masochistic relationships, why she became so infatuated with the therapist.

In the group Gail was boring, dull, and absolutely predictable. Before every utterance she scanned the sea of faces about her looking for clues as to what others wanted and expected. She was willing to be almost anything so as to avoid offending others and possibly driving them away from her. (Of course, it resulted in her driving others away, not from anger but from boredom.) Gail was in chronic retreat from life, and the group tried endless approaches to halt the retreat, to find Gail within the cocoon of compliance she had spun about herself.

However, no progress occurred until the group stopped encouraging Gail, stopped attempting to force her to socialize, to study, to write papers, to pay bills, to buy clothes, to groom herself, but instead urged her to consider the blessings of failure. What was there in failure that was so seductive and so rewarding? Quite a bit, it turned out! Failing kept her young, kept her protected, kept her from deciding. Being infatuated with the therapist served the same purpose. Help was "out there." He knew the answers; her job in therapy was to enfeeble herself to the point where the therapist could not in all good conscience withhold his royal touch.

A critical event occurred when she had a biopsy performed on an enlarged axillary node. She feared cancer and came to the group that day still awaiting the results of the biopsy (which ultimately proved to be benign). She had never been so near to her own death before, and we helped Gail plunge into the terrifying loneliness she experienced. There are two kinds of loneliness—the existential, primordial loneliness that Gail confronted then, and a social loneliness, an inability to "be with." The second, the social loneliness, is commonly and easily worked with in a group therapeutic setting. Basic loneliness is more rarely faced: groups often confuse the two and try to take away one's basic loneliness. But it cannot be taken away, it cannot be resolved, it can only be known.

Rather quickly, then, many things came together for Gail. Far-strewn bits fell into place. She began to make decisions and to take over the helm of her life. She commented, "I think I know what's going on" (I had long forgotten her initial complaint). More than anything else, she had been trying to avoid the specter of loneliness. I think she tried to elude it by staying young, by avoiding choice and decision, by perpetuating the myth that there would always be someone who would choose for her, would accompany her, would always be there for her. Choice and freedom invariably imply loneliness, and as Fromm pointed out long ago, tyranny holds less terror for us than freedom.

Recall the Q-sort item that so many patients found important: "Learning that I must take ultimate responsibility for the way I live my life no matter how much guidance and support I get from others." In a sense, this is a double-edged factor in group therapy. Members learn what they *cannot* obtain from others. It is a harsh lesson and leads both to despair and to strength. One cannot stare at the sun very long, and Gail on many occasions looked away and avoided her dread. Always she came back to it, however, and by the end of therapy had made major shifts within herself.

Therapy groups often tend to water down the tragedy of life. Their natural currency is interpersonal theory, and if care is not taken, they will make the error of translating existential concerns into interpersonal ones, which are more easily grasped in the group. For example, as Gail's case illustrated, existential loneliness may be erroneously translated into social loneliness. Another incorrect translation occurs when we mistake feelings of powerlessness arising from awareness of our basic contingency for a powerlessness based on a sense of social inferiority. The group misses the point completely if it attempts to deal with the first, the fundamental feeling of powerlessness, by attempting to increase the individual's sense of social adequacy.

An extreme experience, for example Gail's encounter with a possibly malignant lymph node, brings us sharply back to reality and places our concerns in their proper perspective. Extreme experience, however, occurs only rarely during the course of the therapy group. Some group leaders attempt to generate extreme experience by using a form of existential shock therapy. With a variety of techniques, they try to bring patients to the edge of the abyss of their existence. I have seen leaders begin groups, for example, by asking each patient to compose the epitaph of their tombstones. "Destination labs" may begin with each member drawing his lifeline and marking upon it his present position: how far are they from their births, how close to their deaths? But our capacity for denial is enormous and it is the rare group that perseveres, that does not slip back into less threatening concerns. Natural events in the course of a group—illness, death of others, and termination and loss—may jolt the group back, but always temporarily.

Some time ago I began a group composed of patients who lived continuously in the midst of extreme experience. All the members had a terminal illness, generally metastatic carcinoma, and all were entirely aware of the nature and implications of their illness. I learned a great deal from that group; I especially learned about the fundamental but concealed issues of life that are so frequently neglected in traditional psychotherapy.

For one thing, the members were deeply supportive to one another and it was extraordinarily helpful for them to be helpful to one another. Offering help so as to receive it in reciprocal fashion was only one and not the most important aspect of the benefits to be gained.

Being useful to someone else drew them out of a morbid self-absorption and provided them with a sense of purpose and meaning. Almost every terminally ill person I have spoken to has expressed deep fear of a helpless immobility—not only of being a burden to others and being unable to care for oneself but of being useless and without value to others. Living, then, becomes reduced to survival, and the individual searches within, ever more deeply, for meaning. The group offered them the opportunity to find meaning outside of themselves. By activity, by extending help to another person, and by caring for others they find the sense of purpose which so often eludes the passive introspective gaze.

The support they offered one another took many forms. They provided transportation to meetings, they maintained telephone vigils when a member was in deep despair, they shared their methods of coping and of gaining strength: one, for example, taught the group meditational procedures, and every meeting thereafter ended with the group, in darkness, meditating over a lighted candle to ease their minds of pain and dread. In a number of ways the group provided the members power to transcend themselves, to extend themselves into others. They welcomed student observers and community interest. They were eager to teach and to share their experiences.

They began the group with a common bond of enmity toward the medical profession. Much time was devoted to disentangling the threads of this anger. Some of the anger was displaced and irrational—anger at fate, envious anger at the living, anger at doctors for not being all-knowing, all-powerful, and all-protecting. Some of the anger was entirely justified—anger at the doctors' lack of sensitivity, at their impersonality, their lack of time, their unwillingness to keep the patient fully informed and to include them in all important management decisions. We attempted to understand the irrational anger and place it where it belonged—on our basic thrownness and on the contingency of our existence. We faced the justifiable anger and attempted to cope with it by striving for effectance, by, for example, inviting oncologists and medical students to the group and by participating in medical school classes and conferences.

All of these approaches, these avenues to the outside of oneself, can, if well-traveled, lead to increased meaning and purpose as well as to an increased ability to bear what cannot be changed. Nietszche, long ago, wrote: He who has a "why" to live can bear with almost any "how."

It was clear to me that the members of this group who plunged most deeply into themselves, who confronted their fate most openly and resolutely, passed into a mode of existence which was richer than that prior to their illness. Their life perspective is radically altered; the trivial, inconsequential diversions of life are seen for what they are. There is a fuller appreciation of the more elemental features of living: the changing seasons, the last spring, falling leaves, the loving of others. Rather than resignation, powerlessness, and restriction, some have experienced a great sense of liberation and autonomy. Most of the group members carry their own time bomb; they keep themselves alive by taking some form of medication, generally a steroid, and thus make a decision daily whether to live or to die. No one takes his life with absolute seriousness until he fully comes to terms with his power to end his life.

We are all very familiar with the centrality of the quality of the therapeutic relationship in the process of change. In group therapy a sound, trusting relationship between the therapist and the patients and between the patients themselves is a necessary mediating condition: it enhances trust, risk-taking, self-disclosure, feedback, constructive conflict, working through problems centering around intimacy, etc. But in addition to these mediating functions, the basic, intimate encounter has an intrinsic value, a value in itself and for itself.

What can the therapist do in the face of the inevitable: I think that the answer lies in the verb "to be." He does by being, by being there with the patient. "Presence" is the hidden agent of help in all forms of therapy. When patients look back on their therapy they rarely remember a single interpretation of the therapist, but they always remember his presence, that he was there with them. It asks a great deal of the therapist to join this group, yet it is hypocrisy not to join. The group configuration is not the therapist and "they," the dying, but it is us, we who are dying, we who are banding together in the face of our common condition. The group so well demonstrates the double meaning of the word apartness: we are separate, lonely, apart from but also a part of. One of my members put it elegantly when she described herself as a lonely ship in the dark. Even though no physical mooring could be made, it was nonetheless enormously comforting to see the lights of other ships sailing the same water.

SELF-UNDERSTANDING

The curative factor Q-sort also underscores the important role that the intellectual component plays in the therapeutic process. Of the twelve categories, the two pertaining to self-understanding ("interpersonal input" and "self-understanding") were ranked first and fourth, respectively, by the patients.

"Interpersonal input" refers to learning how others perceive and experience one. It is the crucial first step in the therapeutic sequence of the curative factor of Interpersonal Learning and was discussed at some length in Chapter 2.

The category of "self-understanding" is more problematic. It was constructed to permit investigation of the importance of derepression and of the intellectual understanding of the relationship between past and present ("genetic insight"). When we examine the five items of this category (Table 1), it is clear that the category is an inconsistent one which contains several very different elements. There is poor correlation among items, some are very heavily valued, and some underchosen. The item #48 referring to discovering previously unknown parts of oneself is the most valued single item of all the sixty. Two items (#46 and #47) which refer to understanding causes of problems and to recognizing the existence of parataxic distortion are also highly valued. The item (#50) most explicitly referring to genetic insight is considered of little value by patients.

When we interviewed patients to learn more about the meaning of their choices, we found that the most popular item (#48—"discovering and accepting previously unknown or unacceptable parts of myself") had a very specific implication to them. More often than not they discovered *positive* areas of themselves—the ability to care for another, to relate closely to others, to experience compassion. There is an important lesson to be learned here. Too often psychotherapy, especially in naïve, popularized, or 1920 conceptualizations, is viewed as a detective search, as a digging or a stripping away. Rogers, Horney, Maslow, and our patients as well remind us that therapy is also exploration horizontally and upward; digging or excavation may uncover our riches and treasures as well as shameful, fearful, or primitive aspects of ourselves. Maslow states that "uncovering psychotherapy *increases* love, courage, creativity and curiosity while it *reduces* fear and hostility. This kind of therapy does not create from nothing; the implication is that it uncovers what was there in the first place." [16]

Thus, one way that self-understanding promotes change is that it encourages individuals to recognize, to integrate, and to give free expression to previously dissociated parts of themselves. When we deny or stifle parts of ourselves, we pay a heavy price—we feel a deep amorphous sense of restriction, we are "on guard," we are often troubled and puzzled by inner, yet alien, impulses demanding expression.

When we can reclaim these split-off parts, we experience a wholeness and a deep sense of liberation.

So far so good. But what of the other components of the intellectual task? For example, how does "learning why I think and feel the way I do" (item 47) result in therapeutic change?

First, we must recognize that there is a heavy press for intellectual understanding in the psychotherapeutic enterprise—a press which comes from both patient and therapist. Our search for understanding is deeply rooted. Maslow,[17] in a treatise on motivation, posited that man has cognitive needs which are as basic as his needs for safety, love, and self-esteem. Monkeys in a solid enclosure will do considerable work for the privilege of being able to look through a window at the laboratory outside; furthermore, they will work hard and persistently to solve puzzles without any reward except for the satisfactions inherent in the puzzle-solving itself. Most children are dangerously curious; in fact, we grow concerned if they lack curiosity about their environment. Considerable observational and experimental evidence indicates that psychologically healthy individuals are positively attracted to the mysterious and unexplained.[16,18]

So patients automatically search for understanding, and therapists who always prize their intellectual capacities join them. Often, it all seems so natural that we lose sight of the raison d'être of therapy. After all, the object of therapy is change, not self-understanding. Or is it? Or are the two synonymous? Or does any and every type of self-understanding lead automatically to change? Or is the quest for self-understanding simply an interesting, appealing, reasonable exercise for patients and therapist to engage in, serving, like mortar, to keep the two joined together while something else, perhaps "relationship," occurs, which is the real mutative force in therapy?

It is far easier to pose these questions than to answer them. I will present some preliminary arguments here, and in the next chapter, after developing some material on the interpretative task and techniques of the therapist, I will attempt to present a coherent thesis.

If we examine the motives behind our curiosity and our proclivity to explore our environment, we shed some light on the process of change. These motives include *effectance* (our desire for mastery and power), *safety* (our desire to render the unexplained harmless through understanding), and *pure cognizance* [16] (our desire for knowledge and exploration for its own sake).

The worried householder who explores a mysterious and frightening noise in his home; the young student who, for the first time, looks through a microscope and experiences the exhilaration of understanding the structure of an insect wing; the medieval alchemist or the New World explorer probing uncharted and proscribed regions—all receive their respective rewards: safety, a sense of personal keenness and satisfaction, and mastery in the guise of knowledge or wealth.

Of these motives, the one least relevant for the change process is the pure cognizance motive. There is little question that knowledge for its own sake has always propelled man; the lure of the forbidden is an extraordinarily popular and ubiquitous motif in folk literature from the story of Adam and Eve to the saga of Peeping Tom. It is no surprise, then, that the desire to know enters the psychotherapeutic arena; yet there is little evidence that understanding for its own sake results in change.

But the desire for safety and for mastery play an important and obvious role in psychotherapy. They are, of course, as White [19] has ably discussed, closely intertwined. The unexplained and especially the fearful unexplained cannot be tolerated for long; all cultures, either through a scientific or a religious explanation, attempt to make sense of chaotic and threatening stimuli.

In the psychotherapeutic situation, information decreases anxiety by removing ambiguity. There is considerable research evidence to document this observation. To cite one well-known experiment: Dibner [20] exposed forty psychiatric patients to a psychiatric interview after dividing them into two experimental conditions. Half were prepared for the interview and given cues about how they should, in a general way, conduct themselves, whereas the other half were given no such cues (high ambiguity situation). The results demonstrated that the subjects in the high ambiguity situation experienced, during the interview situation, a far greater degree of anxiety (as measured by several subjective, objective, and physiological techniques). The converse is, incidentally, also true: anxiety increases ambiguity by distorting perceptual acuteness. Anxious subjects show disturbed organization of visual perception; they are less capable of perceiving and organizing visual cues shown tachistoscopically [21] and are distinctly slower in completing and recognizing incomplete pictures in a controlled experimental setting.[22] Thus, unless the individual is able to order his world cognitively, he may experience anxiety which, if severe, interferes with the perceptual apparatus. Thus, anxiety begets anxiety; the ensuing perplexity and overt or subliminal awareness of perceptual distortion becomes itself a potent secondary source of anxiety.[23]

In psychotherapy, patients are enormously reassured by the belief that their chaotic inner world, their suffering, and their tortuous interpersonal relationships are all explicable and thereby governable. Therapists, too, are made less anxious if, when confronted with great suffering and voluminous, chaotic material, they can believe in a set of principles which will permit an ordered explanation. Frequently, therapists will cling tenaciously to their system in the face of considerable contradictory material; sometimes, ironically, in the case of researcher-clinicians, it is evidence which has issued from their own investigations. A belief system is valuable also in that it enables the therapist to preserve his equanimity in the face of considerable affect. Analysts working with adults who express powerful and primitive emotions maintain their bearings by believing that their patient has regressed to the experiential world and expressive patterns of the infant.

Maslow goes beyond safety, anxiety reduction, and mastery in his explanation of the mutative effects of knowledge. He views psychiatric illness as a knowledge-deficiency disease. "I am convinced that knowledge and action are frequently synonymous, identical in the Socratic fashion. Where we know fully and completely, suitable action follows automatically and reflexly. Choices are then made without conflict, with full spontaneity." [16] Thus, Maslow would support the moral philosophic contention that if we know the good, we will always act for the good; presumably, it follows that if we know what is ultimately good for us, we will act in our own best interests.

There is little, so far, that is controversial. Self-knowledge permits us to integrate all parts of ourselves, decreases ambiguity, permits a sense of effectance and mastery, and allows us to act in concert with our own best interests. An explanatory scheme also permits generalization and transfer of learning from the therapy setting to new situations in the outside world. The great controversies arise not when we discuss the process or purpose or effects of explanation but when we discuss *content* of explanation. As I shall hope to make clear in the next chapter, I think these controversies are irrelevant. When we focus on change rather than on self-understanding as our ultimate goal, we cannot but conclude that an explanation is correct if it strengthens the patient's will and, ultimately, his ability to change. The final common result of all our intellectual efforts in therapy is change; each clarifying, explanatory, or interpretive act of the therapist is ultimately designed to exert leverage on the patient's will to change. More on this later.

IMITATIVE BEHAVIOR

Successfully treated patients rated imitative behavior as the least helpful of the twelve curative factors. However, in retrospect, the five items on imitative behavior seem to have tapped only a limited sector of this curative mode (see Table 1). They failed to distinguish between mere mimicry, which apparently has only a restricted value for patients, and the acquisition of general modes of behavior, which may have considerable value. To patients, conscious mimicry is an especially unpopular concept as a curative mode since it suggests a relinquishing of individuality—a basic fear of many group patients. On the other hand, patients may acquire from others a general strategy which may be used in a number of different situations. They begin to approach problems by considering, not necessarily on a conscious level, what some other member or the therapist would think or do in the same situation. For example, Rosenthal [24] has demonstrated that successful patients adopt the complex value system of the therapist. Sullivan, many years ago in a remarkable passage which adumbrates many of Laing's views of schizophrenia, described the use of imitative behavior by hospitalized schizophrenic patients which resulted in a form of "noblesse oblige sanity." [25]

A study of "social recoveries" in one of our large mental hospitals some years ago taught me that patients were often released from care because they had learned not to manifest symptoms to the environing persons; in other words, had integrated enough of the personal environment to realize the prejudice opposed to their delusions. It seemed almost as if they grew wise enough to be tolerant of the imbecility surrounding them, having finally discovered that it was stupidity and not malice. They could then secure satisfaction from contact with others, while discharging a part of their cravings by psychotic means.

Such a therapeutic result occurs within the confines of the patient's psychotic solution to his life stress. The therapeutic mechanism of imitative behavior in outpatient groups is considerably different. The initial imitation is, in part, an attempt to gain approval; however, it does not end there. The more intact patients retain their reality-testing and flexibility and perceive that change in their behavior elicits favorable and wanted responses from others. Increased acceptance can then act to change one's self-concept and self-esteem in the manner described in Chapter 3, and an adaptive spiral is instigated.

It is also possible for individuals to identify with aspects of two or more individuals, resulting in an amalgam. Although parts of others are imitated, the resultant amalgam may be a novel, innovative pattern of behavior.

What of spectator therapy? Is it not possible that patients may learn much from observing the solutions achieved by others who have similar problems? I have no doubt that this occurs in the therapy group. It seems even more important in the shorter term encounter group. In the Lieberman, Yalom, Miles study,[6] the "significant incident" data indicated that the members undergoing the most change profited heavily from incidents in which they were entirely passive observers but nonetheless acquired some type of cognitive input (self-under-standing, knowledge about the laws of human interaction, etc.).

Not only do patients learn from observing the substantive work of others who are like them, but they also learn from watching the *process* of others working. In that sense, imitative behavior is a transitional curative factor which permits patients subsequently to engage more fully in other aspects of therapy. For example, one of the five imitative behavior items was rated by the patients as the eighth (of sixty) most important curative factor: "Seeing that others could reveal embarrassing things and take other risks and benefit from it helped me to do the same."

FAMILY REENACTMENT

Family reenactment, or the corrective recapitulation of the primary family experience, a curative factor highly valued by many therapists, is not considered helpful by the group patients (see Table 1). Nor did the encounter group members value this factor highly.[6] (However, it is of interest to note that only the successful encounter group members cited this factor as important. See p. 76.)

The fact that this factor is not cited often by patients, though, should not surprise us since the factor is one which operates at a different level of awareness from such explicit factors as catharsis or universality. Family reenactment becomes more a part of the general horizon against which the group is experienced. Few therapists will deny that the primary family of each group member is an omnipresent specter which relentlessly haunts the group therapy room. The patient's experience in his primary family obviously will, to a great degree, determine the nature of his parataxic distortions, the role he assumes in the group, his attitudes toward the group leaders, etc. In other words, there is every reason to believe that the member's early primary family experience influences the nature of his therapy group experience and imbues it with power.

There is little doubt in my mind that the therapy group reincarnates the primary family; an ethos is created which flings patients back several decades and evokes ancient memories and ancient feelings. In my last meeting with a group before departing for a sabbatical to revise this book, a patient related this dream: "My father was going away for a long trip. I was with a group of people. My father left us a 30-foot boat, but rather than giving it to me to steer, he gave it to one of my friends and I was angry about this."

This is not the place to discuss this dream fully. Suffice it to say that the patient's father had deserted the family when the patient was young, leaving him to be tyrannized by an older brother thereafter. The patient said that this was the first time he had thought of his father in years. The events of the group—the therapist's leaving, his place being taken by a new therapist, the patient's attraction to the co-therapist (a woman), his resentment toward another dominating patient in the group—all acted in concert to awaken long slumbering memories.

Thus, the family haunts the group. Group events, member sibling rivalry, therapist-parents, and regressive group fantasies all pitch the patient back to his early life in the family. He reenacts early family scripts in the group and, if therapy is successful, is able to experiment with new behavior, to break free from the locked family role he once occupied. He recaptures the past and, again if therapy is successful, does so, much less arbitrarily; in fact, the patient changes the past by reconstituting it.

I believe these are important phenomena in the therapeutic process, and yet it is altogether a different question to ask if the group should focus explicitly upon these phenomena. I think not. I think that this process is part of the internal, often silent, homework of the group patient. These shifts in our perspective on the past occur because of the vitality of the work in the present; change does not occur through a direct summons and inquiry of the spirits of the past. There are, as we shall discuss in Chapter 5, many overriding reasons for the group to maintain an ahistoric focus. To focus unduly on those who are not present, on parents and siblings, on oedipal strivings, on sibling rivalries, or on incorporative or patricidal desires is to deny the reality of the group and the other members as a living experience in the here-and-now.

CURATIVE FACTORS: MODIFYING FORCES

It is not possible to construct an absolute hierarchy of curative factors; there are many modifying forces. Curative factors are influenced by the type of group therapy, by the stage of therapy, by extragroup forces, and by individual differences.

Curative Factors in Different Group Therapies

Different types of group therapies favor the operation of different clusters of curative factors. For example, Alcoholics Anonymous and Recovery, Inc., primarily encourage the operation of instillation of hope, imparting of information, universality, altruism, and some aspects of group cohesiveness. Discharge planning groups in psychiatric hospitals may use much "imparting of information" and "development of socializing techniques." Intensive interactional group therapy exerts its chief therapeutic power through "interpersonal learning" and "group cohesiveness"; nevertheless, the other curative factors play an indispensable role in the intensive therapy process. To appreciate the interdependence of the curative factors, we must consider the therapeutic process in its longitudinal dimension.

Curative Factors and Stages of Therapy

Many patients expressed difficulty in rank-ordering curative factors because they found various factors helpful at different stages of therapy. Factors of considerable importance early in therapy may be far less salient late in the course of treatment. In the early stages of development the group is chiefly concerned with survival, with establishing boundaries and maintaining membership; in this phase, factors such as the instillation of hope, guidance, and universality seem especially important. A universality phase early in the group is inevitable, as members search out similarities and compare symptoms and problem constellations. The first dozen meetings of the group present a high risk period for potential dropouts, and it is often necessary to awaken hope in the patients in order to keep them attending through this critical phase. Factors such as altruism and group cohesiveness operate throughout the course of therapy; but their nature changes with the stage of the group. Early in therapy altruism takes the form of offering suggestions or helping one another to talk with appropriate questions and attention. Later, it may take the form of a more profound caring and "being with." Group cohesiveness operates as a curative factor at first by means of group support, acceptance, and the facilitation of attendance, and later by means of the interrelation of group esteem and self-esteem and through its role in interpersonal learning. It is only after the development of group cohesiveness that patients may engage deeply and constructively in the self-disclosure, confrontation, and conflict essential in the process of interpersonal learning.

Patients' needs and goals change during the course of therapy. In Chapter 2, I described a common sequence in which patients first seek symptomatic relief and then, during the first months in therapy, formulate new goals—often interpersonal ones: they wish to be able to relate more deeply to others, to be able to love, to be honest with others. As patients' needs and goals shift during therapy, so, too, must the necessary therapeutic processes. Modern enlightened psychotherapy is often termed dynamic psychotherapy because it appreciates the dynamics, the motivational aspects of behavior, many of which are not in awareness. Dynamic therapy may be thought of also as changing, nonstatic, evolving psychotherapy; patients change, the group goes through a predictable developmental sequence, and so, too, the curative factors shift in primacy and influence during the course of therapy.

Curative Factors Outside the Group

Although major behavioral and attitudinal shifts would seem to require a degree of interpersonal learning, this is by no means invariably visible in the group. Occasionally, patients make major changes without making what would appear to be the appropriate investment in the therapeutic process. This brings up an important principle in therapy: the therapist or the group does not have to do the entire job. Personality reconstruction as a therapeutic goal is as unrealistic as it is presumptuous. Our patients have many adaptive coping strengths which may have served them well in the past, and not infrequently, a boost from some event in therapy may be sufficient to help the patient to begin coping in an adaptive manner. We have previously used the term "adaptive spiral" to refer to the process in which one change in the patient begets changes in his interpersonal environment which beget further personal change. The adaptive spiral is the reverse of the vicious circle, in which so many patients find themselves ensnared—a sequence of events in which dysphoria has interpersonal manifestations which weaken or disrupt interpersonal bonds and consequently create further dysphoria.

Documentation of these points comes when we ask patients about other therapeutic influences or events in their lives which occurred concurrently with their therapy course. In one sample [11] of twenty patients, eighteen described a variety of extragroup therapeutic factors. Most commonly cited was a new or an improved interpersonal relationship with one or more of a variety of figures (member of the opposite sex, parent, spouse, teacher, foster family, or a new set of friends). Two patients claimed to have benefited by going through with a divorce that had long been pending. Many others cited success at work or school, which raised their self-esteem as they established a reservoir of real accomplishments: others became involved in some new social venture (YMCA groups or political committee work).

It is possible, of course, that these factors were fortuitous, independent factors which deserve, along with group therapy, credit for the successful outcome. On closer examination, however, it is apparent that usually the external factor was an auxiliary to group therapy. The group mobilized the members to take advantage of environmental resources which, in fact, had long been available. After all, the spouses, relatives, potential friends, social organizations, and academic or job opportunities were always "out there," available, waiting for the patient to seize them. The group may have given the patient only the impetus necessary for a slight boost to allow him to exploit these previously untapped resources. Frequently, the group members and the therapist are unaware of the importance of these factors and view the patient's improvement with skepticism or puzzlement.

A study of encounter group members who had very successful outcomes yielded corroborative results.[6] More often than not, the members did not credit the group for their change. Instead, they described the beneficial effects of new relationships which they had made, new social circles they had created, new recreational clubs they had joined, greater work satisfaction they had found. However, closer inquiry indicated that the relationships, social circles, recreational clubs, and work satisfaction had not suddenly come into being de novo. They had always been available in the life space of the individual. Not until the group experience mobilized him to take advantage of these resources was he able to exploit them for his satisfaction and personal growth.

We have considered, at several places in this text, how the skills which group members acquire prepare them ably for new social situations in the future. Not only are extrinsic skills acquired but intrinsic capacities are released; psychotherapy removes neurotic obstructions which have stunted the development of the patient's own resources. At the risk of belaboring an obvious point, I recall a patient beginning therapy who described a weekend of skiing. What could have been an extraordinarily pleasant experience for him (fine, sunny weather, good snow conditions, agreeable companions) turned into a nightmarish one. He was obsessed by the thought that he would fall on the slopes, lose his skis, and, by the time he had readjusted them, that his friends would decide not to wait for him at the lifts. He had a fear of abandonment which so pervaded all his experience that he could take no pleasure in any solitary activity. Therapy was quite successful in alleviating this fear, and once this obstruction was removed the patient blossomed and found gratification in a diverse number of experiences. If the therapist believes in therapy as "obstruction removal," his burden is lightened and he retains his respect for the rich, never fully knowable capacities of his patients.

Individual Differences and Curative Factors

It is important to note that the rank-ordering of the curative factors in Table 1 is a mean or average value. There was, among the twenty patients studied, considerable individual variation in the ranking of the factors. The investigators explored several possible reasons for these differences. Do patients in one group differ from the patients in another group? Are the differences dependent on age, sex, length of time in treatment, degree of improvement, or the original reasons for seeking therapy? Statistical analysis demonstrated that none of these factors accounted for the individual differences.

Obviously, not everyone needs the same things or responds in the same way to group therapy; there are many therapeutic pathways through the group therapy experience. For example, earlier we described the importance of catharsis; many restricted individuals are benefited by experiencing and expressing strong affect. Others, with contrasting problems of impulse control and great emotional lability may, on the contrary, profit from acquiring an intellectual structuring and from reining in emotional expression. Some narcissistic characters need to learn to share and to give, whereas others, self-defeating in their self-effacement, need to learn to ask for and demand their rights. The manner in which an individual is helped in group therapy is the result of the interplay of several factors: his interpersonal needs, his strengths and weaknesses, his extragroup resources, and the composition and culture of his particular therapy group.

Although these issues require considerable research, certain conclusions seem heavily supported by all available studies. Group therapy draws its unique potency from its interpersonal and group properties. The agent of change appears to be the group and the intermember influence network. The effective group therapist must direct his efforts toward maximal development of these therapeutic resources. The next chapters will consider the role and the techniques of the group therapist from the viewpoint of the curative factors which we have described.

REFERENCES

1. R. Corsini and B. Rosenberg, "Mechanisms of Group Psychotherapy: Processes and Dynamics," *J. Abnorm. Soc. Psychol.*, 51: 406–411, 1955.
2. F. Fiedler, "A Comparison of Therapeutic Relationships in Psychoanalytic, Non-Directive and Adlerian Therapy," *J. Consult. Psychol.*, 14: 436–445, 1950.
3. R. W. Heine, "A Comparison of Patients' Reports on Psychotherapeutic Experience with Psychoanalytic, Non-Directive and Adlerian Therapists," *Am. J. Psychother.*, 7: 16–23, 1953.
4. C. Truax and R. Carkhuff, *Toward Effective Counseling and Psychotherapy* (Chicago: Aldine Press, 1967).
5. H. Strupp, R. E. Fox, and K. Lessler, *Patients View Their Psychotherapy* (Baltimore, Maryland: The Johns Hopkins Press, 1969).
6. M. A. Lieberman, I. D. Yalom, and M. B. Miles, *Encounter Groups: First Facts* (New York: Basic Books 1972).
7. H. Feifel and J. Eells, "Patients and Therapists Assess the Same Psychotherapy," *J. Consult. Psychol.*, 27: 310–318, 1963.
8. G. B. Blaine and C. C. McArthur, "What Happened in Therapy as Seen by the Patient and His Psychiatrist," *J. Nerv. Ment. Dis.*, 127: 344–350, 1958.
9. B. Berzon, C. Pious, and R. Parson, "The Therapeutic Event in Group Psychotherapy: A Study of Subjective Reports by Group Members," *J. Indiv. Psychol.*, 19: 204–212, 1963.

10. H. Dickoff and M. Lakin, "Patients' Views of Group Psychotherapy: Retrospections and Interpretations," *Int. J. Group Psychother., 13:* 61–73, 1963.
11. I. D. Yalom, J. Tinklenberg, and M. Gilula, "Curative Factors in Group Therapy." Unpublished study.
12. I. D. Yalom, P. S. Houts, S. M. Zimerberg, and K. H. Rand, "Prediction of Improvement in Group Therapy," *Arch. Gen. Psychiat., 17:* 159–168, 1967.
13. J. Block, *The Q-Sort Method in Personality Assessment and Psychiatric Research* (Springfield, Ill.: Charles C. Thomas, 1961).
14. E. Jones, *The Life and Work of Sigmund Freud, Vol. 1* (New York: Basic Books, 1953), p. 40.
15. I. D. Yalom, "Existential Factors in Group Therapy," *Strecker Monograph Series,* XI, The Institute of the Pennsylvania Hospital, 1974.
16. A. Maslow, "The Need to Know and the Fear of Knowing," *J. Gen. Psychol., 68:* 111–125, 1963.
17. A. Maslow, *Motivation and Personality* (New York: Harper, 1954).
18. D. Berlyne, *Conflict, Arousal and Curiosity* (New York: McGraw-Hill, 1960).
19. R. W. White, "Motivation Reconsidered: The Concept of Competence," *Psychol. Rev., 66:* 297–333, 1959.
20. A. S. Dibner, "Ambiguity and Anxiety," *J. Abnorm. Soc. Psychol., 56:* 165–174, 1958.
21. L. Postman and J. S. Brunner, "Perception under Stress," *Psychol. Rev., 55:* 314–323, 1948.
22. E. Verville, "The Effect of Emotional and Motivational Sets on the Perception of Incomplete Pictures," *J. Gen. Psychol., 69:* 133–145, 1946.
23. S. J. Korchin *et al.,* "Experience of Perceptual Distortion as a Source of Anxiety," *Arch. Neurol. Psychiat., 80:* 98–113, 1958.
24. D. Rosenthal, "Changes in Some Moral Values Following Psychotherapy," *J. Consult. Psychol., 19:* 431–436, 1955.
25. H. S. Sullivan, cited in E. Goffman, *The Presentation of Self in Everyday Life* (Garden City, N.Y.: Doubleday Anchor Books, 1959), p. 18.

5

THE THERAPIST:
TASKS AND
TECHNIQUES

Now that we have considered *how* people change in group therapy, it is time to turn to the therapist and his role in the therapeutic process. In this chapter we shall consider the basic tasks of the therapist and the techniques by which he may accomplish these tasks.

The previous four chapters contend that therapy is a complex process consisting of a number of elemental factors which interlace in an intricate fashion. The group therapist's job is to create the machinery of therapy, to set it into motion, and to keep it operating with a maximum of effectiveness. Sometimes I think of the group therapeutic process as an enormous dynamo; often the therapist is deep in the interior, working, experiencing, interacting (and is himself influenced by the energy field); other times he dons mechanic's clothes and tinkers about around the exterior, lubricating, tightening nuts and bolts, replacing parts.

Before turning to specific tasks and techniques, I wish to emphasize something to which I will return again and again in the following pages. Underlying all considerations of technique there must be a consistent, positive relationship between therapist and patient. The basic posture of the therapist to his patient must be one of concern, acceptance, genuineness, empathy. Nothing, no technical consideration, takes precedence over this. There will be times when the therapist challenges the patient, shows anger and frustration, suggests that if the patient is not going to work he consider leaving the group. But these efforts (which in the right circumstances may have therapeutic clout) are never effective unless they are experienced against a horizon of an accepting, concernful therapist-patient relationship.

I have chosen to discuss the techniques of the therapist around his three fundamental tasks: (1) Creation and Maintenance of the group, (2) Culture Building, and (3) Activation and Illumination of the here-and-now. We must postpone the bulk of the discussion of the first task, Creation and Maintenance, until much essential background material is presented in Chapters 7, 8, and 9. In this chapter we shall focus primarily on Culture Building and Here-and-Now Activation and Illumination.

Creation and Maintenance of the Group

The leader is, of course, solely responsible for creating and convening the group. His offer of professional help serves as its initial *raison d'être*, and he naturally sets the time and place for meetings. A considerable part of the maintenance task is performed before the first meeting and, as we shall elaborate in later chapters, the leader's expertise in the selection and the preparation of members will greatly influence the group's fate.

Once the group begins he must attend to gate-keeping functions, especially the prevention of member attrition. Occasionally, a patient's unsuccessful group experience resulting in premature termination of therapy may play some useful function in his overall therapy career; for example, a failure or rejection by a group may so unsettle the patient that he is ideally primed for his next therapist. Generally, however, a patient who drops out early in the course of the group should be considered a therapeutic failure. Not only does he fail to receive benefit, but the progress of the remainder of the group is adversely affected. Stability of membership seems to be a sine qua non of successful therapy. If dropouts do occur, the therapist must, unless he is leading a closed group (see Chapter 9), add new members.

Initially, the patients are strangers to one another and know only the therapist, who serves as a transitional object. He is the group's primary unifying force; the members relate to one another at first through their common relationship with him.

The therapist must recognize and deter any forces which threaten group cohesiveness. Continued tardiness, absences, subgrouping, disruptive extragroup socialization, and scapegoating all threaten the integrity of the group and command the intervention of the therapist. Each of these issues will be discussed fully in later chapters. For now, it is only necessary to emphasize the therapist's responsibility to super-individual forces. His first task is to help create a social system. There will be times when he must delay dealing with pressing needs of an individual patient and in fact there will be times when it will be necessary to sacrifice a patient (removing the patient from the group) for the good of the group. More of that later.

Culture Building

Once the group is a physical reality, the therapist turns his energies to shaping the group into a therapeutic social system. He endeavors to establish a code of behavioral rules, or norms, which will guide the interaction of the group. The desirable norms for a therapeutic group follow logically from the discussion of the curative factors.

Consider for a moment the curative factors outlined in the first four chapters. Who is it that provides the support, universality, advice, interpersonal feedback, testing, learning, opportunities for altruism, and hope? Obviously, the other members of the group! Thus, to a very large extent, *it is the group which is the agent of change.*

This makes for a crucial difference in the basic role of the individual therapist and the group therapist. In the individual format the therapist functions as the solely designated direct agent of change; in the group therapeutic format he functions far more indirectly. Thus, if it is the group members who, in their interaction with one another, set into motion the many curative factors, then it is the group therapist's task to create a group culture maximally conducive to the proper type of group interaction.

The game of chess provides a useful analogy. The expert player, in the beginning of the game, does not strive for checkmate or outright capture of a piece, but instead aims at obtaining strategic squares on the board and thereby increasing the power of each of his pieces. In so doing, he is indirectly moving toward his ultimate goal since, as the game proceeds, his superior strategic position will favor an effective attack and ultimate gain of material. So, too, the group therapist methodically builds a culture which will ultimately exert great therapeutic strength.

A jazz pianist, a member of one of my groups, once commented on the role of the leader by reflecting that very early in his musical career he deeply admired the great instrumental virtuosos. It was only much later that he grew to understand that the truly great jazz musicians were those who knew how to augment the sound of others, how to be quiet, how to enhance the functioning of the entire combo.

It is obvious that the therapy group has norms which radically depart from the rules, or etiquette, of typical social intercourse. Unlike almost any other kind of group, the members must feel free to comment on the immediate feelings they experience toward the group, the other members, and the therapist. Honesty and spontaneity of expression must be encouraged in the group. If the group is to develop into a true social microcosm, members must interact freely with one another. In schematic form, the pathways of interaction should appear like the first, rather than the second, diagram, in which communications are primarily to or through the therapist.

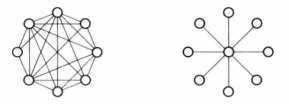

Other desirable norms include high levels of involvement in the group, nonjudgmental acceptance of others, high levels of self-disclosure, a desire for self-understanding, dissatisfaction with present modes of behavior, and an eagerness for change. Norms may be a prescription for as well as a proscription against certain types of behavior. They have an important evaluative element in that members feel the behavior *ought* or *ought not* to be performed. They may be implicit as well as explicit. In fact, generally the members of a group do not consciously formulate the norms of the group. Thus, to learn the norms of a group the researcher is ill-advised to ask the members for a list of the unwritten rules of the group. He does better to present the members with a checklist of behaviors and ask them to indicate which are appropriate and which inappropriate in the group.

Norms invariably evolve in every type of group—social, professional, and therapeutic. But by no means is it inevitable that a therapeutic group will evolve norms which facilitate the therapeutic process. Systematic observation of a number of therapy groups readily reveals that many are encumbered with crippling norms. They may, for example, so value hostile catharsis that positive sentiments are eschewed, they may have a "take turns" format in which the members sequentially describe their problems to the group, they may have norms which do not permit members to question or challenge the therapist. We will return to specific norms which hamper or facilitate therapy, but first let us consider how norms come into being.

THE CONSTRUCTION OF NORMS

Norms of a group are constructed both from expectations of the members for their group and from the explicit and implicit directions of the leader and more influential members. If the members' expectations are not firm, then the leader has even more opportunity to design a group culture which, in his view, will be optimally therapeutic. Obviously, he is the initial seat of influence in the group and the members look to him for direction.

Psathas and Hardert,[1] conducting a careful analysis of the leader's interventions in a training group, demonstrated that the leader's statements to the group play a powerful, though usually implicit, role in determining the norms established in the group. Shapiro and Birk [2] observed that "whenever the leader made a comment following closely after a particular member's actions this person became a center of attention in the group and often assumed a major role in future meetings." Furthermore, the relative infrequency of the leader's comments augmented the strength of his interventions.

By discussing the leader as norm-shaper I am not proposing a new or contrived role for the therapist. He always shapes the norms of the group. It is essential that he be aware of this function because, wittingly or unwittingly, the leader affects the group norms. He cannot *not* influence norms; virtually all of his early group behavior is influential. Moreover, what he does not do is often as important as what he does do; Don Jackson frequently said that "one cannot not communicate." Once I observed a group led by a British group analyst in which a member who had been absent the six previous meetings entered the meeting a few minutes late. The therapist in no way acknowledged the arrival of the patient and after the session explained to the observers that he chose not to influence the group since he preferred that they make their own rules about welcoming tardy or prodigal members. However, it appeared clear to me that his non-welcome was an influential act and very much of a norm-setting message. His group had evolved, no doubt, as a result of many similar directives, into a non-caring, insecure one which sought methods of currying the leader's favor.

Norms are created relatively early in the life of a group and once established are difficult to change. Consider, for example, the small group in an industrial setting which forms norms regulating individual member output, or a delinquent gang which establishes turf codes of behavior, or a psychiatric ward which forms norms of expected staff and patient role behavior. To change entrenched standards is notoriously difficult and requires considerable time and often large turnover in group membership.

An interesting laboratory experiment by Jacobs and Campbell [3] illustrates the tenacity and durability of norms. Group members in a darkened room were asked to estimate how much a point of light (which was, in fact, stationary) moved (the "autokinetic response" [4]). A numerical group norm from which the individual members departed only minimally was rapidly established. The experimenters then replaced members, until there had been several complete turnovers of membership. However, the group norm, which had been established by individuals long since departed from the group, remained fixed.

To summarize: every group evolves a set of unwritten rules or norms which determine the behavioral procedure of the group; the ideal therapy group has norms which permit the curative factors to operate with maximum effectiveness; norms are shaped both by the expectations of the group members and by the behavior of the therapist; the therapist is enormously influential in norm-setting—it is a function that he cannot avoid; norms constructed early in the group have considerable perseverance. The therapist is, thus, well-advised to go about this important function in an informed, deliberate manner.

HOW DOES THE LEADER SHAPE NORMS?

There are two basic roles the therapist may assume in the group: he may be a technical expert and he may be a model-setting participant. In each of these roles he helps to shape the norms of the group.

The Technical Expert. When assuming this role, the therapist deliberately slips into the traditional garb of expert. He employs a variety of techniques to move the group in a direction he considers desirable. He explicitly attempts to shape norms during his early preparation of patients for group therapy. This procedure, described fully in Chapter 9, carefully instructs patients about the rules of the group. The therapist attempts to reinforce the instructions in two ways: by backing it with the weight of his authority and his experience, and by presenting the rationale behind his suggested mode of procedure through which he attempts to enlist the support of the patient's reason.

When the group begins, the therapist has a wide choice of techniques at his disposal to shape the group culture. These range from explicit instructions and suggestions to more subtle reinforcing techniques. For example, as we described earlier, the leader will attempt to create an interactional network in which the members freely interact with one another rather than direct all their comments to or through him. To this end, he may implicitly instruct members in their pre-group interviews or in the first group sessions; he may, repeatedly during the meetings, ask for all members' reactions to another member or toward a group issue; he may wonder why conversation is invariably directed toward himself; he may refuse to answer questions or may even close his eyes when he is addressed; he may ask the group to engage in exercises which teach patients to interact with one another—for example, he may ask each member of the group, in turn, to give their first impressions of every other member; or he may, in a much less obtrusive manner, shape behavior by rewarding members who address one another—he may nod or smile at them, address them warmly, or shift his posture into a more receptive position. Exactly the same principle applies to the myriad of other norms the therapist wishes to inculcate: self-disclosure, open expression of emotions, promptness, self-exploration, etc.

Therapists vary considerably in style. Although many do much of their norm-shaping by explicit methods, all therapists, to a degree often greater than they suppose, perform their tasks through the subtle technique of social reinforcement. Human behavior is continuously influenced by a series of environmental events (reinforcers) which may be positively or negatively valenced and which exert their influence on a conscious or subliminal level.

Advertising science and political propaganda techniques are but two examples of a systematic harnessing of reinforcing agents. Psychotherapy, no less, relies on the use of subtle, often nondeliberate social reinforcers. Although no self-respecting therapist likes to consider himself a social reinforcing agent, nevertheless he continuously exerts influence in this manner, unconsciously or quite deliberately. He may positively reinforce some behavior by numerous verbal and nonverbal acts including nodding, smiling, leaning forward, an interested "Mmm," or a direct inquiry for more information. On the other hand, he may decline to reinforce behavior which he does not deem salubrious by not commenting, not nodding, ignoring the behavior, turning his attention to another patient, looking skeptical, raising eyebrows, etc. Any obvious verbal directive from the therapist is an especially effective reinforcer because of the paucity of his interventions and his refusal to structure the group.

Every form of psychotherapy is a learning process, relying in part on operant conditioning. I agree with Shapiro, who states that "therapy without manipulation is a mirage which disappears on close scrutiny." [2] Marmor,[5] speaking from the vantage point of psychoanalysis, says, "What goes on in the psychotherapeutic 'working through' process is a kind of conditioned learning in which the therapist's overt and covert responses act as 'reward-punishment' cues which reinforce more mature patterns of behavior and inhibit less mature patterns."

There is considerable research to document the efficacy of operant techniques in the shaping of group behavior. Using these techniques deliberately one can reduce silences [6] or increase personal and group comments, expressions of hostility to the leader, or intermember acceptance.[7,8] Though there is evidence that they owe much of their effectiveness to these learning principles, psychotherapists often eschew this evidence because of the unfounded fear that such a mechanistic view will undermine the essential human component of the therapy experience. The facts are compelling, however, and an understanding of his own behavior does not strip the therapist of his spontaneity. The therapist who recognizes that he does exert great influence through social reinforcement and who has formulated for himself a central organizing principle of therapy will be more effective and consistent in his therapeutic interventions. The experienced therapist does not become less spontaneous but acts on these principles reflexly as they become internalized determinants of his behavior.

The Model-Setting Participant. The leader shapes norms not only through explicit or implicit social engineering but through the example he sets in his personal group behavior. The therapy group culture represents a radical departure from the social rules to which the patient is accustomed. The patient is asked to discard familiar social conventions, try out new behaviors, and take many risks. How can the therapist demonstrate to the patient that new behavior will not have the anticipated adverse consequences? One method which has considerable research backing is modeling: the patient is encouraged to alter his behavior by observing the therapist engaging freely and without adverse effects in the behavior under question. Bandura has demonstrated in many well-controlled research endeavors that individuals may be influenced to engage in more adaptive behavior (for example, the overcoming of specific phobias [9,10]) or less adaptive behavior (for example, unrestrained aggressivity [11]) through observing and assuming the therapist's or therapist-surrogate's behavior.

The leader may, by offering a model of nonjudgmental acceptance and appreciation of others' strengths as well as their problem areas, help to shape a group which is health-oriented. If, on the other hand, he conceptualizes his role as that of a detective of psychopathology, the group members will follow suit. For example, one group patient had actively worked on the problems of other members for months but steadfastly had declined to disclose herself. Finally in one meeting she began to discuss her problems and "confessed" that one year previously she had had a two-month stay in a state psychiatric hospital. The therapist responded reflexly, "Why haven't you told us this before?" This comment, perceived as a punitive one by the patient, served only to reinforce her fear and distrust of others. Obviously, there are questions and comments which will close people down and others which will help them to open up. The therapist, for example, might have commented upon the fact that she now seemed to trust the group sufficiently to talk about herself or might have commented about how difficult it must have been for her previously in the group, wanting to share this disclosure and yet being afraid to do so.

The leader sets a model of interpersonal honesty and spontaneity; however, he keeps in mind the current needs of the members and demonstrates behavior which is congruent with the developmental stage of the group. Total disinhibition and unrestrained expression of all feelings is no more salubrious in therapy groups than in other forms of human encounter and if faithfully enacted may lead to ugly, purposeless, destructive interaction, such as Albee portrays in *Who's Afraid of Virginia Woolf*. The therapist must set a model which includes responsibility and appropriate restraint as well as honesty. The concept of the totally analyzed therapist who experiences no destructive feelings and fantasies toward his patients is, in my experience, illusory. But the judicious use of the leader's own feelings is an invaluable part of his armamentarium. Consider the following therapeutically effective intervention:

In the first session of a group of nonpatient business executives meeting for a five-day human relations laboratory, a twenty-five-year-old, aggressive, swaggering member who had obviously been drinking heavily that day proceeded to dominate the meeting and make a fool of himself. He boasted of his accomplishments, belittled the group, monopolized the meeting, interrupted, outshouted, and insulted every other member. All attempts to deal with the situation failed; i.e., feedback as to how angry or hurt he had made others feel, interpretations about the meaning and cause of his behavior. Then my co-leader commented quite sincerely, "You know what I like about you? Your fear and lack of confidence. You're scared here, just like me; we're all scared about what will happen to us this week." That statement permitted the patient to discard his facade and, eventually, to become a valuable group member. Furthermore, the leader, by modeling an empathic nonjudgmental style, helped to establish a gentle accepting group culture.

Interacting as a group member requires, among other things, that the therapist accept and admit his fallibility. The therapist who needs to appear infallible offers a perplexing and impeding example for his patients. He may be so disinclined to admit error that he is withholding or devious in his relationship with the group.

Example: In one group, the therapist, who needed to appear omniscient, was to be out of town for the next meeting. He suggested to the group that they meet without him and tape record the meeting, promising to listen to the tape before the next session. He forgot to listen to the tape but, because of his need not to be wrong, was unable to admit this to the group. Consequently, the subsequent meeting, in which the therapist bluffed by avoiding mention of the previous leaderless session, turned out to be diffuse, confusing, and discouraging.

Another example involved a neophyte therapist with similar needs. A patient attacked him by accusing him of making long-winded, confusing, fly-paper-like statements. Since this was the first confrontation of the therapist in this young group, the members were tense and perched on the edge of their chairs. The therapist responded by wondering whether he didn't remind the patient of someone from the past. The attacking patient clutched at the suggestion and volunteered his father as a candidate; the crisis passed and the group members settled back in their chairs. However, it so happened that previously this therapist had himself been a member of a group (of psychiatric residents) and his colleagues had repeatedly focused on his tendency to make lengthy, convoluted, confused comments. In fact, then, what had transpired was that the patient had seen the therapist quite correctly but was persuaded to relinquish his perceptions. If one of the goals of therapy is to help the patient to test reality and to clarify his interpersonal relationships, then clearly this transaction was antitherapeutic. (This illustrates, too, a point made earlier in regard to "reenactment of the primary family" as a curative factor: undue emphasis on the past may serve to deny the immediate reality of the group.)

Another consequence of the need to be perfect occurs when the therapist becomes overly cautious in his comments. Lest he make an error, he weighs his words so carefully, interacting so deliberately and with such poor timing, that he sacrifices spontaneity and may mold a group which is stilted and lifeless. Often, therapists who maintain an omnipotent, distant role are also saying, in effect, "Do what you will; you can't hurt or touch me." This pose may have the unwanted effect of aggravating a sense of impotence in the patients. This is obviously counterproductive since one of the important norms of an effective therapy group is that the members take very seriously what each says to the other.

In one group, Les, a young male patient, had made little movement for months despite vigorous efforts by the leader. In virtually every meeting the leader attempted to bring Les into the discussion, but to no avail. Instead, Les became more defiant and withholding and the therapist became more active and angry. Finally Joan, another patient, commented to the therapist that he was a stubborn father treating Les like a stubborn son and that he was bound and determined to *make* Les change. Les, she added, was relishing the role of the rebellious son who was determined to defeat his father. This rang true for the therapist; it clicked with his internal experience and he acknowledged this to the group and thanked Joan for her comments. The therapist's behavior in this example was extremely important for the group. In effect, he said, "I value you [the patients], this group, and this mode of learning." Furthermore, he reinforced norms of self-exploration, the interpretative mode, honesty, and confrontation with the therapist. The transaction was helpful to the therapist (it is the unfortunate therapist who cannot learn more about himself in his therapeutic work) and to Les, who explored very fully his delight in defiantly frustrating the therapist.

Occasionally, less modeling is required of the therapist because of the presence of some "ideal" group patients who fulfill this function. In fact, there have been studies in which selected model-setting patients were deliberately introduced into the group. Schwartz and Hawkins [12] introduced a pair of experienced group patients to serve as models in each of two inpatient schizophrenic groups. It was known from their past group behavior that one pair of patients habitually made affect-laden statements whereas the other pair made impersonal non-affect statements. The discussion of the group was recorded and analyzed. The results attest to a significant amount of imitative behavior: the group with the models who expressed affect showed an increment in the amount of affect expressed, whereas the other group increasingly made non-affect, impersonal statements.

Goldstein et al. [13] report an exploratory study in which they introduced a confederate (a nonpatient psychology graduate student) into two outpatient groups. The "plants" pretended to be patients but met regularly in group discussions with the therapists and supervisors. Their role and behavior were planned to facilitate, by their personal example, self-disclosure, free expression of affect, confrontation with the therapists, silencing of monopolists, clique-busting, etc. The two groups were studied (through patient-administered cohesiveness questionnaires and sociometrics) for twenty sessions. The results indicated that the plants, though not the most popular members, were regarded by the other patients as facilitating therapy; moreover, the authors concluded (though there were no control groups) that the plants served to increase group cohesiveness. Although a trained "plant" would contribute a form of deceit incompatible with the process of long-term group therapy, the use of such individuals has intriguing implications. It is entirely feasible, for example, to "seed" new therapy groups with an "ideal" group therapy patient from another group, who then continues therapy in two groups. Or a patient who has recently satisfactorily completed group therapy might serve as a model-setting auxiliary therapist during the formative period of a new group.

Despite these provocative possibilities, it is the therapist who, willingly or unwillingly, will continue to serve as the chief model-setting figure for the group patients. Consequently, it is of the utmost importance that the therapist have sufficient self-confidence to fulfill this function. The less comfortable the therapist feels, the more likely he is to encounter difficulties in this aspect of his role, and he will veer to one extreme or the other in his personal engagement in the group: either he will fall back into a comfortable, concealed professional role or he will escape from the anxiety and responsibility inherent in the leader's role by abdication and becoming simply "one of the boys." Either extreme has unfortunate consequences for the development of group norms. The first helps to create norms of caution and guardedness. The second results in a severe limitation of the therapist's role: he is unable to use the wide range of methods at his disposal for the shaping of norms; furthermore, he creates a confused group which is unlikely to work fruitfully on important transference issues.

The issue of the transparency of the therapist has implications which extend far beyond the task of norm-setting. When the therapist discloses himself in the group, not only does he model behavior but he performs an act which has considerable significance in many other ways for the therapeutic process. Many patients develop conflicted and often distorted feelings to the therapist; the transparency of the therapist plays a crucial role in the working through of transference. We shall discuss the ramifications of therapist transparency in great detail in the next chapter; for the present, let us turn to some specific examples of therapeutic norm-setting.

WHICH NORMS? EXAMPLES OF THERAPEUTIC
GROUP NORMS

The Self-Monitoring Group. It is important that the group begin to assume responsibility for its own functioning. When this norm has failed to develop, the group tends to be passive, the members feel dependent upon the leader to supply movement and direction, and the leader feels increasingly fatigued and irritated by the burden of making everything work. Something has gone awry in the early development of such a group. When I lead groups like this, I often experience the members of the group as moviegoers. They visit the group each week to see what's playing; if it happens to interest them, they will engage in the group. My task in the group, then, is to help members understand that they *are* the movie: if they do not perform, the screen is blank; there is no performance.

From the beginning of its life I attempt to transfer the responsibility of the group to the members. For example, in the very early meetings of a group I may stop the group and remark, "I see that an hour has gone by and I'd like to ask, How has the group gone today? Are you satisfied with it? How does it compare with last week's meeting? What's been the most involving part of the meeting so far today? The least involving part?" The general point is that I endeavor to shift the evaluative function from me to the patients. I say to them, in effect, "You have the ability (and responsibility) to determine when this group is working effectively and when it is wasting its time."

If a member laments, for example, that "the only involving part of this meeting was the first ten minutes—after that we just rapped for forty-five minutes," my reflex response is, "Then why did you let it go on? How could you have stopped it?" Or, "All of you seemed to have known this. What stopped you from acting? Why is it always my job to do what you are all able to do?" One begins to learn that there is generally very good consensus about productive and unproductive group work. (And it is almost invariably related to the presence or absence of the here-and-now focus, which we shall discuss very shortly.) If the group has had a particularly effective meeting, I often label it so and help the patients to do so as well. Such meetings serve as reference points against which they may compare other sessions.

Self-Disclosure. Self-disclosure is a necessary component of the therapeutic process. I prefer to lead groups whose norms say, in effect, that self-disclosure is important, that it is never dangerous, and that it accelerates the work of the group. During pre-group individual meetings, I make these points explicit to patients. If the patient has an important "secret" which involves some central aspect of his life—for example, homosexuality, alcoholism, compulsive shoplifting, or transvestism—I inform the patient that, sooner or later, he will have to share this with the group.

However, it does not follow that intensive self-disclosure, at any time, is always a good thing in the therapy group. The group is not a forced confessional. I prefer a norm that permits, within certain limits, members to set their own pace of disclosure. If a patient is guarded and silent in his early meetings, I try to invite him to participate and later ask how he felt about my invitation. I share with him my dilemma between not wanting to be forcefully intrusive but also wanting to continue to encourage him to participate.

Self-disclosure can often be deepened by asking for meta-disclosures—disclosures about the disclosure. For example, I might say, "John, you've told us several things about yourself today that were obviously difficult for you to say. What was the telling like for you inside? What was the hardest thing to say? What did you feel about the response of the group?" If undue pressure is placed on a member to disclose, I will, depending on the problems of the particular patient and his stage of therapy, respond in one of several ways. For example, I may relieve the pressure by commenting that "there are obviously some things that John doesn't yet feel like sharing; the group seems eager, even impatient to bring John aboard, while John doesn't yet feel safe or comfortable enough." (The word "yet" is important since it conveys the appropriate expectational set.) At other times I may shift the emphasis of the group from "wringing" the disclosure out of the patient to exploring the obstacles to his disclosure. What does he fear? What are the anticipated dreaded consequences? From whom in the group does he anticipate disapprobation?

The patient should never be punished for revealing himself. One of the most destructive events that can occur in a group is for members to use personal, sensitive material which has been disclosed in the group against one another in times of conflict. The therapist should intervene vigorously at this point; not only is it "dirty fighting" but it undermines some important group norms. This "vigorous intervention" can take many forms. In one way or another the therapist must call attention to the violation of trust. Often I will simply "stop action," interrupt the conflict, and point out that something very important has just happened in the group. I ask the offended member for his feelings about the incident, ask others for theirs, wonder whether others have had similar experiences, point out how this will make it difficult for others to reveal themselves, etc. Any other work in the group is temporarily postponed; the important point is that the incident be underscored to reinforce the norm that self-disclosure is not only important but safe.

Procedural Norms. The optimal procedural format in the group is an unstructured, unrehearsed, freely interacting one. At times groups will slip into a restrictive interactive pattern. For example, the group may devote an entire meeting to each of the members in rotation. They may take turns, perhaps the first person to speak obtaining the group floor for the meeting, or the one who presents the most pressing life crisis that week. Some groups have enormous difficulty changing the focus from one member to another, because a norm has somehow evolved whereby a change of topic is considered an interruption and consequently bad form, rude, or very rejecting. Members may lapse into silence, feeling they dare not ask for time themselves yet being unwilling to keep the other member supplied with questions, all the while silently hoping he will soon stop talking.

These patterns hamper the development of a potent group and ultimately result in group frustration and discouragement. I prefer to deal with these antitherapeutic norms by calling attention to them and indicating that, since the group has constructed them, it has the power to change them. For example, I might say, "I've been noticing that over the past four weeks, the entire meeting has been devoted to only one person, often the first one who speaks that day, and also that others seem unwilling to interrupt and are, I believe, sitting silently on many important feelings. I wonder how this practice ever got started and whether or not we want to change it." A comment of this nature may be liberating to the group; the therapist has not only given voice to something that everyone knows to be true but has also the possibility for other procedural options.

The Importance of the Group. The more important the members consider the group, the more effective the group becomes. I believe that the ideal therapeutic posture for patients is for their therapy group experience to be considered the most important event in their lives. The therapist is well-advised to reinforce this belief in any manner available to him. If he is forced to miss or to cancel a meeting, he informs them of it well in advance and conveys to the group his concern about his absence. He arrives punctually for meetings. If he has been thinking about the group between sessions, he may share his thoughts with the members. He reinforces members when they give testimony of the group's usefulness to them or when they indicate they have been thinking about other members during the week.

The more continuity between meetings, the better. A well-functioning group continues to work through issues from one meeting to the next. (This is more easily done if the group meets more than once a week.) The therapist does well to encourage continuity; more than anyone else he is the group "time-binder," connecting events and fitting experiences into the temporal matrix of the group. "That sounds very much like what John was working on two weeks ago," or, "Irene, I've noticed that ever since you and Jill had that run-in three weeks ago you have become more depressed and withdrawn. What are your feelings now toward Jill?" etc.

The group increases in importance when members come to recognize it as a rich reservoir of information and support. When members express curiosity about themselves, I, one way or another, convey the belief that any information members might desire about themselves is present in the group room, provided they learn how to tap it. Thus, when Ken wonders whether he is too dominant and theatening to others, my reflex is to reply, in effect, "Ken, there are many people who know you very well in this room. Ask them."

Events which strengthen bonds between members enhance the potency of the group. It augurs well when group members go out together for post-meeting coffee, hold long discussions in the parking lot, or phone one another during the week in times of crisis. (Such extragroup contact is not without possible complication, however. This topic is a complex one which I shall discuss in detail in Chapter 11.)

Members as Agents of Help. The group functions best if the patients appreciate the valuable help they can provide one another. If the group continues to regard the therapist as the sole source of aid, then the group fails to achieve an optimal level of autonomy and self-respect. To reinforce this norm, the therapist may call attention to incidents demonstrating the mutual helpfulness of members. He may teach members more effective methods of assisting one another. For example, after a patient has been working with the group or some issue for a long portion of a meeting, the therapist may comment, "Reid, could you think back over the last forty-five minutes? Which comments have been the most helpful to you and which the least?" or "Victor, I can see you've been wanting to talk about that for a long time in the group and until today you've been unable to. Somehow Eve helped you to open up. What did she do? And what was it today that Ben did that seemed to close you down rather than open you?" etc.

Behavior undermining the norm of mutual helpfulness should not be permitted to go unnoticed. If, for example, one member challenges another concerning his treatment of a third member by stating, "Fred, what right do you have to talk to Peter about that? You're a hell of a lot worse than he is in that regard," I might intervene by commenting, "Phil, I think you've got some negative feelings about Fred today coming from another source. Maybe we should get into them. I can't agree with you when you say that because Fred is similar to Peter, he can't be helpful. In fact, quite the contrary has been true here in the group; since we *are* similar to one another, we might be especially useful."

Now many of these examples of therapist behaviors may seem deliberate, pedantic, even pontifical. They are not the nonjudgmental, nondirective, mirroring, or clarifying comments so typical of therapist behavior when he is engaged in other aspects of his task in the therapeutic process. However, it is vital that the therapist attend, quite deliberately, to his norm-setting function. It is a task which underlies and, to a great extent, precedes much of the other work of the therapist. Perhaps now, however, we have explored a sufficiently representative sample of those norms which need to be set and associated therapist techniques, and it is time to turn to the other basic tasks of the therapist which can be considered broadly in terms of activation and process illumination of the here-and-now.

The Here-and-Now: Activation and Process Illumination

INTRODUCTION

The major difference between a therapy group which hopes to effect extensive and enduring behavioral and characterological change and such groups as A.A., Recovery Inc., groups of expectant mothers, weight reduction groups, and others is that the therapy group experience, to a large extent, transpires in the here-and-now.

As I have discussed previously, the here-and-now focus, to be effective, consists of two symbiotic tiers, neither of which has therapeutic power without the other. First, the group members must focus their attention on their feelings toward the other group members, the therapist, and the group. This means that the group discourse is an ahistoric one: the immediate events *in* the meeting take precedence over events both in the current outside life and in the distant past of the members. This focus greatly facilitates the development and stark emergence of each member's social microcosm; it facilitates feedback, catharsis, meaningful self-disclosure, and acquisition of socializing techniques. The group becomes more vital and *all* of the members (not only the one who is "working" that session) become intensely involved in the meeting.

But the here-and-now focus rapidly reaches the limits of its usefulness without the second step, which is the illumination of process. If the powerful curative factor of interpersonal learning is to be set into motion, the group must recognize, examine, and understand process. It must examine itself, it must study its own transactions, it must transcend pure experience and apply itself to the integration of that experience.

Thus, the effective use of the here-and-now is dualistic: the group lives in the here-and-now and it also doubles back on itself—it performs a self-reflective loop and examines the here-and-now behavior which has just occurred.

here-and-now self-reflective loop

here-and-now experience

Accordingly, the therapist has two discrete functions in the here-and-now: he must steer the group into the here-and-now and he must guide the self-reflective loop (or "process commentary"); much of the here-and-now steering function can be shared by the group members, but, for reasons we shall examine later, process commentary remains to a large extent the task of the therapist.

"Process" Definition. The term "process," used liberally throughout this text, has a highly specialized meaning in a number of other fields—law, anatomy, sociology, anthropology, psychoanalysis, and descriptive psychiatry. In interactional psychotherapy, "process" refers to the relationship implications of interpersonal transactions. A therapist who is process-oriented concerns himself not solely with the verbal content of the patient's utterance, but with the "how" and the "why" of the utterance, especially insofar as the "how" and "why" illuminate some aspects of the patient's relationship to others with whom he is interacting. Thus, the therapist considers the metacommunicational aspects of the message: * Why, from the relationship

---

* Metacommunication refers to the communication about the communication. Compare, for example: "Close the window!" "Wouldn't you like to close the window? You

aspect, is the patient making the statement at this time, to this person, in this manner? Consider, for example, this transaction: During a lecture a student raised his hand and asked, "What was the date of Freud's death?" The lecturer replied, "1938," only to have the student inquire, "But sir, wasn't it 1939?" The student asked a question the answer to which he already knew presumably for reasons other than a quest for information. ("A question ain't a question if you know the answer.") We might infer that the process of the transaction was that the student wished to demonstrate his knowledge, or that he wished to humiliate or defeat the lecturer. Frequently, in the group therapy setting, the understanding of process becomes more complex; we search not only for the process behind a simple statement but for the process behind a sequence of statements made by a patient or by a number of patients. What does this sequence tell us about the relationship between one patient and the other group members, or between clusters or cliques of members, or between the members and the leader, or, finally, between the group as a whole and its primary task?

Some clinical vignettes may further clarify the concept:

Early in the course of a group therapy meeting, Burt, a tenacious, bulldog-faced, intense graduate student, exclaimed to the group in general and to Rose (an unsophisticated astrologically inclined cosmetologist) in particular, "Parenthood is degrading!" This provocative statement elicited considerable response from the group, all of whom possessed parents and many of whom were parents, and the ensuing donnybrook consumed the remainder of the group session.

Let us consider the various perspectives available to the therapist and the group from which to view Burt's statement.

1. The statement can be viewed strictly in terms of substantive *content*. In fact, this is precisely what occurred in the group; the members engaged Burt in a debate of the virtues versus the dehumanizing aspects of parenthood—a discussion which was affect-laden but intellectualized and which brought none of the members closer to their goals in therapy. Subsequently, the group felt discouraged about the meeting and angry with themselves and with Burt for having dissipated a meeting.

---

must be cold." "I'm cold, would you please close the window?" "Why is this window open?" Each of these statements contains a great deal more than a simple request or command; each conveys a metacommunication—a message about the nature of the relationship between the two interacting individuals.

2. On the other hand, the therapist might have considered the *process* of Burt's statement, from any one of a number of perspectives.

a. Why did Burt attack Rose? What was the interpersonal process between them? In fact, the two had had a smoldering conflict for many weeks, and in the previous meeting Rose had wondered why, if Burt was so brilliant, was he still, at the age of thirty-two, a student. Burt had viewed Rose as an inferior being who functioned primarily as a mammary gland; once, when she had been absent, he had referred to her as a brood mare.

b. Why is Burt so judgmental and so intolerant of nonintellectuals? Must he always maintain his self-esteem by standing on the carcass of a vanquished or humiliated adversary?

c. Assuming that Burt was chiefly intent upon attacking Rose, why did he proceed so indirectly? Is this characteristic of Burt's expression of aggression? Or is it characteristic of Rose that no one dares, for some unclear reason, to attack her directly?

d. Why did Burt, through an obviously provocative and indefensible statement, set himself up for a universal attack by the group? Although the words were different, this was a familiar melody for the group and for Burt, who had on many previous occasions placed himself in this position. Was it possible that Burt was most comfortable when relating to others in this fashion? He once stated that he had always loved a fight; indeed, he almost licks his chops at the appearance of a row in the group. In fact, his early family environment was distinctively a fighting environment. Was fighting, then, a form (perhaps the only available form) of involvement for Burt?

e. The process may be considered from the even broader perspective of the entire group. Other relevant events in the life of the group must be considered. For the past two months the session had been dominated by Kate, a deviant, disruptive, and partially deaf member who had, two weeks previously, dropped out of the group with the face-saving proviso that she would return when she obtained a hearing aid. Was it possible that the group needed a Kate and was Burt merely filling the required role of scapegoat? Through its continual climate of conflict, through its willingness to spend an entire session discussing in nonpersonal terms a single theme, was the group avoiding something—possibly an honest discussion of their feelings concerning Kate's rejection by the group or their guilt or fear of a similar fate? Or were they perhaps avoiding the anticipated perils of self-disclosure and intimacy?

Was the group saying something to the therapist through Burt (and through Kate)? For example, Burt may have been bearing the brunt of an attack that was displaced from the co-therapists. The therapists—bearded, aloof figures with a proclivity for rabbinical-like pronouncements—had, interestingly enough, never been attacked or confronted by the group (although the patients, in private, referred to the group as "the Smith Brothers' group!"). Surely there were strong, avoided feelings toward them, which may have been further fanned by their failure to support Kate and by their complicity through inactivity in her departure from the group.

Which one of these many process observations is correct? Which one could the therapist have employed in an effective intervention? The answer is, of course, that any and all may be correct. They are not mutually exclusive; each may be correct without invalidating the others. Each views the transaction from a slightly different vantage point. By clarifying each of these in turn, the therapist could focus the group on many different aspects of its life. Which one, then, should the therapist choose?

The therapist's choice should be based on one primary consideration—the needs of the group. Where is the group at that particular time? Has there been too much focus on Burt of late with the others feeling bored, uninvolved, and excluded? In that case the therapist might best wonder aloud about what the group is avoiding. He might remind the group of previous sessions spent in similar discussions which left them dissatisfied, or he might help one of the members verbalize this by inquiring about his inactivity or apparent uninvolvement in the discussion. If the group communications have been exceptionally indirect, he might comment on the indirectness of Burt's attacks or ask the group to help, via feedback, clarify what is happening between Burt and Rose. If, as was the case in this group, there was an important group event which was being strongly avoided (Kate's departure), then this should be pointed out. In short, the therapist must determine what he thinks the group needs most at that time and help it move in that direction.

In a T-group of clinical psychology interns, one of the members, Robert, commented that he genuinely missed the contributions of some of the members who had been generally very silent. He turned to two of these members and asked if there was anything he or others could do that would help them participate more. The two members and the rest of the group responded by launching a withering attack on Robert. He was reminded that his own contributions had not been very substantial, that he was often silent for entire meetings himself, that he had never really expressed his emotions in the group, and so forth.

Viewed from the content level, this transaction is bewildering: Robert expressed concern for the silent members and, for his solicitude, was soundly buffeted. Viewed from the process level, however, it made perfectly good sense: the group members were very much involved in a struggle for dominance and their inner response to Robert's statement was, "Who are you to issue an invitation to speak? Are you the host or leader here? If we allow you to comment on our silence and suggest solutions, then we acknowledge your dominion over us," etc.

In another group, Kevin, an overbearing business executive, opened the meeting by asking the other members—housewives, lower income workers, and shopkeepers—for help with a problem confronting him. The problem was that he had received orders to cut his staff immediately by 50 percent—he had to fire twenty out of forty men.

The content of the problem was intriguing and the group spent forty-five minutes discussing such aspects as justice versus mercy—i.e., whether one retains the most competent men or whether one should retain the men with the largest families or those who would have the greatest difficulty in finding another job. Despite the fact that most of the members engaged animatedly in the discussion, which involved important problems in human relations, the therapist strongly felt that the session was an unproductive one: the members remained in "safe" territory and the discussion could have appropriately occurred at a dinner party or any other social gathering; furthermore, as time passed, it became abundantly clear that Kevin had already spent considerable time thinking through all aspects of this problem and no one was able to provide him with novel approaches or suggestions.

The continued focus on content was unrewarding and eventually frustrating for the group. What was the process of this transaction? The therapist had to consider the data available to him. As the meeting progressed, Kevin, on two occasions, revealed the amount of his salary (which was more than twice that of any other member); in fact, the overall interpersonal effect of Kevin's presentation was to make others aware of his affluence and power. The process became even more clear when the therapist recalled the previous meetings in which Kevin had attempted, in vain, to establish a special kind of relationship with the therapist (he had sought some technical information on a projective psychological test for a project on which he was working). Furthermore, in preceding meetings Kevin had been soundly attacked by the group for his intransigent religious convictions and labeled hypocritical because of his propensity for extramarital affairs and compulsive lying. He had also been termed "thick-skinned" because of his apparent insensitivity to the others. One other important aspect of Kevin's group behavior was his dominance; almost invariably he was the most active, central figure in the group meetings.

With this information about process, a number of alternatives were available to the therapist. He might have focused on Kevin's bid for prestige, especially following his loss of face in the previous meeting. Phrased in a nonaccusatory manner, a clarification of this sequence might have helped Kevin become aware of his desperate need for the group members to respect and admire him. At the same time the self-defeating aspects of his behavior could have been pointed out; despite his efforts to the contrary, the group had come to resent and, at times, even scorn him. Perhaps, too, Kevin was attempting to disclaim the appellation of "thick-skinned" by sharing with the group (or dramatizing) the personal agony he experienced in deciding how to cut his staff. The style of the intervention would have depended on Kevin's degree of defensiveness; if he had seemed particularly brittle or prickly, then one might have underscored how hurt he must have been at the previous meeting. If Kevin had been more open, the therapist might have asked him directly what type of response he would have liked from the others. Other therapists might have preferred to interrupt the content discussion and ask the group what Kevin's question had to do with last week's session. Or the therapist might have chosen to call attention to an entirely different type of process by reflecting on the group's apparent willingness to permit Kevin to occupy the group center stage week after week. By encouraging the members to discuss their response to his monopolization, the therapist could have helped the group initiate an exploration of their relationship to Kevin.

Process Focus—The Power Source of the Group. Process focus is not just one of many possible procedural orientations; on the contrary, it is indispensable and a common denominator to all effective interactional groups. One so often hears words to the following effect: "No matter what else may be said about experiential groups (therapy groups, encounter groups, etc.), one cannot deny that they are potent—that they offer a compelling experience for participants." The process focus is the power cell of these groups; it is precisely because they encourage process exploration that they are potent experiences. A process focus is the one truly unique feature of the experiential group; after all, there are many socially sanctioned activities in which the individual can express emotions, help others, give and receive advice, confess and discover similarities between himself and others. But where is it permissible to comment, in depth, on here-and-now behavior, on the nature of the immediately current relationship between people? Possibly only in the parent-young child relationship, and even then the flow is undirectional. The parent is permitted process comments: "Don't look away when I talk to you!" or "Be quiet when someone else is speaking," or "Stop saying 'I dunno.' " But process commentary among adults is tabooed social behavior; it is considered rude, impertinent, shocking, intrusive, flirtatious. It is observed generally in the context of extreme conflict, and when it surfaces, when individuals comment about others' manners, gestures, speech, physical appearance, one can be certain that the battle is bitter and the possibility of conciliation chancy.

Why should this be so? What are the sources of this taboo? Miles,[14] in a thoughtful essay, suggests the following reasons why process commentary is eschewed in social intercourse: socialization anxiety, social norms, fears of retaliation, and power maintenance.

Socialization anxiety. Process commentary evokes early memories and anxieties associated with parental criticism of the child's behavior. Parents comment on the behavior of children, and although some of this process focus is positive, much more is critical and serves to control and alter the child's behavior. Adult process commentary often awakens old socialization-based anxiety and is experienced as critical and controlling.

Social norms. If individuals felt free to comment at all times upon the behavior of others, social life would become intolerably self-conscious, complex, and conflicted. Underlying adult interaction is a shared contract that a great deal of immediate behavior will be invisible to the parties involved. Each party acts in the safety of the knowledge that his behavior is not being noticed (or controlled) by the others; this safety provides an autonomy and a freedom that would be impossible if each continuously dwelled on the fact that the others observe his behavior and are free to comment on it. The Freud-Jung correspondence [15] provides an excellent illustration: toward the end of their relationship both parties so carefully observed and analyzed every nuance of the other's behavior that the relationship became unbearable. Even the reader feels the mounting anxiety and restriction and longs for the liberating final dissolution. Thus, in a Darwinian sense, the pocess commentary taboo has originated and persists to permit survival of the interaction necessary for our social order.

Fears of retaliation. We cannot monitor or stare at another person too closely. Unless the relationship is an exceedingly intimate one, such intrusiveness is almost always dangerous and anxiety-provoking, and we can expect some form of retribution: we will be accused of rudeness, flirtatiousness, or attack, and we may, with some degree of certainty, expect some form of retaliation. If we choose to comment on another's behavior, we do so knowing that our view of the other is always imperfect; there is a distinct risk that our process comment will be inaccurate, leaving us vulnerable to feedback from the other, which by the same token will be imperfect and unjust. Aside from intentional systems such as a therapy group, there is no forum for interacting individuals to test and to correct their observations of one another.

Power maintenance. Process commentary undermines arbitrary authority structure. Industrial organizational development consultants have long known that if a social structure openly investigates its own structure and process, power equalization takes place. High power individuals are not only more technically informed but also possess organizational information which permits them to influence and manipulate. They not only have skills which allowed them to obtain a position of power but, once there, have such a central place in the flow of information that they are able to reinforce their position. The greater the authority structure of an institution, the more stringent are the precautions against open commentary process (viz., military, church). If an individual wishes to maintain a position of arbitrary authority, then it behooves him to inhibit the development of any rules permitting reciprocal process observation and commentary.

THE THERAPIST'S TASKS IN THE HERE-AND-NOW

In the first stage of the here-and-now focus, the therapist's task is to move the group into the here-and-now. By a variety of techniques, many of which we shall discuss shortly, he steers the group members away from discussion of outside material and focuses their energy upon their relationship with one another. He expends more time and effort upon this task early than late in the course of the group. As the group progresses, the members share much of this task with him and the here-and-now focus becomes an effortless and natural part of the group life flow. In fact, many of the norms described in the last section which the therapist must establish in the group are norms which foster a here-and-now focus. For example, when the leader sets norms of interpersonal confrontation, of emotional expressivity, of monitoring their own work, of valuing the group as an important source of information, he is, in effect, reinforcing the importance of the here-and-now. Gradually, members, too, come to value the here-and-now focus and will themselves work in the here-and-now and, by a variety of means, encourage their co-members to do likewise.

It is altogether another matter with the second phase of the here-and-now orientation—process illumination. There are forces preventing members from fully sharing that task with the therapist. The person who comments on process sets himself apart from the others; he is viewed with suspicion, as "not one of us." When a group member makes observations about what is happening in the group, the others often respond resentfully about his presumptuousness in elevating himself above the others. If he comments, for example, that nothing is happening today or that the group is stuck or that no one is revealing himself or that there seem to be strong feelings toward the therapist, then he courts danger; the response of the other members is predictable—they will challenge him to make something happen today, or to reveal himself, or to talk about *his* feelings to the therapist. Only the therapist is relatively exempt from that charge, only he has the right to suggest that others "work," or that others reveal themselves without his having to engage personally in the act which he suggests.

Throughout the life of the group, the members are involved in a struggle for favored positions in the hierarchy of dominance. At times the conflict around control and dominance is quite flagrant, at other times more quiescent. But it never vanishes. Some strive nakedly for power, others subtly; others desire it but are fearful of assertion; others always assume an obsequious, submissive posture. Statements by members which suggest that they place themselves above or outside the group generally evoke responses which emerge from the dominance struggle rather than from consideration of the content of the statement. Therapists are not entirely immune to evoking this response; some patients are inordinately sensitive to being controlled or manipulated by the therapist. They find themselves in the paradoxical position of applying to the therapist for help and yet are unable to accept help because all statements by the therapist are viewed through spectacles of distrust. This is a function of the specific pathology of some patients (and it is, of course, good grist for the therapeutic mill), it is not a global, universal response of the entire group.

By the same token, the therapist has far more freedom than any other member to store information, to make observations about sequences or cyclical patterns of behavior, to connect the events which have occurred over long periods of time.* He is the group historian, only he is permitted to maintain a temporal perspective, and he remains immune from the charge that he removes himself from the group, elevates himself above the others. It is the therapist who keeps in mind the original goals of the patient and the relationship between these goals and the events which gradually unfold in the group.

For example, two patients, Tim and Marjorie, had a sexual affair which eventually came to light in the group. The other members reacted in various ways but none so condemnatory nor so vehemently as Diana, a forty-five-year-old nouveau-moralist, who criticized them both for breaking group rules— Tim, for being "too intelligent to act like such a fool," Marjorie for "her irre-

---

* Stock and Whitman [16] studied, microscopically, a single, crucial incident in a group session. They noted that the therapist's apperception of the group interaction differed from that of the patients in that the therapist "is likely to maintain a 'diagnostic' attitude and to see both the total group and individual dynamics in a fairly broad time perspective. Patients, on the other hand, are more likely to respond with direct affect to immediate group events."

sponsible disregard for her husband and child," and the "Lucifer therapist" who just "sat there and let it happen." The therapist eventually pointed out that in her formidable moralistic broadside some individuals had been obliterated, that the Marjorie and Tim with all their struggles and doubts and fears whom Diana had known for so long had suddenly been replaced by faceless one-dimensional stereotypes. Furthermore, the therapist was the only one to recall the reasons for seeking therapy which Diana had expressed at the first group meeting: namely, that she needed help in dealing with her rage toward a nineteen-year-old rebellious, sexually awakening daughter, who was in the midst of a search for her identity and autonomy! From here it was but a short step for the group and then for Diana herself to enter the experiential world of her daughter and to understand with great clarity the nature of the struggle between mother and daughter.

There are many occasions when the process is rather obvious to all the individuals in the group but members cannot comment on it simply because the situation is too "hot," they are too much a part of the interaction to separate themselves from it. In fact, often, even at a distance, the therapist feels the heat and is himself wary about naming the beast.

One neophyte therapist, when leading a training group of hospital nurses, learned through collusive intermember glances in the first meeting that there was considerable unspoken tension between the young progressive nurses and the older, conservative nursing supervisors in the group. The therapist felt that the issue, one reaching deep into tabooed regions of the authority-ridden nursing profession, was too sensitive and potentially explosive to touch. His supervisor assured him that it was too important an issue to leave unexplored and that he should broach it, since it was highly unlikely that anyone else in the group could do what he dared not. In the next meeting the therapist did so in a manner which is often effective in minimizing defensiveness: he stated his own dilemma about the issue, i.e., he told the group that he sensed a hierarchical struggle between the freshly trained nurses and the powerful senior nurses but that he was hesitant to bring it up for fear that the younger nurses would either deny it or so attack the supervisors that the latter would suffer injury or angrily scuttle the group. His comment was enormously helpful and plunged the group into an open and constructive exploration of a vital issue.

I do not mean that only the leader *should* make process comments. As I shall discuss later, other members are entirely capable of performing this function; in fact, often their process observations are more readily accepted than those of the therapists. What is important is that the commentator not perform this function to avoid the patient role or in any other way to distance himself from or to elevate himself above the other members.

Thus far in this discussion I have, for pedagogical reasons, overstated two fundamental points which I must now qualify. Those points are: (1) the here-and-now approach is an ahistoric one and (2) there is a sharp distinction between here-and-now experience and here-and-now process illumination.

Strictly speaking, an ahistoric approach is an impossibility; every process comment refers to an act already belonging to the past. (Sartre once said, "Introspection is retrospection.") Not only does process commentary involve behavior which has just transpired but it frequently refers to cycles of behavior or repetitive acts which have occurred in the group over weeks or months. Thus, the past of the group, events in which the group members have participated, are a part of the here-and-now and an integral part of the data on which process commentary is based.

My qualification of the ahistoric approach goes even farther. As I shall discuss later in a separate section, no group can maintain a total here-and-now approach. There will be frequent excursions into personal history and into current life situations. In fact, this discourse is so inevitable that one becomes curious at its omission. What is important, however, is the accent: the crucial task is not to uncover, to piece together, and to understand the past, but to use the past for the help it offers in understanding (and changing) the individual's mode of relating to the others in the present.

The distinction between here-and-now experience and process commentary is not a sharp one—there is much overlap. For example, low inference commentary ("feedback") is both experience and commentary. When one member remarks that another refuses to look at him or that he is furious at another for continually deprecating him, he is at the same time commenting on process and involving himself in the affective here-and-now experience of the group. Process commentary, like nascent oxygen, exists for only a short duration; it rapidly becomes incorporated into the experiential flow of the group and becomes part of the data from which future process comments will flow. For example, in a group meeting of mental health trainees one member began the session with an account of some extreme feelings of depression and depersonalization. The group avoided pursuing his dysphoria and instead offered him much practical advice. The leader commented on the process—on the fact that the group veered away from asking the member about his depression and depersonalization—resulting in a considerable increase in emotional involvement on the part of the group and an uncovering of fears about self-disclosure. Soon afterward, however, a couple of counterdependent members objected to the leader's intervention; they felt that the leader was dissatisfied with their performance in the group, that he was criticizing them, and, in his usual subtle manner, was manipulating the group to fit in with his preconceived notions of the proper conduct of a meeting. Thus, the leader's process comments became part of the experiential ebb and flow of the group, and the members' criticism of the leader, at first process commentary, soon became experience, and in itself subject to process commentary, as the group worked not only with the accurate aspects of their observations but also with their tendency to challenge the leader at every step of the way.

Summary. The effective use of the here-and-now focus requires two steps: experience in the here-and-now and process illumination. (Process refers not to the content of a communication but to the implications of that communication about the nature of the relationship between the communicating parties.) It is the combination of these two steps which imbues an experiential group with such compelling potency.

There exist powerful injunctions against process commentary in everyday social intercourse.

The therapist has different tasks in each step. First, he must endeavor to plunge the group into the here-and-now experience. Second, he must help the group observe and understand the process of what has occurred.

The first step becomes part of the group norm structure and the group members ultimately assist the therapist in this chore.

The second task to a much greater extent remains the responsibility of the therapist and consists, as I shall discuss shortly, of a wide and complex range of behaviors ranging from labeling single behavioral acts to juxtaposing several acts to combining acts over time into a pattern of behavior to pointing out the undesirable consequences of the patient's behavioral patterns to more complex inferential explanations, or interpretations, about the meaning and motivation of such behavior.

HERE-AND-NOW ACTIVATION: TECHNIQUES

In this section I wish to describe but not prescribe some techniques: each therapist must develop techniques consonant with his style. More important than mastering any technique, the therapist must fully understand the strategy and theoretical foundations upon which all effective technique must rest.

I suggest that the therapist "think here-and-now." When he does so long enough, he reflexly steers the group into the here-and-now. Sometimes I feel like a shepherd herding a flock into an ever-tightening circle; I head off errant, historical, or "outside" statements like strays and guide them back into the circle. Whenever an issue is raised in the group, I think, "How can I relate this to the group's primary task? How can I make it come to life in the here-and-now?" I am relentless in this effort and I begin it in the very first meeting of the group.

For example, in the first meeting the members generally introduce themselves, tell something about why they have sought therapy, and, often with help from the therapist, may discuss how they are feeling that very day. I often intervene at some convenient point well into the meeting and remark to the effect that, "Many things have been going on here today; you're each gradually becoming part of the group, each gradually telling one another about yourself. But I have a hunch that something else is also going on and that is that you're each sizing one another up, each arriving at some impressions of the other, each wondering how you'll fit in with the others. I wonder now if we could spend some time discussing what each of us has come up with thus far."

The therapist moves the focus from outside to inside, from the abstract to the specific, from the generic to the personal. If a patient describes a hostile confrontation with a spouse or roommate, the therapist may inquire, "If you were to be angry like that with anyone in the group, with whom would it be?" or, "With whom in the group can you foresee getting into the same type of struggle?" If a patient comments that one of his problems is that he lies, or that he stereotypes people, or that he manipulates groups, the therapist may inquire, "What is the main lie you've told in the group thus far?" or, "Can you describe the way you've stereotyped some of us?" or, "To what extent have you manipulated the group thus far?" If a patient complains of mysterious flashes of anger or suicidal compulsions that come over him, the therapist underscores the importance of his signaling to the group the very moment they occur during the session so that the group can track them down and relate them to events that occur in the session.

If a member describes his problem as being too passive, too easily influenced by others, the therapist may move him directly into the issue by asking who in the group could influence him the most and who the least? If a member comments that the group is too polite and too tactful, the therapist may ask, "Who are the leaders of the peace and tact movement in the group?" If a member is terrified of revealing himself and fears humiliation, the therapist may ask him to identify those in the group who he imagines might be most prone to ridicule him.

In each of these instances the therapist can further deepen the interaction by encouraging responses from the others. "How do you feel about the stereotype?" "Can you imagine yourself ridiculing him?" "Does this resonate with feelings that you are indeed influential, angry, too tactful, etc.?" Even simple techniques of asking patients to speak directly to one another, to use second person rather than third person pronouns, and to look at one another are very useful.

Easier said than done! These suggestions are not always heeded. To some patients they are very threatening indeed, and the therapist must here, as always, employ good timing and attempt to experience what the patient is experiencing. Search for methods that lessen the threat. Begin by focusing on positive interaction: "Toward whom in the group do you feel most warm?" "Who in the group is most like you?" or, "Obviously, there are some strong vibes, both positive and negative, going on between you and John. I wonder what you most envy about him? And what parts of him do you find most difficult to accept?" The subjunctive tense often provides some safety and distance. "*If you were* to be angry at someone in the group, at whom would it be?" or, "*If you were* to go on a date with Albert [another group member], what kind of experience would it be?"

Resistance occurs in many forms; often it appears in the cunning guise of total equality. Especially in the early course of the group, patients often respond to the therapist's here-and-now urgings by claiming that they feel exactly the same toward all of the group members. They, in response to the therapist's inquiry, reply that they feel equally warm toward all the members, or feel no anger toward any, or feel equally influenced or threatened by all. Do not be misled by this. It is never true. Depending once again on his sense of timing, the therapist decides how much farther to push his inquiry. Sooner or later he must help members to differentiate one from the other. Eventually the patient will disclose that he does have slight differences of feelings toward some of the members. These slight differences are important and are often the vestibule to full interactional participation. I explore the slight differences (no one ever said they had to be enormous ones); sometimes I suggest that they hold up a magnifying glass to these differences and describe what they then see and feel.

If patients are very frightened of self-disclosure, the therapists may gently prod them along by asking for metadisclosures—disclosure about the disclosure (see pp. 117–118). For example, if a very shy, hidden member is helped by one of the members to share some of his secrets, the therapist might comment, "Joe, what was it like inside when you told us these things?" or, "What's been the hardest thing for you to say so far?" or, "Mary has asked you to tell a great deal about yourself. How did you feel about her questions? Did you welcome them? Resent them? Wish they had even come earlier? How can we know when we're pushing you too much or when you really want us to push?" I remember one variation which proved useful. Once in a T-group of psychiatric residents a member went around the group giving her impressions of each of the other members. When she finished, I asked her to go around again rating (on a 1-10 scale) her disclosures to each person for the amount of risk-taking she had done. The second round gently but significantly deepened her involvement in the process.

Often the resistance is deeply ingrained and considerable ingenuity is required. For example, one patient, Bob, resisted participation on a here-and-now level for months. (Keep in mind that "resistance" does not usually connote conscious obstinacy. More often it stems from sources out of awareness. Sometimes the here-and-now task is so unfamiliar and uncomfortable to the patient that it is not unlike learning a new language; unless maximal concentration is applied, he slips back into his habitual distance-elaborating mode.) Bob's typical mode of relating to the group was to describe some pressing current life problem. Often the problem assumed crisis proportions which placed some powerful restraints on the group. First, they felt compelled to deal immediately with the precise problem he presented, and second, they had to tread cautiously because he explicitly informed them that he needed all his resources to cope with the crisis and could not afford being shaken up by any interpersonal confrontation. "Right now, don't make waves, I'm just hanging on by my fingertips." Efforts to alter this pattern were unsuccessful and the group felt blocked and discouraged in dealing with Bob. They cringed when he brought in problems to the meeting.

One day he opened the group with a typical gambit: after weeks of searching he had obtained a new job but was convinced that he was going to fail and be dismissed. The group dutifully, but warily, investigated the situation. The investigation met with many of the familiar, treacherous obstacles which block the path of work on "outside" problems. There seemed to be no objective evidence that Bob was failing at work. He seemed, if anything, to be trying too hard, working eighty hours a week. The evidence, Bob insisted, simply could not be appreciated by anyone not there at work with him: the glances of his supervisor, the subtle innuendos, the air of dissatisfaction toward him, the general ambience in the office, the failing to live up to his (self-imposed and unrealistic) sales goals. Moreover, Bob was a highly unreliable observer; he always downgraded himself and disregarded his strengths.

The therapist moved the entire transaction into the here-and-now by asking, "Bob, what grade do you think you deserve in the group and what do each of the others get?" Bob, not unexpectedly, awarded himself a "D minus" and staked his claim for at least eight more years in the group. Bob awarded all the other members substantially superior grades. The therapist replied by awarding Bob a "B" for his work in the group and then went on to point out the reasons: Bob's commitment to the group, perfect attendance, willingness to help others, great efforts to work despite anxiety and often disabling depression.

Bob laughed it off; he treated the incident as a gag or a therapeutic ploy. But the therapist held firm and insisted that he was entirely serious. Bob then insisted the therapist was wrong and pointed out his failings in the group (one of which was, ironically, the avoidance of the here-and-now); however, his disagreement with the therapist was very incompatible with his long-held, frequently voiced, total confidence in the therapist. (He had often invalidated the feedback of other members in the group by claiming that he trusted no one's judgment except the therapist's.)

The intervention was enormously useful and it transferred the process of Bob's evaluation of himself from a secret chamber lined with the distorting mirrors of his self-perception to the open vital arena of the group. No longer was it necessary that the members accept Bob's perception of his boss's glares and subtle innuendos. The "boss" (the therapist) was there in group. The transaction, in its entirety, was available to the group.

I never cease to be awed by the rich lode of subterranean data which exists in every group and in every meeting. Beneath each sentiment expressed there are layers of invisible, unvoiced ones. How to tap these riches? Sometimes when there is a long silence in a meeting I express this very thought: "There is so much information that could be valuable to us all today if only we could excavate it. I wonder if we could, each of us, tell the group about some thoughts that occurred to us in this silence which we thought of saying but didn't." The exercise is more effective, incidentally, if the therapist himself starts it or participates. For example, "I've been feeling antsy in the silence, wanting to break it, not wanting to waste time, but on the other hand feeling irritated that it always has to be me doing this work for the group," or, "I've been feeling torn between wanting to get back to the struggle between you and me, Mike. I feel uncomfortable with this much tension and anger but I don't know, yet, how to help understand and resolve it." When I feel there has been a particularly great deal unsaid in a meeting, I have often used, with success, a technique such as this: "It's now six o'clock and we still have half an hour left, but I wonder if you each would imagine that it's already six-thirty and that you're on your way home. What kind of disappointments would you have about the meeting today?"

The therapist must help members discuss their feelings about the group itself as well as those toward individual members. For example, I may ask a new patient in the group how he viewed the previous meeting. If he comments that it was productive, I inquire about the most and the least productive parts of it. Whatever the technique, the aim is to help the patient move more deeply into the interactional flux of the group.

Many of the observations the therapist makes may be highly inferential. Objective accuracy is not the issue; as long as the therapist persistently directs the group from the nonrelevant, from "then-and-there" to "here-and-now," he is operationally correct. If a group spends time in an unproductive meeting discussing dull, boring parties and the therapist wonders aloud if they are indirectly referring to the present group session, there will be no method of ascertaining with any degree of certainty whether or not he is correct. "Correctness" in this instance must be defined relativistically and pragmatically. By shifting the group's attention from "then-and-there" to "here-and-now" material, he performs a service to the group—a service which, consistently reinforced, will ultimately result in a cohesive, interactional atmosphere maximally conducive to therapy. Following this model, the effectiveness of an intervention should be gauged by its success in focusing the group upon itself.

According to this principle, a group which dwells at length on the subject of poor health and the sense of guilt for remaining in bed during times of sickness might be asked if "the group isn't *really* wondering about the therapist's recent absence." Or a group suddenly preoccupied with death and the losses which each member has incurred might be asked whether they are also concerned with the impending four-week summer vacation for the group. One psychotherapy group in a prison which was asked to meet in a different room to permit observation by some visiting psychiatrists began its session with a lengthy discussion of new FBI computers which, at the press of a button, could deliver total information about any individual in a few seconds. The therapist made the useful interpretation that the group was dealing with the issue of being observed; he wondered if they were angry and disappointed with him and suspected that he, like the computer, had little regard for their feelings.

Obviously, these interventions would be pointless if the group had already thoroughly worked through all the implications of the therapist's recent absence, the impending four-week summer break, or the therapist's act of permitting observation. The technical procedure is not unlike the sifting process in any traditional psychotherapy. Presented with voluminous data in considerable disarray, the therapist selects, reinforces, and interprets those aspects which he deems most helpful to the patient at that particular time. Not all dreams and not all parts of a dream are attended to by the therapist; however, a dream theme which elucidates a particular issue on which the patient is currently working is vigorously pursued.

Implicit here is the assumption that the therapist knows the most propitious direction for the group at a specific moment. As we have seen, this is not a precise matter; what is most important is that the therapist has formulated for himself broad principles of ultimately helpful directions for the group and its members—this is precisely where a grasp of the curative factors is essential.

Often when the therapist engages in this activating function, he performs two simultaneous acts: he steers the group into the here-and-now but at the same time he interrupts the content flow in the group. Not infrequently, members feel resentful or rejected by the interruption and the therapist must attend to these feelings for they, too, are part of the here-and-now. This consideration often makes it very difficult for the therapist to intervene. Early in the socialization process we learn not to interrupt, not to change the subject abruptly. Furthermore, there are times in the group when everyone seems keenly interested in the topic under discussion; even though the therapist is certain that the group is not "working," it is not easy to buck the group current. Social psychological small group research strongly documents the compelling force of group pressure. To take a stand opposite to the perceived consensus of the group requires considerable courage and conviction.

My experience is that the therapist, when faced with this type of dilemma, increases the patient's receptivity if he expresses both sets of feelings to the group. For example, "Mary, I feel very strained as you talk. I'm having a couple of strong feelings; one is that you're into something that is very important and painful for you, and the other feeling is that Ed [the new member] has been trying hard to get into the group for the last few meetings and the group seems unwelcoming. This didn't happen when other new members entered the group. Why do you think it's happening now?" or, "Warren, I had two reactions as you started talking; the first is that I'm delighted you feel comfortable enough now in the group to participate, but the other feeling is that it's going to be hard for the group to respond to what you're saying because it's so very abstract and far removed from you personally. I'd be so much more interested in what it's been like inside for you the past weeks in the group; even though you've been silent, I know you've tuned in to many issues."

There are, of course, many more activating procedures, but my goal is not a compendium of techniques. Quite the contrary; I describe the techniques only to illuminate the underlying principle of here-and-now activation. These techniques, or "group gimmicks," are servants not masters. To use them injudiciously, to fill voids, to make the group more jazzy, to acquiesce to the members' demands that the leaders lead is seductive but not constructive for the group. In an encounter group research project [17] (see Chapter 14), one leader leaned too heavily on group gimmicks, employing them without proper timing or a clear conception of his role in the process of change. The outcome of his group was exceptionally poor, without a single member profiting significantly from the experience.

Remember that sheer acceleration of interaction is not the purpose of these techniques; if the therapist moves too quickly, using gimmicks to make interactions, emotional expression, and self-disclosure too easy, he misses the whole point. Resistance, fear, guardedness, distrust, in short, everything which impedes the development of satisfying interpersonal relations must be permitted expression. The goal is not to create a slick-functioning, streamlined social organization, but instead one which functions well enough and engenders sufficient trust for the unfolding of each member's social microcosm. Working through the resistances to change is the key to the production of change. Thus, the therapist does not want to go *around* obstacles but *through* them. (As we shall see in Chapter 14, this is one key difference between the therapy and the encounter group.)

PROCESS ILLUMINATION: TECHNIQUES

As soon as the therapist has been successful in steering patients into a here-and-now interactional pattern, he must concern himself with turning this interaction into therapeutic advantage. This task is complex and consists of several stages. The patient must first recognize what it is that he is doing with other people (ranging from simple acts to very complex patterns unfolding over a long duration of time); he must then appreciate the impact of this behavior upon others; he must understand the influence of his behavior upon other's opinion of him and consequently upon his own self-regard; he must decide whether he is satisfied with his habitual interpersonal style; and lastly he must be helped to exercise his will to change. Even when the therapist has helped the patient transform intent into decision and decision into action, his task is still not complete. He must help the patient solidify the change and he must encourage generalization of the change, from the group setting into the patient's larger life environment.

Each of these stages may be facilitated by some specific cognitive input by the therapist, and I shall describe each step in turn. First, however, there are several prior and basic considerations which I must discuss: How does the therapist recognize process? How can he help the members to assume a process orientation? How can the therapist increase the receptivity of the patient to his process commentary?

Recognition of Process. Before the therapist embarks on any phase of process illumination, he must himself learn to recognize process. The experienced therapist does this naturally and effortlessly; he observes the group proceedings from a perspective which permits him a continuous view of the process underlying the content of the group discussion. He automatically attends to process; he listens not solely to what the patient is telling but also to what the patient is saying through the process of telling it.

Thus in a group meeting, a patient, Pete, discloses much heavy, deeply personal material. The group is moved by Pete's account and devotes much time to listening, to helping him elaborate more fully, and to offering him support. The therapist shares in these activities but he entertains other thoughts as well. For example, he may wonder why of all the members it is invariably Pete who reveals first and most. Why does Pete so often put himself in the role of the group patient whom all the members must nurse? Why must he always display himself as so vulnerable? Why *today?* After the conflict in the group last meeting, one might have expected Pete to be angry; instead, he "shows his throat." Is he avoiding giving expression to his rage? And so forth.

At the end of a session in another group, Mr. Glass, a young, rather fragile patient, had, amidst considerable emotional upheaval, revealed for the first time his preference for homosexual relationships.

At the next meeting the group urged him to continue. He attempted to do so but, nearly asphyxiated with emotion, blocked and hesitated. Just then, with indecent alacrity, Mrs. Plough filled the gap with, "I have a problem." Mrs. Plough, an aggressive forty-year-old cab driver, who sought therapy because of social loneliness and bitterness, proceeded to discuss interminably a complex situation involving an unwelcome house-visiting aunt. For the experienced, process-oriented therapist, the phrase "I have a problem" is a double entendre. Far more trenchantly than her words, Mrs. Plough's behavior says, "I have a problem," and her problem is manifest in her insensitivity to Mr. Glass, who, after months of silence, had finally mustered the courage to speak.

It is not easy to tell the beginning therapist how to recognize process; the acquisition of this perspective is one of the major tasks of his training procedure. And it is an interminable task; throughout his career the experienced therapist increases his ability to penetrate more deeply into the substratum of group discourse. This greater vision increases the keenness of the therapist's interest in the meeting. Generally, beginning students who observe meetings find them far less meaningful, complex, and interesting than the experienced therapist.

There are certain guidelines, though, which may facilitate the neophyte therapist's recognition of process. Note the simple nonverbal sense data available: Who chooses to sit where? Which members sit together? Who chooses to sit close to the therapist? Who far away? Who sits near the door? Who comes to the meeting on time? Who is habitually late? Who looks at whom when they speak? Do some members look at the therapist while speaking to another member? If so, then they are not relating to one another but instead to the therapist through their speech to the other. Are members looking at their watches, slouching in their seats, or yawning? Are the chairs pulled away from the center of the table at the same time great interest is verbally professed in the group? Are coats kept on? When in a single meeting or in the sequence of meetings are they removed? How quickly does the group enter the room? How do they leave it? What about cigarettes; who smokes and when; in what manner? (Berger [18] describes a beautiful, self-possessed woman who smoked not in moments of tension but only when the tension had subsided sufficiently to allow her to light and hold the cigarette with aplomb.) A near-infinite variety of postural shifts may betoken discomfort; foot flexion, for example, is a particularly common sign of anxiety. A change in dress or grooming is not uncommonly an indicator of change in a patient or in the atmosphere of the entire group. The first flicker of resentment toward the leader from an unctuous, dependent male may be a change in group garb from a shirt and tie to an open-necked sport shirt. Indeed, it is common knowledge that nonverbal behavior frequently expresses feelings of which the patient is yet unaware; the therapist, through observing and teaching the group to observe nonverbal behavior, may hasten the process of self-exploration.

Sometimes the process is clarified by attending not only to what is said but to what is omitted: the female patient who offers suggestions, advice, or feedback to the male patients but never to the other women in the group; the group that never confronts or questions the therapist; the topics (e.g., sex, money, death) that are never broached; the patient who is never attacked; or the one who is never supported—all these omissions are part of the transactional process of the group.

Physiologists commonly study the function of a hormone by removing the endocrine gland which manufactures it and observing the changes in the hormone-deficient organism. Similarly, in group therapy, we may learn a great deal about the role of a particular member by observing the here-and-now process of the group when he is absent. For example, if the absent member is an aggressive, competitive individual, the group may feel liberated and other patients, who had felt threatened or restricted in the missing member's presence, may suddenly blossom into activity. If, on the other hand, the group has depended on the missing member to carry the burden of self-disclosure or to coax other members into speaking, then it will feel helpless and threatened when he is absent. Quite often this occurrence elucidates interpersonal feelings which previously were entirely out of the group members' awareness, and the therapist may, with profit, encourage the group to discuss these feelings toward the absent member both at that time and later in his presence.

Similarly, a rich supply of data about feelings toward the therapist often emerges in the leaderless or alternate meeting. One leader led a T-group of mental health professionals composed of one female and twelve males. The woman, though she habitually took the chair closest to the door, felt reasonably comfortable in the group until the therapist was out of town and a leaderless meeting was scheduled. At that meeting the group discussed sexual feelings and experiences far more blatantly than ever before, and she had terrifying fantasies of the group locking the door and descending upon her for a "gang bang." She realized how the therapist's presence had offered her safety against fears of unrestrained sexual behavior by the other members and against the emergence of her own sexual fantasies. (She realized, too, the meaning of her occupying the seat nearest the door.)

Search in every possible way to understand the relationship messages in any communication. Look for incongruence between verbal and nonverbal behavior. Be especially curious when there is something arhythmic about the transaction, when for example the intensity of a response seems disproportionate to the stimulus statement, or if the response seems to be off target or to make no sense. At these times look for several possibilities: for example, parataxic distortion (the responder is experiencing the sender unrealistically) or metacommunications (the responder is responding, accurately, not to the manifest content but to another level of communication) or displacement (the responder is reacting not to the current transaction but to feelings stemming from previous transactions).

Common group tensions. Remember that there are certain tensions always present, to some degree, in every therapy group. Consider, for example, such tensions as the struggle for dominance, the antagonism between mutually supportive feelings and sibling rivalrous ones, between greed and selfless efforts to help the other, between the desire to immerse oneself in the comforting waters of the group and the fear of losing one's precious individuality, between the wish to get better and the wish to stay in the group, between the wish to help others and the fear of being left behind. Sometimes these tensions are quiescent for months until some event wakens them and they erupt into forceful expression.

The therapist must not forget these tensions; they are always there, always subtly fueling the hidden motors of group interaction. The knowledge of these tensions often facilitates the therapist's recognition of process. For example, earlier in this chapter I described an intervention where the therapist, in an effort to steer a patient into the here-and-now, gave him a grade for his work in the group. The intervention was effective for that particular patient but not without repercussions for the rest of the group. The next meeting two patients asked the therapist to clarify some remark he had made to them at a previous meeting. The remarks had been so supportive in nature and so straightforwardly phrased that the therapist was puzzled at the request for clarification. Deeper investigation revealed that the two patients, and later others, too, were requesting grades from the therapist.

In another group of mental health professionals at several levels of training, the leader was deeply impressed at the group skills of Stewart, one of the youngest, most inexperienced members. The leader expressed his fantasy that Stewart was a plant, that he couldn't possibly be just beginning his training since he conducted himself like a veteran with ten years' group experience. The comment evoked a flood of sibling-rivalrous tensions; it was not easily forgotten by the group and for months to come it was periodically revived and angrily discussed. With his comment, the therapist planted the kiss of death on Stewart's brow since thereafter the group systematically challenged and deskilled him. When the therapist makes a positive comment or evaluation of one member, he is apt to evoke feelings of sibling rivalry. When, as in each of these two examples, he makes a comment which has comparative evaluative overtones, he can be certain that he will rake the embers of sibling rivalry into full conflagration.

The struggle for dominace fluctuates in intensity throughout the group. It is much in evidence at the beginning of the group as members jockey for position in the pecking order. Once the hierarchy is agreed upon, the issue may become quiescent with periodic flare-ups, for example, when some member, as part of his therapeutic work, begins to grow in assertiveness and to challenge the established order. When new members enter the group, especially agressive members who do not "know their place," who do not respectfully search out and honor the rules of the group, it is with a high degree of certainty that the leader may expect the dominance struggle to influence much of the group discourse. For example, in one group Betty was much threatened by the entrance of a new, aggressive woman, Rena. A few meetings later, when Betty discussed some important material concerning her inability to assert herself, Rena attempted to help by commenting that she, too, used to be like that, and then she presented various methods she had used to overcome it. Rena reassured Betty that if she continued to talk about it openly in the group she, too, would gain considerable confidence. Betty's response was silent fury of such magnitude that several meetings passed before she could discuss and work through her feelings. To the uninformed observer, Betty's response would appear puzzling, but with the knowledge of Betty's seniority in the group and Rena's vigorous challenge to that seniority, her response was entirely predictable. She did not respond to Rena's manifest offer of help but instead to Rena's metamessage of "I'm more advanced than you, more mature, more knowledgeable about the process of psychotherapy, and more powerful in this group despite your longer presence here."

Primary task and secondary gratification. The concepts of primary task, secondary gratification, and the dynamic tension between the two provide the therapist with a useful guide to the recognition of process (and, as I shall discuss later, a guide as well to the factors underlying the patient's resistance to process commentary).

First some definitions. The *primary task* of the patient is, quite simply, to achieve that for which he originally sought help. He may wish for relief of suffering, better relationships with others, or to live more productively and fully.

It may be much more complicated than this. Sometimes the patient's view of his primary task changes considerably as he progresses in therapy. Sometimes the patient and the therapist have widely different views of his primary task. I have, for example, known patients who verbalize a goal of relief from pain (e.g., from anxiety, depression, insomnia, etc.) but have a deeper and more problematic goal of a different nature; for example, one patient hoped that through therapy he would become so well that he would out-mental health others, become even more superior to his adversaries; another wished to learn how to manipulate others even more effectively. The patient's reality testing may be sufficiently good to keep these goals quite hidden. They are not advanced as part of the initial "contract" he makes with the therapist, and yet they exert a pervasive influence in his work. In fact, much therapy may have to occur before some patients can formulate an appropriate primary task.

The patient, then, is generally aware of what he wishes to achieve in the therapy experience. By methods which we have discussed, the therapist, in his pre-group preparation of the patient and in the first group meetings, makes the patient aware of what he must do in the group if he is to accomplish his primary task. And yet once the group begins, some very peculiar things begin to happen. A number of clinical vignettes illustrate this paradox.

A young female patient enjoyed the attention of all three of the men in the group. She withheld the information from the group that she was engaged to be married, even though her sado-masochistic relationship with her fiancé was an enormous problem for her. After she was married, she misrepresented her husband to the group by portraying him as a passive ne're-do-well rather than an accomplished mathematician. She feared that if the men in the group realized what a formidable competitor her husband was, they would be frightened away. The sham continued for several months.

Bill, a young man in another group, behaved analogously. He was much interested in seducing the women of the group and shaped his behavior in an effort to appear suave and charming. He concealed his feelings of awkwardness, his desperate wish to be "cool," his fear of women, and his envy of some of the men in the group. He could never discuss his compulsive masturbation and occasional voyeurism. Whe another male member discussed his disdain for the women in the group, Bill (pleased at the withdrawal of competition) praised him for his honesty. When another member discussed, with much anxiety, his homosexual fantasies, Bill deliberately withheld the solace he might have offered in sharing his own, similar fantasies. Nothing took precedence over being "cool."

Another patient devoted all her energies to achieving an image of mental agility and profundity. She, often in very subtle ways, continuously took issue with the therapist. She scorned any help the therapist attempted to offer her and took great offense when he attempted to interpret her behavior. When the therapist reflected that she made him feel he had nothing of value to offer her, her finest hour occurred as she beamed that perhaps *he* ought to join a therapy group to work on *his* problems.

Another member enjoyed an enviable position in the group because of his mistress, a beautiful actress, whose picture he delighted to pass around in the group. She was his showpiece, a living proof of his natural superiority. When one day she suddenly and peremptorily left him, he was too mortified to face the group and dropped out of therapy.

These examples have one common feature: in each instance the patient has given priority not to the primary task but to some *secondary gratification* arising in the group: a relationship with another member, an image which he wishes to project, a group role in which he is the most sexually desirous, most influential, most wise, most superior.

In each of these illustrations the patient's pathology obstructed the pursuit of the primary goal. And yet, is this not as it should be? Have we not stressed so often that patients recreate their interpersonal worlds in the social microcosm of the group? To be sure! But in the incidents described here the portrayal of pathology assumed a form which, on a very basic level, opposed the work of therapy. Patients diverted their energies from therapy to the pursuit of some form of gratification in the group. If this here-and-now behavior were avaiable for study, if the patients could, as it were, be pulled out of the group matrix to view in a more dispassionate manner their actions, then the entire sequence would become part of the therapeutic work. But in all these instances the gratification took precedence over the work to be done. Patients concealed information, misrepresented themselves, rejected the therapist's help, and refused to give help to one another.

This is a familiar phenomenon in individual therapy. Long ago, Freud spoke of the patient whose desire to remain in therapy outweighed his desire to be cured. The individual therapist satisfies his patients' wishes to be succored, to be listened to, to be cradled. Yet there is a vast, quantitative difference in this respect between individual and group therapy. The individual therapy format is far more insular; the group situation offers an enormous range of gratifications. To the extent that the group is a social microcosm, it contains the possibil-

ities of satisfying virtually any social need in the individual's life.
Moreover, the gratification offered is often compelling; our social
needs to be dominant, to be admired, to be loved, to be revered are
very powerful indeed.

Is the tension that exists between primary task and secondary gratification nothing more than a sightly different way of referring to the familiar concept of "resistance" and especially of "acting out?" In the
sense that the pursuit of secondary gratification obstructs the therapeutic work, it may generically be labeled as resistance. Yet there is a
shade of difference which I wish to emphasize. Resistance ordinarily
refers to pain avoidance. Freud's original view was that the very same
psychic energies that were responsible for the repression of a noxious
experience act to guard the gateway to the abode of the repressed material and to fend off any inquiry threatening to disturb that material
and to unleash the original dysphoria. The definition has broadened
since then but still retains the general connotation of "protection."
Obviously, resistance in this sense is very much in evidence in group
therapy, both on an individual and, as we shall discuss, on a group
level. What I wish to emphasize is the abundant availability of secondary gratification in the therapy group. Often the therapeutic work in a
group is derailed not because the patient is too defensively anxious to
work but because he finds himself unwilling to relinquish gratification.

Often, when the therapist is bewildered by the course of events in
the therapy group, the distinction between primary task and secondary gratification is most useful. If the therapist asks himself, "Is the
patient working on his primary task?" he has a firm base of departure.
And when the substitution of secondary gratification for primary task
is well-entrenched and resistive to intervention, the therapist has no
more powerful technique than to remind the patient of his primary
task—the original reasons for his seeking therapy.

The same principle applies to the entire group as well. It can be
said that the group has a primary task which consists of the development and exploration of all aspects of the relationship of each member
to each of the others, to the therapist, and to the group as an aggregate.
The therapist and, later, the group members can easily enough sense
when the group is working, when it is involved in its primary task, and
when it is avoiding that task. The leader may be unclear about what it
is that the group is doing, but he does know that it is not involved in
either developing or exploring relationships between members. If the
therapist has been successful in helping the group to identify its task,
then he must conclude that it is actively evading the task either be-

cause of some dysphoria associated with the task itself or because of some form of secondary gratification which is sufficiently satisfying to supplant the therapy work.

Attend to your feelings. All of these guides to the recognition and understanding of process have their usefulness. But the most important clues the therapist has are his own feelings in the meeting, feelings that he comes to trust after repeated episodes of consensual validation from previous similar incidents in his group therapy experience. The experienced therapist learns to listen to his feelings; they are as useful to him as a microscope to a microbiologist. If he feels impatient, frustrated, bored, confused, discouraged—any of the entire panoply of feelings available to an individual—he considers this valuable data and puts it to work, if appropriate.

One does not have to understand his feelings or arrange and deliver a neat interpretive corsage. The simple expression of feelings is often sufficient to help the patient proceed further. One therapist, for example, experienced a forty-five-year-old woman in an unreal, puzzling manner because of her rapidly fluctuating method of presenting herself. He finally commented: "Sharon, I have several feelings about you that I'd like to share. As you talk I often experience you as a competent mature woman, but sometimes I see you as a very young, almost presexual child trying to cuddle, trying to be pleasing to everyone. I don't think I can go any farther with this now, but I wonder what chords this strikes up in you." The observation struck some very deep chords in the patient and helped her to explore her conflicted sexual identity and her anxiety separation.

Sharing feelings of being shut out often proves useful. Consider the following example from a multiple impact therapy session (a psychotherapy teaching format [19] in which one patient meets with several therapists, with procedural rules similar to those of group therapy.)

In her fourth session Mrs. Straw, a severely ill narcotics addict with a marked inability to interact directly with others (a problem which the group had been exploring), began with an involved, detailed account of a family argument. With its endless procession of names of cousins, great aunts, and neighbors, the story, whatever else it meant, had the effect of excluding the therapists from her world during the hour.

Finally, one commented that he felt impatient, frustrated, and very much shut out. She then took a note out of her purse and read something that she said she had written to the group of therapists. It was a long, rather chilling allegory involving her swimming aimlessly in circles, with children nearby trying to swim with weights on their feet which adults had placed there to help them develop power. She shouted for help to passers-by on the shore and they encouraged her to swim harder and to rest in a boat which, however, was full of holes and drew water. She knew that, although it was good to rest, she could never learn to swim in a boat.

The allegory was poignant and intriguing; but the therapists, when they recalled the group's primary task, verbalized once again their feelings of exclusion and frustration. The reading of the allegory had been an entirely autistic affair which effectively kept them at a great distance. Mrs. Straw then remarked that she had to tell the group that she was drowning. A therapist said that he sensed her feeling of drowning in the very first session and wondered why she had to tell them in this beautiful but devious fashion. In an unusual burst of directness, she replied that she wished to pique their interest in her by showing how sensitive and clever she was. Others pointed out that this was unnecessary and that they had, in fact, often thought and talked about her between sessions. They felt that though her strategy was in part successful (they were intrigued and impressed by the allegory), it also resulted in annoying and distancing them; it was after she had unveiled both the allegory and her need to impress them that their interest in her was greatest. Although literary devotees may shudder at this dismissal of her allegory as a much-to-be-eschewed manifestation of interpersonal deviousness, it proved, nonetheless, good medicine for his patient, who had seen Xanadu too often in her beclouded, oblique course through an unpeopled world.

To reply on his feelings in the therapeutic process, the therapist must have a reasonable degree of confidence in the appropriateness of his feelings. If the therapist responds inappropriately to the patient, then that feeling, too, is important but more so to the therapist than to the patient. The more the therapist responds unrealistically to the patient (on the basis of counter-transference or possibly because of pressing personal emotional problems), the less helpful, in fact, the more antitherapeutic, will he be in presenting these feelings as if they were the patient's problem rather than his own. The therapist needs to use the delicate instrument of his own feelings, and he needs to use it frequently and spontaneously. It is of the utmost importance that this instrument be as reliable and accurate as possible. It is for this reason that I believe every therapist should obtain sufficient personal psychotherapy. (More about this in Chapter 15.)

Helping Group Members Assume a Process Orientation. It has long been known that observations, viewpoints, and insights arrived at through one's own efforts are valued more highly than those that are thrust upon one by another. The mature leader resists the temptation to make brilliant virtuoso interpretations; instead, he searches for methods which will permit patients to achieve self-knowledge through their own efforts. As Foulkes [20] put it, "There are times when the therapist must sit on his wisdom, must tolerate defective knowledge and wait for the group to arrive at solutions."

The task, then, is to influence members to assume and to value the process perspective. Many of the norm-setting activities of the leader described earlier in this chapter serve this end. For example, the therapist emphasizes process by periodically tugging the members out of the here-and-now and inviting them to consider more dispassionately the meaning of the transactions which have recently occurred. Though techniques vary depending on the therapist's style, the intent of these interventions is to switch on a self-reflective beacon. The therapist may, for example, interrupt the group at an appropriate interval to comment, in effect, "We are about halfway through our time for today and I wonder how everyone feels about the meeting thus far?"

By no means does the therapist have to understand the process to ask for members' analyses. He may simply say, "I'm not sure what's happening in the meeting but I do see some unusual things; e.g., Bill has been very silent, Jack's moved his chair back three feet, Mary's been shooting glances at me for the past several minutes. What ideas do you all have about what's going on today?"

A process review of a "highly charged" meeting is often necessary. It is important for the therapist to demonstrate that intense emotional expression provides material for significant learning. Sometimes the therapist can divide such a meeting into two parts: the experiential and the analysis of that experience. At other times the therapist may rehash at the following meeting; he can ask about the feelings that members took home with them after the previous meeting or simply solicit further thoughts they've since had about what occurred.

Obviously, the therapist teaches through modeling his own process orientation. There is nothing to lose and much to gain by the therapist sharing whenever possible his perspective on the group. Sometimes he may do this in an effort to clarify the meeting: "Here are some of the things I've seen going on today. . . ." Sometimes he may wish to use a convenient device such as summarizing the meeting to a late arriving co-therapist or member.

In Chapter 13 I describe a technique which, in extreme form, shares the therapist's process observations with the patients. Following each meeting, the therapist writes a detailed summary of the meeting, including a continuous stream of his spoken and unspoken process observations, and distributes these summaries to the patients prior to the next meeting. In this approach the therapist, despite his personal and professional disclosure, seemed to lose none of his effectiveness. Quite the contrary; in a number of ways the therapy work seemed to be facilitated. One particular effect was the increase in the patients' perceptivity to the process of the group.

Facilitating the Patients' Acceptance of Process-Illuminating Com-

ments. F. Scott Fitzgerald once wrote, "I was impelled to think. God, was it difficult! The moving about of great secret trunks." Throughout therapy, patients are asked to think, to shift internal arrangements, to examine the consequences of their behavior. It is hard work and it is often unpleasant, frightening work. It is not enough simply to provide patients with information or explanations; the therapist must also facilitate the assimilation of the new information. He can use a number of strategies to help patients in this work.

Be concerned with the framing of interpretive remarks. No comments, not even the most brilliant ones, can be of value if delivery is not accepted, if the patient rejects the package unopened and uninspected. The relationship, the style of delivery, and the timing are thus as essential as the content of the message. Beware of appellations which are categorizing or limiting; they are counterproductive, they threaten, they raise defenses. Patients reject global accusations: e.g., dependency, narcissism, exploitation, arrogance. And with good reason, since we are always more than any one or any combination of labels. It is far more acceptable (and far more true) to speak of traits or parts of an individual. For example, "I often can sense you very much wanting to be close to others, offering help as you did last week to Mickey, but there are other times, like today, when I see you as aloof, almost scornful of the others. What do you know about this part of you?"

Often in the midst of heavy group conflict, group members hurl important truths at one another. Under these conditions, one cannot acknowledge the truth—it would be aiding the aggressor, committing treason against oneself. If he is to make the conflict-spawned truths available for consumption, the therapist must appreciate and neutralize the defensiveness of the combatants. He may, for example, appeal to a higher power (the patient's desire to know himself) or he may increase receptivity by limiting the scope of the accusation. For example, "Farrell, I see you now closed up, threatened, and fending off everything that Jamie is saying. You've been very adroit in pointing out the weaknesses of her arguments; but what happens is that you (and Jamie, too) end up getting nothing for yourself. I wonder if you could take a different tack for a while and ask yourself this" (and later, "Jamie, I'd like to ask you to do the same"): "is there *anything* in what Jamie is saying that is true for you? What parts seem to strike an inner chord? Could you forget for a moment the things that are *not* true and stay with those that *are* true?"

These are certain repetitive patterns which, if clearly labeled, can be quite useful in the recognition and acceptance of process commentary. Eric Berne described, in extremely accessible and often humorous terms, a number of such repetitive patterns or "games." These are often helpful for a start but like any labeling techniques become restrictive if depended upon so heavily that leaders attempt to fit all human interaction into a few procrustean beds.

Sometimes patients, in an unusually open moment, make a statement which may at some future time provide the therapist with great leverage. The thrifty therapist underscores these comments in the group and stores them for future use. For example, one patient who was both proud of and troubled by his ability to manipulate the group with his social charm pleaded one meeting: "Listen, when you see me smile like this I'm really hurting inside. Don't let me keep getting away with it." Another patient who tyrannized the group with her tears announced one day: "When I cry like this I'm angry, I'm not going to fall apart, so stop comforting me, stop treating me like a child." These moments of truth can be of great value if recalled, in a constructive, supportive manner, at times when the patient is closed and defensive.

Process Commentary—A Theoretical Overview

It is not easy to discuss, in a systematic way, the actual practice of process illumination. How can one propose crisp, basic guidelines for a procedure which has such complexity, such range, such delicate timing, so many linguistic nuances. One is tempted to beg the question by claiming that herein lies the art of psychotherapy: it will come to the therapist as he gains experience; he cannot, in a systematic way, come to it. To a degree, I believe this to be so; yet I also believe that it is possible to blaze crude trails, to provide the clinician with general principles that will accelerate his education without limiting the scope of his artistry.

The approach I shall take in this section closely parallels the approach I used in the beginning of this book to clarify the basic curative factors in group therapy. At that time I asked the questions: How does group therapy help patients? In the group therapeutic process, what is "core" and what is "front"? This approach led to the delineation of a number of basic curative factors and, I believe, did not result in any restraint on the therapist in his choice of methods to implement these factors.

In this section I shall proceed in a similar fashion. Here the issue is not "How does group therapy help?" but "How does the act of process illumination lead to change?" Although the issue warrants considerable attention because of its great complexity, the length of this discussion should not suggest that the interpretive function of the therapist take precedence over his other tasks.

First, let us proceed to view in a dispassionate manner the entire range of interpretive comments. We shall ask of each the simplistic but basic question, "How does this interpretation, this process-illuminating comment, help the patient to change?" Such an approach, consistently followed, leads one to discover a set of basic operational patterns. Despite the vast ideological complexity of clinical interpretations, they all lead into a very few final common pathways to change. I shall in this section describe these pathways, but I wish to emphasize that they are the product of a systems analysis of a process; this section is not to be construed as a recipe or flow chart for interpretation. I do suggest, however, that the analysis offered herein is an accurate and comprehensive representation of the relationship between process commentary and the initiation of change, and that the neophyte therapist may profit from building his interpretive approach upon these basic premises.

Let us begin by studying a series of process comments that a therapist made to a patient over several months of group therapy.

1. You are interrupting me.
2. Your voice is tight and your fists are clenched.
3. Whenever you talk to me you take issue with me.
4. When you do that I feel angry, threatened, and often frightened.
5. I think you feel very competitive with me and are trying to devalue me.
6. I've noticed that you've done the same thing with all the men in the group. Even when they try to approach you helpfully you strike out at them. Consequently, they see you as hostile and threatening.
7. In the three meetings when there were no women present in the group you were more approachable.
8. I think you're so concerned about your sexual attractiveness to women that you view men only as competitors. You deprive yourself of the opportunity of ever getting close to a man.
9. Even though you always seem to spar with me, there seems to be another side to it. You often stay after the group to have a word with me; you frequently look at me in the group. And there's that dream you described three weeks ago about the two of us fighting and then falling to the ground in an embrace. I think you very much want to be close to me but somehow you've got closeness and homosexuality entangled and you keep pushing me away.
10. You are lonely here and feel unwanted and uncared for. That rekindles so many of your bad feelings of unworthiness.

11. So what's happened in the group now is that you've distanced yourself, estranged yourself from all the men here. Are you satisfied with that? (Remember that one of your major goals when you started the group was to find out why you've not had any close men friends and to do something about that.)

Note that the comments form a progression from sense data commentary—observations of single acts—to a description of feelings evoked by that act, to observations about several acts over a period of time, to the juxtaposition of different acts, to speculations about the patient's intentions and motivations, to comments about the unfortunate repercussions of his behavior, to the inclusion of more inferential data (dreams, subtle gestures), to calling attention to the similarity between his behavioral patterns in the here-and-now and in his outside social world.

As the sequence progresses, the comments become more inferentially based. They begin with sense data observations and gradually shift to more complex generalizations based on sequences of behavior, interpersonal patterns, fantasy, and dream material. As the comments become more complex and more inferential, the author of the comments becomes more removed from the other person; in short, more a therapist process-commentator. Members often make some of the earlier statements to one another but, for reasons I have already presented, rarely make the ones at the end of the sequence. There is, incidentally, an exceptionally clear barrier between comments #4 and #5. The first four statements issue from the experience of the commentator. They are his experience; they can be devalued or ignored, but they cannot be denied, they cannot be taken away from him. The fifth statement ("I think you feel very competitive with me and are trying to devalue me") is much more likely to evoke defensiveness and to close down constructive interactional flow. This genre of comment is intrusive; it is a guess about the other's intention and motivation and is often rejected unless an important trusting, supportive relationship has been previously established. If members in a young group make many type #5 comments to one another, they are not likely to develop a constructive therapeutic climate.

But how does this series (or any series of process comments) help the patient change? In making these process comments, the therapist initiates the process of change by escorting his group patient through the following sequence:

1. *Here is what your behavior is like.* Through feedback and, later, through self-observation, the patient learns to see himself as others see him.

2. *Here is how your behavior makes others feel.* Members learn about the impact of their behavior on the feelings of other members.
3. *Here is how your behavior influences the opinions others have of you.* Members learn that, as a result of their behavior, others value them, dislike them, find them unpleasant, respect them, avoid them, etc.
4. *Here is how your behavior influences your opinion of yourself.* Building on the information gathered in the first three steps, patients formulate self-evaluations; they make judgments about their self-worth and their lovability. (Recall Sullivan's aphorism that the self-concept is largely constructed from reflected self-appraisals.)

Once this sequence has been developed and is fully understood by the patient, once he has a deep understanding that his behavior is not in his own best interests, that his relationships to others and to himself are a result of his own actions, then he has come to a crucial point in therapy—he has entered the antechamber of change. The therapist is now in a position to pose a question which initiates the real crunch of therapy. The question, presented in a number of ways by the therapist but rarely in direct form, asks: "Are you satisfied with the world you have created? This is what you do to others, to others' opinion of you, and to your opinion of yourself—*are you satisfied with your actions?*"

When the inevitable negative answer arrives, the therapist embarks on a many-layered effort to transform a sense of personal dissatisfaction into a decision to change and then into the act of change. In one way or another, the therapist's interpretive remarks are designed to encourage the act of change. Only a few psychotherapy theoreticians (e.g., Rank,[21] May,[22] Arieti,[23] Farber [24]) include the concept of "will" in their formulations; yet it is, I believe, implicit in most interpretive systems. The intrapsychic agency which initiates an act, which transforms intention and decision into action, is "will." Will is the primary "responsible mover" within the individual. Although modern metapsychology has chosen to emphasize the "irresponsible movers" [24] of our behavior (i.e., unconscious motivations and drives), it is difficult to do without the idea of "will" in our understanding of change. We cannot bypass it under the assumption that it is too nebulous and too elusive and, consequently, consign it to the black box of the mental apparatus, to which the therapist has no access.

Knowingly or unknowingly, every therapist assumes that each patient has within him the capacity to change through willful choice. The therapist, using a variety of strategies and tactics, attempts to escort the patient to a crossroads where he can choose, choose willfully in the best interests of his own integrity. The therapist's task is not one of creating will or of infusing will into the patient. That, of course, he cannot do. What he can do is to help remove encumbrances from the bound or stifled will of the patient.

The concept of will provides us with a useful construct in understanding the procedure of process illumination. The interpretive remarks of the therapist can all be viewed in terms of how they bear on the patient's will. The most common and simplistic therapeutic approach is an exhortative one. "Your behavior is, as you yourself now know, counter to your best interests. You are not satisfied, this is not what you want for yourself. Damn it, change!" The expectation that the patient will change is simply an extension of the moral philosophical belief that if man knows the good (i.e., what, in the deepest sense, is in his best interest), he will act accordingly. In the words of Aquinas: "Man, insofar as he acts willfully, acts according to some imagined good." And, indeed, for some individuals this knowledge and this exhortation is sufficient to produce therapeutic change. To be sure, this is often the case for individuals who change as a result of some short-term experiential group. However, patients with significant and well-entrenched psychopathology generally need much more.

The therapist, through interpretative comments, proceeds to exercise one of several other options which help the patient to disencumber his will. The therapist's goal is to guide the patient to a point where he accepts one, several, or all of the following basic premises:

1. ONLY I CAN CHANGE THE WORLD I HAVE CREATED FOR MYSELF.
2. THERE IS NO DANGER IN CHANGE.
3. TO ATTAIN WHAT I REALLY WANT, I MUST CHANGE.
4. I CAN CHANGE, I AM POTENT.

Each of these premises, if fully accepted by the patient, can be a powerful stimulant to willful action. Each exerts its influence in a different way. Though I shall discuss each in turn, I do not wish to imply a sequential pattern. Each, depending on the need of the patient and the style of the therapist, may be effective independently of the others.

ONLY I CAN CHANGE THE WORLD I HAVE CREATED FOR MYSELF

Behind the simple group therapy sequence I have described (seeing one's own behavior and appreciating its impact on others and on oneself) there is a mighty overarching concept, one whose shadow touches every part of the therapeutic process. That concept is *responsibility*, and though it is rarely discussed explicitly, it is nonetheless woven into the fabric of most psychotherapeutic systems. "Responsibility" has many meanings: legal, religious, ethical. I shall use it in the sense that one is "responsible for" by being "the basis of," the "cause," the "author" of something.

One of the most fascinating aspects of group therapy is that everyone is born again, born together in the group. Each member starts off on an equal footing. Each, in the view of the others (and, if the therapist does his job, in the view of himself), gradually scoops out and shapes his own life space in the group. *Each, in the deepest sense of the concept, is "responsible" for this space and for the sequence of events which will occur to him in the group.* Once the patient truly appreciates this, it follows that he must accept, too, that there is no hope for change unless he changes. Others will not change him for him, nor will change occur to him. He is responsible for his past and his present life in the group (as well as in the outside world), and he is similarly and totally responsible for his future.

Thus, the therapist helps the patient to understand that the world is arranged in a generally predictable and orderly fashion, that it is not that he *cannot* change but that he *will* not change, that he bears the responsibility for the creation of his world, and therefore, the responsibility for the transmutation of this world.

THERE IS NO DANGER IN CHANGE

These efforts may not be enough. The therapist may tug at his therapeutic cord and learn that the patient, even if he is thus enlightened, still makes no significant therapeutic movement. So the therapist attempts to apply additional therapeutic leverage. He helps his patient face the paradox that he continues to act contrary to his basic interests. The therapist in a number of ways begins to pose the question, "How come? How come you continue to defeat yourself?"

A common method of explaining "How come?" is to assume that there are obstacles to the patient's exercising willful choice, obstacles which prevent the patient from considering in any serious manner altering his behavior. The presence of the obstacle is generally inferred; the therapist makes an as-if assumption: "You behave *as if* you feel there were some considerable danger that would befall you if you were to change. You fear to act otherwise lest some calamity befall you." The therapist assists the patient to clarify the nature of the imagined danger and then proceeds, in a number of ways, to detoxify, to disconfirm the reality of this danger.

The patient's reason may be enlisted as an ally; the process of identifying and naming the fantasied danger may, in itself, enable the patient to understand how far his fears are removed from reality. Another approach is to encourage the patient, in carefully calibrated doses, to commit the dreaded act in the group. The fantasied calamity does not, of course, ensue and the dread is gradually extinguished. For example, a patient may avoid any aggressive behavior because at a very deep level he fears that he has a dammed-up reservoir of homicidal fury and must be constantly vigilant lest he unleash it and eventually face retribution from others. The therapist helps the patient express aggression in small doses in the group: his pique at being interrupted, his irritation at members who are habitually late, his anger at the therapist for charging him money, etc. Gradually, he is helped to relate openly to the other members and to demythologize himself as an alien and homicidal being. Although the language is different, this is precisely the same approach to change used in systematic desensitization—a major technique of behavior therapy.

TO ATTAIN WHAT I REALLY WANT, I MUST CHANGE

Another explanatory approach which many therapists take to deal with the paradox that patients persist in behaving counter to their best interests is to consider the payoffs of their present behavior. Though the behavior of the patient sabotages many of his mature needs and goals, at the same time it satisfies another set of needs and goals. In other words, the patient has conflicting motivations which cannot be simultaneously satisfied. For example, a patient may wish to be able to establish mature heterosexual relationships, but at another, often unconscious, level he may wish to be nurtured, to be cradled endlessly, to assuage castration anxiety by a maternal identification, or, to use another vocabulary, to be sheltered from the terrifying freedom of adulthood.

Obviously, he cannot satisfy both sets of wishes: he cannot establish an adult heterosexual relationship with a woman if he also says (and much more loudly), "Take care of me, protect me, nurse me, let me be a part of you."

The therapist attempts to clarify this for the patient. "Your behavior makes sense if we assume that you wish to satisfy the deeper, more primitive, more infantile need." He tries to help the patient to understand the nature of his conflicting desires, to choose between them, to relinquish those which cannot be fulfilled except at enormous cost to his integrity and autonomy. Once the patient realizes what he "really" wants (as an adult) and that his behavior is designed to fulfill opposing growth-retarding needs, he gradually concludes that "to attain what I really want, I must change."

I CAN CHANGE, I AM POTENT

Perhaps the major therapeutic approach to the question "How come?" ("How come you act in ways counter to your best interests?") is to offer explanation, to attribute meaning to the patient's behavior. The therapist says, in effect, you behave in certain fashions "because . . ." and the "because" clause generally involves motivational factors which lie outside of the patient's awareness. It is true that the previous two options I have discussed also proffer explanation but, and I shall clarify this shortly, the purpose of the explanation (the nature of the leverage exerted on will) is quite different in each of these approaches.

What type of explanation does the therapist offer the patient? And which explanations are correct and which incorrect? Which "deep"? Which "superficial"? It is at this juncture that the great metapsychological controversies arise, since the nature of the therapist's explanation is a function of the ideological school to which he belongs. I think we can sidestep the great ideological struggle by keeping a fixed gaze on the *function* of the interpretation, on the relationship between explanation and the final product—change. After all, it is change that is our goal. Self-knowledge, derepression, analysis of transference, and self-actualization are all worthwhile enlightened pursuits, all quite probably related to change, preludes to change, companions of change, and yet they are not synonymous with change.

Explanation provides us with a system by which we can order the events in our lives into some type of coherent and predictable pattern. To name something, to place it into a logical (or paralogical) causal sequence, is to experience it as being under our control. No longer is our behavior or our internal experience frightening, inchoate, out of control; instead, we behave (or have a particular inner experience) *because. . . .* The "because" offers us mastery (or a *sense* of mastery which, phenomenologically, is tantamount to mastery). It offers us freedom and effectance. As we move from a position of being motivated by unknown forces to a position of identifying and controlling these forces, we move from a passive, reactive posture to an active, acting, changing posture.

If we accept this basic premise—that a major function of explanation in psychotherapy is to provide the patient with a sense of personal mastery—it follows that the value of an explanation should be measured by this criterion. To the extent that it offers a sense of potency, a causal explanation is valid, correct, or "true." Such a definition of "truth" is a completely relativistic and pragmatic one. It argues that no explanatory system has hegemony or exclusive rights; no system is the correct, fundamental one or the "deeper" (and, therefore, better) one.

Therapists may offer the patient any of a number of interpretations to clarify the same issue; each may be made from a different frame of reference, and each may be "true." Freudian, Sullivanian, Horneyan, Existential, Transactional Analytic, and Adlerian explanations—all of these may be true simultaneously. None, despite vehement claims to the contrary, have sole rights to the truth. After all, they are all based on imaginary "as if" structures. They all say, "You are behaving (or feeling) *as if* such and such a thing were true." The super ego, id, ego; the archetypes; the masculine protest; the parent, child, and adult ego state—*none of these really exists;* they are all fictions, all psychological constructs created for our semantic convenience. They justify their existence only by virtue of their explanatory powers.

Does this mean that we abandon our attempts to make precise, thoughtful interpretations? Not at all. Only that we recognize the purpose and function of the interpretation. Some may be superior to others, not because they are "deeper" but because they have more explanatory power, are more credible, provide more mastery, and are, therefore, more useful. Obviously, the interpretations must be tailored for the recipient; in general, they are more effective if they make sense, if they are logically consistent with sound supporting arguments, if they are bolstered by empirical observation, if they are consonant with the patient's frame of reference, if they "feel" right, if they somehow "click" with the internal experience of the patient, and if they have generalizeability and can be applied to many analogous situations in the life of the patient. Higher order interpretations generally offer a novel explanation to the patient for some large pattern of behavior (as opposed to a single trait or act). The novelty of the therapist's explanation stems from his unusual frame of reference, which permits him to unify data about the patient in an original fashion; indeed, often the data is material which is generally overlooked by the patient or is out of his awareness.

If pushed, to what extent am I willing to defend this relativistic thesis? When I present this position to students, they respond with such questions as: does that mean that an astrological explanation is also valid in psychotherapy? These questions make me uneasy, but I have to respond affirmatively. If an astrological or shamanistic or magical explanation enhances a sense of mastery, and leads to inner, personal change, then it is a valid explanation. There is much evidence from cross-cultural psychiatric research to support this position; the explanation must be consistent with the values and with the frame of reference of the human community in which the patient dwells. In most primitive cultures it is often *only* the magical or religious explanation that is acceptable, and hence valid and effective.

An interpretation, even the most elegant one, has no benefit if the patient does not hear it. The therapist should take pains to review some of his evidence with the patient and present the explanation clearly. (If he cannot, it is because the therapist does not himself understand it; it is not, as some claim, because the therapist is speaking directly to the patient's unconscious.)

Do not always expect the patient to accept an interpretation. Sometimes the patient hears the same interpretation many times until one day it seems to "click." Why does it "click" that one day? Perhaps the patient may have come across some corroborating data from new events in his environment or from the surfacing in fantasy or dreams of some previously unconscious material. Sometimes a patient will hear an interpretation from another member that he will accept when he would not accept the identical interpretation from the therapist. (Patients are clearly capable of making interpretations as useful as those of the therapists, and generally other members are quite receptive to these interpretations, *provided the other member has accepted the patient role and does not offer interpretations to acquire prestige, power, or a favored position with the leader.**)

Sometimes the interpretation finally clicks when the patient's relationship to the therapist is just right. Remember that patients respond to the therapist on several levels. It is as though the patient hears the therapist's words through an encoding system which, to a degree consonant with the severity of his pathology, obscures the content of the interpretation and amplifies his idiosyncratic view of the process: e.g., the interpreter is trying to control you, to demonstrate his superiority over you, to entrap you, to objectify you, and so forth. If the rela-

---

* Educators have long been aware that the most effective teacher is often a near peer, an individual who is close enough to the student to be accepted and who, by identifying with the student's mental processes, is hence able to present material in a timely, accessible fashion.

tionship is troubled, these considerations prevail and even the most impeccable interpretation does not succeed; an interpretation becomes maximally effective when it is transmitted against a background of acceptance and trust.

It is not possible to discuss in more detail the types of effective interpretations; to do so would require a description of the vast number of explanatory schools. There are, however, three venerable concepts so deeply associated with interpretation that they deserve some special treatment here. These concepts are the use of the past, mass group interpretations, and transference. I shall turn to the past now and to mass group interpretations in the second part of Chapter 5. So many interpretative systems revolve about the axis of transference (indeed, traditional analytic theory decrees that *only* the transference interpretation can be an effective one), that I shall devote Chapter 6 entirely to the issue of transference and transparency.

The Use of the Past

Too often, explanation is confused with "originology" (the study of origins). We have discussed already that an explanatory system may effectively postulate a "cause" of behavior from any of a large number of perspectives. Still, many therapists continue to believe that to find the "real," the "deepest" causes of behavior, one must refer to the past. This position was staunchly defended by Freud, a committed psychosocial archaeologist. To the end of his life Freud relinquished neither his search for the primordial (i.e., the earliest) explanation nor his tenacious insistence that successful therapy hinged on the excavation of the earliest layers of life's memories.

The powerful and unconscious factors which influence our behavior are by no means limited to the past. As I shall discuss, the future is also a significant determinant of our behavior. In addition to the past and future, there are unconscious field forces in the immediate present which incessantly influence our feelings and actions.

The past may affect our behavior through pathways fully described by traditional Freudian analytic theory and by learning theorists (strange bed fellows). However, the "not yet," the future, is a no less powerful determinant of behavior, and the concept of future determinism is a fully defensible one. We have at all times within us a sense of purpose, an idealized self, a series of goals for which we strive. These factors, both conscious and unconscious, all arch into the future and profoundly influence our behavior. To be cut off from the future is extraordinarily uncomfortable: individuals lose a sense of purpose or meaning in their life and experience a deep anhedonia or a depressive, hopeless despair. Certainly the knowledge of our destiny, our deterioration, and ultimate death deeply influences our conduct and our inner experience. Though we generally keep them out of awareness, the terrifying contingencies of our existence play upon us without end. We either strive to dismiss them by enveloping ourselves in life's many diversions, or we attempt to vanquish death by faith in an afterlife or by striving for symbolic immortality in the form of children, material monuments, and creative expression.

The Galilean concept of causality which stresses current field forces has considerable explanatory potency. As we hurtle through space, not only is our behavioral trajectory influenced by the nature and direction of the original push, and the nature of the goal which beckons us, but it is also influenced by all the current field forces operating upon it. Thus, explanation ensues from the exploration of the concentric rings of conscious and unconscious current motivations which envelop our patients. To cite only one example, patients may have a need to attack, which covers a layer of dependency wishes that are not expressed because of anticipation of rejection. Note that we need not ask, "How did he get to be so dependent?" The past need not be a part of the explanation of his need to attack; in fact, the future (his anticipation of rejection) plays a more central role in the interpretation.

A clinical example of interpretation based on this current field force model occurred in a group in which two patients, Stephanie and Louise, expressed strong sexual feelings toward the male therapist of the group. (Both of them, incidentally, had histories, indeed chief complaints, of masochistic sexual gratification.) One meeting they discussed the explicit content of their sexual fantasies involving him. Stephanie fantasized her husband being killed, herself having a psychotic breakdown, the therapist hospitalizing her and personally nurturing her, rocking her and caring for all her bodily needs. Louise had a different set of fantasies. She wondered if the therapist was well cared for at home. She imagined frequently that something happened to his wife and that she could care for him by cleaning his house and cooking his meals.

The shared "sexual" attraction (which, as the fantasies indicate, was not genital-sexual) had for Stephanie and Louise a very different "explanation." The therapist pointed out to Stephanie that she, throughout the course of the group, had suffered frequent physical illness or severe psychological relapses. He explained that at a deep level she seemed to feel as though she could get his love and that of the other members only by a form of self-immolation. However, it never worked. She never obtained the love she wanted; more often than not, she discouraged and frustrated others. Even more important was the fact that as long as she behaved in ways which caused her so much shame, she could not love herself. He emphasized that it was crucial for her to change the pattern since it defeated her in her therapy: she was frightened to get better since she felt that this entailed an inevitable loss of love and nurturance.

In his comments to Louise, the therapist juxtaposed several aspects of her behavior; she had always derogated herself, refused to assume her rights, and had always complained of being unable to interest men in her. Her fantasy explicated her motivations: if she could be self-sacrificing enough, if she could put the therapist deeply into her debt, then she should, in reciprocal fashion, receive the love she sought. However, Louise's search for love always failed also. Her eternal ingratiation, her dread of self-assertion, her continued self-devaluation succeeded only in making her appear dull and spiritless to those whose regard she most desired. Louise, like Stephanie, whirled about in a vicious circle of her own creation: the more she failed to obtain love, the more frantically she repeated the same self-destructive pattern—the only course of behavior she knew or dared to enact.

These interpretations offered two explanations for a similar behavioral pattern: "sexual" infatuation for the therapist. Two different dynamic pathways to masochism were sketched. In each, the therapist assembled together several aspects of their behavior in the group as well as fantasy material and suggested that, if certain assumptions were made (e.g., that Stephanie acted as though she could only obtain the therapist's love by offering herself as severely damaged; that Louise acted as though she could obtain his love only by so serving him as to place him in her debt), then the rest of the behavior "made sense." Both interpretations were potent and had a significant impact upon future behavior. Yet neither broached the question, "How did you get to be that way? What happened in your earlier life to create such a pattern?" Both dealt instead with currently existing concentric patterns: the desire for love, the conviction it could be obtained only in certain ways, the sacrifice of autonomy, the resulting shame, the ensuing increased need for a sign of love, etc.

One formidable problem with explanations based on the distant past is that they contain within them the seeds of therapeutic despair.

A formidable paradox: if we are fully determined by the past, whence comes the ability to change? As is evident in such later works as *Analysis Terminable and Interminable*, Freud's uncompromising deterministic view of man led him to, but never through, this Gordian Knot.

The past, moreover, no more determines the present and the future than it is determined by them. The "real" past exists for each of us only as we constitute it in the present against the horizon of the future. Frank [25] reminds us that patients, even in prolonged therapy, recall only a minute fraction of their past experience and may selectively recall and synthesize the past so as to achieve consistency with their present view of themselves. (Goffman [26] suggests the term "apologia" for this reconstruction of the past.) As a patient through therapy changes his present image of himself, he may reconstitute or reintegrate his past; for example, he may recall long forgotten positive experiences with parents. He may humanize them and, rather than experience them solipsistically (as figures who existed by virtue of their service to him), he may begin to understand them as harried, well-intentioned individuals struggling with the same overwhelming facts of the human condition that he himself faces. Once one reconstitutes the past, a new past can further influence one's self-appraisal; however, it is the *reconstitution* of the past, not simply the *excavation* of the past, that is crucial.

If explanations are not to be sought from an originological perspective and if the most potent focus of the group is an ahistoric, here-and-now one, does this mean that the past plays no role at all in the group therapeutic process? Not at all! The past is a frequent visitor to the group and an even more frequent visitor to the inner private world of each of the members during the course of therapy. Not infrequently, for example, the past plays an important role in the development of group cohesiveness by increasing intermember understanding and acceptance. The past is often invaluable in conflict resolution. Consider, for example, two members locked in a seemingly irreconcilable struggle, each of whom finds many aspects of the other repugnant. Often a full understanding of the developmental route whereby each arrived at his particular viewpoint can rehumanize the struggle. An individual with a regal air conveying hauteur and condescension may suddenly seem understandable, even winsome, when one learns of his immigrant parents and his desperate struggle to transcend the degradation of his slum childhood. Individuals are benefited through being fully known by others in the group and being fully accepted;

knowing another's process of becoming is a rich and often indispensable adjunct to knowing the person.

An ahistoric "here-and-now" interactional focus is never fully attainable. Discussion of future anticipation, both feared and desired, and past and current experiences are an inextricable part of human discourse. Often the *omission* of the past, or one's current outside life, is important group material. It is worth noting that a certain patient often speaks of his father but never of his mother, or that he never mentions his children to the group and in fact has little integration of his role as a husband or parent, or that he never tells the group of changes in his relationships to other people. Each of these omissions sheds light upon the current experiential world of the patient. What is important is the accent; the past is the servant and not the master. It is important in that it explicates the current reality of the patient as he unfolds himself in relation to the other group members. As Rycroft [27] states, "It makes better sense to say that the analyst makes excursions into historical research in order to understand something which is interfering with his present communication with the patient (in the same way that a translator might turn to history to elucidate an obscure text) than to say that he makes contact with the patient in order to gain access to biographical data."

To employ the past in this manner involves an anamnestic technique differing from that often employed in individual therapy. Rather than a systematic careful historical survey, the therapist periodically attempts a sector analysis in which he explores the development of some particular interpersonal stance. Consequently, there are many other aspects of the patient's past which remain undiscussed. It is not uncommon, for example, for group therapists to conclude a course of very successful therapy with a patient and yet be unfamiliar with such significant aspects of the patient's early life as school history, physical illnesses, occupation of parents, geographical moves, etc.

The explicit mention of the past in the therapy group is not an accurate reflection of the consideration of the past which occurs within each patient during therapy. The intensive focus on the relationship between members does not, of course, have as its goal the formation of enduring relationship between the group members. Instead, it is training, a dress rehearsal for the work that must be done with the truly important individuals in his life. At the end of therapy, patients very commonly report significant additudinal improvements in relationships which have rarely been explicitly discussed in the group;

many of these, of course, involve family members with whom one has had a relationship stretching far back into the past. So the past is part of the working-through process, more often implicitly than explicitly, and the therapist should be aware of this silent important homework. He does not use the group meeting for this function, though, because he cannot afford to sacrifice the therapeutic potency which flows from the here-and-now interactional focus.

5

THE THERAPIST: TASKS
AND TECHNIQUES

(continued)

Mass Group Process Commentary

A specific type of process explanation remains to be discussed. Some leaders choose to focus primarily or entirely on mass group phenomena. They refer, in their statements, to "the group" or "we" or "all of us"; they attempt to clarify the relationship between the group, as an entity, and its primary task (the investigation of intermember—and I include the leader here—relationships), or between the group and one of its members, a subgroup, the leader, or some shared concern. For example, return for a moment to the "parenthood is degrading" incident described on page 123. In that incident the therapist had many process commentary options, some of which were mass group explanations. He might, for example, have raised the issue of whether the "group" needed a scapegoat and whether, with Kate gone, Burt filled the role; or whether the "group" was actively avoiding an important issue—i.e., their guilty pleasure and fears about Kate's departure.

Throughout this text I have interwoven comments related to mass group phenomena: for example, the tasks of the therapist in the construction of a social system, norm-setting, the role of the deviant, scapegoating, emotional contagion, role suction, subgroup formation, group cohesiveness, group pressure, the regressive dependency fostered by group membership, the response of the group toward termination, toward the addition of new members, toward the absence of the leader, etc. There is no question, then, of the importance of group level phenomena. All group leaders would agree that there are forces inherent in a group which significantly influence behavior; individuals behave differently in group than they do in dyads (that is one of the factors that makes group selection difficult). There is wide agreement that an individual's behavior cannot be fully understood without an appreciation of his environmental press.

What leaders do *not* agree about, however, is the application of this knowledge in the group therapeutic process. The controversies between the mass group process oriented leaders and the interpersonal process leaders have become more strident and more polarized. Many leaders—for example, the Tavistock school, which I shall discuss shortly—insist that every statement of the leader consist of (or contain) a mass group interpretation. The issue is sufficiently controversial to demand a detailed discussion.

Rationale of Mass Group Process Commentary

I shall begin by clarifying my position. The therapist uses group level phenomena continuously in the course of therapy: many of the major curative factors, such as cohesiveness, relate to mass group properties. However, it does not follow that the leader need make group level comments. I would maintain that only a very small percentage of the therapist's interventions need be mass group ones. One assists a group to develop cohesiveness in a variety of ways, beginning with the selection and preparation of patients. The therapist may, for example, reinforce self-disclosure, reinforce members bringing in group dreams, clarify how the group goals are confluent with the individual member's goals, or encourage the expression of positive as well as negative intermember affect. In fact, as I shall argue, a role in which the leader focuses exclusively on group level phenomena is restrictive and severely limits the therapist's effectiveness. However, there are times when mass group process commentary is needed. When? Let me suggest a simplifying principle: *The purpose of a mass group interpretation is to remove some obstacle which has arisen to obstruct the progress of the entire group.* The two common types of obstacles are: anxiety-laden issues and antitherapeutic group norms.

ANXIETY-LADEN ISSUES. Often some issue arises which is so threatening that the group, on either a conscious or an unconscious level, refuses to confront the problem and takes some type of evasive action. This avoidance takes many forms, all of which are commonly referred to as "group flight." A clinical example of flight from an anxiety-laden issue may clarify this point:

Six members were present at the sixty-fifth group meeting; one member, John, was absent. For the first time and without previous mention, one of the members, Mary, brought her dog to the meeting. The group, usually an animated, active one, was unusually subdued and nonproductive. Their speech was barely audible and throughout the meeting they discussed safe topics on a level of impersonality appropriate to any large social gathering. Much of the content centered on study habits (three of the members were graduate students), on examinations, and on teachers (especially their failings and untrustworthiness). Moreover, the senior member of the group discussed former members who had long since departed from the group—the "good old days" phenomenon. The dog (a wretched, restless creature who spent most of the group session noisily licking his genitals) was never mentioned and finally the therapist, thinking he was speaking for the group, brought up the issue of Mary's bringing the dog to the meeting. Much to the therapist's surprise, Mary—a highly unpopular, narcissistic member—was unanimously defended; everyone denied that the dog was in any way distracting and left the therapist as a lonely protester.

The therapist considered the entire meeting as a flight meeting and accordingly made appropriate mass group interpretations which we will discuss. But first, what is the evidence that such a meeting is "flight"? And flight from what? We must consider the age of the group; in a young group, meeting, let us say, for the third time, such a session may be a manifestation not of resistance but of the group's uncertainty about their primary task and of their groping to establish procedural norms. However, this group had already met for fourteen months and, furthermore, the previous meetings had been strikingly different in character. Convincing evidence of flight occurs when the preceding group meeting is examined. At this meeting, John, the member absent from the meeting under consideration, had been twenty minutes late and happened to walk down the corridor at the precise moment when the door of the adjoining observation room was opened. John heard the voices of the other group members and saw a room full of observers viewing the group; moreover, the observers at that moment happened to be laughing at some private joke. Although John, like all the group members, had been told that the group was being observed by students, nevertheless this shocking irreverent confirmation stunned him. When John, in the last moments of the meeting, was finally able to discuss it with the other members, they were equally stunned. John, as we have seen, missed the next session.

This event was a catastrophe of major proportion for the group. It would be for any group, for that matter; it would raise serious questions in the minds of the members about the therapeutic situation. Was the therapist to be trusted? Was he, like his colleagues in the observation room inwardly laughing at them? Was anything he said genuinely based? Was the group, once perceived as a human situation, in fact a sterile, contrived, laboratory specimen being studied dispassionately by a therapist who probably felt closer allegiance to "them" (the others, the observers) than to the group? Despite, or, we should say, because of, the magnitude of these painful group issues, the group declined to confront the matter. Instead, they engaged in flight behavior which now begins to be understandable. Exposed to an outside threat, the group banded tightly together for protection; they spoke softly about safe topics so as to avoid sharing anything with the outside menace (the observers and, through association, the therapist). The therapist was unsupported when he asked about the obviously distracting behavior of the dog; the "good old days" was a reference to and yearning for bygone times when the group was pure and the therapist could be trusted. The discussion of examinations and untrustworthy teachers was also a thinly veiled expression of attitudes toward the therapist.

The precise nature and timing of the intervention is largely a matter of individual style. Some therapists, myself included, tend to intervene when they sense the presence of some group flight even though they do not clearly understand its source. The therapist may, for example, comment that he feels puzzled or uneasy about the meeting and inquire as to whether "there is something the group is not talking about today" or whether "the group is avoiding something," or perhaps he might ask about the "hidden agenda." He increases the salience of his inquiry by citing the evidence—e.g., the whispering, the sudden shift toward neutral topics and a noninteractive mode of communication, his experience of being left out or of being deserted by the others in the dog issue. Furthermore, he might add that the group is strangely avoiding all discussion both of the previous meeting and of John's absence today. In our clinical example it would not be a sufficient goal merely to get the group back on the track, back to a discussion of more meaningful material. The issues being avoided are too crucial to the group's existence to be left submerged. This is particularly relevant in a group whose members have insufficiently explored their relation to the therapist. Therefore, the therapist should repeatedly turn the group's attention back onto the main issue and not be misled by substitute behavior—e.g., the group's offering for discussion another theme, perhaps even a somewhat charged one. His task is not simply to circumvent the resistance, to redirect the group to work areas, but to plunge them into the source of the resistance—not *around* anxiety but *through* anxiety.

Another clue to the presence and strength of resistance is the group's response to the therapist's resistance-piercing commentary. If his comments, even when repeated, fall on deaf ears, if he feels ignored by the group, if he has a sense that it would be extraordinarily difficult to influence the group, then he knows that the "group," rather than a few members, is involved and that the underlying dysphoria is considerable.

Another common way in which the group flight manifests itself is through intellectualization. For example, after a meeting in which two members disclosed their homosexuality, a group launched into a discussion of prejudice that lasted for two sessions. Prejudicial feelings in the abstract about Jews, Negroes, Orientals, and homosexuals were discussed. What was avoided, however, was a swarm of deeply personal feelings aroused by the two homosexual patients. The members avoided their scorn, their fears of their own latent homosexual feelings, their anger toward the therapists for having chosen these two when, as one member stated later, "the group so badly needed men." The group may also avoid work by more literal flight, by absences or by tardiness. Whatever the form, however, the result is the same: in the language of the group dynamicist, locomotion toward the attainment of group goals is impeded, and the group is no longer engaged in its primary task.

Not uncommonly, the issue precipitating the resistance is discussed symbolically. Uneasiness over observers may be discussed metaphorically by a group which launches into a long conversation about other types of confidentiality violation: for example, public posting of grades for a school course, or family members opening one another's mail. Hidden anger provoked by the therapist's absence may prompt discussions of parental feelings or death or illness. So, the therapist may learn something of what is being resisted by asking himself, "Why is this particular [non-work] topic being discussed and *why now?*"

ANTITHERAPEUTIC GROUP NORMS

Another type of group obstacle warranting a mass group interpretation occurs when antitherapeutic group norms are elaborated by the group. For example, a group may, as I discussed earlier, establish a "take turns" format in which an entire meeting is devoted, sequentially, to each member of the group. Such a format is undesirable since members are often forced into premature self-disclosure with consequent humiliation at subsequent meetings. Furthermore, members, as their "turn" approaches, may experience extreme anxiety or even decide to terminate therapy. Or a group may have established a pattern of devoting the entire session to the first issue raised in that session; strong invisible sanctions have been erected against changing the subject. Another group may establish a "Can you top this?" format in which the members engage in a spiraling orgy of self-disclosure. Or a group may become tightly knit, offering so hostile a welcome to new members that they soon terminate therapy.

In such instances, the therapist's interpretations about the mass group phenomena are more effective if the process is clearly described, the deleterious effects on the members or the group at large specifically cited, and the implication made that alternatives to these normative patterns may be found.

Frequently, one notes that the group, during its development, bypasses certain important phases or never incorporates certain norms into its culture. For example, a group may develop without ever going through a period of examining its views about the therapist, without ever confronting or attacking him; or a group may develop without a whisper of intermember dissension, without status bids or struggles for control; or a group may meet for a year or more with no hint of real intimacy or closeness arising among the members. Such a collaborative avoidance is a result of the group members collectively constructing norms dictating this avoidance. If the therapist senses that the group is providing a one-sided or incomplete experience for the members, he may then comment on the missing aspect of group life in that particular group. (Such an intervention assumes, of course, that there are regularly recurring, predictable phases of small group development with which the therapist is thoroughly familiar—a topic which I will discuss in Chapter 10.)

Mass Group Interpretations—General Considerations

The general principle advanced earlier—that the purpose of a mass group interpretation is to remove some obstacle which has arisen to obstruct the progress of the entire group—is a deceptively simple one;

from both a theoretical and a practical standpoint, the matter is far more complex.

THE CONCEPT OF THE "GROUP"

Gradually over the years, the myth of the "group" has been elaborated and has generated considerable confusion in the field. As psychoanalysts entered the field of group therapy, they brought with them time-honored concepts and techniques of their discipline.

It was reasoned that traditional psychoanalytic techniques, with some modifications, could be employed in group therapy; however, the group and not the individual was now considered the patient, and vague concepts like "group ego" and "group superego" were formulated. Free association by an individual patient was then replaced by "group association." [28] The "group" became regarded as an autonomous organism: ". . . the group tends to speak and react to a common theme as if it were a living entity, expressing itself in different ways through various mouths. All contributions are variations on this single theme, even though the groups are not consciously aware of that theme and do not know what they are really talking about." [29]

Now obviously, the concept of the group as a system with characteristic properties is a valuable one; however, what has happened is that many workers have tended to anthropomorphize the group. Just as we have instilled life into a stock market which "attempts to fight off a selling wave" or "desperately guards the 700 Dow Jones level," so, too, have we conceptually breathed life into the group. It is not, I feel, fatuous to point out that the group is not a living entity; it is but an abstraction created for our semantic and conceptual convenience. When it becomes so metapsychologized that it promotes not clarity but haziness of thought, then it no longer serves its original function.

As an example of the conceptual pitfalls involved, consider the process of diagnosing the state of the group. How do we know what is the dominant group culture, common group tension, or group mind? How many of the group members must be involved before we conclude it is the "group" speaking? This last question, particularly, is a cause of considerable confusion; Bion and Ezriel, as we shall see, make the dubious assumption that silence by a group member signifies collusion or agreement with the individuals "speaking for the group." This results in a "group mind" or "group culture" interpretation made on the basis of a small percentage of the membership.

THE TIMING OF GROUP INTERVENTIONS

For pedagogical reasons, interpersonal phenomena and mass group phenomena have been discussed as though they were quite distinct; in practice, of course, the two often overlap and the therapist is faced with the question of when to emphasize the interpersonal aspects of the transaction and when to emphasize the mass group aspects. This matter of clinical judgment cannot be neatly prescribed; as in any therapeutic endeavor, judgment develops from experience (particular supervised experience) and from intuition. As Melanie Klein stated, "It is a most precious quality in an analyst to be able at any moment to pick out the point of urgency." [30]

The point of urgency is far more elusive in group therapy than in individual treatment. As a general rule, however, an issue critical to the existence or functioning of the entire group always takes precedence over a narrower interpersonal issue. As an illustration let us return to the group which engaged in whispering, discussion of neutral topics, and other forms of group flight during the meeting after a member had inadvertently discovered the very indiscreet group observers. In the meeting under consideration, Mary (who had been absent at the previous meeting) brought her dog. Under normal circumstances this act would clearly have become an important group issue: Mary had neither consulted with nor informed the therapist or other members of her plans to bring a dog to the group; she was, because of her great narcissism, an unpopular member, and her act was representative of her insensitivity to others. However, in the meeting under consideration, there was a far more urgent issue—one threatening the entire group—and the dog was discussed not from the aspect of facilitating Mary's interpersonal learning but as he was used by the group in their flight. Only later, after the obstacle to the group's progress had been worked through and removed, did the group return to a meaningful consideration of their feelings about Mary bringing the dog.

Total Group Interventions—Other Views

Other group therapists disagree and view the formulation of total group interventions not as a method of removing obstacles but as the chief or even the sole procedural task of the therapist. Systematic and influential approaches to mass group phenomena in therapy groups have been elaborated by Bion, Ezriel, and Whitaker and Lieberman.* These three approaches differ from my own and from one another in (1) the nature of group phenomena described and (2) the use and the rationale of these phenomena in therapy.

BION. Wilfred Bion, a practicing Kleinian analyst, first became interested in group dynamics during the early 1940s when he, together with John Rickman,[33] first experimented with large and small group meetings in a military psychiatric hospital. Later, from 1947 to 1949, Bion conducted two therapy groups and a series of staff discussion groups at the Tavistock Clinic. After 1949 his interest turned to other areas,† and he permanently left the group therapy field.

Nature of the Group Phenomena. Bion studied his groups through holistic spectacles. Searching for total group currents, he noted that at times the group appeared to be pursuing its primary task ‡ in a rational, effective fashion. Bion called this group culture the "work group" culture. At other times he noted that the group no longer seemed to be pursuing its primary task; instead, it appeared to be dominated by certain massive emotional states which resulted in behavior incompatible with the primary task. Three types of basic, recurring emotional states (a "constellation of discrete feelings that permeate all the group's interactions") [34] were described: (1) aggressiveness, hostility, and fear; (2) optimism and hopeful anticipation; (3) helplessness or awe.

From these primary observations [35] Bion postulated that in each of these emotional states the group was acting "as if" the members shared some common belief from which their affect stemmed. For example, while in an optimistic or hopefully anticipatory state, the group acts "as if" its aim is to preserve itself by finding strength or a new leader from its peer membership; when it is in a helpless or awed state, it acts "as if" its aim is to obtain support, nurturance, strength from something outside the group—generally the designated leader. When it is in an aggressive or fearful state, it acts "as if" its aim is to

---

* It is not my intention to present a historical survey of the concept of the "group in the group" therapeutic process, but to describe systems which utilize mass group interpretations in a manner significantly different from the approach I have described. For example, it seems likely that Foulkes antedates most workers in his appreciation of total group forces.[31] However, in his current practice, Foulkes rarely makes a total group intervention, and, when he does, it is in an attempt to remove, in much the manner described here, some obstacle in the path of the group.[32]

† An exceedingly influential figure in the British Psychoanalytic Society, he has been chiefly interested in the development and application of Kleinian principles in psychoanalysis and in the understanding and psychotherapy of the schizophrenias.

‡ Bion considered the primary task of the therapy group to be an exploration of its own intragroup tensions.

avoid something by fighting or running away from it. Bion terms each of these three emotional states "basic assumption cultures" and thus speaks of three types of basic assumption groups: basic assumption pairing, basic assumption dependency, and basic assumption flight-fight, respectively.

Thus, at any given time a group may be described as either a work group, or as one of the three basic assumption groups, or in some transitional phase.

A basic assumption group may have a life span of a fraction of a meeting, or it may persist for several months. Note that the primary observation is the emotional state. "I consider the emotional state to be in existence and the basic assumption to be deductible from it." [36] This means that the basic assumption culture need not necessarily be conscious to the members or even observable to the leader but that if one makes the "as if" assertion (i.e., the group is acting "as if" its purpose is to . . .) then the leader will be able to understand seemingly illogical and unconnected behavior on the part of the members. Thus, the basic assumption hypothesis is simply a construct which permits leaders to organize data into a coherent pattern.

Bion's focus on the individual group member centered on that member's relationship to the group culture. The concept of *valency* was developed to describe an individual's attraction to a particular group culture. This attraction, analogous to tropism in plants,[35] is a force which leads a member into being the chief spokesman or a participant or a major rebel in one of the basic assumption cultures.

One other important aspect of Bion's view of groups is that it is *leader-centered*. All three basic assumption states are oriented around the issue of leadership. Each type of group searches for a leader—one who will meet its needs: the basic assumption dependency group attempts in various ways to coax or coerce the professional leader to guide them; the flight-fight group searches for a member who will lead them in this direction; the pairing group optimistically pairs and waits, hopeful that the leader will "emerge from the offspring of the pair." [35]

Therapeutic Considerations. Bion's views on the technique of group therapy are not explicit in his writings and, with his departure from the field, have never been clarified. Basically, it appears that Bion's ultimate goal was helping patients achieve the ability to become effective members of work groups. All of Bion's interpretations were mass group interpretations and were made immediately upon the therapist's recognition of the group situation. He repeatedly confronted the group with its basic assumption behavior, especially insofar as it related to the therapist. This behavior is depicted by Bion as characteristically illogical, impulsive, and non-reality-oriented. By confronting the group repeatedly in this manner, Bion attempted to reinstate the work group culture. He hoped that patients, as they became aware of the nature and unrealizability of their unrealistic demands, would gradually learn more realistic and adaptive methods of group functioning.

Three specific types of conflict which complicate group functions are described by Bion, who implies that it is the task of the therapist and the work group to expose, clarify, and work through these conflicts: (1) a desire on the part of the individual for "a sense of vitality by total submergence in the group" which exists alongside a desire for "a sense of individual independence by total repudiation of the group"; (2) the conflict between the group and the patient whose desires are often at cross-purposes to the needs of the group; and (3) the conflict between the problem-oriented work group and the basic assumption group.

At other times Bion suggests therapeutic approaches which imply that he places great emphasis on the working through of deeply unconscious material.

I must stress the point that I consider it essential to work out very thoroughly the primitive primal scene as it discloses itself in the group. This differs markedly from the primal scene in its classical description in that it is much more bizarre and seems to assume that a part of one parent, the breast or the mother's body, contains amongst other objects a part of the father . . . the group experience seems to me to give ample material to support the view that these fantasies are of permanent importance for the group. . . . Even in the "stable" group the deep psychotic levels should be demonstrated though it may involve temporarily an apparent increase in the "illness" of the group.[35]

Bion always interpreted the group to the entire group rather than to an individual member. He assumed that the effects would be wide and more effective since each individual would find all interpretations relevant to some degree.[37]

Overview of Bion's Approach. Bion himself seemed far more interested in understanding the dynamics of groups than in elaborating an effective system of group therapy. One of Bion's colleagues, who was associated with Bion while he conducted groups at the Tavistock Clinic (1947–1949) and who inherited his clinical groups, stated that "Bion's group technique seemed primarily suited to staff members whose goal was to understand group dynamics. Patients might be helped provided they had a level of sophistication high enough to grasp the relevance of the mass group interpretations for their own problems. Patients treated in this type of group therapy format without this degree of sophistication often responded with bewilderment and perplexity." [38] I had the opportunity to observe for one year two outpatient neurotic groups led by two highly experienced Tavistock leaders. My impressions were that the groups were singularly ineffective. The patients seemed bewildered by the therapist's interpretations. In fact, the greatly restricted role of the therapist (e.g., his impersonality, his personal disengagement, his making only group process interpretations, etc.) served, in my view, to stifle rather than to augment the therapeutic potential inherent in the small group setting. A recent study by Malan [39] corroborates this impression. In a carefully controlled outcome study of patients in Tavistock therapy groups, Malan and his associates found that there were no differences in outcome between those patients who had had at least two years of group therapy and those patients who had dropped out of therapy after only a few group meetings. Furthermore, they reported that the patients' retrospective evaluation of their therapists' contributions was decidedly negative. Patients commented that the therapists were unhelpful, distant, uncaring, and enigmatic.

Until recently, the Bionic-Tavistock model has had relatively little influence on the practice of group therapy in America, perhaps in part, as Parloff [37] suggests, because of Bion's reliance on Kleinian rather than Freudian concepts. However, with the increased importation and acceptance of Kleinian thought and with the increased exposure of professionals to the Tavistock small group laboratories, there has been a greater use of this model in group therapy. This, in my view, is most unfortunate since the approach so severely restricts the role of the therapist that it has limited therapeutic effectiveness; it clearly flies in the face of the powerful body of research in psychotherapy (see Chapter 3) which demonstrates the crucial importance of "relationship" in the therapeutic endeavor. If the therapist remains impersonal, if he does not provide support, if he does not unconditionally accept the patient, if he chooses to limit his behavior to interpretation (and impersonal mass group interpretation at that) then the burden of proof is on him to demonstrate that even though he violates basic therapeutic dicta, he is nonetheless effective. Research such as Malan's [39] makes that demonstration highly unlikely.

Even though Bion's direct contributions to group psychotherapy technique are not substantial, his influence on the field has nonetheless been considerable. His method of viewing the group as a whole, his focus on the here-and-now, his attempt to understand unconscious forces influencing group texture and activity were indeed innovative.

His ideas have generated considerable interest and research in group dynamics. (A monograph by Stock and Thelen [40] reviews the large number of research inquiries based on Bion's formulations.)

Bion's ingenious and highly original conceptualizations about group dynamics have intrigued many workers. An all-inclusive system satisfies one's need for closure and provides a group leader with a sense of mastery; all of the richly variegated, often confusing aspects of group life can be neatly classified. A citadel of such impregnability is erected that the therapist (as I have observed) can, when the members are engaged in activity not easily classifiable, accuse the "basic assumption fight" group of deliberately attempting to confuse him!

Despite the ingenuity of the system, we must keep in mind that it is a highly speculative one arrived at intuitively by an individual who, though highly astute, did not continue to develop and refine his group observations. Sherwood,[34] in a penetrating critical study of Bion's group theories, has described Bion's method as science by fiat and states that, examined from a logical, scientific vantage point, Bion's methodology and conclusions are wholly indefensible. Certainly many of the group phenomena Bion describes are readily observable in groups. However, there are, after all, only a limited number of ways in which individuals can respond to social or interpersonal stress. Horney pointed out that individuals can move *toward* others (a search for love), *against* others (a search for mastery), *away from* others (resignation, a search for freedom), or *with* others (a cooperative, mature collaboration). This social repertoire seems closely parallel to fight (against), flight (away), dependency (toward), work (with). Furthermore, as Parloff [37] notes, sex (pairing), aggression (fight-flight), and dependency would appear to be an adequate classification of the motivational states of the members of any group. However, the appearance of these phenomena by no means validates the Bionic system. It is not necessary to postulate a highly elaborate system in order to explain the fact that the members of a group may be threatened by their designated task in the group and may engage in avoidance behavior. The degree of the threat and nature of the avoidance behavior is determined by the members' major conflicted areas, preferred styles of behavior, and by the laws of group dynamics.

Bion has proposed a system purported to represent the basic dynamics of all groups, and yet objective group workers will often be unable to classify events in their own groups according to Bionic theory. Bion, it must be remembered, studied group phenomena in a highly specialized type of group—a group which was confronted with a highly ambiguous task and an enigmatic leader. The preoccupation of his groups with leadership phenomena may be an iatrogenic rather than a universal group truth.

EZRIEL. Henry Ezriel, a contemporary of Bion, and a participating observer of some of Bion's early groups at the Tavistock Clinic, viewed group phenomena differently and developed a system of group therapy which, though less heroically group-based than Bion's, nevertheless relies on total group interpretations.[41,42,43,44] Ezriel, in his individual analytic work, advocated a totally here-and-now view of the therapeutic situation. He directed his attention toward the therapist-patient relationship and noted that the patient is required to relate (the *required relationship*) to the therapist in one fashion in order to avoid the occurrence of a second type of relationship (the *avoided relationship*). The patient unconsciously attempts to avoid this second type of relationship because his unconscious fantasies make him believe that if it were to emerge into reality a third type of relationship, some dreaded *calamity*, would occur. Ezriel concludes that a recognition of these three relationships (required, avoided, and calamitous) is essential for the understanding of the dynamics of both individual and group sessions; in groups, however, two further concepts are necessary—the common group tension and the common group structure.

In the group session each patient will give expression to his own three relationships. (He will overtly behave in the required manner and provide the perceptive analyst with clues about his unconsciously avoided relationship and the equally unconscious feared calamity.) The set of three relationships will differ from one patient to another and set up a tension in the group—the *common group* tension:

> . . . which may be regarded as consisting of the various unconsciously determined pushes and pulls exerted by the members of the group on one another and on the therapist which make the patients react to one another, make them select, reject, and distort one another's remarks, model and remodel one another's interventions, until gradually a certain *common group structure* emerges. The common group structure is thus a vector, the resultant of the individual contributions of all members of the group. It contains the dynamically essential features of the three relationships of each patient, and so might be described as their common denominator.[45]

Ezriel thus attempts to understand the common group tension and common group structure in terms of the required, avoided, and calamitous relationships for the entire group as well as for each of the individual members. In one group, for example, the members may bid for his attention and favors, setting up a common group structure of considerable intermember rivalry and obsequiousness to the leader. If the appropriate data are available from the material of the current session, the therapist will know, for example, that the group curries his favors (required relationship) in order to avoid attacking him because of their intense envy of him (avoided relationship) for fear that he might massively retaliate by injuring them or throwing them out of the group (calamity). After having clarified the common group structure and the three group relationships, the therapist can focus on the three relationships of individual members. For example, some of the male patients may be envious and angry because the therapist has a special relationship with the women in the group; secretly they would like to attack or banish the therapist but fear the calamitous consequences of such an act. A female patient may envy him his penis, which would result in the calamity of her losing the therapist on whom so much depends.[41]

Therapeutic Considerations. Ezriel's views about therapeutic mechanisms and techniques, though disputable, are nonetheless stated with remarkable clarity. The aim of both individual and group therapy is thought to be "the removal of unconscious conflicts and needs (and thus of the source of transference)." [46] The therapist should be *"nothing but a passive projection screen except for his one active step of interpretation."* [46] The therapeutic process thus consists of the therapist helping the patient, through interpretation, to understand his transference distortions toward the therapist. The form of the interpretation is clearly stated: a three-part statement with a "because clause" joining the second and third parts—i.e., "You are behaving in one way to avoid behaving in another *because* you fear. . . ." The essence of the therapeutic process is the *reality testing* which is induced by the interpretive process. Through the therapist's continued willingness to verbalize and to confront the calamity calmly, patients gradually realize the irrationality of the feared calamity. In the group therapy format the therapist first identifies the common group structure and interprets the three relationships for the group as a whole; then he makes a separate three-part interpretation for each of the group members, pointing out their overt contribution to the group structure (required relationship) and, insofar as the therapist perceives it, the patient's avoided relationship and the anticipated calamity. Thus, every interpretation made by the therapist (and Ezriel suggests that the therapist participate in no other fashion in the group) is both a mass group interpretation and an individual interpretation.

Overview. Although beautiful in its simplicity and consistency, this approach to group therapy has several significant encumbrances.

Chief among these is a rigidity in the conception of the therapist role that prevents the therapist from fulfilling the many other vital functions of the leader. Ezriel firmly advocates the blank projection screen therapist role and considers any therapist participation, other than interpretation or asking for repetition of a statement he has not heard, an error. In one group, in which the majority of members remained in therapy for nine years and three for eleven years, the members at the end of therapy discussed the changes that had occurred in each person; they all agreed that, aside from being a decade older, Dr. Ezriel had not changed whatsoever. "That," states Dr. Ezriel, "is good technique." [41] This rigidity of therapist role may be too high a price to pay for the dubious and unsubstantiated rewards of a purely interpretive approach. Besides, if, as Ezriel states, the essence of psychoanalytic treatment is reality testing, then the "projective screen" therapist role may be a logical inconsistency. For example, on one occasion Ezriel, in giving an interpretation to a patient, stated merely, "I know you want to bite me"; it was not necessary to say more since the remainder of the interpretation was nonverbal: the therapist by his accepting, understanding manner disconfirmed the patient's fantasied dreaded calamity.[41] If this is the central curative factor, why so severely limit the therapist? Why may not the therapist manifest himself more honestly so as to enhance the reality testing? The types of feared calamities are finite; the great majority of Ezriel's interpretations center about three calamities—the therapist will (1) be destroyed by the patient, (2) retaliate massively toward the patient, or (3) reject and abandon the patient. Surely an open, accepting, more transparent therapist will demonstrate the unrealistic nature of these fears by his actions more rapidly than will an impersonal opaque therapist by his words!

Not only is the therapist's role restricted, but the group, too, may become restricted. The therapist-centered interpretations of Ezriel (and Bion) may result in a leader-centered group with limited member-member interpersonal interaction, limited cohesiveness, and an unfavorable climate for interpersonal learning. Note that I have no quarrel with Ezriel's formulation of the analytic interpretation; the tripartite (required, avoided, and calamitous relationships) formulation is a clear and, in my opinion, a sound approach to one aspect of human relationships. To therapists whose background is not in Freudian psychoanalysis, the content of Ezriel's interpretations may be unacceptable; he generally couches the avoided and calamitous relationships in the stark language of unconscious oedipal or pre-oedipal infantile sexuality. Nevertheless, the tripartite system is adaptable to other frames of reference. Our patients whose interpersonal relationships are maladaptive find themselves compelled by internal reasons to relate to others in relatively fixed ways; their styles are determined by a fear of some calamity (for example, rejection, scorn, derision, engulfment, their own uncontrollable rage) should they attempt to relate differently. The choice of interpretive language is arbitrary and incidental.

The mass group interpretation is central to Ezriel's approach. Recall that each of his interpretations first describes the group structure and then each member's contribution to that structure. The requirement that the therapist wait until he understands (or thinks he understands) the group structure vastly complicates life for the therapist; not only is he restricted from usefully participating at other times but he is also burdened with the task of diagnosing, with exceedingly indistinct guidelines, the group structure. The recognition of the common group structure is, no less than with Bion's basic assumption cultures, a very arbitrary process. Ezriel, like Bion, suggests that the total material produced by all the members of the group is handled by the therapist as though it had been produced by one patient. Unanimity of the group membership is not necessary to enable the therapist to judge what the "group" is doing. Ezriel may, for example, diagnose the group structure on the basis of the verbal productions of only three out of nine members.[41] The silent members are adjudged, by dint of their silence, to be in agreement with the others ("communication by proxy").[41] Why it is that disagreement must actively be verbalized is unclear.

Given these objections, why bother with the mass group interpretation? What purpose does it serve? Ezriel states that one member's behavior is not understandable out of the context of the entire group. Furthermore, an interpretation about the entire group and each member's contribution to the group is one that compels interest in all the members. Most important of all, however, is that through a total group focus the therapist avoids the pitfall of engaging in individual therapy with any of the group members. This danger is more apparent than real, however, if the therapist has the mobility and flexibility of role which will enable him to deal with issues of favoritism and rivalry as they arise.

WHITAKER AND LIEBERMAN. Whitaker and Lieberman have applied Thomas French's focal conflict theory to therapy groups. Their position is clearly stated in a series of propositions.[47]

Proposition 1: Successive individual behaviors are linked associatively and refer to a common underlying concern about the here-and-now situation.

The comments and activities of a group therapy session are not diverse; they all hang together in relationship to some underlying issue. Seemingly unrelated acts gain coherence if one assumes that there is some concern which is shared by the members of the group.

Proposition 2: The sequence of diverse events which occur in a group can be conceptualized as a common, covert conflict (the group focal conflict) which consists of an impulse or wish (the disturbing motive) opposed by an associated fear (the reactive motive). Both aspects of the group focal conflict refer to the current setting.

For example, the members of a group may share a common wish to be singled out by the therapist for special attention (the disturbing motive) and yet they fear that such a wish will result in disapproval by the therapist and by other patients (reactive motive). The interaction between the wish and the fear is the group focal conflict.

Proposition 3: When confronted with a group focal conflict, the patients direct efforts toward establishing a solution which will reduce anxiety by alleviating the reactive fears and, at the same time, satisfy to the maximum possible degree the disturbing impulse.

In the group just described the members may arrive at the solution of searching for similarities among themselves; it is as if each were saying, "We are all alike, no one is asking for special favors." This solution, though it temporarily relieves tension, is by no means productive of growth; instead, the disturbing wish (to be unique and be singled out by the therapist for special gratification) is merely suppressed in the service of comfort. Other solutions, however, may be more enabling of group and personal growth.

Proposition 4: Successful solutions have two properties. First, they are shared; the behavior of all members is consistent with or bound by the solution. Second, successful solutions reduce reactive fears; individuals experience greater anxiety prior to the establishment of a successful solution, less anxiety after the solution is established.

Proposition 5: Solutions may be restrictive or enabling in character. A restrictive solution is directed primarily to alleviating fears and does so at the expense of satisfying or expressing the disturbing motive. An enabling solution is directed toward alleviating fears and, at the same time, allows for some satisfaction or expression of the disturbing motive.

For example, the disturbing motive in one group was the wish to express angry destructive feelings toward the therapist. The reactive motive (fear) was that the therapist would punish or abandon the group members. The group solution was to band together to express anger toward the therapist. Following one meeting they discussed the matter and found strength in an implicit agreement that each would express his anger toward the therapist.

However, the specific group focal conflict is not within the conscious awareness of the group members who are most involved, and the solution is not deliberately planned but is a vector, a course of action which "clicks" with the unconscious wishes and fears of each member. Should the solution be clearly unsatisfactory to one of the members, a new group conflict is created which culminates in a modified group solution. In this instance, the reactive fear was alleviated by the mutual support of the group members, and the disturbing wish was therefore expressed. Such a solution will, over the long term, be enabling for the patients since only by gradual exposure and expression of their disturbing wishes can the necessary reality testing occur.

As Whitaker and Lieberman recognize, there is an overlapping between their tripartite schema and that of Ezriel's. Ezriel's required relationship is analogous to the group solution, the avoided relationship to the disturbing motive, and the calamitous relationship to the reactive motive. However, Ezriel considers the required relationship (group solution) to be a defensive, restrictive posture while Whitaker and Lieberman's focal conflict theory includes solutions which allow gratification of the disturbing motive while alleviating fears; thus the solution (required relationship) may be enabling rather than purely defensive and thereby subject to interpretation.

There is, however, a major difference between Ezriel's and Whitaker and Lieberman's therapeutic application of their group concepts. In their therapeutic approach Whitaker and Lieberman are most concerned with the nature of the group solution. Therapeutic intervention is required when a group solution appears which is restrictive to the group and to the members. Furthermore, an interpretation which elucidates the total group configuration is only one of a number of mechanisms which may be employed to influence the group. They suggest, for example, that the therapist may, with efficacy, deal with a restrictive solution by modeling for the patients a different form of behavior.[31] Thus, the role of the therapist is a flexible one: he may ask questions, he may report on his personal reactions, he may focus on an individual's idiosyncratic mode of operating within the group, or, as we have seen, he may focus on total group movement.

Whitaker and Lieberman do not lose sight of the fact that the tripartite (disturbing motive, reactive motive, and solution) system is but an abstraction rather than an entity in the animistic sense. Its purpose is to clarify the meaning and origin of behavior patterns which are restrictive for the group. Thus in their views about total group phenomena and in their application of this information to the therapy process, Whitaker and Lieberman's approach, despite a semantic difference, overlaps significantly with the approach I have discussed earlier in this chapter.

To summarize, the problem of the mass group therapist orientation is more one of omission than of commission. I do not quarrel with the importance of mass group phenomena in the behavior and experience of the members. What I do strenuously disagree with is a restriction of the therapist role. Interpretation, as I have indicated, does play an important role in therapy, but it is by no means the only ingredient in successful therapy. Most of the curative factors are mediated through other activities of the therapist, especially his norm-shaping activities.

An examination of a recent statement [48] by Horwitz, a leading spokesman for the mass group oriented approach, may clarify these points. He lists several advantages of the group centered approach:

1. It helps avoid the "squeaky wheel getting the grease" pitfall. The therapist avoids the hazard of favoring one patient over another; he searches for the common elements shared by all.
2. The therapist views an individual's behavior as a piece of the whole, as embedded in a group context.
3. The patient is supported by perceiving that his central anxieties and conflicts are part of the human condition and shared by the other members. As a result of this discovery, the patient is able with less anxiety to express these concerns.
4. The group-as-a-whole interpretive technique fosters a therapeutically useful regression.

Let us consider each of these concepts. They are, I trust, familiar ones by now—I have discussed each many times throughout this text. Though they are put as justification for the mass group interpretive approach, yet it is my view that none of them requires substantial mass group process commentary or restricts the therapist's role to interpretation. In the interactional approach I have described, there is little possibility of one patient being substantially favored over another since the therapist always considers the process of a transaction; if one patient speaks, the therapist considers the interactional context of the act—"Why now? What does his act tell us about his relation to the others? Why are the others silent after he speaks?" The interactional therapist always views each member's behavior as embedded in a group context. "Universality"—the discovering of the shared nature of one's deepest concerns—has been amply considered. The last point—the fostering of regression—is more complex. My experience is that regression invariably occurs in an interactional group; an approach which encourages members to display in ever-deepening fashion their basic interpersonal behavior always fosters regression. The more disturbed, distorted interpersonal modes always emerge in a context which permits free, disinhibited affect and behavioral expression. No semi-deliberate mystification, no impersonal therapist behavior is needed to encourage regression either in intermember or in member-therapist transactions. Regression is most commonly seen in the patients' distorted view of the therapist. As we shall examine in the next chapter, transference does not have to be coaxed into being: it is a ubiquitous phenomenon in group therapy. Indeed, the task in group therapy is more one of resolution than of evocation of regression.

REFERENCES

1. G. Psathas and R. Hardert, "Trainer Interventions and Normative Patterns in the T-group," *J. Appl. Behav. Sci.*, 2: 149–169, 1966.
2. D. Shapiro and L. Birk, "Group Therapy in Experimental Perspective," *Int. J. Group. Psychother.*, 17: 211–224, 1967.
3. R. C. Jacobs and D. T. Campbell, "The Perpetuation of an Arbitrary Tradition through Several Generations of a Laboratory Microculture," *J. Abnorm. Soc. Psychol.*, 62: 649–658, 1961.
4. M. Sherif, "Group Influences upon the Formation of Norms and Attitudes," in E. E. Maccoby, T. M. Newcomb, and E. L. Hartley (eds.), *Readings in Social Psychology* (New York: Holt, Rinehart, and Winston, 1958), pp. 219–232.
5. J. Marmor, cited in R. Liberman, "Social Reinforcement of Group Dynamics: An Evaluative Study," presented at American Group Psychotherapy Association Convention, Chicago, January 1968.
6. R. V. Heckel, S. L. Wiggins, and H. C. Salzberg, "Conditioning Against Silences in Group Therapy," *J. Clin. Psychol.*, 18: 216–217, 1962.
7. M. Dinoff, R. Horner, D. B. Kuppiewski, H. Rikard, and O. Timmons, "Conditioning the Verbal Behavior of a Psychiatric Population in a Group Therapy-Like Situation," *J. Clin. Psychol.*, 16: 371–372, 1960.
8. M. A. Lieberman, "The Implications of a Total Group Phenomenon: Analysis for Patients and Therapists," *Int. J. Group. Psychother.*, 17: 71–81, 1967.
9. A Bandura, "Modelling Approaches to the Modification of Phobic Disorders," presented at the Ciba Foundation Symposium: The Role of Learning in Psychotherapy, London, 1968.
10. A Bandura, J. Grusec, and F. Menlove, "Vicarious Extinction of Avoidance Behavior," *J. Personal. Soc. Psychol.*, 5: 16–23, 1967.
11. A. Bandura, D. Ross, and J. Ross, "Imitation of Film Mediated Aggressive Models," *J. Abnorm. Soc. Psychol.*, 66: 3–11, 1963.
12. A. M. Schwartz and H. L. Hawkins, "Patient Models and Affect Statements in Group Therapy," paper read at American Psychological Association Meetings, Chicago, September 1965.
13. A. Goldstein, S. Gassner, R. Greenberg, A. Gustin, J. Land, R. Liberman, and D. Steiner, "The Use of Planted Patients in Group Psychotherapy," *Am. J. Psychother.*, 21: 767–774, 1967.
14. M. Miles, "On Naming the Here-and-Now": Unpublished essay.

15. Freud-Jung correspondence.
16. D. Stock and R. W. Whitman, "Patients' and Therapists' Apperceptions of an Episode in Group Psychotherapy," *Human Relations, 10:* 367–383, 1957.
17. M. Lieberman, I. Yalom, and M. Miles, *Encounter Groups: First Facts* (New York: Basic Books, 1973).
18. Milton Berger, "Nonverbal Communications in Group Psychotherapy," *Int. J. Group Psychother., 8:* 161–178, 1958.
19. I. D. Yalom and J. H. Handlon, "The Use of Multiple Therapists in the Teaching of Psychiatric Residents," *J. Nerv. Ment. Dis., 141:* 684–692, 1966.
20. S. H. Foulkes and E. J. Anthony, *Group Psychotherapy: The Psychoanalytic Approach* (2nd ed.; Baltimore: Penguin Books, 1965), p. 153.
21. O. Rank, *Will Therapy and Truth and Reality* (New York: Alfred A. Knopf, 1950).
22. R. May, *Love and Will* (New York: W. W. Norton, 1969).
23. S. Arieti, *The Will to be Human* (New York: Quadrangle Books, 1972).
24. L. Farber, *The Ways of the Will* (New York: Basic Books, 1966).
25. J. Frank, *Persuasion and Healing* (New York: Schocken Books, 1963), p. 161.
26. E. Goffman, "The Moral Career of the Mental Patient," *Psychiatry, 22:* 123–142, 1959.
27. C. Rycroft, *Psychoanalysis Observed* (London: Constable, 1966), p. 18.
28. Foulkes and Anthony, *op. cit.*, p. 29.
29. *Ibid.*, p. 238.
30. J. Strachey, "The Nature of the Therapeutic Action of Psycho-Analysis," *Int. J. Psychoanal., 15:* 127–159, 1934.
31. S. H. Foulkes, "A Memorandum on Group Therapy," British Military Memorandum ADM 11, BM (mimeographed), July 1945.
32. S. H. Foulkes, personal communication, April 1968.
33. W. Bion and J. Rickman, "Intra-Group Tensions in Therapy," *Lancet,* November 27, 1943.
34. M. Sherwood, "Bion's Experiences in Groups: A Critical Evaluation," *Human Relations 17:* 113–130, 1964.
35. W. R. Bion, *Experiences in Groups and Other Papers* (New York: Basic Books, 1959).
36. *Ibid.*, p. 94.
37. M. B. Parloff, "Advances in Analytic Group Therapy," in J. Marmor (ed.), *Frontiers of Psychoanalysis* (New York: Basic Books, 1967).
38. J. Sutherland, personal communication, 1968.
39. D. Malan, personal communication, 1974.
40. D. Stock and H. Thelen, *Emotional Dynamics and Group Culture* (New York: New York University Press, 1958).
41. H. Ezriel, personal communication, 1968.
42. H. Ezriel, "A Psycho-Analytic Approach to Group Treatment," *Brit. J. Med. Psychol., 23:* 59–74, 1950.
43. H. Ezriel, "Notes on Psycho-Analytic Group Therapy: Interpretation and Research," *Psychiatry, 15:* 119–126, 1952.
44. H. Ezriel, "Experimentation Within the Psycho-Analytic Session," *Brit. J. Philos. Sci., 7:*29–48, 1956.
45. H. Ezriel, "The First Session in Psycho-Analytic Group Treatment," *Nederlands Tydskrift voor Geneeskunde, 111:* 711–716.
46. H. Ezriel, "The Role of Transference in Psychoanalytic and Other Approaches to Group Treatment," *ACTA Psychotherapeutica, Supplementum, Vol. 7,* 1957.
47. D. S. Whitaker and M. Lieberman, *Psychotherapy through the Group Process* (New York: Atherton Press, 1964).
48. L. Horwitz, "Group-Centered Interventions in Therapy Groups," *Comprehensive Group Studies, Vol 2:* 311–331, 1971.

6

THE THERAPIST: TRANSFERENCE AND TRANSPARENCY

❧

In the first five chapters we have discussed the mechanisms of therapeutic change in group therapy, the tasks of the therapist, and the techniques by which he accomplishes his tasks. We shall in this chapter turn from what the therapist must *do* in the group to how he must *be*. Does he play a role? To what degree is he free to be "himself"? How "honest" can he be? How much transparency can he permit himself?

Any discussion of therapist "freedom" does well to begin with transference, which can be either an effective tool for the therapist or a set of shackles which encumbers his every movement. In his first and extraordinarily prescient essay on psychotherapy (the final chapter of *Studies in Hysteria* [1895[1]]), Freud noted several possible impediments to the formation of a good working relationship between patient and therapist. Most of these could be resolved easily, but one stemmed from deeper sources and resisted efforts to banish it from the therapeutic work. Freud labeled this impediment "transference," since it consisted of attitudes toward the therapist which he believed had been "transferred" from earlier attitudes toward important figures in the patient's life. These feelings toward the therapist were "false connections," new editions of old impulses.

Only a few years passed before Freud realized that transference was far more than an impediment to therapy; if used properly it could be the therapist's most effective tool.[2] What better way to help the patient recapture the past than to allow him to reexperience and reenact ancient feelings toward parents in his current relationship to the therapist? Furthermore, the conflicted relationship with the therapist, the transference neurosis, was amenable to reality testing; the therapist could treat it, and in so doing he simultaneously treated the infantile conflict. Considerable evolution in psychoanalytic technique has occurred over the last half century, but until recently certain basic principles regarding the role of transference in psychoanalytic therapy have endured with relatively little change:

1. Analysis of transference is the major therapeutic task of the therapist;
2. Since the development (and, then, the resolution) of transference is crucial, it is important that the therapist facilitate its development by concealing his real self so that the patient can encloak him in transference much as he might dress a clothing store mannequin (this is, of course, the rationale behind the traditional "blank screen" role of the analyst).
3. The most important type of interpretation the therapist can make is one which clarifies some aspect of transference (Strachey's "mutative interpretation").

Within the past few years, however, many analysts have perceptibly shifted their position as they have recognized the importance of other factors in the therapeutic process. For example, a lead article in the *American Journal of Psychiatry* [3] by a prominent analyst stated: "Psychoanalysts have begun, in general, to feel more free to enter into active communicative exchanges with patients instead of remaining bound to the incognito 'neutral mirror' model of relative silence and impassivity." He continues by pointing out that therapy is a learning process wherein patients acquire new models of thinking, feeling, and behavior:

Moreover, these new models are not always achieved cognitively and consciously; as often as not they are acquired subtly, as a result of overt or covert suggestion, unconscious identification with the therapist, corrective emotional experiences in the interaction with him, and a kind of operant conditioning via implicit or explicit expressions of his approval or disapproval. In this process, the nature and quality of the patient-therapist interaction, the real personalities of both patient and doctor, and the degree of faith, hope, trust, and motivation that the patient brings to the therapeutic situation are of paramount importance in enabling the new learning to take place successfully.

Few would quarrel with the importance of the development, appreciation, and resolution of transference in individual dynamically oriented therapy.* What is at issue, however, is the priority of the

* In the psychoanalytic literature, definitions of transference differ from one another in their degrees of freedom.[4,5] The more rigorous definition of transference is that it is a state of mind of a patient toward his therapist produced by displacement onto the thera-

transference work relative to other curative factors in the therapeutic process. The problem is a substantial one since the tasks are not complementary but, to an extent, mutually exclusive—the therapist cannot focus his attention sheerly upon transference and at the same time hope to utilize the large number of other potential curative factors.

These problems are troublesome to the individual therapist, but they constitute an issue of great urgency to the group therapist who, as we have seen in these many pages, has such a variety of tasks to perform that he cannot afford to limit his activities to an investigation of transference.

The difference between therapists who consider the resolution of therapist-patient transference as the paramount curative factor and therapists who attach equal importance to the interpersonal learning ensuing from member-member relationships and from the many other curative factors is more than a theoretical difference; in practice, marked differences of technique ensue. These two vignettes from a group led by a therapist-centered leader illustrate this point.

The members of a group meeting for the twentieth time discussed at great length the fact that they did not know one another's first names. They then dealt with the general problem of intimacy, discussing, for example, how difficult it was to meet and really know people today. How does one make a really close friend? Now, on two occasions during the course of this discussion members erred or forgot the surname of another member. From this data the group leader made a transference interpretation; namely, that by forgetting the others' names the members were each expressing a wish that all the other members would vanish so that each alone could have the therapist's sole attention.

In another group during a session in which two male members were absent, four women bitterly criticized the one male patient present, a homosexual, for his detachment and narcissism, which precluded any interest in the lives or problems of others. The therapist suggested that the women attacked the male patient because he did not desire them sexually; moreover, he was an indirect target—the women really wanted to attack the therapist for his refusal to engage them sexually.

In each instance the therapist selectively attended to the data and, from the vantage point of his conception of the paramount curative factor, made an interpretation which was pragmatically correct since it focused the members' attention upon their relationship with the

pist of feelings, ideas, etc., which derive from previous figures in the patient's life. Others extend "transference" to apply not only to the analyst-analysand relationship but to other interpersonal situations. In this discussion, as elsewhere in this text, I use the term liberally to refer to the irrational aspects of any relationship between two people. In its clinical manifestations the concept is synonymous with "parataxic distortion." As we shall discuss, there are more sources of "transference" than the simple transfer or displacement of feeling from a prior to a current object.

leader. However, in each instance the therapist-centered interpretation was an incomplete one and denied the important reality of inter-member relationships; in fact, the members of the first group, in addition to their wish for the therapist's sole attention, *were* considerably conflicted about intimacy and about their desires and fears of engaging with one another. In the second group the homosexual patient *had* in fact been narcissistic and detached in his relationship to the women in the group, and it was exceedingly important for him to recognize and understand his behavior.

Any mandate which limits the group therapist's flexibility renders him less effective. I have seen some therapists hobbled by a conviction that they must at all times be totally "honest" and transparent and others by the dictum that they must make only transference or only mass group interpretations or, even worse, make only mass-group-transference interpretations.

This chapter attempts to clarify the following issues related to transference:

1. Transference *does* occur in therapy groups; indeed, it is omnipresent and radically influences the nature of the group discourse.
2. Without an appreciation of transference and its manifestations, the therapist will often not be able to understand the process of the group.
3. If he ignores transference considerations in his relationship with patients, he may seriously misunderstand some transactions and confuse rather than guide his members; if he sees *only* the transference aspects of his relationships with members, he does violence to their autonomy.
4. There are some patients whose therapy hinges on the resolution of transference distortion; there are others whose improvement will depend upon "interpersonal learning" stemming from work not with the therapist but with another member; and there will be many patients who choose alternate therapeutic pathways in the group and derive their primary benefit from other curative factors.
5. Attitudes toward the therapist are not all transference based: many are reality based and others are irrational but flow from other sources of irrationality inherent in the dynamics of the group. (As Freud knew, not all group phenomena can be explained on the basis of individual psychology.[6])
6. If the therapist maintains his flexibility, he may make good therapeutic use of these irrational attitudes toward him without at the same time neglecting his many other functions in the group.

Transference in the Therapy Group

Every patient, to a greater or lesser degree, perceives the therapist in-correctly because of transference distortions. Few are conflict-free in their attitudes toward such issues as parental authority, dependency, God, autonomy, and rebellion—all of which often come to be per-sonified in the person of the therapist. These distortions are con-tinually at play under the surface of the group discourse; indeed, hardly a meeting passes without some clear token of the powerful feelings embodied in the therapist. Witness the difference caused by the therapist's entrance. The group is often engaged in animated con-versation only to lapse into complete silence when the therapist enters the room. (Someone once said that the group therapy meeting officially begins when suddenly nothing happens!) The therapist's ar-rival is not only a reminder to the group of its task, but it also evokes early constellations of feelings about the adult, the teacher, the eval-uator. Without him the group can frolic; his presence is experienced as a stern reminder of the responsibilities of adulthood.

Observations of seating patterns often reveal some of the complex and powerful feelings toward the leader. Frequently, the members at-tempt to sit as far away from him as possible; a paranoid patient often takes the seat directly opposite him, perhaps in order to watch him more closely; a dependent patient generally sits close to the therapist. If co-therapists sit close to each other with only one vacant chair be-tween them, the members may be disinclined to occupy it. One mem-ber, after eighteen months of group therapy, still described a feeling of great oppression when seated between the therapists.

Over a couple of years I, for research purposes, asked group members to fill out a questionnaire following each meeting. One of their tasks was to rank order every member for activity (according to the total number of words spoken). There was excellent intermember reliability in their ratings of the other group members but exceedingly poor reliability in their ratings of the group therapist. In the same meetings some patients rated the therapist as the most active member, whereas others considered him the least active. The powerful and unrealistic feelings of the members toward the therapist prevented an accurate appraisal, even on this relatively objective dimension. Some techniques to demonstrate this phenomenon have been developed for group dynamic classroom teaching. One non-subtle but effective pro-cedure consists of each member estimating the amount of money the group leader has in his pocket. The estimates vary enormously, but generally they show a concordance with transference set.

One patient, when asked to discuss his feelings toward me, stated that he disliked me greatly because I was cold and aloof. He reacted immediately to his disclosure with intense discomfort. He imagined a number of possible repercussions: I might be too upset by his attack to be of any help to the group any longer, I might retaliate by kicking him out of the group, I might humiliate him by mocking him for some of the homosexual fantasies he had shared with the group, or I might use my psychiatric wizardry to harm him in the future. On another occasion a group noted that I was wearing a copper bracelet. When they learned it was for tennis elbow, their reaction was extreme. They felt angry that I should be superstitious or ascribe to any quack cures. (They had berated me for months for not being human enough!) Some mused that if I would spend more time with my patients and less time on the tennis court, we would all be better off. One patient who always idealized me said that she had seen copper bracelets advertised in *Sunset Magazine* but she guessed that mine was more special—perhaps something I had bought in Switzerland!

Some members characteristically address all their remarks to the therapist, or they may speak to other members only to glance furtively at the therapist at the end of their statement. It is as though they speak to others in an attempt to reach the therapist, seeking his stamp of approval for all their thoughts and actions. They forget, as it were, their reasons for being in therapy, as they continuously seek to gain a conspiratorial eye contact with him, to be the last one to leave the session, to be, in a multitude of ways, his favorite child. One middle-aged woman described a dream to the group in which the group therapy room was transformed into the therapist's living room, which was quite bare and unfurnished. Instead of the other members, the room was crowded with the therapist's family, which consisted of several sons. He introduced her to them and she felt an intense degree of warmth and pleasure. Her association to the dream was that she was overjoyed at the thought there was a place for her in the therapist's home. Not only could she furnish and decorate his house (she was a professional interior decorator) but, since he had only sons, there was room for a daughter.

In the last chapter we described the group's strong response to any indication that the leader favors any one member of the group. In a T-group of psychiatry residents one member, Stewart, was so shaken by a very stormy meeting that, as the members were leaving the room, the leader suggested to him that he phone if he needed to talk about what had happened (there was a two-week Christmas break following the meeting). Stewart did phone for a brief conversation with the leader, who forgot, when the group reconvened three weeks later, to mention this to the other members. Weeks later, when the group was attacking the leader for his inaccessibility, Stewart defended the leader by mentioning, in passing, the phone call. The response of the group was fierce: they felt betrayed, they mocked the leader's remark that the invitation to Stewart to call was only a natural, human gesture without great moment and that he had simply forgotten to mention it to the group. "Where is your unconscious?" they jeered. "Innocent" surface acts by the leader often have deep implications for the members and huge underground neural cables may soon be crackling with affect.

Transference is so powerful and so ubiquitous that the dictum "the leader shall have no favorites" seems to be essential for the stability of every working group. Freud [6] suggested that group cohesiveness, curiously, derives from the universal wish to be the favorite of the leader. The prototypic human group, the sibling group, was dominated by intense feelings of rivalry. Every child wished to be the favorite and resented his rivals for their claims to maternal love. The older child wished to rob the younger of his privileges or to eliminate him altogether. And yet each realized that his rival was equally loved by his parents; therefore, he could not destroy his sibling without incurring parental wrath and thus destroy himself. The only possible solution was to insist on equality: if one could not be the favorite, then there must be no favorite at all. Everyone is granted an equal investment in the leader and out of this demand for equality is born what we have come to know as group spirit. (Freud at this juncture is careful to remind us that the demand for equality applies only to the other members. They do not wish to be equal to the leader, but quite the contrary; they have a thirst for obedience and wish to be ruled. We shall return to this shortly.)

Freud was very sensitive to the powerful and irrational manner in which group members view their leader and made a major contribution by systematically analyzing this phenomenon and applying it to psychotherapy. Obviously, however, the psychology of member and leader has existed since the earliest human grouping and Freud was not the first to note it. To cite only one example, Tolstoy in the nineteenth century was keenly aware of the subtle intricacies of the member-leader relationship in the two most important groups of his day: the church and the military. His insight into the overevaluation of the leader gives *War and Peace* so much of its pathos and richness. Consider Rostov's regard for the Tsar: [7]

He was entirely absorbed in the feeling of happiness at the Tsar's being near. His nearness alone made up to him by itself, he felt, for the loss of the whole day. He was happy, as a lover is happy when the moment of the longed-for meeting has come. Not daring to look around from the front line, by an ecstatic instance without looking around, he felt his approach. And he felt it not only from the sound of the tramping hoofs of the approaching cavalcade, he felt it because as the Tsar came nearer everything grew brighter, more joyful and significant, and more festive. Nearer and nearer moved this sun, as he seemed to Rostov, shedding around him rays of mild and majestic light, and now he felt himself enfolded in that radiance, he heard his voice—that voice caressing, calm, majestic, and yet so simple. . . . And Rostov got up and went out to wander about among the campfires, dreaming of what happiness it would be to die—not saving the Emperor's life—(of that he did not dare to dream), but simply to die before the Emperor's eyes. He really was in love with the Tsar and the glory of the Russian arms and the hope of coming victory. And he was not the only man who felt thus in those memorable days that preceded the battle of Austerlitz: nine-tenths of the men in the Russian army were at that moment in love, though less ecstatically, with their Tsar and the glory of the Russian arms.

(Indeed, it would seem that submersion in the love of a leader seems almost a prerequisite for war. How ironic that more killing has probably been done under the aegis of love than under the banner of hatred!)

Napoleon, that consummate leader of men, was according to Tolstoy not ignorant of "transference"; nor did he hesitate to utilize it in the service of victory. In *War and Peace* Tolstoy had him deliver this dispatch to his troops on the eve of battle: [8]

Soldiers! I will myself lead your battalions. I will keep out of fire, if you, with your habitual bravery, carry defeat and disorder into the ranks of the enemy. But if victory is for one moment doubtful, you will see your Emperor exposed to the enemy's hottest attack, for there can be no uncertainty of victory, especially on this day, when it is a question of the honor of the French infantry, on which rests the honor of our nation.

As a result of transference the therapy group may grant the leader superhuman powers. His words are given more weight and imbued with more wisdom than they possess. Equally austute contributions made by other members are ignored or distorted. All progress in the group is attributed to him. Errors, faux pas, and absences of the therapist are seen as deliberate techniques which he employs to stimulate or provoke the group for its own good. Groups, including groups of professional therapists, overestimate his presence and knowledge. They believe that there are great calculated depths to each of his interventions, that he predicts and controls all the events of the group. Even when he confesses puzzlement or ignorance, that, too, is regarded as part of his technique, deliberately intended to have a particular effect on the group.

Who shall be the leader's favorite son? For many group members this longing serves as an internal horizon against which all other group events are silhouetted. No matter how much each cares for the other members of the group, no matter how much each is pleased to see others work and receive help, there is a background of envy, of disappointment that he is not basking alone in the light of the leader. The desire for sole possession of the leader and the ensuing envy and greed lie deeply embedded in the substructure of every group. An old colloquialism for the genital organs is "privates." However, today therapy groups discuss genitality and sexuality with much ease, even relish. The "privates" of a group are more likely to be the fee structure, because often money and fees act as electrodes upon which much of the feeling toward the leader is condensed. The fee structure is an especially charged issue in many mental health clinics which charge members of the group different fees dependent upon income. How much one pays is often one of the group's most tightly clenched secrets, since differences in payment by the members (and the silent insidious corollary, differences in rights, in the degree of ownership) threaten the very cement of the group: equality for all members.

Members often expect the leader to sense their needs; often, that is most clearly apparent to them when the group has an alternate (leaderless) meeting (see Chapter 13) in which they may feel unprotected and uncared for; there is no one there who will know, without their having to ask, what they are feeling and what they wish from the group. One member wrote a list of major issues that troubled him; he brought it to meeting after meeting, waiting for the therapist to divine its existence and to ask him to read it. Obviously, the content of the list meant little. If he had really wanted to work on the problems enumerated there, he could have taken the initiative himself to present the list to the group. No, what was important was the therapist's presence and nurturance. His transference was such that he had incompletely differentiated himself from the therapist; their ego boundaries were blurred; if he knew or felt something, that was tantamount to the therapist's knowing and feeling it. Patients carry the therapist around with them, he is in them, he observes their actions, he engages in imaginary conversations with them.

When several members of the group share this desire for an all-knowing, all-caring leader, then the meetings take on a characteristic flavor. The group seems helpless and dependent. The members de-skill themselves and seem unable to help themselves or others. De-skilling is particularly dramatic in a group composed of professional therapists who suddenly seem unable to ask even the simplest questions of one another. For example, in one meeting the group talked about loss. One member mentions, for the first time, the recent death of his mother. Then silence. There is a sudden group aphasia. No one is even able to say, "Tell us more about it." They are all waiting—waiting for the touch of the therapist. No one wants to encourage anyone else to talk for fear of lessening his chance of obtaining the leader's ministrations.

Then, too, the opposite occurs. Members appear to challenge the leader continuously. He is distrusted, his motivations are misunderstood, he is treated as though he were the enemy. Examples of such negative transference are very common. One patient, just beginning the group, expended considerable energy in an effort to dominate the other members. Whenever the therapist attempted to point this out, the patient regarded his intentions as malicious: the therapist was interfering with his growth, the therapist was threatened by him and was attempting to keep him subservient, or, finally, the therapist was deliberately blocking his progress lest he improve too quickly and thus diminish the therapist's income. Another paranoid patient who had a long history of broken leases and lawsuits brought against her by irate landlords recapitulated her litigiousness in the group. She refused to pay her small clinic bill because she claimed that there was an error in the account. However, she could not find the time to come to talk to the clinic administrator. When the therapist on a number of occasions reminded her of the account, the ungrateful wench compared him to a Jew slumlord or a greedy capitalist who would have liked her to damage her health permanently by slaving forty hours a week in a coal mine. Another patient habitually became physically ill with flu symptomatology whenever she grew depressed. It was impossible for the therapist to work with her without her feeling that he was accusing her of malingering in much the same way that her parents had done. One therapist on a couple of occasions accepted a cigarette from a female member; another member responded very strongly and accused him both of "mooching" and of exploiting the women in the group.

Many reasons exist for the unrealistic attack upon the therapist, but some stem from the same feelings of helpless dependency which result in such worshipful obedience described above. Some patients ("counterdependents") respond counterphobically to their dependency by incessantly defying the leader. There are others who validate their integrity or potency by attempting to triumph over the big adversary; a sense of exhilaration and power ensues from twisting the tail of the tiger and emerging unscathed.

The most common charge that members levy against the leader is that he is too cold, too aloof, too inhuman. In part, this is reality based. For reasons, both professional and personal, which we shall discuss shortly, many therapists do keep themselves hidden from the group. Furthermore, their role of process commentator requires a degree of distance from the group. But there is more to it. Although the members insist that they wish the therapist to be more human, they have the simultaneous counter wish that he be more than human. Freud often made this observation and eventually based his explanation for religious belief in *The Future of an Illusion* on man's thirst for a superbeing. It seemed to him that the group integrity depended upon the existence of some superordinate figure who, as we have discussed, fosters the illusion of loving each member equally. Solid group bonds become chains of sand if the leader is lost. If the general perishes in battle, it is imperative that the news be kept secret lest panic ensue. So, too, for the leader of the church. Freud was fascinated by a 1903 novel, *When It Was Dark*,[6] in which Christ's divinity was questioned and ultimately disproved. The work depicted the catastrophic effects on Western European civilization; previously stable social institutions deconstituted like parts of a model airplane whose glue has suddenly deteriorated.

And so we note great ambivalence about the members' directive to the leader to be more human. They claim that he tells them nothing of himself, yet they rarely make explicit inquiry. They demand that he be more human yet excoriate him for wearing a copper bracelet, mooching a cigarette, or forgetting to tell the group that he had conversed with a member over the phone. They prefer not to believe him if he professes puzzlement or ignorance. The illness or infirmity of a therapist always arouses considerable discomfort among the members; somehow the therapist should be beyond biological limitation. When a leader abandons his role, his followers are much distressed. When Shakespeare's Richard II laments his "hollow crown" and gives vent to his discouragement, and need for friends, his court bids him to be silent.

A group of psychiatric residents I once led put the dilemma very clearly. They often discussed the "big people" out there in the world—their therapists, group leaders, supervisors, and the adult community of senior practicing psychiatrists. The closer they came to the completion of their training, the more important and problematic did the "big people" become. I wondered, was it possible that they too would soon become some of the big people? Could it be that even I had my big people? There were two opposing sets of concerns about the big people and both were equally frightening: first, that the big people were real; that they possessed superior wisdom and knowledge and would dispense an honest but terrible justice to the young, presumptuous frauds who tried to join their ranks; or, secondly, that the big people themselves were frauds, that the members were all Dorothys facing the Oz wizard. The second possibility had more frightening implications than the first: it brought them face to face with their intrinsic loneliness and apartness. It was as if for a brief time life's illusions were stripped away, exposing to view the naked scaffolding of existence—a very terrifying sight, one that we conceal from ourselves with the heaviest of curtains. The "big people" are one of our most effective curtains: as frightening as their judgment may be, it is far less terrible than that other alternative—that there are no big people and that one is finally and utterly alone.

The leader is thus seen unrealistically by members for many reasons: true transference or displacement of affect from some prior object is one source; conflicted attitudes toward authority, dependency, autonomy, rebellion, etc., which become personified in the therapist are another; and still another source is the tendency to imbue the therapist with superhuman features so as to use him as a shield against existential (or ontological) anxiety. One further source issues from the members' explicit or intuitive appreciation of the great power of the group therapist. His presence and his impartiality are, as we have already discussed, essential for group survival and stability. He cannot be deposed; he has at his disposal enormous power; he can expel members, add new members, mobilize group pressure against anyone he wishes.

In fact, the sources of intense, irrational feelings toward the therapist are so varied and so powerful that transference will occur, come what may. I do not believe the therapist need unduly concern himself with the task of generating or facilitating the development of transference. He need not, for example, assume a pose of unflinching neutrality. Better that he spend his time attempting to turn the transference to therapeutic account. A clear illustration of transference occurred with a patient who attacked me often for aloofness, deviousness, and hiddenness. He accused me of manipulation—of pulling strings to guide each member's behavior. I was not clear and open. I never really came out and told the group exactly what I was trying to do in therapy. The striking part of this illustration is that this patient was a member of a group in which, for experimental purposes (see Chapter 13), I had been writing very clear, very honest, very transparent group summaries and mailing them to the members before the next meeting. Never has any therapist, I believe, made a more earnest attempt to demystify the therapeutic process. Yet earlier in the very meeting in which he attacked me, he informed the group that he doesn't read the summaries and in fact had a large number of them unopened lying on his desk!

As long as a leader assumes the responsibility of leadership, transference will occur. I have never seen a group without a rich and complex underpinning of transference. The problem is, thus, not *evocation* but, on the contrary, *resolution* of transference. If the therapist is to make therapeutic use of transference, he must help the patient to recognize, to understand, and to change his distorted attitudinal set toward the leader.

There are two major approaches to facilitate transference resolution in the therapy group: consensual validation and increased therapist transparency. The therapist may encourage the patient to validate his impressions of the therapist against those of the other members. If many or all of the group members concur in the patient's view of and feelings toward the therapist, one may conclude either that the reaction to the therapist stems from global group forces related to his role in the group or that the reaction is not an unrealistic one at all—the patients are perceiving him accurately. If, on the other hand, one member alone of all the group members possesses a particular view of the therapist, then he may be helped to examine the possibility that he sees the therapist, and perhaps others, too, through an internal distorting prism.

Thus, one method of facilitating reality testing is to encourage patients to check out their perceptions with one another. The other major method calls for the use of the therapist's person; he allows the patient to confirm or disconfirm impressions of him by gradually revealing more of himself. He presses the patient to deal with him as a real person in the here-and-now. He responds to the patient, he shares his feelings, he acknowledges or refutes motives or feelings attributed to him, he looks at his own blind spots, he demonstrates respect for the feedback the members offer him. In the face of the increasing amount of data the patient has about the therapist, it becomes increasingly difficult to maintain a fictitious belief system concerning him.

The group therapist undergoes a gradual metamorphosis: in the beginning he busies himself with the many functions necessary in the creation of the group, the development of a social system in which the many curative factors may operate, and in the activation and illumination of the here-and-now. Gradually, the therapist begins to interact with each of the members; as time progresses he relates more personally to them and the early stereotypes the patient cast onto the therapist become more difficult to maintain. This process between the therapist and each of the members is not qualitatively different from the interpersonal learning which ensues as a result of each member's relationship with other members. After all, the therapist has no monopoly on authority, dominance, sagacity, or aloofness and many of the members work out their conflicts in these areas not with the therapist (or *only* with the therapist) but with other members who have these attributes. This change in the degree of transparency of the therapist is by no means limited to group therapy; someone once said that when the analyst tells the analysand a joke, you can be sure the analysis is approaching its end. However, the pace, the degree, the nature of the therapist transparency and the relationship between this activity of the therapist and his other tasks in the group is problematic and deserves careful consideration. More than any other single characteristic, the nature and the degree of therapist self-disclosure differentiates the various schools of group therapy.

The Psychotherapist and Transparency

Major "lasting" psychotherapeutic innovations appear and vanish with bewildering rapidity; only a truly intrepid observer would attempt to differentiate evanescent from potentially important and durable trends in the diffuse, heterodox American psychotherapeutic scene. Nevertheless, it seems that there are stirrings, in widely varying settings, of a shift in the therapist's basic presentation of himself. Consider the following vignettes:

The staff and the sixty acute and chronically ill patients of a state hospital meet together for a community meeting in which problems of a specific patient as well as those of the entire community are discussed. Following this, the entire ward, the professional staff (psychiatrists, psychologists, nurses, social workers) and the auxiliary staff (occupational and recreational therapists, etc.) meet for an hour to discuss staff relationships. In this meeting personal grievances are aired; for example, how the authoritarianism of a particular nurse or doctor is undermining others on the ward, or how a staff member is so anxious to be liked by the patients that he competes with other members of the staff for the patients' attention. They may additionally vent their collective feelings of frustration, puzzlement, or discouragement about a particular patient, a ward situation, or, for that matter, the field in general. This type of staff meeting is no longer unusual; the professional staff including the trained psychotherapists has, since the innovative writings of Maxwell Jones [9] and Stanton and Schwartz,[10] recognized the necessity of working out intrastaff tensions. What *was* unusual, however, was that most of the sixty patients were sitting around the periphery listening to and watching the staff group.

Therapists leading therapy groups which are observed through a one-way mirror reverse the roles at the end of the meeting. The patients are permitted to observe while the therapist and the students discuss or "rehash" the meeting.

At a university training center, a tutorial teaching technique has been employed in which four psychiatric residents meet regularly with an experienced clinician who conducts an interview in front of a one-way mirror. The patient is often invited to observe the post-interview discussion.

Similarly, I have for many years used as a teaching vehicle a multiple therapy format [11] in which one patient is treated simultaneously by several therapists (usually four psychiatric residents and two experienced clinicians). One of the important ground rules is that there is no post-session rehash; everything that is said must be said in the presence of the patient, including disagreements about diagnosis, the appropriate plan of therapy, as well as criticism of one therapist by another.

A group therapist began a meeting by asking a patient who had been extremely distressed at the previous meeting how he was feeling today and whether the therapy session had been helpful to him. His co-therapist then said to him, "Tom, I think you're doing just what I was doing a couple of weeks ago—pressing the patients to tell me how effective my therapy is. We both seem on a constant lookout for reassurance. I think we are reflecting some of the general discouragement in the group. I wonder whether the members may be feeling pressure that they have to improve to keep up our spirits."

In several groups at an outpatient clinic, the therapists write a detailed summary (see Chapter 13) after each meeting and mail it to the patients before the next session. The summary contains many things such as a narrative account of the meeting, a running commentary on process, each member's contribution to the session, but it also contains much therapist disclosure—his ideas about what was happening to everyone in the group that meeting; a relevant exposition of the theory of group therapy; exactly what he was attempting to do in the meeting; his feelings of puzzlement or ignorance about some events in the group; his own personal feelings including both those said and unsaid in the session. These summaries are virtually indistinguishable from summaries the therapists had previously written for their own private records.

Without discussing the merits or disadvantages of the approaches demonstrated in these vignettes, it can be said for now that there is no evidence that the therapeutic relationship or situation became corroded. On the psychiatric ward in the tutorial and in the therapy groups, the patients, rather than lose faith in their all too human therapists, developed more faith in a process in which the therapists were willing to immerse themselves. The patients who observed their therapists in disagreement learned that, although "no one true way" exists, the therapists are nonetheless dedicated and committed to finding ways of helping their patients.

In each of these vignettes the therapists abandon their traditional role and share some of their many uncertainties with their patients. Gradually, the therapist is defrocked, the therapeutic process demystified. The past decade has witnessed the demise of the concept of psychotherapy as an exclusive domain of psychiatry. A short time ago therapy was indeed a private closed-shop affair. Psychologists were under surveillance lest they be tempted to practice "therapy" rather than "counseling"; social workers could do "casework" but not psychotherapy. The eggshell era of therapy, in which the patient was considered so fragile and the mysteries of technique so deep that only the individual with the ultimate diploma dared treat him, is gone forever. Instead, the past few years have witnessed the establishment of diverse programs, many sponsored by the National Institute of Mental Health, designed to train nonprofessionals to do psychotherapy. For example, Rioch [12] has, under the auspices of the Washington School of Psychiatry, established courses to train housewives in both individual and group therapy. Psychiatric technicians are being trained by intensive NIMH-sponsored courses to be group therapists in psychiatric hospitals.[13] Well-integrated college students have been successfully used as psychotherapists for disturbed adolescents at both Stanford University [14] and Berkeley.[15] Ex-addicts, with only brief training, have been widely used as therapists for groups of addicts.

The recent groundswell of interest in leaderless or patient-led groups is another case in point. Within the past few years many publications have described the rationale and course of these self-directed interactional groups [16,17,18,19] (not to be confused with nonprofessional groups, such as Alcoholics Anonymous or Recovery, Inc., which are primarily suppressive and inspirational). The most thorough and systematic approach to patient-led groups has been made by Berzon,[18,19] who for several years has attempted to program leadership functions into a group through a written or tape-recorded instructional manual to be used at each meeting. (This work is of such interest and significance that it will be discussed in detail in Chapter 13.) Though we have little reliable information about the process of leaderless women's lib groups, it is safe to say that they are extremely widespread, have had significant impact on a large number of women, and are likely to become more prevalent in the future.

Nor is this reevaluation of the therapist's role solely a modern phenomenon. There were adumbrations of such experimentation among the earliest dynamic therapists. Ferenczi, for example, because of his dissatisfaction with the therapeutic results of psychoanalysis, continually challenged the aloof, omniscient role definition of the classical psychoanalyst. During his last several years he openly acknowledged his fallibility to patients and, in response to a just criticism, felt free to say, "I think you may have touched upon an area in which I am not entirely free myself. Perhaps you can help me see what's wrong with me." [20] Foulkes [21] stated thirty years ago that the mature group therapist was a truly modest one—one who could sincerely say to his group, "Here we are together facing reality and the basic problems of human existence. I am one of you, not more and not less."

All of these approaches argue that therapy is a rational, explicable process. They espouse a humanistic attitude to therapy, in which the patient is considered a full collaborator in the therapeutic venture. No mystery need surround the therapist or the therapeutic procedure; aside from the ameliorative effects stemming from expectations of help from a magical being, there is little to be lost and perhaps much to be gained through the demystification of the therapy process. A therapy based on a true alliance between therapist and enlightened patient reflects a greater respect for the capacities of the patient and, with it, an increased reliance on self-awareness rather than on the easier but more precarious comfort of self-deception.

Greater therapist transparency is, in part, a reaction to the old authoritarian medical healer who, for many centuries, has colluded with distressed man's wish for succor from a superior being. Healers have harnessed and indeed cultivated this need as a powerful agent of treatment. In countless ways they have encouraged and fostered a belief in their omniscience: Latin prescriptions, specialized language, secret institutes with lengthy and severe apprenticeships, imposing offices, and pyramids of diplomas—all have contributed to the image of the healer as a powerful, mysterious, and prescient figure.

In unshackling himself from his ancestral role, the therapist of today has at times sacrificed his effectiveness at the altar of self-disclosure. However, the dangers ensuing from indiscriminate therapist transparency (which we shall consider shortly) should not deter us from exploring the judicious use of therapist self-disclosure.

THERAPIST TRANSPARENCY AND ITS EFFECT
ON THE THERAPY GROUP

The primary sweeping objection to therapist transparency is, as we
have discussed, based on the traditional analytic belief that the paramount curative factor is the resolution of patient-therapist transference. From this point of view it is necessary for the therapist to remain
relatively anonymous or opaque in order to foster the development of
unrealistic feelings toward him. It is my position, however, that other
curative factors are of equal or greater importance and that the therapist who judiciously uses his own person increases the therapeutic
power of the group by encouraging the development of these factors.
He gains considerable role flexibility and maneuverability and may,
without concerning himself about role spoilage, directly attend to
group maintenance, to the shaping of the group norms, and to here-
and-now activation and process illumination. By decentralizing his
position in the group, he hastens the development of group autonomy
and cohesiveness.

One objection to self-disclosure, a groundless objection I believe, is
the fear of escalation, the fear that once the therapist reveals himself,
the group will insatiably demand even more. Recall that there are
powerful forces in the group which oppose this trend. The members
are extraordinarily curious about the therapist, yet, at the same time,
they wish him to remain unknown and powerful. My own clinical
work is at times complicated by my occasionally leading human development laboratories (intensive T-groups). The "reentry phenomenon" (discussed in Chapter 14) often results in abrupt but transient
shifts in my role as a leader; yet I find that my therapy groups are neither confused nor, later, more personally demanding of me.

As a clinical illustration of this point, consider a group therapy session which I held immediately after returning from a week-long residential human relations laboratory.

Four members, Don, Charles, Janice, and Martha, were present at
the twenty-ninth meeting of the group. One member and the co-
therapist were absent; one other member, Peter, had at the previous
meeting dropped out of the group. The first group theme that emerged
was the group's response to Peter's terminating. The group discussed
this very gingerly from a great distance, and I commented that we had,
it seemed to me, never honestly discussed our feelings about Peter
when he was present and that we were avoiding them now even after

his departure. Among the responses was Martha's comment that she was glad he had left, that she had felt they couldn't reach him, and that she didn't feel it was worth her while to try. She then commented on his lack of education and noted her surprise that he had even been included in the group—a thinly veiled swipe at the therapists. I felt that Martha's judgmentalism and her immediate rejection of others had never been openly discussed in the group, and I thought I might help Martha and the group confront this issue by asking her to go around the group and describe those aspects of each person she found herself unable to accept. This proved to be very difficult for her, and she generally avoided the task by phrasing her objections in the past tense— i.e., "I once disliked some trait in you but now it's different." When she had finished with each of the patients, I pointed out that she had left me out; indeed, she had never expressed her feelings toward me except through indirect attacks. She proceeded to compare me unfavorably with the co-therapist, stating that she found me too retiring and ineffectual; with dispatch she then attempted to undo the remarks by commenting that "still waters run deep" and recalling a number of examples of my sensitivity to her.

The other members suddenly stated that they'd like to tackle the same task and did; in the process they revealed many long-term group secrets, such as Don's effeminacy, Janice's slovenliness and desexualized grooming, and Charles's lack of empathy with the women in the group. Martha was compared to "a golf ball, tightly wound up with an enamel cover." I was attacked by Don for my deviousness and lack of interest in him. The group then asked me also to go around the group in this manner; being fresh from a seven-day T-group, and no admirer of the Duke of Playa Toro who led his army from the rear, I agreed. I told Martha that her quickness to judge and condemn others made me reluctant to show myself to her, lest I, too, be judged and found wanting. I agreed with the golf ball metaphor and added that her judgmentalism made it difficult for me to approach her, save as an expert technician. I told Don that I felt his gaze on me constantly; I knew he desperately wanted something from me, and that the intensity of his need and my inability to satisfy that need often made me very uncomfortable. I told Janice that I missed a spirit of opposition in her, she tended to accept and exalt everything that I said so uncritically that it became difficult at times to relate to her as an autonomous adult. The meeting continued at an intense involved level, and after its end the observers expressed grave concerns about my behavior. They felt that I had irrevocably relinquished my leadership role and become a group member; that the group would never be the same; and that, furthermore, I was placing my co-therapist, who would return the following week, in an untenable position.

In fact, none of these predictions materialized. In subsequent meetings the group plunged more deeply into work; several weeks were required to assimilate the material generated in that single meeting. In addition, the group members, following the model of the therapist, related to one another far more forthrightly than before and made no demands on the therapist for escalated self-disclosure.

There are many different types of therapist transparency depending upon the therapist's personal style and his particular goals in the group at that time. Is he trying to facilitate transference resolution? Is he model-setting in an effort to set therapeutic norms? Is he generally attempting to assist the interpersonal learning of the members by working upon their relationship with him? Is he attempting to support and demonstrate his acceptance of members by saying in effect: "I value and respect you and demonstrate this by giving of myself?"

An incident of therapist disclosure that was enormously helpful to the group occurred in a meeting when all three women members discussed their strong sexual attraction to one of the group therapists. Much work was done on the transference aspects of the situation, on the women being attracted to a man who was obviously unattainable, older, in a "superior" position, etc. The therapist then pointed out that there was still another side of it. None of the women had expressed similar feelings toward the other therapist (also male), and, furthermore, other female patients who had been in the group previously had had the same feelings. He could not deny that it gave him pleasure to hear these sentiments expressed to him, and he asked them to help him look at his blind spots—i.e., what he was doing unbeknownst to himself to encourage this? His request opened up a long and fruitful discussion by the group members of a number of important feelings about both therapists. There was much agreement that the two were very different: the one who was the object of the women's affection was more vain, took much more care about his physical appearance and clothes, and had an exactitude and preciseness about his statements which created about him an attractive aura of suave perfection. The other therapist was sloppier in appearance and behavior: he spoke more often when he was unsure of what he was going to say, he took more risks, was willing to be in error, and in so doing was more often helpful to the patients. The feedback sounded right to the therapist who had requested it; he had heard it before and so informed the group. He thought about their comments during the week and at the following meeting thanked the group and told them that they had been helpful to him.

The therapist may facilitate the group work by responding to the patients' perception of him simply by reflecting on how the patients' statement makes him feel. Or he may report whether the patients' comments "fit," whether they click with his internal experience: "There are times when I feel irritated with you but at no time do I feel I want to impede your growth, or see you work in a coal mine, or want to slow your therapy so as to earn more money from you. That simply isn't a part of my experience of you." Or "I feel very uncomfortable by your deference to me—I always feel that you've put yourself down very low and that you're always looking up at me." Or "I've never heard you challenge me so directly before. Even though it's a bit scary for me, it's also very refreshing." Or "I feel restrained, very unfree with you because you give me so much power over you. I feel I have to check every word I say because you give so much weight to all of my statements."

Note that these therapy disclosures are all part of the here-and-now of the group. In each the therapist discloses something of the inner world which he experiences in the group. Most therapists prefer not to reveal aspects of their personal life to the group, though there are some who choose to do so in the service of providing a model for the patients. For example, Berger states, "It is at times very helpful for the therapist to share some past or current real-life problem and to afford a model for identification through his capacity to come through such a problem constructively." [22]

Many therapists shrink away from self-disclosure without being clear about their reasons for doing so. Too often, perhaps, therapists rationalize by cloaking their personal inclinations in professional garb. There is little doubt, I believe, that the personal qualities of the therapist influence both his professional style and his choice of ideological school.

An incident which occurred at a group therapy workshop aptly illustrates some of these issues. An experienced, competent group therapist brought up the following dilemma: several months after the completion of group therapy a patient had invited him to dine at his home. He wanted the therapist to meet his new wife; he had spoken of her much during his stay in the group and married her shortly after termination. The therapist felt that this patient had had a very successful course of therapy: he had worked exceedingly well and resolved many important issues (including transference distortions); in fact the therapist could not remember having had a patient with a more successful course of therapy. Moreover he liked the patient, would have enjoyed seeing him, and was curious to meet his wife.

Yet he declined the invitation. He felt that it would be professionally improper and unwise but had much difficulty being more explicit than that. Several themes emerged in the workshop discussion. Would it not totally undermine the therapeutic relationship? Suppose the patient might need the therapist again? Should the therapist not rotate in a professional orbit around the patient so as to be available for immediate recall? (Yet the therapist felt the patient had had a completely successful course of therapy and there was no reason to suspect further treatment would be necessary.) Would it not, in some ill-defined way, retrospectively undo some of the therapeutic work? Would it not be unsettling for the patient to see the therapist in a different light? (Yet the patient had worked on and resolved transference issues. This was no tenuous cure on the basis of suggestion, a "transference cure," or "crooked cure," as Freud put it.) Was the therapist denying termination by continuing to see the patient? (Often this is the case. Yet this patient worked long and well on termination.) Is it not bad practice from the standpoint of the other members of the group? Is favoritism not fractionating? (True enough, yet the patient terminated therapy many months ago and, since many other members were ready to terminate in the next months, the group ended and was now no longer in existence.) Does the therapist not have to protect his private time? Does it not immeasurably complicate life and therapy to mix social and professional roles? (Most certainly. Yet the patient was no longer a patient. Moreover the therapist *wanted* to dine with him.)

It seemed that every "professional" reason for the therapist's behavior proved to be rationalization. The closest the therapist could come to the truth, he said, was that he was made very uncomfortable at the prospect of the patient seeing him eat, or seeing him feel uncomfortable in social conversation—not skillfully engaging in the introductions, not adeptly taking his leave at the end of the evening. The truth was, of course, that the therapist wanted to protect not the patient but himself! To protect himself from the odious charge of being human— of eating, of faltering, in short of being less than Godlike.

Many therapists decline to reveal themselves to the group because of their fears about where it will lead. What further information will the patients demand? I have often posed this question to successfully treated patients at the end of therapy. Most express a wish that the therapist had been more open, more personally engaged in the group. None would have wanted the therapist to have discussed more of their private life or personal problems with the group. The therapist, I think, need not fear that he will be stripped and asked to stand shivering and naked before the group.

The real fear lies elsewhere. One group patient (the same one who likened the therapist to a Jew slumlord) had this dream: "We [the group] were all sitting around a long table with the therapist at the head. He had in his hand a slip of paper with something written on it. I tried to snatch it away from him but he was too far away." Months later as she was approaching the crisis and turning point of her therapy, she recalled the dream and added that she knew all along what was written on the paper but hadn't wanted to say it in front of the group. It was his answer to the question: "Do you love me?" I think this is the question which is so enormously threatening to the therapist. Even worse perhaps is the group question: "How much do you love each of us?" These questions threaten the very frame of the psychotherapeutic contract. They challenge some tenets that both parties have agreed to keep invisible. They are but a step away from a commentary upon the "purchase of a friendship" model. "If you really care for us, would you see us if we had no money?" They come perilously close to the ultimate, terrible secret of the psychotherapist, which is that the intense drama in the group room plays a very small compartmentalized role in his life. As in *Rosencrantz and Guildenstern*, key figures in one drama rapidly become shadows in the wings as the therapist moves immediately onto the stage of another drama.

Only once have I been blasphemous enough to lay this bare before a group. A therapy group of psychiatric residents was dealing with my departure (for a several month sabbatical). My personal experience during that time was one of saying goodbye to a number of patients and to several groups, some of which were more emotionally involving for me than the resident group. Termination work was difficult and the group members attributed much of the difficulty to the fact that I had been so involved in the group that I was finding it difficult to say goodbye. I acknowledged my involvement in the group but presented to them the fact which they knew but refused to know, i.e., that I was vastly more important to them than they were to me. They were clearly aware of this unbalanced pseudo-mutuality in psychotherapeutic work with their own patients, and yet they had never applied it to themselves. There was a gasp in the group as this truth, this denial of specialness, this inherent cruelty of psychotherapy, came home to them.

Does this discussion lead to the conclusion that there is no place in therapy for concealment? That the most helpful therapist is the one who is most fully and most consistently self-disclosing? Let us turn our attention to the limitations of transparency.

Pitfalls Involved in Therapist Transparency

Some time ago I observed a group led by two neophyte group therapists who were at that time much dedicated to the ideal of therapist transparency. They formed an outpatient group and conducted themselves in an unflinchingly honest fashion, expressing openly in the first meetings their uncertainty about group therapy, their self-doubts, and personal anxiety. In so doing, however, they jettisoned their group maintenance function; the majority of the members dropped out of the group within the first six sessions.

The new time-extended "marathon groups" (see Chapter 9) which meet from twenty-four to forty-eight consecutive hours place paramount emphasis on self-disclosure. The sheer physical fatigue wears down defenses and abets maximal disclosure by both members and therapist. For those still encumbered by scraps of physical or psychological concealment, many psychotherapists have reported enthusiastically on "group therapy in the nude," and the mass media (for example *Time Magazine* [23]) have given considerable coverage to Southern California * nude marathons. Indeed, at an American Psychiatric Association convention, fifteen hundred people tried to cram into an auditorium seating seven hundred in order to watch a movie of nude marathon therapy. Specialized methods have evolved in these groups which, short of proctoscopy, carry disclosure to its ultimate (e.g., the group may "spread-eagle" a member to afford maximal genital disclosure).

Many untrained leaders undertake to lead groups with the monolithic credo "Be yourself" as a central organizing principle around which all other technique and strategy is shaped. Yet what has happened is not freedom for the therapist but tyranny. The paradox is that freedom and spontaneity in extreme form can result in a leadership role which is as narrow and restrictive as the tradional blank screen

---

* Many of the wilder innovations in therapy have sprung from Southern California. It brings to mind the fanciful notion in Saul Bellow's *Seize the Day* [24] of someone tilting the large flat map of the United States and observing that "everything that wasn't bolted or screwed down slid into Southern California."

leader. Under the present-day banner of "anything goes if it's genu-ine" (at any time, to any degree), the leader sacrifices flexibility in his role. Consider the issue of timing. In the first example, the neophyte, fully honest, therapists overlooked the fact that leadership behavior which may be appropriate at one stage of therapy may be quite inap-propriate at another. If patients need initial support and structure to remain in the group, then it is the therapist's task to provide it. There are situations when, as Maslow [25] puts it, "The good leader must keep his feelings to himself, let them burn out his own guts, and not seek the relief of catharting them to followers who cannot at that time be helped by an uncertain leader."

The leader who strives only to create a mystique of egalitarianism between member and leader may in the long run provide no leader-ship at all. It is a naïve misconception to view effective role behavior of the leader as unchanging; as the group develops and matures, dif-ferent forms of leadership are required. Furthermore, the "honest" comment of the dedicated leader may be the pragmatically correct response, rather than an indiscriminate expression of what may be the therapist's distortions or misperceptions. After all, as Parloff [26] states, "The honest therapist is one who attempts to provide that which the patient can assimilate, verify and utilize." * Ferenczi years ago under-scored the necessity for proper timing. The analyst, he said, must not admit his flaws and uncertainty too early. First the patient must feel sufficiently secure in his own abilities before he is called upon to face defects in the one on whom he leans.[20]

In a sense, what may happen is that leader transparency becomes so cherished and romanticized that it achieves an independent au-tonomy; it is then considered as an end rather than as a means to an end. There has been an attempt to dignify this transformation by workers such as Mowrer [16] and Stoller,[28] who present self-disclosure as the keystone of an oversimplified approach to psychopathology and therapy. Jourard states, for example, that "people become clients be-cause they do not disclose themselves in some optimal degree to the people in their life." [29] The corollary is that psychotherapy should re-

---

* A rich example of this principle is found in the novel *Magister Ludi*,[27] in which Hermann Hesse describes an event in the lives of two renowned healers. Joseph, one of the healers, severely afflicted with feelings of worthlessness and self-doubt, sets off on a long journey to seek help from his rival, Dion. At an oasis Joseph described his plight to a stranger, who turns out to be Dion; whereupon Joseph accepts Dion's invitation to go home with him in the role of patient and servant. In time Joseph regains his former se-renity, zest, and effectance and becomes the friend and colleague of his master. Only after many years have passed and Dion lies on his deathbed does he reveal to Joseph that when the latter encountered him at the oasis, he, Dion, had reached a similar im-passe in his life and was en route to request Joseph's assistance.

verse this process, with the therapist leading the way by his own personal example.

Thus, it is argued that the therapist sets an invaluable model for patients by fully disclosing himself. Yet who ever said that full disclosure was possible or desirable in the therapy group or in the outside world? On the contrary, personal and interpersonal concealment and deception seem to be an integral ingredient of any functioning social order. O'Neill illustrated this in dramatic form in *The Iceman Cometh*. In that play a group of derelicts live, as they have for twenty years, in the back room of a bar. The group is an exceedingly stable one with many well-entrenched group norms. Each man maintains himself by a set of illusions ("pipe dreams," O'Neill labels them). One of the most deeply entrenched group norms is that no member challenge another's pipe dreams. Then enters Hickey, the iceman, a traveling salesman, a totally enlightened enlightening therapist, a false prophet who believes he brings fulfillment and lasting peace to each man by forcing him to shed his self-deceptions and stare with unwinking honesty at the sun of his life. Hickey's surgery is deft. He forces Jimmy Tomorrow (whose pipe dream was to unhock his suit, sober up, and get a job "tomorrow") to act now. He gives him clothes and sends him, and then the others, out of the bar to face today. The effects on each man and upon the group are calamitous. One member commits suicide, others grow severely depressed, the "life goes out of the booze," members attack each others' illusions, the group bonds disintegrate, and the group veers toward dissolution. In a sudden, last minute convulsive act, the group labels Hickey psychotic, banishes him, and gradually reestablishes its old norms and cohesion. These "pipe dreams" or "vital lies," as Ibsen calls them in *The Wild Duck*, are often essential to personal and social integrity. They should not be taken lightly or impulsively stripped away in the service of honesty.

Commenting on the social problems of the United States, Victor Frankl once suggested that the Statue of Liberty on the East Coast be balanced by a Statue of Responsibility on the West Coast. In the therapy group freedom becomes possible and constructive only when it is coupled with responsibility. None of us is free from impulses or feelings which, if expressed, could be destructive to another. I suggest that we encourage patients and therapists to speak freely, to shed all their internal censors and filters save one—the filter of responsibility.

This does not mean that no unpleasant sentiments are expressed; indeed, growth cannot occur in the absence of conflict. It does mean, however, that responsibility, not freedom, is the superordinate principle. The therapist has a particular type of responsibility

—responsibility to his patients and to his therapy task. Patients have a human responsibility toward one another and, as therapy progresses, as solipsism diminishes, as empathy increases, they come to exercise that responsibility in their interactions with one another.

Thus, the therapist is not in the group primarily to be honest or to be authentic. In times of confusion about his behavior, the therapist may profit from a momentary stepping back and a reconsideration of his primary tasks in the group. Therapist self-disclosure is an aid to the group because it sets a model for the patients and because it assists some patients to reality-test their feeling toward the therapist. The therapist may ask himself, where is the group now? Is it a concealed, overly cautious group which may profit from a leader who models personal self-disclosure? Or is it a group which has already established vigorous self-disclosure norms and is in need of other assistance? The therapist must, as we have noted, consider whether his behavior will interfere with his group maintenance function. He must know when to recede into the background. Unlike the individual therapist, the group therapist does not have to be the axle of therapy. In part, he is midwife to the group: he must set a therapeutic process in motion and may, if he insists on centrality, inhibit the progress of the group.

An overly restricted definition of the role of the group therapist, whether it be based on transparency or, for that matter, on any other criterion, may cause the leader to lose sight of the individuality of each patient's needs. The same caveat applies to leaderless groups or groups in which there is an attempt to create an automated leader. Despite his group orientation, the leader must retain some individual focus; not all patients need the same thing. Some, perhaps most, patients need to relax controls; they need to learr how to express their affect—anger, love, tenderness, hatred. Others, however, need the opposite; they need to gain impulse control because their life styles are already characterized by labile and immediately acted-upon affect.

One final consequence of more or less unlimited therapist transparency is that the cognitive aspects of therapy may be completely neglected. As we have noted previously, mere catharsis is not in itself a corrective experience. Cognitive learning or restructuring (much of which is provided by the therapist) seems necessary for the patient to be able to generalize his group experiences to his outside life; without this transfer or carryover, we have succeeded only in creating better, more gracious therapy group members. Without the acquisition of some knowledge about general patterns in his interpersonal relationships, the patient may, in effect, have to discover the wheel anew in each of his subsequent interpersonal transactions.

REFERENCES

1. Breuer and Freud, *Studies in Hysteria.*
2. S. Freud, "Five Lectures on Psychoanalysis," Standard Edition, Vol. 2 (London: Hogarth, 1955).
3. J. Marmor, "The Future of Psychoanalytic Therapy," *American Journal of Psychiatry, Vol. 130*, Nov. 1973, pp. 1197–1202.
4. Rycroft, C. *A Critical Dictionary of Psychoanalysis* (New York: Basic Books, 1968).
5. J. Sandler, G. Dave, and A. Holder, "Basic Psychoanalytic Concepts: III Transference." *Brit. J. Psychiatry, 116:* 667–72, 1970.
6. S. Freud, *op. cit.*, No. 2, "Group Analysis."
7. L. Tolstoy, (1865–69) *War and Peace* (New York: The Modern Library, Random House, Inc.,) p. 231.
8. L. Tolstoy, *op. cit.*, p. 245.
9. M. Jones, *The Therapeutic Community* (New York: Basic Books, 1953).
10. A. H. Stanton and M. S. Schwartz, *The Mental Hospital* (New York: Basic Books, 1954).
11. I. D. Yalom and J. H. Handlon, "The Use of Multiple Therapists in the Teaching of Psychiatric Residents," *J. Nerv. Ment. Dis., 141:* 684–692, 1966.
12. M. J. Rioch, E. Elkes, A. A. Flint, B. S. Usdansky, R. G. Newman, and E. Silber, "National Institute of Mental Health Pilot Study in Training Mental Health Counselors," *Am. J. Orthopsychiat., 33:* 678–689, 1963.
13. G. O. Ebersole, P. H. Leiderman, and I. D. Yalom, "Training and Non-Professional Group Therapist: A Controlled Study," *J. Nerv. Ment. Dis.*, in press.
14. J. R. Hilgard and U. S. Moore, "Affiliative Therapy in the Treatment of Withdrawn Young Adolescents," *J. Acad. Child Psychiat.*, in press.
15. G. Goodman, "Companionship as Therapy: The Use of Non-Professional Talent," in J. T. Hart and T. M. Tomlinson (eds.), *New Directions in Client-Centered Psychotherapy* (Boston: Houghton-Mifflin, 1968).
16. O. H. Mowrer, *The New Group Therapy* (Princeton: D. Van Nostrand, 1964).
17. M. Harrow *et al.*, "Influence of the Psychotherapist on the Emotional Climate in Group Therapy," *Human Relations, 20:* 49–64, 1967.
18. B. Berzon and L. N. Solomon, "The Self-Directed Therapeutic Group: Three Studies," *J. Counsel. Psychol., 13:* No. 4, 1966.
19. B. Berzon, "Self-Directed Small Group Programs: A New Resource in Rehabilitation," *Final Narrative Report, Vocational Rehabilitation Administration Project #RD1748*, January 1968, (La Jolla, California: Western Behavioral Science Institute), pp. 1–107.
20. M. Green (ed.), *Interpersonal Analysis: The Selected Papers of Clara M. Thompson* (New York: Basic Books, 1964).
21. S. H. Foulkes, "A Memorandum on Group Therapy," *British Military Memorandum, ADM.*, July 1945.
22. M. M. Berger, "The Function of the Leader in Developing and Maintaining a Working Therapeutic Group," unpublished mimeograph, 1967.
23. *Time,* February 23, 1968, p. 42.
24. S. Bellow, *Seize the Day* (New York: Viking Press, 1956).
25. A. H. Maslow, "Notes on Unstructured Groups at Lake Arrowhead," unpublished mimeograph, 1962.
26. M. Parloff, "Discussion of Accelerated Interaction: A Time-Limited Approach Based on the Brief Intensive Group," *Int. J. Group Psychother., 28:* 239–244, 1968.
27. H. Hesse, *Magister Ludi* (New York: Frederick Unger, 1949), pp. 438–467.
28. F. Stoller, "Accelerated Interaction: A Time-Limited Approach Based on the Brief Intensive Group," *Int. J. Group Psychother., 28:* 220–235, 1968.
29. S. Jourard, *The Transparent Self* (Princeton: D. Van Nostrand, 1964), p. 21.

7

THE SELECTION

OF PATIENTS

The fate of a group therapy patient and of a therapy group may, in large measure, be determined before the first group therapy session. Unless careful selection criteria are used, the majority of patients assigned to group therapy may terminate treatment discouraged and without benefit. Research on small groups, to be described in Chapter 8, suggests that the initial composition of the group has a powerful influence on the ultimate outcome of the entire group.

In this chapter I will consider the clinical consensus and research evidence bearing upon the selection of group therapy patients. How can the therapist determine whether or not a given patient is a suitable candidate for group therapy? The following chapter considers the task of group composition. Once it has been decided that the patient is a suitable group therapy candidate, then into which specific group shall he go? Some of the research cited in Chapters 7 and 8 has little immediate clinical relevance; nor is it definitive work. Instead, I describe the research because selection and composition are areas in which research can make a significant contribution, and much of the research methodology used in laboratory and T-group work is clearly applicable to the study of therapy groups.

The first consideration in the determination of group therapy suitability is the type of group therapy available. Selection criteria vary widely depending upon the structure, procedure, and goals of the therapy group. In most inpatient settings, in which small groups are an important treatment modality, all patients are assigned (often at random) to small groups. Grossly disturbed patients are usually excluded until their behavior has been modified to the point where it will no longer disrupt group integrity. For therapy groups with specialized goals, patient selection is relatively uncomplicated; the admission criteria may be simply the existence of the target symptom—obesity, alcoholism, or addiction, for example.

The question is more difficult for the therapist dealing with intensive, dynamic outpatient group therapy, and his selection criteria will be less obvious. Some of the complications become apparent merely through an examination of the selection criteria cited in the clinical literature. We will note first that the colorful descriptive terminology is so highly individualized that it is difficult to establish any consensus. Undesirable candidates include schizoid personalities, chaotic and inchoate egos, emotional illiterates, monopolists, depressives, true hysterics, and psychopaths. This potpourri of symptomatic, characterologic, behavioral, and folk nomenclature is evidence of the need for a system of classification which can convey relevant, predictive information about interpersonal behavior.

Secondly, we will be struck by the contradictions which abound in the clinical literature. There are few conditions cited as contraindications for group therapy for which an opposing opinion or anecdotal report cannot be found. Homosexuality or psychosomatic conditions, for example, which are anathema to some experienced group therapists, have been successfully treated in group therapy by others. Such contradictions are not surprising considering the diversity in training, professional background, and theoretical orientation of therapists; all these factors would, of course, lead to great variations in diagnostic and therapeutic style. With these opposing clinical opinions and a paucity of relevant, controlled research, the neophyte group therapist, especially the professionally agnostic one, will have few firm guidelines for his patient selection.

Finally, one notes that, with a few exceptions, the emphasis in selection criteria is on excluding unsuitable patients from group therapy. It would seem that it is easier to identify characteristics which weigh against the admission of a patient to a therapy group than to establish clear indications for such treatment.

Exclusion Criteria

CLINICAL CONSENSUS

There is considerable clinical consensus that patients are poor candidates for outpatient intensive group therapy if they are: brain damaged,[1,2] paranoid,[3] extremely narcissistic,[4] hypochondriacal,[5] suicidal,[5,4] addicted to drugs or alcohol,[1,2] acutely psychotic,[5,6,7] or sociopathic.[8,9]

These patients seem destined to fail because of their inability to participate in the primary task of the group; they soon construct an interpersonal role which proves to be detrimental to themselves as well as to the group. Consider the sociopathic patient, an exceptionally poor risk for outpatient, interactional group therapy. Characteristically, these patients are destructive in the group. Although early in therapy they may become important and active members, they will eventually manifest their basic inability to relate, often with considerable dramatic and destructive impact. To cite a clinical example:

Mr. Glebe, a thirty-five-year-old highly intelligent patient with a history of alcoholism, great mobility, and impoverished interpersonal relationships, was added with two other new patients to an ongoing group, which had been reduced to three by the recent graduation of members. The cotherapists sensed that he was a poor risk, but because the group was an observed teaching group, they were anxious to reestablish its size; he was one of the few potential patients available. In addition, they were somewhat intrigued by his alleged determination to change his life style. The classic sociopath is forever reaching a turning point in his life. Mr. Glebe, by the third meeting, had clearly become the social-emotional leader of the group—seemingly able to feel more acutely and suffer more deeply than the other members. He presented the group, as he had the therapists, with a largely fabricated account of his background and current life situation. By the fourth meeting, as the therapists learned later, he had seduced one of the female members, and by the fifth meeting spearheaded a discussion of the group's dissatisfaction with the brevity of the meetings. He proposed that the group, with or without the permission of the therapist, meet more often, perhaps at one of the members' homes, without the therapist. By the sixth meeting he had vanished, without prior notification to the group. The therapists learned later that he had suddenly decided to take a two-thousand-mile bicycle trip, hoping to sell the trip journal to a magazine.

This rather extreme example demonstrates many of the reasons why inclusion of a sociopathic individual in a heterogeneous outpatient group is ill-advised: his social "front" is deceptive; he often consumes such an inordinate amount of group energy that his departure leaves the group bereft, puzzled, and discouraged; he rarely assimilates the group therapeutic norms and instead often exploits other members and the group as a whole for his more immediate gratification. This does not mean that group therapy is contraindicated for these patients. In fact, a specialized form of group therapy [10] with a more homogeneous population and a sagacious utilization of strong group and insitutional pressure may well be the treatment of choice. This principle also applies to many of the other contraindications listed above. Thus, it is far more accurate to speak of contraindications for a specified type of group therapy. For example, specialized groups have been shown to be quite effective with mentally defective patients,[11] chronic aftercare patients,[12] and patients addicted to alcohol [13],[14] or other drugs.[15]

SYSTEMATIC STUDIES—REASON FOR FAILURE IN GROUP THERAPY

Almost all the systematic studies of group therapy selection have attempted to elaborate exclusion criteria; they have focused on the failures in group therapy rather than the successes. From the standpoint of research methodology, it is more feasible to establish failure criteria than success criteria.

The study of one obvious failure criterion, premature termination of therapy, has been a rich source of information bearing on the selection process. There is evidence that early terminators do not benefit from their brief stay in the group. In a study of thirty-five patients who dropped out in twelve or fewer meetings, only three reported themselves as improved; [16] moreover, even those three patients were adjudged to have made only marginal symptomatic improvement. In each instance, therapy was discontinued because the patient sought to flee from group stress and not because of the natural conclusion of successful therapy. Premature group terminators have, in addition, an adverse effect on the remaining members of the group, who are threatened and demoralized by the early dropouts. The work phase of the group which requires membership stability may be delayed for months.

Early group termination is thus a failure for the patient and a detriment to the therapy of the remainder of the group. It is also a very common phenomenon. Dropout rates reported in the literature are: 57 percent (three or fewer meetings—university outpatient clinic); [1] 51 percent (nine or fewer meetings—Veterans Administration outpatient clinic); [17] 35 percent (twelve or fewer meetings—university outpatient clinic); [16] 30 percent (three or fewer meetings—clinic and private outpatient groups); [18] 25 percent (twenty or fewer meetings—inpatient and outpatient groups); [19] 35 percent (twelve months or less—long term analytic group therapy).[20]

A study of these early dropouts may help to establish sound exclusion criteria and, furthermore, may provide an important goal for the selection process. The refinement of the selection process, if only to reduce the early dropout rate, would be a significant achievement. Note that although the early terminators are not the only failures in group therapy, they are unequivocal failures. (We may, I think, dismiss as unlikely the possibility that they have gained something positive which will manifest itself later. A recent outcome study of encounter group participants [21] noted that individuals who had a negative experience in the group did not, when studied six months later, "put it all together" and enjoy a delayed benefit from the group experience. If they left the group shaken or discouraged, they were apt to remain that way.) Keep in mind that the study of group dropouts tells us nothing about the group continuers; group continuation is a necessary but not sufficient factor in successful therapy. However, this research strategy circumvents some taxing problems of methodology, especially the critical problem of defining and measuring success in psychotherapy. Let us now consider some of the reasons that patients prematurely terminate therapy which have relevance for the selection process.

Kotkov [22] compared twenty-eight continuers and twenty-eight dropouts (seven meetings or less) in a Veterans Administration outpatient clinic on the basis of data collected at the initial interview. The dropouts significantly differed, in several respects, from those who continued. The former, at their initial interview, were either more "spontaneous-composed," more hostile, or, on the other hand, were more placid and needed prodding. They complained less frequently of tension and more often demonstrated somatization of conflicts rather than "emotional reactivity." They complained of headaches, severe insomnia, and demonstrated motor restlessness. Often, they appeared to be less motivated toward treatment and were less psychologically minded.

In other studies, [23] also in Veterans Administration outpatient clinics, dropouts were studied with the Rorschach projective test. They had less capacity to withstand stress, less desire for empathy, and less ability to achieve emotional rapport.* However, the discriminating power of the Rorschach in the task was modest, scarcely better than the crudest interview screening. (To the best of my knowledge, no predictive Rorschach studies have been done.) The dropouts had a lower Wechsler verbal scale I.Q. and came from a lower socioeconomic class.†

Nash and his co-workers [1] studied a group of forty-eight patients in a university outpatient clinic; the patients had been randomly assigned to individual therapy (N = 18) or to one of three therapy groups (total N = 30). The seventeen dropouts (three or fewer meetings) differed significantly from the thirteen continuers in several respects. Dropouts were more socially ineffective than continuers, and the few continuers who were socially ineffective scored exceptionally high on discomfort; the continuers had a history of fluctuating illness (which implies that the dropouts more likely experienced their illness as progressive and urgent); the dropouts were high deniers and often terminated therapy as their denial crumbled in the face of confrontation by the group.

These studies then suggest that, on initial interview, patients destined to drop out of groups are likely to have the following characteristics: high denial; high somatization; lower motivation; lower psychological mindedness; lower socioeconomic class, social effectiveness, and I.Q. Grotjahn [20] studied his outpatient analytic groups and noted that over a six-year period 43 patients (35 percent) dropped out within the first twelve months of therapy. He felt that in retrospect approximately 40 percent of the dropouts were predictable and fell into three categories: (1) patients with diagnoses of manifest or threatening psychotic breakdowns either depressive, paranoid, or, in one instance, catatonic in nature; (2) patients who used the group for crisis resolution and dropped out when the emergency had passed; (3) highly schizoid, sensitive, isolated individuals who needed more careful, intensive preparation for group therapy.

I shall discuss one final study [16] in greater detail since it has considerable relevance for the selection process. I studied the first six months of life of nine therapy groups in a university outpatient clinic and investigated all patients who terminated in twelve or fewer meetings. A total of ninety-seven patients were involved in these groups (seventy-one original members and twenty-six later additions); of

---

* The form-color/color-form ratio contributed most to this differentiation.
† That dropouts (from any psychotherapeutic format) are disproportionately high amongst the lower socioeconomic class is a finding corroborated by many other studies. [24,25,26]

these, thirty-five were early dropouts. Considerable data were generated from interviews and questionnaire studies of the dropouts and their therapists, as well as from the records and observations of the group sessions and historical and demographic data from the case records.

Reasons for Premature Termination. An analysis of the data suggested nine major reasons for the patients' dropping out of therapy:

1. External factors
2. Group deviancy
3. Problems of intimacy
4. The fear of emotional contagion
5. Inability to share the doctor
6. Complications of concurrent individual and group therapy
7. Early provocateurs
8. Inadequate orientation to therapy
9. Complications arising from subgrouping

Usually more than one factor is involved in the decision to terminate. Some factors are more closely related to external circumstances or to enduring character traits which the patient brings with him to the group (and thus relevant to the selective process), whereas others are related to problems arising within the group; these latter are more relevant to the discussion of therapist technique in Chapters 9 and 10. Most relevant to the establishment of selection criteria are the patients who dropped out because of external factors, group deviancy, and problems of intimacy.

EXTERNAL FACTORS. 1. *Physical reasons for terminating therapy* (e.g., irreconcilable scheduling conflicts, moving out of the geographic area) played a negligible role in decisions to terminate. When this reason was offered by the patient, closer study usually demonstrated the presence of group-related stress more pertinent to his departure. Nevertheless, in the initial screening session the therapist should always inquire about any such pending major life changes. There is considerable evidence to suggest that dynamic group therapy is not a brief form of therapy and that patients should not be accepted into a group if there is a considerable likelihood of forced termination within the next several months.

Invariably, patients encounter periods of discouragement and frustration in the course of the group. There will be many days when they will have a strong disinclination to come to the meeting. If their commute to the group is long or complicated or if their transportation depends upon other people, there is a greater likelihood of absenteeism or drop out. Obviously, there are many exceptions to this: some therapists tell of patients who faithfully fly to meetings from remote regions month after month. However, as a general rule the therapist does well to heed this factor. If patients live at considerable distance and there are equivalent groups closer to him, everyone's interests are served by a judicious referral.

2. *External stress* was considered a factor in the premature drop out of several patients who were so disturbed by external events in their lives that it was difficult for them to expend the energy for involvement in the group. They could not explore their relationships with other group members while they were consumed with the threat of disruption of relationships with the most significant people in their lives. It seemed especially pointless and frustrating to these patients to hear other group members discuss their problems when their own problems seemed so compelling. Among the external stresses were: severe marital discord with impending divorce, initial heterosexual exploration, impending academic failure, and disruptive relationship with parents.

The importance of external stress as a factor in premature group termination was difficult to gauge, since often it appeared secondary to internal forces. A patient's psychic turmoil may cause disruption of his life situation so that secondary external stress occurs; or a patient may focus on an external problem, magnifying it as a means of escaping anxiety originating from the group therapy. Several patients considered external stress as the chief reason for termination, but in each instance careful study indicated that external stress seemed at best a contributory but not sufficient cause for the drop out. Undue focusing on external events often seemed to be one manifestation of a denial mechanism which was helping the patient to avoid something he perceived as dangerous in the group. The patients use the external stress as a rationalization for termination in order to avoid the anticipated dangers of self-disclosure, aggression, intimacy, or facing unknown aspects of themselves.

In the selection process, therefore, an unwarranted focusing on external stress may be an unfavorable sign, whether it represents an extraordinary amount of stress or whether it is a manifestation of denial. Another unfavorable type of referral is the patient who has been propelled into therapy by an external crisis and has well-delineated goals; for example, a person distressed by a recent major loss through death or rejection. If a patient has a recurrent problem—for example, a severe reaction to a heterosexual rejection—and has had successful brief individual therapy in a similar instance in the past and seeks similar therapy again, he is in my experience also a poor candidate for group therapy.

GROUP DEVIANCY. The study of patients who drop out of therapy because they are group deviants offers a rich supply of information relevant to the selection process; but first the term "deviant" must be carefully defined. Almost each group patient represents an extreme in at least one variable—i.e., he is the youngest, the only unmarried member, the sickest, the only Oriental, the only nonstudent, the angriest, or the quietest. However, there were a large number of patients (33 percent of the dropouts) who deviated significantly from the rest of the group in several areas crucial to their group participation, and this deviancy and the consequent repercussions were considered as the primary reason for their premature termination. The patients' roles varied from those who were silent nonparticipators to those who were loud, angry, group disruptors, but always they were isolates and were perceived by the therapists and by the other members as retarding group locomotion.

It was said of all these patients by the group, by the therapists, and sometimes by the patients themselves that they just "didn't fit in." This distinction is difficult to translate into objectively measurable factors. The most commonly described characteristics are: a lack of psychological sophistication, a lack of interpersonal sensitivity, and a lack of personal psychological insight manifested in part by the common utilization of denial. The patients were often of a lower socioeconomic status and educational level than the rest of the group. The therapists, when describing their group behavior, emphasized that these patients retarded the group by functioning on a different level of communication from that of the rest of the group. They tended to remain at the symptom-describing, advice-giving and seeking, or judgmental level and avoided discussion of immediate feelings and here-and-now interaction.

There was an important subcategory of five patients who were chronic schizophrenics and, after individual treatment, were making a borderline adjustment. They had "sealed over" and were utilizing much denial and suppression. Their peculiarity was quite obvious to the other group members by their bizarre dress, mannerisms, and verbal content.

Two other patients in the study differed from the other members of their group in their style of life. One had a history of prostitution and had an illegitimate child; another had a history of narcotic addiction—with the inevitable underworld contacts. However, these two patients did *not* differ from the others in ways that impeded group locomotion (psychological insight, interpersonal sensitivity, and effective communication) and never became group deviants.

One other patient became an extreme deviant in his group because of his moral and religious norms. His therapy group was one of young college students who spoke freely of intimate areas and often acted out sexual concerns. The patient was a Quaker and was currently a conscientious objector doing alternative service as a hospital orderly. His moral views differed so extremely from those of the other group members that he became an isolate and terminated. The therapists stated that the group felt relieved when he left because he had "put a clamp on the group's feelings."

There is considerable social-psychological data from research with laboratory groups which helps us to understand the fate of the deviant in the therapy group. Group members who are unable to participate in the group task and who impede group locomotion toward the completion of the task are much less attracted to the group and are motivated to terminate membership.[27] Individuals whose contributions fail to match high group standards have a high rate of group drop out,[28] and this is particularly marked when the individuals have a lower level of self-esteem.[29] The task of therapy groups is to engage in meaningful communication with the other group members, to reveal oneself, to give valid feedback, and to examine the hidden and unconscious aspects of one's feelings, behavior, and motivation. The individuals who fail at this task are those who lack the requisite skills or motivation. They lack the required amount of psychological-mindedness, are less introspective, less inquisitive, and more apt to utilize self-deceptive defense mechanisms, or they are reluctant to accept the role of patient and the accompanying implication that some personal change is necessary. They may, for example, persist in the expectation that a change in others will be forthcoming. Lundgren and Miller [30] have shown in research upon Bethel T-groups that the individuals who are most satisfied with themselves and who are inclined to overestimate others' opinion of them tend to profit less from the group experience. The Lieberman, Yalom, Miles encounter group study [31] demonstrated that the group members who did not highly value or desire personal change were likely to terminate prematurely. The ability to face one's deficiencies, even to the point of undue self-criticism, and a degree of sensitivity to the feelings of others seem to be requisite skills for successful group membership. Similarly in group therapy, members who on post-group questionnaires cannot accurately perceive how others view them are more likely to remain, at best, peripheral members.[32]

What happens to individuals who are unable to engage in the basic group task and who are perceived by the group and, at some level of awareness, by themselves as impeding the group? Schachter [33] has demonstrated that, in a small group, communication toward a deviant is very great initially and then drops off sharply as the group rejects the deviant. The rejection (on sociometric measures) was proportional to the extent to which the deviancy was relevant to the purpose of the group. Much research has demonstrated that one's position in the group communication network significantly influences his satisfaction with the group.[34] Jackson [35] has shown also that an individual's attraction to a group is directly proportional to the extent to which this individual is considered valuable by the other members of the group. It also has been demonstrated [36] that the ability of the group to influence an individual is dependent partly on the attractiveness of the group for that member and partly on the degree to which the member communicates with the others in the group. It is also well known from the work of Sherif [37] and Asch [38] that an individual will often be made exceedingly uncomfortable by a deviant group role, and there is recent evidence [39] that individuals in a deviant or isolate group role, who cannot or do not verbally express anxiety, may experience physiological anxiety correlates. Lieberman, Miles, and I demonstrated that encounter group members who were deviants (members considered "out of the group" by the other members or those individuals who grossly misperceived the group norms) had virtually no chance of benefiting from the group and an increased likelihood of suffering negative consequences.[40]

There is experimental evidence, then, that the group deviant derives less satisfaction from the group, experiences anxiety, is less valued by the group, is less prone to be influenced or benefited by the group, is more likely to be harmed by the group, and is far more prone than nondeviants to terminate membership.

These experimental findings coincide notably with the experience of deviants in the therapy groups studied. Of the eleven deviants, there was only one who did not terminate prematurely. This patient managed to continue in the group because of massive support he received in concurrent individual therapy. However, he not only remained an isolate in the group but, in the opinion of the therapists and other members, he impeded the progress of the group. What happened in that group was remarkably similar to the phenomena described above by Schachter [33] in experimental groups: at first considerable group energy was expended on the deviant, then the group gave up; he was, to a great extent, excluded from the communicational network, but the group could never entirely forget him, and he slowed the pace of the work. If there is something important going on in the group that cannot be talked about, there will always be a degree of generalized communicative inhibition. With a disenfranchised member, the group is never really free; in a sense, it cannot move much faster than its slowest member.

These findings bear heavily upon the selection process. The patients who will assume a deviant role in therapy groups are not difficult to identify in screen interviews. The denial, the de-emphasis of the intrapsychic and interpersonal factors, the tendency to attribute dysphoria to somatic and external environmental factors are often quite evident.

The sample of chronic "sealed over" schizophrenic patients was particularly recognizable. These patients maintained a precarious adjustment and could not intimately involve themselves in a rapidly moving interactional group without seriously threatening this adjustment. The chronic schizophrenic patients were all introduced into the group for similar reasons: their individual therapists had felt that they had probably reached a plateau in treatment and that they now needed to develop socializing skills; in some instances, a transfer to group therapy was utilized as a method of gradual termination without arousal of guilt in the therapist. The error thus occurs not in the identification of these patients but in the assumption that, even if they will not "click" with the rest of the group, they will, nevertheless, still benefit from the overall group support and the opportunity to improve their socializing techniques. In our experience, this expectation is not realized. The referral is a poor one, with neither the patient nor the group profiting. Eventually, the group will extrude the deviant. They may smile at one another when he speaks or behaves irrelevantly; they will mascot him, they will ignore him rather than invest the necessary time to understand his interventions. In short, an environment will be created which can only be inimical to the therapeutic process.

Rigid attitudes coupled with proselytizing desires may rapidly propel an individual into a deviant position. One of the most difficult patients for me to work with in groups is the individual who employs fundamentalist religious views in the service of denial. The defenses of this patient are often impervious to the ordinarily potent group pressures because they are bolstered, in his self system, by the norms of another anchor group—his particular sect. The interpretation that he is employing certain basic tenets with unrealistic literalness is often not effective, and a frontal assault on these defenses merely rigidifies them.

It is important that the therapist attempt to screen out patients who will become marked deviants *relative to the goals of the particular group for which they are being considered.* As I have suggested, other forms of deviancy, unrelated to the group task, are irrelevant. An individual who is deviant in sexual object choice is a case in point. Consider those with a homosexual orientation; some do very poorly in therapy groups composed of heterosexual males and females. They do poorly, however, not because of their deviant sexual style but because of interpersonal behavior in the group which is counter to the group task. They may be so guarded and secretive that they cannot establish even minimal reciprocity of trust with other members; they may use the group as a platform to eulogize the gay liberation front and refrain from looking inward and sharing personal concerns; or they may be so sexually driven and their drive so egosyntonic that they can only use their interpersonal contact for overt or thinly sublimated sexual purposes. However, I have found that the majority of homosexuals who seek treatment voluntarily (rather than through external pressures) respond very well in group therapy. It does not matter whether the patient initially seeks treatment to change his sexual orientation to a heterosexual one or whether he wishes to acquire greater comfort and self-understanding within his homosexual orientation. Either goal is an entirely appropriate one in a therapy group, provided that a group climate of respect for individual differences has been established. (See Chapter 12 for a more complete discussion of the group therapy approach to the patient with a homosexual orientation.)

Patients, then, become deviants because of their interpersonal behavior in the group sessions and not because of a deviant life style or past history. There is no type of past behavior too deviant for a group to accept once therapeutic group norms are established. I have seen individuals with life styles including prostitution, exhibitionism, voyeurism, kleptomania, fragging, infanticide, and histories of various other heinous criminal offenses accepted by a middle class "straight" group. Alcoholics, to cite another example, often do poorly in mixed intensive outpatient groups, not because of their drinking but because of their interpersonal behavior. Not infrequently an individual with a serious drinking problem manifests oral character traits which in the group setting take the form of insatiable demands for support, confirmation, and reassurance. He often is fixed upon receiving nurturant supplies from the therapist, whom he is unable to share with the other members. Frustration tolerance is low, and when his threshold is reached, the alcoholic may respond in ways that are inaccessible to group influence, usually through some type of motoric expression—

for example, by increased drinking, absenteeism, tardiness, and drunken arrivals at meetings. (A cautionary note. To the extent that a single appellation such as "alcoholic" fails to render a whole person, these remarks are generalizations and many group therapists have treated individuals with alcoholic problems quite successfully.[14])

Although the dropout category of "group deviancy" is the most significant one from the standpoint of the initial selection procedure, some of the other categories are also relevant.

PROBLEMS OF INTIMACY.* Conflicted feelings about intimacy represent a common reason for premature termination. The dropouts manifested their intimacy conflicts in various ways: (1) schizoid withdrawal, (2) maladaptive self-disclosure (promiscuous self-disclosures or pervasive dread of self-disclosure), and (3) unrealistic demands for instant intimacy.

Several patients diagnosed as schizoid personality pattern disturbances, because of their interpersonal coldness, aloofness, introversion, and tendency toward autistic preoccupation, experienced considerable difficulty relating and communicating in the group. Each had begun the group with a resolution to express his feelings and to correct previous maladaptive patterns of relating. They failed to accomplish this and experienced frustration and anxiety, which in turn further blocked their efforts to speak. Their therapists described their group role as: "schizoid-isolate," "silent member," "nonentity," "peripheral," "nonrevealer," "doctor's helper." Attributing the cause of the failure to themselves, most of these patients terminated treatment thoroughly discouraged as to the possibility of ever obtaining help from group therapy.

Another schizoid patient, whose diagnosis lay closer to the nebulous boundary between schizophrenia and schizoid personality, dropped out for different reasons—his fears of his own aggression against other group members. He originally applied for treatment because "of a feeling of wanting to explode . . . a fear of killing someone when I explode . . . which results in my staying far away from people." He participated intellectually in the first four meetings he attended but was frightened by the other members' expression of emo-

---

* The dropout categories are heavily overlapping. For example, the chronic schizophrenic "group deviants" were also, undoubtedly, heavily conflicted in the area of intimacy and would have encountered considerable difficulty in this area in the group, had not their deviant group role forced their drop out earlier. Conversely, many of the patients who dropped out because of problems of intimacy began to occupy a deviant role because of the behavioral manifestations of their problems in intimacy. Had the stress of the internal intimacy conflict not forced them to terminate, it is most likely that the inherent stresses of the deviant role would have created pressures leading to termination.

tion. In the fifth meeting one patient monopolized the entire meeting with a repetitive, tangential discourse. The patient became extremely angry with the monopolizer and with the rest of the group members for their complacency in allowing this to happen; with no previous communication to the therapists, he abruptly terminated.

Other patients manifested their problems with intimacy in other ways: some experienced a constant, pervasive dread of self-disclosure which precluded their participation in the group and ultimately resulted in their dropping out; others engaged in premature, promiscuous self-disclosure and abruptly terminated, whereas still others made such inordinate demands on the other group members for immediate, prefabricated intimacy that they created an inviable group role for themselves.

This entire category of patients with severe problems in the area of intimacy presents a particular challenge to the group therapist both in the area of selection and in the area of therapeutic management (to be considered in Chapter 12). The irony is that these patients whose attrition rate is so high are the very ones for whom a successful group experience could be particularly rewarding. Harrison and Lubin [41] reported that, in a human relations laboratory (see Chapter 14), individuals designated as "work-oriented" (as opposed to "person-oriented") learn more and change more as a result of their group experience even though they are significantly more uncomfortable in the group. Harrison and Lubin do not use the label "schizoid," but their description of "work-oriented" indivduals suggests a strong overlap: ". . . constriction of emotionality . . . threatened by expression of feelings by others . . . hard for them to experience and express their own emotional reactions." Therefore, these patients, whose life histories are characterized by ungratifying interpersonal relationships, stand to profit much from successfully negotiating an intimate group experience; and yet if their past interpersonal history has been too deprived, the group will prove too threatening for them and they will drop out of therapy more demoralized than before.

Thus, this general category represents at the same time a specific indication and counterindication for group therapy. The problem, of course, is one of early identification and screening out of those who will be overwhelmed in the group. If only we could, with accuracy, quantify this critical cut-off point! The prediction of group behavior from pretherapy screening sessions is quite a complex task which I will discuss in detail in the next chapter. However, it may be noted here that an individual who, in the screening procedure, is a severely schizoid, isolated individual with a pervasive dread of self-disclosure is an unfavorable candidate for interactional group therapy. Mildly or moderately schizoid patients, on the other hand, are excellent candidates for group therapy and rarely fail to benefit therefrom. Great caution should be exercised when the therapist is seeking a replacement member for an already established, fast-moving group. If the therapist decides on a therapeutic trial, then he should adequately prepare the schizoid patient for the group (see Chapter 9) and consider also the possibility of short-term individual therapy conducted concurrently with the early phases of group therapy.

THE FEAR OF EMOTIONAL CONTAGION. Several patients who dropped out of group therapy reported that they had been extremely adversely affected by hearing the problems of the other group members. One patient stated that during his three weeks in the group, he was very upset by the others' problems, dreamed about them every night, and relived their problems during the day. Others reported being upset by one particularly disturbed patient in each of their groups; they were all frightened by seeing aspects of the other patient in themselves, fearing that they too might become as mentally ill as the severely disturbed patient or that continued exposure to this patient would evoke a personal regression. Another patient in this category experienced a severe revulsion toward the other group members, stating, "I couldn't stand the people in the group. They were repulsive. I got upset seeing them trying to heap their problems on top of mine. I didn't want to hear their problems. I felt no sympathy for them and couldn't bear to look at them. They were all ugly, fat, and unattractive." She bolted the first group meeting thirty minutes early and never returned. She had a lifelong history of being upset by other people's illnesses and avoiding sick people; once when her mother fainted, she "stepped over her" to get away rather than trying to help. Others also, as Nash *et al.*[1] reported in an earlier study, had a long-term proclivity to avoid sick people. They reported a lack of curiosity about others and, if they had been present at an accident, were "the first to leave" or tended to "look the other way." Most of them report being very upset at the sight of blood. They became especially disturbed if another person discussed problems which were similar to their own.

A fear of emotional contagion, unless it is extremely marked and very clearly manifest in the pretherapy screening procedure, is not a terribly useful index for group inclusion or exclusion. Generally, it is difficult to predict this behavior from screening interviews; furthermore, a fear of emotional contagion was not, in itself, sufficient cause for failure. If the therapist is sensitive to the problem, he can deal with it effectively in the therapeutic process. Occasionally, patients must gradually desensitize themselves; I have known patients who dropped out of several therapy groups before finally persevering. The therapist may help by clarifying for the patient the crippling effects of his attitudes toward others' failings. Logic thus dictates that these attitudes do not rule out group therapy. Quite the contrary; if the discomfort can be contained, the group may very well offer the ideal therapeutic format for the patient.

The other reasons for group therapy dropouts—"inability to share the doctor," "complications of concurrent individual and group therapy," "early provocateurs," "problems in orientation to therapy," and "complications arising from subgrouping"—are generally a result not so much of faulty selection but of faulty therapeutic technique and will be discussed in later chapters. None of these categories, though, belongs purely to the "selection" or "therapy technique" rubric. For example, some patients terminated because of an inability to share the therapist. They never relinquished the notion that progress in therapy was dependent solely upon the amounts of goods (time, attention, etc.) they received from the group therapist. Although it may have been true that these patients tended to be excessively dependent and authority-oriented, it was also true that they had been incorrectly referred to and prepared for group therapy. They had all been in individual therapy, and the group was considered as a method of therapy-weaning. Obviously, group therapy is not a modality to be used in the termination phase of individual therapy, and the therapist, in his pretherapy screening, should be alert to the rationale behind the referral of the patient to group therapy.

Inclusion Criteria

The most important criterion for inclusion is the most obvious one— motivation. The patient must be highly motivated for therapy in general and for group therapy in particular. It will not do for the patient to start group therapy because he was "sent"—sent by a spouse, a probation officer, an individual therapist, any individual or agency outside himself. To permit a patient to enter the group with this reluctant motivational set is to curtail greatly his chances for success. Many of the patient's erroneous prejudgments of the group may be corrected in the preparation procedure (see Chapter 9), but if the therapist discerns a very deeply rooted unwillingness to accept responsibility for treatment or a deeply entrenched unwillingness to enter the group, he should not accept the patient. If, on the other hand, the therapist senses that the patient is willing to regard the group experience as the most important of his current activities, the therapist may regard this as a propitious sign. In general, however, inclusion criteria play little role in the selection process for group therapy; most group therapists adhere to the dictum that all patients, aside from the specific exceptions enumerated above, are suitable for group therapy. In other words, if none of the exclusion criteria applies to the patient, he may be started in group therapy.

Although this policy is not satisfactory, its source is obvious: inclusion criteria are far more difficult to elaborate. For one thing, inclusion criteria must be more comprehensive; one striking feature can point to exclusion, whereas many factors must be considered in reaching a decision about suitability. Any systematic approach to the definition of inclusion criteria must issue from the study of successful group therapy patients, who theoretically should offer valuable information for the selection process. Imagine a rigorously controlled study in which a large number of patients are systematically studied before entering therapy and then followed and evaluated after a year or two of group therapy. There should, of course, be a differential rate of success, and by correlating the pretherapy data with outcome, we should be able to determine those patient characteristics predictive of favorable outcome. Unfortunately, there are extreme difficulties inherent in such a study: patients drop out of therapy, many obtain ancillary individual therapy, group therapists vary in competence and techniques, and initial diagnostic technique is unreliable and often idiosyncratic.

A team of researchers (Houts, Zimerberg, Rand, and myself) attempted, nonetheless, in 1965, to study factors evident in pretherapy which might predict successful outcome in group therapy.[42] Forty patients * (in five outpatient therapy groups) were followed through one year of group therapy. Outcome was evaluated † and correlated with many variables studied before the onset of therapy. The results indicated that a large number of factors were *not* predictive of success in group therapy, including: level of psychological sophistication,‡ the

---

* The patients studied were adult, middle-class, well-educated, psychologically sophisticated outpatients who suffered from neurotic or characterologic problems.

† By a team of raters who, on the basis of a structured interview, evaluated (with excellent reliability) change in symptoms, functioning, and relationships. The patients also independently rated their own outcome, using the same scales.

‡ Measured by the psychological-mindedness subscale of the California Personality

therapists' prediction of outcome,* previous self-disclosure,† and demographic data. In fact, the only variables predictive of success were the patients' attraction to the group ‡ and the patients' general popularity § in the group (both measured at the sixth and twelfth meetings). The finding that popularity correlated highly with successful outcome has some implications for selection, because the researchers found that high previous self-disclosure, activity in the group, and the ability to introspect were some of the prerequisites for group popularity.

The Lieberman, Yalom, Miles encounter group study [44] demonstrated that, on pre-group testing, those who were to profit most from the group were those who highly valued and desired personal change; who viewed themselves as deficient both in understanding their own feelings and in their sensitivity to the feelings of others; who had a high expectational set for the group, anticipating that it would provide relevant opportunities for communication and help them correct their deficiencies. No other systematic outcome studies exist which bear on inclusion criteria—a glaring defect and one that must be corrected before a sound scientific base for group therapy can be established.

Other inclusion criteria become evident when we also consider the members of the group into which the patient will be placed. Thus far, for pedagogical clarity, I have oversimplified the problem by attempting to identify only absolute criteria for inclusion or exclusion. Unlike individual therapy recruitment, where we need only consider the questions of whether or not the patient will profit from therapy and whether or not he and a specific therapist can establish a working relationship, recruitment for group therapy cannot, in practice, ignore the remainder of the group members. It is conceivable, for example, that a patient such as a dependent alcoholic, compulsive talker, or sociopath might derive some benefit from a group but also that his presence would render the group less effective for several other members. Conversely, there are patients who would do well in a variety of treatment modalities but are placed in a slowly moving group because of their catalytic qualities or because of some specific need of a particular group. For example, some groups at times seem to need an aggressive member, or a strong male, or a soft feminine member. Borderline

---

Inventory and by the therapists after an initial screening interview. These measures were probably too insensitive for a population already screened clinically for this variable.

* The therapist rated each patient on a 7-point scale after the initial interview for how well he thought the patient would do in therapy.

† Measured by a modification of the Jourard Self-Disclosure Questionnaire.[43]

‡ Measured by a group cohesiveness questionnaire (see Chapter 3).[42]

§ Measured by a sociometric questionnaire.[42]

schizophrenic patients,* despite their stormy course of therapy and the absence of outcome studies validating the efficacy of group therapy for them, very often find their way into therapy groups. In fact, I have often searched for them because of their beneficial influence on the therapy process. These patients have a greater awareness of their unconscious, less dedication to formal social inhibitory techniques, and very often lead the group into a more candid and eventually intimate culture. Considerable caution must be exercised, however, in including a member whose ego strength is significantly less than that of the other members. If they have socially desirable behavioral traits and if they are valued by the other members because of this openness and deep perceptivity, they will generally do very well. If, however, their social behavior alienates others and if the group is so fast moving or threatening that, rather than lead, they retard the group, then they will be driven into a deviant role and their experience is likely to be a counter-therapeutic one.

One final, and important, criterion for inclusion is the therapist's personal feeling toward the patient. Regardless of the source, if the therapist experiences a strong dislike for or disinterest in the patient, he should refer the patient elsewhere. This caveat is obviously a relative one and each therapist must establish for himself the intensity of such feelings which would preclude effective therapy. It is my impression that the issue is a somewhat less crucial one for group therapists than for individual therapists; with the consensual validation available in the group from the other patients and from the co-therapist, many therapists find that they are more often able to work through initial negative feelings toward patients in group therapy than in individual therapy.

An Overview of the Selection Procedure

The material thus far presented about selection of patients has a disturbingly disjunctive nature. We can, I believe, introduce some order by applying to this material a central organizing principle—a simple punishment-reward system. Members are prone to terminate membership in a therapy group, and are thereby poor candidates, when the

* To be distinguished from the chronic schizophrenic patient in partial remission who uses repressive and suppressive defenses, described as a poor candidate in the section on deviants.

punishments or disadvantages of group membership outweigh the rewards or anticipated rewards. When speaking of punishments or disadvantages of group membership, I refer to the price the patient must pay for group membership. This includes an investment of time, money, energy, as well as a variety of dysphorias arising from the group experience, including anxiety, frustration, discouragement, and rejection.

The patient should play an important role in the selection process. It is preferable for him to deselect himself before entering the group than to undergo the discomfort of dropping out of the group. He can only make a judicious decision, however, if the therapist provides him with the necessary information: e.g., nature of the group experience, anticipated length of therapy, his expected behavior in the group, etc. There will be more about this in the discussion on preparation of the group patient in Chapter 9.

The rewards of therapy group membership consist of the various types of satisfactions members obtain from the group. Let us consider those rewards, or determinants of group cohesiveness, that are relevant to the selection of patients for group therapy.[45]

Members are satisfied with their groups (attracted to their groups and prone to continue membership in their groups) if:

1. They view the group as meeting their personal needs (i.e., their goals in therapy).
2. They derive satisfaction from their relationships with the other members.
3. They derive satisfaction from their participation in the group task.
4. They derive satisfaction from group membership vis-à-vis the outside world.

Each of these factors, if absent or of negative valence, may outweigh the positive valence of the others and result in group termination.

DOES THE GROUP SATISFY PERSONAL NEEDS?

The explicit personal needs of group therapy members are at first expressed in their "chief complaint"—their purpose for seeking therapy. These personal needs are usually couched in terms of relief from suffering, less frequently in terms of self-understanding or personal growth. Several factors are important here: there must be a significant personal need; the group must be viewed as an agent with the potential of meeting that need; and the group must be seen in time as making progress toward meeting that need. There must be a reasonable degree of discomfort, of course, to provide the required motivation for change. The relationship between discomfort and suitability for group therapy is not a linear one but a curvilinear one. *Patients with too little discomfort* (coupled with only a modest amount of curiosity about groups or themselves) are usually unwilling to pay the price for group membership.

Patients with moderately high discomfort may, on the other hand, be willing to pay a high price provided they have faith or evidence that the group can and will help. This faith may derive from a number of sources: e.g.,

1. Endorsement of group therapy by the mass media, by friends who have had a successful group therapy experience, or by a previous individual therapist
2. Explicit preparation by the group therapist (see Chapter 9)
3. Unquestioned belief in the omniscience of authority figures
4. Observing or being told about improvement of other group members
5. Observing small changes in himself occurring early in group therapy

Patients with exceedingly high discomfort stemming from either extraordinary environmental stress, internal conflicts, inadequate ego strength, or some combination of these, may be so overwhelmed with anxiety and realistic management of the external stress that the group goals and activities seem utterly irrelevant. Initially many groups are unable to meet highly pressing personal needs. Greatly disturbed patients may be unable to tolerate the frustration which occurs as the group gradually evolves into an effective therapeutic instrument. They may demand instant relief, which the group cannot supply, or they may develop anxiety-binding defenses which are so interpersonally maladaptive (for example, extreme projection or somatization) as to make the group socially nonviable for them. Individuals who are acutely psychotic are, as we have indicated, generally to be excluded from outpatient interactional group therapy. I refer to the initial selection criteria; established group members who become psychotic during the course of treatment may often be managed in the group setting (see Chapter 12).

Individuals who have been described as "psychologically insensitive," "nonpsychologically minded," "nonintrospective," "high deniers," "psychological illiterates," and "psychologically insensitive" may be unable to perceive the group as meeting their personal needs. In fact, they may perceive an incompatibility between their personal needs and the group goals. How can the exploration of the interpersonal relations of the group members help them with their "bad nerves"? These individuals, too, may have few sources of group satisfaction available to them. Not only does the group not satisfy their personal needs, but they cannot satisfactorily engage in the group activities (which require the very abilities they lack—introspection, sensitivity, etc.), and they eventually are further burdened with the anxiety inherent in the group deviant role. There is a need here for sensitive clinical judgment since some highly motivated, more flexible individuals with these characteristics may be taught by the group to become working patients in the group. As a general rule, however, I have found that patients who utilize denial or other self-deceptive defense mechanisms, who tend to somatize psychological conflicts, or to deal with them in a nonpsychological mode, are usually poor group referrals. The possible benefits derived from their learning the patient role are, in my experience, outweighed by the negative balance of the group reward-punishment system, and they terminate group membership.

SATISFACTION FROM INTERMEMBER RELATIONSHIPS

Group members derive satisfaction from their relationship with other group members, and often this source of attraction to the group may dwarf the others. The importance of intermember relationships both as a source of cohesiveness and as a curative factor was fully discussed in Chapter 3, and we need only pause here to reflect that it is rare for a member to continue membership in the prolonged absence of interpersonal satisfaction.

The development of interpersonal satisfaction may be a slow process. Frank [45] has pointed out that mentally ill patients are often contemptuous of themselves and therefore prone to be initially contemptuous of their fellow patients. They have had, for the most part, few gratifying interpersonal relationships in the past and have little trust or expectancy of gaining anything from close relationships with the other group members. Often, the patients may use the therapist as a transitional object. By relating positively to him at first, they may more easily grow closer with one another. Parloff [46] has demonstrated that group patients who established closer relationships with the group therapist were significantly more inclined to perceive other group members as socially attractive.

SATISFACTION FROM PARTICIPATION IN THE GROUP ACTIVITIES

The satisfaction that patients derive from participation in the group task is largely inseparable from the satisfaction derived from the relationships with the other group members. The group task (to achieve a group culture of intimacy, acceptance, introspection, understanding, and interpersonal honesty) is, in essence, an interpersonal one. However, research with a wide variety of groups has demonstrated that satisfactory participation in the group task, regardless of its nature, is an important source of satisfaction from the group membership.[47] Therapy group members who cannot introspect, reveal themselves, care for others, or manifest their feelings will derive little gratification from their participation in the group activities. These include many of the types of individuals discussed earlier, for example, the schizoid personality, those patients with other types of overriding intimacy problems, the deniers, the somatizers, and the mentally retarded.

SATISFACTION FROM PRIDE IN GROUP MEMBERSHIP

Members of many groups derive satisfaction from membership because the outside world regards their group as highly valued or prestigious. Therapy groups obviously are at a disadvantage in this regard, and generally this source of attraction to the group is not readily available. However, therapy group members will generally develop some pride in their group; for example, they will defend the group if it is attacked by new members. They may feel a sense of superiority over outsiders (A.A. calls them "earth creatures")—people who are as troubled as they but lack the good sense to join a therapy group. If patients manifest extraordinary shame at membership and are reluctant to reveal their membership to intimate friends or even spouses, then obviously therapy group membership must appear to them dissonant with the values of other important anchor groups, and it is not likely that they will develop a high attraction to the group. Occasionally, as Frank [45] and Ends [13] point out, outside groups (for example, family, military, or more recently, industry) will exert pressure on the individual to seek therapy group membership. Groups held together only by this coercion are tenuous, but as the group process evolves, other sources of cohesiveness may be generated.

Summary

In summary, the guidelines for selection stem primarily from the study of group therapy failures. If followed, these guidelines will improve our selection criteria by screening out (and assigning to another type of therapy group or to another therapy modality) patients destined to fail early in the course of group therapy. Using these criteria, the Stanford Psychiatric Outpatient Clinic reduced their dropout rate from 35 percent to 10 percent over a three-year period. [16,42,48,49] Although part of this reduction may have been due to improvement in therapist technique, the major reason for the reduction was a refinement in selection criteria. Nevertheless, this approach to selection is a distinctly limited one. For purposes of exposition we have approached the problem, thus far, in an unidimensional manner. We have attempted to delineate selection criteria for patients posited in absolute terms, or, if the rest of the group has been considered, it has been a phantom anonymous group with a narrowly limited range of members' traits and behavior. In practice, of course, the members of the group into which the patient may go must be reckoned with in vivo; and it is not simply a matter of "Shall the patient enter group therapy?" but also "Shall he enter therapy in that particular group?" This problem, one of a higher order of complexity, is one to which we shall now turn our attention.

REFERENCES

1. E. Nash, J. Frank, L. Gliedman, S. Imber, and A. Stone, "Some Factors Related to Patients Remaining in Group Psychotherapy," *Int. J. Group Psychother.*, 7: 264–275, 1957.
2. J. A. Johnson, *Group Psychotherapy: A Practical Approach* (New York: McGraw-Hill, 1963).
3. I. W. Graham, "Observations on Analytic Group Therapy," *Int. J. Group Psychother.*, 9: 150–157, 1959.
4. S. R. Slavson, *A Textbook in Analytic Group Psychotherapy* (New York: International Universities Press, 1964).
5. S. R. Slavson, "Criteria for Selection and Rejection of Patients for Various Kinds of Group Therapy," *Int. J. Group Psychother.*, 5: 3–30, 1955.
6. R. Corsini and W. Lundin, "Group Psychotherapy in the Mid West," *Group Psychother.*, 8: 316–320, 1955.

7. M. Rosenbaum and E. Hartley, "A Summary Review of Current Practices of Ninety-Two Group Therapists," *Int. J. Group Psychother.*, *12*: 194–198, 1962.

8. J. Abrahams and L. W. McCorkle, "Group Psychotherapy at an Army Rehabilitation Center," *Dis Nerv. Sys.*, *8*: 50–62, 1947.

9. G. Bach, *Intensive Group Therapy* (New York: Ronald Press, 1954).

10. I. D. Yalom, "Group Therapy of Incarcerated Sexual Deviants," *J. Nerv. Ment. Dis.*, *132*: 158–170, 1961.

11. R. Kaldeck, "Group Psychotherapy with Mentally Defective Adolescents and Adults," *Int. J. Group Psychother.*, *8*: 185–192, 1958.

12. M. Scher, "Observations in an Aftercare Group," *Int. J. Group Psychother.*, *23*: 322–337, 1974.

13. E. J. Ends and C. W. Page, "Group Psychotherapy and Psychological Change," *Psychol. Monogr.*, *73*, No. 480, 1959.

14. I. D. Yalom, "Group Therapy and Alcoholism," *Annals of the New York Academy of Sciences*, Vol. 233, pp. 85–103, 1974.

15. E. A. Willett, "Group Therapy in a Methadone Treatment Program," *Internat. J. of Addiction*, *8*: 33–34, 1973.

16. I. D. Yalom, "A Study of Group Therapy Dropouts," *Arch. Gen. Psychiat.*, *14*: 393–414, 1966.

17. B. Kotkov, "The Effect of Individual Psychotherapy on Group Attendance," *Int. J. Group Psychother.*, *5*: 280–285, 1955.

18. E. Berne, "Group Attendance: Clinical and Theoretical Considerations," *Int. J. Group Psychother.*, *5*: 392–403, 1955.

19. Johnson, *op. cit.*, p. 144.

20. M. Grotjahn, "Learning From Dropout Patients: A Clinical View of Patients Who Discontinued Group Psychotherapy," *Int. J. Group Psychother.*, *22*: 306–319, 1972.

21. M. A. Lieberman, I. D. Yalom, M. B. Miles, *Encounter Groups: First Facts* (New York: Basic Books, Inc., 1972).

22. B. Kotkov, "Favorable Clinical Indications for Group Attendance," *Int. J. Group Psychother.*, *8*: 419–427, 1958.

23. B. Kotkov and A. Meadow, "Rorschach Criteria for Continuing Group Psychotherapy," *Int. J. Group Psychother.*, *2*: 324–331, 1952.

24. L. H. Gliedman, A. Stone, J. Frank, E. Nash, and S. Imber, "Incentives for Treatment Related to Remaining or Improving in Psychotherapy," *Am. J. Psychother.*, *11*: 589–598, 1957.

25. J. Frank, L. H. Gliedman, S. Imber, E. Nash, and A. Stone, "Why Patients Leave Psychotherapy," *Arch. Neurol. Psychiat.*, *77*: 283–299, 1957.

26. D. Rosenthal and J. Frank, "The Fate of Psychiatric Clinic Outpatients Assigned to Psychotherapy," *J. Nerv. Ment. Dis.*, *127*: 330–343, 1958.

27. M. Horwitz, "The Recall of Interrupted Group Tasks: An Experimental Study of Individual Motivation in Relation to Group Goals," in D. Cartwright and A. Zander (eds.), *Group Dynamics: Research and Theory* (New York: Row, Peterson, 1962), pp. 370–394.

28. L. Coch and J. R. French, Jr., "Overcoming Resistance to Change," in Cartwright and Zander, *op. cit.*, pp. 319–341.

29. E. Stotland, "Determinants of Attraction to Groups," *J. Soc. Psychol.*, *49*: 71–80, 1959.

30. D. Lundgren and D. Miller, "Identity and Behavioral Changes in Training Groups," *Human Relations Training News*, Spring 1965.

31. Lieberman, Yalom, Miles, *op. cit.*, p. 324.

32. I. D. Yalom and P. Houts, unpublished data, 1966.

33. S. Schachter, "Deviation, Rejection, and Communication," in Cartwright and Zander, *op. cit.*, pp. 260–285.

34. H. F. Leavitt, "Group Structure and Process: Some Effects of Certain Communication Patterns on Group Performance," in E. E. Maccoby, T. M. Newcomb, and E. L. Hartley (eds.), *Readings in Social Psychology* (New York: Holt, Rinehart and Winston, 1958), pp. 175–183.

35. J. M. Jackson, "Reference Group Processes in a Formal Organization," in Cartwright and Zander, *op. cit.*, pp. 120–140.

36. L. Festinger, S. Schachter, and K. Back, "The Operation of Group Standards," in Cartwright and Zander, *op. cit.*, pp. 241–259.
37. M. Sherif, "Group Influences upon the Formation of Norms and Attitudes," in Maccoby, Newcomb, and Hartley, *op. cit.*, pp. 219–232.
38. S. E. Asch, "Interpersonal Influence: Effects of Group Pressure upon the Modification and Distortion of Judgments" in Maccoby, Newcomb, and Hartley, *op. cit.*, pp. 175–183.
39. P. H. Leiderman, "Attention and Verbalization: Differentiated Responsivity of Cardiovascular and Electrodermo Systems," *J. of Psychosomatic Research, 15:* 323–328, 1971.
40. Lieberman, Yalom, and Miles, *op. cit.*, pp. 342–344.
41. R. Harrison and B. Lubin, "Personal Style, Group Composition and Learning— Part I," *J. Appl. Behav. Sci., 1:* 286–294, 1965.
42. I. D. Yalom, P. S. Houts, S. M. Zimerberg, and K. H. Rand, "Prediction of Improvement in Group Therapy," *Arch. Gen. Psychiat., 17:* 159–168, 1967.
43. S. Jourard, "Self-Disclosure Patterns in British and American College Females," *J. Soc. Psychol., 54:* 315–320, 1961.
44. Lieberman, Yalom, and Miles, *op. cit.*, pp. 315–355.
45. J. D. Frank, "Some Determinants, Manifestations, and Effects of Cohesiveness in Therapy Groups," *Int. J. Group Psychother., 7:* 53–63, 1957.
46. M. B. Parloff, "Therapist-Patient Relationships and Outcome of Psychotherapy," *J. Consult. Psychol., 25:* 29–38, 1961.
47. R. Heslin and D. Dunphy, "Three Dimensions of Member Satisfaction in Small Groups," *Human Relations, 17:* 99–112, 1964.
48. I. D. Yalom, P. S. Houts, G. Newell, and K. H. Rand, "Preparation of Patients for Group Therapy," *Arch. Gen. Psychiat., 17:* 416–427, 1967.
49. A. Sklar, I. D. Yalom, S. Zimerberg, and G. Newell, "Time Extended Group Therapy: A Controlled Study," *Comparative Group Studies,* pp. 373–386, Nov. 1970.

8

COMPOSITION OF
THERAPY GROUPS

Imagine the following situation: a psychiatric outpatient clinic with ten group therapists ready to form groups and seventy patients who, on the basis of the selection criteria outlined thus far, are suitable group therapy candidates. How should the triage proceed and what bearing will it have on the outcome of treatment?

A second, more common clinical problem is closely related. Assume that there is one patient who has been deemed a suitable group therapy candidate and that there are several therapy groups, each with one vacancy. Into which group should the patient go? The solution to this problem is to be found in the solution to the first. If valid principles about the effective total composition of a group can be established, the corollaries of these principles may provide the guidelines for adding new members or replacing members who leave the group. We grope in the dark if we try to replace a missing unit without any knowledge of the organization of the total social organism.

In this chapter we shall examine research evidence and clinical observations bearing on group composition. Is it possible that the proper blend of individuals will form the ideal group? That the wrong blend remains an inharmonious aggregate, never coalescing into a working group?

First, we must be clear about the ingredients of our blend. Of the infinite number of human characteristics, which are germane to the task of composing a therapy group? The essence of the therapy group is interaction: each member must continually communicate and interact with the other members. Regardless of any other consideration, it is the actual behavior of the members of the group that dictates the fate of the group. Therefore, if we are to talk intelligently about group composition, we must speak of composing the group in such a way that the members will interact in some desired manner. The entire procedure of group composition and selection of group patients is thus based on a very important assumption. That assumption is that we can, with some degree of accuracy, predict the group behavior of an individual from our pretherapy screening. If we cannot predict group behavior from our screening procedure, then all of our preceding pronouncements about group selection and our subsequent remarks about group composition will have little meaning.

The Prediction of Group Behavior

The previous chapter advises against the inclusion of certain patients in the group because they behave in a manner which has undesirable effects on themselves and the group. For example, alcoholic, sociopathic, and floridly psychotic individuals are, it is suggested, best excluded from an outpatient interactional group. Generally, predictions limited to individuals with such extreme, fixed, maladaptive interpersonal behavior are reasonably accurate; the grosser the pathology, the greater the predictive accuracy. There is scarcely any room for error when considering a paranoid schizophrenic with an active, expanding, persecutory delusional system. He will soon grow to distrust the group members, become secretive, suspicious, perhaps openly accusatory, and then, as the delusional system generalizes, will ultimately regard the group members as inimical. Ordinarily, in clinical practice the problem is a far more subtle one; most patients who apply for treatment have a wide repertoire of behavior, and their ultimate group behavior is far less predictable.

A number of pretherapy screening procedures have been employed to predict future behavior in group therapy. Before discussing the behavior variables which are most salient to group composition, let us examine screening practices to determine precisely what they do predict about the future group behavior of patients.

THE PREDICTIVE VALUE OF THE
STANDARD DIAGNOSTIC INTERVIEW

The most common method of screening patients is the individual interview. Quite often the interview is the routine one used at intake with all patients applying for treatment to a practitioner or clinic. The interviewer, in addition to acquiring information about such topics as motivation for treatment, ego strength, environmental stresses, past history, etc., attempts to make predictions as to how the patient may behave in the group. These predictions are often highly remote inferences stemming from observations of the patients' behavior in the dyadic situation.

One of the traditional end products of the mental health interview is a diagnosis which, in capsule form, is meant to summarize the patient's condition and convey useful information to another practitioner. The psychiatric diagnosis based on the American Psychiatric Association official manual [1] is, as most group therapists will attest, spectacularly useless as an indicator of interpersonal behavior. It was never meant for this purpose; it stemmed from a disease-oriented medical discipline and is primarily etiologically and symptomatically based.

Although a disease-oriented classification system serves many purposes, it has serious shortcomings which are especially evident to those practitioners who work primarily with individuals with relatively minor maladjustments. The typical clinician in an outpatient clinic or the private practitioner finds that the great majority of his patients have some characterologic disturbance classifiable only in some vague way in the official nomenclature. A few, but only a few, of the categories or subcategories are useful in predicting interpersonal behavior. A person labeled as a schizoid personality will most likely behave in a roughly predictable manner: he will probably remain detached, perhaps intellectualizing, be unable to reach and share his feelings with others, and be percieved by others as cold, uncaring, and distant. However, what can be predicted about the group behavior of an individual labeled as "psychoneurotic reaction, anxiety type" or "phobic type" or, for that matter, "personality disorder, sexual deviation" or "emotionally unstable personality"? Two individuals with an anxiety reaction can manifest entirely different interpersonal styles. Expanding their diagnosis to include their personality type is of little help because of the inadequacy of the available personality description labels.

Even if the American Psychiatric Association classificatory system were useful in predicting the group behavior of an individual, its value would still be limited because of its poor reliability, as attested by two controlled studies of the diagnostic procedure. Ash [2] studied the agreement between pairs of psychiatrists who examined fifty-two outpatients and found that a pair of psychiatrists tended to agree about the diagnostic subcategory (i.e., type of neurosis, psychosis, or personality disorder) in approximately 40 percent of the cases. There was only 64 percent agreement about the major divisions (psychotic reactions, neurotic reactions, personality disorders). Beck,[3] studying the diagnostic agreement between six pairs of senior clinicians, found a concordance rate which ranged from 33.3 percent to 61.4 percent. When the diagnostic categories were analyzed separately, the researchers found a higher rate of agreement for some than for others. For example, there was a rate of agreement of 63 percent for neurotic depression, 55 percent for anxiety reaction, 53 percent for schizophrenia, and only 38 percent for personality trait disturbance. When we place this final figure in juxtaposition with the fact that a large percentage of our outpatients fall into the personality trait category, and consider also that the category has little predictive value, we begin to appreciate the magnitude of the diagnostic folly.

Diagnostic formulations which require even greater inference than the standard nosological categories are even less useful. Exclusion criteria cited in the clinical literature,[4] such as "inadequate ego strength" or "sexual life deviant" or "charged with anxiety or guilt" or "inability to relinquish egocentricity," lack clear definitions; furthermore, interclinician reliability would no doubt be so low as to invalidate their general usefulness. That a diagnostic label fails to predict very much about human behavior should neither surprise nor chagrin us. No label or phrase can adequately encompass an individual's essence or entire range of behavior. Any limiting categorization is not only errorful but offensive as well, and stands in opposition to the basic human foundations of the therapeutic relationship. (Camus [5] once described Hell as a place where one's identity was eternally fixed and displayed on personal signs: Adulterous Humanist, Christian Landowner, Jittery Philosopher, Charming Janus, etc. Hell is to have no way of explaining oneself, to be fixed, to be classified once and for all time.)

PREDICTIVE VALUE OF STANDARD
PSYCHOLOGICAL TESTING

Several investigators have sought to use standard psychological diagnostic tests as predictors of group behavior. These have most prominently included the Rorschach, the MMPI, the TAT, the Sentence Completion, and Draw-a-Person tests.[6,7,8] All these tests failed to yield valid predictions, with the single trivial exception [7] that individuals using considerable denial (as evidenced by the Rorschach and TAT) more often made positive, agreeing statements in group therapy.

PREDICTIVE VALUE OF SPECIALIZED
DIAGNOSTIC PROCEDURES

The lack of success that these standard diagnostic procedures have demonstrated in predicting anything at all about group behavior suggests that new procedures which focus primarily on interpersonal behavior must be developed. Recent clinical observations and research have suggested several promising directions. I will discuss these under two headings:

1. A formulation of an interpersonal nosological system.
2. New diagnostic procedures which directly sample group-relevant behavior

An Interpersonal Nosological System. The first known attempt to classify mental illness dates back to 1700 B.C., [9] and the intervening years have seen a bewildering number of systems advanced, each unacceptable, each beset with its own form of internal inconsistency. The central plan in the great majority of systems has been disease-based: either etiological, descriptive, or some combination of the two. With the advent of the object relations and the interpersonal systems of conceptualizing psychopathology, as well as an increased exposure to individuals seeking treatment for less severe problems in living, have come rudimentary attempts to classify individuals according to interpersonal styles of relating.

For example, Karen Horney [10] views troubled individuals as moving exaggeratedly and maladaptively *toward, against,* or *away* from other people and has described interpersonal profiles of these types and various subtypes. Individuals who chiefly move toward others invoke the "self-effacing solution" and deal with others in a currency of love. Those who move against others (the "expansive solutions") engage in an interpersonal search for mastery and are subdivided into three subgroups: the narcissistic, the perfectionistic, and the arrogant vindictive. The third maneuver, moving away from people, is labeled "resignation," and individuals so designated handle interpersonal relationships by withdrawal, by "a search for freedom." Horney's formulations have been influential and valuable for a large number of American clinicians. It is always a singularly rewarding experience to encounter a stereotyped patient who fits flush into one of Horney's character types. One has a keen sense of recognition as well as a firm conviction that, with rather great accuracy, one shall be able to predict much of the course of therapy. Unfortunately, these stereotypes appear uncommonly, and Horney's nosological types are, as she recognized, highly caricaturized and composite profiles; there has been, to my knowledge, no attempt to systematize and quantify this approach to diagnosis. Much the same can be said for Erich Fromm's [11, 12] attempts to formulate nosological categories on the basis of the individual's basic interpersonal orientation (the marketing, receptive, hoarding, and exploitative personalities). These and other classificatory systems developed by interpersonally oriented clinicians may provide a philosophical background for the study of personality but have not been organized and systematized with the precision necessary for the development of a methodology for the scientific study of personality.

There have been two recent noteworthy attempts to arrive at a comprehensive, quantified interpersonal diagnostic system; the interpersonal circular grid of Timothy Leary [13] and the FIRO-B system of William Schutz.[14] * Of these two, the FIRO-B system has been more influential in stimulating group therapy relevant research.

THE INTERPERSONAL CIRCULAR GRID OF LEARY. Leary and his collaborators (Coffey, Freedman, and Ossorio) [15] developed a system of describing personality based on the theoretical formulations of Harry Stack Sullivan. The total personality is considered on three levels: the public, the conscious, the private. These levels are defined by the sources of data which contributed to each level: the public level is derived from objective ratings of the person's behavior (e.g., his statements during group therapy sessions about himself and others); the

* It is curious that these two researchers, William Schutz and Timothy Leary, who devoted so much of their early careers to painstaking, quantified, systematic efforts to describe human behavior, departed so radically from this orientation later in their lives. Schutz, who has worked at Esalen for many years, has been deeply involved in encounter groups, structural integration, and a variety of efforts designed to help individuals recognize and integrate affect. Leary has pursued quite another career.

TABLE 8–1[13]

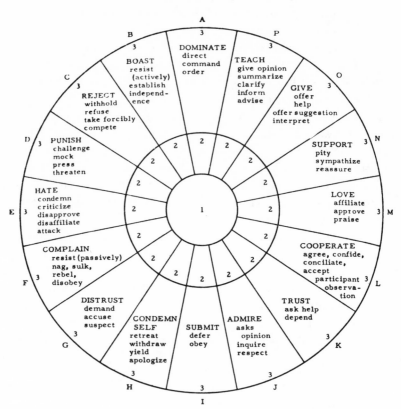

Level I variables: interpersonal mechanisms with illustrative verbs. Intensity ratings: 3, intense or extreme; 2, average or appropriate; 1, mild intensity.

conscious level is derived from self-descriptions; the private level from ratings of projective material of his views of himself and of others. The data on the public level, for example, are then categorized into one of sixteen interpersonal mechanisms (Table 1), which Leary considered sufficient for systematizing all interpersonal behavior. The raters also rated each act on a three-point scale for intensity. The sixteen interpersonal mechanisms were arranged in a circular grid with the two primary axes of love-hate and domination-submission.[15] By applying trigonometric formulas, one can represent the interpersonal behavior of the individual as a point in the circle. Similar principles apply to the other levels: level—conscious, and level—private.*

Although there were some early attempts to use this system for

* Leary[13] later expanded the system to five levels: (1) public communication, (2) conscious descriptions, (3) preconscious symbolizations, (4) unexpressed unconscious, and (5) ego ideal.

prediction of group behavior and for group composition (which will be described shortly), these have remained rudimentary,[16] and the system, perhaps because it is so complex and cumbersome, has not been widely used by other workers for this purpose.

FIRO. The FIRO ("Fundamental Interpersonal Relations Orientation") system [14] was first described by Schutz in 1958. Schutz reviewed a large number of studies of interpersonal behavior from the child development field, social psychological research, and the clinical field and concluded that control, inclusion, and affection are the three basic interpersonal needs and that others described could be reasonably considered within the framework of these three. Using these three needs, an interpersonal profile of an individual may be constructed. The profile attempts to describe the valence of the individual toward each of these needs. Does he very much wish to control others, to be controlled, or is he relatively unconflicted in this area? Does he wish to be included in social activities or excluded? Does he very much desire intimacy or desire to avoid intimacy? The data is derived from a self-administered questionnaire, the FIRO-B (the B stands for behavior), which consists of fifty-four items, each one answered on a six-point scale, and which takes approximately fifteen to twenty minutes to complete. The questions are so superficial and repetitious that it is not uncommon for sophisticated patients to be irritated and insulted by the questionnaire.* The test seems to tap such superficial aspects of a human being that one is inclined to dismiss it; †yet there are a large number and variety of studies attesting to its validity.

One such study examined the selection of roommates among college fraternity members.[14] The FIRO theory allows one to predict the amount of attraction between two individuals. For example, one individual who wishes very much to control and another who wishes very much to be controlled would be highly compatible (if their other two need areas also intermeshed). The selection of roommates by the college students was significantly predicted by this compatibility score.

---

* For example, four typical questions among the fifty-four are: (1) I like people to invite me to things: usually—often—sometimes—occasionally—rarely—never. (2) I like people to include me in their activities: usually—often—sometimes—occasionally—rarely—never. (3) I like people to invite me to things: most people—many people—some people—a few people—one or two people—nobody. (4) I like people to invite me to join their activities: most people—many people—some people—a few people—one or two people—nobody.

† Indeed Schutz, in the preface to the 1966 edition, stated, "My feelings about the material in this book range from thinking it is not only a remarkable system, but a way of life, to wondering how anyone can take it seriously." [14]

There is evidence suggesting that the FIRO-B predicts interpersonal behavior on a psychiatric ward. Gard and Bendig [17] explored the relationship between the FIRO-B score (what patients say about their interpersonal behavior) and their actual behavior. In a well-designed project, they studied 112 male Veterans Administration patients who were hospitalized for a psychotic or neurotic illness or some orthopedic disorder. Behavior ratings along a specially designed scale relevant to inclusive, affectionate, and control behavior were made by nursing personnel over a five-day period. They found that the "traits measured by Schutz's self-report questionnaire are expressed in the behavior of psychiatric subjects and can be objectively reported by observers."

Although the FIRO-B has been used in much small group research, there have been, to my knowledge, no direct attempts to assess its ability to predict interpersonal behavior in small groups. A relevant study,[18] however, demonstrated that when four groups (at a human relations laboratory) were deliberately composed from FIRO scores of individuals with similar interpersonal needs, they were able to identify significantly better than chance their own groups from the description of what these groups should be like from their FIRO composition.

New Diagnostic Procedures Which Directly Sample Group Relevant Behavior. Goldstein, Heller, and Sechrest,[19] in their scholarly consideration of this topic, suggest that the prediction of within-group behavior will be most accurate when it is based on direct behavioral measurement of the individual when he is engaged in a task closely related to the group therapy situation. In other words, the closer we can approximate actual observation of the individual in his subsequent therapy group, the more accurate will be our prediction of his behavior. There is abundant research evidence to support this thesis. If an individual is kept in the same interpersonal format, his behavior will show a consistency over time even though the individuals with whom he must interact are rotated. Research demonstrating this has used children-adult interaction,[20] therapist-patient interaction,[21] and small group interaction.[7, 22] For example, Moos and Clemes [21] have demonstrated that a patient seen by several individual therapists in rotation will not only be consistent in his behavior but will change the behavior of each of the therapists!

The implications of these findings are that, since we cannot accurately predict group behavior from behavior in an individual interview, we should consider obtaining data about the patient's behavior in a group setting. Indeed, there has been some practical application of this principle. For example, in screening applicants for positions which require group-related skills, a procedure for observing their behavior in related group situations has been used. Thus, a group interview test has been used to select officers for the German Air Force,[23] shipyard foremen,[24] Public Health Officers,[25] as well as many types of public and business executives.[26]

This general principle can be refined further, however, since there is additional research which demonstrates that behavior in one group is especially consistent with behavior in previous groups if the groups are similar with regard to composition,[27] group task,[28, 29] group norms,[30] expected role behavior,[30] or global group characteristics (e.g., climate, cohesiveness).[31] In other words, although an individual's behavior is broadly consistent from one group to the next, nevertheless there is still a wide range of behavior at his disposal. The individual's specific behavior in the new group is influenced by the task and the structural properties of the group and by the specific interpersonal styles of the other group members. The further implication, then, is that we can obtain the most relevant data for prediction of subsequent group behavior by observing an individual behave in a group which is as similar as possible to the one for which he is being screened. The most literal application of this principle is to predict the behavior of the applicant by arranging for him to meet with the therapy group for which he is being considered and to observe his behavior in this setting. In fact, Foulkes [32] and Bach [33] suggest that prospective members visit the group on a trial basis so that the group members may carry out their own selection. Although there are several advantages to this format (which we shall discuss in Chapter 10), the procedure is often clinically inefficient: there is considerable disruption to the group; the members are disinclined to reject a prospective member unless there is some glaring incompatibility; furthermore, the prospective member is "on trial," as it were, and a representative sample of his behavior may not be obtained.

A promising development with implications for both research and clinical practice is the test group or waiting list group, a temporary group constituted from a clinic waiting list. The prospective group therapy patient is placed in the test group, his behavior is observed, and on the basis of this data he is then referred to a specific therapy or research group. In an exploratory study Stone, Parloff, and Frank [34] formed four groups of fifteen patients each from the group therapy waiting list which met weekly from four to eight times. Observers noted that the waiting group behavior of the patients was predictive of their behavior in their subsequent long-term therapy group. These workers found, as did Abrahams and Enright,[35] who used a group diagnostic procedure for all patients applying for treatment, that the procedure is clinically benign; patients did not react adversely to the waiting list group. Malamud and Machover [36] organized large groups of approximately thirty patients from the clinic waiting list. These groups were seen for fifteen sessions of highly structured workshops designed to prepare them for therapy. This preparatory group proved very successful; not only were the patients tided over the waiting period, but many reported significant benefit from the experience.

The definitive clinical research study demonstrating that patient behavior in waiting groups will be similar to later behavior in therapy groups has yet to be done. There is, however, so much corroborating evidence from human relations group research * that we can accept this hypothesis with a reasonable degree of certainty.[37,38]

There have been several attempts to design new psychological tests to predict subsequent group behavior. Variants of the Thematic Apperception Test,[41] Sentence Association Test,[42] Sentence Completion Test,[43] and a sixty-item, self-report Q-sort [44] have all been used for this purpose with only equivocal results.

Traditional psychological tests which measure traits or personality needs invariably yield only low-level correlations with subsequent group behavior; they are weak because behavior is multidetermined and heavily influenced by the social press as well as by internal factors. A comprehensive predictive system which attempted to take into consideration several salient determinants was used by Couch [45,46] to demonstrate the predictability of the individual's behavior in laboratory task groups.† Couch studied four determinants of interpersonal behavior:

1.   The personality needs ‡
2.   The concealment defenses §—a measure of the degree to which an indi-

* Generally, the research procedure is to assigne subjects to groups meeting for a predetermined number of meetings and to systematically observe their behavior. At this point, the researchers regroup the members into new groups according to the particular aspect of behavior under the study. Since the bulk of the research has been done by nonclinicians, the attitudes and behaviors are described in non-clinical but nevertheless clinically relevant terms. Subjects may thus be placed in groups according to whether they prefer high or low structure, or positive or negative affect, or whether they are active or passive or high or low participators, or assume or shun leadership.[37, 38] The trial groups may be discontinued at this point or they may serve as a control group against which to compare the experimentally composed group.

† These task groups were five-member Harvard University undergraduate volunteer leaderless groups which were asked to discuss and solve some problem in human relations.

‡ Obtained from a battery of psychological assessment questionnaires.

§ Obtained from clinical assessment in combination with objective psychological tests.

vidual would tend to conceal his underlying needs from overt manifestation

3. The apperceived press *—the individual's perception of the attitude and emotional feelings toward him
4. The behavioral press,† the overt behavioral acts directed toward the individual

These four determinants were then correlated with the individual's actual behavior.‡ Each of the determinants separately showed a positive correlation with the individual's group behavior,§ and summed together they have an impressively high correlation coefficient. The research illustrates, in the author's words, "that individual behavior is multiply determined and can be explained with considerable completeness if the several psychological determinants are considered in combination with one another in an integrated explanatory framework." [45]

Another possible approach to initial screening may be through the use of a simulated group test. A simulated group has been used in social psychological research design to establish unity of environment. For example, a subject is told that he is listening through earphones to a group discussion in the adjoining room and asked for his reactions to the group. The "group" is a tape-recorded simulation of a group. (This approach has also been used to test the effects of group pressure on the autokinetic estimation task.[47]) Clinicians, to my knowledge, have not employed this technique. However, it may not be utterly fantastic to use as a diagnostic tool a movie or a videotape of a therapy group of patients (with proper permission, of course) or a simulated therapy group of actors following a script. At various points the film could be stopped and the patient queried about his emotional response, his ideas about what's happening, or what he might say or do if he were in the group. Strupp and Jenkins [48] have used films of simulated individual interviews as a teaching technique and as an examination for students of psychiatry.

For practitioners or clinics with limited waiting lists and facilities, the concept of trial groups may be only an intriguing, perhaps fanciful, research idea. A less accurate but more accessible method of obtaining similar data is an interpersonally oriented initial interview. In-

* Obtained from a self-administered questionnaire.
† Obtained from objective ratings of behavior.
‡ Rated by objective raters along the dimensions of interpersonal dominance, affect, involvement, and hostility.
§ Of the four, "behavioral press" showed by far the highest correlation with the patient's behavior; this is further evidence for the general principle that the closer the testing situation is to the subsequent clinical situation, the more accurately can subsequent behavior be predicted.

stead of conducting the traditional psychiatric diagnostic interview, the therapist shifts to an interpersonal focus when examining prospective group patients. The therapist should test the patient's ability to deal with the interpersonal reality of the interview. Is he able, for example, to comment upon the process of the interview in which he is engaged, or to understand or accept the therapist's process commentary? Is he obviously tense but denies it when the therapist inquires? Will he identify the most uncomfortable or pleasant parts of the interview? What does he wish the therapist to think of him? Detailed inquiry should be made into the patient's interpersonal and group relationships, his relationships with early chums, closest prolonged friendships, and degree of intimacy with members of both sexes. Many of Sullivan's interview techniques [39] are of great value in this task. It is informative, for example, when inquiring about friendships to ask for the names of best friends and what has become of them. A detailed history of formal and informal groups is valuable, of childhood and adult cliques, of fraternities, of club memberships, of gangs, of teams, of elected offices, and informal roles and status positions. The validity of this type of interview is yet to be determined, but, to my mind, it seems far more relevant to subsequent group behavior than an intrapsychically focused interview.

Powdermaker and Frank [40] described an interpersonal relations interview which, along with a standard psychiatric interview and psychological testing, comprised their pretherapy diagnostic work-up. From this information, conjectures about the patients' subsequent ingroup behavior were made, many of which were correct. Examples of accurate predictions were: "will dominate the group by a flood of speech and advice" or "will have considerable difficulty in showing feelings but will have compulsion to please the doctor and other members," will be "bland and socially skillful, tending to seek the doctor's attention while ignoring the other members," "will have a wait-and-see attitude," "will have a sarcastic, superior 'show-me' attitude and be reluctant to discuss his problems."

In summary, the prediction of certain salient parameters of subsequent group behavior from a pretherapy diagnostic procedure seems completely feasible. Of all the prediction methods, the traditional intake individual interview appears the least accurate and yet the most commonly used. An individual's group behavior will vary depending on his internal psychological needs, his manner of expressing them, and the task, interpersonal composition, and norms of his social environment. A general principle, however, is that the more similar the intake procedure is to the actual group situation, the more accurate will be the prediction of his behavior. The most promising single clinical method may be the observation of the patient's behavior in an intake or waiting list group. If facilities do not permit this, it is recommended that group therapists modify their intake interview and focus on the patient's interpersonal functioning.

Principles of Group Composition

To return now to the central question: given the most ideal circumstances—a large number of patient applicants and a wealth of information by which we can predict behavior—how shall we compose our therapy group?

Perhaps the reason for the scarcity of interest in the prediction of subsequent group behavior is that the amount of information about group composition is even more rudimentary. Why, indeed, bother refining tools to predict group behavior if we lack the knowledge of how to use this information? Although most clinicians sense that the composition of a group profoundly influences its character, the actual mechanism of influence has eluded clarification. I have had the opportunity to study closely the conception, birth, and development of approximately eighty therapy groups—my own and my students'—and have been struck repeatedly by the fact that some groups seem to "jell" immediately and some more slowly, whereas other groups founder painfully, spinning off members, and only emerge as working groups after several cycles of attrition and addition of members. It has been my impression that whether or not the group "jells" is only in part related to the competence or efforts of the therapist or to the number of "good" patients in the group; to a degree, the critical variable is some, as yet unclear, blending of the members.

A recent clinical experience brought this principle home to me quite vividly. I was scheduled to lead a T-group of mental health professionals, all at the same level of training and approximately the same age. At the first meeting over twenty participants appeared—too many for one group. We decided that I should lead two groups but could not arrive at a satisfactory method of dividing the participants. Finally, the participants agreed simply to move in Brownian fashion around the room for five minutes and at that time find themselves in one of the two ends of the room. (A few of the members made this decision on the basis of scheduling convenience.) Each group met for an hour and a half, one group immediately following the other.

Although superficially it might appear that the groups had similar compositions, the subtle blending of personalities resulted in each group having a radically different character. The difference was apparent in the first meeting and persisted throughout the life of the group.

One group assumed an extraordinarily dependent posture. In the first meeting I arrived on crutches with my leg in a cast because I had injured my knee. The group made no inquiry into my condition. They did not by themselves arrange the chairs in a circle. (Remember that all were professional therapists and most had led groups!) They asked my permission for such common acts as opening the window and smoking. Most of the group life was spent analyzing their fear of me, the distance between me and the members, my aloofness and coldness.

In the other group that same day, I had not gone halfway through the door when several members asked, "Hey, what happened to your leg?" The group moved immediately into hard work, and each of the members used his professional skills in a constructive manner. The chief failing I had in this second group was one of feeling unnecessary to its work, and, during the course of the group, it was only with considerable effort that I could focus the group's attention on their disregard of me.

So without doubt the composition of the two groups dramatically influenced the character of their subsequent work. If the groups were ongoing rather than time-limited (sixteen session) T-groups, it is possible that the different environments might have made little eventual difference in the beneficial effect of the group on each of its members. In the short run, however, the members of the first group felt more tense, more deskilled, more restricted and, because of the narrower range of experience of the group, learned less about themselves.

A similar example may be drawn from the Lieberman, Yalom, and Miles [49] encounter group study. Two groups, randomly composed, had an identical leader—a tape recording (the "Encountertape Program") which gave the group instructions about how to proceed at each meeting. Within a very few meetings two very different cultures emerged. One group was dependably obedient to the taped instructions and faithfully followed all the prescribed exercises. The other group developed a disrespectful tone to the "leader," soon referring to him as "George." It was common for members to mock the tape; for example, when the tape gave an instruction to the group, one member commented derisively, "That's a great idea, George." Not only was the culture different for these short-term groups but the outcome was as well. (At the end of the thirty-hour group experience [ten meetings], the irreverent group had an appreciably better outcome.)

Thus, we can be certain that composition affects the character and process of the group. Still, however, we are a long way from concluding that a given method X is a more effective method of composing a group than method Y. The problem rests, of course, in the assessment of effectiveness. Group therapy outcome studies are crude, and no rigorous study exists which investigates the relationship between group composition and the ultimate criterion—long-term therapy outcome. We must therefore rely on nonsystematic clinical observations and studies which, though relevant to composition, stem from nontherapy settings.

CLINICAL OBSERVATIONS ABOUT GROUP COMPOSITION

The impressions of individual clinicians regarding the effects of group composition must be evaluated with caution. The lack of a common language describing behavior, the problems of outcome evaluation, the theoretical biases of the therapist, and the limited number of groups that any one clinician may treat all limit the validity of clinical impressions in this area.

There appears to be a general clinical sentiment that heterogeneous groups have advantages over homogeneous groups for intensive interactional group therapy.[33,50,51,52] Homogeneous groups are believed to "jell" more quickly, to become more cohesive, to offer more immediate support to the group members, to have better attendance, less conflict, and to provide more rapid symptomatic relief. On the other hand, however, clinicians widely believe that the homogeneous group, in contrast to the heterogeneous group, tends to remain at superficial levels and is an ineffective medium for the altering of character structure.

The issue becomes clouded when we ask, "Homogeneous for what?" "Heterogeneous for what?" For age? Sex? Symptom complex? Marital status? Education? Socioeconomic status? Verbal skills? Psychosexual development? Psychiatric diagnostic categories? Interpersonal needs? Which are the critical variables? Is a group composed of mothers with infanticidal obsessions [53] a homogeneous group because of the shared symptom, or a heterogeneous group because of the wide range of personality traits of the members?

Whitaker and Lieberman [54] help to clarify the issue by suggesting that the group therapist strive for maximum heterogeneity in the patients' conflict areas and patterns of coping, and at the same time strive for homogeneity of the patients' degree of vulnerability and capacity to tolerate anxiety. For example, they state that a homogeneous group of individuals, all with major conflicts about hostility which were dealt with through denial, could hardly offer therapeutic benefit to its members. However, a group with a wide range of vulnerability (loosely defined as ego strength) will, for different reasons, also be retarded; the most vulnerable patient will place limits on the group, which will become highly restrictive to the less vulnerable ones. In the same vein, Foulkes and Anthony [55] suggest blending together a "mixed bag of diagnoses and disturbances" to form a therapeutically effective group. "The greater the span between the polar types, the higher the therapeutic potential, if the group can stand it."

Unfolding from these clinical observations is the rule that a degree of incompatibility must exist between the patient and the interpersonal-need culture of the group if change is to occur. This principle— that change is preceded by a state of dissonance or incongruity—has considerable clinical and social psychological research backing and is a concept to which we will return later. However, group members cannot profit from the dissonance in the absence of adequate ego strength; therefore, *heterogeneity for conflict areas*, and *homogeneity for ego strength*.

Heterogeneity must not proceed at the price of creating a group isolate. Consider the age variable: if there is one fifty-year-old member in a group of very young adults, that individual may choose or be forced to assume the role of the personified older generation. Stereotyping of his role (and of those of the younger patients) occurs, and the required interpersonal honesty and intimacy fails to materialize. A similar process may occur in an adult group with a lone late adolescent who assumes the unruly teenager role. Yet there are advantages to having an age spread in the group: patients, through working out their intermember relationships, will come to understand their past, present, and future relationships with a wider range of significant people—parents, peers, and children.

One solution to the problem of maintaining heterogeneity without creating isolates may be to provide some pairing for each patient. One group therapist [56] suggested the "Noah's Ark" principle of group composition, in which each member should have his compeer. Another [57] suggests a composition technique of "group balance," in which the therapist attempts to balance the group for such factors as transference toward the therapist, countertransference, passive-aggressivity, ability to express affect, insight or introspective ability, homosexuality-heterosexuality, and ego strength.

The concept of heterogeneity even with pairing or balance is not without its limitations. For example, if the group has too extreme an age range, the life-stage problems of some members may be so alien to others that cohesivenss is seriously impaired. Aged individuals concerned about subsistence and the process of disengagement are sometimes irreconcilably distant from late adolescents and young adults dealing urgently with identity crises.

Bach [58] employs the concept of role heterogeneity in his approach to composition. In adding a new member, his primary consideration is, "What role is open in the group?" In his view the therapist should strive to increase the group's "role repertoire, in order to obtain better complementation between roles." Theoretically, such an orientation seems quite desirable. Practically, however, it suffers from a lack of clarity. What are the roles in a therapy group? Bach [59] mentions the "guardian of democracy," the "time keeper," the "aggressive male," the "leader," and the individual who provides humorous tension release. We might add: the provocateur, the scapegoat, the doctor's helper,[60] the help-rejecting complainer,[60] the self-righteous moralist,[61] the "star," the fight, flight, dependency, or pairing leaders, the group hysteric, the technical executive leader, the social secretary, the group stud, the group critic, the group romantic, the social emotional leader, etc., etc.

Can we expand the list arbitrarily and indefinitely by listing behavior trait constellations, or are there fixed roles or desirable group facilitating roles, constant from group to group, which members are forced to fill? Until we have some satisfactory frame of reference to deal with these questions, the query, "What role is open in the group?" will contribute little toward an effective approach to group composition.

One final clinical observation. As a supervisor and researcher, I had an opportunity to study closely the entire thirty-month course of an outpatient group led by Dr. R. and Dr. M., two competent psychiatric residents. The group consisted of seven members, all in their twenties, six of whom could be classified as schizoid personalities. The one patient who was considerably different, a passive-aggressive woman, was frightened by the prospects of intimacy and dropped out of the group after five months. Another patient was called for military duty at the end of a year. Two new patients were brought in to replace the losses.

The most striking feature of this homogeneous schizoid group was that it was extraordinarily dull. Everything associated with the group—the meetings, the tape recordings, the written summaries, the supervisory sessions—were low-keyed, affectless, plodding, and dull. Nothing seemed to be happening; there was no discernible movement individually among the patients or in the group as a whole. And yet the attendance was near perfect and the group cohesiveness extraordinarily high.* Since all the group patients in the Stanford clinic over this period of time were subjects in outcome research,[62,66] thorough evaluations of clinical progress were available both at the end of one year and at the end of thirty months. The patients in this group, both the original members and the replacements, did extraordinarily well and underwent substantial characterologic changes as well as complete symptomatic remission. In fact, very few other groups I have studied have had comparably good results. My views about group composition were influenced by this group, and I have come to attach overriding importance to group stability, attendance, and cohesiveness.

Although in theory I agree with the concept of composing a group of individuals with varied interpersonal stresses and needs, I feel that in practice it may represent a spurious issue. Given the limited predictive value of our traditional screening interview, it is probable that we delude ourselves if we think we can achieve the type of subtle balance and personality interlocking necessary to make a real difference in group functioning. For example, although six of the seven patients in Dr. R. and Dr. M.'s group were diagnosed as schizoid personalities, they differed far more than they resembled one another. This apparently "homogeneous" group, contrary to the clinical dictum, did not remain at a superficial level and affected very significant personality changes in its members. Although I have studied many so-called homogeneous groups (e.g., ulcer patients, dermatological patients, obese women, parents of delinquent children) which have remained superficial, I felt that this was the effect not of homogeneity but of the set of the therapist and the restricted culture which he helped fashion. The organization of a group of individuals around a common symptom

---

* Many of the outpatient groups in the Stanford outpatient clinic were involved in research involving the measurement of group cohesiveness.[62,63,64,65] The group led by Dr. R. and Dr. M. scored higher on cohesiveness (measured by self-administered questionnaires) than any other group.

or around their children's problems may convey powerful implicit culture-relevant messages which generate group norms of restriction, a search for similarities, a submergence of individuality, and a discouragement of self-disclosure and interpersonal honesty. Norms, as we elaborated in Chapter 5, once set into motion, may become self-perpetuating and difficult to change.

SYSTEMATIC STUDIES OF GROUP COMPOSITION

As I have already discussed, there are no research studies which directly investigate the effect of group composition on group therapy outcome. However, there is one slightly peripheral study which is relevant to group composition. In this study Yalom and Rand [65] demonstrated the effect of group composition on group cohesiveness. Although group cohesiveness is by no means synonymous with therapy outcome, there is considerable evidence (summarized in Chapter 3) that cohesiveness is positively related to outcome and may be considered a way station or an intervening variable.* The Yalom-Rand project studied forty outpatients shortly before they began therapy in five newly forming therapy groups led by leaders with very similar training and supervision. The FIRO-B test was administered and the interpersonal compatibility of each member vis-à-vis each other member of his group was calculated. Furthermore, by summing all the dyads of the group, a total group compatibility [14] score was obtained for each group. These group and individual compatibility scores were then correlated with individual and total group cohesiveness scores obtained at the sixth and twelfth meetings. The results demonstrated that:

1. FIRO-B compatibility of the group correlated significantly with group cohesiveness.†
2. The patients who dropped out of therapy early in the course of the group had lower FIRO-B compatibility than the group continuers.
3. Any two members who showed extreme incompatibility with each other were significantly less satisfied with the group.

* From the standpoint of research methodology, an intervening variable is a simplifying device; it may be measured soon after the beginning of the group and many of the problems of long-term follow-up circumvented.

† This finding must be interpreted with caution; it has not yet been replicated, and Koran,[67] working with a similar patient population, failed to demonstrate a correlation between FIRO-B compatibility and group cohesiveness. The therapists in Koran's study did not, however, have uniform training. It may be that for compositional factors to emerge, they must not be dwarfed by more powerful variables like markedly different leader styles. It is for this reason that careful clinical observations made by one leader about differences in a large number of his groups are particularly important.

In other words, by giving a rather superficial interpersonal inventory questionnaire to a group of patients before their first contact with one another, one is able to make a reasonably accurate prediction about the cohesiveness of their therapy group six weeks and twelve weeks later. Clinically, this study suggests that a certain type of homogeneity * enhances the formation of group cohesiveness and that patients who are markedly dissonant with the rest of the group in that regard tend to be dissatisfied with the group and to leave therapy prematurely.

There have been several attempts to study the relationship between composition and outcome in human relations groups. I shall merely summarize the finding of these studies here; interested readers should refer to the articles cited for details of the study. First, let us examine the general research procedure of these studies in order to determine their relevance to group therapy.

The subjects are usually participants in a human relations laboratory (generally from the fields of education, industry, or behavioral science) or college student volunteers; they may be broadly considered "normals," although no psychiatric screening is performed. Usually, homogeneous or heterogeneous groups are formed on the basis of some cluster of personality variables which are obtained from psychological tests or from behavioral observations of the subjects in trial groups. The groups are short-term, meeting for six to fifteen sessions, generally over a short period (one to two weeks) of time. Outcome of the groups and of the individuals is assessed by some observational method and/or by subject-administered questionnaires. The personality variables most often used are:

1. "Person-oriented" individuals or "task-oriented" individuals. "Person-oriented" individuals value such characteristics as warmth, openness, sympathy, and genuineness; "task-oriented" individuals value competence, ability, responsibility, initiative, and energy. A similar, overlapping dichotomy used in other studies is the "low structure" versus the "high structure" individual [38,68]—"high structure" characteristics include a preference for clarity and order with less interest in personal feelings and a tendency to defer to authority figures; "low structure" characteristics include a readiness to recognize and examine positive and negative feelings and interpersonal relationships.

2. FIRO-B characteristics.

3. Group culture preference (Bionic basic assumption cultures of depen-

---

* Several types of compatibility may be computed from the FIRO-B profiles. This study used "interchange compatibility"—the type postulated by Schutz as most relevant for small groups—and is a measure of how much intermember agreement there is about the amount of interchange that should occur in each of the interpersonal need areas (affection, control, exclusion).[14]

dency, flight, fight, pairing) obtained from a self-administered questionnaire.[69]

In general the group composition experimental work is of poor quality, the highly sophisticated statistical technique and conclusive findings reported by several reviews [38,68,70,71] notwithstanding. Observer bias is often uncontrolled; subjects are often asked to compare
experimental groups with a previous group without controls for the
length of time in each group or the sequence of the two experiences;
in addition, the experimental groups are often very short-term, and the
effects of the developmental stage of the group may have been overlooked. The most serious shortcoming is in the measurement of individual outcome. Often, the measures consist only of a few questions,
the reliability and validity of which were unevaluated, asked of the
subjects or other group members. The follow-up interval is, with one
exception,[72] quite brief, and evaluation of change usually immediately follows the group experience (always a questionable procedure
since the wave of positive sentiment at the termination of the group
often obviates individual objectivity). With these reservations, let us
consider the research findings:

1. Homogeneous groups of task-oriented, high structure, impersonal individuals function as effective human relations groups which produce
   change in the members. Apparently, these groups offer a combination of
   support and challenge. The members are supported by their perceived
   similarity and challenged by the task of the group, which demands that
   they interact more intensively and intimately than is their wont. The
   groups tend to be highly cohesive.[37,73,74]
2. Homogeneous groups of person-oriented, low structure individuals do not
   function as effective human relations groups, although the groups are interactive and initially stimulating. Apparently, these groups offer too little
   challenge to the members, who are comfortable with the group task and
   with the other members.[37,75]
3. Homogeneous groups of individuals with the same attitudes toward dominance produce less change than groups which are heterogeneously composed for the same variable.[76]
4. Heterogeneous encounter groups (incompatible on FIRO affection scale)
   are more effective in producing greater self-actualization of members,[77,78]
5. There is a lack of consensus about mixed half-and-half (person-oriented
   and task-oriented) groups. They have been generally found to be ineffective, incompatible, poorly cohesive groups, which do not move toward the
   goals of exploration, sharing, and intimate interaction.[38,79] On the other
   hand, there is some modest evidence from one study that they induce
   greater change in the members.[68]
6. Task groups which are homogeneous (FIRO-B compatibility) are more
   productive and more cohesive than heterogeneous groups.[80]
7. Task groups which are homogeneous for culture preference (flight or pair-

ing) [73] are more efficient than mixed groups. There is a suggestion that the mixed groups suffer from the lack of a liaison person to bridge the two subgroups.

8. In general, the atmosphere of groups is predictable from the composition.[18,81]

Overview of Group Composition

It would be most gratifying at this point to integrate these clinical and experimental findings, to point out hitherto unseen lines of cleavage and coalescence, and to emerge with a crisp theory of group composition which has not only firm experimental foundations but also immediate practical applicability. Unfortunately, the insubstantial nature of the data does not permit such a synthesis.

Let us consider, however, the most unequivocal findings. The composition of the group makes a difference; it influences many aspects of group function. A group can be composed which will have certain predictable short-term characteristics: for example, high cohesion, high conflict, high flight, high dependency. Furthermore, we can, if we choose to use available procedures, predict to some degree the group behavior of the individual.

What we do *not* know, however, is the relationship between any of these group characteristics and the ultimate therapy outcome of the group members. Furthermore, we are unclear about the degree to which the group leader may alter these characteristics of the group and we do not know how long the ongoing group will manifest them. A consideration of the theoretical underpinning of the two general approaches to group composition may help clarify the issue. Underlying the heterogeneous approach to composition are two theoretical rationales which may be labeled the "social microcosm theory" and the "dissonance theory." Underlying the homogeneous group composition approach is the "group cohesiveness" theory.

The "social microcosm" theory postulates that since the group is regarded as a miniaturized social universe in which patients are urged to develop new methods of interpersonal interaction, the group should thus be a heterogeneous one in order to maximize learning opportunities. It should resemble the real social universe by being composed of individuals of different sexes, professions, ages, socioeconomic and educational levels; in other words, it should be a demographic heterodox.

The dissonance theory, as applied to group therapy, also suggests a heterogeneous compositional approach, but for a somewhat different reason. Learning or change is likely to occur when the individual, in a state of dissonance, acts to reduce that dissonance. Dissonance creates a state of psychological discomfort and propels the individual to attempt to achieve a more consonant state. If individuals find themselves in a group in which membership has many desirable features (for example, hopes of alleviation of suffering, attraction toward the leader and other members) but which, at the same time, makes tension-producing demands (for example, self-disclosure or interpersonal confrontation), then they will experience a state of imbalance, or to use Newcomb's term, "asymmetry." [82] Similarly, a state of discomfort occurs when the individual, in a valued group, finds that his interpersonal needs are unfulfilled, or when his customary style of interpersonal behavior produces discordant effects. The individual in these circumstances will search for ways to reduce his discomfort. For example, he may leave the group or, preferably, he may begin to experiment with new forms of behavior. To maximize these developments, the heterogeneous argument suggests that the patient be exposed to other individuals in the group who will not fulfill his interpersonal needs (and thus reinforce his neurotic position) but will frustrate him, challenge him, make him aware of different conflict areas, and who will also demonstrate alternative interpersonal modes. Therefore, it is argued, members with varying interpersonal styles and conflicts should be included in a group. If the frustration and challenge is too great, however, and the staying forces (the attraction to the group) too small, no real asymmetry or dissonance occurs; the individual does not change but instead physically or psychologically leaves the group. (Here we see the interface between the dissonance theory and the next model, the cohesiveness theory.) If, on the other hand, the challenge is too small, no learning occurs either; members will collude, and exploration will be inhibited. The dissonance theory thus argues for a broad personality heterodox.

The cohesiveness theory, underlying the homogeneous approach to group composition, posits, quite simply, that attraction to the group is the critical intervening variable to outcome and that composition should proceed along the lines of assembling a cohesive, compatible group.

How can we reconcile or judge these approaches? First, let me point out that, for purposes of clarity, I have focused sharply on the differences between them; in fact, however, there is a permeable interface between each of the three. Thus, the "social microcosm" model may demand personality heterogeneity as well as demographic heterogeneity if the group is to be a simulated social universe; the "dissonance" model demands a degree of cohesiveness and does not exclude demographic heterogeneity in its search for personality heterogeneity.

Second, there is no group therapy research support for the dissonance model. There is great clinical consensus (my own included) that group therapy patients should be exposed to a variety of conflict areas, coping methods, and conflicting interpersonal styles, and that conflict in general is essential to the therapeutic process; [83] however, there is no evidence that deliberately heterogeneously composed groups facilitate therapy, and, as cited above, there is some modest evidence to the contrary.

On the other hand, there is a body of small group research evidence which supports the cohesiveness concept. Interpersonally compatible therapy groups (homogeneous for FIRO interchange compatibility) will develop greater cohesiveness; members of cohesive groups have better attendance, are more able to express and tolerate hostility; are more apt to attempt to influence others, and are in turn themselves more influenceable; members with greater attraction to their group have better therapeutic outcome; patients who are less compatible with the other members tend to drop out of the therapy group as do any two members with marked mutual incompatibility; members with the greatest interpersonal compatibility become the most popular group members, and group popularity is highly correlated with successful outcome.

The fear that a homogeneous group will be unproductive, constricted, or conflict-free, or will deal with a narrow range of interpersonal concerns, is unfounded for several reasons. First, there are few individuals whose pathology is indeed monolithic; few individuals who, despite their chief conflict area, do not also encounter conflicts in intimacy or authority, for example. Secondly, the group developmental process may demand certain role assumption. For example, the laws of group development (see Chapter 10) demand that the group deal with issues of control, authority, and the hierarchy of dominance. In a group with several control-conflicted individuals, this phase may appear early or very sharply. In a group with an absence of these individuals, other members who are less conflicted in the area of dependency and authority may be forced to deal with this area as the group inevitably moves into this phase of development. If certain roles are not filled in the group, most leaders, consciously or unconsciously, alter their behavior to fill the void.[81]

We must also keep in mind that the group experience is a subjective and individualized one. Patients, according to their assumptive worlds, may experience the same incident in different, highly personalized ways. A therapist or an observer often fails to appreciate the personal salience of certain issues for some patients. It is not easy to enter the experiential world of the patients. Often, when reviewing the course of therapy with patients, I have been impressed by their citing, as a critical incident in their therapy, some event which to others appears trivial or inconsequential.

Furthermore, no therapy group with proper leadership can be too comfortable or fail to provide dissonance for its members because the members must invariably clash with the group task. To develop trust, to disclose oneself, to develop intimacy, to examine oneself, to confront others, are all discordant tasks to individuals who have chronically encountered problems in interpersonal relationships.

The nonproductive homogeneous group of person-oriented individuals reported in T-group research is not relevant to group therapy because of the exceedingly low probability that such a group of individuals would seek psychiatric aid. It is my impression that the homogeneous group of individuals, placed together because of a common symptom or problem which remains on a shallow, restricted level, is entirely an iatrogenic phenomenon—a self-fulfilling prophecy on the part of the therapist.

On the basis of our present state of knowledge, therefore, I propose that cohesiveness be our primary guideline in the composition of therapy groups. The hoped-for dissonance will unfold in the group, provided the therapist functions effectively in the pretherapy orientation of patients and during the early group meetings. Group integrity should be a primary concern, and we must select patients with the lowest possible likelihood of premature termination. Patients with a high likelihood of being incompatible with the prevailing group culture or of being markedly incompatible with at least one other member should not be included in the group. Group cohesiveness, be it noted, is not synonymous with group comfort or ease. Quite the contrary; it is only in a cohesive group that conflict can be tolerated and transformed into productive work.

A cohesiveness frame of reference for group composition is by no means inconsistent with the notion of demographic heterogeneity; however, it does set limits for the degree of heterogeneity. Group therapy clarifies interpersonal relationships within the group and provides the members with carryover into their external lives. It makes eminently good sense to suppose that the greater the range of interpersonal relationships clarified within the group, the more universal the carryover will be. Some patients with restricted social environments derive great benefit from interacting with individuals from different cultural, economic, or educational strata. Knowing and accepting an individual previously deemed alien or unacceptable is a source of great therapeutic benefit. However, the demographic variation must be conceived within the general rubric of cohesiveness; too extreme a variation breeds deviancy and undermines cohesiveness.

In summary, it would appear that the group therapist has only rough guidelines, based on the cohesiveness principle, for group composition. His major task is to form a group which will cohere. Time and energy spent on delicately casting and balancing a group is not justified given our current state of knowledge; the therapist does better to invest that time and energy in careful selection of patients for group therapy and in their pretherapy preparation (to be discussed in the next chapter). There is no question that composition radically affects the group character, but, if the group holds together, and if the therapist has an appreciation of the curative factors and is flexible in his role, he can make therapeutic use of any conditions (other than lack of motivation) which arise in the group.

REFERENCES

1. *Diagnostic and Statistical Manual of Mental Disorders,* (2nd ed.; Washington, D.C.: American Psychiatric Association, 1968).
2. P. Ash, "The Reliability of Psychiatric Diagnosis," *J. Abnorm. Soc. Psychol., 44:* 272–276, 1949.
3. A. T. Beck, C. H. Ward, M. Mendelson, J. E. Mock, and J. R. Erbaugh, "Reliability of Psychiatric Diagnoses: 2. A Study of Consistency of Clinical Judgments and Ratings," *Am. J. Psychiat., 119:* 351–357, 1962.
4. S. R. Slavson, "Criteria for Selection and Rejection of Patients for Various Kinds of Group Therapy," *Int. J. Group Psychother., 5:* 3–30, 1955.
5. A. Camus, *The Fall* (New York: Knopf, 1956).
6. J. Deer and A. W. Silver, "Predicting Participation and Behavior in Group Therapy from Test Protocols," *J. Clin. Psychol., 18:* 322–325, 1962.
7. C. Zimet, "Character Defense Preference and Group Therapy Interaction," *Arch. Gen. Psychiat., 3:* 168–175, 1960.
8. E. F. Borgatta and A. E. Esclenbach, "Factor Analysis of Roschach Variable and Behavior Observation," *Psychol. Rep., 3:* 129–136, 1955.
9. K. Menninger, M. Mayman, and P. Pruyser, *The Vital Balance* (New York: Viking Press, 1963).
10. K. Horney, *Neurosis and Human Growth* (New York: W. W. Norton, 1950).
11. E. Fromm, *Man for Himself* (New York: Rinehart, 1947).

12. E. Fromm, *Escape from Freedom* (New York: Farrar and Rinehart, 1941).

13. T. Leary, *Interpersonal Diagnosis of Personality* (New York: Ronald Press, 1957).

14. W. Schutz, *The Interpersonal Underworld* (Palo Alto, Calif.: Science and Behavior Books, 1966).

15. M. Freedman, T. Leary, A. Ossorio, and H. Coffey, "The Interpersonal Dimension of Personality," *J. Personal.*, *20:* 143–161, 1951.

16. H. Coffey, personal communication, 1967.

17. J. G. Gard and A. W. Bendig, "A Factor Analytic Study of Eysenck's and Schutz's Personality Dimensions and Psychiatric Groups," *J. Consult. Psychol.*, *28:* 252–258, 1964.

18. W. Schutz, "On Group Composition," *J. Abnorm. Soc. Psychol.*, *62:* 275–281, 1961.

19. A. Goldstein, K. Heller, and L. Sechrest, *Psychotherapy and the Psychology of Behavior Change* (New York: John Wiley and Sons, 1966), p. 329.

20. B. M. Bishop, "Mother-Child Interaction and the Social Behavior of Children," *Psychol. Monogr.*, *65:* No. 11, 1, 1951.

21. R. H. Moos and S. R. Clemes, "A Multivariate Study of the Patient-Therapist System," *J. Consult. Psychol.*, *31:* 119–130, 1967.

22. G. B. Bell and R. L. French, "Consistency of Individual Leadership Position in Small Groups of Varying Membership," in A. P. Hare, E. F. Borgatta, and R. F. Bales (eds.), *Small Groups* (New York: Knopf, 1955), pp. 275–280.

23. P. M. Fitts, "German Applied Psychology During World War II," *Am. Psychol.*, *1:* 151–161, 1946.

24. M. Mandell, "Validation of Group Oral Performance Test," *Personnel Psychol.*, *3:* 179–185, 1950.

25. B. M. Bass, "The Leaderless Group Discussion Technique," *Personnel Psychol.*, *3:* 17–32, 1950.

26. H. Fields, "The Group Interview Test: Its Strength," *Publ. Personnel Review*, *11:* 139–146, 1950.

27. E. F. Borgatta and R. F. Bales, "Interaction of Individuals in Reconstituted Groups," *Sociometry*, *16:* 302–320, 1953.

28. E. F. Borgatta and R. F. Bales, "Task and Accumulation of Experience as Factors in the Interaction of Small Groups," *Sociometry*, *16:* 239–252, 1953.

29. B. M. Bass, "Leadership," in *Psychology and Organizational Behavior* (New York: Harper, 1960).

30. V. Cervin, "Individual Behavior in Social Situations: Its Relation to Anxiety, Neuroticism and Group Solidarity," *J. Exper. Psychol.*, *51:* 161–168, 1956.

31. R. B. Cattell, D. R. Saunders and G. F. Stice, "The Dimensions of Syntality in Small Groups," *J. Soc. Psychol.*, *28:* 57–78, 1948.

32. S. H. Foulkes and E. J. Anthony, *Group Psychotherapy—The Psychoanalytic Approach* (Harmondsworth, Middlesex: Penguin Books, 1957).

33. G. Bach, *Intensive Group Therapy* (New York: Ronald Press, 1954).

34. A. Stone, M. Parloff, and J. Frank, "The Use of Diagnostic Groups in a Group Therapy Program," *Int. J. Group Psychother.*, *4:* 274–284, 1954.

35. D. Abrahams and J. Enright, "Psychiatric Intake in Groups: A Pilot Study of Procedures, Problems and Prospects," *Am. J. Psychiat.*, *122:* 170–174, 1965.

36. D. Malamud and S. Machover, *Toward Self-Understanding* (Springfield, Ill.: Charles C. Thomas, 1965).

37. H. Baumgartel, unpublished research report (Washington, D.C.: National Training Laboratories, 1961).

38. R. Harrison, "Group Composition Models for Laboratory Design," *J. Appl. Behav. Sci.*, *1:* 409–432, 1965.

39. H. S. Sullivan, *The Psychiatric Interview* (New York: W. W. Norton, 1954).

40. F. Powdermaker and J. Frank, *Group Psychotherapy* (Cambridge, Mass.: Harvard University Press, 1953), pp. 553–564.

41. P. J. Aston, "Behavioral Correlates of Thematic Apperception Responses," unpublished manuscript, 1966.

42. J. Sutherland, H. S. Gill, and H. Phillipson, "Psychodiagnostic Appraisal in the Light of Recent Theoretical Developments," *Brit. J. Med. Psychol.*, *40:* 299–315, 1967.

43. S. Ben-Zeev, "Sociometric Choice and Patterns of Member Participation," in D.

Stock and H. A. Thelen (eds.), *Emotional Dynamics and Group Culture* (New York: New York University Press, 1958), pp. 84–91.

44. W. F. Hill, "The Influence of Subgroups on Participation in Human Relations Training Groups," unpublished doctoral dissertation, University of Chicago, 1955.

45. A. Couch, "The Psychological Determinants of Interpersonal Behavior," Proceedings of the XIV International Congress of Applied Psychology, Copenhagen, August 13–19, 1961.

46. A. Couch, "Psychological Determinants of Interpersonal Behavior," unpublished doctoral dissertation, Harvard University, 1959–1960.

47. R. R. Blake and J. W. Brehm, "The Use of Tape Recording to Simulate a Group Atmosphere," *J. Abnorm. Soc. Psychol.*, 49: 311–313, 1954.

48. H. Strupp and J. Jenkins, "The Development of Six Sound Motion Pictures Simulating Psychotherapeutic Situations," *J. Nerv. Ment. Disease, 136:* 317–328, 1963.

49. M. A. Lieberman, I. D. Yalom, and M. B. Miles, *Encounter Groups: First Facts* (New York: Basic Books, Inc., 1972).

50. H. D. Mullan and M. Rosenbaum, *Group Psychotherapy* (New York: Free Press of Glencoe, 1962).

51. N. Locke, *Group Psychoanalysis* (New York: New York University Press, 1961).

52. Powdermaker and Frank, *op. cit.*, pp. 66–112.

53. H. M. Feinstein, N. Paul, and P. Esmiol, "Group Therapy for Mothers with Infanticidal Impulses," *Am. J. Psychiat.*, 120: 882–886, 1964.

54. D. Whitaker and M. Lieberman, *Psychotherapy Through the Group Process* (New York: Atherton Press, 1964).

55. Foulkes and Anthony, *op. cit.*, p. 94.

56. F. K. Taylor, *The Analysis of Therapeutic Groups* (London: Oxford University Press, 1961).

57. A. S. Samuels, "The Use of Group Balance as a Therapeutic Technique," *Arch. Gen. Psychiat., 11:* 411–420, 1964.

58. Bach, *op. cit.*, p. 25.

59. *Ibid.*, pp. 331–332.

60. J. Frank *et al.*, "Behavioral Patterns in Early Meetings of Therapeutic Groups," *Am. J. Psychiat., 108:* 771–778, 1952.

61. D. Rosenthal, J. Frank, and E. Nash, "The Self-Righteous Moralist in Early Meetings of Therapeutic Groups," *Psychiatry, 17:* 215–223, 1954.

62. I. D. Yalom, P. S. Houts, S. M. Zimerberg, and K. H. Rand, "Prediction of Improvement in Group Therapy," *Arch. Gen. Psychiat., 17:* 159–168, 1967.

63. I. D. Yalom, P. S. Houts, G. Newell, and K. H. Rand, "Preparation of Patients for Group Therapy: A Controlled Study," *Arch. Gen. Psychiat., 17:* 416–427, 1967.

64. A. D. Sklar, I. D. Yalom, S. M. Zimerberg, and G. Newell, "Time Extended Group Therapy: A Controlled Study," *Comparative Group Studies,* in press.

65. I. D. Yalom and K. H. Rand, "Compatibility and Cohesiveness in Therapy Groups," *Arch. Gen. Psychiat., 13:* 267–276, 1966.

66. I. D. Yalom, J. Tinklenberg, and M. Gilula, "Curative Factors in Group Therapy," Unpublished study.

67. L. M. Koran and R. M. Costell, "Early Termination from Group Psychotherapy," *Int. J. Group Psychother., 23:* 346–359, 1973.

68. R. Harrison and B. Lubin, "Personal Style, Group Composition and Learning—Part 2," *J. Appl. Behav. Sci., 1:* 294–301, 1965.

69. Stock and Thelen, *op. cit.*, pp. 50–64.

70. R. Harrison and B. Lubin, "Personal Style, Group Composition and Learning—Part 1," *J. Appl. Behav. Sci., 1:* 286–294, 1965.

71. D. Stock, "A Survey of Research on T-Groups," in L. P. Bradford, J. R. Gibb, and K. D. Benne (eds.), *T-Group Theory and Laboratory Method* (New York: John Wiley and Sons, 1964), pp. 401–406.

72. M. A. Lieberman, "The Influence of Group Composition on Changes in Affective Approach," in Stock and Thelen, *op. cit.*, pp. 131–139.

73. I. Gradolph, "The Task Approach of Groups of Single-Type and Mixed-Type Valency Compositions," in Stock and Thelen, *op. cit.*, pp. 127–130.

74. T. C. Greening and H. Coffey, "Working with an 'Impersonal' T-Group," *J. Appl. Behav. Sci., 2:* 401–411, 1966.

75. D. Stock and J. Luft, "The T-E-T Design," unpublished manuscript (Washington, D.C.: National Training Laboratories, 1960).
76. H. Pollack, "Change in Homogeneous and Heterogeneous Sensitivity Training Groups," unpublished doctoral dissertation (University of California at Berkeley, 1966).
77. W. B. Reddy, "Interpersonal Compatibility and Self-Actualization in Sensitivity Training." *J. Appl. Behav. Sci.*, 8: 237, 1972.
78. W. B. Reddy, "On Affection, Group Composition and Self-Actualization in Sensitivity Training," *J. Consulting and Clinical Psychology, 38:* 211–214, 1971.
79. D. Stock and W. F. Hill, "Intersubgroup Dynamics as a Factor in Group Growth," in Stock and Thelen, *op. cit.*, pp. 207–221.
80. W. Schutz, *Interpersonal Underworld* (Palo Alto, Calif: Science and Behavior Books, 1966), pp. 120–143.
81. M. A. Lieberman, "The Relationship of Group Climate to Individual Change," unpublished doctoral dissertation (University of Chicago, 1958).
82. T. M. Newcomb, "The Prediction of Interpersonal Attraction," *Am. Psychol., 11:* 575–586, 1956.
83. J. Frank, "Some Values of Conflict in Therapeutic Groups," *Group Psychother., 8:* 142–151, 1955.

9

CREATION
OF THE GROUP:
PLACE, TIME, SIZE,
PREPARATION
❧

The Physical Setting

Prior to convening the group, the therapist must make some important decisions about the setting. He must secure an appropriate meeting place and establish policy about the life span of the group, admission of new members, frequency of meetings, duration of each session, and size of the group.

Group meetings may be held in any setting, provided that the room affords privacy and freedom from distraction. Some therapists prefer to have the members seated about a large circular table (a rectangular table is unwieldy since members on one side may be unable to see each other). Others prefer to have no central obstruction so that the patient's entire body is visible and his nonverbal or postural responses are more readily observable.

If the group session is to be tape recorded or viewed through a viewing screen by students, the group's permission must be obtained in advance and ample opportunity provided for discussion of the procedure. A group which is to be observed continuously appears to forget about the viewing screen after a few weeks, but, often in the context of working through authority issues with the leader, members return to it with renewed interest periodically throughout the course of therapy. If there are to be only one or two student observers, they are best seated in the room, though out of the group circle; this proves, in the long run, less distracting than the viewing screen and allows the students to sample more of the group affect, which in some inexplicable manner is often filtered out by the screen. The observers, if they are to be silent, should be cautioned to remain so; the group often attempts to draw them in, and once they have spoken, they find it increasingly difficult to be silent thereafter.

Open and Closed Groups

At their inception groups are designated by their leader as open or closed: a closed group, once begun, shuts its gates, accepts no new members, and meets usually for a predetermined number of sessions; an open group maintains a consistent size by replacing members as they leave the group. An open group, too, may have a predetermined life span; for example, groups in a university student health service may plan to meet only for the nine-month academic year. Usually, open groups continue indefinitely, even though every couple of years there may be a complete turnover of group membership and even of leadership. I have known of therapy groups in psychiatric training centers which have endured for twenty years, being bequeathed every two to three years by a graduating therapist to an incoming student.

Though a closed group with total stability of membership has much to recommend it, the exigencies of outpatient practice diminish its feasibility. Invariably, members will drop out, move away, or face an unexpected scheduling incompatibility; new members must be added at these times lest the group perish from attrition. A closed group format may, however, be practical in a setting in which one is assured of considerable stability, such as a prison, a military base, a long-term psychiatric hospital, or occasionally an outpatient analytic group in which all members are concurrently in individual analysis with the group leader. Ordinarily, the great majority of outpatient groups are conducted as open groups.

Duration and Frequency of Meetings

Until the mid-1960s, the length of the session seemed fixed in psycho-therapy; the fifty-minute individual hour and the eighty-to-ninety-minute group therapy session were part of the entrenched folk wis-dom of the field. Most group therapists agree that, even in well-es-tablished groups, a period of at least sixty minutes is required for the warm-up interval and for the unfolding and working through of the major themes of the session. There also is some consensus among therapists that after about two hours a point of diminishing returns is reached; the group becomes weary, repetitious, and inefficient. Fur-thermore, many therapists appear to function best in segments of eighty to ninety minutes; longer sessions often result in fatigue, which renders the therapist less effective in his remaining therapy sessions that day.

The frequency of meetings varies from one to five times a week. I prefer a twice-weekly schedule. It is generally difficult to assemble outpatients more frequently than that. A once-weekly schedule is the most common format in outpatient work, but in my experience the group often suffers from the long interval between meetings. Often, much has occurred in the life of the members that cannot be ignored, and the group veers away from an interactional mode into a crisis-resolution format. When the group meets more than once weekly, it increases in intensity, the meetings have more continuity, the group continues to work through issues raised the previous week, and the entire process takes on the character of a continuous meeting.

Recently, there has been considerable experimentation with the time variable. This experimentation or reaction to conventional modes of therapy has at times been so extreme as to border on proce-dural anarchy. Groups are reported which meet regularly for four-, six-, or eight-hour sessions. Some therapists choose to meet less frequently but for longer periods—for example, a six-hour meeting every other week; some psychiatric wards have instituted an intensive group therapy week, during which the patients meet in small groups for eight hours a day for five consecutive days; another program offers sixteen hours of group therapy each weekend for sixteen weeks.

A widely publicized new format has been the "marathon" group, which has been described in many popular American magazines, newspapers, and fictionalized accounts.[1,2,3] The marathon group, so christened by Bach,[4] meets for a prolonged session, perhaps twenty-four to forty-eight hours in duration, with little or no time permitted for sleep. The participants are required to remain together for the entire designated time; meals are served in the room, and sleep, if required, comes during short naps in the session or in short, scheduled sleep breaks. The emphasis of the group is on total self-disclosure, intensive interpersonal confrontation, and affective involvement and participation.

The time-extended therapy session has several roots. Undoubtedly, psychotherapy has been influenced by the sensitivity training field and its frequent use of intensive residential workshops in which the participants live together and meet in groups for several hours daily over several days (see Chapter 14). Another influence stems from recent developments in the therapeutic use of the inpatient psychiatric community. Clinicians have increasingly come to regard the psychiatric ward as a potential twenty-four-hour-a-day therapy group and have sought ways to harness the powerful interpersonal forces for therapeutic gain. Intensive family therapy techniques may also have helped set the stage; MacGregor, in 1962, described a mode of multiple impact therapy [5] in which a psychiatric team devoted its total attention to one family for two to three full days.

Time-extended group therapy has been used in clinical practice in several different formats. Patients who may or may not be in other therapy spend a weekend in a marathon group with a leader about whom they first learned from a friend or professional advertisement. If they are in therapy, occasionally their individual therapist may recommend such a group. Some group therapists refer their entire group for a weekend with another therapist or, more commonly, may themselves conduct a marathon meeting with their own group sometime during the course of therapy. Often, hospital wards or correctional agencies schedule a marathon group either as part of an ongoing group or as a discrete experience.

Proponents of the time-extended group claim that the procedure has several advantages: [4,6,7,8,9,10,11] the development of the small group is greatly accelerated; members undergo a more intense emotional experience; the entire course of therapy may take only twenty-four to forty-eight hours. The social microcosm of the group is said to unfold more quickly; if patients are in the group as they are in the world, the group will replicate the real world more rapidly, with patients eating, sleeping, crying, and living together continuously in a setting in which there is no place to hide. The fatigue resulting from lack of sleep doubtlessly contributes to the abandonment of social facades. (As one marathon group leader stated, "Tired people are truthful; they do not have the energy to play games." A ninety-minute session is not long enough to compel people to "take off their masks.") [9]

The results of marathon group therapy reported in the mass media and in scientific journals have been so extraordinary that they boggle the mind. Eighty percent of the participants undergo significant change as the result of a single meeting; [10] thirty-six hours of therapy have proved comparable to several years of conventional ninety-minute weekly group therapy sessions; [8] 90 percent of 400 marathon group members considered the meeting as "one of the most significant and meaningful experiences" of their lives.[12] Marathon group therapy represents a breakthrough in psychotherapeutic practice.[13] The marathon group has become a singular agent of change which allows rapidity of learning and adaptation to new patterns of behavior not likely to occur under traditional arrangements, etc.[4] "If all adults had been in a marathon, there would be no more war; if all teenagers had been in a marathon, there would be no more juvenile delinquency," [14] etc., etc.

This lack of objectivity and the indiscriminating embrace of the latest therapeutic fad are characteristics of the field of psychotherapy in general and of group therapy in particular. Parloff, discussing the claims of marathon group therapists, states, "No sooner does a new group therapy Tinker Bell appear on the scene then a number of practitioners will offer to sustain its weak and flickering light by life-supporting shouts of 'I believe! I believe.' " [7]

The results, to date, are entirely based on anecdotal reports of various participants or questionnaires distributed shortly after the end of the meeting, an exceedingly untrustworthy approach to evaluation. In fact, any outcome study based entirely on interviews, testimonials, or patient self-administered questionnaires obtained at the end of the group is of questionable value. At no other time is the patient more loyal, more grateful, and less objective about his group than at the point of termination; at this juncture there is a powerful tendency to recall and to express only the positive, tender feelings. Experiencing and expressing negative feelings about the group at this point would be unlikely for at least two reasons: (1) there is strong group pressure at termination to participate in positive testimonials; few individuals, as Asch has shown, can maintain their objectivity in the face of apparent group unanimity; and (2) the individual rejects critical feelings toward the group at this time to avoid a state of cognitive dissonance. He has chosen to invest considerable emotion and time in the group; he has often developed strong positive feelings toward other members. To question the value or activities of the group would be to thrust himself into a state of dissonance.

Although the format of the encounter group is especially well suited to controlled research investigation, there has been no evidence to document the many extravagant claims. In a comprehensive review of over 200 articles on marathon practice and research,[11] not one acceptable research inquiry of outcome is described; the attempts either deal with a nonpatient population, lack adequate controls, or employ crude, easily biased measures of outcome.

In 1967 my co-workers and I [15] tested the hypothesis that a time-extended group session accelerates the life cycle of the group. Specifically, we explored the effect of a six-hour, time-extended meeting * on the development of cohesiveness (operationally defined as member-member and member-group involvement) and on the development of a here-and-now, interactive communicational mode.

Six newly formed groups in a psychiatric outpatient department were studied for their first sixteen sessions. Three of these groups held a six-hour first session, while the other three held a six-hour eleventh session. During the period of their first sixteen meetings, each group thus had a six-hour session and fifteen meetings of conventional length (ninety minutes). Tape recordings of the second, sixth, tenth, twelfth, and sixteenth meetings were analyzed to classify the verbal interaction.† (The six-hour meeting itself was not analyzed, since we were primarily interested in studying its effect on the subsequent course of therapy.) Post-group questionnaires measuring group involvement and member-member involvement were obtained at these same meetings.

The results show that the time-extended meeting did *not* influence the communicational patterns in a favorable direction in meetings subsequent to the marathon session. In fact, there was a trend in the opposite direction—i.e., the groups, following the six-hour meetings, appeared to engage in *less* here-and-now interaction. The influence of the six-hour meeting on cohesiveness was quite interesting. In the three groups which held a six-hour initial meeting, there was a trend toward *decreased* cohesiveness in subsequent meetings. However, in the three groups which held a six-hour eleventh meeting, there was a significant *increase* in cohesiveness in the subsequent meetings.

* It is possible that a six-hour meeting may have an entirely different effect from a twenty-four-hour meeting. However, many of the claims cited above also are reported by clinicians using shorter marathon group sessions in outpatient clinics.[8]

† The Hill Interaction Matrix [16] method of scoring interaction was used. The middle thirty minutes of the meeting was systematically evaluated by two trained raters who were naïve about the design of the study.

The implication of these results is that timing must be taken into consideration. It is entirely possible that, at the correct juncture in the course of the group, a time-extended session may help increase member involvement in the group. The therapists of the six groups, when questioned, were not impressed by any significant changes in the development of the group that may have been attributable to the time-extended meeting.

It would be naïve to assume, however, that forthcoming research will greatly influence the tide of interest in the marathon group: I believe that the marathon will be part of the American psychotherapy scene for quite some time to come. With continued publicity, the hope of instant therapy will continue to flourish, and group therapists will, no doubt, be pressured by many of their groups for a marathon experience. The lure of accelerated therapy and instant intimacy is highly resonant with the American penchant for prefabrication. Today in our culture instant, foundationless homes and cities arise de novo; romances and marriages issue from the matchmaker computer; timeless truths of religion are dispensed at a drive-in church service or via dial-a-prayer phone service; even tradition is born fully formed, fully clothed, and fully pedigreed in the guise of the London Bridge bought and transported stone by stone by an American real estate developer to span an artificial waterway in a newly constructed resort city.

It is thus no surprise that the marathon is an American invention. But our unbridled impatience, our "crash program" mentality so effective in nuclear of space research, may come a cropper in psychotherapy. The passage of time may be essential to the psychotherapeutic process, and such experiences as commitment, responsibility, intimacy, and trust cannot be compressed without grotesquely distorting their nature.

Objective appraisal of the time-extended format has been confounded by the tendency of many workers to equate emotional impact or "potency" and therapeutic effectiveness. My own experience as a participant and leader of marathon groups has taught me that the intensive, prolonged transetiquette experience can be a powerful and moving one. There are very few other settings in our culture in which individuals can so unabashedly release pent-up emotion, reveal themselves, cry, and express intense love and hate. At the termination of the session there is no end to such testimonials as "Walking on clouds," "Never felt closer to myself and to others," "People are so beautiful," "Feel stronger than I have ever felt," "My life has been changed," and so on.

And yet we must ask: what does this have to do with therapy? We must again be mindful of the difference between an emotional experience and a corrective emotional experience. Most of all we must consider questions of temporality in therapy: does a change in one's behavior in the group invariably and simultaneously betoken a change in one's outside life? How enduring is change which occurs in a short-term experience? Clinicians have long known that change in the therapy session is not tantamount to therapeutic success; carryover into important outside interpersonal relationships and endeavors is required. Despite our impatience, the laborious process of carryover demands a certain irreducible temporal segment of life.*

Consider the patient who, because of his early experience with an authoritarian, distant, and harsh father, tends to see all other males, especially those in a position of authority, as having similar qualities. In the group he may have an entirely different emotional experience with a male therapist and perhaps one of the male members. What has he learned? Well, for one thing he has learned that not all men are frightening bastards; at least there are one or two who are not. Of what lasting value is this experience to the patient? Probably very little unless the experience is generalizable for future situations. As a result of the group, the individual learns that at least some men in authority positions can be trusted. But which ones? He must learn how to differentiate between people so as not to perceive all men in a predetermined manner. A new repertoire of perceptual skills is needed. Once he is able to make the necessary discriminations, he must learn how to go about making relationships on an egalitarian, distortion-free basis. For the individual whose interpersonal relationships have been impoverished and maladaptive, these are formidable and lengthy tasks which often require the continual testing and reinforcement available in the therapeutic relationship. When a time-extended meeting is scheduled during the course of a long-term group, it is important that the leader provide the proper perspective. The marathon does not provide change; what it does provide is an arena for heightened emotional interaction and for the generation of data which the group and each member will need to work through in future sessions. If the pa-

---

* Lorr [17] reviewed the pertinent clinical research on intensity and duration of treatment and concluded that "duration of treatment is a more influential parameter than the number of treatments . . . change would appear to require the passage of time. Insights are put into practice in daily living. New ways of reacting interpersonally must be tested again and again in natural settings before what has been learned becomes consolidated. Trial and error testing seems a prerequisite for the process of growth and change."

tients have unjustifiably grand expectations for the group, they may begin to "store up" for the marathon and then, afterward, suffer disappointment and discouragement.

Thus, we question whether or not the marathon group precludes the use of long-term therapy; we do not deny its impact. It is an engrossing human experience—perhaps the most sophisticated and compelling of all adult games. Its psychotherapeutic potential is still unknown; clearly it cannot be dismissed summarily on the basis of any of the objections I have raised. One must somehow heed the patients who claim, months after the single extended session, that they experienced an important and durable therapeutic change; one must also heed the psychiatrists who report that some of their long-term patients who engaged in a time-extended group session suddenly became mobilized and their subsequent psychotherapy vastly facilitated. Undoubtedly, as our experience increases and as research is undertaken and evaluated, the time-extended meeting will be allocated an appropriate position in our therapeutic armamentorium. The time-extended meeting may, I believe, have considerable potential as a facilitating procedure in the course of ongoing therapy rather than as an isolated procedure. The danger at present is, as with any new technique, the tendency to consider it a panacea—effective for all patients at all times.

Size of the Group

My own experience and a consensus of the clinical literature suggest that the ideal size of an interactional therapy group is approximately seven, with an acceptable range of five to ten members. The lower limit of the group is determined by the fact that a critical mass is required for an aggregation of individuals to become an interacting group. When a group is reduced to a size of four or three, it often ceases to operate as a group; member interaction diminishes, and therapists often find themselves engaged in individual therapy within the group. Many of the advantages of a group—the opportunity for broad consensual validation, the opportunity to interact and to analyze one's interaction with a large variety of individuals—are compromised as the group size diminishes.

The upper limit is determined by sheer economic principles; as the group increases in size, less and less time is available for the working

through of any individual's problems. Although most outpatient therapists set an upper limit of eight or nine on their groups, sensitivity
training groups generally include more members, usually twelve to
sixteen. It is possible to conduct a face-to-face group with this
number—each member may interact in a meaningful way with each of
the other members—however, there will be insufficient time to work
through with any thoroughness the problem areas which are identified. Such large groups may offer a therapeutic experience to those
members who choose to take advantage of the opportunity, but their
size precludes intensive psychotherapeutic work with each of the
members. Still larger groups ranging from twenty to eighty are conducted by Alcoholics Anonymous, Recovery, Inc., and therapeutic
communities. However, these groups rely on different curative factors; the A.A. and Recovery, Inc., groups use inspiration, guidance,
and suppression, whereas the large therapeutic community relies on
group pressure and interdependence to encourage reality testing, to
combat regression, and to instill a sense of individual responsibility
toward the social community.

To some extent, the optimal group size is a function of the duration
of the meeting: the longer the meeting, the larger the number of patients who can profitably engage in the group. Thus, many of the
"marathon" therapy groups include up to sixteen members. Innumerable variations of group size and duration of meetings are currently
being explored; one therapist in California, for example, has adopted
the procedure of seeing all of his individual patients (and their
spouses) in a fifty-member, six-hour weekly meeting. Others report
short-term intensive groups ranging in size from 70 to 1,000 members.[11]

Little research has been done to explore the relationship between
size and group effectiveness. Castore [18] investigated the relationship
between the size of the group and the number of different member-to-
member verbal relationships initiated (i.e., the number of other
members to whom each individual directed at least one remark—a
measure of the spread of interpersonal interaction in the group) in
fifty-five inpatient therapy groups with a range in size from five to
twenty patients. The results indicated a marked reduction in interactions between members when the group's size reached nine members
and a second marked reduction when seventeen or more members
were present. The implication of the research is that, in inpatient settings, groups of five to eight offer a greater opportunity for total patient
participation.

An observation by Asch [19] is noteworthy. Group pressure, as we have noted, may be harnessed in the service of therapy. Long-cherished but self-defeating beliefs and attitudes may waver and decompose in the face of a dissenting majority. Asch investigated the influence of the size of the majority on group pressure and found a major gradient between a majority of two and three (i.e., a four-member group is significantly more able to influence than a three-member group); but an increase of the majority to four, eight, and even sixteen did not produce effects greater than a majority of three.

Several studies suggest that, from the perspective of the group member, five-member groups are the most harmonious problem-solving groups.[20] Other studies show that as the size of the group increases there is a corresponding tendency for cliques and disruptive subgroups to form.[21] A comparison between twelve-member and five-member problem-solving groups indicates that the larger groups are more dissatisfied and show less consensus.[22] As the group increases in size, research demonstrates, too, that only the more forceful and aggressive members are able to express themselves, whereas the less forceful members are unable to express their ideas or abilities.[23]

Since one must anticipate that one or, possibly, two patients will drop out of the group in the course of the initial meetings, it is advisable to start with a group slightly larger than one's preferred size; thus, to obtain a seven-member group, many therapists start a new group with eight or nine members.

Preparation for Group Therapy

There is great variation in clinical practice regarding the interviewing of patients prior to group therapy. Some therapists, after seeing the patient once or twice in selection interviews, do not meet with the patient individually again, whereas other therapists continue individual sessions with the patient until he starts in the group. Often, it requires several weeks to assemble seven patients for a group, and, to avoid losing the early candidates, the therapist must continue to meet with them periodically. The chief purpose, though, of the post-selection, pre-group interviews is, in my view, to prepare patients for the impending group experience. I would agree with Foulkes [24] that there is little purpose in pretherapy anamnestic interviews, since any truly relevant material will be forthcoming in the group setting. There is some value in considering the pre-group individual sessions as an opportunity to build rapport with the patient, which may prove helpful in keeping him in the group during periods of discouragement and disenchantment early in the course of group therapy. It is my clinical impression that the more often a patient is seen pretherapy, the less likely he is to terminate prematurely from the group. Often, the first step in the development of intermember bonds is their mutual identification with a common shared object—the therapist.

The preparatory process for group therapy has several aspects: the therapist clarifies misconceptions, unrealistic fears and expectations; he provides support; he anticipates and thus diminishes group therapy problems; and he provides patients with a cognitive structure which will enable them to participate more effectively in the group.

MISCONCEPTIONS ABOUT GROUP THERAPY

Certain misconceptions and fears about group therapy occur with such great regularity that the therapist can, with a reasonable degree of certainty, take their presence for granted; and if they go unmentioned by the patient, he should introduce them as potential problems. Despite recent sympathetic presentation by the mass media, there is still a widespread belief among prospective patients that group therapy is second-rate therapy—i.e., that it is cheap therapy, sop provided for those who cannot afford individual therapy; that it is diluted therapy because each patient has only twelve to fifteen minutes of the therapist's time each week; that it exists only because the number of patients greatly exceeds the supply of therapists.

These misconceptions may produce a set of expectations so unfavorable to group therapy that successful outcome becomes unlikely. There is convincing research evidence that the patient's initial expectations of and faith in therapy and in the therapist are positively and significantly related to his remaining in treatment and to an ultimately favorable outcome.[25,26,27]

In addition to evaluative misconceptions, patients are usually further encumbered with burdens of procedural misconceptions and unrealistic interpersonal fears. Many of these are evident in the following dream which a patient reported at her second pre-group individual session shortly before she was to attend her first group meeting.

I dreamed that each member of the group was required to bring cookies to the meeting. I went with my mother to buy the cookies that I was to take to the meeting. We had great difficulty deciding which cookies would be appropriate. In the meantime, I was aware that I was going to be very late to the meeting, and I was becoming more and more anxious about getting there on time. We finally decided on the cookies and proceeded to go to the group. I asked directions to the room where the group was to meet and was told that it was meeting in Room 129A. I wandered up and down a long hall in which the rooms were not numbered consecutively and in which I couldn't find a room with a number A. I finally discovered that 129A was located behind another room and went into the group. When I had been looking for the room, I had encountered many people from my past, many people whom I had gone to school with and many people whom I had known for a number of years. The group was very large, and about forty or fifty people were milling around the room. The members of the group included members of my family: most specifically, two of my brothers. Each member of the group was required to stand in front of a large audience and say what they thought was their difficulty and why they were there and what their problems were. The whole dream was very anxiety-provoking, and the business of being late and the business of having a large number of people was very distracting.

Although time did not permit intensive analysis of the dream, several themes were abundantly clear. The patient anticipated the first group meeting with considerable dread. Her concern about being late reflected a fear of being excluded or rejected by the group. Furthermore, since she was starting in an ongoing group—one which had already met for several weeks—she feared that she would be left behind, the others having progressed far past her position. (She could not find a room with an "A" marked on it.) She dreamed that the group would number forty or fifty. Concerns about the size of the group are common; patients fear that their unique individuality will be lost as they become one of the mass. Moreover, patients erroneously apply the model of the economic distribution of goods to the group therapeutic experience, assuming that the size of the crowd is inversely proportional to the goods received by each individual.

The dream image of each member confessing his problems to the group audience reflects one of the most basic and pervasive fears of individuals entering a therapy group: the anticipation of having to reveal oneself and to confess shameful transgressions and fantasies to an alien audience. Further inquiry reveals the expectation of a critical, scornful, ridiculing, or humiliating response from the other members. The experience is fantasied as an apocalyptic trial before a stern, uncompassionate tribunal. The dream also suggests that pre-group anticipation resulted in a recrudescence of anxiety linked to a number of early group experiences in the patient's life, including those of school, family, and play groups. It is as if her entire social network, all the significant people and groups she has encountered in her life, will be present in this group. (In a metaphorical sense this is true: to the degree that she has been shaped by other groups and other individuals, to the degree that she internalizes them, she will carry them into the group with her since they are part of her character structure; furthermore, she will, through paratoxic distortions, recreate in the therapy group her early significant relationships.)

It is clear from the reference to Room 129 (an early schoolroom in her life) that the patient associates her impending group experience with a time in her life when few things were more crucial than the acceptance and approval of a peer group. Her expectation of the therapist is that he will be like her early teachers—an aloof, unloving evaluator.

Closely related to the dread of forced confession is the concern about confidentiality. The patient anticipated that there would be no group boundaries, that every intimacy she disclosed would be known by every significant person in her life.

Other common concerns, not evident in this dream, include a fear of mental contagion, of being made sicker through association with other psychiatric patients. Often, but not exclusively, this is a preoccupation of schizophrenic or borderline patients. In part, this concern is a reflection of the self-contempt of psychiatric patients who project onto others their feelings of worthlessness and their imagined proclivity to besmirch others with whom they relate. Such dynamics underlie the frequently posed query, "How can the blind lead the blind?" Convinced that they themselves have nothing of value to offer, patients find inconceivable the notion that they might profit from others like themselves. Other patients fear their own hostility: that, if they ever unleashed their rage, it would engulf themselves as well as others. The notion of a group where anger is freely expressed is terrifying to them as they think silently, "If they only knew. . . ."

The unrealistic expectations which, unchecked, would lead to a rejection or a blighting of group therapy can be allayed by an adequate preparation of the candidate. Before outlining a preparation procedure, we shall consider some problems commonly encountered early in the course of the group which may also be ameliorated by pre-therapy preparation.

THE ANTICIPATION OF GROUP PROBLEMS

One important source of perplexity and discouragement for patients early in the course of therapy is a perceived goal incompatibility; they will often be unable to discern the congruence between group goals (e.g., group integrity, construction of an atmosphere of trust, and an interactional confrontive focus) and their individual goals (relief of suffering). What bearing, they wonder, does a discussion of their interpersonal reactions to other members have on their symptoms of anxiety, depression, phobias, impotence, or insomnia?

A high turnover in the early stages of the group is, as we have already shown, a major impediment to the development of an effective group. The therapist, from his very first contacts with the patient, should discourage irregular attendance and premature termination. The issue is a more pressing one than in individual therapy, where absences and tardiness can be profitably investigated and worked through. In the initial stages of the group, irregular attendance results in a discouraged and disjunctive group; there is so much pressing business which the group as a whole must do that resistance expressed through physical absence is especially destructive.

"Subgrouping and extragroup socializing," which has been referred to as the "Achilles heel of group therapy," is a problem that may be encountered at any stage of the group. The issue is a complex one which we shall consider later in detail in Chapter 11. For the present, it is sufficient to point out that the therapist may begin to shape the group norms regarding subgrouping in his very first contacts with the patients.

A SYSTEM OF PREPARATION

I have come to employ a procedure of systematic preparation of group therapy patients which is designed to address each of the foregoing misconceptions, erroneous expectations, and initial problems of group therapy. The misconceptions and expectations should be explored in detail with the patients and corrected not by empty exclamation but by an accurate and complete discussion of each. Early problems in therapy may be predicted by the therapist in the preparatory session, and a conceptual framework and clear guidelines to effective behavior presented to the patients. Although each patient's preparation must be individualized according to his presenting complaints and level of sophistication regarding the therapy process, I have found that a preparatory interview following the general outline below is of considerable value.

Patients are presented with a brief explanation of the interpersonal theory of psychiatry, beginning with the statement that although each manifests his problems differently, all who seek help from psychotherapy have in common the basic problem of difficulty in establishing and maintaining close and gratifying relationships with others. They are reminded of the many times in their lives that undoubtedly they have wished to clarify a relationship, to be really honest about their positive and negative feelings with someone and get reciprocally honest feedback. The general structure of society, however, does not often permit totally open communication; feelings are hurt, relationships fractured, misunderstandings arise, and, eventually, communication ceases. The therapy group is described as a special microcosm in which this type of honest interpersonal exploration vis-à-vis the other members is not only permitted but encouraged. If people are conflicted in their methods of relating to others, then obviously a social situation which encourages honest interpersonal explorations can provide them with a clear opportunity to learn many valuable things about themselves. It is emphasized that working on their relationships directly with other group members will not be easy; in fact, it may be very stressful, but it is crucial because if one can completely understand and work out one's relationships with the other group members, there will be an enormous carryover. They will then find pathways to more rewarding relationships with significant people in their lives now and with people they have yet to meet. The therapist emphasizes that the therapy group does not eventuate in a single ejaculation of "honest disclosure"; instead, it offers a new social contract which encourages both disclosure and a responsibility to continue communication despite pain and anxiety.

The patients are advised that the way in which they can help themselves most of all is to be honest and direct with their feelings in the group at that moment, especially their feelings toward the other group members and the therapists. This point is emphasized many times and is referred to as the "core of group therapy." They are told that they may, as they develop trust in the group, reveal intimate aspects of themselves, but that the group is not a forced confessional and that people have different rates of developing trust and revealing themselves. It is suggested that the group be seen as a forum for risk-taking and that, as learning progresses, new types of behavior may be tried in the group setting.

Certain stumbling blocks are predicted. Patients are forewarned about a feeling of puzzlement and discouragement in the early meetings. It will, at times, not be apparent how working on group problems and intragroup relationships can be of value in solving the problems which brought them to therapy. This puzzlement, they are told, is to be expected in the typical therapy process, and they are strongly urged to stay with the group and not to heed their inclinations to give up therapy. It is almost impossible to predict the eventual effectiveness of the group during the first dozen meetings, and they are asked to suspend judgment, to make a commitment of at least twelve meetings before even attempting to evaluate the ultimate usefulness of the group. They are told that many patients find it painfully difficult to reveal themselves or to express directly positive or negative feelings. The tendencies of some to withdraw emotionally, to hide their feelings, to let others express feelings for them, to form concealing alliances with others, are discussed. The therapeutic goals of group therapy are ambitious because we desire to change behavior and attitudes many years in the making; treatment is therefore gradual and long; no important changes will occur for months, and at least a year of treatment will be required. I discuss with them the likely development of feelings of frustration or annoyance with the therapist, and how they will expect answers from him that he cannot supply. The source of help will often be the other patients, although it may be difficult for them to accept this fact.

Next they are told about the history and development of group therapy—how group therapy passed from a stage during World War II, when it was valued because of its economic features (i.e., it allowed psychiatrists to reach a large number of patients) to its present position in the field, where it is clearly seen as having something unique to offer and is often the treatment of choice. Results of psychotherapy outcome studies are cited in which group therapy is shown to be as efficacious as any mode of individual therapy.[28,29,30] My remarks in this area are focused toward instilling faith in group therapy and dispelling the false notion that group therapy is "second-class therapy."

Confidentiality, patients are told, is as essential in group therapy as it is in any form of doctor-patient relationship; for members to speak freely, they must have confidence that their statements will remain within the group. In my group therapy experience, I can scarcely recall a single serious breach of confidence and can therefore reassure patients on this matter with considerable conviction. Occasionally, members may inquire whether they can discuss aspects of the group therapy experience with a spouse or confidant. The best policy for the therapist to follow is never to "ban" anything but instead to provide sufficient information to the patient so that he shares in the construction of procedural guidelines. Often, a decision is made which permits the patient to share his own experience with another but to keep others' experiences, and certainly their names, in strictest confidence.

The issue of extragroup socializing may be tactfully and effectively approached in preparatory sessions from two standpoints:

1. The group provides an opportunity for learning about one's problems in social relationships; it is not an assembly for meeting and making social friends, and it is the experience of therapists that if used in this manner the group loses its therapeutic effectiveness. In other words, the therapy group teaches one *how to develop intimate, long-term relationships, but it does not provide these relationships.*
2. However, if by chance or design, members do meet outside the group, it is their responsibility to discuss the salient aspects of the meeting inside the group.

It is particularly useless for the therapists to lay down rules prohibiting extragroup socializing; almost invariably during the course of the therapy, group members will engage in some extragroup socializing and, in the face of prohibitions, may be reluctant to disclose this in the group. As we shall elaborate further in the next chapter, the extragroup relationships are not harmful per se (in fact, they may be extremely important in the therapeutic process); what impedes therapy is the conspiracy of silence which often surrounds such meetings. Furthermore, such rules may involve patients in a nonproductive discussion of rule-breaking, whereas the statement that it is the therapist's experience that such activity impedes therapy may, with greater profit, confront patients with the issue of why they act to sabotage their own therapy. Once again, it is advisable to provide ample information to the patient rather than to hand down *ex cathedra* proclamations. For example, the therapist may explain that friendships among certain group members may prevent them from speaking openly to one another in the group, that members may develop a sense of loyalty to a dyadic relationship which conflicts with the openness and candor so essential to the therapy process.

This preparatory procedure consists of more than mere transmission of information from leader to member. The process underlying the content conveys an even more important message—that the therapist respect the patient's judgment and intelligence, that therapy is a collaborative venture, that the therapist is an expert who operates on a rational basis and who is willing to share his knowledge with the patient.

RESEARCH EVIDENCE

In 1966 my co-workers and I [31] tested the effectiveness of such a preparatory session in a controlled experiment. Of a sample of sixty patients awaiting group therapy, half were seen in a thirty-minute preparatory session, whereas the other half were seen for an equal period of time in a conventional interview dedicated primarily to history-taking. Six therapy groups (three of prepared patients, three of unprepared patients) were organized and led by group therapists unaware that there had been an experimental manipulation. A study of the first twelve meetings demonstrated that the prepared groups had more faith in therapy (which in turn positively influences outcome [25,26,27]) and engaged in significantly more group and interpersonal interaction than the nonprepared groups,* and that this difference was as marked in the twelfth meeting as in the second. The research design required that identical preparation be given to each patient; we may surmise that if the preparation were more thorough and more individualized for each patient, its effectiveness might have been further enhanced. Although the information imparted may appear elaborate, the procedure of preparation, be it noted, is a simple one and can easily be accomplished in a single interview.

Heitler [32] used an "anticipatory socialization interview" [33] to prepare lower-class patients for interactional group therapy. The experimental sample consisted of fifty-five patients entering a V.A. group therapy program. Patients alternately were given a preparatory interview or a traditional initial interview. Trained observers rated the groups (which met daily) for two weeks and concluded that the prepared patients participated to a greater extent, were more proactive, and engaged in more self-exploratory behavior. The group therapist rated the prepared patients as more involved, as closer to his ideal of model group therapy patients, and as more initiative in self-exploratory efforts. Though controls are not rigorous in this experiment, and two weeks is too brief a time to state definitively that the preparation would significantly improve outcome, there is, nonetheless, evidence that the patients' initial phase of therapy was greatly facilitated. We gain even more confidence in the findings by noting that there is convincing corroborative evidence regarding the effectiveness of a pre-

---

* The interaction of the groups was measured by scoring each statement during the meeting on a sixteen-cell matrix (Hill Interaction Matrix [16]). Scoring was performed by a team of raters naïve to the experimental design. Faith in therapy was tested by postgroup patient-administered questionnaires.

paratory interview in the individual psychotherapy research literature.[33,34]

THE RATIONALE OF GROUP THERAPY PREPARATION

I have deliberately devoted considerable space to the preparation of
the patient because I believe it is a crucial but oft-neglected function
of the therapist. Let us consider briefly the rationale for a preparatory
process. The first dozen meetings of the therapy group are precarious
and at the same time vitally important: many members are unnecessarily discouraged and terminate therapy; the group is in a highly
fluid state and maximally responsive to the influence of the therapist,
who, if he is sensitive, can take giant strides in influencing the group
to elaborate therapeutic norms. The early meetings are a time of considerable patient anxiety, both intrinsic unavoidable anxiety and extrinsic unnecessary anxiety.

The intrinsic anxiety issues from the very nature of the group; an individual who has encountered lifelong disabling difficulties in his interpersonal relationships will invariably be stressed by a therapy
group which demands not only that he attempt to relate deeply to
other members but that he discuss these relationships with great candor. In fact, as we have noted from group research cited in Chapter
8,[35,36,37] anxiety seems to be an essential condition for the initiation
of change. In group therapy, anxiety arises not only from interpersonal
conflict but from dissonance, which springs from a desire to remain in
the group while at the same time experiencing an incompatibility
with the group task.

There is an imposing body of evidence,[38,39,40] however, which
demonstrates that there are limits to the adaptive value of anxiety in
therapy. An optimal level of anxiety enhances motivation and increases vigilance, but an excessive degree of anxiety will obstruct
one's ability to cope with stress. White notes, in his masterful review
of the evidence supporting the concept of an exploratory drive,[40] that
anxiety and fear are the enemies of environmental exploration; they
retard learning and result in decreased exploratory behavior to an extent correlated with the intensity of the fear. In group therapy, crippling amounts of anxiety may prevent the introspection, interpersonal
exploration, and testing of new behavior so essential to the process of
change.

Much of the anxiety experienced by patients early in the group is
not anxiety intrinsic to the group task but is unnecessary, extrinsic,

and sometimes iatrogenic. This anxiety is a natural consequence of being placed in a group situation in which one's expected behavior, the group goals, and their relevance to one's personal goals are exceedingly unclear. Research with laboratory groups demonstrates that if the group's goals, the methods of goal attainment, and expected role behavior are ambiguous, the group will be less cohesive, less productive, and its members more defensive, anxious, frustrated, and prone to terminate membership.[41,42,43,44,45] An effective preparation for the group will reduce the extrinsic anxiety which stems from uncertainty. By clarifying the group goals, by explaining that group and personal goals are confluent, by presenting unambiguous guidelines for effective behavior, by providing the patient with an accurate formulation of the group process, one reduces uncertainty and the accompanying extrinsic anxiety.

A systematic preparation for group therapy by no means implies a rigid structuring of the group experience. I do not propose a didactic, directive approach to group therapy but, on the contrary, suggest a technique which will enhance the formation of a freely interacting, autonomous group. By averting lengthy ritualistic behavior in the initial sessions and by diminishing initial anxiety stemming from ambiguity, the group is enabled to plunge into group work more quickly. In my view, anxiety caused by deliberate ambiguity is not necessary in order to prevent the group from becoming too socially comfortable. Patients, by definition, are highly conflicted about their interpersonal relationships, and groups which have an increased rate of interpersonal interaction will continually present challenging and anxiety-provoking interpersonal confrontations. Therapy groups which are too comfortable are groups which avoid the task of direct interpersonal confrontation.

Although a systematic consideration of the preparatory process is rare (most group therapy texts omit any mention of it), nevertheless all group therapists do attempt to clarify the therapeutic process and the behavior which is expected of patients; the difference between therapists or between therapeutic schools is largely a difference in timing and style of preparation. Some group therapists initially prepare the new patient by providing him with written material about group therapy,[46] or by having him hear a tape of a model group therapy work meeting,[47] or by having him attend a trial meeting,[48] or by a long series of individual introductory lectures or an instrumented program of therapy and insight aids.[49,50] However, even the therapists who deliberately avoid initial preparation and orientation of the patient nevertheless have in mind goals and preferred modes of group procedure which eventually are transmitted to the patient. By subtle or even subliminal verbal and nonverbal reinforcement, even the most non-directive therapist attempts to persuade his group to accept his values as to what is important and what is unimportant in the group process.[51,52] To cite a clinical example, consider this transcribed statement made in the second meeting by a nondirective British group analyst * who engages in no pretherapy preparation.

Isn't there something noteworthy in what you have done in the last thirty or forty minutes? Because having had this uneasy silence, at first, and then my having commented on that, you began looking at some of the ways that you were facing the problems here . . . it was almost as though you had looked and seen the situation in a more realistic way after that, because since that time you might say you have been exploring each other. You see, Miss H. started to ask Miss A. a lot about herself and this started to show that perhaps you can say something about yourself and people won't be hostile about it. So you could explore each other's attitudes in a way that might even be helpful. But it was quite a striking change from what you had done in the first few minutes, as though you had started a process of, well, perhaps you can feel about each other, perhaps you can think about each other, perhaps you can even look inside each other's thoughts and feelings in a way that might lead to something. Certainly quite a lot of exploration is going on of your own attitudes. This is done in a conventional way up to a point, but perhaps also for the purpose of indicating where you stood with each other, so that you might be more personal about your difficulties.

In this statement the group therapist did much more than merely summarize the events of the previous thirty minutes. He ignored certain activities, he reinforced others, he suggested behavior which would be desirable in future sessions.

Some therapists staunchly oppose preparation of the patient and hold that ambiguity of both patient and therapist role expectation is a desirable condition of the early phases of therapy.[53,54] Their argument is that the development and eventual resolution of patient-therapist transference distortions is a key curative factor in therapy, and that one should seek, in the early stages of therapy, to enhance the development of transference. Enigma, ambiguity, absence of cognitive anchoring, and frustration of conscious and unconscious wishes all facilitate a regressive reaction to the therapist and help create an atmosphere favorable to the development of transference. These therapists wish to encourage such regressive phenomena and the emergence of unconscious impulses so that they may be identified and worked through in therapy.[55]

As I emphasized in Chapter 6, I do not deny the importance of trans-

* Courtesy of Dr. John Sutherland, Tavistock Clinic, London.

ference in the therapy group. The issue is one of priority and technique. Transference is a hardy organism; it takes root and flourishes whether or not we prepare the soil and will not be smothered by adequate preparation for therapy. Furthermore, as we have so often emphasized, transference resolution and interpersonal learning are not the only therapeutic pathways through the therapy group. An opportunity to facilitate the development of the other curative factors should not be sacrificed to the dubious assumption that it would impede the germination of transference.

Two practical observations about preparation are in order. First, the therapist should deliberately repeat and emphasize the essential points of the preparation. Patients, in part because of high anxiety levels immediately before therapy, have an unbelievable tendency to inattend selectively, or to misunderstand key aspects of the therapist's initial comments. Some of my patients have forgotten they were told that observers would be viewing the group through a one-way mirror screen; others who were asked to remain in the group for at least twelve sessions before attempting to evaluate group therapy understood the therapist to say that the group's entire life span would be twelve meetings. Therapists doing time-limited individual therapy often encounter the patient who, toward the end of therapy, denies that the therapist had preset a limited number of sessions.

The second observation is that group therapists often find themselves pressed to find group members. A sudden loss of members may provoke therapists into hasty activity to rebuild the group, often resulting in the selection of unsuitable, inadequately prepared members. The therapist then has to assume the position of selling the group to the patient—a position generally obvious to the patient. The therapist does better to continue the group with reduced membership, to select his additions very carefully, and then to present the group in such a way as to maximize the patient's desire to join the group. In fact, research [56] indicates that the more difficult the entrance procedure and the greater an individual's desire to join, the greater his subsequent attraction to the group. This is the general principle underlying initiation rites to fraternities or arduous selection and admission criteria for many organizations. The applicant cannot but reason that if the group is so difficult to join, it must be very valuable indeed.

REFERENCES

1. R. Adler, "Reporter at Large," *New Yorker*, April 15, 1967, pp. 55–58.
2. *The New York Times*, December 20, 1970.
3. J. Sohl, *The Lemon Eaters* (New York: Simon and Schuster, 1967).
4. F. Stoller, "Marathon Group Therapy," in G. M. Gazda (ed.), *Innovations to Group Psychotherapy* (Springfield, Ill.: Charles C. Thomas, 1968).
5. R. MacGregor, "Multiple Impact Therapy with Families," *Family Process, 1:* 15–29, 1962.
6. E. Mintz, "Time-Extended Marathon Groups," *Psychother. Res. and Practice, 4:* 65–70, 1967.
7. M. Parloff, "Discussion of F. Stoller's Paper," *Int. J. Group Psychother., 18:* 239–244, 1968.
8. B. Navidzadeh, "The Application of Marathon Group Psychotherapy in Outpatient Clinic Settings," paper presented at American Group Psychotherapy Association Convention, Chicago, January 1968.
9. S. B. Lawrence, cited in *Palo Alto Times*, January 3, 1967.
10. F. Stoller, "Accelerated Interaction: A Time-Limited Approach Based on the Brief Intensive Group," *Int. J. Group Psychother., 18:* 220–235, 1968.
11. N. G. Dinges and R. G. Weigel, "The Marathon Group: A Review of Practice and Research," *Comparative Group Studies*, Vol.. 2, No. 4, Nov. 1971, pp. 339–458.
12. G. Bach, "Marathon Group Dynamics," *Psych. Reports, 20:* 1147–1158, 1967.
13. A. W. Rachman, "Marathon Group Psychotherapy" *J. of Group Psychoanalysis and Process, 2:* 57–74, 1969.
14. G. Bach and F. Stoller, "The Marathon Group," cited by N. G. Dinges and R. G. Weigel, *Comparative Group Studies*, Vol. 2, No. 4, Nov. 1971, pp. 339–458.
15. A. D. Sklar, I. D. Yalom, S. M. Zimerberg, and G. L. Newell, "Time-Extended Group Therapy: A Controlled Study," *Comparative Group Studies*, in press.
16. W. F. Hill, *HIM: Hill Interaction Matrix* (Los Angeles: Youth Study Center, University of Southern California, 1965).
17. M. Lorr, "Relation of Treatment Frequency and Duration to Psychotherapeutic Outcome," in H. Strupp and L. Luborsky (eds.), *Conference on Research in Psychotherapy* (Washington, D.C.: American Psychological Association, 1962), pp. 134–141.
18. G. F. Castore, "Number of Verbal Interrelationships as a Determinant of Group Size," *J. Abnorm. Soc. Psychol., 64:* 456–457, 1962.
19. S. E. Asch, "Effects of Group Pressure upon the Modification and Distortion of Judgments," in D. Cartwright and A. Zander (eds.), *Group Dynamics: Research and Theory* (Evanston, Ill.: Row, Peterson, 1962).
20. A. Goldstein, K. Heller, and L. Sechrest, *Psychotherapy and the Psychology of Behavior Change* (New York: John Wiley and Sons, 1966), p. 341.
21. A. P. Hare, *Handbook of Small Group Research* (New York: Free Press of Glencoe, 1962), pp. 224–245.
22. A. P. Hare, "A Study of Interaction and Consensus in Different Sized Groups," *Am. Soc. Rev., 17:* 261–267, 1952.
23. L. F. Carter *et al.*, "The Behavior of Leaders and Other Group Members," *J. Abnorm. Soc. Psychol., 46:* 256–260, 1958.
24. S. H. Foulkes, oral communication, April 1968.
25. A. P. Goldstein, *Therapist/Patient Expectancies in Psychotherapy* (New York: Pergamon Press, 1962).
26. S. Lipkin, "Clients' Feelings and Attitudes in Relation to the Outcome of Client-Centered Therapy," *Psychol. Monogr., 68:* No. 374, 1954.
27. H. L. Lennard and A. Bernstein, *The Anatomy of Psychotherapy* (New York: Columbia University Press, 1960).
28. R. Bednar and G. F. Lawlis, "Empirical Research in Group Therapy," in A. E. Bergin and S. L. Garfield (eds.), *Handbook of Psychotherapy and Behavior Change* (New York: John Wiley & Sons, Inc., 1971).
29. J. Mann, "Evaluation of Group Psychotherapy," in J. L. Moreno (ed.), *The Inter-*

national Handbook of Group Psychotherapy (New York: Philosophical Library, 1966), pp. 129–148.

30. A. Bergin, "The Implications of Psychotherapy Research for Therapeutic Practice," *J. Abnorm. Psychol.*, 71: 235–246, 1966.

31. I. D. Yalom, P. S. Houts, G. Newell, and K. H. Rand, "Preparation of Patients for Group Therapy," *Arch. Gen. Psychiat.*, 17: 416–427, 1967.

32. J. B. Heitler, "Clinical Impressions of an Experimental Attempt to Prepare Lower-Class Patients for Expressive Group Psychotherapy," *Int. J. Group Psychother.*, 29: 308–322, 1974.

33. M. Orne and P. Wender, "Anticipatory Socialization for Psychotherapy: Method and Rationale," *Amer. J. of Psychiatry*, 124: 88–98, 1968.

34. R. Hoehn-Saric, *et al.*, "Systematic Preparation of Patients for Psychotherapy," *J. Psychotherapy Res.*, 2: 267–281, 1964.

35. I. Gradolph, "The Task-Approach of Groups of Single-Type and Mixed-Type Valency Compositions," in D. Stock and H. Thelen (eds.), *Emotional Dynamics and Group Culture* (New York: New York University Press, 1958).

36. D. Stock and J. Luft, "The T-E-T Design," unpublished manuscript (Washington, D.C.: National Training Laboratories, 1960).

37. D. Stock and W. F. Hill, "Intersubgroup Dynamics as a Factor in Group Growth," in Stock and Thelen, *op. cit.*, pp. 207–221.

38. I. L. Janis, *Psychological Stress: Psychoanalytic and Behavioral Studies of Surgical Patients* (New York: John Wiley & Sons, 1958).

39. H. Basowitz *et al.*, *Anxiety and Stress* (New York: McGraw-Hill, 1955).

40. R. W. White, "Motivation Reconsidered: The Concept of Competence," *Psychol. Rev.*, 66: 297–333, 1959.

41. B. H. Rauer and J. Reitsema, "The Effects of Varied Clarity of Group Goal and Group Path Upon the Individual and His Relation to His Group," *Human Relations*, 10: 29–45, 1957.

42. D. M. Wolfe, J. D. Snock, and R. A. Rosenthal, *Report to Company Participants at 1960 University of Michigan Research Project* (Ann Arbor, Mich.: Institute of Social Research, 1961).

43. A. R. Cohen, E. Stotland, and D. M. Wolfe, "An Experimental Investigation of Need for Cognition," *J. Abnorm. Soc. Psychol.*, 51: 291–294, 1955.

44. A. R. Cohen, "Situational Structure, Self-Esteem and Threat-Oriented Reactions to Power," in D. Cartwright (ed.), *Studies in Social Power* (Ann Arbor, Mich.: Research Center for Group Dynamics, 1959), pp. 35–52.

45. Goldstein, Heller, and Sechrest, *op. cit.*, p. 405.

46. H. Martin and K. Shewmaker, "Written Instructions in Group Therapy," *Group Psychother.*, 15: 24, 1962.

47. B. Berzon and L. Solomon, "Research Frontiers: The Self-Directed Group," *J. Counsel. Psychol.*, 13: 491–497, 1966.

48. G. Bach, *Intensive Group Therapy* (New York; Ronald Press, 1954).

49. D. I. Malamud and S. Machover, *Toward Self-Understanding: Group Techniques in Self-Confrontation* (Springfield, Ill.: Charles C. Thomas, 1965).

50. M. D. Bettis, D. Malamud, and R. F. Malamud, "Deepening a Group's Insight into Human Relations," *J. Clin. Psychol.*, 5: 114–122, 1949.

51. Goldstein, Heller, and Sechrest, *op. cit.*, p. 329.

52. E. J. Murray, "A Content Analysis for Study in Psychotherapy," *Psychol. Monogr.*, 70: No. 13, 1956.

53. L. Horwitz, "Transference in Training Groups and Therapy Groups," *Int. J. Group Psychother.*, 14: 202–213, 1964.

54. A. Wolf, "The Psychoanalysis of Groups," in M. Rosenbaum and M. Berger (eds.), *Group Psychotherapy and Group Function* (New York: Basic Books, 1963), pp. 273–328.

55. S. Schiedlinger, "The Concept of Repression in Group Psychotherapy," paper presented at American Group Psychotherapy Association Conference, New York, January 1967.

56. E. Aronson and J. Mills, "The Effect of Severity of Initiation on Liking for a Group," *J. Abnorm. Soc. Psychol.*, 59: 177–181, 1959.

10

IN THE BEGINNING
❦

The work of the group therapist begins long before the first group meeting: indeed, as we have already emphasized, successful group outcome depends largely on the therapist's effective performance of his pretherapy tasks. In previous chapters I have discussed the crucial importance of proper group selection, composition, setting, and preparation. In this chapter I will consider the birth and development of the group: first I will describe the natural history of the therapy group and then problems of attendance, punctuality, membership turnover, and addition of new members—important issues in the life of the developing group.

Formative Stages of the Group

INTRODUCTION

Every group, with its unique cast of characters, all interacting complexly with one another, undergoes a highly individualized development. Each member begins to manifest himself interpersonally and to create his own social microcosm; in time, if the therapist does his job, each will begin to analyze his interpersonal style and eventually to experiment with new behavior. Considering the complexity and richness of human interaction compounded further by the grouping of several individuals with maladaptive styles, it is obvious that the course of the group, over many months or years, will be complex and, to a great degree, unpredictable. Nevertheless, there are mass forces operating in all groups which broadly influence their course of development and which provide us with a crude but nonetheless useful schema of developmental phases.

There are compelling reasons for the therapist to familiarize himself with the developmental sequence of groups. If he is to perform his task of assisting the group to form therapeutic norms and to prevent the establishment of norms which hinder therapy, then obviously the therapist must have a clear conception of the natural, optimal development of the therapy group. If he is to diagnose group blockage and to intervene in such a way as to allow the group to proceed, he must have a sense of favorable and of flawed development. Furthermore, a knowledge of broad developmental sequence will provide the therapist with a sense of mastery and direction in the group, and prevent a feeling of confusion and anxiety, which would only compound similar feelings in the patients.*

Our knowledge of group development stems from a few systematic research inquiries with laboratory task groups and many observational studies of encounter and therapy groups. Although the descriptive language, of course, varies, there is considerable consistency regarding the basic phases of early group development. Broadly, groups go through an initial stage of orientation, characterized by a search for structure and goals, a great dependency on the leader, and a concern about the group boundaries. Next they encounter a stage of conflict, as the group deals with issues of interpersonal dominance. Following this, the group becomes increasingly concerned with intermember harmony and affection, while intermember differences are often submerged in the service of group cohesiveness. Much later, the fully developed work group emerges, which is characterized by high cohesiveness, considerable inter- and intrapersonal investigation, and full commitment to the primary task of the group and of each of the members.

THE FIRST MEETING

The first group therapy session is invariably a success! Patients (and neophyte therapists) generally anticipate the initial meeting with a degree of dread so extreme that it is always allayed by the actual event. Some therapists choose to begin the meeting with a brief intro-

---

* An analogy may be made to the practice of psychoanalysis. There are many reasons for the analyst to be thoroughly familiar with the developmental phases of the analytic process; perhaps one of the more important reasons is that the knowledge forestalls such incapacitating feelings in the analyst as frustration, discouragement, rage, and bewilderment.

ductory statement about the purpose and method of the group (especially if they have not prepared the patients beforehand); others may simply mention one or two basic ground rules—for example, honesty and confidentiality. The therapist may suggest that the members introduce themselves, or he may remain silent. Invariably, some member will suggest that they introduce themselves, and usually within minutes, in American groups, the norm of using first names is established. Following this, a very loud silence ensues, which, like most psychotherapy silences, seems eternal but in actuality lasts only a few seconds. Generally, the silence is broken by the patient destined to dominate the early stages of the group, who will say, "I guess I'll get the ball rolling," or words to that effect. Usually, he then recounts his reasons for seeking therapy, which often elicit similar descriptions from other patients. An alternative course of events occurs when a member (perhaps spurred by the therapist's remark about the tension of the group during the initial silence) comments on his social discomfort or fear of groups. This often stimulates similar comments from other patients about first-level interpersonal pathology.

As I stressed in Chapter 5, the therapist willingly or unwillingly begins to shape the norms of the group at its very conception. Furthermore, he is more efficient in this task when the group is yet young. The first meeting is, therefore, no time for the therapist to be inactive; there are many techniques, some described in Chapter 5, available for effective early intervention.

THE INITIAL STAGE—ORIENTATION, HESITANT PARTICIPATION, SEARCH FOR MEANING

Two tasks confront members of any newly formed group: first, they must determine a method of achieving their primary task—the purpose for which they joined the group; second, they must attend to their social relationships in the group so as to create a niche for themselves which will not only provide the comfort necessary to achieve their primary task but will also result in additional gratification from the sheer pleasure of group membership. In many groups, such as athletic teams, college classrooms, and work details, the primary task and the social task are well differentiated; in therapy groups, although this is not often appreciated at first by members, the tasks are confluent—a fact vastly complicating the group experience of socially ineffective individuals.

Several simultaneous concerns are present in the initial meetings.

Members, especially unprepared members, search for the rationale of therapy; they may be quite confused about the relevance of the group's activities to their personal goals in therapy. The initial meetings are often peppered with questions reflecting this confusion, and even months later members wonder aloud: "How is this going to help? What does all this have to do with my problems?"

At the same time, the members are sizing up one another and the group. They search for a viable role for themselves and wonder if they will be liked and respected or ignored and rejected. Although patients ostensibly come to a therapy group for treatment, social forces are such that they invest most of their energy in a search for approval, acceptance, respect, or domination. To some, acceptance and approval appear so unlikely that they defensively reject or depreciate the group by silently derogating the other members and by reminding themselves that the group is an unreal artificial one, or that they are too special to care about a group membership which requires sacrificing even one particle of their prized individuality. Members wonder what membership entails. What are the admission requirements? How much must one reveal himself or give of himself? What type of commitment must one make? At a conscious or near conscious level they seek the answers to questions such as these and maintain a vigilant search for the types of behavior which the group expects and approves.

If the early group is a puzzled, testing, hesitant group, so too is it a dependent one. Overtly and covertly, members look to the leader for structure and answers, as well as for approval and acceptance. Many of the comments in the group are directed at or through the therapist; surreptitious reward-seeking glances are cast at him, as members demonstrate behavior which in the past has gained approval from authority. The leader's early comments are carefully examined for directives about desirable and undesirable behavior. Patients appear to behave as if salvation emanates solely or primarily from the therapist, if only they can discover what he wants them to do. There is considerable realistic evidence for this belief; the therapist's professional identity as a healer, his host role in providing a room for the group, and his preparing the patients and charging a fee for his services all reinforce the patients' expectations that the therapist will care for them. Some therapists unwittingly compound this belief by behavior which offers unfulfillable promise of succor.

However, the existence of initial dependency cannot be totally accounted for by the situation, by the therapist's behavior, or by a morbid dependency state on the part of the patient. We discussed in

Chapter 6 the many irrational sources of the members' powerful feelings toward the group therapist. Among the strongest of these is man's
need for an omnipotent, omniscient, omnicaring parent, which
together with his infinite capacity for self-deception creates a yearning for and a belief in a superbeing. In young groups the members'
fantasies play in concert to result in what Freud referred to as the
group's "need to be governed by unrestricted force . . . it's extreme
passion for authority . . . it's thirst for obedience." [1] (Yet, who is
God's God? I have often thought that the inordinantly high suicide
rate among psychiatrists [2] was one tragic commentary on this dilemma. Psychotherapists who are deeply depressed and who know
that they must be their own superbeing, their own intercessor, are
more apt to plunge into final despair.)

The content and communicational style of the initial phase is relatively stereotyped and restricted. The social code is consistent with
that of a cocktail party or similar transient social encounters. Problems
are approached rationally; the irrational aspects of the patient who
presents a problem are suppressed in the service of support, etiquette,
and group tranquillity. Semrad [3] suggests the phrase "goblet issues"
to refer to early group communication. The analogy refers to the process of picking up a cocktail goblet at a party and figuratively using it
to peer at and size up the other guests. Thus at first, groups may endlessly discuss topics of apparently little substantive interest to any of
the participants; these "goblet issues," however, serve as vehicles for
the first interpersonal exploratory forays. A member discovers who
responds favorably to him, who sees things the way he does, whom to
fear, whom to respect; gradually he begins to formulate a picture of
the role he will play in the group. These "goblet issues" in social settings include such burning subjects as the weather, "Do you know
what's-his-name?" and "Where are you from?" In therapy groups
symptom description is a favorite early issue, along with previous
therapy experience, medications, and the like.

One common process of early groups is the search for similarities.
Patients are intrigued by the notion that they are not unique in their
misery, and most groups invest considerable energy in demonstrating
how the members are similar. This process often offers considerable
relief to members (see the discussion of "universality," Chapter 1)
and provides part of the foundation on which group cohesiveness will
be erected.

Giving and seeking advice is another characteristic of the early
group; patients present the group with the problems of dealing with
their spouses, children, employers, etc.; the group then attempts to

provide some type of practical solution. As we discussed it in Chapter 1, this guidance rarely is of any functional value but serves as a vehicle through which members can express mutual interest and caring.

Many of these concerns are so characteristic of the initial stage of therapy that their presence can be used to estimate the age of a group. If, for example, one observes a group in which there is considerable advice giving and seeking, a search for similarities, symptom description, the meaning of therapy, and "goblet issues," then one may conclude that the group is either a very young one or an older group with a serious maturational block.

SECOND STAGE—CONFLICT, DOMINANCE, REBELLION

If the first core concern of the group is with "in or out," then the next is with "top or bottom." [4] The group shifts from preoccupation with acceptance, approval, commitment to the group, definitions of accepted behavior, and the search for orientation, structure, and meaning to a preoccupation with dominance, control, and power. The conflict characteristic of this phase is between members or between members and the leader. Each member attempts to establish for himself his preferred amount of initiative and power, and gradually a control hierarchy, a social pecking order, is established.

Negative comments and intermember criticism are more frequent; members often appear to feel entitled to a one-way analysis and judgment of others.[5] As in the first stage, advice is given but in the context of a different social code; social conventions are abandoned and members feel free to make personal criticism about the complainant's behavior or attitudes. Judgments are made of past and present life experiences and styles; it is a time of "oughts" and "shoulds" in the group, a time when the "peer-court," as Bach [5] phrased it, is in session. Members make suggestions or give advice, not as a manifestation of acceptance and understanding—sentiments yet to emerge in the group—but as part of the process of jockeying for position.

The struggle for control is part of the infrastructure of every group: it is always present, sometimes quiescent, sometimes smoldering, sometimes in full conflagration. If there are members with strong needs to dominate, it may be the major theme of the early meetings. The dormant struggle for control often becomes more overt when new members are added to the group, especially new members who do not "know their place" and, instead of making obeisance to the older members in accordance with their seniority, make strong early bids for dominance.

The emergence of hostility toward the therapist is an inevitable occurrence in the life sequence of the group. A large number of observers have emphasized an early stage of ambivalence to the therapist coupled with a resistance to self-examination and self-disclosure.[5,6,7,8] In a research project previously described (Chapter 5), Liberman [9] attempted, through social reinforcement, to hasten therapeutic group development. He chose to reinforce two types of behavior, each of which reflects a "widely accepted" task of the early group. The "expression of hostility toward the leader" was one of the two behaviors chosen for reinforcement. (The other was the expression of intermember concern and acceptance, which will be discussed in our consideration of the next phase.)

The sources of hostility toward the leader are obvious when we recall the unrealistic, indeed magical, attributes with which patients secretly imbue the therapist. Their expectations are so limitless that, regardless of the therapist's competence, he will disappoint them; gradually, as the recognition of his limitations becomes apparent, the process of disenthrallment commences. By no means is this a clearly conscious process; the members may intellectually advocate a democratic group which draws on its own resources but nevertheless may, on a deeper level, crave dependency and attempt first to create and then to destroy an authority figure. Group therapists refuse to fill the traditional authority role: they do not lead in the ordinary manner, they do not provide answers and solutions, they urge the group to explore and to employ its own resources. The members' wish lingers, however, and it is usually only after several sessions that the group comes to realize that the therapist will frustrate their yearning for an "old time" leader.

Yet another source of resentment toward the leader derives from the gradual recognition by each member that he will not be the leader's favorite child. During the pretherapy session, each member comes to harbor the fantasy that the therapist is his very own therapist, intensely interested in the finest details of his past, his present, and his fantasy world. In the early meetings of the group, however, each member begins to realize that the therapist is no more interested in him than in the others; seeds are sown for the emergence of rivalrous, hostile feelings toward the other members. The therapist, in some unclear manner, is thought to have been deceitful.

These unrealistic expectations of the leader and consequent disenchantment are by no means a function of childlike mentality or psychological naïveté. The same phenomenon occurs, for example, in groups of professional psychotherapists. In fact, there is no better way for the trainee to appreciate the group's proclivity both to elevate and to attack the leader than to experience the feelings as a group member.

Some workers [10] who have taken Freud's *Totem and Taboo* [11] extremely literally regard the group's pattern of relationship with the leader as a recapitulation of the primal horde patricide. Freud does indeed suggest at one point that modern group phenomena have their prehistoric analogues in the ancient, misty events of the primal horde: "Thus the group appears to us as a revival of the primal horde. Just as primitive man survives potentially in every individual, so the primal horde may arise once more out of any random collection; insofar as men are habitually under the sway of group formation, we recognize in it the survival of the primal horde." [11] The primal horde, not unlike the chorus in Sophocles' *Oedipus Tyrannus,* is able to free itself from restrictive growth-inhibiting bonds and progress to a more satisfying existence only after the awesome leader has been removed.[12,13]

The patients are never unanimous in their attack upon the therapist; invariably, some champions of the therapist will emerge from the group. The lineup of attackers and defenders may serve as a valuable guide for the understanding of characterologic trends useful for future work in the group. Generally, the leaders of this phase, those members who are earliest and most vociferous in their attack, are heavily conflicted in the area of dependency and have dealt with intolerable dependency yearnings by reaction formation. These individuals, sometimes labeled counterdependents, [14] are inclined to reject prima facie all statements by the therapist and to entertain the fantasy of unseating and replacing the leader.

For example, in the first meeting of a group I asked, at approximately three-fourths of the way through the session, for the members' reflections on the meeting; how had it gone for them? disappointments? surprises? One member who was to control the direction of the group for the next several weeks commented that it had gone precisely as he had expected; in fact, it had been almost disappointingly predictable. The strongest feeling, he added, he had had thus far was one of anger toward me because I had asked one of the members a question that evoked a brief period of weeping. He had felt then, "They'll never break *me* down like that." His first impressions were very predictive of his behavior for quite some time to come. He strove to be never surprised, to be self-possessed and in control at all times. He regarded me not as an ally but as an adversary and was sufficiently forceful to lead the group into a major emphasis on control issues for the first months. If therapy is to be successful, counterdependent members must at some point experience their flip side and recognize and work through deep dependency cravings.

There are other members who immediately side with the therapist; they must be helped to investigate their need to defend him at all costs, regardless of the issue involved. Occasionally, patients defend the therapist because they have encountered a series of unreliable objects and misperceive him as extraordinarily frail; others need to preserve him because they fantasy an eventual alliance with him against other powerful members of the group. The therapist must beware lest he unknowingly transmit covert signals of personal distress to which the rescuers appropriately respond. Many of these conflicted feelings crystallize around the issue of the leader's name. Is he to be referred to by professional title (Dr. Jones or, even more impersonally, "the Doctor") or is he to be called by his first name? Some patients will use the therapist's first name or even a diminutive of the name immediately, before inquiring as to the therapist's preference. Others, even after the therapist has indicated that he feels entirely comfortable on a first name basis, still cannot bring themselves to mouth such irreverence and continue to separate themselves from him with the bundling of a professional title.

Although we have posited disenchantment and anger with the leader as an ubiquitous feature of small groups, by no means is the process constant across groups in form or degree. The therapist's behavior may potentiate or mitigate both the experience and the expression of rebellion. Thus, one prominent sociologist who has for many years led sensitivity training groups of college students reports that inevitably there is a powerful insurrection against the leader, culminating in his being removed bodily by the members from the group room.[15] I, on the other hand, have led similar groups for more than a decade and have never encountered a rebellion which was so extreme that members physically ejected me from the room. Such a difference can only be due to differences in leader styles and behavior. Invoking greater negative response are those therapists who are ambiguous or deliberately enigmatic, who are authoritative yet offer no structure or guidelines for patients, and who covertly make unfulfillable promises to the group early in therapy.

This stage is often difficult and personally unpleasant for group therapists. The neophyte therapist should be reminded, however, that he is essential to the survival of the group; the members cannot afford to liquidate him and he will always be defended. However, for his own comfort, he must learn to discriminate between an attack on his person and an attack on his role in the group. The group's response to the leader is similar to transference distortion in individual therapy in that it is not directly related to his behavior, but its source in the group must be understood both from an individual psychodynamic and from a group dynamic viewpoint.

Therapists who are particularly threatened by a group attack protect themselves in a variety of ways. Once I was asked to act as a consultant for two therapy groups, each approximately twenty-five sessions old, which had developed similar problems: both groups seemed to have reached a plateau, no new ground appeared to have been broken for several weeks, and the patients seemed to have withdrawn interest in the groups. A study of current meetings and past protocols revealed that neither group had yet directly dealt with any negative feelings toward the therapists. However, the reason for this inhibition was quite different in the two groups. In the first group, the two co-therapists (who were leading their first group) had rather clearly shown their throats, as it were, to the group and through their obvious anxiety, uncertainty, and avoidance of hostility-laden issues had pleaded frailty. In addition, they both desired to be loved by all the members and had been at all times so benevolent and so solicitous that an attack by the patients would have appeared unseemly and ungrateful.

The therapists of the second group had forestalled an attack in quite a different fashion: they remained aloof Olympian figures whose infrequent interventions were oracular in their ambiguity and ostensible profundity. At the end of each meeting they summarized the predominant themes and each member's contributions. To attack them would have been perilous as well as impious and futile. In the words of one patient, "It would have resembled shaking one's fist at a lofty mountain peak."

These developments are inhibitory for the group; suppression of important ambivalent feelings about the therapist results in the formation of a counter-productive taboo which opposes the desired norm of interpersonal honesty and emotional expressivity. Furthermore, an important model-setting opportunity is lost; the therapist who withstands an attack without being either destroyed or destructive in retaliation but instead responds by attempting to understand and work through the sources and effects of the attack demonstrates to the group that aggression need not be lethal and that it can be expressed and understood in the group.

One of the consequences of suppression of therapist-directed anger for the two groups in question, and for most groups, is the emergence of displaced, off-target aggression. For example, one group persisted for several weeks in attacking "doctors." Previous unfortunate experiences with doctors, hospitals, and individual therapists were described in detail, often with considerable group consensus on the injustices and inhumanity of the medical profession. In one group, a member attacked the field of psychotherapy by bringing in an article by Eysenck which purported to prove that psychotherapy is ineffective. At other times, police, teachers, and other representatives of authority are awarded similar treatment.

Scapegoating of other members is another "off-target" manifestation and may reach such proportions that unless the therapist intervenes to direct the attack onto himself, the sacrificial patient may be driven from the group. Other groups covertly appoint a leader from their ranks to replace the therapist—always an unsatisfactory process which leaves the group and the patient-leader discouraged and confused. Sensitivity training groups usually resolve the issue by defining the leader's role as that of a specialized member with certain technical skills. It is hoped that the group will learn to evaluate his contributions for their intrinsic value rather than to accept them because of the authority behind them. Therapy groups do not resolve the problem for many months or years; again and again the group returns to the issue as members at a differential rate, according to their degree of dependency conflict, gradually work through their attitudes toward the therapist. It is essential, if this work is to be done, that the group feel free to confront the therapist, who must not only permit, but encourage, such confrontation.

THIRD STAGE—DEVELOPMENT OF COHESIVENESS

The third widely recognized phase of the early formative group is the development of group cohesiveness. Following the previous period of conflict, the group gradually develops into a cohesive unit. Many varied phrases with similar connotations have been used to describe this phase: in-group consciousness; [14,16] common goal and group spirit; [17,18] consensual group action, cooperation, and mutual support; [7,19] group integration and mutuality; [20,21,22,23] we-consciousness unity; [24] external rivalry; [8] and support and freedom of communication.[25] During this phase there is an increase of morale, mutual trust, and self-disclosure. Some members reveal the "real" reason why they have come for treatment; sexual secrets may be shared, long-buried past transgressions are publicly unearthed. Post-group coffee meetings may be arranged; attendance improves and patients evince considerable concern about missing members.

The chief concern of the group is with intimacy and closeness. Schutz,[4] who characterizes patients' concerns in the first phase as "in or out" and in the second as "top or bottom," characterizes the third phase as "near or far"; the primary anxieties have to do with not being liked or close enough to people, or with being too intimate.

Although there may be greater freedom of self-disclosure in this phase, there may also be communicational restrictions of another sort: often the group suppresses all expression of negative affect in the service of cohesion. Compared with the previous stage of group conflict, all is sweetness and light, and the group basks in the glow of its newly discovered unity. The members, in a sense, unite against the rest of the world, with much intermember support, much pride in the group, and much condemnation of the members' adversaries outside the group. Eventually, however, the glow will pale and the group embrace will seem ritualistic unless the hostility in the group is permitted to emerge. Only when all affects can be expressed and constructively worked through in a cohesive group does the group become a mature work group—a state lasting for the remainder of the group's life, with periodic short-lived recrudescences of each of the earlier phases. To underscore this transition, some have suggested a division of this stage into two: a stage of cohesiveness (group against the external world) and a stage of advanced group work or true teamwork in which the tension is between "work," or progress, and regression to an earlier stage.[8]

DEVELOPMENTAL STAGES—OVERVIEW

Now that we have outlined the early stages of group development, let us consider a series of qualifying conditions lest the novice take the proposed developmental sequence too literally. The developmental phases are rarely well demarcated; there is considerable overlap and the boundaries between them are, at best, dim. The evidence for developmental stages of therapy groups stems from nonsystematic clinical observational studies—virtually no controlled research exists which substantiates this developmental sequence. Group developmental research in sensitivity groups has been rudimentary and inconclusive. For example, Bennis *et al.*[26] in a study of six sensitivity groups, tested the hypothesis that the groups would move through two developmental phases: a primary concern with authority and then a primary concern with intimacy. Of these six groups studied, only one showed such a sequence; the other five showed a continuous dealing and redealing with the two problems. More confirmatory evidence arises from research with task groups. For example, Runkel et al.[27] studied twelve small groups who had the task of designing and executing some project related to the relationship between social conditions and learning on a university campus. Results indicated that the groups progressed cyclically through Tuckman's [6] stages of: (1) testing and dependence, (2) intragroup conflict, (3) group cohesion, and (4) functional role-relatedness (mature problem-solving group).

Rarely does the group permanently graduate from one phase. In describing group development, Schutz [4] uses the apt metaphor of tightening the bolts one after another just enough so that the wheel is in place; then the process is repeated, each bolt tightened in turn, until the wheel is entirely secure. In a similar way, phases of a group emerge, become dominant, and then recede, only to have the group return again later to deal with the same issues with greater thoroughness. Perhaps, given these considerations, it would be more accurate to speak of developmental tasks rather than developmental phases or developmental sequence. Hamburg [28] suggests the term "cyclotherapy" to refer to this process of returning to the same issues but each time from a different perspective and each time in greater depth. Often, the therapy group will spend considerable time discussing some issue, such as fees, student observers in the group, the relationship between the co-therapists, and then, months later, return to the same topic yet from an entirely different perspective. Thus, observers may be discussed at first as a threat to confidentiality; later they may be attacked as agents of the therapists who enjoy a greater degree of the therapist's confidence; later the group may sincerely consider formats by which the members may profit from the knowledge, expertise, or special vantage point of the observers.

The determination of the natural history of the therapy group is made even more complex when one considers that leaders may anticipate a certain development phase and, unbeknownst to themselves, firmly guide the group through the predicted stages. Lieberman [29] demonstrated that the leader unknowingly fills a gap in the group. He systematically composed a T-group from which were excluded all individuals with a need for pairing behavior and compared its development during a three-week human relations laboratory with a control group, a naturally composed group. He found that the leaders of the control group expressed the same amount of pairing behavior throughout the course of the group; however, the leader of the experimental group expressed five times more pairing in the third week than in the first. Apparently, he was attempting to fill the need for warmth which had developed in the experimental group. With no control over the highly influential behavior of the leader, the determination of the "natural" developmental sequence becomes very difficult indeed.

A study by Psathas and Hardert [30] is illustrative of the quandary posed for researchers. They collected the group leaders' statements which the members had considered most significant in the initial, middle, and late stages of a sensitivity group and found that statements concerned with acceptance were far more frequent in the final stages than in earlier stages.* However, the interpretation of these results is problematic. It is possible that the members were indeed intrinsically more concerned with affection late in the course of the group and the leaders' statements about intimacy were simply a reflection of this trend. However, it is also possible that the leaders had predetermined that intimacy should be dealt with in the last part of the group and thus influenced the group by making a large number of statements to that effect.

Impact of the Patients on Group Development. The developmental sequence I have described perhaps accurately portrays the unfolding of events in a theoretical, unpeopled therapy group. This developmental scheme is much like the major theme of an ultramodern symphony which is unintelligible to the untrained ear. In the group, the obfuscation derives from the richness and unpredictability of human interaction, which complicates the course of treatment and yet contributes to the excitement and challenge of the therapy group.

Generally, the course of events in the early meetings is heavily influenced by the group member with the "loudest" interpersonal pathology. By "loudest" I refer not to severity of pathology but to pathology which is most immediately manifest in the group: for example, monopolistic proclivities, exhibitionism, promiscuous self-disclosure, easily expressed anger, judgmentalism, or an unbridled inclination to exert control. Not infrequently these patients receive covert encouragement from the therapist and the other group members. The therapists value these patients because they provide a focus of irritation in the group, stimulate the expression of affect, and enhance the interest

---

* Seven two-week training groups at the human relations laboratory were studied, all sessions were recorded, and members at the end of each session were asked to recall the leaders' statements which seemed most significant. The verbatim statement was then transcribed from the tape and categorized according to a list of twelve norm categories selected from the literature. In the early and middle stages "acceptance" was ranked fourth, whereas in the final stage it was ranked first of the twelve categories.

and excitement of the meeting. The other patients initially often welcome the opportunity to hide behind the protagonist as they themselves hesitantly examine the terrain.

In a study of the therapy dropouts of nine outpatient groups,[31] I found that in five groups a patient with a very characteristic pattern of behavior fled the therapy group within the first dozen meetings. These patients ("early provocateurs") differed from one another dynamically but assumed a similar role in the group; they stormed in, furiously activated the group, and then vanished. The therapists described their role in the group in such terms as "catalysts," "targets," "hostile interpreters," "the only honest one," etc. Some of these early provocateurs were active counterdependents and challenged the therapist early in the group. One, for example, who asked in the third meeting why the session has to end when the therapist decrees, attempted to rally interest in a leaderless meeting or, only half-jokingly, in an investigation of the leader's personal problems. Others prided themselves on their honesty and bluntness, mincing no words in giving the other members candid feedback; while others, heavily conflicted in intimacy, both seeking it and fearing it, engaged in considerable self-disclosure and exhorted the group to reciprocate. Although the early provocateurs usually claimed that they were impervious to the opinions and evaluations of others, in fact they cared very much, and in each instance deeply regretted the nonviable role they had created for themselves in the group.

The therapist must recognize this phenomenon early in the group and, through clarification and interpretation of their role, help prevent them from committing social suicide. Perhaps, even more importantly, he must recognize and discontinue his own covert encouragement of their behavior. It is not uncommon for the therapist to be stunned at the early provocateur's dropping out; he so welcomed the behavior of these patients that he failed to appreciate both their distress and his own dependence on them for keeping the group alive. It is useful for the therapist to take note of his reactions to the absence of the various members of his group. (If some patients are never absent, he may fantasize their absences and his reaction to it.) If he dreads the absence of certain patients, if he feels there would be no life in the group that day, then it is likely that there is too much burden on that patient and so much secondary gratification that the patient will not be able to deal with his primary task in therapy.

The development of a group may also be heavily influenced by the presence of members who are experienced therapy group patients. For example, one group which had shrunk to a size of three members was rebuilt after a three-month summer vacation by adding four new members (none of whom had ever been in a group before) and a new co-therapist. The three members were powerful culture bearers who enabled the group and the new members to move very quickly, by-passing such early developmental stages as symptom description, suggestions and advice, and search for structure.

Despite these shortcomings, the proposed developmental sequence has much to recommend it. Common sense decrees that a group first deal with its raison d'être and boundaries, then with dominance and submission, and later, as shared experience increases, with issues of intimacy and closeness. Some time ago at a two-week group workshop I took part in an intergroup exercise in which the sixty participants were asked to form four groups in any manner they wished and then to study the ongoing relationships between groups. The sixty partici-pants, in near panic, stampeded from the large room toward the four rooms designated for the four small groups. The panic, an inevitable part of this exercise,[32] probably stems from primitive fears of exclu-sion from the group. In the group in which I participated, the first words spoken after approximately sixteen members had entered the room were, "Close the door. Don't let anyone else in!" The first act of the group was to appoint an official doorkeeper. Once the group's boundaries were defined and its identity vis-à-vis the outside world established, the group turned its attention to regulating the distribu-tion of power by speedily, before multiple bids for power could im-mobilize the group, electing a chairman. Only much later did the group experience and discuss feelings of trust and intimacy.

Once the therapist has a concept of the developmental sequence, he is more easily able to maintain his objectivity and to appreciate the course the group pursues despite considerable yawing. He may note that the group never progresses past a certain stage or may omit oth-ers. At times, therapists may demand something for which the group is not yet ready. For example, some neophyte therapists feel angry at the group members for their seeming lack of concern for one another. One student therapist compared the members of his group to the thirty-eight silent witnesses [33] who, several years ago in New York City, remained uninvolved as they witnessed a young woman being mur-dered. What he did not appreciate is that mutual caring and concern develop late in the group; in the beginning, members are more apt to view one another as interlopers or rivals for the royal touch of the ther-apist.

Membership: Dropouts, Absences, Tardiness, Addition of New Members

The early developmental sequence of the therapy group is heavily influenced by membership problems. Turnover in membership, tardiness, and absence are facts of life in the developing group and often
threaten its stability and integrity. Considerable absenteeism may redirect the group's attention and energy from its developmental tasks
to the problem of maintaining membership. It is the therapist's task to
discourage irregular attendance and, when necessary, to replace dropouts by adding new members.

MEMBERSHIP TURNOVER

In the normal course of events, 10 to 35 percent of the members
drop out of the group in the first twelve to twenty meetings; if two or
more members drop out, new members are usually added and often a
similar percentage of these additions drop out in their first dozen or so
meetings. Only after this does the group solidify and begin to engage
in matters other than those which concern group stability. Generally,
by the time patients have remained in the group for approximately
twenty meetings, they have made the necessary long-term commitment. In one attendance study [34] of five outpatient groups, there was
considerable turnover in membership over the first twelve meetings, a
settling in between the twelfth and twentieth, and near-perfect attendance, with excellent punctuality and no dropouts, between the twentieth and forty-fifth meetings (the end of the study).

ATTENDANCE AND PUNCTUALITY

Despite the therapist's initial encouragement of regular attendance
and punctuality, difficulties usually arise in the early stages of the
group. At times the therapist, buffeted by gusts of excuses—baby-
sitting problems, vacations, transportation difficulties, work emergencies, out-of-town guests, etc.—becomes resigned to the impossibility
of synchronizing the schedules of seven busy individuals. Resist that
conclusion! Tardiness and irregular attendance usually signify resistance to therapy and should be regarded in the same way in which one

regards these phenomena in individual therapy. When several members are often late or absent, one must look for the source of the group resistance; for some reason, cohesiveness is limited and the group is foundering. When a group has solidified into a hard-working cohesive group, many months may go by with perfect attendance and punctuality.

At other times, the resistance is individual rather than group based. I am continually amazed by the transformation which occurs in some patients who for long periods of time are tardy because of absolutely unavoidable contingencies—for example, periodic business conferences, classroom rescheduling, baby-sitting emergencies. These patients, after recognizing and working through the resistance, may become the most punctual members for months on end. Thus, one periodically late member hesitated to involve himself in the group because of his shame about his impotence and homosexual fantasies. After he disclosed these concerns and worked through his feelings of shame, he found that the crucial high-priority business commitments responsible for his lateness (commitments, which he later disclosed, consisted of perusing his afternoon mail) suddenly ceased to exist.

Whatever the basis for resistance, it is behavior which must, for several reasons, be modified before it can be understood and worked through. For one thing, irregular attendance is destructive to the group; it is, in a sense, contagious and begets group demoralization and further absences. Obviously, it is impossible to work on an issue in the absence of the relevant patients; there are few exercises more futile than addressing the wrong audience by deploring irregular attendance with the group members who are present—the regular, punctual patients.

Various methods of influencing the attendance rate have been adopted by various therapists. Many stress the importance of regular attendance during pretherapy interviews. Patients who appear likely to have scheduling or transportation problems are best referred for individual therapy, as are patients who must be out of town every four weeks or who, a few weeks after the group begins, plan an extended out-of-town vacation. Charging full fees for missed sessions is standard practice unless there is an extraordinary excuse for absence explained to the therapist well in advance. Many group therapists charge patients a set fee per month, which is not reduced for missed meetings regardless of the reason.

It is extremely important that the therapist himself be utterly convinced of the importance of the therapy group and of regular attendance. If so, and if he acts accordingly, he will transmit these values to the patients. Thus, he arrives punctually, awards the group high priority in his own schedule, and, if he must be absent, takes his own absence seriously and informs the group weeks in advance. The importance he places on attendance may be manifested in his reactions to a number of group situations. For example, in a new group one member, Dan, was consistently late or absent. Whenever the therapists discussed his attendance, it was clear that Dan had exceedingly valid excuses: his life and his business were in such crisis that unexpected circumstances repeatedly arose that made attendance impossible. The group as a whole had not jelled; despite the therapist's efforts, other members were often late or absent and there was considerable flight during the sessions. At the twelfth meeting the therapist decided that decisive action was necessary, and he asked Dan to leave the group, explaining that Dan's schedule was such that the group could be of little value to him. He suggested to Dan that he seek individual therapy which would provide greater scheduling flexibility. Although the therapist's motives were not punitive ones and although he was thorough in his explanation and offered to arrange a referral, his action was an unpopular one. Dan was deeply offended and, in anger, walked out midway through the meeting; the other members, extremely threatened, supported Dan to the point of questioning the therapist's authority to ask a member to leave.

Despite this initial reaction of the group, it was soon clear that the therapist had made the proper intervention. The therapist phoned Dan and saw him individually for a few sessions and then referred him for long-term therapy. Dan soon appreciated that the therapist was acting, not punitively, but in his best interests. Irregular attendance at a therapy group would not have been effective therapy for him. The group was immediately affected. Attendance abruptly improved and remained near-perfect over the next several months. The members, once they had recovered from their fear of similar banishment, gradually disclosed their approval of the therapist's act and their great resentment toward Dan and, to a lesser extent, toward some of the other members for having treated the group in such a cavalier fashion.

Other therapists attempt to harness group pressure by, for example, refusing to hold the meeting until a predetermined number of members (usually three or four) are present. Even if not formalized in this manner, the pressure exerted by the other members is the most effective lever brought to bear on errant members. The group is often frustrated and angered by the repetitions and false starts necessitated by irregular attendance; the therapist should encourage the members to express their reactions to late or absent members. Be mindful, though, that the therapist's concern about attendance is not always shared by the members; a young or immature group often welcomes the small meeting, regarding it as an opportunity for more individualized attention from the leader.

Like any event in the group, absences or latenesses are forms of behavior which reflect the individual's characteristic patterns of relating to others. If he comes late, does he apologize? Does he enter in an obtrusive, exhibitionistic manner? Does he ask for a recap of the events of the meeting? Is his relation with the group such that they provide him with a recap? If he is absent, does he phone in advance to let the group know? Does he offer complex overelaborate excuses as though he is convinced he will not be believed? Not infrequently, the patient's psychopathology is responsible for poor attendance. For example, one patient who sought therapy because of a crippling fear of authority figures and a pervasive inability to assert himself in interpersonal situations was frequently late because he was unable to muster the courage to interrupt a conversation or conference with a business associate.

Thus, this behavior is part of the patient's social microcosm and, if handled properly, may be harnessed in the service of self-understanding; but for both the group's and the individual's sake it must be corrected before being analyzed. No interpretation can be heard by the absent patient. In fact, the therapist must time his comments to the returning patient with care. Often patients who have been absent or late return to the meeting with some defensive guilt and are not in an optimal state of receptiveness for observations about their behavior. It is as if they experience a recrudescence of archaic concerns about arriving late at school and have an expectational set of being scolded or punished. The therapist often does well to attend to his group maintenance and norm-setting tasks first and then, later, when the timing seems right and defensiveness diminished, attempt to help the patient explore the meaning of his behavior.

It is helpful to the group if patients phone the therapist in advance, should they find they must miss a meeting or arrive late; without this notification the group may spend considerable time expressing curiosity or concern about the missing member. Often, in advanced groups, the fantasies of the patients about why a member is absent provide the group with valuable material for the therapeutic process; however, in early groups the speculations are often superficial and unfruitful.

Occasionally, though, the absence of members may result in certain important shifts of behavior and in the emergence and expression of feelings which facilitate therapy.

For example, a group composed of four women and three men met for its eighth meeting one day when two of the men were unable to attend. Albert, the remaining male, had previously been withdrawn and submissive in the group. In the meeting in which he was alone with the four women, a dramatic transformation occurred: Albert suddenly erupted into activity, talked about himself, questioned the other members, spoke loudly and forcefully, and on a couple of occasions challenged the therapist. His nonverbal behavior was saturated with quasi-courtship bids directed at the women members—for example, frequent adjustment of his necktie knot and preening of the hair at his temples. Later in the course of the meeting the group focused on Albert's change, and he realized and expressed his fear and envy of the two missing males, both of whom were aggressive, assertive men. He had long experienced a pervasive sense of social and sexual impotence which had been reinforced by his feeling that he had never made a significant impact on the group of people and especially a group of women. In subsequent weeks Albert did much valuable work on these issues—issues which might not have become accessible for many months without the adventitious absence of the two other members.

My clinical preference is to encourage attendance in most of these ways but never, regardless of how small the group, to cancel a session. There is considerable therapeutic value in the patients' knowing that the group is always there, stable and reliable; its constancy will in time beget constancy of attendance. Furthermore, I have had many group sessions with small membership, even at times with a single member, that have proven to be critical meetings for the patients involved. The technical problem with small meetings, especially of three or fewer members, is that the therapist may revert to focusing on intrapsychic processes in a manner characteristic of individual therapy and abandon his focus on group and interpersonal issues. It is far more therapeutically consistent and technically undemanding to focus in depth on group and interpersonal processes even in the smallest of sessions. Consider the following clinical example from a ten-month-old group:

For various reasons—vacations, illnesses, and resistance—only two members (and the therapist) attended: Mary, a thirty-eight-year-old depressed borderline schizophrenic, who on two previous occasions had required hospitalization; and Edward, a twenty-three-year-old schizoid, psychosexually immature individual with moderately severe ulcerative colitis.

Mary spent much of the early part of the meeting describing the depth of her despair, which during the past week had reached such proportions that she had been preoccupied with suicide and, since the group therapist had been out of town, had visited the emergency room at the hospital. While there, she had surreptitiously read her medical chart and seen a consultation note written a year previously by the group therapist in which he had diagnosed her as borderline schizophrenic. She said that she had been anticipating this diagnosis and now wished the therapist to hospitalize her. Edward then recalled a fragment of a dream which he had dreamed several weeks before but had not discussed: the therapist was sitting at a large desk interviewing him; he, Edward, stood up and looked at the paper on which the therapist was writing. There he saw in huge letters one word which covered the entire page: IMPOTENT. The therapist helped him to discuss their feelings of awe, helpless dependence, and resentment toward him, as well as their inclination to shift responsibility and project their bad feelings about themselves onto him.

Mary proceeded to underscore her helplessness by describing her inability to cook for herself and her delinquency in paying her bills, which was so extreme that she now feared police action against her. The therapist and Edward both commented on her persistent reluctance to comment on her positive accomplishments—for example, her continued high-level performance in her teaching profession. The therapist wondered if her presentation of herself as helpless was not designed to elicit responses of caring and concern from the other members and the therapist, which she felt would not be forthcoming in any other way.

Edward then mentioned that he had gone to the medical library the previous day to read some of the therapist's professional articles. In response to the therapist's question about what he really wanted to find out, Edward answered that he guessed he really wanted to know how the therapist felt about him and later described, for the first time, his longing for the therapist's sole attention and love.

Later the therapist expressed his dismay at Mary's reading his note in her medical record. Since there is a realistic component to a patient's anxiety upon learning that her therapist has diagnosed her as "borderline schizophrenic," the therapist discussed, quite candidly, his own discomfort at having to use diagnostic labels for hospital records and conveyed to the patient the confusion surrounding psychiatric nosological terminology; he recalled as best he could his reasons for using that particular label and its implications.

Mary then commented upon the absent members and wondered if she had driven them from the group (a common reaction to the absence of members). She dwelled on her unworthiness and, at the therapist's suggestion, made an inventory of her baleful characteristics, citing her slovenliness, selfishness, greed, envy, and hostile feelings toward all those in her social environment. Edward both supported Mary and resonated with her by identifying many of these feelings in himself. He discussed how difficult it was for him to reveal himself in the group (Edward had disclosed very little of himself previously in the group). Later he discussed his fear of getting drunk or losing control in other ways; for one thing he might become indiscreet sexually. Edward then discussed, for the first time, his fear of sex, his impotence, his inability to maintain an erection, and his last-minute refusals to take advantage of sexual opportunities. Mary empathized deeply with Edward and, although she had for some time regarded sex as abhorrent, expressed the strong feeling that she would like to help him by offering herself to him sexually. Edward then described his strong sexual attraction to Mary, and later both he and Mary discussed their sexual feelings toward the other members of the group. The therapist made the observation, one which proved subsequently to be of great therapeutic importance to Mary, that her interest in Edward and her desire to offer herself to him sexually belied many of the items in her inventory: her selfishness, greed, and ubiquitous hostility to others.

The aspects of this meeting relevant to the present discussion are self-evident. Although only two members were present, they met as a group and not as two individual patients. The other members were discussed *in absentia*, and previously undisclosed interpersonal feelings between the two patients and toward the therapist were expressed and analyzed. It was a valuable session, deeply meaningful to both participants.

THE ADDITION OF NEW MEMBERS

Whenever the group census falls to undesirably low levels (generally five or less), the therapist should introduce new members. This may occur at any time during the course of the group, but often there are major junctures in the group when new parients are added: during the first twelve to twenty meetings (to replace early dropouts) and after approximately one and a half years (to replace improved, graduating members).

Timing. The success of this operation depends, in part, upon proper timing; there are favorable and unfavorable times to introduce new members into a group. Generally, a group which is in crisis, or is actively engaged in an internecine struggle, or has suddenly entered into a new phase of development is an unfavorable group for the addition of new members; often it will reject the newcomers or else will evade confrontation with the pressing group issue and instead redirect its energy toward the incoming members. An example might be a group which is, for the first time, dealing with hostile feelings toward a controlling, monopolistic patient or a group which has recently developed such cohesiveness and trust that a member has, for the first time, shared an extremely important secret with the group. Some therapists postpone the addition of new members even when the census of the group is down to four or five if the group is working well. I prefer not to delay and promptly begin to screen prospective candidates. Small groups, even highly cohesive ones, will eventually grow smaller yet through absences or termination and soon the group will lack the interactional interplay necessary for effective work.

The most auspicious period for adding new members is during a phase of stagnation in the group. Many groups, especially older ones, sensing the need for new stimulation, actively encourage the therapist to add members.

Response of the Group. A *Punch* cartoon, cited by Foulkes,[35] portrays a harassed woman and her child trying to push their way into a crowded train compartment. The child looks up at his mother and says, "Don't worry, Mother, at the next stop it will be our turn to hate!" The parallel to new patients entering the group is trenchant. Hostility to the newcomer is evident even in the group which has beseeched the therapist to add new members. A content analysis of the session in which a new member or members are introduced reveals several themes which are hardly consonant with benevolent hospitality. The group suddenly spends far more time than in previous meetings discussing "the good old days." Long-departed group members and events of bygone meetings are avidly recalled, as new members are guilelessly reminded, lest they have forgotten, of their novitiate status.

Similarly, members may express resemblances they perceive between the new member and some member no longer present in the group. I once observed a meeting in which two members were introduced; the group noted a similarity between one of them and Matthew, a patient who (the newcomer shortly learned) had committed suicide a year before; the other patient was compared with Roger, a patient who had dropped out, discouraged and unimproved after three months of therapy. These groups, be it noted, were unaware of the acerbity of their greetings and consciously felt that they were extending a welcome to the newcomers. The group may also express its ambivalence by discussing, in the newcomer's first meeting, threatening, confidence-shaking issues. For example, in the seventeenth session (one in which two new members entered) one group discussed for the first time the co-therapists' competence. They noted that the therapists were listed in the hospital catalogue as resident-students and suspected they might be leading their first group. This issue, a valid and important one which must be discussed, was nonetheless highly threatening to new members. It is of interest that the information was already known to several group members but until that meeting had never been broached in the group.

There are, of course, simultaneous feelings of welcome and support for new members which are particularly marked if the group has been searching for new members. The members may exercise great gentleness and patience in dealing with new members' initial fear or defensiveness. The group, in fact, may collude in many ways to increase the attractiveness of the group for the newcomer. Often, patients may gratuitously offer testimonials and describe the various improvements they have experienced. In one such group, the newcomer asked a disgruntled, resistive member about her progress; and, before she could reply, two other members, sensing that she would devaluate the group, interrupted and described their own progress. Although groups may unconsciously wish to discourage newcomers, they would seem to prefer to do so by threatening the new member or by severe initiation rites; members are not willing to deter new members by so devaluating their group that the candidates choose not to join it.

Reasons for the Group's Response. There are several reasons for the group's ambivalent response to new members. Some members who highly prize the solidarity and cohesiveness of the group may consider any proposed change as a threat to the status quo. Others may envision the new members as potential rivals for the therapist's and the group's attention; they perceive their own fantasied role as favored child to be in jeopardy. Still other members, particularly those conflicted in the area of control and dominance, may regard the new member as a threat to their position in the hierarchy of power.

A dream by a group patient is illustrative. The patient, George, was a highly narcissistic individual who had been in the group for sixteen months. A sophisticated group member, he was capable of making perceptive, helpful comments to the other members, who treated him with much deference. He had a strong sense of being favored by the therapist over the other group patients. When the group had only five members, two new male patients were introduced, both intelligent and forceful, who immediately challenged George's role in the group. The night after the meeting in which the new members were introduced, George dreamed:

I was in a group with three women, one man and the therapist. One of the men was typing and the therapist threw him out. (N.B., one of the new members was a newspaper writer.) I tried to talk to the others but they wouldn't listen to me. Then I tried to talk to Dr. ———— but he also ignored me. I got up, told the group I was quitting, and walked out the door. No one tried to stop me.

Once outside I didn't know what to do. I stuck my head back in but was still ignored. I left again with the feeling I was all alone.

Similarly, in another group in which a new female patient was being introduced, the two incumbent female members, desperately protecting their stake, employed many prestige-enhancing devices, including the recitation of poetry. When John Donne is quoted in a therapy group as part of the incoming ritual, it is hardly for an aesthetic end.

A common concern of the group is that, even though new members are needed, they will nonetheless slow up the group. The group fears that familiar material will have to be repeated for the newcomers and that the group must recycle, as it were, and relive the stages of gradual social introduction and ritualistic etiquette. This expectation proves to be unrealistic; new patients introduced into an ongoing group generally move quickly into the prevailing level of group communication and bypass the early testing phases characteristic of members in a newly formed group. One additional but less frequent source of ambivalence to the newcomer issues from the threat posed by these individuals to group patients who have improved and who fear to see in the newcomers themselves as they were at the beginning of their own therapy. In order to avoid reexposure to painful, past periods of life, they will frequently shun new patients who appear as reincarnations of their earlier selves.

A baptism by fire suffered by one new patient in a group illustrates many of these dynamics. Katherine, a fifty-five-year-old woman, depressed about her mother's terminal illness, was introduced into a group of six members, all between twenty-five and thirty-five years of age. The group had been a highly sexualized one, with two of the members involved in a sexual relationship (see Chapter 11 for a more detailed description of this group) and the others deeply involved in sexual issues evoked by this relationship. The therapist was concerned that the group existed on such a narrow, genital band of life that the opportunities for learning were severely compromised; he quite deliberately introduced a member with a different set of life concerns in the hope of introducing, at one stroke, such issues in the group as aging, death, parents, and loss.

The group greeted Katherine with a withering barrage; before her first meeting had ended, some members had shouted at her and others had delivered the ultimatum that either she or they would have to leave the group.

The analysis during the following meetings of the group behavior uncovered several causes for their reaction. Much of it was anger displaced from the therapist. The group felt betrayed; they sensed that the therapist, by introducing Katherine, was condemning and controlling their behavior. They had considered it their group and resented having had no voice in the selection of a new member. Some anger was transference-based as members unrealistically responded to Katherine as though she were a rejecting, disapproving elder. Some of the anger, though, belonged to Katherine; she entered the group aggressively, did not wait to be asked why she was there, and proffered much advice to the other members. Ordinarily, new members are expected to attempt to get the "lay of the land," to discover the group norms before venturing in. New members who defy or ignore this convention do not often have an untrammeled entry.

Therapeutic Guidelines. New members entering an ongoing group need to be prepared by the therapist for the therapy experience. In addition to preparing these patients in the standard manner (see Chapter 9), the therapist should also attempt to help them deal with the unique stresses accompanying entry into an established group. I prefer to anticipate for patients their feelings of exclusion and bewilderment at entering an unusual culture which they have not helped to build. They may be reassured that they will be allowed to enter and participate at their own rate. New patients entering established groups may be daunted by the sophistication, openness, interpersonal facility, and daring of more experienced members; they may also be frightened or fear contagion, since they are immediately confronted with patients revealing "sicker" sides of themselves than are revealed in the first meetings of a new group. These contingencies should therefore be discussed with the patient. It is generally helpful to describe the major events of the past few meetings to the incoming patients. If the group has been going through some particularly intense, tumultuous events, it is wise to brief the new patient even more thoroughly.

Many therapists prefer to introduce two new members at a time. Such a practice may have advantages both for the group and for the new members. The group conserves energy and time by assimilating two patients at once; the new patients may ally with each other and thereby feel less alien. Although introduction in pairs does not result in a statistically lower dropout rate [31] and occasionally, if one patient integrates himself into the group with much greater facility than the other, may backfire and create even greater discomfort for a newcomer, nevertheless introduction in pairs has much to recommend it.

The number of new patients introduced into the group heavily influences the pace of absorption. A group of six or seven can generally absorb a new member with scarcely a telltale ripple; the group continues their work with only the briefest of pauses and rapidly pulls the new member along. On the other hand, a group of four confronted with three new members often comes to a screeching halt as all ongoing work ceases and the group devotes all its energy to the task of incorporating the new members. The old members will wonder how much they can trust the new ones. Dare they continue with the same degree of self-disclosure and risk-taking? To what extent will their familiar, comfortable group be changed forever? The new members will be searching for guidelines to behavior. What is acceptable in this group? What is forbidden? If their reception is not a gracious one, they may seek the comfort inherent in an alliance of the newcomers. The therapist will note frequent "we" and "they," or "old members" and "new members" statements. He should heed these signs of schism; until incorporation is complete, little further therapeutic work can be done. A similar situation often arises when therapists attempt to amalgamate nuclei of two groups which have been reduced in number. It is my clinical impression that this procedure is unsound; too often a culture clash and clique formation along lines of the previous groups may persist for a remarkably long period of time.

An interesting strategic variation on the process of adding new members consists of including the group in the selection decision. For example, the therapist may permit the entire group to interview prospective members and, after the candidate leaves, vote on his inclusion. This may sound like a frightening ordeal for the new patient but it need not be. The therapist, in an initial individual screening session, may prepare the patient for the group interview. He may present the procedure from the perspective of finding the proper "fit" between patient and group; furthermore, the procedure may be a two-way interview—the candidate may assess the group as well as be assessed by them. Of course, should the group decide not to accept the patient (and that occurs very rarely), then the therapist assumes full responsibility for placing the patient in another group. This procedure is cumbersome and time-consuming and should only be used with a group that has matured into a seasoned work-group. However, it offers several advantages to both patient and group. The patient having had to overcome barriers to joining the group comes to value it more highly. Is this not the principle behind fraternity initiations, free masonry noviate study, and long, costly apprenticeships in such organizations as psychoanalytic societies? The group members, on the other hand, having had an active role in the decision-making process, will assume responsibility for its decision and invest considerable energy to help the new member become a part of the group. Is this not the principle behind all forms of the democratic group process?

The introduction of new patients may, if properly considered, enhance the therapeutic process of the old members who may respond to a newcomer in highly idiosyncratic styles. An important principle of group therapy that we have discussed on several previous occasions is that every major stimulus presented to the group elicits a variety of responses by the group members. The investigation of the reasons behind these differential responses is generally a rewarding pursuit which clarifies aspects of character structure. To observe that others respond to a situation in a manner markedly different from one's own is an arresting experience which can provide considerable insight into one's behavior. Such an opportunity is unavailable in individual therapy but constitutes one of the chief strengths of the group therapeutic format. An illustrative clinical example may clarify this point.

A new member, Alice—a forty-year-old divorcee—was introduced at a group's eighteenth meeting. The three men in the group greeted her in strikingly different fashions.

Peter arrived fifteen minutes late and thereby missed the introduction. For the next hour he was active in the group, discussing issues left over from the previous meeting as well as events occurring in his life during the past week. He totally ignored Alice, avoiding even glancing at her—a formidable feat in a group of six people in close physical proximity. Later in the meeting, as others attempted to help Alice participate, he, still without introducing himself, fired questions at her in a prosecuting, attorney-like fashion. Peter, a twenty-eight-year-old devout Catholic father of four, had sought therapy because he, as he phrased it, loved women too much and had had a series of extramarital love affairs. In subsequent meetings the group used the events of Alice's first meeting to help Peter investigate the nature of his "love" for women. Gradually, he came to recognize how he used women, including his wife, as part objects, valuing them for their genitals only and remaining insensitive to their feelings and experiential world.

The two other men in the group, Brian and Arthur, on the other hand, were preoccupied with Alice during her first meeting. Arthur, a twenty-four-year-old homosexual who sought therapy in order to change his sexual orientation, reacted strongly to Alice and found that he could not look at her without experiencing the strongest sense of embarrassment. His discomfort and blushing were apparent to the other members, who helped him explore far more deeply than he had previously his relationship with the women in the group. Arthur had desexualized the other two women in the group by establishing in his fantasy a brother-sister relationship with them. Alice, who was sexually attractive, divorced and "available," and at the same time old enough to evoke in him affect-laden feelings about his mother, presented a special problem for Arthur, who had previously been settling down into a too comfortable niche in the group.

Brian, on the other hand, transfixed Alice with his gaze and delivered an unwavering broad smile to her throughout the meeting. An extraordinarily dependent twenty-three-year-old, Brian had sought therapy for depression following the breakup of a love affair. Having lost his mother in infancy, he had been raised by a succession of governesses and had had only occasional contact with an aloof, powerful father of whom he was terrified. His romantic affairs, always with considerably older women, had invariably collapsed because of the insatiable demands he made on the relationship. The other women in the group in the past few meetings had similarly withdrawn from him, and with progressive candor had confronted him with, as they termed it, his puppy-dog presentation of self. Brian thus welcomed Alice, hoping to find in her a new source of succor. Alice in subsequent meetings proved to be quite helpful to Brian, as she revealed her feeling during her first meeting of extreme discomfort at his beseeching smile and her persistent feeling that a relationship with Brian would totally empty her.

In the next three chapters we will discuss later stages of therapy. Freud once compared psychotherapy to chess in that far more is known and written about the opening and the end game than the middle game. Accordingly, the opening stages of therapy and termination may be discussed with some degree of exactness, but the vast bulk of therapy cannot be systematically described. Thus, the following chapters deal in a more generalized way with issues and problems of later stages of therapy and with some specialized therapist techniques.

REFERENCES

1. S. Freud, *Group Psychology and the Analysis of the Ego* (New York: Bantam Books, 1960), p. 76.
2. P. Blachly, paper presented at National Conference of Suicidology, Chicago, 1968.
3. E. Semrad, cited by W. Schutz, *The Interpersonal Underworld* (Palo Alto: Science and Behavior Books, 1966), p. 170.
4. Schutz, *op. cit.*, p. 24.
5. G. Bach, *Intensive Group Therapy* (New York: Ronald Press, 1954).
6. B. Tuckman, "Developmental Sequences in Small Groups," *Psychol. Bull.*, 63: 384–399, 1965.
7. S. Parker, "Leadership Patterns in a Psychiatric Ward," *Human Relations*, 11: 287–301, 1958.
8. B. Berkowitz, "Stages of Group Development," unpublished manuscript.
9. R. Liberman, "Social Reinforcement of Group Dynamics," paper delivered at American Group Psychotherapy Association Convention, Chicago, January 1968.
10. P. Slater, *Microcosm* (New York: John Wiley & Sons, 1966).
11. S. Freud, *Totem and Taboo*, trans. J. Strachey (London: Routledge and Kegan Paul, 1950).
12. J. Friedman and S. Gassell, "The Chorus in Sophocles' *Oedipus Tyrannus*," *Psychoanal. Quart.*, 19: 213–226, 1950.

13. S. H. Foulkes and E. J. Anthony, *Group Psychotherapy—the Psychoanalytic Approach* (Harmondsworth, Middlesex: Penguin Books, 1957).
14. W. G. Bennis, "Patterns and Vicissitudes in T-Group Development," in L. P. Bradford, J. R. Gibb, and K. D. Benne, *T-Group Theory and Laboratory Method: Innovation in Re-education* (New York: John Wiley & Sons, 1964), pp. 248–278.
15. T. Mills, personal communication, April 1968.
16. H. I. Clapham and A. B. Sclare, "Group Psychotherapy with Asthmatic Patients," *Int. J. Group Psychother.*, 8: 44–54, 1958.
17. F. K. Taylor, "The Therapeutic Factors of Group-Analytic Treatment," *J. Ment. Sci.*, 96: 976–997, 1950.
18. H. Coffey, M. Freedman, T. Leary, and A. Ossorio, "Community Service and Social Research—Group Psychotherapy in a Church Program," *J. Soc. Iss.*, 6: 14–61, 1950.
19. R. S. Shellow, J. L. Ward, and S. Rubenfeld, "Group Therapy and the Institutionalized Delinquent," *Int. J. Group Psychother.*, 8: 265–275, 1958.
20. D. Whitaker and M. A. Lieberman, *Psychotherapy Through the Group Process* (New York: Atherton Press, 1964).
21. J. Mann and E. V. Semrad, "The Use of Group Therapy in Psychoses," *J. Soc. Casework*, 29: 176–181, 1948.
22. M. Grotjahn, "The Process of Maturation in Group Psychotherapy and in the Group Therapist," *Psychiatry*, 13: 63–67, 1950.
23. A. P. Noyes, *Modern Clinical Psychiatry* (4th ed.; Philadelphia: Saunders, 1953), pp. 589–591.
24. J. Abrahams, "Group Psychotherapy: Implications for Direction and Supervision of Mentally Ill Patients," in T. Muller (ed.), *Mental Health in Nursing* (Washington, D.C.: Catholic University Press, 1949), pp. 77–83.
25. J. J. Thorpe and B. Smith, "Phases in Group Development in Treatment of Drug Addicts," *Int. J. Group Psychother.*, 3: 66–78, 1953.
26. W. Bennis, R. Burke, H. Cutter, H. Harrington, and J. Hoffman, "A Note on Some Problems of Measurement and Prediction in a Training Group," *Group Psychother.*, 10: 328–341, 1957.
27. P. Runkel, M. Lawrence, S. Oldfield, M. Rider, and C. Clark, "Stages of Group Development; An Empirical Test of Tuckman's Hypothesis," *J. Appl. Behav. Sci.*, 7: 180–193, 1971.
28. D. A. Hamburg, personal communication, 1968.
29. M. A. Lieberman, "The Relationship of Group Climate to Individual Change," unpublished doctoral dissertation, University of Chicago, 1958.
30. G. Psathas and R. Hardert, "Trainer Interventions and Normative Patterns in the T-Group," *J. Appl. Behav. Sci.*, 2: 149–169, 1966.
31. I. D. Yalom, "A Study of Group Therapy Dropouts," *Arch. Gen. Psychiat.*, 14: 393–414, 1966.
32. K. Rice, *Learning for Leadership* (London: Tavistock Publications, 1965).
33. A. M. Rosenthal, *Thirty-Eight Witnesses* (New York: McGraw-Hill, 1964).
34. I. D. Yalom, P. S. Houts, S. M. Zimerberg, and K. H. Rand, "Prediction of Improvement in Group Therapy: An Exploratory Study," *Arch. Gen. Psychiat.*, 17: 159–168, 1967.
35. Foulkes and Anthony, *op. cit.*, p. 137.

11

THE ADVANCED GROUP

Once the group has survived its first few months, it is no longer possible to describe discrete stages of development. When a group achieves a degree of stability, the long working-through process begins and the major curative factors described in the earlier chapters operate with increasing force and effectiveness. Each member, as he engages more deeply in the group, reveals to others and to himself his problems in living, and there is no limit to the richness and complexity which may characterize the sessions of the group.

No one, therefore, can offer specific procedural guidelines for each contingency. In general, the therapist must strive to encourage development and operation of the curative factors. The application of the basic principles of the therapist's role and technique to specific group events and to each patient's therapy (as discussed in Chapters 5 and 6) constitutes the art of psychotherapy, and for this there is no substitute for experience, supervision, and intuition.

Certain issues and problems occur, however, with sufficient regularity to warrant discussion. This chapter considers the phenomena of subgrouping, self-disclosure, conflict, and termination of therapy; and Chapter 12, "The Problem Patient," deals with certain recurrent behavioral configurations which present a challenge to the therapist and to the group.

Subgrouping

Fractionalization—the splitting off of sub-units—occurs in every social organization. The process may be transient or enduring, helpful or harmful, for the parent organization. Therapy groups are no exception; subgroup formation is an inevitable and often disruptive event in the life of the group; and yet there, too, the process, if understood and harnessed properly, may further the therapeutic work.

Subgroup formation in the therapy group arises from the belief of two or more members that they can derive more gratification from a relationship with each other than from a relationship with the entire group. Extragroup socializing is often the first stage of subgrouping. A clique of three or four members may begin to visit each others' homes, to have lengthy telephone conversations, or to engage in business ventures with one another. Occasionally, two members will become sexually involved. Subgroup formation may occur, however, completely within the confines of the group therapy room, as members who perceive themselves to be similar form coalitions. There may be any number of common bonds: a comparable educational level, similar values, similar age, marital status, or group status (e.g., the "old-timer" original members). Social organizations, especially those larger than a therapy group, will characteristically develop opposing factions—two or more conflicting subgroups—but such is not the case in therapy groups, where one clique forms but the remaining group members, excluded from the clique, do not often coalesce into a second subgroup.

The members of the subgroup may be identified by a general code of behavior: they agree with one another regardless of the issue and avoid confrontations among their own membership; they may exchange knowing glances when a non-clique member speaks; they may arrive and depart from the meeting together.

EFFECTS OF SUBGROUPING

Subgrouping can have an extraordinarily disruptive effect on the course of the therapy group. In a study [1] of thirty-five patients who prematurely dropped out from group therapy, I found that eleven (31 percent) dropped out largely because of problems arising from subgrouping. Complications arise whether the patient is included or excluded from a subgroup.

Inclusion. Those included in a dyadic or larger subgroup often find that group life is vastly more complicated and less rewarding. As a patient transfers his allegiance from the group goals to the subgroup goals, loyalty becomes a major issue. Should he abide by the group procedural rules of free and honest discussions of feelings if, in so doing, he would be breaking a confidence established secretly with another member? For example, two group members, Christine and Jerry, often met after a therapy session to have long, intense conversations. Jerry had remained withdrawn in the group and had sought out Christine because, as he informed her, he felt that she alone could understand him. After obtaining her promise of confidentiality, he soon was able to reveal to her his homosexual obsessions and occasional pedophilic involvements. Back in the group, Christine felt restrained by her promise and avoided interaction with Jerry, who eventually dropped out unimproved. Ironically, Christine was an exceptionally sensitive member of the group who might have been particularly useful to Jerry by encouraging him to participate in the group had she not been restrained by the antitherapeutic subgroup norms (i.e., her promise of confidentiality). Another example of the conflict between group and subgroup norms is cited by Lindt and Sherman:[2]

An older, paternal man had been giving two other patients a ride home and had invited them to see television at his house. The visitors witnessed an argument between the older patient and his wife, and at a subsequent group session told him that they felt he was mistreating his wife. The older patient, evidently feeling betrayed and considering the group his enemy rather than his friend, seemed to develop feelings of rejection and dropped out of treatment.

Similar and very severe problems occur when group members engage in sexual relations: they often hesitate to "besmirch" (as one patient phrased it) an intimate relationship by giving it a public airing. Freud, who never practiced clinical group therapy, wrote in 1921 a prescient essay on group psychology [3,4] in which he underscored the incompatibility between a sexual love relationship and group cohesiveness. Though we may disagree with the cornerstone of his argument (that inhibited sexual instincts contribute to the cohesive energy of the group), his conclusions are compelling: i.e., no group tie, be it race, nationality, social class, or religious belief, can remain unthreatened by the overriding importance that two people in love can have for each other. Obviously, the ties of the therapy group are no exception. Members of a therapy group who become involved in a love-sexual relationship will almost inevitably come to award their dyadic relationship higher priority than their relationship to the group. They sacrifice their value for each other as helpmates in the group; they refuse to betray confidences; in their efforts to be charming to one another they affect poses in the group; they perform for one another, blurring out the therapists, other members of the group, and, most importantly, their primary goals in therapy. Often the other group members are dimly aware that someting important is occurring which is being actively avoided in the group discussion—a state of affairs which usually results in global group inhibition.

Chance once provided us with some empirical evidence to substantiate these comments. A research team [5] happened to be studying closely a therapy group in which two members developed a sexual relationship. Since the study began months before the liaison occurred, good baseline data is available. Several observers (as well as the patients themselves in post-group questionnaires) rated each meeting along a seven-point scale for: amount of affect expressed, amount of self-disclosure, and general value of the session. In addition, the communication flow system was recorded with the number and direction of each patient's statements charted on a who-to-whom matrix. During the course of the observation period two patients, Bruce and Geraldine, developed a sexual relationship which, we learned later, was kept secret from the therapist and the group for three weeks. During these three weeks there was a steep downward gradient in the scoring of the quality of the meetings, with particularly limited expression of affect and diminished self-disclosure. Moreover, the overall verbal activity of the group decreased and scarcely a single verbal exchange between Geraldine and Bruce was recorded! The couple resolved the problem by deciding that one of them would drop out of the group (not an uncommon form of resolution). Geraldine dropped out, and in the following meeting Bruce discussed the entire incident with relief and with great candor. (The ratings by both patients and observers indicated this meeting to be valuable, with strong affect expression, high disclosure from others as well as Bruce, and an active interactional flow.)

Exclusion. Exclusion from the subgroup also complicates group life. Anxiety associated with earlier exclusion experiences is evoked which, if not discharged by working through, may reach disabling levels. Often it is exceptionally difficult for members to comment on their feelings of exclusion; they may be disinclined to intrude into a relationship or to risk incurring the wrath of the involved members by discussion of the subgroup in the session.

Nor are therapists immune to this problem. Recently, one of my supervisers observed two of his group patients (both married) walking arm in arm along the street. The therapist found himself unable to comment on this and supplied a number of rationalizations: the therapist should not place himself in the position of spy or disapproving parent in the eyes of the group; the therapist is not free to bring up nongroup material; the involved members will, when they are psychologically ready, discuss the problem. However, these are rationalizations; there is no more important issue than the interrelationship of the group members. If the therapist is unwilling to bring in all material which bears on member relationships, he can hardly expect members to do so. If the therapist feels himself trapped in a dilemma—on the one hand, needing to bring in these observations and, on the other, unhappy about seeming like a spy—then often the best approach is to share with the group both his observations and his personal uneasiness and reluctance to discuss them. The therapist may wish to inquire why it is his responsibility alone to bring in these observations so imporant to therapy: why have the involved parties avoided their responsibility to their own therapy?

One college student group had a disproportionately high number of dropouts. Through a variety of factors, including poor selection and subgrouping complications, five of the original eight members dropped out. The remaining members badly shaken by the threat to the existence of the group, banded together and excluded several newcomers, each of whom dropped out after a few meetings. As Frank [6] has pointed out, this is a form of group suicide since, if continued, the group will perish from attrition. Many groups at this juncture will elaborate initiation rites. In this group the rites were particularly severe; the new members felt excluded and attacked. As one patient put it, "The group received me like, 'Who the heck are you?' I felt it was a closed corporation and I was an interloper." The culture that the original group had established was a playfully hostile one with much bantering, sarcasm, and little expression of support or positive feelings. To new members who had had no share in the creation of the culture, the atmosphere seemed exceedingly threatening and destructive. Their fears and feelings of isolation were greatly accentuated by the knowledge that the core members met socially at informal meetings to which the new members were not welcome.

CAUSES OF SUBGROUPING

Subgrouping is caused by both group and individual forces. Some groups (and some therapists) have a disporportionately high incidence of subgrouping; some individuals will invariably become involved in subgrouping in whatever group they are placed.

Subgrouping may be a manifestation of a considerable degree of undischarged hostility in the group, especially toward the leader. In their classic research on three different styles of leadership, White and Lippit [7] noted that the group was more likely to develop disruptive in-group and out-group factions under an authoritarian, restrictive style of leadership. The members, unable to express their anger and frustration directly to the leader, released these feelings obliquely by binding together and mobbing or scapegoating one or more of the other members.

I have in my discussion of primary task and secondary gratification (in Chapter 5) already presented one of the major dynamics underlying subgrouping. When patients violate group norms by secret liaisons, they are opting for need gratification rather than for pursuit of personal change—their primary reason for being in therapy. Need frustration occurs early in therapy; for example, patients with strong needs for intimacy, dependency, sexual conquests, or dominance may soon sense the impossibility of gratifying these needs in the group and often attempt to gratify them outside of the formal group. In one sense, these patients are "acting out" in that, outside the therapy setting, they engage in an organized, symbolically determined form of behavior which relieves inner tensions. It is exceptionally difficult to discriminate, except in retrospect, "acting out" from acting or participation in the therapy group. The course of the therapy group is a continual cycle of action and analysis of this action. The social microcosm concept depends on patients engaging in their habitual patterns of behavior, which are then examined by the patient and the group. "Acting out" as a form of resistance to therapy occurs only when the patient refuses to examine and to allow the group to examine his behavior. Extragroup behavior which is *not* examined in the group becomes then a particularly potent form of resistance, whereas extragroup behavior which is subsequently brought back into the group and worked through may prove to be of considerable therapeutic import.

THERAPEUTIC CONSIDERATIONS

By no means, then, is subgrouping, with or without extragroup socializing, invariably disruptive. If the goals of the subgroup are consonant with the goals of the parent group, subgrouping may ultimately enhance group cohesiveness; for example, a coffee group or a bowling league may operate successfully within a larger social organization. In therapy groups, some of the most significant incidents in therapy occur as a result of some extragroup member contacts which are then fully worked through for therapy. For example, two members who went to dinner together after the meeting discussed new observations and sets of feelings that arose in the social setting. One of the pair had been far more flirtatous, even openly seductive, than she had been in the group; furthermore, much of this was "blind spot" behavior—out of her awareness.

Another group scheduled a beer party for one member who was terminating. Unfortunately, he had to leave town unexpectedly and the party was canceled. The member acting as social secretary notified the others of the cancellation but by error neglected to contact one member, Jim. On the night of the party Jim waited, in vain, at the appointed place for two hours reexperiencing many familiar feelings of rejection, exclusion, and bitter loneliness. The discussion of these reactions and of Jim's lack of any annoyance or anger and his feeling that his being excluded was natural, expected, "the way it should be," led to much fruitful therapeutic work for him. When the party was finally held, considerable data was generated for the group. Members displayed different aspects of themselves. For example, the member who was least influential in the group because of his affect isolation and his inability or unwillingness to disclose himself assumed a very different role because of his wit, store of good jokes, and easy social mannerisms. Another, who was an experienced and sophisticated group patient, reencountered his dread of social situations, his inability to make small talk, and took refuge behind the role of host, devoting his time busily to refilling empty glasses.

In another group a dramatic example of effective subgrouping occurred when the patients became concerned about one member who was in such despair that she considered suicide. Several group members maintained a week-long telephone vigil, which proved to be beneficial both to the patient and to the cohesiveness of the entire group.

Thus the principle is clear: any type of extragroup contact may prove to be of considerable usefulness provided that the goals of the parent group are not relinquished. If such meetings are viewed as part of the group rhythm of behaving and understanding this behavior, much valuable information can be made available to the group. For this to occur, the involved members must inform the group of all important extragroup events. If they do not, the disruptive effects on cohesiveness we have described will take place. *It is not the subgrouping per se that is destructive to the group but the conspiracy of silence that generally surrounds it.*

In practice, groups which meet only once weekly often experience more of the disruptive effects of subgrouping than the beneficial ones. Much extragroup socializing never comes directly to the group's attention, and the behavior of the involved members is never made available for analysis in the group. For example, the extragroup relationship described earlier between Christine and Jerry in which Jerry revealed in confidence his homosexual behavior never was made known to the group. Christine disclosed the incident over a year later to a research psychiatrist who interviewed her in a psychotherapy outcome study.

The therapist should, then, encourage open discussion and analysis of all extragroup contacts and all in-group coalitions. It may be emphasized in the pre-group preparation that it is the patient's responsibility to bring extragroup contacts into the group. If the therapist surmises from glances between two members in the group or from their appearance together outside the group that a special relationship exists between them, he should not hesitate to present his feeling to the group. No criticism or accusation is implied, since the investigation and understanding of an affectionate relationship between two members may be as therapeutically rewarding as the exploration of a hostile impasse. The therapist must attempt to disconfirm the misconception that psychotherapy is reductionistic in its ethos, that all experience will be reduced to some fundamental (and base) motive. Furthermore, other members must be encouraged to discuss their reaction to the relationship, whether it be one of envy, jealousy, rejection, or vicarious satisfaction.

One practical caveat: patients engaged in some extragroup relationship which they are not prepared to discuss in the therapy group may request the therapist for an individual session and ask that the material discussed not be divulged to the rest of the group. The therapist who gives such a promise of confidentiality soon finds that he is in an untenable collusion from which it is difficult to extricate himself. I would suggest that the group therapist *never* offer a promise of confidentiality; instead, he should only assure the patients that he will be guided by his professional judgment and act in their therapeutic behalf.

Therapy group members may establish sexual relationships with one another but not with any great frequency. The therapy group is not a prurient group; patients have severe sexuals conflicts resulting in such problems as impotence, frigidity, social alienation, and sexual guilt. Probably far less sexual involvement occurs in a therapy group than in a social or professional group with a similar longevity.

The therapist cannot, by edict, prevent the formation of sexual relations or any other form of subgrouping. I agree with Wolf, who states:

> . . . men and women who become so engaged do so compulsively and generally drift into physical familiarity whether the physician forbids it or not. Then the therapist is faced with their sense of guilt, a tendency to hide aspects and a secret defiance that complicates and obscures the significance of the act. Furthermore, patients who leap into bed with one another do so rather extensively with people outside the group. In the therapeutic setting, the repetition of the sexual act has the advantage of subjecting compulsive promiscuity to examination under the microscope.[8]

Consider the clinical example (described in Chapter 2) of Mrs. Cape, Charles, and Louis. Recall that Mrs. Cape seduced Charles and Louis as part of her struggle for power with the group therapist. The episode was, in one sense, disruptive for the group; Mrs. Cape's husband learned of the incident and threatened Charles and Louis, who, along with other members, grew so distrustful of Mrs. Cape that dissolution of the group appeared imminent. The crisis was resolved by the group's expelling Mrs. Cape (who continued therapy in another group). Despite these complications, some benefits occurred. The episode was thoroughly explored within the group, and the participants obtained considerable help with their sexual pathology. For example, Charles, who had a history of a Don Juan style of relationships with women, at first disclaimed all responsibility in the matter. He washed his hands of the incident by pointing out that Mrs. Cape had asked him to go to bed, and, as he phrased it, "I don't turn down a piece of candy when it's offered." Louis also tended to disclaim responsiblity for his relationships with women and customarily regarded them as objects or "pieces of tail." Both Charles and Louis were presented with powerful evidence of the implications of their act—the effects on Mrs. Cape's marriage and the effects on their own group—and so came to appreciate their personal responsibility for their acts. Mrs. Cape, for the first time, realized the sadistic nature of her sexuality; not only did she employ sex as a weapon against the therapist but, as we have already described, as a means of depreciating and humilating Charles and Louis.

If the therapist cannot forbid subgrouping, neither should he encourage it. I have found it most helpful to make my position on this problem explicit to patients in the preparatory or initial sessions. I tell them that it has been my experience that extragroup activity often impedes therapy and, if necessary, I describe some of the complications we have discussed. I underscore that if extragroup meetings occur, fortuitously or by design, then it is their responsibility to the members and to the group to keep the others fully informed. The therapist must help the patient understand that the group therapy experience will provide him with the skills necessary to establish durable relationships but will not provide him with the relationships. If patients do not transfer their learning, they derive their social gratification exclusively from the therapy group and therapy becomes interminable.

It is my experience that it is unwise to include two members in an out-patient group who already have a long-term special relationship: husband and wife, roommates, business associates, etc. It is perfectly possible to focus group therapy on the improvement of a long-term relationship, but that entails a different kind of therapy group (e.g., marital couples' group, conjoint family therapy, social network therapy) than the type described in this book.

In inpatient psychotherapy groups, the problem is even more complex since the group members spend their entire day in close association with one another. For example, in a group in a psychiatric hospital for criminal offenders, a subgrouping problem had created great divisiveness. Two members, who were by far the most intelligent, articulate, and best-educated members of the group, had formed a close friendship and spent much of every day together. The group sessions were characterized by an inordinate amount of tension and hostile bickering, much of it directed at these two men, who by this time had lost their separate identities and were primarily regarded, and regarded themselves, as a dyad. Much of the attacking was off-target, and the therapeutic work of the group had become overshadowed by the attempt to destroy the dyad. As the situation progressed, the therapist, with good effect, helped the group explore several themes. First, the group had to consider that the two members could scarcely be punished for their subgrouping since everyone had an equal opportunity to form such a relationship. The issue of envy was thus introduced, and gradually the members discussed their own longing and inability to establish a friendship. Furthermore, they discussed their feelings of intellectual inferiority to the dyad, as well as their

sense of exclusion and rejection by them. The two members had, however, augmented these responses by their actions; both had, for years,
maintained their self-esteem by demonstrating their intellectual superiority whenever possible. When addressing other members, they deliberately used polysyllabic words and maintained a conspiratorial attitude which accentuated the others' feelings of inferiority and
rejection. Both profited from the group's description of the subtle re-
buffs and taunts they had meted out and came to realize that others
had suffered painful effects from their behavior.

ILLUSTRATIVE CLINICAL EXAMPLE

I shall end this discussion with a rather lengthy clinical illustration.
It is the longest clinical tale told in the book and I include it because it
not only illustrates in depth many of the issues involved in subgrouping but also other aspects of group therapy discussed in other chapters, including the differentiation between primary task and secondary gratification and the issue of assumption of responsibility in
therapy.

The group, an outpatient one led by two male co-therapists, met
twice weekly. The patients were young, ranging in age from twenty-
five to thirty-five years. At the time we shall join the group, two
women recently graduated, leaving only four male patients (and, of
course, the two therapists). One of the men was Bill, the male lead in
the drama which unfolded. Bill, a tall, handsome thirty-two-year-old
divorced dentist, had been in the group for approximately eight
months without significant progress. He originally sought therapy because of chronic anxiety and episodic depressions. He was socially
self-conscious to the degree that simple acts, for example, saying good
night at a party, caused him much torment. If he could have been
granted one wish by some benevolent therapeutic muse, it would
have been "to be cool." He was dissatisfied with work, he had no male
friends and a Don Juan pattern of relating to females. Though he had
been living with one woman for a few months, he had no commitment
to her and considered the relationship as highly tenuous.

The group, waiting for new members, met for several sessions with
only four men and established a virile, Saturday night, male-bonded
subculture. Issues which had rarely surfaced while women were in
the group occupied much of the center stage; the men discussed mas-
turbatory practices and fantasies, fighting, feelings of cowardice, concerns about physique, feelings about the large breasts of a former

group member, and their fantasies of a group gang-bang with the bearer of those large breasts.

Two women were then introduced into the group, and never have I seen a well-established culture disintegrate so quickly. The Saturday night camaraderie was swept away by a flood of male dominance behavior. Bill boldly, brazenly competed not for one but for both of the women. The other men in the group reacted to the first meeting with the two women members in accordance with their dynamic patterns. One, a twenty-five-year-old graduate student, arrived at the meeting in short pants (lederhosen), the only time in eighteen months of therapy he thus bedecked himself, and during the meeting was quick to discuss, in detail, his homosexual proclivities. Another made an appeal to the maternal instincts of the new patients by presenting himself as a fledgling with a broken wing. The remaining member removed himself from the race by remarking, after the first forty minutes, that he wasn't going to join the others in the foolish game of competing for the women's favors; besides, he had been observing the new members and concluded that they had nothing of value to offer him.

One of the women was Jan, an attractive twenty-eight-year-old divorceé with two children. She was a language teacher who sought therapy for many reasons: depression, promiscuity, infanticidal obsessions, loneliness. She complained that she could not say "no" to an attractive man. Men used her sexually: they would make a sexual call at her home for an hour or two in the evening but would not be willing to be seen with her in the daylight. There was an active willful part of it, too, as she boasted of having had sexual relations with most of the heads of the departments at the college where she taught. Because of poor judgment she was in deep financial trouble. She had written several bad checks and was beginning to flirt with the idea of prostitution: if men were exploiting her sexually, then why not charge them for her favors?

In the pre-group screening interviews and preparatory sessions, the therapists realized that her great promiscuity made her a likely candidate for self-destructive sexual acting out in the group. Therefore, they took much greater pains than usual to emphasize that outside social involvement with other group members would not be in her or the group's best interests.

After the entrance of the two women, Bill's group behavior altered radically: he disclosed himself less, he played a charming, seductive role, he became far more deliberate and self-conscious in his actions. In short, in pursuit of secondary sexual gratification he appeared to lose all sense of why he was in a therapy group. Rather than welcome the therapist's comments to him, he resented them: he felt they made him look bad in front of the women. He rapidly jettisoned his relationship to the men in the group and thenceforth related to them dishonestly. For example, in the first meeting, when one of the members told the women he felt they had nothing of value to offer him, Bill rushed in to praise him for his honesty though his primary feelings at that point was one of exhilaration that the other had folded his tent and left him in sole possession of the field of women. At this stage Bill was resistive to any interventions. The therapists tried many times during these weeks to illuminate his behavior for him, but they felt as though they were attempting to strike a match in the midst of a monsoon.

After approximately three months Jan made an overt sexual proposition to Bill which the therapists learned of in a curious way. Bill and Jan chanced to arrive early in the group room, and in their conversation Jan invited Bill to her apartment to view some pornographic movies she had recently obtained. Observers viewing the group through a one-way mirror had also arrived early, overheard the proposition, and related it to the therapists after the meeting. The therapists, feeling uneasy about Big Brotherism, brought up the incident in the next meeting only to have Jan and Bill deny that there was a sexual invitation involved. The discussion ended with Jan angrily stomping out midway through the meeting. In succeeding weeks, after each meeting she and Bill met in the parking lot for long talks and embraces. Jan brought these incidents back into the meeting but in so doing incurred Bill's anger at her for betraying him. Eventually, Bill made an overt proposition to Jan, who, on the basis of much work done in the group, decided it would be against her best interests. For the first time she said "no" to an attractive, interested, attentive man and received much group support for her stance.

(I am reminded of an episode Victor Frankl once told me of a patient who had consulted him on the eve of his marriage. He had had a sexual invitation from a strikingly beautiful women, his fianceé's best friend, and felt he could not pass this up. When would such an opportunity come his way again? It was, he insisted, a unique once-in-a-lifetime opportunity! Dr. Frankl, quite elegantly I think, pointed out that he did indeed have a unique opportunity and indeed it was one that would never come again. It was the opportunity to say "no" in the service of his responsiblity to himself and his chosen mate!)

Bill, meanwhile, was finding life in the group increasingly complex; not only was he pursuing Jan but also Carrie, who had entered the group with Jan. At the end of each meeting Bill struggled with such conundrums as how to walk out of the group alone with each woman at the same time. Jan and Carrie were, at first, very close, almost huddling together for comfort when entering an all-male group. It was to Bill's advantage to separate them, and in a number of ways he contrived to do so. Not only did Bill have a "divide and seduce" strategy, but he also found something intrinsically pleasurable in the process of splitting. He had had a long history of splitting and seducing roommates and, before that, of investing energy in order to interpose himself between his mother and sister.

Carrie had passed through, with the help of much prior therapy, a period of promiscuity similar to Jan's. She was more desperate for help, more committed to therapy than Jan, and very committed to a relationship with her boyfriend. Consequently, she was not eager to consumate a sexual relationship with Bill; but as the group progressed she developed a strong attraction to him and an even stronger determination that if she could not have him, neither should Jan. One day in the group Carrie quite unexpectedly announced that she was getting married in three weeks and invited the group to the wedding. She described her husband-to-be as a rather passive, clinging, ne'er-do-well; it was only many months later that the group learned he was a gifted mathematician who was considering faculty offers from a number of leading universities. Thus, Carrie, too, often pursued secondary gratification rather than her primary task. In her efforts to keep Bill interested in her and to compete with Jan, she misrepresented her relationship with another man, underplaying the seriousness of her involvement until her marriage forced her hand. Even then, she presented her husband in a fraudulently unfavorable light so as to nourish Bill's hopes that he still had an opportunity for a liaison with her. In so doing, Carrie sacrificed the opportunity to work on her relationship with her fiancé—one of the very urgent tasks for which she had sought therapy!

After several months in the group, Jan and Bill decided upon a sexual relationship and announced to the group their planned assignation two weeks later. The group members reacted strongly. The two women (another had entered the group by this time) were angry. Carrie felt secretly hurt at Bill's rejection of her; in the group she expressed much anger at their threatening the integrity of the group. The new patient, who had a relationship with a man similar to Bill, identified with Bill's girlfriend. Some of the men participated vicariously; they perceived Jan as a sexual object and rooted for Bill to score! Another said (and as time went by in the group, this sentiment was heard more often) that he wished Bill would hurry up and screw her so that they could talk about something else in the group. He was an anxious, timid individual who had had no heterosexual experience whatsoever; the sexual goings-on in the group were, as he phrased it, so much out of his league that he could not participate in any way. Rob, another man in the group, silently wished that the heterosexual preoccupation of the group were different. He had been having increasing concern about homosexual obsessions; yet he delayed discussing this in the group for many weeks because of his sense that the group would be unreceptive to his needs and that he would lose the respect of the members who placed such extraordinary value on heterosexual prowess. Eventually, however, he did discuss these issues with some relief. (It is of importance to note that Bill, aside from advice and solicitude, offered Rob very little. Some ten months later, after Rob left the group and after the Bill-Jan pairing had been worked through, Bill disclosed his own homosexual concerns and fantasies. Had Bill, whom Rob admired very much, shared these at the appropriate time, they would have offered Rob considerable help. Bill would not at that time, however, disclose anything which might encumber his campaign to seduce Jan—another instance of secondary gratification that rendered the group less effective.)

After their sexual liaison began, the Jan-Bill relationship became even more inaccessible for group scrutiny and for therapeutic work. They began speaking of themselves as "we" and resisted all exhortations of the therapists or other members to learn about themselves by analyzing their behavior. At first it was difficult to know what was operating between the two aside from powerful lust. The therapists knew that Jan's sense of personal worth was outwardly based. To keep others interested in her she needed, she felt, to give gifts—especially sexual ones. Furthermore, there was a vindictive aspect: she had triumphed over important men previously (department chairmen and, prior to that, her father) by sexual seduction. It seemed likely that Jan felt powerless in her dealings with the therapists; her chief interpersonal coinage—sex—afforded her no significant influence over them, but it did permit an indirect victory through the medium of Bill. We learned much later how she and Bill would gleefully lie in bed together relishing the thought that they had put something over on the therapists. Bill not only recapitulated in the group his sexualization of relationships, his repetitive efforts to prove his potency by yet another seduction, but found particularly compelling the opportunity for oedipal mastery—the taking of women away from the leader.

Thus, Bill and Jan, in a rich behavioral tapestry, displayed their dynamics and recreated their social environment in the group. Bill's narcissism and his inauthentic mode of relating to Jan was clearly portrayed. He often made innuendos to the effect that his relationship to the girl with whom he lived was deteriorating, thus planting a seed of marital hope in Jan's imagination. Bill's innuendos colluded with Jan's enormous capacity for self-deception: she alone of any of the group members considered marriage a serious possibility. When the other members tried to help her hear Bill's primary message—that she was not important to him, that she was a sexual object and merely another conquest—she reacted defensively and angrily. Gradually, the dissonance between Bill's private statements and the group's interpretations of Bill's intentions created so much discomfort that Jan considered leaving the group. The therapists reminded Jan that this was precisely what they had warned her about before she entered the group; if she dropped out of therapy, all that had happened in the group would come to naught. She had had many brief and unrewarding relationships in the past; the group offered her a unique opportunity, i.e., the opportunity to stay with a relationship and, for once, play the drama through to its end. Jan decided to stay, perhaps as much to prove the therapists wrong as for any other self-serving reason.

Jan and Bill's relationship was an exclusive one: neither related in any significant way to anyone else in the group, except that Bill attempted to keep erotic channels open to Carrie ("to keep his account open at the bank," as he put it). Carrie and Jan persisted in a state of unrelenting enmity so extreme that they both had homicidal fantasies toward the other. (When Carrie married she invited everyone in the group to the wedding save Jan. Only when a boycott was threatened by the others was a frosty invitation proffered to Jan.) Bill's relationship to the therapists had been very important to him before Jan's entry; during the first months of his liaison with Jan, he seemed to forget their presence. Gradually, however, his concern about them returned. One day, for example, he brought in a dream in which the therapists escorted all the members, save him, into an advanced postgraduate group. He, Bill, was demoted to a more elementary, retarded group.

Jan and Bill's relationship consumed enormous amounts of group energy and time. Relatively few unrelated themes were worked on in the group, but all of the members worked on personal issues which related to the pairing; e.g., sex, jealousy, envy, fears of competition, concerns about physical attractiveness. There was a sustained high level of emotionality in the group. Attendance was excellent: over a thirty-meeting stretch there was not a single absence!

Gradually their relationship began to sour. Jan had always maintained that all she wanted from Bill was his sheer physical presence—one night a month with him was what she required. Now she was forced to realize that she wanted much more. She felt pressured in life: she had lost her job and was beset by financial concerns; she had given up her promiscuity but felt sexual pressures and now began to say to herself, "Where is Bill when I really need him?" She grew depressed, but, rather than work on the depression in the group, she minimized it. Once again secondary considerations were given priority over primary, therapeutic ones, for she was reluctant to give Carrie and the other members the satisfaction of seeing her depressed: they had warned her months ago that a relationship with Bill would ultimately be self-destructive.

And where, indeed, was Bill? That question plunged us into the core issue of Bill's therapy: responsibility. As Jan grew more deeply depressed (a depression punctuated by accident proneness, e.g., an automobile accident and a kitchen accident in which she burned herself), the group confronted Bill with an awesome question: had he known in advance the outcome of the adventure, would he have done anything different? Bill said that he would not have. "If I do not look after my own pleasure, who will?" he rejoined. The other members of the group and now Jan, too, attacked him for his self-indulgence and his lack of responsibility for others. Bill pondered over this confrontation only to advance a series of rationalizations at the subsequent meeting. He was not irresponsible; he was high-spirited, impish, a life-loving Peer Gynt. Life contains little enough pleasure; why is he not entitled to take what he can? He insisted that the group members and therapists, guilefully dressed in the robes of responsibility, were, in fact, trying to rob him of his freedom.

For many sessions the group plunged into the issues of love, freedom, and responsibility. Jan, with increasing directness, confronted Bill. She jolted him in the group by asking exactly how much he cared for her. He squirmed and alluded both to his love for her and to his unwillingness to establish an enduring relationship with any woman. In fact, he found himself turned off to any woman who wanted a long-term relationship. I was reminded of a comparable attitude toward love in the novel *The Fall*, where Camus expresses Bill's paradox with shattering clarity.

It is not true, after all, that I never loved. I conceived at least one great love in my life, of which I was always the object . . . sensuality alone dominated my love life. . . . In any case, my sensuality (to limit myself to it) was so real that even for a ten-minute adventure I'd have disowned father and mother, even were I to regret it bitterly. Indeed—*especially* for a ten-minute adventure and even more so if I were sure it was to have no sequel.

The group therapist, if he was to help Bill, had to make certain that there was to be a sequel.

Bill did not want to be burdened with Jan's depression. He had women in various cities around the country who loved him (and whose love made him feel alive); yet for him these women did not have an independent existence. He preferred to think that his women came to life only when he appeared to them. Once again, Camus said it for him:

I could live happily only on condition that all the individuals on earth, or the greatest possible number, were turned toward me, eternally in suspense, devoid of independent life and ready to answer my call at any moment, doomed in short to sterility until the day I should deign to favor them. In short, for me to live happily it was essential for the creatures I chose not to live at all. They must receive their life, sporadically, only at my bidding.

Jan pressed him relentlessly. She told him that there was another man who was seriously interested in her and she pleaded with Bill to level with her, to be honest about his feelings to her, to set her free. By now Bill was quite certain that he no longer desired Jan. (In fact, as we were to learn later, he had been gradually increasing his commitment to the girl with whom he lived.) Yet he could not allow the words to pass through his lips. A strange type of freedom then, as Bill himself gradually grew to understand: the freedom to take but not the freedom to relinquish. (Camus wrote, "Believe me, for certain men at least, not taking what one doesn't desire is the hardest thing in the world!") He insisted he be granted the freedom to choose his pleasures, yet as he came to see, he had not the freedom to choose for himself; his choice was almost invariably one which resulted in his thinking less well of himself, and the greater his self-hatred, the more compulsive, the less free, was his mindless pursuit of sexual conquests which afforded him only an evanescent balm.

Jan's pathology was equally patent. She ceded her freedom to Bill (a logical paradox); only he had the power to set her free. The therapists confronted her with her pervasive refusal to accept her freedom: why could she not say "no" to a man? How could men use her sexually unless she chose that they use her? It was evident, too, that she punished Bill in an inefficient, self-destructive manner: accidents, depression, lamentations that she had trusted a man who had then betrayed her and that she would now be ruined for life.

Bill and Jan circled these issues for months. From time to time they

would reenter their old relationship but always with slightly more sobriety and slightly less self-deception. During a period of non-work
the therapists, sensing that the timing was correct, confronted them in
a forcible manner. Jan arrived late at the meeting complaining about
the disarray of her financial affairs. She and Bill giggled as Bill commented that her irresponsibility about money made her all the more
adorable. The therapist stunned the group by observing that Jan and
Bill were doing so little therapeutic work that he wondered if it made
sense for them to continue in the group. Jan and Bill accused the therapist of hypermoralism. Jan said that for weeks she only came to the
group to see Bill and to talk to him after the group—if he left she did
not think she would continue. The therapists reminded her that the
group was not a dating bureau: there were far more important tasks for
her to pursue. Bill, the therapists continued, would play no role in the
long scheme of her life and would shortly fade from her memory. Bill
had no commitment to her and if he were at all honest he would tell
her so. Jan rejoined that Bill was the only one in the group who truly
cared for her. The therapist disagreed and said that Bill's type of caring for her was clearly in her worst interests.

Bill left the meeting furious at the therapists (especially at their
comment that he would soon fade from Jan's mind). For a day he fantasized marrying Jan to prove them wrong but returned to the group to
plunge into serious work. As his honesty with himself deepened, as he
faced a central feeling of emptiness which a woman's love had always
temporarily filled, he entered and worked his way through a painful
depression. Jan was acutely despondent for two days following the
meeting and then made some significant decisions for herself about
work, money, men, and therapy.

The group then entered a phase of productive work which was further deepened when the therapist introduced a patient much older
who brought with her many neglected themes in the group: parents,
death, marriage, physical deterioration. Jan and Bill fell out of love,
they began to examine their relationships to others in the group, including the therapists, Bill stopped lying, at first to Jan, then to Carrie,
then to the other members, and, finally to himself. Jan continued in
the group for six more months and Bill for another year.

The outcome for both Jan and Bill was, regardless of the severity of
outcome criteria engaged, stunning. In interviews nine months after
their termination, both showed impressive changes. Jan was no longer
depressed, self-destructive, or promiscuous. She was involved in the
most lengthy, stable, and satisfying relationship with a man she had
ever had. The infanticidal obsessions had disappeared (with, in-

cidently, scarcely a mention of them during her entire course of therapy). She had gone into a different and, for her, more rewarding professional career. Bill, once he understood that he had made his relationship with his girlfriend a tenuous one to allow him to seek that which he really didn't want, allowed himself to feel more deeply and married shortly before leaving the group. His anxious depressions, his tortured self-consciousness, his pervasive sense of emptiness had all been replaced by their respective, vital counterparts.

I am not able in these few pages to sum up all that was important in the therapy of Jan and Bill. Obviously, there was much more to it, including many important interactions with other members and with the therapists. The development and working through of their extragroup relationship was, I believe, not a complication but an indispensable part of their therapy. It is unlikely that Jan would have had the motivation to remain in therapy if Bill were not present in the group. It is unlikely that, without Jan's presence, Bill's central problems would have surfaced clearly and become so accessible for therapy. The price paid by the group was enormous, however. Vast amounts of group time and energy were consumed by Jan and Bill. Other members were neglected, many important issues untouched, It is most unlikely that a new group or a group that met less frequently than twice a week could have afforded the price.

Conflict in the Therapy Group *

Conflict cannot be eliminated from human groups, whether we consider dyads, small groups, macrogroups, or such megagroups as nations and blocs of nations. If conflict is denied or suppressed, invariably it will manifest itself in oblique, corrosive, and often ugly ways. Although our immediate association with conflict is negative—destruction, bitterness, war, violence—a moment of reflection brings to mind positive associations; conflict brings drama, excitement, change, and development to human life and societies. Therapy groups are no exception. Conflict is inevitable in the course of the group's development; its absence, in fact, suggests some impairment of the developmental sequence. Furthermore, conflict can be harnessed in the

* This discussion draws heavily from essays by Jerome Frank [9] and Carl Rogers.[10]

service of the group; the group members can, in a variety of ways, profit from conflict, provided its intensity does not exceed their tolerance and provided that proper group norms have been established. This section will consider conflict in the therapy group—its sources, its meaning, and its value in therapy.

There are many sources of hostility in the therapy group. There are antagonisms based on mutual contempt, a contempt which arises from the patient's own self-contempt. Indeed, often months pass before some patients really begin to hear and respect the opinions of other members; they have so little self-regard that it is at first inconceivable that others, similar to themselves, have something valuable to offer.

Transference or parataxic distortions often generate hostility in the therapy group. A patient may respond to others, not on the basis of reality but on the basis of an image of the other distorted by his own past relationships and his current interpersonal needs and fears. Patients may see in others aspects of significant individuals in their lives. Should the distortion be a negatively charged one, then a mutual antagonism may be easily initiated.

The "mirror reaction" [11] is a form of parataxic distortion and a particularly common source of hostility in the therapy group. Individuals may have suppressed, for years or their entire lives, some traits or desires of which they are much ashamed; when they encounter another person who embodies these very traits, they generally shun him or experience a strong but inexplicable antagonism toward him. The process may be close to consciousness and recognized aasily with guidance by others, or it may be deeply buried and understood only after many months of investigation. For example:

One patient, Vincent, a second-generation Italian-American who had grown up in the Boston slums and obtained a good education with great difficulty, had long since dissociated himself from his roots. Having invested his intellect with considerable pride, he spoke with care to avoid any nuance of his background. In fact, he abhorred the thought of his lowly past and feared that he would be found out—that others would see through his front to his core, which he regarded as ugly, dirty, and repugnant. In the group Vincent experienced extreme antagonism for another member, also of Italian descent, who had, in his values and in his facial and hand gestures, retained his identification with his ethnic group. It was through his investigation of his antagonism toward the other that Vincent arrived at many important insights about himself.

Frank [9] described a similar, double mirror reaction:

. . . in one group a prolonged feud developed between two Jews, one of whom flaunted his Jewishness while the other tried to conceal it. Each finally realized that he was combatting in the other an attitude he repressed in himself. The militant Jew finally understood that he was disturbed by the many disadvantages of being Jewish, and the man who hid his background confessed that he secretly nurtured a certain pride in it.

In a group of psychiatric residents, one member, Pat, agonized over a decision of transferring to another more academically oriented residency. The group, led by one particular member, Louis, was singularly unsympathetic to his plight. They resented his taking group time, they rebuked him for his weakness and indecisiveness, they insisted that he "crap or get off the pot." When the therapist guided the group into an exploration of the sources of their anger toward Pat, many dynamics became evident (several of which I shall discuss in Chapter 15). One of the strongest sources was uncovered by Louis, who discussed his own paralyzing indecisiveness. He had, a year previously, dealt with the same decision that Pat faced and, unable to make an active decision, had resolved the dilemma by passively deciding not to decide and by suppressing the entire problem. Pat's behavior reevoked the whole agonizing problem for Louis, who resented Pat not only for disturbing his uneasy slumber but also for struggling with the issue more honestly and more courageously than he had.

Projective identification is a mechanism closely related to the mirror reaction. It is an unconscious process which consists of projecting some of one's own (but disowned) attributes onto another, toward whom one subsequently feels an uncanny attraction—repulsion. Projective identification is generally more autonomous than mirroring: the other individual need not closely personify the projected aspects of oneself. The difference is only a relative one, however; the vessel into which one projects must be a suitable container. A stark literary example of projective identification occurs in Dostoievski's nightmarish tale *The Double*, in which the protagonist encounters a man who is his double physically and yet the personification of all the dimly perceived, hated aspects of himself. The tale depicts with astonishing vividness the uncanny attraction and the horror and hatred which developed between the protagonist and his double.

Rivalry may be yet another source of conflict, as patients compete with one another in the group. They may vie for the largest share of the therapist's attention or for some particular role: the most powerful, respected, sensitive, disturbed, or needy person in the group.

In the fiftieth meeting of one group, a new member, Ginny, was added. In many aspects she was quite similar to Douglas, one of the original members: they were both artists, mystical in their approach to life, often steeped in fantasy, and both too familiar with their unconscious. It was not an affinity, however, but an antagonism which developed between the two. Ginny immediately established the role she invariably assumed with others: she behaved in a spiritlike, irrational, and disorganized fashion in the group. Douglas, who saw his role as the sickest and most disorganized member being usurped, reacted to her with less tolerance and understanding than to any of the "squarer" members of the group. Only after active interpretation of the role conflict and Douglas's assumption of a new role ("most improved member") was an entente between the two members achieved.

Occasionally, antagonisms may also develop on the basis of differences in outlook based on differing life experiences. Members of different generations may dispute the drug issue or the new sexual code. Liberals and conservatives may develop considerable heat around civil rights or political issues.

As the group progresses, the members may grow increasingly impatient and angry at patients who have not adopted the group's norms of behavior. If one member, for example, continues to hide behind a facade, the group may coax him, attempt to persuade him, and finally angrily demand that he be honest with himself and the others in the group.

Obviously, certain patients because of their character structure will invariably be involved in conflict and will engender conflict in any group to which they belong. Consider the paranoid personality.[12] His assumptive world is that there is danger in the environment. He is eternally suspicious and vigilant. He examines all experience with an extraordinary bias as he searches for clues. He misses the obvious in his quest for signs of danger underneath. He is tight, ready for an emergency. He does not play or permit himself abandonment and looks suspiciously upon these behaviors in others. Obviously, these traits will not endear the paranoid patient to the other group members; sooner or later anger will erupt all around him, and the more severe and rigid the character structure, the more extreme will be the conflict.

Chapter 10 discusses another source of hostility in the group: the growing disenchantment and disappointment with the therapist for frustrating the patients' unrealistic expectations of him. If the group is unable to confront the therapist directly, it may create a scapegoat, which further increases the general level of conflict in the group.

Regardless of its source, the discord, once begun, follows a predictable sequence. The antagonists develop the belief that they are right and the others are wrong, that they are good and the others bad. Moreover, although it is not recognized at the time, these beliefs are characteristically held with equal conviction and certitude by each of the two opposing parties. Where such a situation of opposing beliefs exists, we have all the ingredients for a deep and continuing tension.

Generally, a breakdown in communication ensues. The two parties cease to listen to each other with any degree of understanding. Often, if the social situation permits, the two opponents completely rupture their relationship at this point and the correction of misunderstandings is thus permanently prevented. The analogy to international relations is all too obvious.

Not only do the opponents stop listening, but they also may unwittingly distort their perceptions of one another. Perceptions are filtered through a screen of stereotype. The opponent's words and behavior are shaped to fit a preconceived view of him. Contrary evidence is ignored or distorted; conciliatory gestures may be perceived as deceitful tricks.

Distrust is the basis for this sequence; opponents view their actions as honorable and reasonable and the behavior of others as scheming and evil. If this sequence, so common in human events, were permitted to unfold in therapy groups, little opportunity for change or learning would be available to the group members. A group climate and group norms which can preclude such a sequence must be established early in the life of the group.

Cohesiveness is the prime prerequiste for the successful management of conflict. Members must develop a feeling of mutual trust and respect and must come to value the group as an important means of meeting their personal needs. The patients must understand that communication must be maintained if the group is to survive; all parties must continue to deal directly with one another, no matter how angry they become. Furthermore, everyone is to be taken seriously; when a group treats one patient as a mascot whose opinions and anger are lightly regarded, the hope of effective treatment for that patient has all but officially been abandoned. Moreover, group cohesiveness will have been seriously compromised, since the next most peripheral member will have reason to fear similar treatment. The cohesive group in which everyone is taken seriously soon elaborates norms which obligate members to go beyond name-calling. Each member must pursue and explore derogatory labels; he must be willing to search more deeply within himself to understand his antagonism and to make explicit those aspects of others which anger him. Norms must be established which make it clear that group members are there to understand themselves, not to defeat or ridicule others.

Once a member realizes that others accept him and are trying to understand him, then he finds it less necessary to hold rigidly to his own beliefs, and he may be willing to explore previously denied aspects of himself. Gradually, he may develop motivational insight. He "comes to recognize that not all of his motives are those he has proclaimed and that some of his attitudes and behaviors are not so fully justified as he has been maintaining to his opponent and to the world." [10] When this step has been achieved, a breakthrough may occur in which the individual changes his perception of the situation and realizes that the problem can be viewed in more than one way.

Empathy is an important element in conflict resolution and facilitates a humanization of the struggle. Often, the understanding of the past plays an important role in the development of empathy; once an individual appreciates the aspects of his opponent's earlier life which have resulted in his current stance, the position of the other not only makes sense but may even appear right for him. *Tout comprendre, c'est tout pardonner.*

Conflict resolution is often impossible in the presence of off-target or oblique hostility. For example:

In one group a patient began the session by requesting and obtaining the therapist's permission to read a letter she was writing in conjunction with a court hearing on her impending divorce, which involved considerable property settlement and custodianship of children. The letter-reading consumed considerable time and was eventually interrupted by the therapist and then the patients, who disputed the content of the letter. The sniping by the group and defensive counterattacks by the protagonist continued until the group atmosphere was crackling with irritability. The group made no constructive headway until the therapist explored with the patients the process of the meeting. The therapist was annoyed with himself for having permitted the letter to be read and with the patient for having put him in that position. The group members were angry at the therapist for having given permission and at the patient both for consuming so much time and for relating to them in the frustrating impersonal manner of letter-reading. Once the anger had been directed away from the oblique target of the letter's contents onto the appropriate targets of the therapist and the letter-reader, steps toward conflict resolution could begin.

Permanent conflict abolition, let me note, is not the final goal of the therapy group; conflict will continuously recur in the group despite successful resolution of past conflicts and despite the presence of considerable mutual respect and warmth. However, neither is unrestrained expression of rage a goal of the therapy group. The therapeutic use of conflict, like all other behaviors, is a two-step process: experience and integration of that experience. In a variety of ways the therapist helps patients both experience and understand conflict.

Almost invariably, two group members who feel considerable mutual antagonism have the potential to be of the greatest value to each other. Each obviously cares about how the other regards him. Generally, there is much envy and much mutual projection and thus the opportunity to uncover hidden parts of oneself. In their anger each will tell the other important (though unpalatable) truths about the other. The self-esteem of the antagonists may be increased by the conflict; when people become angry at one another, this in itself may be taken as an indication that they are important to one another and take one another quite seriously. At other times patients learn that although others may respond negatively to some trait, mannerism, or attitude, they themselves are valued.

For patients who have been unable to express anger, the group may serve as a testing ground for taking risks and learning that such behavior is neither dangerous nor necessarily destructive. Chapter 2 described a number of incidents cited by patients as turning points in their therapy; a majority of these critical incidents involved the expression, for the first time, of strong negative affect. It is also important for patients to learn that they can withstand attacks and pressure from others. Overly aggressive patients may learn some of the interpersonal consequences of blind self-assertion. Through feedback, they appreciate their impact on other individuals and gradually come to terms with the self-defeating pattern of their behavior. For many, angry confrontations may provide valuable learning opportunities since therapy group members learn to remain in mutually useful contact despite their anger.

Patients may be helped to express anger more directly and more fairly. Even in all-out conflict there are tacit rules of war which, if violated, make satisfactory resolution all but possible. For example, in therapy groups combatants will occasionally take information disclosed by the other in a previous spirit of trust and use it later to scorn or humiliate the other. Or they may refuse to examine the conflict because they claim to have so little regard for the other they do not wish to waste any further time. These postures require vigorous intervention by the therapist. One of the most common indirect and self-defeating modes of fighting is the one used by Jan in the clinical description earlier in this chapter. This strategy calls for the patient, in one form or another, to injure himself in the hope of inducing guilt in the other—the "see what you've done to me" strategy. Usually, much therapeutic work is required to change this pattern; it is generally deeply engrained with roots stretching back to earliest childhood. (Remember the common childhood fantasy of one's imagined funeral with anguished parents and other tormentors beating their breasts in endless guilt.)

In the process of disagreeing, each patient may learn more about the reasons for his position and may, in fact, discover new and more valid reasons. He may also understand that, despite the source of his anger, he expresses himself in self-defeating, maladaptive ways. Some may learn from feedback that they habitually display scorn, irritation, or disapproval. Our sensitivity to facial gestures and nuances of expression far exceeds our proprioceptive sensitivity; [13] only through feedback do we learn that we communicate something which is not intended or, for that matter, even consciously experienced.

Patients who do not experience anger are common and always challenging in therapy. They learn that others in their situation would feel angry; they learn to read their own body language ("my fists are clenched so I *must be* angry"); they learn to magnify rather than suppress the first flickerings of anger; they learn that it is safe, permissible and in their best interests to feel and express anger.

Strong shared affect may enhance the importance of the relationship. Chapter 3 described how group cohesiveness is increased when members of a group go through intense emotional experiences together, regardless of the nature of the emotion. "In this manner," as Frank says, "members of a successful therapy group are like members of a closely knit family who may battle each other, yet derive much support from their family allegiance." [9] A dyadic relationship, too, which has weathered much stress is apt to be an especially rewarding one. An experience in which two individuals in group therapy experience an intense mutual hatred and then, through some of the mechanisms we have described, resolve the hatred and arrive at some mutual understanding and respect is always of great therapeutic value.

Self-Disclosure

Self-disclosure—both feared and valued by participants—plays an integral part in all group therapies. Culbert [14] offered the following definition.

Self-disclosure refers to an individual's explicitly communicating to one or more others some personal information that he believes these others would be unlikely to acquire unless he himself discloses it. Moreover, this information must be "personally private"; that is, it must be of such a nature that it is not something the individual would disclose to everyone who might inquire about it.

The content of the self-disclosure may include past or current events in one's life, fantasy or dream material, hopes or aspirations for the future, and current feelings toward other individuals. In group therapy the latter category (feelings toward other members) often assumes major importance.

RISK

Obviously, self-disclosure requires the presence of at least one other person and must be examined within the context of that relationship. Every self-disclosure involves some risk on the part of the discloser. The degree of risk depends on several factors: [14]

1. The nature and intensity of the disclosed material. If the disclosure is of a highly personal nature, emotionally charged and previously undisclosed, obviously the risk is greater. First-time disclosures (i.e., the first time the individual has shared this information with anyone) are especially charged.
2. The probability that the receiver will receive the disclosure as the communicator intends. The risk is diminished if the discloser is certain that the receiver shares similar concerns and that he is sensitive to the communicator's needs.
3. The probability that the receiver will react as the communicator intended. The self-discloser always has some hopes and expectations of a specific type of response from the receiver. The more familiar the receiver, the more frequently they have had similar transactions in the past, the less the risk. If the receiver is vulnerable with respect to the discloser, then, too, the risk is less. For example, the receiver may have previously disclosed himself to the communicator; in such an instance the communicator has a degree of leverage and may, with little risk, reciprocate.

SEQUENCE OF SELF-DISCLOSURE

In conventional social relationships, in which one participant has an inclination for self-disclosure, a predictable sequence usually occurs. The discloser begins by making low level disclosures. The receiver who is involved in a lasting relationship with the discloser (and not merely a casual acquaintance at a cocktail party) is likely to consider himself charged with certain responsibilities or obligations to the discloser. He generally responds to the disclosure by some appropriate

comment, depending on the nature of the disclosure, and then recip-
rocates with some disclosure of his own. The receiver now, as well as
the original discloser, is vulnerable, and a deepening relationship
usually continues, with the participants making slightly more open
and intimate disclosures in turn until some optimal level for that relationship is reached.

ADAPTIVE FUNCTIONS OF SELF-DISCLOSURE

Self-disclosure is a prerequisite for the formation of meaningful interpersonal relationships in a dyadic or in a group situation. As disclosures proceed in the group, the entire membership gradually increases its level of involvement, responsibility, and obligation to one
another. If the timing is right, there is nothing which will commit an
individual to a group more than to receive or to reveal some intimate
secret material. There is nothing more exhilarating than for a member
to disclose for the first time some material which has burdened him for
years and to be understood and fully accepted. If, as interpersonalists
such as Sullivan and Rogers have maintained, self-acceptance must be
preceded by acceptance by others, then the individual, if he is to accept himself, must gradually permit others to know him as he really is.

Research evidence validates the importance of self-disclosure in
group therapy. Chapter 3 described the relationship between self-
disclosure and popularity in the group. Popularity (determined from
sociometrics) correlates positively with the therapy outcome;[15] patients who are high disclosers in the early meetings often assume high
popularity in their groups.[16] Peres [17] demonstrated that successfully
treated patients in group therapy had made almost twice as many self-
disclosing personal statements during the course of therapy as did unsuccessfully treated patients. Truax and Carkhuff [18] also found that patients' success in group therapy correlated with their transparency
during the course of the group. Lieberman, Yalom, and Miles [19] found
that, in encounter groups, individuals who had negative outcomes
revealed less of themselves than the other participants.

The concept of carryover is vital here; not only are patients rewarded by the other group members for self-disclosure, but the behavior, thus reinforced, is integrated into the individual's relationships outside the group, where it is similarly rewarded. Often, the
first step in revealing to a spouse or a potential close friend is the
"first-time" disclosure in the therapy group.

MALADAPTIVE SELF-DISCLOSURE

Self-disclosure is related to optimal psychological and social adjustment in a curvilinear fashion: too much or too little self-disclosure signify maladaptive interpersonal behavior.

Too little self-disclosure usually results in severely limited opportunity for reality testing. If an individual fails to disclose himself in a relationship, he generally forfeits an opportunity to obtain valid feedback. Furthermore, he prevents the relationship from developing further; without reciprocation, the other party will either desist from further self-disclosure or else rupture the relationship entirely.

The individual who does not disclose himself in the group has little chance of genuine acceptance by the other members and therefore little chance of experiencing a rise in self-esteem. Vosen has demonstrated this very point experimentally. In his study, "a self-perceived lack of self-disclosure resulted in reduced self-esteem." [20] Should it occur that an individual is accepted on the basis of a (false) image he attempts to project, no enduring boost in self-esteem occurs; moreover, he is even less likely at this point to engage in valid self-disclosure since he now runs the added risk of losing the acceptance he has gained through his false presentation of self. [14]

Some individuals dread self-disclosure, not primarily because of shame or fear of nonacceptance but because they are heavily conflicted in the area of control: to them self-disclosure is dangerous because it makes them vulnerable to the control of others. When others in the group have made themselves exceedingly vulnerable through self-disclosure, then and only then are they willing to reciprocate.

Self-disclosure blockages will impede individual members as well as entire groups. If an individual has an important secret which he feels he dare not reveal to the group, he may find participation on any but a superficial level very difficult because not only must he conceal the secret but he must also conceal all possible leads to the secret. In Chapter 9, I discussed in detail how, in the early stages of therapy, the therapist might best approach the patient with a top secret. To summarize, it is advisable for the therapist to counsel the patient that he must, if he is to benefit from therapy, share the secret with the group. The pace and timing are up to the patient, but the therapist may offer to make the act easier in any way the patient wishes. These are times when the therapist, unwittingly, discourages self-disclosure. The most terrifying secret I have known a patient to possess occurred in a newly formed group led by a neophyte therapist. The patient had, one year previously, murdered her two-year-old child and then failed in a suicide attempt. (The court ruled her insane and released her on the provision that she be in therapy.) After fourteen weeks of therapy, not only had the patient told nothing of herself but by her militant promulgation of denial and suppressive strategies (such as astrological tables and ancient mystical sects) had impeded the entire group. Despite his supervisor's counsel, the group therapist could find no method to help the patient (or the group) move into therapy. The supervisor then observed some group sessions and noted that the patient provided the therapist with a vast number of opportunities to help her discuss the secret. A productive supervisory session was devoted to the therapist's avoidance of the patient; his feelings about his own two-year-old child, his horror (despite himself) at her act, colluded with her guilt to silence her in the group. In the following meeting the gentlest question by the therapist was sufficient to free the patient's tongue and to change the entire character of the group.

In some groups (and I find this frequently in groups of mental health professionals) self-disclosure is discouraged by a general climate of judgmentalism. Members are reluctant to disclose "shameful" aspects of themselves lest others lose respect for them. In groups of mental health professionals this issue is even more pressing. Since our chief professional instrument is our own person, a professional as well as a personal loss of respect is at risk. In one group, for example, a psychiatric resident discussed her homosexuality, while another discussed his lack of confidence as a physician and his panic whenever he is placed in a life or death situation. Bob, another member, reported that their fears of revealing this material were well-founded since he did lose respect for them and doubted whether he would, in the future, refer patients to them. The group continued, with the other members condemning Bob for his judgmentalism and suggesting that they would be reluctant to refer patients to him. And so the serpent could continue to swallow its tail ad infinitum unless the therapist makes a vigorous process intervention.

One must differentiate, too, between a healthy need for privacy and neurotic compulsive secrecy. There are some individuals, not often likely to find their way into groups, who are private individuals in an adaptive way; they share intimacies with only a few intimate friends and shudder at the thought of self-disclosure in a group. Moreover, they enjoy private self-contemplative activities. This is a far different thing from privacy which is based on fear, shame, or crippling social inhibitions. In fact, as Maslow [21] suggests, the resolution of neurotic privacy may be an essential first step toward the establishment of a healthy desire for privacy. Many patients who are nondisclosers have at the same time a fear of being alone and involve themselves in many unrewarding dependent relationships; they so dread loneliness that they can no longer experience the pleasures of privacy. Their sense of self is so stunted that the world takes on a reality only as it is perceived through the experience of another. Thus, they cannot enjoy a movie alone or a play or a sporting event: they await the newspaper review or the reactions of others to experience the realness of the event. They may be so sensitized to rejection or abandonment that the experience of being alone fills them with dread. Others are so painfully self-conscious that they torture themselves while alone by dwelling on how they appear to others: do others think them friendless, lonely, pitiable, etc.?

Too much self-disclosure can be as maladaptive as too little. Indiscriminate self-disclosure is not a goal of mental health nor a pathway to it. Some patients make the grievous error of reasoning that if self-disclosure is good, then total and continuous self-disclosure must be a very good thing indeed. But, as Goffman [22] notes, urban life would become unbearably sticky if every contact between two individuals entailed a sharing of personal concerns and secrets. Obviously, the type of relationship that exists between the discloser and the receiver should be the major factor in determining the pattern of self-disclosure. Several research investigations have demonstrated this experimentally: individuals disclose different types and amounts of material, depending on if the receiver is a mother, father, best male friend, female friend, work associate, or spouse.[23,24,25]

However, some maladaptive disclosers disregard and thus jeopardize their relationship to the receiver. The individual who in his self-disclosure fails to discriminate between intimate friends and more distant acquaintances perplexes his associates. We have all, I am certain, experienced a feeling of confusion or betrayal upon learning that supposedly intimate material confided to us has been shared with many others. Furthermore, a great deal of self-disclosure may frighten off an unprepared recipient. In a rhythmic, flowing relationship, one party leads the other in self-disclosures, but never by too great a gap.

In group therapy, members who reveal early and promiscuously will often drop out early in the course of therapy. Patients should be encouraged to take risks in the group; such behavior change results in positive feedback and reinforcement and encourages further risk-taking. But if they reveal too much too early, they may exceed their tolerance: they feel so much shame that any interpersonal rewards are offset; furthermore, they may threaten others willing to support them but not yet prepared to reciprocate. The discloser is then placed in a position of such great vulnerability in the group that he often chooses to flee.

All of these observations suggest that self-disclosure is a complex, social act which is situation and role bound. One does not self-disclose in solitude; time, place, and person must always be considered. What is appropriate self-disclosure in a therapy group, for example, may be disastrously inappropriate in other situations. (This failure to demarcate boundaries—and the ensuing grief therefrom—is characteristic of many individuals who have had an exhilarating short-term experience in an encounter group [see Chapter 14]).

What is appropriate self-disclosure for one stage of a therapy group may be inappropriate for another stage. These points are particularly evident in the case of self-disclosure of one's feelings toward other members ("feedback"). It is my belief that the therapist should help the members be guided as much by responsibility to others as by freedom of expression. I have seen some very vicious, destructive events occur in groups under the aegis of honesty and self-revelation. "You told us that we should be honest about expressing our feelings, didn't you?" But in fact we always selectively reveal our feelings. There are always layers of reactions which we rarely share: feelings about unchangeable attributes, physical characteristics, deformity, professional or intellectual mediocrity, social class, lack of charm, etc. For some individuals, disclosure of overt hostile feelings is "easy—honest." What about the underlying meta-hostile feelings—feelings of envy, guilt, concern, empathy, brotherhood, one's sadistic pleasure in vindictive triumph?

In Chapter 6, I discussed some of the role bound characteristics of group leader self-disclosure. The leader must place other considerations first. The general who, after having made an important tactical decision, goes around wringing his hands and verbally expressing his uncertainty is certain to undercut the morale of his entire command.[21] The therapy group leader does not disclose those feelings which would undermine the effectiveness of the group: his impatience with the group, his desire to get home to dinner, his preoccupation with the patient or group seen earlier in the day, his list of favorites in the group, and a host of other deeply personal concerns.

Termination

Termination is more than an act signifiying the end of therapy; it is an integral part of the process of therapy and, if properly understood and managed, may be an important force in the instigation of change. There are at least three common forms of termination in the therapy group: (1) the termination of the unsuccessful patient, (2) the termination of the successful patient, and (3) the termination of the entire group.

THE UNSUCCESSFUL PATIENT

Generally, unsuccessful patients who drop out of group therapy leave the group within the first twenty meetings; research has indicated that there are far fewer dropouts between the twentieth and fiftieth meetings and furthermore that patients who remain in the group for as long as fifty meetings have a high likelihood of improvement (85 percent in one study).[15]

The reasons for premature termination have been discussed elsewhere in this book. In general, they stem from problems caused by deviancy, subgrouping, conflicts in intimacy and disclosure, the role of the early provocateur, external stress, complications of concurrent individual and group therapy, inability to share the leader, inadequate preparation, and emotional contagion. Underlying all these reasons is the fact that there is considerable stress early in the group; patients who have maladaptive interpersonal patterns are exposed to unaccustomed demands for candor and intimacy, they are often confused about procedure, they suspect that the group activities bear little relevance to their problem, and, finally, too little support occurs for them in the early meetings to sustain their hope.

The general principles of preventing dropouts have been discussed in Chapters 9 and 10. One important approach to decreasing the dropout rate is, in the pretherapy preparation, to anticipate major group concerns and problems. This anticipation makes clear to the patient that periods of discouragement are expected in the therapy process. Patients are less prone to lose confidence in a therapist who appears to have the foreknowledge which stems from experience.

Some groups contain experienced group members who assume some of this predictive function. For example:

One group which graduated several members but which contained three old members was reconstituted with five new members. In the first two meetings the old members briefed the new ones and, among other information, told them that by the sixth or seventh meeting some patient would decide to drop out and then the group "would have to drop everything for a couple of meetings to persuade him to stay." The old members went on to predict which of the new members would be the first to decide to terminate. This form of prediction is a most effective manner of ensuring that the prediction does not come to pass.

Even despite painstaking preparation, however, many patients will consider dropping out. When a patient informs a therapist that he wishes to leave the group, the traditional approach is to urge him to return to the group to discuss it with the other group members. Underlying this practice is the assumption that the group will help the patient work through his resistance and thereby dissuade him from terminating. This approach, however, is rarely successful. In one study [1] of thirty-five dropouts from nine therapy groups (with an original membership of ninety-seven patients), I found that every one of the dropouts was urged to return for another meeting; not once was this effective in averting the premature termination. (Furthermore, there were no group continuers who threatened to drop out and were salvaged by this technique.) When the patient did return to a final meeting, he did not amplify his reasons for leaving the group because in each instance he was no longer committed to the group or to the group norms; generally, he communicated in a defensive, guarded manner, and neither he nor the group benefited from the exchange.

Generally, the therapist is well-advised to see a potential dropout for a short series of individual interviews in which the sources of group stress are discussed. An accurate penetrating interpretation by the therapist may be extremely effective in keeping the patient in therapy.

For example, one schizoid, alienated patient announced in the eighth meeting that he felt he was getting nowhere in the group and had decided to terminate. In an individual session the patient stated something he had never been able to say in the group; namely, that he had many positive feelings toward a couple of the group members. Nevertheless, he insisted that the therapy was ineffective and that he desired a more accelerated and more relevant form of therapy. The therapist correctly interpreted the patient's intellectual criticsm of the group therapy format as a rationalization; he was, in fact, fleeing from the closeness he had felt in the group. The therapist again explained the social microcosm phenomenon and clarified for the patient that in the group he was repeating his lifelong style of relating to others; he had always avoided or fled from intimacy and no doubt would always do so in the future unless he stopped running and allowed himself the opportunity to explore his interpersonal problems in vivo. The patient returned to the group and eventually made considerable gains in therapy.

The inexperienced group therapist is often highly threatened by the patient who threatens to drop out. Often during the second or third month of therapy several patients simultaneously consider termination; at this point the neophyte therapist may suffer considerable discomfort and experience the fantasy of standing alone in the group with everything crumbling away underneath. In time he will learn that early dropouts are inevitable in the group * and that they do not signify a personal failure on his part. If the therapist panics and puts undue pressure on the patient to continue in the group, the patient will generally perceive that he is being asked to do something not for himself but for the therapist or for the group, and will almost certainly leave therapy.

Some highly experienced group therapists rarely have dropouts. Not only are they more skilled in the selection process but they have a degree of confidence in the group which, in a number of ways, is transmitted to the group members. They are able to predict even after a few sessions which patients will be unable to work in the group and, rather than go through a dropout process which is demoralizing for the patient and group, they inform the patient that, in their best judgment, the group will not be useful to him and that another form of therapy be considered. This method of reducing dropouts is more than a specious form of bookkeeping (conversion of "dropouts" to "thrownouts") analogous to the procedure used by some hospitals to inflate survival rate of various surgical procedures (transferring terminal patients to affiliated institutions). It reflects a posture of the therapist which increases the commitment to work and the value of the group.

When a patient, despite the therapist's best efforts, does choose to leave the group, then it is up to the therapist to make the experience as constructive as possible; such patients ordinarily are considerably demoralized and tend to view the group experience as "one more failure." Even if the patient denies this feeling, the therapist should still assume that it is present and in a private discussion with the patient should advance alternative methods of viewing the experience. For

* In fact, an escape hatch is essential to the group process; its presence allows some patients to make their first tentative commitments to the group. The group must have some decompression mechanism; mistakes in the selection process are inevitable, unexpected events in the lives of the new members occur, unanticipated group incompatibilities develop. Some intensive week-long human relations laboratories meeting at a geographically isolated locale lack such an escape hatch, and on several occasions I have observed psychotic reactions stemming from the forced continuation in an incompatible group.

example, he may present the notion of "readiness" or "group fit." Some patients are able to profit from group therapy only after a period of individual therapy; others, for reasons unclear to us, are never able to work effectively in therapy groups. It is also entirely possible that the patient may have a successful course of therapy in another group, and this possibility should be explored. In any case, the patient should be helped to understand that it is not *he* who has failed but that, due to a number of possible reasons, a form of therapy has failed.

The therapist may use the final interview to review in detail the patient's experience in the group in a manner useful for the patient. Occasionally, the therapist is uncertain about the usefulness or advisability of confronting patients who are terminating therapy. Should he, for example, confront a denying patient who attributes his dropping out of the group to his hearing difficulties when in fact he had been an extreme deviant and was clearly rejected by the group? As a general principle, it is useful to view the patient from the perspective of his entire career in therapy. If he is very likely to reenter therapy, a constructive confrontation will, in the long run, enable him to use his next therapy more effectively. If, on the other hand, there is little likelihood that the patient will pursue a dynamically oriented therapy, there is little point in presenting a final interpretation which the patient will never be able to use or to extend; there is little point in undermining defenses, even self-deceptive ones, if one cannot provide a satisfactory substitute.

TERMINATION OF THE SUCCESSFUL PATIENT

Throughout, this book has emphasized that group therapy is a highly individualized process. Each patient will enter, participate in, use, and experience the group in a highly personal manner. The end of therapy is no less an individualized matter. Only very general assumptions about the length and overall goals of therapy may be made. Most patients require approximately twelve to twenty-four months to undergo substantial and durable change, although it is possible to resolve crises and achieve symptomatic relief in far briefer periods of time. The goals of therapy have never been stated more succinctly than in Freud's "to be able to love and to work." Some would, today, add a third, "to play," and others would hope, too, that the patient would be able to love himself, to allow others to love him, to be more flexible, and to search for and trust his own values. Some patients may achieve a great deal in a few months, whereas others require years of group therapy. Some patients have far more ambitious goals than others; it would not be an exaggeration to state that some patients, satisfied with their therapy, terminate in approximately the same state in which others may begin therapy. Some patients may have highly specific goals in therapy and, because much of their psychopathology is ego-syntonic, choose to limit the amount of change they are willing to undertake. Others may be hampered by important external circumstances in their lives. All therapists have had the experience of helping a patient improve to a point at which further change would make him worse. For example, a patient might, with further change, outgrow, as it were, his spouse; continued therapy would result in the rupture of an irreplaceable relationship unless concomitant changes occur in the spouse. If that contingency is not available, the therapist may be well-advised to settle for the positive changes that have occurred, even though the personal potential for greater growth is clearly evident.

Termination of professional treatment is but a stage in the individual's career of growth; termination is not tantamount to stagnation. Patients continue to change, and one important effect of successful therapy is to enable patients to use constructively the resources in their personal environment. I have seen many successful patients in long-term follow-up interviews who have not only continued to change post-termination but who, after they have left the group, recall months later an observation or interpretation made by another member or the therapist which has suddenly become meaningful to them. Not only growth but setbacks occur following termination; many successfully treated patients will encounter stress in excess of their coping ability and need temporary help. In addition, all patients experience anxiety and depression following departure from the group; a period of mourning is an inevitable part of the termination process.

The timing of termination is as inexact and as individualized a matter as the criteria for termination. Some therapists find that termination from group therapy is less problematic than termination from long-term individual therapy, in which patients often become so dependent on the therapeutic situation that they are loath to part with it. Group therapy patients are usually more aware that therapy is not a way of life but a process with a beginning, middle, and end. In the therapy group there are many living reminders of the therapeutic sequence. Patients see new members enter therapy and improved members terminate; they observe the therapist beginning the process over and over again as he helps the beginners over difficult phases of therapy. Through this they realize the bittersweet fact that though the therapist is a person with whom they have had a real and meaningful relationship, he is also a professional: he must shift his attention to others; he will not remain as a permanent and bottomless source of gratification for them.

Not infrequently, the group places subtle pressure on a member not to terminate; not only will the remaining members miss him but they will miss his contributions. There is no doubt that patients who have worked in a therapy group for many months or years acquire interpersonal and group skills which make them particularly valuable members. (I think that this may be one important *qualitative* difference between group therapy and individual therapy outcome. Perhaps it could be demonstrated by testing patients with film or video-taped group segments and obtaining their observations about the underlying process.)

For example, a terminating patient pointed out in his final meeting that in four of the last five sessions it was Albert who started the meeting but that rapidly the group switched over to Dave, who was more entertaining and engaging. Following that, he noted that Albert, aside from occasional sniping, slumped into silence for the rest of the meeting. He also remarked that two other members never communicated directly to each other; instead, they always used a third party mediator. Another patient in her last meeting remarked that she had noted the first signs of the breakdown of a long-term collusion between two patients in which they had, in effect, agreed never to say anything challenging or unpleasant to the other. In the same meeting she chided the members of the group who were asking for clarification about the group ground rules regarding subgrouping. "Answer it for yourselves. It's your therapy. You know what you want to get out of the group. What would it mean to you? Will it get in your way or not?" All of these comments are highly sophisticated—worthy of any experienced group therapist.

The therapist may so highly value these members' contributions that at times he shares in the members' reluctance to allow a patient to terminate; there is, of course, no justification for such a posture and the therapist should explore this openly as soon as he becomes aware of it. I have, incidentally, noted a role suction operative at such times. Once the senior member leaves, another moves into a position wherein he is able to exercise the skills he has acquired.

Some socially isolated patients may postpone termination because they use the therapy group as a social group rather than as a means for developing the skills to create a social life for themselves in their home environment. The therapist must in this instance focus on transfer of learning and encourage risk-taking outside the group. Others may prolong unduly their stay in the group by hoping for some type of guarantee that they are indeed safe from future difficulties; they may suggest that they remain in the group for a few more months until they start a new job, or get married, or graduate from college. If the improvement base seems secure, however, these delays are generally unnecessary: we can never be certain, we are always at risk.

Not infrequently, patients experience a brief recrudesence of their original symptomatology shortly before termination. Rather than prolong their stay in the group, the therapist should help the patients understand this event for what it is—a protest against termination. One patient, three meetings before termination, reexperienced much of the depression and meaninglessness that had brought him into therapy. The symptoms rapidly disappeared with the therapist's interpretation that he was searching for reasons not to leave the group. That evening he had a dream which he brought into the next meeting: "You [the therapist] offered me a place in another group in which I would receive training as a therapist. I felt that I had duped you into thinking I was better." The dream represents an ingenious strategem to defeat termination: it offers two alternatives—the first is that the patient goes into another of the therapist's groups in which he receives training as a therapist; the second is that he has duped the therapist and has not really improved (and thus should continue in the group). Either way the dream is taken, the patient does not have to terminate.

Some patients improve gradually and consistently during their stay in the group. Others go about things more disrhythmically and improve in bursts. I have known many patients who, though committed to the group and hard-working, make no apparent progress whatsoever for six, twelve, even eighteen months and then suddenly in a short period of time seem to transform themselves. (What do we tell our students? That they should not look for immediate gratifications from their patients but instead, if they build solid, deep therapeutic foundations, change is sure to follow. So often we think of this as a sop—a platitude designed to bolster therapists' morale—that we forget it is true.) There are certain patients for whom this is especially true: these patients are particularly sensitized to abandonment, they have a low self-regard, and feel that their only currency in their traffic with the therapist and group is their illness. If they were to improve, the therapist would leave them; therefore, they must minimize or conceal progress. Of course, it is not until much later that they discover the key to the absurd paradox: once they truly improve, they will no longer need the therapist!

One useful sign suggesting readiness for termination is that the group becomes less important to the patient. One terminating member commented that Mondays and Thursdays (the days of the group meetings) were now like any other day of the week. When she began in the group, she lived for Mondays and Thursdays with the rest of the days inconsequential padding between meetings.

I have made a practice of recording the first therapy interview with the patient. Not infrequently, these tapes are useful in arriving at the termination decision. By listening, many months later, to their initial session, patients can obtain a clearer perspective of what they have accomplished and what remains to be done. Therapists who use alternate sessions report that when a patient's behavior in the leaderless meeting is identical to his behavior in the presence of a therapist, the optimal time for termination may be at hand.

The group members are an invaluable resource in helping one another decide about termination, and a unilateral decision made by a patient without consulting the other members is often a premature one. Generally, a well-timed termination decision will be discussed for a few weeks in the group, during which time the patient works through his feelings about leaving the group. Not infrequently, patients make an abrupt decision to terminate their membership in the group immediately; I have found that these patients find it difficult to express gratitude and positive feeling, hence they attempt to abbreviate the separation process as much as possible. These patients must be helped to understand and correct their jarring, unsatisfying method of ending relationships. To ignore this phase of interpersonal relationships is to neglect an important area of human relations. Termination is, after all, a part of almost every relationship, and throughout one's life one must, on many occasions, say goodbye to important people.

Many terminating patients attempt to lessen the shock of departure by creating bridges to the group which they can use in the future. They seek assurances that they may return, collect telephone numbers of the other members, or arrange social meetings so as to keep themselves informed of important events of the group. These efforts are only to be expected and yet the therapist must not collude in such a way as to deny termination. On the contrary, he must help the members to explore it to its fullest extent. The patient is truly leaving, he cannot really return, the group will be irreversibly altered, new members will replace him, the present cannot be frozen, time flows on cruelly and inexorably. These facts are evident to the remaining members as well; there is no better stimulus than a departing member to encourage the group to deal with issues around separation, loss, death, aging, the contingencies of existence, and the passing of time. Termination is thus more than an extraneous event in the group; it is the microcosmic representation of some of the most crucial and painful issues of all.

The group may need some sessions to work on their loss and to deal with many of these termination issues. After a member leaves the group, it is generally wise not to introduce new patients into the group without a hiatus of one or more meetings. A member's departure is often an appropriate time for others to take inventory of their own progress in therapy. Members who entered the group together with the terminating patient may feel some pressure to move more quickly. Other reactions are a function of conflict areas. Some members may misperceive the member's leaving as a forced departure and may feel a need to reaffirm a secure place in the group—by regressive means if necessary. Other more competitive members may rush toward termination prematurely.

The therapist must also look to his own feelings during the termination process because occasionally he unaccountably and unnecessarily delays the patient's termination. Some perfectionistic therapists may unrealistically expect too much change in their patients and refuse to accept anything less than total recovery; moreover, they lack faith in the patient's ability to continue growth following the termination of formal therapy. Other patients bring out Pygmalion pride in us; we find it difficult to part with someone who is, in part, our own creation: saying goodbye to some patients is saying goodbye to a part of ourselves. Furthermore, it is a permanent goodbye; if the therapist has done his job properly, the patient no longer needs him and breaks all contact. Nor, of course, is the therapist exempt from feelings of loss and bereavement. There are many members to whom he has grown close. He will miss them as they him. To the therapist as well as the patient, termination is the jolting reminder of the inbuilt cruelty of the psychotherapeutic process.

THE TERMINATION OF THE GROUP

Groups terminate for various reasons. Some therapists set a time limit at the beginning of the group. Often, external circumstances dictate the end of the group; for example, groups in a university mental health clinic usually run for eight to nine months and disband at the beginning of the summer vacation. Other groups end when the therapist leaves the area, although this is not inevitable since the co-therapist, if present, may continue the group, or the group may be transferred to another therapist (who may, incidentally, aid in the transition by attending the original therapist's last few meetings). Occasionally, a therapist may decide to end a group because the great majority of patients all are ready to terminate at approximately the same time.

Often, the group avoids the difficult and unpleasant work of termination by ignoring or denying their concerns, and it is the therapist who must keep the task in focus for them. The end of the group is a real loss; patients gradually come to realize that it can never be reconvened, that even if they continue a relationship with one member or a fragment of the group, nevertheless the entire group will be gone forever.

The therapist must often repeatedly call the members' attention to the impending termination. If avoidance is extreme—manifested, for example, by an increased absence rate—the therapist must confront the group with their behavior. Usually with a mature group the best approach is a direct approach; the members can be reminded that it is their group and they must decide how they want to end it. Irregularly attending members must be helped to understand their behavior. Do they feel their absence makes no difference to the others or do they so dread expressing positive feelings toward the group or perhaps negative feelings to the therapist for ending it that they avoid a confrontation? Pain over the loss of the group is, in part, dealt with by a sharing of past experiences; exciting and meaningful past group events are remembered, patients remind one another of "the way you were then"; personal testimonials are invariably heard in the final meetings. It is important that the therapist not bury the group too early, otherwise the group is in for several ineffective "lame duck" sessions. One must find a way to hold the issue of termination before the group and yet help it keep working until the very last minute.

Throughout, the therapist facilitates the group work by disclosing his own feelings about separation. The therapist, no less than the patients, will miss the group. For him, too, it has been a place of anguish, conflict, fear, and also of great beauty; some of life's truest and most poignant moments occur in the small and yet limitless microcosm of the therapy group.

REFERENCES

1. I. D. Yalom, "A Study of Group Therapy Dropouts," *Arch. Gen. Psychiat.*, *14*: 393–414, 1966.
2. H. Lindt and M. Sherman, "Social Incognito," in "Analytically Oriented Group Psychotherapy," *Int. J. Group Psychother.*, *2*: 209–220, 1952.
3. S. Freud, *Group Psychology and the Analysis of the Ego* (New York: Bantam, 1960).
4. I. Yalom, "Group Psychology and the Analysis of the Ego: A Review," *Internat. J. Group Psychother.*, XXIV No. 1, Jan. 74, pp. 67–82.
5. I. D. Yalom and P. Houts, unpublished data, 1965.
6. J. D. Frank, "Some Determinants, Manifestations, and Effects of Cohesiveness in Therapy Groups," *Int. J. Group Psychother.*, *7*: 53–63, 1957.
7. R. White and R. Lippit, "Leader Behavior and Member Reaction in Three 'Social Climates,'" in D. Cartwright and A. Zander (eds.), *Group Dynamics: Research and Theory* (New York: Row, Peterson, 1962), pp. 527–553.
8. A. Wolf, "The Psychoanalysis of Groups," in M. Rosenbaum and M. Berger (eds.), *Group Psychotherapy and Group Function* (New York: Basic Books, 1963), p. 320.
9. J. D. Frank, "Some Values of Conflict in Therapeutic Groups," *Group Psychother.*, *8*: 142–151, 1955.
10. C. Rogers, "Dealing with Psychological Tensions," *J. Appl. Behav. Sci.*, *1*: 6–24, 1965.
11. S. H. Foulkes, *Therapeutic Group Analysis* (New York: International Universities Press, 1964), p. 81.
12. D. Shapiro, *Neurotic Styles* (New York: Basic Books, 1965).
13. E. Berne, *Games People Play* (New York: Grove Press, 1964).
14. S. A. Culbert, *The Interpersonal Process of Self-Disclosure: It Takes Two to See One* ("Explorations in Applied Behavioral Science," No. 3 [New York: Renaissance Editors, 1967]).
15. I. D. Yalom, P. S. Houts, S. M. Zimerberg, and K. H. Rand, "Prediction of Improvement in Group Therapy: An Exploratory Study," *Arch. Gen. Psychiat.*, *17*: 159–168, 1967.
16. S. Hurley, "Self-Disclosure in Small Counseling Groups," unpublished Ph.D. dissertation, Michigan State University, 1967.
17. H. Peres, "An Investigation of Non-Directive Group Therapy," *J. Consult. Psychol.*, *11*: 159–172, 1947.
18. C. Truax and R. Carkhuff, "Client and Therapist Transparency in the Psychotherapeutic Encounter," *J. Couns. Psychol.*, *12*: 3–9, 1965.
19. M. Lieberman, I. Yalom, M. Miles, *Encounter Groups: First Facts* (New York: Basic Books, 1973).
20. L. M. Vosen, "The Relationship Between Self-Disclosure and Self-Esteem," unpublished Ph.D. dissertation, University of California at Los Angeles, 1966; cited by Culbert, *op. cit.*
21. A. H. Maslow, unpublished mimeographed material, 1962.
22. E. Goffman, *The Presentation of Self in Everyday Life* (Garden City, N.Y.: Doubleday Anchor Books, 1959).
23. M. Rickers-Ouiankina, "Social Accessibility in Three Age Groups," *Psychol. Rep.*, *2*: 283–294, 1956.
24. S. M. Jourard and P. Lasakow, "Some Factors in Self-Disclosure," *J. Abnorm. Soc. Psychol.*, *56*: 91–98, 1950.
25. D. E. Bugenthal, R. Tannenbaum, and H. Bobele, unpublished manuscript cited by Culbert, op. cit.

12

PROBLEM PATIENTS

The Monopolist

The *bête noire* of many group therapists is the habitual monopolist, an individual who seems compelled to chatter on incessantly. These patients are anxious if they are silent; if others get the floor, the monopolists reinsert themselves with a variety of techniques: they rush in indecently to fill the briefest silence, they respond to every statement in the group, they continually note similarities between the problems of the speaker and their own, with the recurring refrain, "I'm like that, too." The monopolist may persist in describing, in endless detail, conversations with others (often taking several parts in the conversation) or in presenting accounts of newspaper or magazine stories which may be only slightly relevant to the group issue. Some hold the floor by assuming the role of the interrogator, and still others capture the members' attention by enticing them with bizarre or sexually piquant material. I have known some patients who monopolized by puzzling the others: they described rare, "out of the blue" déjà vu or depersonalization episodes, often omitting mention of important clarifying details such as severe precipitating stress. Grand hysterics may monopolize the group by means of the crisis method: they regularly present the group with major life upheavals, which always seem to demand urgent and lengthy attention. Others members are cowed into silence since their problems seem trivial in comparison. ("It's not easy to interrupt *Gone With the Wind*," as one of my patients put it.)

EFFECTS ON GROUPS

Although the group may in the initial meetings welcome and perhaps encourage the monopolist, the mood rapidly turns to one of frustration and anger. New group members are often disinclined to silence a member for fear that they will thus incur an obligation to fill the silence. There is the obvious rejoinder of, "All right, I'll be quiet. You talk." And, of course, it is not possible to talk easily in a tense, guarded climate. Unless the group has some particularly assertive members, it may not deal directly with the monopolist for some time; instead, it may smolder quietly or make indirect hostile forays. Generally, oblique attacks on the monopolist will only aggravate the problem and fuel a vicious circle. The monopolist's compulsive speech is an attempt to deal with anxiety; as he senses the rising group tension and resentment, his anxiety rises and his tendency to speak compulsively is correspondingly increased. Some monopolists are consciously aware, at these times, of throwing up a smoke screen of words in order to divert the group from making a direct attack.

Eventually, this source of unresolved tension will have a detrimental effect on cohesiveness, manifested by such signs of group disruption as indirect, off-target fighting, absenteeism, dropouts, and subgrouping. When the group does confront the monopolist, it is often in an explosive, brutal style; the spokesman for the group usually receives unanimous support. (I have seen him receive a round of applause.) The monopolist may then sulk, enforce complete silence on himself for a meeting or two ("See what they do without me"), or leave the group. In any event, little that is therapeutic has been accomplished.

THERAPEUTIC CONSIDERATIONS

The overall task of the therapist is to interrupt the behavioral pattern of the monopolist in a therapeutically effective fashion. Despite the strongest provocation and temptation to shout the patient down or to silence him by edict, such an assault has little value except as a temporary catharsis for the therapist. The patient is not helped: no learning has accrued; the anxiety underlying the monopolist's compulsive speech persists and will erupt again in further monopolistic volleys or, if no outlet is available, will force the patient to drop out of the group. Neither is the group helped; regardless of the circumstances, the others are threatened by the therapist's silencing, in a heavy-handed manner, one of the members. Therapy is perceived as potentially dangerous, and a crystal of caution and fear is implanted in the mind of each member lest a similar fate befall him.

Nevertheless, the monopolistic behavior must be checked, and generally it is the therapist's task to do this. Often, with good reason, the therapist does well to wait for the group to handle a group problem;

however, the monopolistic patient is one problem that the group, and especially a young group, often cannot handle. The monopolistic patient seems to pose a threat to the basic procedural underpinnings of the group: group patients are encouraged to speak in a group, yet this patient who speaks a great deal must be silenced. The therapist must address himself to this issue, he must prevent the elaboration of therapy-obstructing norms, and in addition he must intervene to prevent the monopolistic patient from committing social suicide. A two-pronged approach is most effective: the therapist must consider both the monopolizing patient and the group which has allowed itself to be monopolized.

From the standpoint of the group, the therapist should bear in mind the principle that, by definition, no monopolistic patient may exist in a vacuum; he always abides in a dynamic equilibrium with a group which permits or encourages his behavior. The therapist may thus inquire why the group permits or encourages one member to carry the burden of the entire meeting. Such an inquiry may startle the members, who had only perceived themselves as passive victims of the monopolist. After the initial protestations are worked through, the group may then, with profit, examine their exploitation of the monopolist; for example, they may have been relieved by not having to participate verbally in the group. They may have permitted the patient to do all the self-disclosure, or to make a fool of himself, or to act as a lightning rod for the group's anger, while they themselves assumed little responsibility for the therapeutic goals of the group. Once the members disclose and discuss their reasons for inactivity, their personal commitment to the therapeutic process is augmented. They may, for example, discuss their fears of assertiveness, or of harming the monopolist, or of a retaliatory attack by some specific member or by the therapist; they may wish to avoid seeking the group's attention lest their greed be exposed; they may secretly revel in the monopolist's plight and enjoy being a member of the victimized and disapproving majority. A disclosure of any of these issues by a hitherto uninvolved patient signifies progress and greater engagement in therapy.

The group approach to this problem must be complemented by work with the monopolistic patient. The basic principle is a simple one: the therapist does not want to silence the monopolist; *he does not want to hear less from the patient but, instead, wants to hear more.* The seeming contradiction is resolved when we consider that the monopolist conceals himself behind his compulsive speech. The issues he presents to the group do not reflect deeply felt personal concerns; they are selected for other reasons: to entertain, to gain attention, to justify his position, to present grievances, etc. Thus the monopolist sacrifices his opportunity for therapy to his insatiable need for attention and control. Although each therapist will fashion his intervention according to his own style, the essential message to the monopolist must be that, through his compulsive speech, he holds the group at arm's length and prevents others from relating meaningfully to him. He is offered not rejection but an invitation to engage more fully in the group. If the therapist harbors only the singular goal of silencing the patient, then he has, in effect, abandoned the therapeutic goal and may as well remove the patient from the group.

In addition to his grossly deviant behavior, the monopolist has a major impairment of his social sensory system. He seems peculiarly unaware both of his interpersonal impact and of the response of others to him; moreover, he lacks the capacity or inclination to empathize with others in his social setting. Data from an exploratory research endeavor [1] support this conclusion. Patients and student observers were asked to fill out questionnaires at the end of each group meeting. One of the areas explored was activity; the participants were asked to rank the group members, including themselves, for the total number of words uttered during the meeting. There was excellent reliability in the activity ratings among patients and observers, with two exceptions: (1) the ratings of the therapist's activity by the patients showed large discrepancies (a function of transference; discussed in Chapter 6) and (2) monopolistic patients placed themselves far lower on the activity rankings than did the other members, who were often unanimous in ranking the monopolist as the most active member in the meeting.

The therapist must, then, help the monopolist observe himself by encouraging the group to provide continual feedback for him; without the leader's encouragement the group may, as we have shown, provide the feedback only in a disjunctive, explosive manner, which elicits only a defensive posture. Such a sequence has little therapeutic value and merely recapitulates a drama in which the patient has performed far too often. For example, in the initial interview one male monopolist complained about his relationship with his wife, who, he claimed, often abruptly resorted to such "sledgehammer tactics" as publicly humiliating him or accusing him of infidelity in front of his children. The sledgehammer approach accomplished nothing durable for this patient; once his bruises had healed, he and his wife began the cycle anew. Within the first few meetings of the group a similar sequence unfolded: because of his monopolistic behavior, judgmentalism, and inability to hear the members' response to him, the group pounded harder and harder until finally, when he was forced to listen, the message was a cruel and destructive one.

The therapist must help to increase the patient's receptivity to feedback. He may have to be forceful and directive, saying, for example, "Mark, I think it would be best now for you to stop speaking because I sense there are some important feelings about you in the group which I think would be very helpful for you to know." The therapist should also help the group disclose their responses to Mark rather than their interpretations of his motives. Far more useful and acceptable is a statement such as "When you speak in this fashion I feel . . ." rather than, "You are behaving in this fashion because. . . ." The patient may often perceive motivational interpretations as accusatory but can hardly reject the validity of others' subjective responses to him.

Too often we confuse or interchange the concepts of interpersonal manifestation, response, and cause. The cause of monopolistic behavior may vary considerably from patient to patient: some individuals speak in order to control others, many so fear that they will be influenced or penetrated by others that they compulsively defend each of their statements; others so overrevaluate their productions that delay is impossible and all thoughts must be immediately expressed. Generally, the cause of the monopolist's behavior is not well understood until much later in therapy and interpretation of the cause offers little help in the early management of the disruptive behavior patterns. It is far more effective to concentrate on the patient's manifestation of self in the group and the other members' response to his behavior. Gently but repeatedly, the patient must be confronted with the paradox that, however much he may wish to be accepted and respected by others, he persists in behavior which generates only irritation, rejection, and frustration.

A clinical illustration of many of these issues occurred in a therapy group in a psychiatric hospital in which sexual offenders were incarcerated:

Ron, who had been in the group for seven weeks, launched into a familiar lengthy tribute to the remarkable improvement he had undergone. He described in exquisite detail how his chief problem had been that he hadn't understood the damaging effects his behavior had on others, and how now, having achieved such understanding, he was able to leave the hospital. The therapist observed that some of the members were restless, one softly pounded his fist into his palm, while others slumped back in a posture of indifference and resignation. He stopped the monopolist by asking the group how many times they had heard Ron relate this account. The group members agreed that they had heard it at every meeting, in fact, they had heard Ron speak this way in the first meeting he attended; furthermore, they had never heard Ron talk about anything else and knew him only as a "story." The members discussed their irritation with Ron, their reluctance to attack him for fear of seriously injuring him, of losing control of themselves, or of painful retaliation. Some spoke of their hopelessness about ever reaching Ron, and of the fact that he related to them only as a matchstick figure without flesh or depth. Still others spoke of their terror of speaking and revealing themselves in the group; therefore, they welcomed Ron's monopolization. A few members expressed their total lack of interest or faith in therapy and therefore failed to intercept Ron because of apathy.

Thus the process was overdetermined; a host of interlocking factors resulted in a dynamic equilibrium called monopolization. By halting the runaway process, uncovering and working through the underlying factors, the therapist obtained maximum therapeutic benefit from a potentially crippling group phenomenon. Each member moved closer to group involvement; Ron was no longer permitted or encouraged to participate in a fashion that could not possibly be helpful to him or the group.

It is essential to enlist the patient as an ally in the therapeutic work. He must have some reasons for wishing to change his monopolistic patterns, especially since he does not enter therapy with this complaint. For example, he may be helped to consider the sequence of events in the group. When he entered the group, what kind of response was he hoping to get from the group members? What has actually transpired? How does he explain the discrepancy? One must help him generalize beyond the group. He might devaluate the importance of learning about the group's reaction to him, or suggest that the group consists of disturbed people. He may protest: "This is the first time something like this has ever happened to me." If the therapist is sufficiently on top of things to have prevented scapegoating, then this is always untrue; the patient is in a very familiar place—vis-à-vis others. What is different in the group is the presence of norms which permit the others to comment openly on his behavior. The therapist is in a much stronger position if he can help the patient examine and discuss his interpersonal difficulties (the fact that he feels lonely, that he has no close friends, no one ever listens to him, that he is shunned without reason, etc.). Once these are made explicit, one can, more convincingly, demonstrate to the patient the importance and relevance of examining his in-group behavior. Good timing is necessary; there is no point in attempting to do this work with a closed defensive patient in the midst of a fire storm. Repeated, gentle, reasoned interventions are required.

The Schizoid Patient

The schizoid condition, the malady of our times, perhaps accounts for more patients entering psychotherapy than any other psychopathological configuration. These patients are emotionally blocked, isolated, distant individuals who often seek group therapy because of a vague sense that something is missing: they cannot feel, cannot love, cannot play, cannot cry. They are spectators of themselves, they do not inhabit their own bodies, they do not experience their own experience.

Sartre in *The Age of Reason* vividly describes the experiential world of such an individual:[2]

. . . He closed the paper and began to read the special correspondent's dispatch on the front page. Fifty dead and three hundred wounded had already been counted, but that was not the total, there were certainly corpses under the debris. . . . There were thousands of men in France who had not been able to read their paper that morning without feeling a clot of anger rise in their throat, thousands of men who had clenched their fists and muttered: "Swine!" Mathieu clenched his fists and muttered: "Swine!" and felt himself still more guilty. If at least he had been able to discover in himself a trifling emotion that was veritably if modestly alive, conscious of its limits. But no: he was empty, he was confronted by a vast anger, a desperate anger, he saw it and could almost have touched it. But it was inert—if it were to live and find expression and suffer, he must lend it his own body. It was other people's anger. "Swine!" He clenched his fists, he strode along, but nothing came, the anger remained external to himself. . . . Something was on the threshold of existence, a timorous dawn of anger. At last! But it dwindled and collapsed, he was left in solitude, walking with the measured and decorous gait of a man in a funeral procession in Paris. . . . He wiped his forehead with his handkerchief and he thought: "One can't force one's deeper feelings." Yonder was a terrible and tragic state of affairs that ought to arouse one's deepest emotions. . . . "It's no use, the moment will not come. . . ."

The schizoid patient often finds himself in a similar predicament in the therapy group. In virtually every group meeting the patient, unless he selectively inattends to the proceedings, has confirmatory evidence that the nature and intensity of his emotional experience differs considerably from that of the other members. The patient may be puzzled at this discrepancy, he may conclude that the other members are melodramatic, excessively labile, phony, overly concerned with trivia, or simply of a different temperament. Eventually, however, schizoid patients begin to wonder about themselves; like Sartre's

Mathieu, they become aware that somewhere inside themselves is a vast reservoir of feeling that they cannot reach.

In one way or another, by what he says or what he does not say, the schizoid patient conveys his emotional isolation to the other members. Chapter 2 described a patient who could not understand the members' concern about the therapist's leaving the group or a member's obsessive fears about her boyfriend being killed. He saw people as interchangeable. He had his need for a M.D.R. (minimum daily requirement) of affection (without, it seemed, proper concern about the source of affection). He would be "bugged" by the departure of the therapist because it would slow up his therapy. He would be annoyed with himself for not having made better use of the therapist. But he did not share in the feeling expressed by the others: grief at the loss of the person who is the therapist. In defense of himself, he maintained, "There's not much sense to my having any strong feelings about the therapist's leaving since there is nothing I can do about it." Another patient, chided by the group because of his lack of empathy toward two highly distressed members, responded, "So, they're hurting. There are millions of people hurting all over the world at this instant. If I let myself feel badly for everyone who was hurting, I'd find it a full-time occupation." In other words, feelings are awarded priority according to the dictates of rationality; they must be justified pragmatically—if they serve no purpose, why have them?

The group is often keenly aware of a discrepancy between the patient's words, his experience, and his emotional response. One patient, who had been criticized for withholding information from the group about his relationship with a girlfriend, frostily asked, "Would you like to bring your camera and climb into bed with us?" When questioned, however, he denied any feeling of anger and could not account for the tone of sarcasm. At other times the group reads the schizoid patient's emotions from postural or behavioral cues. Indeed, the patient may relate to himself in a similar way and join in the investigation, commenting, for example, "My heart is beating fast, so I must be frightened" or "My fists are clenched, so I must be angry."

The response of the other members is characteristic and proceeds from curiosity and puzzlement through disbelief, solicitude, irritation, and frustration. They will repeatedly ask the patient, "What do you *feel* about . . . ?" and only much later come to realize that they were demanding that he quickly learn to speak a foreign language. Soon, members become increasingly active in helping to resolve what at first appears to be a minor affliction. They begin to tell him what he *should* feel and what *they* would feel were they in his situation. Even-

tually, frustration sets in. The group tries even harder, almost always
with no noticeable results. Soon a sledgehammer approach may be
used as members try to force an affective response by increasing the
intensity of the stimulus. Meetings may become very predictable and
very discouraging. Sometimes the group mascots the patient: he becomes the source of much amusement to the group. (Henri Bergson [3]
felt that a central aspect of the comic situation was man as machine.
There seems to be something intrinsically comic in the spectacle of
man acting in a routinized, mechanical manner [viz., much Chaplin-
esque humor or Laurel and Hardy slapstick]. I think it is this dimension which leads the group to find humor in what would appear to be
an unfunny situation.)

   The therapist must avoid joining in the quest for a "breakthrough."
I have never seen a schizoid patient significantly change by virtue of a
dramatic incident; the change is a prosaic process of grinding labor,
repetitive small steps, and almost imperceptible progress. It is tempting to employ some activating, nonverbal, or Gestalt techniques to
hasten the patient's movement. At times these approaches may hasten
the patient's recognition and expression of nascent or repressed feelings; but the therapist must not lose sight of the price he must pay as a
result of excessive, one-to-one directive work—the group may become
less potent, less autonomous, more dependent and leader-centered.
(We shall discuss these issues at length in Chapter 13.) In Chapter 5, I
described several here-and-now activating techniques which are useful in work with the schizoid patient. Encourage him to differentiate
between members; despite his protestations, he does not feel precisely the same way toward everyone in the group. Help him to move
into feelings he passes off as inconsequential. When he admits, "Well,
I may feel slightly irritated or slightly hurt . . . ," suggest that he stay
with these feelings; no one ever said that he need discuss only big
feelings. "Hold up a magnifying glass to the hurt; describe exactly
what it is like." Try to cut off his customary methods of avoidance:
"Somehow, you've gotten away from something that seemed important. Can we go back to where we were five minutes ago? When you
were talking to Julie, I thought you looked near tears. Something was
going on inside." He must be encouraged to observe his body; often
he may not experience affect but will be aware of the affective autonomic equivalents: tightness in the stomach, sweating, throat constriction, flushing, sweating, etc. Gradually, the group may help him
to translate those into their psychological meaning; they may, for example, note the timing of his reactions and their appearance in conjunction with some event in the group.

The therapist should also beware of assessing events solely according to his own experiential world. As we have shown previously, patients may experience the same event in totally different manners; a seemingly trivial event to the therapist or to one patient may represent an exceedingly important experience to another. A slight show of irritation by a restricted schizoid patient may represent for him a major breakthrough; it may be the first time in adulthood that he has expressed anger and may further enable him to test out new behaviors both in and out of the group.

In the group, the schizoid patient is both a high risk and a high reward patient. If he can manage to persevere, to continue in the group and not be discouraged by his inability to change his relationship style quickly, he is almost certain to profit considerably from the group therapy experience.

The Silent Patient

The converse of the monopolist, the silent member, represents a less disruptive but often equally challenging problem to the therapist. Is the silent member always a problem in the group? Perhaps he profits silently. A story, probably apocryphal, which has circulated among group therapists for years is the account of the patient who attended a group for a year without uttering a word. At the end of the fiftieth meeting, he announced to the group that he would not return; his problems had been resolved, he was due to get married the following day, and he wished to express his gratitude to the group for the help they had given him.

Some reticent patients may profit from vicariously engaging in treatment through identifying with active patients with similar problems; it is possible that changes in behavior and risk-taking can gradually occur in their relationship outside the group while they remain silent and seemingly unchanged in the group. The encounter group research project of Lieberman, Yalom, and Miles [4] indicated that some of the participants who changed the most seemed to have a particular ability to maximize their learning opportunities in a short-term group (thirty total hours) by engaging vicariously in the group experience of other members. There was evidence, though, that, in general, the *more active and the more influential the member in the group matrix, the more likely he was to benefit.* Lundgren and Miller [5] have demonstrated in T-groups that, regardless of what the participants said, the more words they spoke, the greater the positive change in their picture of themselves.

There is much clinical consensus that in long-term therapy, the silent patient does not profit from the group. The greater the verbal participation, the greater the sense of involvement, and the more the patient is valued by others and ultimately by himself. I would suggest, then, that we do not be lulled by the apocryphal story of the silent patient who got well. A silent patient is a problem patient; he rarely benefits from the group.

Patients may be silent for many reasons. Some may experience a pervasive dread of self-disclosure; every utterance, they feel, may commit them to progressively more disclosure. Others may feel so conflicted about aggression that they cannot undertake the self-assertion inherent in speaking. Others who demand nothing short of perfection in themselves never speak for fear of falling short when they open their mouths, whereas others keep their distance from the group or manage to control it by maintaining a lofty superior silence. Some patients are especially threatened by a particular member in the group and habitually speak only in the absence of that member. Others participate only in smaller meetings or in alternate (leaderless) meetings. Some are afraid of displaying weakness and remain silent lest they chink, plead, or cry. Others may lapse into a periodic silent sulk in an effort to punish others or to force the group to attend to them.

The important point though is that silence is never silent; it is behavior and, like all other behavior in the group, has meaning both in the framework of the here-and-now and as a representative sample of the patient's typical way of relating to his interpersonal world. The therapeutic task, therefore, is not only to change the behavior (that is essential if he is to remain in the group) but to help the patient learn about himself from his behavior.

Proper management depends in part on the dynamics of the silence, which the therapist ascertains from the pregroup individual interviews and from the patient's nonverbal cues, as well as from his few verbal contributions. A middle course must be steered between placing undue pressure on the patient and, on the other hand, allowing him to slide into an extreme isolate role. The therapist may still maintain an attitude of allowing each patient to modulate his own degree of participation and yet periodically including the silent patient by commenting on his nonverbal behavior when, by gesture or demeanor, he is evincing interest, tension, sadness, boredom, or amusement. Often he may hasten the member's participation by encouraging the other members to reflect on their perceptions of him and then asking the

silent member to validate these perceptions. Even if repeated prodding, cajoling, inviting is necessary, it is still possible to avoid making
the patient a passive object by repeated process checks. "Is this a
meeting when you want to be prodded? How did it feel when Mike
put you on the spot? Did he go too far? Can you let us know when we
make you uncomfortable? What's the ideal question we could ask you
today to help you come into the group?" In these and other ways one
enlists the patient as active collaborator in the campaign against his
silence. If a patient resists all these efforts and his participation remains very limited even after three months of meetings, my experience has been that the prognosis is poor. The group will become increasingly frustrated and puzzled at vainly coaxing, encouraging, or
challenging a silent, blocked patient to participate. In the face of
group discouragement and disapprobation, his position in the group
becomes even more nonviable and the likelihood of participation ever
more remote. Concurrent individual sessions may be useful in helping the patient at this time; if this fails, the therapist should seriously
consider withdrawing the patient from the group.

The Psychotic Patient in the Group

The therapy group is severely challenged when a member develops a
psychosis during the course of treatment. The fate of the psychotic patient, the response of the other members, and the effective options
available to the therapist all depend, in part, upon when the psychosis
occurs in the history of the group. In general, the older the group and
the more well-established the affected member, the more tolerant
and effective will the therapy group be in the crisis.

THE PSYCHOTIC PATIENT IN THE
EARLY PHASES OF THE GROUP

In Chapter 7 ("The Selection of Patients") I emphasized that the
grossly psychotic patient should be excluded in the initial screening
process from outpatient, interactional group therapy. If, by accident or
design, such a severely ill patient is included in the group, both the
group and the patient almost invariably suffer. The group is impeded
in its progress in a manner which will be illustrated shortly; the pa-

tient soon slides into a deviant role in the group and eventually terminates treatment, often much the worse for his experience.

At times, despite cautious screening, a patient, because of unanticipated stress from his life circumstances or from the group, becomes
psychotic in the early stages of therapy. In these instances the problems created for the newly formed group are very considerable. This
book has repeatedly stressed that the early stages of the group are a
time of great flux and great importance. The young group is easily influenced, and the norms which are established early are often exceedingly durable. A rather intense sequence of events occurs as, in a few
weeks, an aggregate of frightened, distrustful strangers evolves into an
intimate, mutually helpful group. Any event which, in the early part of
the group, consumes an inordinate amount of time and which diverts
energy from the tasks of the developmental sequence is potentially
destructive to the group. A number of the relevant problems are illustrated by this clinical example:

Joan, a thirty-seven-year-old housewife who had once, several years before,
been hospitalized and treated with electro-convulsive therapy for depression,
sought group therapy at the insistence of her individual therapist, who
thought that an understanding of her interpersonal relationships would help
her to improve her relationship with her husband. In the early meetings of the
group she was an active member who tended to reveal far more intimate details of her past history than the other members. Occasionally, she expressed
anger toward another member and then engaged in excessively profuse apolo-
gies coupled with self-depreciatory remarks. By the sixth meeting her behavior became still more inappropriate. For example, she discoursed at great
length on her son's urinary problems and described, with intricate detail, the
surgery that had been performed to relieve urethral stricture. At the following
meeting she noted that the family cat had also developed a blockage of the
urinary tract; she then pressed the other members of the group to describe
their pets.

In the eighth meeting, Joan disorganized completely. She behaved in a
bizarre, irrational manner, insulting members of the group, openly flirting
with the male members to the point of stroking their bodies, and finally lapsed
into punning, klang associations, and inappropriate laughter and tears. One of
the therapists then escorted her from the room, phoned her husband, and arranged for immediate psychiatric hospitalization. Joan remained in the hospital in a hypomanic psychotic state for a month, and then gradually recovered.

The members during the meeting were obviously extremely uncomfortable, their feelings ranging from bafflement and fright to annoyance. After
Joan left they expressed feelings of guilt for, in some unknown manner, having triggered her behavior. Others spoke of their fear, and one recalled another person who had acted in a similar fashion but, in addition, had bran-
dished a gun.

During the subsequent meeting, the members discussed many feelings
related to the incident. One member expressed his conviction that no one

could be trusted; even though he had known Joan for seven weeks, her behavior proved to be totally unpredictable. Others expressed their relief that they were, in comparison, psychologically healthy; others, in response to their fears of similarly losing control, employed considerable denial and veered away from discussing these problems. Some expressed a fear of Joan's returning and making a shambles of the group. A lack of faith in the effects of hospitalization was expressed. "What good," they asked, "could a hospital do for Joan?" Others expressed their diminished faith in group therapy; one member asked for hypnosis, and another brought to the meeting an article from a scientific journal claiming that psychotherapy was ineffective. A loss of faith in the therapists was expressed in the dream of one member, in which the therapist was in the hospital and was rescued by the patient.

In the next few meetings, all these themes went underground; the meetings became listless, shallow, and intellectualized. Attendance dwindled and the group seemed resigned to its own impotence. At the fourteenth meeting, the therapists announced that Joan was improved and would return the following week. A vigorous, heated discussion ensued. The members feared that:

1. They would upset her, that an intense meeting would make her ill again, and that therefore the group would be forced to move slowly and superficially.
2. Joan would be unpredictable; at any point she might lose control and display dangerous frightening behavior.
3. Joan would, because of her lack of control, be untrustworthy; nothing in the group would remain confidential.

At the same time, the members expressed considerable anxiety and guilt for wishing to exclude Joan from the group, and soon tension and a heavy silence prevailed. The extreme reaction of the group persuaded the therapist to delay for a few weeks the reintroduction of Joan (who was, incidentally, in concurrent individual therapy).

When Joan reentered the group, she was treated as a fragile object, and the entire group interaction was guarded and defensive. By the twentieth meeting, five of the seven members had dropped out of the group, leaving only Joan and one other member.

The therapists reconstituted the group by adding five new members. It is of interest to note that, despite the fact that only two of the old members and the therapists continued in the reconstituted group, the old group culture persisted: Joan was treated so delicately and so obliquely by the new members that the group moved slowly, floundering in its own politeness and social conventionality. Only when the therapists openly confronted this issue and discussed in the group their own fears of upsetting Joan and thrusting her into another psychosis were the members able to deal with their feelings and fears about her. At that point the group moved ahead more quickly; Joan remained in the new group for a year and made decided improvements in her ability to relate with others and in her self-concept.

THE PSYCHOTIC PATIENT LATER IN THE
COURSE OF THE GROUP

An entirely different situation often presents itself when a patient who has been an involved, active group member develops a sudden and severe worsening of his clinical condition. The concern of the other members may be primarily for the patient rather than for themselves or for the group. Since they had previously known and understood the now psychotic patient as a person, they often react with great concern and interest; the patient is less likely to be viewed as a strange and frightening object to be avoided. The popular stereotype of the insane person includes a strong element of differentness; the patient's appearance and behavior seem totally dissimilar to anything the observer has experienced within himself.*

Although perceiving similarity may enhance the other members' ability to continue relating to the distressed patient, it also creates a personal upheaval in some members, for they begin to fear that they, too, can lose control and slide into a similar abyss. It is most important for the therapist to anticipate this reaction so as to enable the others to work through their dread.

When faced with a psychotic patient in a group, many psychiatrists reflexly revert back to their early medical model and symbolically "dismiss" the group by intervening forcefully in a one-to-one fashion. In effect, they say to the group, "This is too serious a problem for you to handle"; such a maneuver, however, is often antitherapeutic: the patient is frightened and the group emasculated.

It has been my experience that a mature group is perfectly able to deal with the psychiatric emergency and, although there may be false starts, the group will be able to consider every contingency and take every action that the therapist might have considered. Consider the following clinical example:

In the forty-fifth meeting Rhona, a forty-three-year-old divorcee, arrived a few minutes late in a disheveled, obviously disturbed state. Over the previous few weeks she had gradually been sliding into a depression, but the process

---

* Moos and Yalom [6] demonstrated, for example, that medical students assigned for the first time to a psychiatric ward regarded the psychotic patients as extremely dangerous, frightening, unpredictable, and dissimilar to themselves. At the end of their five weeks' assignment, these attitudes underwent considerable change; the students grew less isolated and frightened of their patients, as they learned that "psychotics" were but confused, deeply anguished human beings, more like themselves than they had previously thought.

had clearly suddenly accelerated. She was tearful, despondent, and evidenced a degree of psychomotor retardation. During the early part of the meeting she wept continuously and expressed feelings of great loneliness, hopelessness, and inability to love, hate, or, for that matter, to have any deeply felt emotion; she described her feeling of great detachment from everyone, including the group, and when prompted, discussed her suicidal ruminations.

The group members responded to Rhona with great empathy and concern. They inquired about events during the past week and helped her discuss two important occurrences which seemed related to the depressive crisis: (1) she had for months saved money and planned a summer trip to Europe; her seventeen-year-old son had, during the past week, decided to decline a summer camp job which had been offered him and refused to search for other jobs—a turn of events which, in Rhona's eyes, jeopardized her trip; (2) she had after months of hesitation decided to attend a dance for divorced middle-aged people which proved to be a disaster: no one had approached her to dance and she had left for home consumed with feelings of total worthlessness.

The group helped her to explore her relationship with her son: she for the first time expressed rage at him for his lack of concern for her. With the group's assistance she attempted to define the limits of her responsibility toward him. It was difficult for Rhona to discuss the dance because of the amount of shame and humiliation she felt. Two other women in the group, one single and one divorced, empathized deeply with her and shared their experiences and reactions to the scarcity of males. Rhona was also reminded by the group of the many times she had, during sessions, interpreted every minor slight as a total rejection and condemnation of herself. Finally, after much attention, care, and warmth had been offered her, one of the members pointed out to Rhona that the experience of the dance was being disconfirmed right in the group: several people who knew her well were deeply concerned and involved with her. Rhona rejected this by claiming that the group, unlike the dance, was an artificial, unreal situation in which people followed artificial, unnatural rules of conduct. The members quickly pointed out that quite the contrary was true: the dance, the contrived congregation of strangers, was the artificial situation and the group was the real one, since it was there that she was truly and completely known.

Rhona, consumed with the conviction of her own worthlessness, then berated herself for her inability to feel reciprocal warmth and involvement with the group members. One of the members then quickly intercepted this maneuver by pointing out that this was a familiar and repetitive pattern of hers: that she experienced some feelings toward the other members which were evidenced by her facial expression and body posture, but then her "shoulds" took over and tortured her by insisting that she "should" feel more, "should" feel more warmth and more love than anyone else. The net effect was that the real feeling she did have was rapidly extinguished by the winds of her impossible self-demands.

In essence, what then transpired was Rhona's gradual recognition of the discrepancy between her public and private esteem (described in Chapter 3). At the end of the meeting, Rhona responded by bursting into tears and crying for several minutes. The group was reluctant to leave but did so when they had all convinced themselves that suicide was no longer a serious consideration. Throughout the next week the members maintained an informal vigil; each phoned Rhona at least once.

Rather early in the session the therapist realized the important dynamics operating in Rhona's depression and, had he chosen, might have made the appropriate interpretations to allow the patient and the group to arrive much more quickly at a cognitive understanding of the problem—but at considerable cost to the meaningfulness and value of the meeting both to the protagonist and to the other members. For one thing, the group would have been deprived of an opportunity to experience its own potency; every success adds to the group's cohesiveness and enhances the self-regard of each of the members. It is difficult for some therapists to do this, and yet it is essential that the therapist learn to sit on his wisdom. There are times when it is foolish to be wise and wise to be silent. The therapist must find other, more productive ways of satisfying his need for public acclamation.

At times, as in this clinical episode, the group chooses and performs the appropriate action; at other times, the group may decide that the therapist must act. One must differentiate between a hasty decision stemming from infantile dependence and an unrealistic appraisal of the therapist's powers and, on the other hand, a decision based on a thorough investigation of the situation and a mature appraisal of the therapist's expertise.

These points lead us to an important principle of group dynamics, one which is substantiated by considerable research. A group which reaches an autonomous decision based on a thorough exploration of the pertinent problems will employ all of its resources in support of its decision; a group which has a decision thrust upon it is likely to resist that decision and be even less effective in making valid decisions in the future.*

A widely cited study by Coch and French [8] is relevant here. The authors studied a pajama-producing factory in which periodic changes in jobs and routine were necessitated by advances in technology. For many years these changes were resisted by the employees; with each change there was an increase in absenteeism, turnover, aggression to the management, as well as decreased efficiency and output. An experiment was designed to test various methods of overcoming the employees' resistance to change. The critical variable studied was the degree of participation of the group members (the employees) in the planning of the change. The employees were divided into three

---

* Hardly a hypermodern principle! Thomas Jefferson once stated that "that government is the strongest of which every man feels a part." [7]

groups and three variations were tested: (1) the first variation involved no participation by the employees in planning the changes, though an explanation was given to them; (2) the second variation involved participation through elected representation of the workers in designing the changes to be made in the job; (3) the third variation consisted of total participation by all the members of the group in designing the changes. The results showed conclusively that, on all measures studied (aggression toward management, absenteeism, efficiency, number of employees resigning from the job), the success of the change was directly proportional to the degree of participation of the group members.

The implications for group therapy are apparent: members of a therapy group who personally participate in the planning of a course of action will be more committed to the enactment of the plan. They will, for example, invest themselves more fully in the care of a psychotic member if they recognize that it is their problem and not the therapist's alone.

At times, as in the clinical example cited above, the entire experience is beneficial to the development of group cohesiveness; sharing intense emotional experiences usually strengthens intermember ties. The danger to the group occurs when the psychotic patient consumes a massive amount of energy for a prolonged period of time. At this point other members may drop out of the group, and the group may deal with the disturbed patient in a cautious, concealed manner or attempt to ignore him; all of these methods never fail to aggravate the problem further. In such critical situations, one important option always available to the therapist is to see the disturbed patient in individual sessions for the duration of the crisis (this will be dealt with more fully in the discussion of concurrent individual therapy). However, here too the group should explore the implications thoroughly and share in the decision.

One of the worst calamities that can befall a therapy group is the presence of a manic-depressive member. A patient in the midst of a severe hypomanic thrust is perhaps the single most diruptive problem for a group. (In contrast, a full-blown manic episode presents little problem since the decision is clear: hospitalization is required.)

One of my therapy groups attempted to deal with a manic-depressive patient for over a year. Most of the time the patient was an extraordinarily valuable member; she was fully committed to the group, insightful, sensitive, and provocative. When she became depressed, the group was deeply concerned for her, feared suicide, and devoted many hours to bolstering her self-concept and dissuading her from resignation or suicide. When she grew manic she dominated the group; she could not refrain from responding to every comment made in the meeting, she interrupted other members continuously, and she also stirred up great concern on the part of the other members, who grew alarmed at the many unwise and impulsive economic and personal life decisions she made. Gradually, the depressive and manic episodes grew more severe and the lucid interval between episodes shorter. Eventually, hospitalization was required and she left the group with no benefit from her experience.

There is clinical evidence to indicate that the classic manic-depressive patient is best managed pharmacologically and is probably impervious to psychologically based treatment, even when the therapy is carried out by the most experienced clinicians.[9] It is obviously unwise, then, to allow the group to invest so much time in treatment which has such little likelihood of success. There are times when a patient, for his own sake and certainly for the other members' sakes, should be removed from the group. The problem lies, of course, in ascertaining when that time has arrived; generally, we are certain only when viewing the situation retrospectively. The manic-depressive patient, however, represents a clearer indication than most. Such a decision, too, should be shared with the group, even though the therapist must actively take the lead. It is important for the therapist to take the responsibility for arranging for the patient's future treatment. Otherwise, patients may be extraordinarily threatened at the prospect of similar abandonment.

The Narcissistic Patient

A healthy love of oneself is essential to the development of self-respect and self-confidence; an excessive degree of narcissism takes the form of loving oneself to the exclusion of others, of losing sight of the fact that others are sentient beings; that others, too, are constituting egos, each constructing and experiencing their unique world. In short, the narcissist is a solipsist who experiences the world and other individuals as existing solely for him.

A number of different personality styles may be grafted onto a narcissistic trunk-root structure; hence, I cannot describe the typical group therapy pilgrimage of the narcissistic patient. However, there are issues stemming from the core narcissistic posture which assume similar form in the group.

The narcissistic patient generally has a stormier time of it in group therapy than in individual therapy. In fact, the individual format provides so much gratification that the core problem emerges much more slowly: the patient's every word is listened to, every feeling, fantasy, and dream examined, everything is given him, little demanded from him. In the group, however, the patient is expected to share time, to understand, to empathize with and to help other patients, to form relationships, to be concerned with the feelings of others, to receive feedback which often may be critical.

One patient, Hazel, frequently criticized the group format by commenting on her preference for the one-to-one format. She often supported her position by citing psychoanalytic literature critical of the group therapy approach. She felt bitter at sharing time in the group. For example, one day three-fourths of the way through a meeting, the therapist remarked that he perceived Hazel and John to be under much pressure. They both admitted that they needed and wanted some help from the group; after a moment's awkwardness John gave way, saying he thought his problem could wait till the next session. Hazel consumed the rest of the meeting and, at the following session, continued where she left off. When it appeared that she had every intention of using the entire meeting, one of the members commented that John had been "left hanging" last session. But there was no easy transition since, as the therapist pointed out, only Hazel could release the group and she gave no sign of doing so graciously (Hazel had lapsed into a sulking silence). Nonetheless, the group turned to John, who was in the midst of a major life crisis. John presented his situation but no good work was done. At the very end of the meeting Hazel began weeping silently and the group, thinking that she wept for John, turned to her. On the contrary, however, she wept, she said, for all the time, which she could have used, that was wasted on John. What Hazel could not appreciate for at least a year in the group was that this type of incident did not support her request for individual therapy—quite the contrary; the fact that such difficulties arose in the group was precisely the reason that the group format was especially indicated for her.

Another narcissistic patient, Ruth, who sought therapy for her inability to maintain deep relationships, participated in the group in a highly stylized fashion: she insisted on filling in the members every week on the minute details of her life and especially on her relationships to men—her most pressing problem. Many of these details were extraneous, but she was insistent (much like the "watch me" phase of early childhood); aside from "watching her," there seemed no way the group could relate to Ruth without her feeling deeply rejected. She insisted that friendship consisted of sharing intimate details of one's life; yet we learned through a follow-up interview with a member who terminated the group that Ruth frequently called her for social evenings but she could no longer bear to be with Ruth because of her propensity to use friends in the same way one might use an analyst: as an ever-patient, ever-solicitous, ever-listening ear.

Some narcissistic patients who have a deep sense of specialness feel that not only do they deserve maximum group attention but that it should be forthcoming without any effort expended on their part. They expect the group to care for them, to reach out for them despite the fact that they reach out for no one, they expect gifts, surprises, compliments though they give none, they expect concern though they are not themselves concernful, they expect to be able to express anger and scorn but to remain immune from retaliation, they expect to be loved and admired for simply being there. I have seen this posture especially pronounced in beautiful women who had been beautiful children and who had been praised all their lives simply by virtue of their appearance and their presence.

The lack of concern or empathy for others is very obvious in the group. After several meetings members begin to note that although the patient may work on himself in the group, he never questions, supports, or assists others. One member felt no hesitation at asking openly for a transfer from the group. After eight months he had overcome much of his problem with shyness, had learned what the other members thought about him, and he felt that now he was reaching a point of diminishing return in the group: for the most part he had gotten what he could from the other members. This same member gave virtually nothing to the group, not even information about himself; the group often remarked on his parsimoniousness; he did not speak to them, they said, but sent verbal telegrams wasting as few words as possible. The group honed in on this trait, causing the patient to look deeply at his narcissistic assumptive world. When the group confronted him with the fact that only a mother would continue to give without reciprocation, he was deeply moved and, by way of assent, noted that customarily he would send letters of a few sparse lines to his mother and receive in return several generous pages with sentences overflowing into all margins. The trait applied to his academic work as well, since he could never write a luxuriant colorful essay; instead, he turned in terse outlines and was bewildered at his instructor's lack of appreciation for his efforts.

In the last chapter, I described, in the long account of Bill and Jan's relationship, many of Bill's narcissistic modes of relating to other people. Much of his failure to view the world from the position of the other was summed up in a statement he made to the "other woman" in the group, Carrie, after sixteen months together. He once wistfully said that he regretted that "nothing ever really happened" between them. Carrie sharply corrected him: "You mean nothing sexual, but a great deal has happened for me. You tried to seduce me. For once I refused. I didn't fall in love with you and I didn't go to bed with you. I didn't betray myself or my husband. I learned to know you and to care for you very deeply with all your faults and with all your assets. Is that nothing happening?" Several months after the end of therapy I asked Bill in a follow-up interview to recall some of the most significant events or turning points in therapy. He described a session late in therapy when the group watched a video tape of the previous session. Bill was stunned to learn that he had completely forgotten most of the session, remembering only those few points in which he was centrally involved. His egocentricity was brought home to him in a powerful way and affirmed what the group had been trying to tell him for months.

The Boring Patient

Rarely does anyone seek therapy because he is boring. Yet in thinly disguised garb the complaint is not uncommon. Patients complain that they never have anything to say to others, that they are left standing alone at parties, that no member of the opposite sex will take them out more than once, that others use them only for sex, that they are inhibited, shy, socially awkward, empty, or bland.

In the social microcosm of the therapy group these patients recreate these problems, and the members of the group (and the therapists) find them boring. The signs are obvious: after the first few times they have spoken, there is no clear interest in them, the therapist dreads a small meeting in which only two or three boring members will be present; if they were to leave the group they would simply glide out leaving nary a ripple in the pond of the group.

Boredom is a highly individualized experience. Not everyone is bored by the same situation, and it is not easy to make generalizations. In general, though, the boring patient in the therapy group is one who is massively inhibited. He lacks spontaneity, he never takes risks, his utterances are always "safe" (and, alas, always predictable), he is obsequious and carefully avoids any sign of aggressivity, he is often masochistic (rushing to pummel himself before anyone else might make the attempt), he says what he believes the social press requires—he scans the social field to determine what he ought to say and any contrary sentiment coming from within is squelched. The particular social style of the individual varies considerably: some may be silent, others stilted and hyperrational, others timid and self-effacing, others dependent, demanding, or pleading.

The group members often escalate their efforts to encourage spontaneity in the boring patient. They ask the patient to share his fantasies about members, to scream, to curse—anything to pry something unpredictable from the patient.

One of my patients, Nora, drove the group to despair by her constant cliches and self-deprecatory remarks. After many months in the group her outside life began to change for the better, but each report of success was accompanied by the inevitable self-derogatory neutralizer. She was accepted by an honorary professional society (that was good, she said, because it was one club that couldn't kick her out), she received her graduate degree (but she should have finished earlier), she had gotten all A's (but was a child for bragging about it to the group), she looked better physically (shows you what a good sunlamp can do), she had been asked out by several new men in her life (sheer luck), she obtained a good job (it fell into her lap), she had had her first vaginal orgasm (give the credit to marijuana).

The group tried to tune her in to her self-effacement; one engineer suggested bringing an electric buzzer to the group to ring each time Nora knocked herself. One member, trying to shake her into a more spontaneous movement, commented on her bra, which he felt could be improved. (This was Ed, discussed in Chapter 2, who generally related only to the sexual parts of women.) He said he would bring her a present, a new bra, next session. Sure enough, the following session he arrived with a present, a huge box, which Nora said she would prefer to open at home. So there it sat, looming in the group and, of course, inhibiting any other topic. Nora was asked at least to guess what it contained, and she ventured, "A pair of falsies." She was finally prevailed upon to open the gift and did so laboriously and with enormous embarrassment. The box contained nothing but styrofoam stuffing. Ed explained that this was his idea for Nora's new bra: that she should wear no bra at all. Nora promptly apologized to Ed (for guessing he had given her falsies) and thanked him for the trouble he had taken. The incident launched much work for both members. (I shall not here discuss the sequel for Ed.) The group held up for Nora the fact that she had been humiliated and embarrassed, and yet she responded by apologizing to Ed. She had politely thanked someone who had just given her a gift of precisely nothing! The incident created the first robust spark of self-observation in Nora. She began the next meeting with: "I've just set the world ingratiation record. Last night I received an obscene phone call and I apologized to the man!" (She said, "I'm sorry you must have the wrong number.")

The underlying dynamics of the boring patient vary enormously from individual to individual. Many have a core dependent position and so dread rejection and abandonment that they eschew any aggressive remark that might initiate retaliation. Unfortunately, they mistakenly confuse healthy self-assertion with aggression and by refusing to grow, to present themselves as full, differentiated individuals with their own desires, interests, and opinions, they bring to pass (by boring others) the very rejection and abandonment they had hoped to forestall. Some seem trapped between a life-death dichotomy: on the one hand, they dread autonomy with its fearful loneliness and freedom; on the other, they dread dependency with its stagnation and permanence.

The important point for the therapist to keep in mind is that, like silence, narcissistic selfishness or monopolization, boredom is to be taken seriously. It is an important problem for the patient whether or not he identifies it as a problem. No urgent "breakthrough" technique is indicated: The therapist has much time, since the boring patient is tolerated by the group much better than the patient with abrasive, narcissistic, or monopolistic trends. In fact, the group, because they come to know him more deeply, find him less boring than does his outside social environment. Lastly, keep in mind that the task is not one of inspiriting the patient, of injecting color, spontaneity, richness *into* him, but instead of asking why he has squelched all the creative, vital, childlike parts of himself and of encouraging him to allow these qualities, which reside in all of us, to find expression.

The Help-Rejecting Complainer

The help-rejecting complainer,[10,11,12,13,14] a variant of the monopolist, was first identified and christened by Frank [10] in 1952; since then the behavior pattern has been recognized by many group clinicians, and the eponym appears frequently in psychiatric literature. In this section I shall discuss the rare, fully developed, help-rejecting complainer; however, this pattern of behavior is not an all-or-nothing distinct clinical syndrome. Patients may arrive at this style of interaction

through various psychodynamic pathways and may persistently manifest this behavior in an extreme degree with no external provocation;
others may demonstrate only a trace of this pattern, whereas still
others may become help-rejecting complainers only at times of particular stress.

DESCRIPTION

The help-rejecting complainer (hereafter HRC) has a very distinc-
tive behavioral pattern in the group: he implicitly or explicitly
requests help from the group by presenting problems or complaints
and then rejects the help which is offered. He continually brings environmental or somatic problems to the group and often describes them
in a manner which causes them to appear insurmountable; in fact, the
HRC seems to take pride in the insolubility of his problems. Often he
directs all of his attention toward the therapist in a tireless campaign
to elicit medication or advice from him. Clearly his behavior indicates
a need not for approval or respect but for help. He seems oblivious to
the group's reaction to him and apparently is willing to appear ludi-
crous so long as he is allowed to persist in his search for help. He
bases his relationship to the other members along the singular dimension of establishing that he is more needy of aid than they. The HRC
rarely shows competitiveness in any area except when another
member makes a bid for the therapist's or group's attention by presenting a problem; at this juncture he often attempts to belittle others'
complaints by comparing them unfavorably with his own. One such
patient stated quite explicitly, "It seems like such a waste to me listening to you when my problems involve life and death and yours
seem so superficial." [12] The HRC seems entirely self-centered in that
he speaks only of himself and his problems. In fact, however, his
problems are not clearly formulated to the group or to himself; they
are obscured by his propensity to exaggerate them and to affix blame
on others in his environment, often on authority figures on whom he
is dependent in some fashion.

When the group and the therapist respond to his plea, the entire
bewildering configuration takes form, as the patient rejects the help
offered him. The rejection is unmistakable, though it may assume
many varied and subtle forms; sometimes the advice is rejected
overtly, sometimes indirectly, sometimes it may be accepted verbally
but is never acted upon or, if acted upon, inevitably fails to improve
the plight of the patient.

EFFECTS ON THE GROUP

The effects on the group are obvious: the other members become bored and irritated, then frustrated and confused. The HRC appears to them as a greedy whirlpool, sucking down the group's energy. Worse yet, no deceleration of the HRC's demands is evident. Faith in the group process suffers, as members experience a sense of impotence and, further, as they despair of making their own needs appreciated by the group. Cohesiveness is undermined as absenteeism occurs or as patients subgroup in an effort to exclude the HRC.

DYNAMICS

The behavioral pattern of the HRC appears to be an attempt to resolve highly conflicted feelings about dependency. On the one hand, the patient feels helpless and insignificant and experiences himself as totally dependent on others, especially on the therapist, for a sense of personal worth. If the therapist notices and ministers to him, his sense of significance and self-acceptance is augmented. His entire identity has become inextricably interwoven with his claim for attention due him because of his suffering; he may feel alive and important only when he functions as a "crisis-creator." On the other hand, however, his dependent position is vastly confounded by a pervasive distrust and enmity toward authority figures. A vicious circle results, one which has been spinning for much of the patient's life: consumed with need, he turns for help to a figure whom he anticipates as unwilling (or unable) to help him; his anticipation of refusal so colors his style of requesting help that his prophecy is fulfilled, and further evidence is accumulated for his belief in the malevolence of the potential care-giver.

The characteristic pattern of behavior in the group both expresses and attempts to resolve this predicament. The HRC manifests and at the same time denies his dependency by exaggerating his helplessness while blaming others for his difficulties; he asks for help only indirectly through an interminable presentation of problems and avoids an overt supplicant posture. He then presents these problems in such form as to preclude effective help, thus denying his helplessness by defeating the potential care-givers.[3] The victory is, of course, a Pyrrhic one since the HRC destroys others through first destroying himself.

Berger and Rosenbaum, who report several cases,[12] particularly emphasize the HRC's latent motivation to frustrate and defeat the group and the therapist. Their series of HRC's were subject to severe deprivation early in life; parents were either absent or seriously disturbed. Often marked depressive trends were evident as well as a pervasive need to deprive others of pleasure as they themselves had been deprived. Should an HRC undergo some positive change, it will often be withheld from the group until several months after the fact.

GUIDELINES FOR MANAGEMENT

A severe HRC is an exceedingly difficult clinical challenge, and many such patients have prevailed over therapist and group by failing in therapy. It would thus be presumptuous and misleading to attempt to prescribe a careful therapeutic plan; however, certain generalizations may be posited. Surely it is a blunder for the therapist to confuse the help requested for the help required. The HRC solicits advice not for its potential value but in order to spurn it; ultimately, the therapist's advice, guidance, and medication will be rejected, forgotten, or, if used, will prove ineffective or, if effective, will be kept secret. It is also a blunder for the therapist to unburden himself of his growing frustration and resentment to the patient. Retaliation merely completes the vicious circle; the patient's anticipation of ill-treatment and abandonment is once again realized and he finds justification for his own anger. Once again he is able to affirm that no one can ever really understand him.

What course, then, is available to the therapist? One clinician suggests, perhaps in desperation, that the therapist interrupt the vicious circle by indicating that he "not only understands but shares the patient's feelings of hopelessness about his situation, thus refusing to perpetuate his part in a futile relationship." [10] Although, in the case described, this strategy resulted in the HRC's breaking off therapy, there was a suggestion that the patient, in an effort to prove the doctor wrong, experienced considerable improvement.

In general, however, the therapist should attempt to mobilize the major curative factors in the service of the patient. Once a cohesive group has been formed and the patient, through universality, identification, and catharsis, has come to value his membership in the group, then the therapist can encourage interpersonal learning by continually focusing on feedback and process in much the same manner as that described in the discussion of the monopolistic patient. Once the patient cares about his interpersonal impact on the other members, then he should be helped to recognize his characteristic pattern of relationships. One therapist, having once identified the process, called the group's attention to it by humming the tune "Nobody Knows the Trouble I've Seen" [10] when the HRC engaged in his typical behavior. Eric Berne,[15] who considers the HRC pattern as the most common of all social and psychotherapy group games, has christened it "Why don't you—yes but." The use of such easily accessible descriptive labels often makes the process more transparent and acceptable to the group members.

An example of a critical incident which initiated an adaptive spiral occurred in the sixtieth meeting of a therapy group. Mrs. Gaul, the help-rejecting complainer, was an obese, poorly groomed, thirty-seven-year-old housewife who had originally been a monopolist in the group but had gradually altered this aspect of her behavior. Her participation, though more constructive, was still HRC in style. For the two previous meetings the group had worked hard on Mrs. Gaul's disinclination to accept help—a discussion initiated by Mrs. Gaul's ambivalently declining an offer of chewing gum which one of the members passed around the group; when pressed she finally relented but insisted on accepting only half a stick. In the current meeting Mrs. Gaul began all over again, with a repetitious account of the malfeasance of her husband (now threatening to leave her again) and of her rare metabolic abnormality which made it impossible for her either to lose weight or to refrain from compulsive midnight eating. Finally Mr. Grady, an ally of hers on previous occasions and the group member whom she most liked and respected, erupted to tell her how she evoked feelings of futility and despair in him. He boomed out then in his heavy Irish brogue, "You, Mrs. Gaul, by your whole demeanor, render me impotent, and I must get away from you!" With that he strode out of the room, although the meeting was not yet over. Subsequently her demeanor, her behavior, as well as her grooming changed considerably and the single incident seemed to consolidate a great deal of previous work in the group. Certainly the social microcosm concept became abundantly clear; only too obvious was the parallel between Mr. Grady and her husband, who had also had to leave her and who, incidentally, had also been rendered impotent.

Generally, however, the treatment of a patient with an extreme HRC behavior pattern is an extraordinarily difficult and unrewarding task. If possible, such patients should not be included in a therapy group. Unfortunately, the prediction of this pattern of group behavior is difficult with standard pretherapy screening techniques. Occasionally, these patients can be recognized from their waiting group behavior, or from records of their experience in a previous therapy group, and at that point referred to individual therapy. If the HRC pattern is present but less extreme and fixed, the patient may well be accessible to group therapy, though, as Frank [10] suggests, he should be introduced into an ongoing rather than a beginning therapy group; the

advanced group will be able to offer the patient more understanding
and acceptance and at the same time be less disrupted than the young,
developing group.

The Self-Righteous Moralist

The self-righteous moralist (SRM), first described by Rosenthal,
Frank, and Nash,[16] evinces a pattern of behavior evident in the early
group meetings. The most outstanding characteristic of the self-righteous moralist is the need to be right and to demonstrate that the other
person is wrong, particularly when some moral issue is involved. His
interpersonal motives differ from those of patients evincing other behavioral patterns we have discussed. The monopolist wants to control
others for sundry reasons. The help-rejecting complainer wants to solicit help and then to defeat the benefactor. The self-righteous moralist, on the other hand, is relatively unconcerned about being liked or
respected; above all, he wishes to be right, to be respected for his
moral integrity, and to be successful in imposing his values on other
people.

In the first meeting the SRM usually presents himself as calm and
self-assured, demonstrating his superiority by his poise. He is often
silent at first until he is clear about the group or some member's position. He then usually becomes the key figure in the discussion because of the intensity of his convictions and his propensity to belabor
his viewpoint indefatigably. Characteristically, he refuses to concede
any points, to admit any error, or to make any modification of his original formulation.[16] When others discuss problems, he participates in a
manner which will enhance his status. He may point out that he has
survived greater environmental stress, that he has continued to succeed despite manifold handicaps, and that his solutions may serve as
models for others. Although the group may empathize with him when
he first presents his problems, the empathy is soon transformed into irritation when the members realize that his primary interest is in at-
taining a position of moral superiority rather than in sharing experiences. If another member attempts to assume a position of superiority
in the group, the self-righteous moralist feels challenged and engages
the interloper by attempting to prove him wrong. The therapist, too, is
challenged, though often only obliquely; the patient may express
doubts about therapy and refer to the opinions of other experts in the

field or cite reputable authorities in other fields. When particularly threatened, he may challenge and attack the therapist's moral values.

Patients with this behavioral pattern are deeply troubled by feelings of shame and anger. Rosenthal *et al.*[16] report that their four patients all experienced an early loss of the parent of the opposite sex which resulted in deprivation and loss of social status. Blame for these events is affixed to the parent of the same sex, but the patients, for fear of retaliation, are unable to express their anger. Each responded by attempting to show up the parent of the same sex by assuming and "correctly" filling the parental role. However, instead of gratitude from the concerned parties, the patients received indifference and hostility. So gradually, as manifested in the group, they have come to experience themselves as much maligned figures who have sacrificed themselves for others. This lifetime of sacrifice accounts for the SRM's failure to achieve status and has provided him with a special understanding of life. "His attitude has become one of righteous indignation, his mien is that of one who has suffered nobly. He seeks recognition for his nobility of character rather than for his achievements." [16] The anticipated recognition, however, does not materialize, a fact which merely reinforces the patient's view of himself as long-suffering and unrewarded. His pride in his noble character, his only perceived virtue, is reinforced and more vigorously claimed in his interpersonal dealings. Thus the vicious process comes full circle.

The recognition of the role that shame and lowered self-esteem play in the dynamics of these patients is important in formulating a therapeutic plan. Unless the therapist intervenes, the self-righteous moralist mobilizes so much resentment that he is soon forced out of the group. Not only must the patient be protected but the group must be helped to deal with his provocative behavior. Shame is perhaps the key concept in the successful therapeutic approach. If the group can be helped to sense the shame which underlies the angry self-righteous polemics of the patient, their response to him will be constructive. The therapist, once attuned to the patient's deep sense of failure and shame, will respond accordingly rather than be drawn into the same catastrophic interpersonal sequence that the patient creates in his customary way of relating to the world.

Often, however, before the therapist fully recognizes the pattern, the entire malignant sequence has unfolded and reached a point of irreversibility; the group has responded to the self-righteous moralist at first with patience, then with irritation, at times with studied indifference, and finally with fury. The patient often defends himself and rationalizes the fact that he has not attained the respect he desired by devaluating the group and by convincing himself that the group's opinion is of little import.

Many of these principles are illustrated in this clinical vignette.

Stewart, a twenty-nine-year-old male who sought therapy because of intense sexual urges toward adolescent girls, immediately slid into the self-righteous moralist pattern in the group. He established his moral superiority by an ingenious maneuver: he underscored his ability to lead a good Christian life despite the handicap of ego-alien sexual impulses. His behavior in the group conformed closely to the pattern described above, and he especially berated the group and the therapists for their personal disregard of Christian ethics. The group's response to him, particularly their pointing out that his contempt and scorn for them was not only infuriating but highly un-Christian, apparently went unheeded. The feelings of the members toward him degenerated to the point of name-calling, and three members expressed deep, ungovernable feelings of hatred toward Stewart.

Stewart expressed little concern for the opinions of pagans and, by the twentieth meeting, when the situation became unbearable, he dropped out of the group. To the casual observer, his experience in the group was not only not helpful but indeed catastrophic. However, he immediately began therapy in a married couples' group and proved to be far more receptive when he received the same feedback from his wife and from other couples. Follow-up interviews confirmed that he had learned a great deal in the group but had reflexly locked himself into a relationship with the group which precluded experimentation with new behavior. His behavior, however, in the initial meetings of the second group was considerably different from his behavior in the first.

This vignette illustrates a point I have made elsewhere in the text: therapy does not terminate with termination from the group. Successful patients may continue to grow and to integrate new eperiences for the rest of their lives. Unsuccessful patients who, because of a "role-lock," found their position in the group to be nonviable and who were thus unable to change (or to admit change), are sometimes able to profit from their experience nonetheless and to use their subsequent therapy more effectively.

The Homosexual in the Group *

There is a certain inconsistency in including a section on the homosexual as a problem patient since one of the major points I wish to make is that the homosexual can be successfully treated only when he and the group no longer consider him as a special problem. When the person emerges from "the homosexual," the special problem no longer exists. However, there are so many stereotypes about the homosexual that these patients will encounter certain predictable problems in the therapy group, problems generated by ingrained responses of other members as well as by the patient's own highly stylized self-image.

INCLUSION CRITERIA

In the chapter on selection for group therapy, I made the point that homosexuality is not a criterion for exclusion from group therapy; neither is it a criterion for inclusion. An individual is incompletely described by his sexual behavior alone, and the same criteria must be evaluated in the homosexual as with any candidate: e.g., interpersonal style, psychological sensitivity, and motivation for therapy. It has been my experience with a large number of patients that individuals with homosexual problems can be treated very effectively in an outpatient heterogeneous group. Whether or not a homosexual applying for therapy wishes to change his sexual orientation and "switch" to heterosexuality is irrelevant to the selection process. Individuals who are quite committed to a homosexual style of sexual relations can nonetheless benefit greatly from group therapy. In fact, a homosexual who is confirmed in his sexual orientation but markedly symptomatic is a more suitable candidate than a rather comfortable individual who desires to alter his sexual orientation because of pressures placed upon him from outside agencies. Other therapists disagree [17] and rarely recommend that a homosexual patient be treated in a predominantly heterosexual group. They feel that the group constantly, subtly, often unawares, invalidates the gay patient's identity, and they suggest that if the patient works in a straight group, he also have strong gay support from concurrent membership in other therapy or affinity groups.

* This section deals almost exclusively with the male homosexual patient in heterogenous therapy groups. My experience with female homosexual patients in group therapy is so limited that I am obliged to remain silent on the subject.

A particularly unsuitable candidate is an asymptomatic individual whose homosexual style of life is egosyntonic and who requests therapy in order to reassure himself of the immutability of his life patterns—i.e., he goes through the motions of obtaining therapy to satisfy his superego that no stone has been left unturned in his attempt to conform. Such a patient derives a sufficient amount of gratification from his life style so that he will thwart his own therapy. Perhaps the most unsuitable of all candidates is the individual who has been legally prosecuted for some sexual offense and must obtain psychotherapy as a condition of his probation or parole status. Although there are exceptions, these patients generally are not helped in an outpatient heterogeneous therapy group.

Although individuals with a homosexual proclivity may come to therapy with the same broad spectrum of complaints and precipitating stress as nonhomosexual patients, there are nevertheless certain recurring configurations which stem from characteristic features of their life style. Most commonly such patients experience anxiety and depression related to a confrontation between their homosexuality and their social environment. Compulsive "cruising" which has become so indiscriminate and so flagrant that exposure and jeopardy of the patient's professional and social life are imminent is a frequent complaint. Others seek help after exposure has tumbled down their professional and, if they are married, their family lives. Others apply for treatment in an exceedingly distraught state, following a disruption or a threatened disruption of a love relationship. Middle-aged homosexuals often seek help for a pervasive sense of emptiness and futility; the chief currency in some of the gay world is youthful beauty, and with its passing, individuals feel bankrupt and unable to raise capital once more for an interpersonal investment. Sometimes a "last leaf on the tree" feeling prevails; the patient's realization of his biological sterility adds to his despair.

As a general rule, the more acute the presenting symptoms, the more distinct the precipitating stress; and the more the homosexual patient views his salvation in the hands of others, the *less* favorable a candidate he is for group therapy. Acute stress rapidly vanishes: anxiety stemming from the disruption of a love relationship dissipates with the return of a lover or the acquisition of another; the humiliation and pain of exposure soon diminish, as do family and social pressures to seek therapy. As these forces which once propelled the patient to therapy lose their vigor, so too the patient's commitment to therapy wanes. If, on the other hand, the patient's decision to enter therapy has been a more deliberate judgment, if he has a clear sense of personal responsibility for the origin and solution of his life predicament, if he experiences guilt, self-hatred, and concern that his life has escaped his conscious control, the outlook is more favorable.

THE PATIENT IN THE GROUP

The first important task for the homosexual patient is self-disclosure. For him to become a working, engaged member of the therapy group, he must disclose himself to the other members and preferably he should do so early in the course of the group. Otherwise, it is very likely that the patient will drop out of the group in the early months of therapy, since he will be merely recapitulating the highly dishonest, unsatisfying social relationships which he experiences outside the group.

Good public relations work in the past few years has fostered a less judgmental attitude toward homosexuality. (There was, for example, much sympathetic press coverage of the 1974 American Psychiatric Association's decision to remove the label of "Sexual Deviate" from the homosexually oriented individual.) Despite the growing public acceptance, the gay individual nonetheless remains estranged from the "straight" world. So often he considers homosexuality as the matrix of his identity and yet must conceal this very aspect of himself from family, teachers, business associates, and many "front" male and female friends. He therefore has a sense of sham and deceit about his presentation of self; lest his "real self" leak out, he must maintain a constant vigilance and suppression of spontaneity. The resulting mental fatigue and tension is stoically borne by the secret homosexual until it reaches such proportions that symptomatology ensues. Some open homosexuals gain periodic release in the company of other homosexuals in the gay social world. (The term "gay" is well-chosen, for it *is* a gay world in which the fetters of conventionality are cast off in a spirit of reckless abandon. One of my patients described the gay world as a "magic wonderful fairyland in which secret notes, affairs, rendezvous, and intrigues are everywhere. It is like eating forever the frothy icing of a cake; only one must never notice that there is no cake underneath.")

The therapy group offers such individuals an opportunity for rapprochement with his environment. Simply to be known fully and accepted by representatives of the straight world has great therapeutic value for many homosexuals. Some profess scorn for the straight world, but long to be accepted by it. Often the group's acceptance is a novel type of acceptance for him, based neither on his youth, physical attributes, nor on the achievements of his sham self.

The therapy group offers the homosexual patient a valuable opportunity, unavailable elsewhere, to explore his attitudes and relationships to women. Not infrequently, many such patients have a heterosexual phobia of such magnitude that they have in their adult life avoided virtually all close contact with women; and the therapy group, with mandatory heterosexual interaction, may appear initially threatening on this basis. A dream reported at the twelfth meeting by a gay patient clearly illustrates this conflict:

> I was in a Greyhound bus with some other people. I didn't know who they were. There were two handsome male drivers. I don't know why there were two of them. We were on a trip. At first it was a trip to someplace very beautiful; there was ocean on both sides and beautiful trees with Spanish moss. And then suddenly we ended up on an island on which there were a lot of trapped people. There were some vampire bats, and we had to drive them off. We even crushed them under our feet—they made a crunching sound! There was also a woman who was knitting and had a child and who was like Ann (a group member). She had leprosy, and I couldn't get too close to her.

The dream was a therapist's treasure trove and the patient produced many relevant associations: the two bus drivers seemed like the two (male) co-therapists, the bus of people like the therapy group, the trip like the course of therapy which at first, with the sweet honeyed taste of approval and acceptance, seemed idyllic but now grew increasingly threatening and was finally experienced as a terrifying entrapment on an island. The knitting woman was overtly a group member who often brought knitting to the group. (Knitting also culled forth the association of Mme La Farge.) The vampire bats reminded him of another woman in the group who seemed caustic and intrusive. All of these primitive phantoms—a bloodsucking vampire; a leprous, defiled, contagious hag; a guillotine-tending necrophiliac—had contributed to a phobic avoidance of women.

Often the gay patient must be pressed to discuss his feelings toward the women members; generally, his fear of them is not conscious initially; instead, he experiences revulsion, indifference, or minor irritation. Only as he relates closely to several women in the group and recognizes their individuality, their similarity to himself, their own longings to accept themselves and be accepted by others, will he be able to relinquish these irrational stereotypes.

Some driven, gay patients may, when particularly stressed, respond by a compulsive, promiscuous sexual acting out, often cruising such familiar homosexual locales as gay bars, lavatories, or certain public parks. After repeated acting-out cycles, the therapist and the group gradually arrive at an understanding of the stress and the subsequent sequence of events; often, with forceful interpretive intervention, the group is able to terminate such a cycle early in its development. Generally, the sequence is initiated by an event which produces an intense feeling of alienation, loneliness, or self-hatred. The patient responds by seeking immediate refutation; he demonstrates to himself that, corporally, he is loved, admired, and "in touch" with others. The reassurance is short-lived, since his behavior is but a caricature of intimacy and love; presently he is flooded with even more shame and estrangement as his critical, ego-observing faculties respond to the gulf between his actual and his idealized behavior. The additional shame and estrangement cause again the same fixed acting-out patterns, thus perpetuating the vicious circle.

Jed, a twenty-two-year-old male, who had been in the group for a year and had done no cruising for several months, attended a college graduation banquet the night before the group session. During the course of the evening he experienced an overwhelming desire to cruise and left the dinner early to drive about in a frenzied, aimless search for a sexual contact. As Jed described these still present feelings, the group members helped him explore the precipitating event—the graduation banquet. He recalled his feelings of great loneliness and unworthiness as he witnessed the "good people" of his class relating warmly to one another; he reflected on the squandered opportunities for closeness and was overcome by the abyss that he felt existed between himself, the pariah, and his classmates. The group helped Jed both cognitively and emotionally. They pointed out that his frantic search for a man, any man, was an attempted solution to his feelings of exclusion and self-hatred; he had, they recalled, gone through similar sequences previously in the group. Furthermore, Jed's picture of the entire class, save himself, as one closely bonded circle of brotherhood was illusory; the group reminded him of the universality of many of his feelings of alienation and uniqueness. The group's display of interest, affection, and respect for him during the meeting allowed him to disconfirm the very feelings which had launched the compulsion to cruise. The effect of the meeting was to de-energize the compulsion and to allow Jed to regain willful control of his behavior.

THE RESPONSE OF THE GROUP

Patients with homosexual problems vary as widely in their presentation of self as do heterosexual individuals, and the response of the group to them is equally varied. There are, however, certain characteristic responses of the group to the issue of homosexuality. The members' initial response to the disclosure by a patient that he is a homosexual is invariably sympathetic and accepting. Very often they will attempt to put the discloser at ease by revealing their own homosexual fantasies and experiences; in fact, the group members often welcome the opportunity to unburden themselves.

De-individualization of the patient sometimes follows, in which the group discusses their best friends who are homosexuals and the "homosexual problem" in society. Voyeurism is another form of de-individualization, with some members delving into the patient not because of an interest in him but to peer into the life and the sexual practices of the homosexual. Early in the group, the presence of a homosexual often stimulates members to "figure him out." Homosexual psychodynamics seem particularly clear and enticing, and the group members may launch an historical inquiry into the events of his early psychosexual development. This exploration, too, seems curiously unrelated to the patient and often represents a flight from more immediate feelings on the part of the group.

A therapy group rarely expresses moral condemnation or attempts to make normative judgments of the gay patient, and yet it does not easily relinquish the goal of "converting" the patient to a heterosexual pattern. Although the group appears to accept the patient's own goal of making a better homosexual adjustment, they will, often months or years later, express disappointment at anything less than a shift to a heterosexual orientation.

Individual members, according to their own dynamics, may have extreme responses to a gay patient in the group. Some male patients who have considerable doubts about their sexual adequacy may experience particular discomfort in the presence of a homosexual. They avoid interaction with him in the group lest they be confronted with their own secret fears that they, too, are homosexual. Indeed, there are few males who escape this uncertainty. (Ovesey,[18] in his essay on "pseudohomosexuality," suggests reasons for the prevalence of this uncertainty: too often in our culture we erroneously equate homosexuality with nonaggressive behavior, avoidance of the opposite sex, or the use of the genitals to satisy nonsexual drives like dependency or power.) One member with doubts about his sexual identification was told by a homosexual patient that his dress and grooming were slightly feminine. The patient brooded over this for a couple of days and then dismissed it by reminding himself that he must "consider the source." Subsequently in the group he found himself audibly muttering "goddamned queer" every time the homosexual patient spoke. It is the patient with the severest, yet unrecognized, conflicts of sexual identity who responds most adversely to the overt homosexual. In fact, the gay patient may be most useful to the group in this regard; he may help the male group members recognize and deal with their homophobia— their avoidance of positive feelings and physical contact of any nature with other males.

One of the therapist's chief tasks is to re-individualize the patient who has a homosexual sexual orientation. Patients do not seek therapy because they are "homosexuals"; they request help instead because of profound problems in relating to others, reflected, in part, by problems in their sexual orientation. As therapy proceeds and the group and the patient himself lay aside the appelate of "homosexual," the patient's manifold problems of dependency, self-contempt, and fear of competition become evident and accessible for therapy. The same type of schematization operates as other members ruminate at length about whether or not they are homosexuals; as they realize the universality of so-called perverse behavior, they begin to understand that labels are irrelevant and dehumanizing. Thus, in this way the patient with a homosexual orientation often adds breadth and depth to the group.

REFERENCES

1   I. D. Yalom and P. Houts, unpublished data, 1965.
2. J. Sartre, *The Age of Reason*, trans. Eric Sutton (New York: Alfred A. Knopf, 1952), p. 144. © 1947 by Eric Sutton.
3. H. Bergson, *Laughter* (Garden City, N.Y.: Doubleday, 1956).
4. M. Lieberman, I. Yalom, and M. Miles, *Encounter Groups: First Facts* (New York: Basic Books, 1973).
5. D. Lundgren and D. Miller, "Identity and Behavioral Changes in Training Groups," *Human Relations Training News*, Spring 1965.
6. R. H. Moos and I. D. Yalom, unpublished data, 1963.
7. B. B. Wassel, *Group Analysis* (New York: Citadel Press, 1966), p. 148.
8. L. Coch and J. R. French, "Overcoming Resistance to Change," *Human Relations*, 1: 512–532, 1948.
9. M. B. Cohen *et al.*, "An intensive Study of 12 Cases of Manic Depressive Psychosis," *Psychiatry*, 17: 103–137, 1954.
10. J. D. Frank *et al.*, "Behavioral Patterns in Early Meetings of Therapeutic Groups," *Am. J. Psychiat.*, 108: 771–778, 1952.
11. J. D. Frank *et al.*, "Two Behavior Patterns in Therapeutic Groups and their Apparent Motivation," *Human Relations*, 5: 289–317, 1952.
12. M. Berger and M. Rosenbaum, "Notes on Help-Rejecting Complainers," *Int. J. Group Psychother.*, 17: 357–370, 1967.
13. S. Brody, "Syndrome of the Treatment-Rejecting Patient," *Psychoanal. Rev.*, 51: 75–84, 1964.

14. Correspondence by Dr. Derbolowsky, *Group Analysis*, 1: No. 1, 13–16, 1967.
15. E. Berne, *Games People Play* (New York: Grove Press, 1964).
16. D. Rosenthal, J. Frank, and E. Nash, "The Self-Righteous Moralist in Early Meet-ings of Therapeutic Groups," *Psychiatry*, 17: 215–223, 1954.
17. Donald Clark, Ph.D. Personal communication, 1975.
18. L. Ovesey, "The Pseudohomosexual Anxiety," *Psychiatry*, 18: 17–25, 1955.

13

TECHNIQUE
OF THE THERAPIST:
SPECIALIZED
FORMATS AND
PROCEDURAL AIDS

The standard group therapy format in which one therapist meets with six to eight patients is often complicated by other factors: the patient may be in concurrent individual therapy; there may be a co-therapist in the group; occasionally the group may meet without the therapist—in fact, some groups operate completely without the presence of a therapist. This chapter will discuss these contingencies and will in addition describe some specialized techniques and approaches which, though not essential, may at times facilitate the course of therapy.

Concurrent Individual and Group Therapy

Many different combinations of group and individual therapy may be practiced. There are no systematic data which permit firm conclusions about the effectiveness of any of these combinations. Guidelines must thus be formulated from clinical judgment and from deductive reasoning based on the posited curative factors. My own clinical experience leads me to conclude that concurrent individual therapy is neither necessary nor helpful except in certain instances. If members are selected with a moderate degree of care, a therapy group meeting once or, preferably, twice a week is ample therapy and should provide benefit to the great majority of patients. Optimal combinations in order of my personal preference are: (1) all patients exclusively in group therapy; (2) all group members in concurrent individual therapy with the group therapist; (3) all or some members in concurrent individual therapy with other therapists; (4) some members in concurrent individual therapy with group therapist.

The realities of clinical practice are such that the ideal format for the patient is not always ideal or even feasible for the therapist. Psychotherapists in solo private practice generally must form their groups from the ranks of their individual patients, and some or most continue in individual therapy. Therapy groups in clinics or in cooperative practices are, because of the large available pool of patients, far easier to form and consequently far more common. However, busy, overtaxed clinics have other prevailing exigencies: often there is too little therapist time available for careful screening and preparation of patients, for individual crisis sessions, and for groups meeting more than once weekly.

Occasionally, individual therapy is required to keep a member in the group: the patient may be so fragile, anxious, or threatened that the risk of drop out is very high.

For example, Ginny,* a young, borderline schizophrenic participating in her first group, was considerably threatened by the first few meetings. She had felt increasingly alienated because her bizarre fantasy and dream world seemed so far from the experience of the other members. In the fourth meeting she attacked one of the members and was in turn attacked. For several nights thereafter she had terrifying nightmares, the main themes of which were: (1) her mouth turning to blood (which appeared related to her fear of aggressing verbally because of her world-destructive fantasies); (2) walking along the beach and being engulfed by a huge wave (related to her fear of losing her boundaries and identity in the group); and (3) being picked up and then held down by several men while the therapist performed an operation on her brain; his hands were, however, guided by the men holding her down (obviously related to her fears of therapy and of the therapist's being overpowered by the members).

Her hold on reality grew more tenuous and it seemed unlikely that she could continue in the group without added support. Concurrent individual

* This is Ginny Elkin (pseudonym) with whom I co-authored the book: *Every Day Gets a Little Closer* (Basic Books, 1975).

therapy with another therapist was arranged; it enabled her to remain in the group and to derive much support therefrom.

Some patients may go through a severe life crisis which requires considerable individual temporary support in addition to their group therapy. Occasionally, individual therapy is required in order to enable a patient to use the group; a patient may be so blocked by anxiety or fear of aggression that he is unable to participate effectively in the group therapeutic process. Active intervention may be necessary to escort the patient into a therapeutic position in the group; otherwise, he may become locked into a cramped role and, as some studies [1,2] suggest, will find the group therapy experience unrewarding or even injurious.

Concurrent individual therapy can complicate life in the therapy group in several ways. When there is a marked difference in the individual therapist's and the group therapist's basic approach, the two therapies may work at cross-purposes. If, for example, the individual approach is oriented toward understanding genetic causality and delves deeply into past experiences while the group focuses primarily on here-and-now material, the patient is apt to become confused and to judge one approach on the basis of the other. Generally, patients beginning group therapy are discouraged and frustrated by the initial group meetings, which offer less support than their individual therapy hours, where their narcissistic needs are gratified by the therapist's exclusive attention and by the exploration of the minute details of their past and present life, dreams, and fantasies. Sometimes such patients, when attacked or stressed by the group, may defend themselves by unfavorably comparing their group to their individual experience; such an attack on the group invariably results in further attacks on the individual and further deterioration of the situation. Later in the course of therapy, patients often reverse their comparative evaluations of the two modes. Some therapists [3] have noted that, as therapy progresses, patients may terminate their individual therapy and rely solely on the group; moreover, at the conclusion of therapy, patients, when reviewing their therapy experience, may state that they wished they had begun the group earlier or that much of their individual therapy was unnecessary.

Another complication of concurrent therapy occurs when patients use their individual therapy to drain off affect from the group. The patient may interact like a sponge in the group, taking in feedback and reacting to it in the safer domain of his individual therapy hour. The patient has a powerful rationalization available with which he can support this resistance: he altruistically proclaims, "I will allow the others to have the group time since I have my own hour." When this pattern is pronounced, the group therapist, in collaboration with the individual therapist, may insist that either the group or the individual therapy be terminated. I have known several patients whose involvement in the group dramatically accelerated when their concurrent individual therapy was stopped.

If two conditions are met, the individual and the group therapeutic approaches may complement each other. First, the individual and the group therapist must be in frequent communication with each other—a condition often recognized but rarely realized because of the time pressures of clinical practice. Second, the individual therapy must complement the group approach by being itself here-and-now oriented and by furthering the work of the group. Group patients can make good use of their individual hour to explore, in depth, their feelings toward the group members and toward incidents and themes of current meetings. Such an exploration can serve as a testing ground for further involvement in the life of the group. The patient is often able to examine an uncomfortable, turbulent relationship in the individual setting long before he is able to confront the issue in the group. The individual therapist can with great profit focus on transfer of learning, on helping the patient apply what he has learned in the group to new situations—for example, to the patient's relationship with the individual therapist as well as to important figures in his outside life. It is obvious, too, that the therapists must avoid undermining the other therapy format. An effort by the individual therapist to explore the group experience in the individual therapy hour is viewed by the patient as a vote of confidence in the group.

Many of these potential complications can be avoided if the group therapist serves also as the individual therapist. Clearly, he then has control over the type of individual therapy conducted. Similarly, a group in which all members are in concurrent individual therapy with the group leader is generally a stable group with few dropouts from therapy. However, this format has its own inherent complications. Some therapists become confused about confidentiality: it becomes increasingly difficult to remember who said what in which setting. Can the therapist repeat in the group some intimate material which was revealed in an individual session? Or must he couch his remark in vague language only identifiable by the one patient? As a general rule, it is ill-advised to make any contract of confidentiality regarding the individual sessions; the therapist should retain the privilege of bringing up any individual material in the group, according to his professional judgment.

We shall discuss co-therapists in the next section. For now I wish to point out that if two therapists lead the group and some patients see one therapist individually, some another, and some neither, the complexities are compounded. To the extent that special exclusive relationships exist and that group material is removed from the center of the group, to that same extent is the group rendered less potent and effective.

At times factionalism and sibling rivalry are pronounced in a group in which the members see the leader in concurrent individual therapy; intermember resentment may be particularly extreme if some of the members are not in concurrent therapy because they cannot afford the fee. Occasionally, it may be necessary for the therapist to see a group member who is in crisis for a few individual sessions. For example, patients who are severely stressed by a loss (such as death, separation, or divorce) or by some other major environmental stress (such as academic or job failure) or are on the verge of dropping out of the group may need some temporary support, guidance, or medication. The individual attention the patient receives in this instance rarely arouses any resentment from other members, particularly if they have shared in the decision that the extra help is needed at this time.

Concurrent group and individual therapy may present some special problems for neophyte group therapists. Some find it difficult to see the same patient in two formats since they customarily assume a different role in the two types of therapy; in group they tend to be more informal, more open, more actively engaged with the patients; in individual therapy they remain more impersonal, more distant, and assume a pose of confident omniscience. Often therapists in training prefer that the patients have a "pure" treatment experience—i.e., that they be solely in group therapy without concurrent individual therapy with themselves or other therapists. This is probably a realistic concern since it enables them to establish a base line of expectations about the effects of each type of therapy.

Co-Therapists

Some group therapists choose to meet alone with a group but the majority prefer to work with a co-therapist.[4] No research has been conducted to determine the relative efficacy of the two methods, and clinicians differ in their opinions.[4,5] My clinical experience has taught me that the co-therapy approach may have some special advantages but potential hazards as well.

A co-therapy arrangement of anything other than two therapists of completely equal status is, in my experience, inadvisable. Some training programs have utilized an apprenticeship format in which a neophyte therapist participates as a junior therapist in a group led by a senior clinician; however, the status differential often results in tension and unclarity about the leadership role for both therapists and patients. If two therapists of markedly different levels of experience do co-lead a group, it is important that each be mature, comfortable with each other, and comfortable in their roles as co-workers and as teacher and apprentice. The senior leader teaches by modeling and by encouraging his co-leader to participate in every way possible. The student strives to avoid destructive competition as well as obsequious non-assertiveness.

A partnership in which the two therapists are of nominally equal status but are in actuality widely different in competence and sensitivity will almost invariably result in serious difficulty for the group. After a few meetings the members are clearly aware of any strain between the two leaders and this, if marked, leads to a tense, inhibited group. If is therefore of utmost importance that the therapists feel comfortable and open with each other.

The choice of a co-leader is, thus, an important step and not to be taken lightly. I have seen many classes of psychiatric residents choose co-leaders and have had the opportunity to follow the progress of these groups. I am convinced that the ultimate success or failure of the group depends to a large part upon the correctness of that choice. If the co-leaders are uncomfortable with each other, are closed, competitive, in wide disagreement about style and strategy (and if these differences are not resolvable in supervision), there is little likelihood that their group can develop into an effective work group. Consultants or supervisors called in to assist with a group that is not progressing satisfactorily can often offer the greatest service by directing their attention to the relationship between co-therapists. (I shall discuss this fully in Chapter 15.)

Co-therapist choice should not be made blindly—do not agree to co-lead a group with someone you do not know well. Do not make the choice on an inability to say no to an invitation: it is far too important and too binding a relationship for that.* If the therapists are themselves in an experiential group, they have an ideal opportunity to see one another's group behavior, and I suggest to my students that they delay decisions about co-therapists until after such a group. One does well to select a co-leader toward whom one feels close but who is dissimilar to oneself: such complementarity enriches the experience of the group. There are, as I shall discuss, advantages in a male-female team, but one does far better to lead a group with someone compatible of the same sex than with an opposite sexed colleague with whom one does not work well. Husbands and wives quite frequently co-lead a marital couples group (generally of short term and focused on improvement of dyadic relationships); co-leadership, however, of a long-term singles group requires an unusually mature and stable marital relationship. I advise therapists who are involved in a newly formed intense relationship, romantic or otherwise, with each other, not to lead a group together; it is far more advisable to wait until the relationship has developed more stability and permanence.

It is essential that the co-therapists have a period of time together, even fifteen minutes, at the end of each session to discuss the meeting and their reflections about the other's behavior. If the group is supervised, both therapists should attend the supervisory session.

Whether or not co-therapists should openly express disagreement during the group session is an issue of some controversy. I have generally found co-therapist disagreement unhelpful to the group in the first few meetings; at that point the group is too unstable and pre-cohesive to tolerate such a division of leadership. Later, however, therapist disagreement may contribute a great deal to therapy. In one study [7] I asked twenty patients who had concluded long-term group therapy about the effects of therapist disagreement on the course of the group and on their own therapy. The patients were unanimous in their judgment that it was beneficial. It was a model-setting experience for some patients: they observed individuals whom they re-

---

* In Evelyn Waugh's *Brideshead Revisited* [6] the protagonist, as he departed for his first year of college, was counseled by his father that if he were not circumspect, a considerable part of his second year at college would be devoted to getting rid of undesirable friends he had made during his first year.

spected disagree openly and resolve their differences with dignity and tact. Others found it most useful in working through some of their feelings about authority figures: they witnessed the therapists make mistakes, differ with their colleagues, and experience discomfort, without permanently harming themselves. In short, the therapists are experienced as humans who, despite their imperfections, are genuinely attempting to help the patients. Such a humanization process is inimical to irrational stereotyping, and patients learn to differentiate others according to their individual attributes rather than to their roles.

Some patients were made uncomfortable by co-therapist disagreement and likened it to the witnessing of parental conflict; nonetheless, it strengthened the honesty and the potency of the group. On many occasions I have observed stagnant groups spring into life when the two therapists differentiated themselves as individuals.

Splitting is another phenomenon often occurring in groups led by co-therapists. Some patients respond to their feelings of impotence and helplessness in the presence of adults by attempting to split the therapists, in much the same way as they may have, in their primary family, attempted to split their parents. They may attempt in a variety of ways to undermine the therapists' interrelationship and to intrude between them. Some are quite perceptive about tensions in the co-therapists' relationship and will, in a destructive fashion, play upon these tensions. For example, if a senior therapist feels threatened by his younger co-therapist, the member might scheme to be influenced by anything the younger therapist said and inattend to the contributions of the other, regardless of the content of their offerings. Such a process should be noted and interpreted; it is usually an indication of highly conflicted attitudes toward authority images.

Some groups become split into two factions, with each co-therapist having its own "team" of patients with whom he has a special relationship. Sometimes this split has its genesis in the relationship which the therapist and those patients established before the onset of the group, when he saw them in prior individual therapy or in consultation. (For this reason, it is advisable that both therapists interview the patient, preferably simultaneously, in the pre-group screening. I have noted patients who have continued to feel a special bond throughout their entire group therapy course with the member of the co-therapy team who first interviewed them.) Other patients align themselves with one therapist because of his personal characteristics, or because they feel he is more intelligent, more senior, more sexually attractive, or more ethnically or personally similar to them. Whatever the reasons for the subgrouping, the process should be noted and openly discussed. Transference distortions may become quite evident, as several patients discuss widely varying perceptions of the two therapists. A survey of a highly experienced sample of group therapists revealed considerable consensus that the co-therapy format encourages the development and the working through of transference.[4]

Most co-therapy teams deliberately or, more often, unwittingly split roles: one therapist assumes a more provocative role—much like a Socratic gadfly—while the other is more supportive and serves as a harmonizer in the group.* When the co-therapists are male and female, the roles are usually (but not invariably) assumed accordingly. There is much agreement among clinicians [4] that a male-female co-therapist team may have some unique advantages: the image of the group as the primary family may be more strongly evoked; many fantasies and misconceptions among the group members about the relationship between the two therapists occur and may, with profit, be worked through. Many patients may benefit from the model setting of a male-female pair working together collaboratively with mutual respect without the destructive competition, mutual derogation, exploitation, or pervasive sexuality too often associated with male-female pairings by the patients.

A father-son (both psychiatrists) co-therapy team has been described with interesting results.[9] The therapists concluded that the presence of a parent and a son working together harmoniously was a living demonstration to the patients of the successful resolution of parent-child conflicts. Patients at first distorted and misperceived the relationship in several ways: they interpreted benign remarks by the father as criticism or attacks on the son; they refused to believe that the son made independent interpretations in the group; they felt that he had to "clear" them first with his father. By working through such issues, the members were helped to understand their own relationship with parents and parental imagos.

From my observations of over sixty therapy groups led by neophyte therapists, I consider the co-therapy format to have special advantages for the beginning therapist. For one thing, the presence of a co-therapist lessens initial anxiety and permits the therapist greater

* This split is consonant with findings by Robert Bales in some well-known research on group leadership.[8] Bales studied laboratory task groups of college students discussing some problem in human relations. Almost invariably two types of leaders (as determined by activity ratings and sociometric rankings) emerged from the membership: (1) a "task-executive" leader, the most active member who spurs the group on and who helps them perform the primary task; and (2) a social-emotional leader who attends to the group's emotional needs and reduces tension sufficiently to allow the group to proceed.

equanimity and objectivity in his efforts to understand the meeting. In the post-meeting rehash, the co-therapists can provide valuable feedback about each other's behavior. Until the therapist obtains sufficient experience to be reasonably clear of his presentation of self in the group, this co-therapist feedback is vital in enabling him to differentiate what is real and what is transference distortion in the patients' perceptions of him. The presence of a co-therapist often increases the usefulness of the supervisory session (see Chapter 15). Often, much professional and personal growth is generated by the therapist (often with the supervisor's aid) working through his relationship with his co-leader.

It is especially difficult for beginning therapists to maintain their objectivity in the face of massive group pressure. For example, one group unanimously prescribed for one young male member that he take advantage of several available casual sexual opportunities in an effort to work through his sexual timidity. In actuality, the advice was destructive for the patient, who was, with great difficulty, working on his relationship to his newly wedded wife; however, unable to oppose the group current, the therapist found himself agreeing with the group's advice to the patient—a type of advice that would have been unthinkable to him were he seeing the patient in individual therapy. In such a situation the presence of a co-therapist may be an excellent stabilizer.

One of the more unpleasant and difficult chores for the neophyte therapist is to weather a group attack upon himself and to help the group make constructive use of it. When under the gun, he may be too threatened either to clarify the attack or to encourage further attack without appearing defensive or condescending. There is nothing more squelching than an individual, under fire, saying, "It's really great that you're attacking me. Keep it going!" A co-therapist may prove invaluable here; he may help the members express and work through their anger and at the same time encourage further exploration of all feelings toward the therapist.

The Leaderless Group

Leaderless groups have been used in group psychotherapy in two major forms: (1) the occasional or regularly scheduled leaderless meeting which serves as an adjunct to traditional therapist-led therapy groups and (2) the self-directed group—a group which meets for its entire lifespan without a designated leader.

THE LEADERLESS MEETING

In 1949 Alexander Wolf, a pioneer in the development of group therapy, first suggested the use of regularly scheduled "alternate" meetings without the therapist.[10] His groups, which met three times weekly, were asked to meet an additional two or three times without him at one of the members' homes. Since then, other therapists have reported the use of alternate meetings in a variety of temporal arrangements: some suggest two therapist-led meetings and one alternate meeting weekly, whereas others, myself included, prefer only an occasional leaderless meeting. Although some therapists have spoken out vociferously against the leaderless meeting, describing the chaotic acting out and disruption which may ensue,[11,12] the general clinical consensus is that such fears are unfounded.

Even though we cannot be certain about the efficacy of the alternate meeting in the overall course of therapy, there is little doubt that the events and reactions surrounding it have important implications for the understanding of the dynamics of the member-leader relationship. Members generally do not initially welcome the suggestion of the leaderless meeting; many unrealistic fears and consequences of his absence are evoked. In one study [7] I asked a series of patients who had been in group therapy for at least eight months, "What would have happened in the group if the group therapists were absent?" (This is another way of asking what function the group therapists perform in the group.) The replies were varied. Although a few patients stated they would have welcomed leaderless meetings, most of the others expressed, in order of frequency, these general concerns:

1. *The group would stray from the primary task.* A cocktail hour atmosphere would occur, problems would be avoided, long silences would transpire, the discussions would become increasingly irrelevant. "We would end up in left field without the doctor to keep us on the track!" "I could never express my antagonisms without the therapist's encouragement." "We need him there to keep things stirred up." "Who else would bring in the silent members?" "Who would make the rules? We'd spend the entire meeting simply trying to make rules."
2. *The group would lose control of its emotions.* Anger would be unrestrained and there would be no one available either to rescue the damaged members or to help the aggressive ones maintain control.
3. *The group would be unable to integrate its experiences and to make con-*

structive use of them. "The therapist is the one who keeps track of loose ends and makes connections for us." "He helps clear the air by pointing out where the group is at a certain time." He was viewed by the members as the time-binder—the group historian who sees patterns of behavior longitudinally and who points out that what a member did today, last week, and last month fits into a coherent pattern. The members say, in effect, that though they may have a great deal of action and involvement without the therapist, they will be unable to make use of it.

Many of the concerns are clearly unrealistic and reflect an infantile, dependent posture on the part of the members. It is for this very reason that a leaderless meeting may play an important role in the therapy process. The members are helped to experience themselves as autonomous, responsible, and resourceful adults who, though they may profit from the therapist's expertise, are nevertheless able to control their emotions, to pursue the primary task of the group, and to integrate their experience. In a sense, the rationale is identical to that underlying the therapeutic community. Jones,[13] Daniels,[14] and many others have pointed out that the traditional authority-bound mental hospital not only fails to counteract feelings of helplessness and inadequacy on the part of hospitalized patients but, by its authoritarian total-care structure, reinforces these very features. Thus, it is reasoned, a new patient-directed intentional social system which encourages patients' personal growth and decision-making capacity must be constructed.

Few would extend the analogy in group therapy to the conclusion that the therapist should be permanently excluded. The outpatient therapy group, unlike the therapeutic community, does not consider the assumption of responsibility to be the overriding goal in therapy since all outpatients assume sufficient responsibility to, at least, maintain themselves out of a hospital. Nevertheless, it remains an important minor theme in the treatment of many patients—a theme which is highlighted by the patients' reactions to the absence of the therapist.

If the leaderless meeting is to be a constructive experience, it is important that the patients' unrealistic predictions about their own helplessness are not realized. Proper timing is important in constructive meetings; the therapist must be certain that the therapy group has developed cohesiveness and has established productive norms before suggesting that alternate meetings be considered.

The leaderless meeting not only fosters a sense of autonomy and responsibility but has several other advantages. Issues arise in the alternate meetings which yield important insights about each patient's relation to the therapist(s). Some patients feel liberated and are far more active and uninhibited in the absence of the therapist; others are, for the first time, able to express critical feelings toward him; still others display their contempt for their peers (and thus their self-contempt) by refusing to participate, on the grounds that all benefit emanates solely from the therapist.*

Although many therapists fear that intense sexual acting out will occur in leaderless meetings, experience has shown the fear to be unfounded. However, it is very common for groups to assume a more playful (often sexually tinged) character in the absence of the leader. The transformation is often startling in its abruptness; no sooner does the teacher leave the room than the class erupts into unrestrained, mirthful play. One group planned a party on a nearby nude beach, another discussed a nude swimming party, another (a group of alcoholics) talked about a marijuana party, another burlesqued the mannerisms, beard, and careful carelessness of the therapist's grooming and clothing.

In assessing the possible hazards of leaderless meetings we must keep in mind the distinction between acting and acting out. Acting out is, by definition, a resistance to therapy; it is action concealed from the group's analytic eye; patients discharge through action those impulses which should be discussed and examined in therapy. Acting is far different; as Lieberman states, "For acting read trying out, reality testing, practice, and the distinction becomes clear." [15] All change must be preceded by action, and all action in therapy meetings which is available for the group's analytic scrutiny may be useful in the process of change. "Rightly understood and accepted, all experiences are good and the bitter ones best of all." [16]

How the group chooses to communicate the events of the alternate meeting to the therapist is often of great interest. Do they attempt to conceal or distort information or do they compulsively brief him on all details? Sometimes the ability of a group to withhold information from the therapist is in itself an encouraging sign of group maturation, although therapists are usually uncomfortable at being excluded. In the group, as in the family, not only must the individual strive for autonomy but the leader must be willing to allow him to do so. Often the

---

* The alternate meeting becomes divisive if all members do not attend. If a patient steadfastly refuses to come to leaderless meetings, it is a significant matter and deserves much attention in the group. If this cannot be resolved and if the therapist is firmly committed to the group's holding alternate meetings, he should consider transferring the patient to another group; his chances for improvement in a group wherein he holds only partial membership are poor.

leaderless session and subsequent events allow the therapist to experience and understand his own desires for control and his feelings of being threatened as his patients grow away from him.

SELF-DIRECTED GROUPS

The alternate session has two primary goals: to increase the group's and the members' sense of personal responsibility and autonomy and to hasten the emergence of several important themes for subsequent working through with the therapist's help. The self-directed group operates on another principle: the primary healing forces are inherent in the group and may be evoked and harnessed without the presence of a formal leader. In part, the self-directed group has sprung into being as a result of the shortage of professional manpower; in part, it is a reflection of a humanistic trend which decries the need for an authority structure that is perceived as restrictive and growth-inhibiting.

Although no formal inventory of self-directed groups exists, there is no doubt that it is a movement of considerable magnitude; Mowrer [17] in 1961 reported 265 self-directed groups in America. Alcoholics Anonymous has an enormous membership with chapters meeting in virtually every major city of the world. Other well-known groups include Synanon (drug addiction); Mattachine, Daughters of Bilitis, and Gay Liberation groups (homosexuality); TOPS and Weight Watchers (obesity); Grow Groups, Schizophrenics Anonymous, Neurotic Anonymous, Recovery Incorporated (mental illness); etc. Women's consciousness-raising groups have sprung up all over the country: they have, in addition to their social, political and economic concerns, a personal growth objective and will, most likely, grow even more numerous in the future. Self-directed groups are a heterogeneous lot; few are, in actuality, leaderless but rely instead on leaders drawn from the ranks of former members—for example, Synanon, Alcoholics Anonymous, or Recovery, Inc. Some may remain nominally leaderless, such as a self-led group of mental health professionals or a women's consciousness-raising group, but yet be guided by a natural leader who has emerged from the ranks.

One of the more interesting action-research ventures into the self-directed group field was conducted by Berzon and her associates.[18] Their work began with groups of physically or psychiatrically disabled subjects referred by the Division of Vocational Rehabilitation and with groups of subjects from the community or college campus who have volunteered for a group therapy experience. Their methods were later adapted for use with groups in hospitals, prisons, educational institutions, and for groups of individuals searching for a personal growth experience.[19]

Berzon at first organized groups which, with no further instructions, were asked to meet for a series of twelve to eighteen meetings. (There was a buzzer placed in the center of the room which could be used to signal a group leader when the group desired help. The buzzer was not often used and was later discontinued.) It soon became clear that the leaderless group needed more direction, and a booklet of programmed instructions was prepared for the group's use. Later, this was changed to a series of audio tapes. The tapes were designed to help the group members accomplish certain goals: to encourage participation, to focus attention on the here-and-now, and to encourage helping behavior.

Berzon's work clarifies the role of the leader in the group by eliminating him and building in his functions artificially, using some rather ingenious techniques. For example, in a ten-session program [18] three basic stages were proposed: (1) group building (first four sessions); (2) intensification of feelings (fifth through ninth sessions); and (3) separation (last session). A task was designated and an exercise assigned, via an audio tape, for each session according to the principles of group development. Following each exercise, the group spent the remainder of the time discussing their reactions to it.

Session 1: Activities are proposed which make the participants aware of the boundaries of the group. For example, the members of the group stand in a circle and one at a time one member steps out of the circle and then tries to break into the group.

Session 2: The basic ground rule of discussing the here-and-now is presented to the group. A tape of two groups is presented, one which is tuned in to this principle and one which is not. The group is asked to break into pairs to practice this type of participation.

Session 3: Another norm is instituted: the principles of facilitative feedback are explained and members asked to practice in a go-around.

Session 4: A review session. Members evaluate themselves about their progress in employing group principles thus far presented.

Session 5: Top secret exercise (described in Chapter 1).

Session 6: Members form a circle with a member in the center who attempts to break out. The group is to be experienced as standing between him and his freedom. Each member attempts this and then discusses his feelings about the exercise.

Session 7: Each member goes around the group and describes the other members metaphorically—as an animal, a piece of furniture, a car, etc.

Session 8: Each group member in turn spends three minutes telling the group of his strengths and five minutes listening to feedback from the others of his strengths.

Session 9: The group selects three members who have kept the others farthest away from them. They go one at a time to the center of the group and then each member expresses, nonverbally, positive feelings to him. The task is assigned as an exercise in the reception of positive feelings.

Session 10: A series of short exercises is followed by a discussion of the changes that have occurred in members. Unfinished business is attended to and the members say goodbye to one another.

Berzon has reported on several evaluative studies of versions of this program. These studies indicate that members of the self-directed therapy groups become more interpersonally sensitive, self-accepting, and self-reliant than no-treatment controls. One study [18] compared seventy-five subjects in self-directed groups to forty-four comparable subjects who had no group experience. Self-concept (measured by a semantic differential rating scale) [20] was significantly higher at the end of the ten meetings in the group members than for the controls after a comparable period of time. No change occurred on the other measure, "personal efficacy" (a five-item forced-choice instrument).[21]

In 1965 an evaluative study [18] was carried out comparing the results of professionally directed groups ($N = 34$), self-directed groups ($N = 29$), and control groups (no group experience; $N = 20$). All subjects were vocational rehabilitation patients. An eighteen-session self-directed program was used which was similar in concept to the ten-session program described above. The professionally directed groups and the self-directed groups, but not the control group members, showed a significant increase in self-concept. Both professionally directed and self-directed members showed a significant increase in the ratings of vocational rehabilitation counselors; one year later the positive changes persisted for the professional-directed groups but not for the self-directed groups. On a therapeutic climate scale (measuring self-exploration and facilitative behavior) the professionally-directed but not the self-directed groups showed an increase in the last nine group sessions. The dropout rate was slightly higher in the self-directed groups. It would seem then that both professionally-directed and self-directed groups showed positive change but that the changes in the professionally directed groups were more marked and durable.

Lieberman, Yalom, and Miles [22] studied the outcome of a ten-session leaderless, programmed encounter group of normal college students. In the entire project seventeen groups were studied, fifteen led by leaders of varying ideological schools (see Chapter 14) and two groups led by the "Encounter Tape Program." Of the twenty-two members who began these two leaderless groups, one dropped out, one had a negative outcome, thirteen (60 percent) were unchanged, five (22.5 percent) had a positive outcome, and two (9 percent) a very positive outcome. Although these are, at best, modest results and unacceptable outcomes for most group therapists, the two groups nevertheless compared favorably to leader-led groups in the project. (Their six months follow-up placed the two groups third and eighth most effective of the seventeen groups.) Keep in mind, however, that these were short-term (thirty hour total) groups of nonpatients; the extrapolation of these results to therapy group outcome is difficult.

My impression of the two groups from my observation of the meetings and interviews with the members was that they were safe, supportive, low-key groups. The type of learning available was highly selective in that little opportunity existed for investigation of attitudes toward either conflict or authority. For example, in one meeting a member grew very angry at another and, weeping, ran out of the meeting. Next week she returned, the tape provided an agenda for that meeting, and the incident was permanently buried. There was no leader present to bring the group back to the issue; no one took the responsibility of insuring that the group not only resolved the conflict but also learned from it. Similarly, there was no one who occupied a designated leadership position, and thus no investigation of the entire area of authority could be pursued.

A group in which the leader is replaced by some mechanical device is an entirely different type of leaderless group from such groups as A. A. or Recovery Incorporated, which do not abolish authority but, on the contrary, derive their strength from a heavily ritualized tradition in which authority is embedded. The first two of the A. A. twelve steps, for example, ask the members to recognize that they are powerless over alcohol and to give themselves up to a power greater than themselves. The many self-help groups differ so considerably in goals and mechanisms of change employed that there is little justification for the concept of a leaderless group movement. The automated tape recorder leader is a particularly curious development emerging, as it does, from a tradition whose ethos is so vitalistic and anti-mechanistic. I consider the trend as a bizarre mutation of the humanistic psychological movement. One of the members of a tape-led group presented the paradox clearly when he said, "There's something very odd about that goddamn machine teaching me to be more human."

Dreams

The number and types of dreams that patients bring to their therapy is very largely a function of the therapist's behavior. His response to the first dreams presented by patients will influence the choice of dreams subsequently presented. The intensive, detailed, personalized investigation of dreams practiced in analytically oriented individual therapy is hardly feasible in group therapy. For groups meeting once or twice weekly, such a practice would demand that a disproportionate amount of time be spent on one patient; the process would, furthermore, be minimally useful to the remaining members who would become mere bystanders.

What useful role, then, can dreams play in group therapy? In individual analysis or analytically oriented treatment, the therapist is usually presented with a large number of dreams and dream fragments. He never strives for a complete analysis of the dream. (Freud always held that a total dream analysis should be a research, not a therapeutic endeavor.) Instead, the therapist, in a variety of ways, elects to work on dreams or aspects of dreams which he deems most pertinent to the current phase of therapy. He may ignore some dreams, he may ask for extensive associations to others, he may establish connections with a previous dream or issue in therapy. Generally, the therapist will use dreams to pursue the current theme in individual therapy: for example, if a patient who is currently working on his concerns about his sexual identity brings in a dream with male-female doubles as well as a heavily disguised patricidal theme, the therapist will generally select the former theme for work and ignore or postpone the second theme for later work. Moreover, the process is a self-reinforcing one; it is well-known that patients who are deeply involved in therapy will dream or remember dreams compliantly—i.e., they will produce dreams which corroborate the current thrust of therapy and reinforce the theoretical framework of the therapist. ("Tag along" dreams, Freud termed them.)

Substitute "group work" for "individual work" and the group therapist may use dreams in precisely the same fashion. The investigation of certain dreams accelerates the group therapeutic work. Most valuable are group dreams—dreams which involve the group as an entity—or dreams which reflect the dreamer's feelings toward one or more members of the group. Either of these types may elucidate not only the dreamer's but other members' concerns which are until then not yet fully conscious. Sometimes the dream introduces, in disguised form, material which is conscious but which members have, for various reasons, been reluctant to discuss in the group. In either case, the dream may be used in the service of a primary task of the group; to explore the here-and-now interpersonal relationships of the group members.

Some illustrative examples of members' dreams in group therapy may clarify these points.

In the sixth meeting of a group a patient related a dream fragment: "We [the group] were in a strange large room. We were expected to undress. Everyone else took off their clothes. I was afraid and ran out of the room."

In discussing her dream, the patient, who had until then been an almost completely silent member, spoke of her great fears of self-disclosure and her feeling that once she began to participate in the group in any manner she would be humiliated by being forced to disrobe completely. As the group encouraged her to explore her fear more deeply, she spoke of her particular dread of one of the co-therapists and one of the dominant members of the group; she dreaded, especially, their disapprobation of her current extramarital sexual activities. The dream thus enabled her both to enter the group and to forewarn the group about her great sensitivity and vulnerability to criticism.

At the twentieth meeting a patient related this dream: "I was walking with my younger sister. As we walked she grew smaller and smaller. Finally I had to carry her. We arrived at the group room where the members were sitting around drinking tea. I had to show the group my sister. But this time she was so small she was in a package. I unwrapped the package but all that was left of her was a tiny bronze head."

The investigation of this dream clarified several previously unconscious concerns of the patient. The dreamer, Miss Sands (see Chapter 2), had been extraordinarily lonely and had immediately become deeply involved in the group; in fact, it represented her only important social world. At the same time, however, she feared her intense dependence on the group; it had become too important to her. She modified herself rapidly to meet with group expectations and, in so doing, lost sight of her own needs and identity. The rapidly shrinking sister symbolized herself becoming more infantile, more undifferentiated, and finally inanimate as she sacrificed herself in a frantic quest for the group's approval. Some of the manifest content of the dream becomes clearer through a consideration of the content of the meeting preceding the dream: the group had spent considerable time discussing her body—she was moderately obese—and finally one member had offered her a diet she had recently seen in a magazine. Thus her concerns about losing her personal identity took the dream form of shrinking in size.

Shortly afterwards in the same group another patient brought in this dream fragment: "I brought my sister in to meet the group. She was beautiful and I wanted to show her off to the members."

This patient, Mr. Farr (Chapter 2), had had many dreams involving his family members, all of whom had died at Auschwitz, but he had never before had a dream involving the group. His Don Juan style of life had for many years served to bolster his self-esteem by enabling him to possess beautiful women whom other men would desire. The dream helped to uncover these dynamics as they operated in the microcosm of the group. He dreamed of eliciting respect and admiration from the members by showing off his possession, his beautiful (but dead) sister; behind this desire was the conviction that he had little intrinsic personal substance for which other members would value him.

The following dream illustrates how the therapist may shift the material and selectively focus on those aspects which further the group work:

My husband locked me out of our grocery store. I was very concerned about the perishables spoiling. He got a job in another store, where he was busy cleaning out the garbage. He was smiling and enjoying this, though it was clear he was being a fool. There was a young, attractive clerk there who winked at me and we went out dancing together.

The patient was the middle-aged woman who was introduced into a younger group in which two members, Jan and Bill (see Chapter 11), were involved in a sexual relationship. From the standpoint of her personal dynamics, the dream was highly meaningful. Her husband, a distant, work-oriented individual, locked her out of his life; she had a strong feeling of her life slipping by unused (perishables spoiling). She had referred to her own sexual fantasies as "garbage"; she felt considerable anger toward her husband to which she could not give vent (in the dream she made an absurd figure of him). Yet the therapist chose to refrain from tasting these tempting dream-morsels and instead focused on the parts which had greater group relevance. She had many concerns about being excluded from the group; she felt older, less attractive, and very isolated from the other members. Accordingly, the therapist focused on the theme of being "locked-out" and on her desire for more attention from the men in the group (one of whom resembled the clerk who took her dancing at the end of the dream).

The following is an example of a dream which clarifies a previously undisclosed fact of a patient's interpersonal behavior.

A female patient dreamed: "I went to a dance recital given by Joyce [one of the members]. Jim was there; I went over to him at intermission and asked him where he was sitting. He stammered and hesitated so that I grew uncomfortable and ran away."

Jim, a homosexual, responded to this dream by commenting that it was prophetic: if he were to see any members of the group at a social event, he would be so ashamed of their meeting any of his homosexual friends that he would go to any lengths to avoid encountering the group members. The other member's dream thus enabled Jim to plunge into the crucial issue of his shame and his need to conceal himself continually from the straight world.

The following three dreams illustrate how conscious but avoided material may, through dreams, be brought into the group for examination.

"There were two rooms side by side with a mirror in my house. I felt there was a burglar in the next room. I thought I could pull the curtain back and see a person in a black mask stealing my possessions."

This dream was brought in at the twentieth meeting of a therapy group which was observed through a one-way mirror by the therapist's students. Aside from a few comments in the first meeting, the group members had never voiced and explored their feelings about the observers. A discussion of the dream led the group into a valuable discussion of the therapist's relationship to the group and to his students. Were the observers "stealing" something from the group? Was the therapist's primary allegiance toward his students and were the group members merely a means of presenting a good show or demonstration for them?

"It was session time. The session took place in a big blue bathroom like the therapist's. We all sat down around the bathtub, in a circle, with our feet in the water. We all had our shoes on, so the water in the bathtub became very dirty. The faucet was opened to clean up the water. Someone suggested that we should take our shoes off. Some agreed with this, but others did not. I was ashamed because my feet are ugly, so I had to agree with those who wanted to keep their shoes on. To solve the problem, someone brought some wooden mats to put under our feet, but there were too few mats and we began to argue and quarrel. At this moment, I woke up full of anguish." [23]

The group listened to this dream and reported that following the previous meeting, four of the seven members had gone to a bar and formed two heterosexual couples. To them the bathtub represented the group, in which they deposited their dirty feelings (all four of the involved members had a history of homosexual difficulties). Later in the session one of the members mentioned that he could never profit from the sessions because whenever he talked, someone always interrupted him. The group then began to argue about how various members usurped the others' time, and several illustrative episodes from recent meetings were recalled. The dream image of the members fighting for the few wooden mats of the therapist brought to light long-smoldering feelings of rivalry and competition for the therapist's attention.

A patient in another group presented a similar dream fragment: "The whole group was sitting around the bathtub washing their feet. The dirt slowly went down the drain."

This was the group which, two sessions previously, had expelled Mrs. Cape (see Chapter 2) because she had, by breaking rules of confidentiality, become exceedingly disruptive to the group. The meeting immediately prior to the dream was a breast-beating session in which all members, including the therapists, had felt extraordinarily guilty at expelling her. The dream, by its stark and cruel symbolism, "washing the dirt out of the group," reminded the members not to become overwhelmed by their guilt; there had been a very valid reason for their drastic action.

FANTASY

Waking dreams or fantasies may play an important role in the therapeutic process. A great wealth of material exists just below consciousness and, if made available to the therapy process, greatly enriches the work. Some therapists regularly ask for recall of fantasy material. They encourage members to discuss the fantasies they have had about the group or the members during the interval since the previous meeting. They may, for example, ask members to share the fantasies about the group they have had on the way to the meeting that day. Others may guide fantasy formation during the group. For example, if two members are deeply involved, the therapist may clarify the relationship by asking not for their feelings toward each other (often these are not clearly known) but for a fantasy of doing something with each other. One twenty-eight-year-old woman was told by a male member that he would simply like to walk alone with her in the woods with his head on her shoulder. Since one of her primary problems centered about her inability to attract men to her, it proved of great benefit to her to discover how she had been manifesting herself maternally rather than sexually to the other member.

The Use of Videotape in the Therapy Group

Modern scientific technology, which has so largely contributed to the dehumanization of present-day society and, consequently, to the necessity for group therapy, has at the same time created an instrument—the videotape recorder—which has considerable potential benefit for the teaching, practice, and understanding of group therapy.

Videotape recording has proven its value in the teaching of all forms of psychotherapy. Students and supervisors are permitted to view the session with a minimum of distortion. Important nonverbal aspects of behavior of both students and patients which may be completely missed in the traditional supervisory format become available for study. The student-therapist has a rich opportunity to observe his own presentation of self and his own body language. Confusing aspects of the meeting may be viewed several times until some order appears. Valuable teaching sessions which clearly illustrate some basic principles of therapy may be stored and a teaching videotape library created. These features suggest that videotapes are a significant advance over older methods of observation such as audiotapes, closed-circuit television, or one-way mirrors.

The potential benefit for the group therapy patient is self-evident. Do we not wish patients to obtain a more accurate view of their behavior? Do we not search for methods to encourage self-observation and to make the self-reflective aspect of the here-and-now as salient as the experiencing aspect?

Though these potential benefits seem formidable, the proper role and application of this new technique in ongoing therapy is far from settled. Some therapists make the videotape recording a central feature and, in a sense, structure the group around it; others, myself included, find the technique of value and periodically make use of it as an auxiliary aid in the therapeutic process; others, frustrated by the mechanical difficulties and disappointed that the technique failed to live up to expectations (often unrealistic ones), have abandoned video recording entirely.

Many clinicians stress the importance of immediate playback; they arrange for the patient to view the tape as soon as possible after the experience. This necessitates great instrumental flexibility: camera, tape deck, and monitor must be in the group room and the tape rewound on the spot for viewing and commentary by members and therapists. Obviously, certain segments must be selected for this type of viewing ("focused feedback" [24,25]); selection may be made by the group or by the therapist. Some therapists use an auxiliary therapist whose chief task is to operate the camera and associated gadgetry and to select suitable portions for playback. Other therapists prefer the less complicated method of videotaping an entire meeting and devoting the following session for playback and reactions to it. Some therapists schedule an extra playback meeting in which most of the previous tape is observed; others tape the first half of the meeting and observe the tape during the second half.

Patient response depends upon the timing of the procedure. Berger [26,27] notes that the patient's response to his first playback session differs from his response to later sessions. In the first playback patients attend primarily to their own image and are relatively less involved with the process of the group. Later they may be more attentive to their styles of responding and relating to others. For this reason, it is far more efficient, later in therapy, to select certain important segments for viewing rather than to view, indiscriminately, an entire session.

Often a patient's long-cherished self-image is radically challenged by a first videotape playback. It is not unusual for him to recall and to accept previous feedback he had gotten from other members; often with dramatic impact he understands that the group had been honest and, if anything, overprotective in previous confrontations. The group is no longer experienced as a critical or destructive tribunal, and the patient may become more amenable to future interpretations. Although feedback about our behavior from others is important, it is not as convincing as information we discover for ourselves; videotape provides feedback which is not mediated through a second person. Often profound self-confrontations occur; one cannot hide from oneself and patients may subsequently abandon defensive and incogruent facades. My initial playback reactions are concerned with the presence or absence of sex appeal in women and masculinity in men.[26] In subsequent playback sessions patients note their interactions with others, their withdrawal, self-preoccupation, hostility, or aloofness. They are far more able to be self-observant and objective than when actually involved in the group interaction.

I have on occasion found video recording to be enormously useful in crisis situations. For example, one alcoholic patient arrived at the group intoxicated and proceeded to be monopolistic, insulting, and crude. Any work done during such a meeting is in vain since the patient's mental status renders him incapable of retention and integration. However, the meeting was videotaped and a subsequent viewing of the meeting was enormously helpful to the patient: he had been told but really never knew how destructive alcohol was to himself and to others. On another occasion in an alcoholic group, a patient arrived intoxicated and in deep despair. He lost consciousness and lay stretched out on the sofa while the group, encircling him, discussed what to do with him. Some time later the patient viewed the tape with profound effect. He had often been told, but without impact, that he was self-destructive, that he was killing himself with alcohol. The sight of himself laid out as if on a bier brought his suicidal life pattern and his death home to him with undeniable force. Berger [26] describes a similar episode. A periodically manic patient, who had never accepted that her behavior was unusual, had an opportunity to view herself in a particularly high, disorganized state. In each of these instances, the videotape provided a powerful self-observatory experience—a necessary first step in the therapeutic process.

Many therapists are reluctant to inflict a TV camera on the group; they feel that it will inhibit the group's spontaneity and that the group will resent, though not necessarily overtly, the intrusion. In my opinion the situation is virtually identical to the introduction of the audio tape recorder into psychotherapy in the 1950s. The person who appears to experience the most discomfort is the therapist. If he regards the camera as an intrusion and alters his behavior accordingly, obviously the technique will obstruct therapy. Many therapists who have become accustomed to videotapes report that, after the initial adjustment, the process of the meeting is not altered; [28] other therapists dispute that point and claim that the sound and sight of the machinery, the presence of a cameraman, the interruptions to the group, and the unnatural seating pattern (if only one camera is used, the group must, for everyone to be seen, sit in a horseshoe pattern) are always an interference in the group. Patients, especially if they will view the playback, are almost always receptive to the suggestion of videotaping. Often, however, they are concerned about confidentiality and need reassurance on this issue. If the tape will be viewed by anyone other than the group members (for example, students or supervisors), the therapist must be very explicit about the purpose of the viewing and the identity of the viewers and must obtain written permission from all the members.

The technique is still so new that we will for some time be unable to evaluate its overall importance in the psychotherapy process. We may expect, as with any new technique, overstated claims. The process is a self-reinforcing one since the enthusiasm engendered by the innovators will itself have a salutory effect on therapy outcome. There is little doubt that self-observation plays a role in the therapy process; however, it is a precondition for therapeutic change, not synonymous with change. Videotaping is but a technique, to be employed only insofar as it facilitates the operation of the basic curative factors. It may complement but it is not an alternative for sound clinical training.

Written Summaries

Over the past two years my colleagues and I have experimented with a technique which provides the patient with a detailed overview (from the therapists' perspective) of each meeting. The technique is still in its early stages (I have used it in approximately two hundred group meetings), but I believe it has sufficient theoretic and practical implications to merit a brief description here. (It is more fully described elsewhere.[29])

The technique is a simple one. At the end of each meeting the therapist dictates a narrative account of the meeting to which he adds a mélange of editorial commentary. The summaries are typed and mailed to the group members before their next session. Dictation of the summaries (three to seven double-spaced pages) requires approximately twenty to thirty minutes of the therapist's time.

The summaries were first used in a group of alcoholic patients. As my co-therapist and I plunged the members into an interactional focus, anxiety levels rose to the point that maladaptive anxiety-reducing methods of coping were in evidence (absenteeism, increased drinking, massive denial, etc.). We sought for techniques to modulate anxiety: increased structure, a suggested (written) agenda for each meeting, video playback, and written summaries distributed after each meeting. The latter technique was by far the most efficacious one and soon replaced the others. Subsequently, I have used the summaries in other groups including a twice-weekly highly sophisticated outpatient neurotic group. The summary soon assumed a number of tasks; it provided understanding of the events of the session, noted and rewarded patient gains, predicted (and thus prevented) undesirable developments, brought in silent members, increased cohesiveness (by underscoring similarities and caring in the group, etc.), provided interpretations (either repetition of interpretations made in the group or new interpretations occurring to the therapist later), and provided hope to the patients (helping them realize that the group was an orderly process and that the therapists had some coherent sense of the group's long-term development).

The summaries should be honestly straightforward about the process of therapy. They are virtually identical to summaries I make for my own files (which provide most of the clinical material for this book) and are based on the assumption that the patient be a full collaborator in the therapeutic process, that psychotherapy is strengthened not weakened by demystification.

The summaries serve a number of functions; in fact, they may be used to augment every one of the group leader's tasks in the group. Patient reactions to the summaries (gathered from questionnaires and interviews) underscore several of these functions. I shall, when applicable, present illustrative excerpts from the summaries.

REVIVIFICATION

The summary becomes another group contact; the meeting is revivified, the group is more likely to assume continuity, each meeting continues the theme of the previous one.

SELF-REFLECTION

The patients are helped to reexperience and to assimilate important events of a meeting. Often, group sessions may be so threatening or unsettling that members move into a defensive, survival position. Only later (often with the help of the summary) can they review the significant events and convert them into constructive learning experiences. The therapist's interpretations (especially complex ones) delivered in the midst of a melee often fall on deaf ears. The interpretations when repeated in the summary were often far more effective since the patient could consider them at length far from the heat of battle.

SHAPING OF GROUP NORMS

We have used the summaries to reinforce norms both implicitly and explicitly. For example, the following excerpt reinforced the here-and-now norm.

Phil's relationship with his boss is very important and difficult for him at this time, and as such is certainly material for the group. However, the members do not know the boss, what he is like, what he is thinking and feeling—and thus are limited in offering help. However, they are beginning to know one another and can be more certain of their own reactions to one another in the group. They can give more accurate feedback about feelings that occur between them rather than trying to guess what the boss may be thinking.

Or consider the following excerpt which encourages the patients to make process commentary and to approach the therapist in an egalitarian manner. (In the excerpt Irv is the therapist.)

Jed did something very different in the group today, which was to make an observation about the bind that Irv was in. He noted, quite correctly, that Irv was in a bind of not wishing to change the topic from Dinah because of Irv's reluctance to stir up any of Dinah's bad feelings about being rejected or abandoned in the group, but on the other hand Irv wanted very much to find out what was happening to Pete, who was obviously hurting today.

THERAPEUTIC LEVERAGE

The therapist may, in the summary, keep the patient's primary task in front of him: he may remind him of his original purpose in coming to therapy or he may take care to repeat statements by patients that will offer leverage in the future. For example:

Lucille began weeping at this point but when Ed tried to console her she snapped, "Stop being so kind. I don't cry because I'm miserable, I cry when I'm pissed off. When you console me or let me off the hook because of my tears, you always stop me from looking at my anger."

NEW THOUGHTS

Often the therapist understands an event after the fact; on other occasions the timing is not right for him to make a clarifying remark—too much cognition might squelch the emotional experience, or there is simply no time for him to contribute to the group, or a patient is so defensive that he would reject any efforts at clarification. The summaries provide an excellent vehicle in which the therapist can convey his remarks.

TRANSMISSION OF TEMPORAL PERSPECTIVE OF THE THERAPIST

Far more than any member of the group, the therapist maintains a long-range temporal perspective. He is cognizant of subtle changes occurring over months in the group as well as in the course of each member's therapy. There are many times when the sharing of these observations offers hope, support, and meaning for the members. For example:

Seymour spoke quite openly in the group today about how hurt he was by Jack and Burt switching the topic off him. We were struck by the ease with which he was able to discuss these feelings. We can clearly remember his hurt, passive, silence in similar situations in the past, and are impressed with how markedly he has changed his ability to express his feelings openly.

Or again:

Delores described the despair she has been experiencing. In some ways it sounded almost identical to the kinds of despair Delores described in the group when she first entered—having to do with loneliness, with the feeling that there was no one in the world who cared about her, with the feeling that she always had to ask people to be with her and to do things with her, that no one ever sought her out. However, there was an important difference in her state now and her condition at that time. The major difference was that several months ago Delores presented these things as though that's the way the world *was*—that there really *was* no one in the world for her. This time she has much more of a realistic view of it. She realizes that this is the way she is thinking right now. She feels badly and angry because she experiences the fact that there is so much more work to do. She is upset at the fact that her center of self-regard is not inside of her but still outside of her, and that she allows others to define her, to tell her whether she is worthwhile or not, rather than having a stable sense of self-worth inside of her.

The summaries provide temporal perspective in yet another way. The patients almost invariably save and file the reports; they thus have a comprehensive account of their progression through the group to which they may, with great profit, refer in the future.

THERAPIST SELF-DISCLOSURE

The therapist, in the service of the patients' therapy, may use the summary as a vehicle to disclose a great deal of his here-and-now feelings (of puzzlement, of discouragement, of irritation, of pleasure) and of his views about the theory and meaning underlying his behavior in the group. Consider these illustrative excerpts (Irv and Louise are the therapists.)

Irv and Louise both felt considerable strain in the meeting. We felt caught between our feelings of wanting to continue more with Dinah, but also being very much aware of Al's obvious hurting in the meeting. Therefore, even at the risk of Dinah's feeling that we were deserting her, we felt strongly about bringing in Al before the end of the meeting.

We felt very much in a bind with Seymour. He was silent during the meeting. We felt very much that we wanted to bring him into the group and help him talk, especially since we knew that the reason he had dropped out of his previous group was because of his feeling that people were uninterested in what he had to say. On the other hand, today we decided to resist the desire to bring him in because we knew that by continually bringing Seymour into the group, we are infantalizing him, and sooner or later it will be much better if he were able to do it by himself.

Irv had a definite feeling of dissatisfaction with his own behavior in the meeting today. He felt he dominated things too much, that he was too active, too directive. No doubt this is due in large part to his feeling of guilt at having missed the previous two meetings and wanting to make up for it today by giving as much as possible.

Louise wondered whether the fact that Sarah was leaving the group was only due to her new work schedule or whether she was leaving the group because in fact she was considerably improved. It is striking that Louise said this only a few seconds before Irv was going to say it. The therapists are always looking for reassurances about their patients feeling better.

FILLING GAPS

An obvious and important function of the summary was to fill gaps in for patients who miss meetings because of illness or vacation. The summaries kept them abreast of events and enabled them to move more quickly back into the group.

NEW PATIENTS

The entrance of new patients may be facilitated by providing them with summaries of the previous few meetings.

Our initial impressions of the technique are that it facilitates therapy. The patients have been unanimous in their positive evaluation: most read and consider the summary very seriously, many reread it several times, almost all file them for future use, their therapeutic perspective and commitment is deepened, the patient-therapist relationship is strengthened, and no serious transference complications occur. Like any event in the group, the summaries will generate differential responses: for example, those patients with severe dependency yearnings will cherish every word, those with severe counterdependent postures will challenge every word or, in one instance, be unable to spare the time to read them at all, obsessive patients obsess over the precise meaning of the words, and paranoid patients search for hidden meanings. Thus, although they provide a clarifying force, they do not thwart the formation of the distortions so necessary to therapy.

Structured Exercises

I shall use the term "structured exercise" to denote any of the large number of activities in which the group follows some specific set of orders. The exercise is generally prescribed by the leader, but occasionally by some experienced member. The precise rationale of the procedures vary, but in general they are thought to be accelerating devices: they attempt to speed up the group with "warm-up" procedures which bypass the hesitant, uneasy first steps of the group; they speed up interaction by assigning tasks to interacting individuals which circumvent ritualized, introductory social behavior; and they speed up individual work by techniques designed to help members move quickly to "get in touch with" suppressed emotions, with unknown parts of themselves, and with their physical body.

The structured exercise may require only a few minutes or it may consume the entire meeting; it may be predominantly a verbal procedure or a nonverbal one (almost all nonverbal procedures, however, include a verbal component; generally, the exercise generates data which is subsequently discussed). The exercise may involve the entire group as a group (the group may be asked, for example, to build something or to plan an outing) or one member vis-à-vis the group (one member stands, eyes closed, in the center and falls, allowing the group to support him and then to cradle and rock him) or the entire group as individuals (each member may be asked to "go around" and to give his initial impressions, off the top of his head, of everyone else in the group) or the entire group as dyads (the blind walk—the group is broken into dyads and each pair takes a walk with one member blindfolded, led by the other) or a single, particular dyad (two members locked in a struggle may be asked to take turns pushing the other to the ground and then lifting him again) or each of the members of the group independently (the members may be asked to imagine themselves as a tiny microbe entering, traveling through, and experiencing all the parts of their own body) or one particular member (a member working in the "hot seat" may be asked to have an internal dialogue giving voice to two or more conflicting forces within him).

Structured exercises were first described in group work in the T-groups of the 1950s and became even more common and variegated with the evolution of the encounter group (see Chapter 14). In recent years the gestalt therapy field has provided an additional source of structured procedures. The use of these procedures has grown to the extent that many group leader training programs are technique-oriented and novitiates lead groups clutching only a grab bag of gimmicks into which they reach whenever the proceedings flag. Many recent articles and texts for group leaders devote disproportionate space to group exercises; in fact, some texts are little more than a compendium of "self-actualizing" structured procedures.[30,31]

This development is most unfortunate and a gross miscarriage of the intent of the approaches which originally spawned these techniques. The T-group field formulated exercises which were designed to demonstrate principles of group dynamics (both intra- and intergroup). They also fashioned accelerating aids; since the typical T-group met for a sharply limited period of time, the trainers sought methods which would speed the group past the initial reserve and the traditional social ritualized behaviors. Their intent was that members experience as much as possible of the developmental sequence of the small group. With the hypertrophy of these techniques within the laboratory came a reaction against the practice by many of the more experienced leaders. Argyris,[32] for example, has argued for years that prescriptive leader behavior deprives the group of the opportunity to assume these functions and leads to an unproductive learning climate. Consequently, over the past decade, in many T-group laboratories there has been less emphasis on structured experiences for groups and a shift away from a packaged learning model.

Gestalt therapy, another major source of structured exercises, is a therapy approach based firmly on existential roots. Transcripts of Fritz

Perls' sessions with patients [33,34] as well as his theoretical essays [35] demonstrate that Perls was basically concerned with problems of existence, of self-awareness, of responsibility, of contingency, of wholeness both within one individual and within the individual's social and physical universe. Although Perls' approach was novel, his conception of man's basic dilemma is one which he shares with a long skein of philosophers of life stretching back to the beginning of recorded thought. Paradoxically, gestalt therapy has come to be considered by some as a speedy, pre-packaged, gimmick-oriented therapy, whereas in fact it offers a therapeutic approach based on the deepest and most unpalatable of truths. Unlike the brief therapies, it attempts to penetrate denial systems and to bring patients to a new perspective on their position in the world. Rather than being technique-based, it basically decries a technical, packaged, deindividualized approach. And yet some gestalt therapy trainees do not progress past technique, do not grasp the theoretical assumptions upon which all technique must rest.

How has it come about that so many have mistaken the substance for the essence of the gestalt approach? The cornerstone for the error was, unwittingly, laid by the founder of gestalt therapy, Fritz Perls, who had a creative, technical virtuosity which acted in such consort with his flair for showmanship so as to lead many to mistake the medium for the message. Perls had to do battle with the hyperintellectualized emphasis of the early analytic movement and often overreacted and overstated his opposition to theory. "Lose your mind and come to your senses," Perls proclaimed. Consequently, he did not write a great deal and taught by illustration, trusting that his students would discover their own truths through experience rather than through intellectual thought. Yet in his few expository essays [33] it is clear that Perls read and thought deeply and extensively; much of his work rests on the basic assumptions of such thinking men as Husserl, Heidigger, and Sartre. The many half day or whole day workshops afforded by gestaltists which consist of the same tired string of audience exercises ("Finish the sentence, 'I am aware . . .' " "Think of an incomplete decision in your life, give a voice to the opposing forces, and let those voices have a dialogue") only perpetuate the erroneous view that gestalt therapy is a series of structured exercises.

What do we know about the effects of these procedures upon the process and outcome of the group? The encounter group project [22] (see Chapter 14 for details) of Lieberman, Yalom, and Miles studied the impact of the structured exercise quite closely and came to the following conclusions. The leaders who used large numbers of exercises were popular with their group. The members regarded them as more competent, more effective, and more perceptive than leaders who used these techniques sparingly. Yet the members of the high exercise groups had a significantly *lower* outcome than did the members of the low exercise groups. (The high exercise groups had fewer high changers, fewer total positive changers, and more negative changers. Moreover, the high changers of the high exercise groups were *less* likely to maintain their change over time.) In short, the moral of this story is that if you want your group members to think you're competent and that you know what you're doing, then use an abundance of structured interventions; in doing so, in "leading," in providing explicit directions, in assuming total executive function, you fulfill their fantasies of what a leader should do. However, the outcome of the group experience for the members will not be improved; in fact, there is evidence that these techniques are less effective than more unstructured approaches.

The research looked at other differences between high and low exercise groups. There were no differences in the amount of self-disclosure nor were there differences in emotional climate between high and low exercise groups. There were a number of differences in the themes emphasized: the high exercise groups focused on the expression of positive and negative feelings; the low exercise groups had a greater range of thematic concerns: the setting of goals, the selection of procedural methods, closeness vs. distance, trust vs. mistrust, genuineness vs. phoniness, affection, and isolation. It would seem, then, that many common themes which groups must deal with are simply not considered in high exercise groups; the leader's active approach settles these issues for the group. The exercises appear to plunge the members more quickly into a greater degree of expressivity, but the group pays a price for its speed; it circumvents many group developmental tasks and it does not develop a sense of autonomy and potency.

It is not easy for the group clinician to evaluate his own use of structured techniques. In the encounter group project almost all leaders used some structured exercises. Some of the more effective leaders attributed their success in large measure to these techniques. To take one example, many leaders used the "hot seat" technique (a format in which one member occupies the "hot seat" and the leader, in particular, and the other members focus on that member exclusively and exhaustively for long periods of time). However, the approach was as highly valued by the most ineffective leaders as by the effective leaders. Obviously, there were other aspects of leader behavior accounting for the effective leaders' success, but if they erroneously credit their effectiveness to the structured exercise, then it is given a value it does not deserve (and is unfortunately passed on to students as the central feature of the change process).

The Lieberman, Yalom, Miles encounter group project also demonstrated the central importance of psychosocial forces in the change process: change was heavily influenced by the individual's role in the group (centrality, level of influence, value congruence, activity) and by characteristics of the group (cohesiveness, climate of intensivity and harmoniousness, norm structure). In other words, the data failed to support the leader's belief in the importance of his centrality, of the necessity of his direct therapeutic interaction with each member.

Though these findings issue from short-term encounter groups, they have much relevance for the therapy group. First, consider the concept of "acceleration." In that they bypass early, "slow" stages of the group interaction, in that they plunge members more quickly into an expression of positive and negative feelings, structured exercises do indeed "accelerate" interaction. But do they accelerate the process of therapy? I think that, in general, they do not. In short-term T-groups it is often legitimate to employ techniques to bypass certain difficult stages, to help the group flit on when it is mired in an impasse. In long-term therapy groups the "by-pass" is less germane; the leader more often wishes to guide the group *through* anxiety, *through* the impasse or difficult stages rather than around them. Resistance is not an impediment to therapy but is the stuff of therapy. The early psychoanalysts conceived of the analytic procedure as a two-stage process: the analysis of resistance and then the "true" analysis (which consisted of strip-mining the infantile unconscious roots of behavior). Later they realized that the analysis of resistance, if pursued thoroughly, was sufficient unto itself. Interactional group therapy, as I have indicated throughout, functions similarly: there is more to be gained by experiencing and exploring great timidity or suspiciousness or any of a vast number of dynamics underlying a member's initial guardedness than by providing him with a vehicle which plunges him willy-nilly into deep disclosure or expressivity. Acceleration which results in material untimely wrenched from individuals may be counterproductive if the proper context of the material is not yet constructed. To illustrate this point, consider the following intervention from a gestalt therapy group: [36]

One medical student in a group punctuated almost every remark (made in a very intense voice) with a flick of his head to the right. I had another student stand behind him and hold his head fairly tightly. After a minute or two, the head movement disappeared and the man began to flick his right wrist slightly at the end of each comment. Another student held his wrist. Soon a fairly noticeable shrug of the right shoulder appeared to replace that. At this point, I had him then exaggerate the shrug extensively, turning it into an entire body movement; within a minute or two, he was able to put this gesture into the words "who cares?" This was the miniaturized organismic counterpoint to his overtly expressed close interest in what I was saying.

It would appear that the leader accelerated the surfacing of feelings of indifference or cynicism, and the emergence of these feelings is cited as a validation of the technique. I would argue, though, that if this patient were in a therapy group in which proper norms were established—norms of trust, risk-taking, free interpersonal exploration—then without question these attitudes would emerge in a number of ways without some dazzling accoucheur aide. Furthermore, as time progressed, as he deepened his interaction with each of the members and as each became more important to him, the "who cares?" would become even more meaningful. Because the patient works in a group for weeks or months before these feelings fully surface, one cannot conclude that these weeks or months were time wasted. On the contrary; they may represent essential time, time spent in building the social and interpersonal context which makes their subsequent emergence and working through "therapeutic."

I would urge caution in the use of structured exercises in therapy groups for yet another reason. The leader who prescribes structured tasks for his group may pay a high price for his approach. He runs the risk of establishing norms which hamper the development of the group into a potent therapeutic force. Members begin to feel that help (all help) emanates from the leader, they await their turn to work with him, they deskill themselves, they cease to avail themselves of the help and resources available in the group. They divest themselves of responsibility. This is a curious development since Perls was so acutely aware of the necessity for each individual to assume responsibility for himself and his therapy. Much of Perls' modus operandi was, in fact, explicitly directed toward that end. Yet beneath the technique, beneath the imperative to assume responsibility, the gestalt therapist creates a bewildering paradox: on the one hand, he exhorts the patient to be, do, act for himself, while, on the other hand, he says, through his leadership style: "I will take charge, I will lead you. Depend on me to provide energy and ingenious techniques." In a group the paradox is even more striking as the members wait their turn to work and are deprived of the opportunity to be autonomous as a group and to be helpful to one another. In short, the group is infantalized, and rather than a therapy group they become a congregation of individuals, each of whom does individual therapy in the presence of the other supplicants.

To the gestalt therapist this poses no problem since he never intended to use the group as a therapeutic agent; Perls always did individual therapy in a group—members came up one by one to occupy the "hot seat" and to work with him. Why, then, bother with a group at all? Perls employed the group as an omnipresent Greek chorus—when individuals work in the presence of others, they work with greater seriousness and with greater commitment. And so the group is used as a presence, as a symbolic equivalent of the watchful eyes of one's entire human community. At times, too, observing members do some significant silent, internal work which is instigated by some aspect of the work of another. Occasional group interactions are encouraged, which the gestalt therapist may use to collect data about the individual. Sometimes other members may make useful observations or comments, but often the leader specifically asks them not to interfere in the "work." (It is this formalized, gestalt therapy concept of "individual therapy in a group" which accounts for my not considering gestalt therapy at length in this text.* Though I agree with many of the goals and underlying assumptions of the gestalt school, I feel that their group therapy technique is ill-founded and makes extraordinary inefficient use of the therapeutic potential of the group.)

In voicing these objections to the excessive use of structured exercises, I have overstated the case. Surely there is a middle ground—a middle ground between, on the one hand, allowing the group to flounder and mire profitlessly in some unproductive sequence and, on the other hand, to assume a frenetically active, structured leadership

---

* It is for the same reason that I have not fully discussed transactional analytic group therapy, which also uses an individual-therapy-in-a-group model. T.A., as compared with gestalt therapy, is a less novel, less original movement in psychotherapy. In fact, its basic concerns, view of man, goals, and therapeutic approach are conventional; without exception, each of T.A.'s major concepts are to be found in the traditional psychological literature stretching back over the last forty years. What is most novel and most useful about the T.A. methodology is its vocabulary: arresting, lucid terminology for such concepts as interpersonal transactions ("games"), conflicting inner constellations of motives and drives ("parent, child, and adult ego states"), goals and therapy commitment ("contract"), genetic determinants of ego restrictions ("archaic decisions"); guiding fictions, life-style ("scripts"), parental expectations, super ego (parental injunctions), and the like. To the extent that this vocabulary has made it possible for mental health workers (and especially those with little professional background) to obtain a more rapid and more incisive grasp of intra- and interpersonal transactions, T.A. has made a very significant contribution to the field. However, to the extent that it has restricted understanding by, for example, stuffing all the complexities of human behavior into a limited number of games, ego states, and scripts and to the extent that it has overemphasized the member-leader helping relationship to the neglect of the many other curative factors in group therapy, the T.A. approach has not been productive.

role. The Lieberman, Yalom, and Miles encounter group study [22] reached that very conclusion. It was demonstrated that the degree to which leaders assumed an "executive," managerial function was related to outcome in a curvilinear fashion—i.e., too much and too little were negatively correlated with good outcome; too much executive function created the types of problems I have discussed in the preceding section (leader-centered, dependent groups); too little (a laissez faire approach) resulted in plodding, unenergetic, high attrition groups.

Indeed, many of the techniques I described in Chapter 5 which the leader employs in his norm-setting, here-and-now activation and process-illumination functions have a prescriptive quality. ("Toward whom in the group do you feel closest?" "Can you look at Mary as you talk to her?" "If you were going to be graded for your work in the group, what grade would you receive?" etc.) The matter is, then, one of degree, accent, and purpose. If structured interventions are suggested which are designed to help mold an autonomously functioning group, or to steer the group into the here-and-now, or to explicate process, they may be of value. If used, they should be properly timed; nothing is as disconcerting as the right idea in the wrong place at the wrong time. It is a mistake to use exercises as emotional space filler, i.e., something interesting to do when the group seems at loose ends. A properly led therapy group should not need energizing from without; if there seems insufficient energy in the group, if meetings seem listless, if time and time again the therapist feels he must inject voltage into the group, there is, most likely, a significant developmental problem which the increased use of accelerating devices only compounds. One, instead, should explore the obstructions, the norm structure, the members' passive posture toward the leader, the relationship of each member to his primary task, and so forth. My experience is that if the therapist prepares his patients adequately, if he actively shapes expressive, interactional, self-disclosing norms in the manner described in Chapter 5, there will be no paucity of activity and energy in the group.

REFERENCES

1. J. Frank, L. H. Gleidman, S. Imber, E. Nash, and A. Stone, "Why Patients Leave Psychotherapy," *Arch. Neurol. Psychiat.*, 77: 283–299, 1957.

2. E. Nash, Frank, L. Gleidman, S. Imber, and A. Stone, "Some Factors Related to Patients Remaining in Group Psychotherapy," *Int. J. Group Psychother., 7:* 264–275, 1957.

3. G. Bach, *Intensive Group Therapy* (New York: Ronald Press, 1954).

4. H. Rabin, "How Does Co-Therapy Compare With Regular Group Therapy," *Am. J. Psychother., 21:* 244–255, 1967.

5. H. Spitz and S. Kopp, "Multiple Psychotherapy," *Psychiat. Quart. Supple., 31:* 295–331, 1957.

6. E. Waugh, *Brideshead Revisited* (Boston: Little, Brown, 1945).

7. I. D. Yalom, J. Tinklenberg, and M. Gilula, unpublished data. 1967.

8. R. F. Bales, "The Equilibrium Problem in Small Groups," in T. Parsons, R. F. Bales, and E. A. Shils (eds.), *Working Papers in the Theory of Action* (Glencoe, Ill.: Free Press, 1953), pp. 111–161.

9. J. Solomon and G. Solomon, "Group Therapy with Father and Son as Co-therapists: Some Dynamic Considerations," *Int. J. Group Psychother., 13:* 133–140, 1963.

10. A. Wolf, "The Psychoanalysis of Groups," *Am. J. Psychother., 3:* 529–557, 1949.

11. S. R. Slavson, *A Textbook in Analytic Group Psychotherapy* (New York: International Universities Press, 1964), pp. 398–399.

12. J. Johnson, *Group Therapy: A Practical Approach* (New York: McGraw-Hill, 1963), pp. 56–57.

13. M. Jones, *The Therapeutic Community* (New York: Basic Books, 1953).

14. D. Daniels, "Milieu Therapy of Schizophrenia," in C. P. Rosenbaum, *Perspectives on the Schizophrenias: Phenomenology, Sociology, Biology and Therapy* (New York: forthcoming Science House).

15. M. A. Lieberman, D. S. Whitaker, and M. Lakin, "Groups and Dyads: Never the Twain Shall Meet," unpublished mimeograph, University of Chicago, 1967.

16. Anonymous, from *Calendar of Health* (New York: League for Right Living, 1908), cited in *J. Appl. Behav. Sci., 3:* 101, 1967.

17. O. H. Mowrer, *The New Group Therapy* (Princeton, New Jersey: D. Van Nostrand Co., Inc., 1964).

18. B. Berzon, "Final Narrative Report: Self-Directed Small Group Programs," NIMH Project RD 1748, mimeographed material, Western Behavioral Science Institute, 1968.

19. R. B. Morton, "The Uses of the Laboratory Method in a Psychiatric Hospital—Section A: The Patient Training Laboratory; An Adaptation of the Instrumented Training Laboratory," in E. H. Schein and W. G. Bennis (eds.), *Personal and Organizational Change Through Group Methods: The Laboratory Approach* (New York: John Wiley & Sons, 1965), pp. 114–151.

20. E. G. Aiken, "Alternate Forms of a Semantic Differential for Measurement of Changes in Self-Description," *Psychol. Rep., 16:* 177–178, 1965.

21. G. Gevrin, "JOBS Project Report," Institute for Social Research, University of Michigan, 1967.

22. M. Lieberman, I. Yalom, and M. Miles, *Encounter Groups: First Facts* (New York: Basic Books, 1973).

23. D. Zimmerman, "Some Characteristics of Dreams in Group-Analytic Psychotherapy," *Int. J. Group Psychother., 17:* 524–535, 1967.

24. D. Miller, "The Effects of Immediate and Delayed Audio and Videotaped Feedback on Group Counseling," *Comparative Group Studies, 1:* 19–47, 1970.

25. M. Robinson "A Study of the Effects of Focused Videotaped Feedback in Group Counseling," *Comparative Group Studies, 1:* 47–77, 1970.

26. M. Berger, "The Use of Video Tape with Psychotherapy Groups in a Community Mental Health Program," paper delivered at the American Group Psychotherapy Conference, Chicago, January 1968.

27. M. Berger, *Videotape Techniques in Psychiatric Training and Treatment* (New York: Brunner/Mazel, 1970).

28. H. Langee, G. Newell, and S. MacIntosh, "Effects of Video Tape Replay on Group Process and Group Members," in preparation.

29. I. Yalom, S. Brown, and S. Bloch, "The Written Summary as a Group Psychotherapy Technique," *Archives of General Psychiatry*, in press.

30. H. Otto, *Group Methods to Actualize Human Potential* (Beverly Hills, Calif.: Holistic Press, 1970).

31. W. Schutz, *JOY: Expanding Human Awareness* (New York: Grove Press, 1967.).

32. C. Argyris, "On the Future of Laboratory Education," *J. Appl. Behav. Sci., 3:* 153–183, 1967.

33. F. Perls, *The Gestalt Approach and Eye Witness to Therapy,* (Ben Lomond, Calif.: Science and Behavior Books, 1974).

34. F. Perls, *Gestalt Therapy Verbatim* (Moab, Utah: Real People Press, 1969).

35. F. Perls, *Ego, Hunger and Aggression* (New York: Vintage Books, Random House, 1969).

36. Enright, J. "Awareness Training in the Mental Health Professions," in J. Fagan and I. L. Shepherd (eds), *Gestalt Therapy Now* (Palo Alto, California: Science and Behavior, 1970).

14

GROUP THERAPY AND
THE NEW GROUPS

Group therapists who wish to stay abreast of their field and attend major educational meetings of professional group therapy organizations are faced with a bewildering array of training opportunities. A sprinkling of workshop titles at the American Group Psychotherapy Annual Convention conveys current flavors:

> Marathon Multimedia Group Therapy
> Transactional Analysis and Contract Therapy in Groups
> Encounter-Gestalt Techniques in Analytic Group Therapy
> Nonverbal Gestalt and Encounter Games in Group Therapy
> Combined Gestalt-Transactional Analysis in Group Therapy
> Nude Marathon Group Therapy
> Body Movement in Group Therapy
> Touching in Group Therapy
> And one (my favorite) in which the chairman states, "I use experiential gestalt methods and Kleinian concepts within a structured transactional analysis framework. And you?"

If each of these titles represents a substantial and important new trend in group therapy technology, it would appear that group therapy is experiencing a renaissance and that, even running as fast as possible, one cannot stay abreast of all the new developments.

But are these new developments? Do these new trends represent a coherent intellectual thrust into the future? Are these major changes in substance as well as form? I think not, and this chapter will suggest that rather than a renaissance we are in the midst of a manneristic period with undue emphasis on technique and style. If this is true, it raises the interesting question of why the youthful and robust group therapy field is veering so quickly into a high baroque phase.

Of all the current influences on group practice, none is as obvious as the encounter group movement, as evidenced by the workshop titles quoted above. The task of this chapter is to examine the important relationship between encounter groups and the group therapy field. First, we need to discuss, with as much precision as possible, the encounter group: what is it? Who goes to it? How effective is it? Where does it come from?

What Is an Encounter Group?

"Encounter groups" is a rough, inexact generic term which encompasses a great variety of forms. Consider some of its many aliases: human relations groups, training groups, T-groups, sensitivity groups, personal growth groups, marathon groups, human potential groups, sensory awareness groups, gestalt groups, Synanon, basic encounter groups, psychological Karate, truth labs, experiential groups, confrontation groups, etc.

Although the nominal plumage is dazzling in its diversity, there are several common denominators shared by all these groups. They range in size between eight and twenty members—large enough to encourage face to face interaction, yet small enough to permit all members to interact; they are generally time limited, often compressed into hours or days; they focus to a large extent on the here-and-now; they are trans-etiquette and encourage the doffing of traditional social facades; they value interpersonal honesty, exploration, confrontation, heightened emotional expressiveness, and self-disclosure. The goals of the group are often vague. Occasionally, they stress merely the provision of an experience—joy, a state of being "turned on," entertainment—but more often they implicitly or explicitly strive for some type of change—change in behavior, attitudes, values, life-style, degree of self-actualization, change in one's relation to others, to nature, to one's physical being, or change in one's way of being-in-the world. The participants are not generally labeled "patients"; the experience is not considered therapy but "growth."

Who Goes to Them?

No one knows how many individuals have participated in encounter groups. The setting—informal, non-institutionalized, non-registered, often recreational—and the inexact definition and boundaries make an accurate census impossible, but experts estimate that five million individuals in the United States have participated in one or another form of encounter group in the past fifteen years. A study of institutions offering encounter group experiences provides some scope of the magnitude of the movement. Scarcely a week goes by without my receiving in the mail notification of some new organization offering a group experience or training in group methods. One organization, Synanon (originally established to treat drug addicts but subsequently offering help in the form of a new life-style to any troubled individual), conducted, in 1970, weekly groups at its Oakland branch for over 1,500 non-addict, non-Synanon dwellers ("square games").

The best known of the growth centers, Esalen at Big Sur, California, began in 1960 with an offer of occasional weekend groups. Each year the number of participants has grown, and in 1974 over 5,300 individuals [1] engaged in one of the many personal growth group activities sponsored by Esalen encounter groups. In 1969 at least seventy-five other growth centers, many modeled after Esalen, were operating throughout the country.

Has the encounter group movement already peaked? Again, we can only guess. In 1975, compared with 1967, encounter groups seem less visible: University bulletin boards and underground newspapers do not advertise them so blatantly; some growth centers have gone out of business while those that survive hawk other wares—Rolfing, TM (transcendental meditation), Tai Chi, Bioenergetics, Arica, Sufi. My opinion is that they have not died, that they will be with us for a long time to come; but their plumage has faded, and they are less visible, having become an unobtrusive part of the background. An encounter group is no longer news; it does not command attention. Yet there is no evidence that over the last few years there have been fewer people attending encounter groups. Although it is true that many growth centers have folded, this may be simply another reflection of the ubiquity of encounter groups: people simply do not need to leave home to find them. Those growth centers that do not change, that continue to offer only the same program, rapidly lose their constituency. (Indeed, NTL, the founder and the behemoth of the T-group movement, remained dependent on an unchanging group format and has recently fallen upon hard times.) The growth centers that continue in operation have been the ones which have been most creative and innovative in introducing fetching new formats. (Do not mistake this changing pattern of growth techniques for some logical progression based on accretion of knowledge or technical evolution; the explanation rests on economic factors—novelty is essential for solvency.) This does not mean that encounter groups are not present at growth centers, only that they do not receive star billing; they have been incorporated into other formats and the encounter group culture has become part of the general growth center ambience.

The encounter group does not seem destined, like Dianetics and Dada, to burn itself out. It is not simply part of the evanescent California youth culture; participants, for the large part, come from the influential, middle-aged, upper-middle-class, well-educated (the "great washed white") segment of the population. By no means are the groups limited to California; they are to be found in virtually every large urban area and university campus in the United States and in many European countries as well (i.e., especially West Germany, the Netherlands, the Scandinavian countries, and Great Britain). Indeed, the encounter group movement, if we may call it that, seems so robust that Carl Rogers has referred to it as "one of the most rapidly growing social phenomena in the United States . . . perhaps the most significant social invention of this century." [2]

The proliferation and tenacity of encounter groups suggest that they have not been foisted upon society but arose in response to a pressing cultural need. More about that later. On a narrower scope the phenomenon has deep implications for the mental health field. Although some participants may attend for stimulation, novelty, "mind expansion," social and sexual contacts, a large number attend to obtain help with long-standing, severe, psychological problems.[3]

Where Do They Come From? Antecedents and Evolution of the Encounter Group [4,5,6,7,8]

"Encounter group" is a recent term for an experiential group and was coined by Carl Rogers in the 1960s. The most common term prior to that was T-group ("T" for training—training in human relations).* The first T-group, the ancestor of most modern experiential groups, was held in 1946.

THE FIRST T-GROUP

In 1946 Frank Simpson, the executive director of the Connecticut Interracial Commission, which had been created to implement the new Connecticut Fair Employment Practices Act, asked Kurt Lewin for help in training leaders who could deal effectively with intergroup tensions. Kurt Lewin at that time was the director of the Commission of Community Interrelations, an undertaking of the American Jewish Congress, as well as the director of the Massachusetts Institute of Technology's new Research Center for Group Dynamics. Simpson requested help in training a wide range of community leaders— businessmen, labor leaders, schoolteachers—to deal more effectively with interracial tensions and to use their knowledge to change racial attitudes in other people.

Kurt Lewin organized a workshop in June 1946 at New Britain, Connecticut, in which three group leaders, Leland Bradford, Kenneth Benne, and Ronald Lippit—all destined to exert great influence in the nascent field of human relations training—led groups of ten members each. Kurt Lewin headed a small team of social psychologists who researched the process and outcome of the conference experience. The small groups were led in the traditional manner of the day; they were basically discussion groups which analyzed "back-home" problems presented by the group members. Some role-playing techniques were used to diagnose behavioral aspects of the problems and to practice alternative problem solving techniques.

A research observer whose task was to record and code behavioral interactions and sequences was assigned to each of the small groups. Evening meetings were held in which the group leaders and the research observers met and pooled their observations of leader, member, and group behavior. Soon some participants learned of these evening meetings and asked permission to attend. Lewin agreed, but the

---

* In this chapter I shall use the terms "T-group" and "encounter group" loosely interchangeably. As I shall discuss, the field is so sprawling that no single term is entirely satisfactory. Even in my usage I shall retain a nuance of difference: "T-group" when I want to accent the more traditional human relations flavor, "encounter group" when I wish to accent the more unconventional personal growth aspect.

other staff members were at first reluctant to allow the members to overhear the staff's private discussion of the member's behavior; the staff feared that their own inadequacies might be revealed, and, furthermore, they were extremely uncertain about the effects on the members of hearing direct commentary about their behavior. The members were finally permitted to attend the open meetings on a trial basis. Observers who have written about the experiment all report that the effect on both participants and staff was "electric." [8] There was something galvanizing about witnessing an in-depth discussion of one's own behavior. Soon the format of the evening meetings was widened to permit the participants to respond to the observations, and shortly thereafter all parties were involved in the analysis and interpretation of their interaction. Before many evenings had passed, all the participants were attending the evening meetings, which were often continued for as long as three hours; there was widespread agreement that the meetings offered the participants a new and rich understanding of their own behavior. The staff immediately realized that they had, somewhat serendipitously, discovered a powerful technique of human relations education—experiential learning. Group members learn most effectively by studying the very interactional network in which they themselves are enmeshed. They profit enormously by being confronted, in an objective manner, with on-the-spot observations of their own behavior and its effects on others; they may learn about their interpersonal styles, the responses of others to them, and about group behavior and development in general.

From this beginning the T-group, as a technique of education, has undergone considerable change. This development can be understood more fully if we first backtrack even farther to consider the question of why Kurt Lewin was asked to perform this task and why he accepted.

THE INFLUENCE OF KURT LEWIN

Although he died only a few months after the Connecticut experience, Kurt Lewin, through his students and his ideas, exerted a mighty influence on the future development of the T-group and the human relations field. Lewin, a German psychologist, well-known for his work in field theory, visited America on a lecture tour before World War II. Once out of Germany, he recognized more clearly the impending Nazi calamity and, after helping his family escape, took up permanent residence in the United States. Lewin accepted a visiting professorship at Harvard for a short time, and, while there, he lectured at Springfield College, where he met Lawrence Hall, who was teaching a course in group work and provided Lewin with his first introduction to the small group field. (During this time Lewin also had some brief contact with Samuel Slavson, one of the pioneers in group therapy.) When, a short time later, Lewin accepted a professorship at the University of Iowa, he was accompanied by Ronald Lippit, one of Hall's students, whose major field of interest was small groups.

At the same time as Lewin was growing more interested in group dynamics (a term which he coined), he became increasingly dedicated to changing behavior. Much of the impetus for his action orientation arose from his observation of Nazi Germany, which stimulated a deep interest in such problems as the reeducation of the Hitler youth and the changing of anti-Semitic attitudes. His interest in the effect of the social climate on individual attitudes led him to such research as the classic experiment with Lippit and White on the effects of three types of leadership: authoritarian, democratic, and laissez-faire.[9] During the war he explored methods of changing attitudes toward foods and attempted, through group methods, to persuade individuals to increase their intake of such available foods as brains and kidneys.[10] He became interested in retaining individuals who were, for example, ineffective, authoritarian group leaders to perform a task more effectively. Although he was aware that such retraining might result in broad characterologic change, he never researched this possibility,[5] nor did he give serious consideration to the possibility that the authoritarian characterologic traits were present from early life and resistant to change. Toward the end of his career, Lewin and his students moved to M.I.T., where he headed the Research Center for Group Dynamics. After Lewin's death his students, who include many of the prominent contemporary social psychologists,* moved to the Institute for the Study of Group Dynamics at the University of Michigan.

Lewin's research had led him to several conclusions about changing behavior, conclusions which were instrumental in the Connecticut laboratory. He believed that long-held beliefs can be changed only when individuals are able to examine them personally and conclude that they are unsatisfactory. Methods of changing attitudes, or retraining, therefore, are effective if trainees are provided with opportunities for discovering the deleterious effects upon themselves and others of their customary behavior. Thus, the trainee must be helped to see himself as others see him. Only when the individual himself discovers

---

* John French, Dorwin Cartwright, Alex Bavelas, Ronald Lippit, R. K. White, Leon Festinger.

these facts will his attitudes and subsequent behavior change. As Lewin put it, "This result occurs when the facts become really *their* facts (as against other people's facts). An individual will believe facts he himself has discovered in the same way he believes in himself." [6]

Lewin's dedication to both action and research and his principle of "no research without action, no action without research" left an indelible impression on the entire development of the T-group. From the very beginning, as exemplified in the Connecticut laboratory, research has been woven into the fabric of the T-group. I refer not only to formal research but to a research attitude on the part of the leader; he and the group members are collaborators in a research inquiry designed to enable each participant to experience, understand, and change his behavior. This feature, together with the concept of the T-group as a technique of education, is essential, as we shall shortly show, in the differentiation of the T-group from the therapy group. It was a principle, however, that was gradually abandoned in the later metamorphosis of T-group to encounter group.

DEVELOPMENT OF THE NATIONAL TRAINING LABORATORY (NTL)

After the Connecticut workshop, Leland Bradford, Ronald Lippit, and Kenneth Benne, who fully realized the important implications of the experience, made plans for a similar three-week laboratory the following summer at the Gould Academy in Bethel, Maine. Sixty-seven participants and thirty-seven staff members participated in a heavily researched laboratory. The laboratory plan consisted of morning small discussion groups and afternoon and evening large group meetings and theory sessions. The small discussion groups, the ancestor of the encounter group, were called "basic skill training groups" (shortened in 1949 to "T-group") and met with a leader, called the trainer, and an observer; the first part of the meeting was a discussion of some substantive issue or "back-home" problem; the second part was a feedback session in which the observer reported his process observations to the group and led the ensuing discussion. The laboratory was so successful that similar laboratories were held in 1948 and 1949. The T-group soon became the central and dominant function of the laboratory. Gradually its format altered: the feedback process became less formalized and more integrated into the matrix of the T-group, and the feedback observer became, correspondingly, an assistant trainer.

By 1950 the sponsoring organization, the National Training Laboratory (NTL), was established within the National Education Association (NEA) as a permanent year-round organization. Leland Bradford, who at that time was chief of the NEA Division of Adult and Veteran Education, became the executive director of the NTL and guided it in its development from the fledgling institute which sponsored the 1947 summer lab for sixty-seven participants to its heyday in the 1960s when it employed over sixty-five full-time professional and administrative staff, had a network of six hundred NTL trained leaders, and in 1967 alone held human relations laboratories for over 2,500 participants. From his earliest student days, Bradford has been deeply interested in methods of education. As a teaching assistant in the 1930s he made effective use of the informal discussion group and sought to decrease the emotional distance between teacher and student. T-groups have always been for him part of a technology of education.

In the first Bethel laboratories it soon became clear that the T-group was overloaded with tasks: it was asked not only to teach members about their interpersonal behavior but also to explicate group dynamic theory, to discuss members' problems in their home organizations, to help them develop leadership skills, and to aid in the transfer of T-group learning to the "back-home" situation. The trainer, correspondingly, was asked to assume too many disparate roles. The NTL human relations laboratories in the 1950s (and still to some extent today) were characterized by efforts to unburden the T-group so that it could fulfill its central purpose more effectively. The laboratory day was generally divided between the T-group and other functions. For example, A-groups (action groups) composed of individuals of the same occupation were sociologically oriented and focused on problems and methodologies of change in larger social systems. Often supplementary reading material was distributed to members of the A-groups, short lectures were given, and outside cases were presented for analysis. Application groups were created which attempted to build bridges between T-group learning and "back-home" settings. Very frequently T-group members experienced a sense of let-down and were disillusioned when they attempted to apply their T-group learning to their work situation; the application group dealt with the "reentry phenomenon" and such problems as how to improve staff meetings, how to increase the influence and morale of subordinates, and how to initiate constructive organizational change.

The problem with A-groups, application groups, theory groups, etc., was that the members attempted to turn all such sessions into additional T-groups. The pull of the T-group was of such magnitude that it tended to eat up the entire human relations laboratory, and consequently the staff was often faced with the problem of how to ensure that other types of learning were not ignored.

In the early 1950s more of the training staff were clinically oriented, and the language of interpretation and clarification gradually grew less Lewinian and more Rogerian and Freudian. The founders of the field expressed some concern at this point lest the T-group turn into a therapy group. They underscored both the fact that participants had contracted for an educational experience in human relations and not for psychotherapy and that there was not sufficient time available in a laboratory to resolve deeper therapeutic issues.[8]

Throughout, the NTL human relations laboratories have been characterized by their great flexibility and their willingness to research their own activities * and to use the findings of such research to modify subsequent laboratories. In 1952 sociologists were invited to study the development of the social organization of the entire laboratory community. Later a large group exercise was instituted in many labs, and the differences in dynamics between the large group and the small T-group were thoroughly studied. In 1957 the intergroup task was introduced: a series of exercises were developed in which T-groups competed or interacted with one another; the researchers and participants studied both the intergroup relationship and the intragroup repercussions of this relationship.[12]

DEVELOPMENT OF THE T-GROUP

As the nature of the entire human relations laboratory evolved, so, too, did the character of the T-group. As other exercises were developed to take over the cognitive and transfer of learning functions, the T-group increasingly came to focus on interpersonal behavior. Obviously, the character of the group depends greatly upon the techniques of its trainer, compositional factors, and the raison d'être of the group. For example, beginning in the late 1950s, trainers were often asked to be change agents by organizations such as business corporations, school systems, branches of government, and often they conducted groups in the work unit of the consulting institution. T-groups composed of work group peers or of the entire hierarchical structure of a work unit obviously will differ from T-groups composed of strangers who will have no further contact once the group ends. The goal of the group may vary enormously; for example, an institution may be pri-

* See Stock (1964) [11] for a summary of much of the NTL research.

marily concerned not with self-awareness but with team building and lubrication of the interpersonal relationships in a work unit so as to ensure greater productivity.

Generally, the T-group moved in the direction of ever greater emphasis on feedback, interpersonal honesty, self-disclosure, unfreezing, and observant participation. Discussion of outside material ("there-and-then") including "back-home" current problems or past personal history, was discouraged, whereas here-and-now material was highly prized.

*Feedback.** This term, borrowed from the electrical engineers, was first applied to the behavioral sciences by Lewin (it is no accident that he was teaching at M.I.T. at the time).[13] The early trainers realized that an important flaw in society was that too little opportunity exists for individuals to obtain accurate feedback from their back-home associates: bosses, fellow employees, wives, teachers, students, etc. Feedback became an essential ingredient of all T-groups; without it the here-and-now focus has little meaning or vitality. Feedback seems most effective in the group when it stems from here-and-now observations and when it follows the generating event as closely as possible. Furthermore, the feedback should be checked out with other group members to establish its validity and reduce perceptual distortion.

*Unfreezing.** This term, also adopted from Lewinian change theory, refers to the process of disconfirming an individual's former belief system. The individual must be primed and his motivation for change must be generated before change can occur. He must be helped to reexamine many cherished assumptions about himself and his relations to others. The familiar must be made strange; [14] many common props, social conventions, status symbols, and ordinary procedural rules are eliminated from the T-group, and the individual's values and beliefs about himself are challenged. This may create a state of considerable discomfort for the individual, a state which he is willing to tolerate only under certain conditions: he must experience the group as a refuge wherein he is safe, wherein he can entertain new beliefs and experiment with new behavior without fear of reprisal.

*Observant Participation.** Most trainers considered observant participation as the optimal method of involvement for all group participants. Members must both participate emotionally in the group and observe themselves and the group objectively. Often this is a difficult

---

* We have discussed elsewhere the importance of feedback, unfreezing (dissonance, conflict), and observant participation (the dual nature of the here-and-now) in the advanced work of the therapy group.

task to master and members chafe at the trainer's attempts to subject the group to objective analysis. Yet the dual task is essential to learning; either action or intellectual scrutiny alone produces a low yield for learning. Camus once wrote, "My greatest wish: to remain lucid in ecstasy." [15] So, too, the T-group (and the therapy group) is most effective when its members can couple cognitive appraisal with an emotional experience.

Cognitive Aids. Cognitive guides around which T-group participants (or delegates, as they are often called) can organize their experience are often presented in brief "lecturettes" by the T-group leader or another staff member. One example of such a cognitive guide is the Johari window,* a four-celled personality paradigm which clarifies the function of feedback and self-disclosure.

	Known to Self	Unknown to Self
Known to Others	A	B
Unknown to Others	C	D

Cell A, "Known to Self and Known to Others," is the public area of the self; Cell B, "Unknown to Self and Known to Others," is the blind area; Cell C, "Known to Self and Unknown to Others," is the secret area; Cell D, "Unknown to Self and Unknown to Others," is the unconscious self. The goals of the T-group, the trainer suggests, are to increase the size of Cell A by decreasing Cell B (blind spots) through feedback and Cell C (secret area) through self-disclosure. In traditional T-groups, Cell D (the unconscious) was considered "Out of Bounds."

The use of such cognitive aids, lectures, reading assignments, and theory sessions demonstrates that the basic allegiance of the T-group was to the classroom rather than to the consulting room. The participants were considered students; the task of the T-group was to facilitate learning for its members. Different trainers emphasized different types of learning: some focused primarily on group dynamics and helped the members to understand group development, group pressures, the leadership role, and common group tensions and obstacles; others emphasized personal learning and focused on the interpersonal style and communication of the members. These two emphases be-

---

* Named after Joe Luft and Harry Ingram, who first described the window.[16]

came more polarized until a formal distinction was made in laboratory planning between group process groups (which were more concerned with group properties, group functioning, and, on a larger scale, with organization development) and personal development groups. I shall pursue the evolution of the T-group most concerned with personal development, since it is this form of T-group which most closely resembles the therapy group and which has spawned the many varieties of encounter groups.

From T-Group to Encounter Group

GROUP THERAPY FOR NORMALS

In the 1950s the NTL established several regional branches, and each of the various sectors gradually developed its own T-group emphasis. It was the West Coast and particularly Southern California which pursued the "personal development" model most vigorously. A 1962 article by Southern California trainers [17] which presented a model of a T-group as "group therapy for normals" clearly signaled the change in emphasis from group dynamics to individual dynamics, from stress on the development of interpersonal skills to a greater concern with personal growth. The experiential group was still considered an instrument of education—not therapy. However, a broader, more humanistically based definition of education was proposed: education is not, they argued, the process of acquiring interpersonal and leadership skills, not the understanding of organizational and group functioning; education is nothing less than full self-discovery, the mining of untapped resources, the development of one's full potential.

THE STRESSES OF NORMALITY

These group leaders worked with normal healthy members of society, indeed with individuals who by most objective standards had achieved a considerable degree of success. Yet they learned that inwardly, in deep contrast to their external success, their group members lived with a fairly continuous level of tension, insecurity, and value conflict.

In most respects we seem adjusted in our day-by-day activities. We appear to behave appropriately with regard to the demands made upon us by our families, friends, and jobs. Yet this appearance is deceptive. Internal doubts and schisms persist. As no convenient learning vehicle is typically available to the "pseudo-healthy" person, tensions below the surface debilitate realization of potential capacities, stunt creativity, infuse hostility into a vast range of human contact, and frequently generate hampering psychosomatic problems.[17]

The highly competitive American culture, many behavioral scientists have noted, encourages facade building. The man who is considered successful by his peers too often strives to protect his public image at all cost. If he has doubts about his adequacy, he swallows them and maintains a constant vigilance lest any personal uncertainty or discomfort slip through. This process is an isolating and crippling one since it curtails communication not only with others but with oneself. Gradually, in order to eliminate a perpetual state of self-recrimination, the successful individual comes to believe in the reality of his facade and attempts through unconscious means to ward off internal and external attacks on his self-image. Thus a state of equilibrium is reached but at a costly price: considerable energy is invested in maintaining intra- and interpersonal separations, energy which might otherwise have been used in the service of self-actualization; creativity and self-knowledge are sacrificed as the individual turns his gaze outward in a never-ending search for peer validation; interpersonal relationships are shallow and unrewarding; he squelches spontaneity so that his studied facade remains unruffled; he avoids self-disclosure, and he refrains from confronting others lest he be similarly challenged.

THE T-GROUP AS A SOCIAL OASIS

The T-group was promulgated as a respite from this "culture game." [17] It offered an oasis in which many of the restrictive norms described above were unnecessary, in fact not permitted; the accoutrements which in the outside world symbolize success and normality had to be deposited at the door of the T-group. Individuals were no longer rewarded for their material success, for their hierarchical position, for their unruffled aplomb, for their efficiency, or for their expertise in their area of specialization; instead, they were exposed to the totally different values of the T-group and were rewarded for interpersonal honesty, for disclosure of self-doubts and perceived weaknesses. Gradually, they discovered that in the T-group their pretense of self-satisfaction was not only unnecessary but an encumbrance. For years they had operated on the assumption that there would be a high cost to pay if they lowered their facade; the cost was envisioned as humiliation, rejection, and loss of social or professional status. Their experience in the T-group helps to challenge these assumptions and enables them to experiment with openness and to differentiate its real costs from its pseudo-costs. Obviously, there are some real risks in the disclosure of all our thoughts and feelings: "The realities of living, of sensible interpersonal strategy and tactics, clearly dictate the advisability of keeping some things as part of our private selves." [17] But many of the pseudo-costs are exposed. Lowering of the facade does not result in rejection; in fact, members find themselves more completely accepted since they are accepted on the basis of a fully disclosed self rather than on the basis of a false projected image. Moreover, their deep sense of isolation is assuaged, as each becomes aware of the universality of his secret doubts and fears. These processes are self-reinforcing since the experience of universality encourages each to reveal even more of himself. Members who have previously regarded interpersonal relationships as automated or threatening are able to sample the inherent richness and depth of human intimacy.

As communication becomes more open in the group and members "level" with one another, sharing their positive and negative perceptions with one another, they become more familiar with their "blind selves," those aspects of their personality of which they were previously unaware. Generally, the more an individual has disengaged himself from honest interpersonal confrontations, the grosser are his blind spots. Often this process is a painful and threatening one; but once a member realizes that others are nonjudgmental and desire reciprocal feedback, his defensiveness diminishes.

Thus the T-group sought to reverse the restricting and alienating effects of the "culture game." Both internal and external separations were removed as the individual learned to relate honestly to himself and to others. As the goal of the group shifted from education, in a more traditional sense, to personal change, the name of the group shifted from T-group (training in human relations) or sensitivity training group (training in interpersonal sensitivity), to a name more consonant with the basic thrust of the group. Several labels were advanced: Personal Growth Groups, Human Potential Groups, Human Development Groups, Basic Encounter Groups. "Encounter Group," which stresses the basic authentic encounter between members (and between leader and members and between the disparate parts of each member), has had the most staying power and has become the most popular name for the modern, swinging, let-it-all-hang-out experiential group which attracts many deeply troubled individuals and bears some resemblance to the therapy group.

Other factors, then prevalent in the California counterculture, heavily influenced the form of the encounter group. The anti-intellectualism, the bitter disappointment in and opposition to scientific technology resulted in a marked emphasis on experiencing and expressing feelings, on a renewed interest in intuitive knowledge, in the wisdom of the body, in mysticism and a marked distrust in the inductive sequence—members railed at "head trips" and "mind-fucking."

Anti-authoritarianism accompanied anti-intellectualism. Traditional ritualistic barriers were flattened in the spirit of "anything goes." Novelty was valued for its own sake and even more so if it constituted a triumph over the old order. A friend of mine, an art critic, recently visited Southern California for the first time. When I asked for his impressions, he described a visit to a Los Angeles hamburger stand. He was given a small plastic container filled with ketchup. Elsewhere in the country these containers have a dotted line with instructions, "tear here." The California container had no lines, only the simple inscription, "tear anywhere."

The "third force" in psychology (third after Freudian analysis and Watsonian-Skinnerian behaviorism), which emphasized a holistic, humanistic concept of the person, provided impetus and form to the encounter group from yet another direction. Psychologists such as Maslow, Allport, Fromm, May, Perls, Rogers, Bugenthal (and the philosophers behind them—Sartre, Tillich, Jaspers, Heidigger, and Husserl) rebelled strongly against the mechanistic model of behaviorism, the psychic determinism and reductionism of classical analytic theory. "Where," they asked, "is the person? Where is consciousness, will, decision, responsibility, and a recognition and concern for the basic and tragic dimensions of existence?"

All of these influences resulted in groups with a much broader, and vaguer, goal—nothing less than "total enhancement of the individual." [17] Time in the group was set aside for reflective silence, for listening to music or poetry; members were encouraged to give voice to their deepest concerns—to reexamine these basic life values and the discrepancies between these values and their life-styles, to encounter their many false selves, to explore, for example, the softer, long-buried feminine parts of themselves.

The collision course with psychotherapy now grows increasingly apparent. The groups claim that they offer group therapy for normals yet also that normality today is a sham, that we are all patients: the disease is a dehumanized runaway technocracy, the remedy a return to grappling with basic problems of the human condition and the vehicle of remedy, the experiential group. The medical model could no longer be applied to mental illness. The differentiation between mental illness and health grew as vague as the distinction between treatment and education. Encounter group leaders claimed at the same time that patienthood is ubiquitous and that "one need not be sick to get better."

How Effective Is the Encounter Group?

In its early days the T-group was heavily researched. The social psychologists and sociologists associated with the National Training Laboratories generated an enormous amount of rigorous research into the process and outcome of the T-group. As the T-group evolved into the encounter group, the quantity and quality of research declined sharply. The reasons for this are many: the encounter group leaders often come from a non-academic background; research and quantification run counter to the humanistic, often antirationalistic, encounter group ethos. (Both leaders and members have proven uncooperative with the intrusion of research.) Many goals of the encounter group (self-awareness, self-realization, fulfillment of potential, being in touch with self, etc.) are so subjective that they discourage research investigation.

The first large-scale controlled research inquiry into effectiveness of encounter groups was conducted by Lieberman, Yalom, and Miles in 1973. Since I have drawn from this study in several places in this book, I shall describe the design and method before reporting the results. The project is extensive and complex and I can only touch upon major features relevant to our present discussion; I refer interested readers to the text fully describing the project.[18]

We offered an encounter group experience as an accredited one-quarter course at Stanford University. Two hundred and ten participants (all undergraduate students, aged eighteen to twenty-two) signed up for the course and were then randomly distributed (aside from sex, race, and previous encounter group experience) to one of eighteen groups, each of which met for a total of thirty hours over a twelve-week period of time. Sixty-nine subjects, similar to the participants but who did not have a group experience, were used as a control population and completed all the outcome research instruments.

THE LEADERS

Since a major intent of the study was to investigate the effect of leader technique upon outcome, we sought to diversify leader style by employing leaders from several ideological schools. We selected representation from ten such schools and, prior to the experiment, had certain expectations about the style of each of the leaders:

1. *Traditional NTL* (T-groups). We expected the leader to help members understand themselves and others within and through a study of the group process. We expected the leaders to help members learn something about group dynamics including power and work distribution, cohesiveness, group pressure, attitudes toward leadership, subgrouping, and scapegoating.

2. *Encounter Groups* (Personal Growth Group). We expected the leader to focus on interpersonal and intrapersonal themes, to have a liberating model of personal development, to strive to increase the personal growth of each member.

3. *Gestalt Groups*. We expected the leader to work, primarily on an intra-psychic level, with each of the members in turn, to inattend to group and (to a large extent) intermember dynamics as he pursued one-to-one work with the members.

4. *Sensory Awareness Groups* (Esalen group). We expected the leader to use many structured exercises, to emphasize the experiencing and deepening of interpersonal relations, to encourage members to break free from social and muscular inhibitions, to experience their bodies in a different, richer sense, to emphasize doing, to deemphasize intellectual integration of the experience.

5. *Transactional Analytic Groups*. We expected the leader to work, one-to-one with each of the members of the group, to disregard group dynamics, to focus to some extent on interpersonal interaction ("games") but heavily on intrapsychic learning. (Transactional analysis refers more to transactions between ego states—parent, child, and adult—*within* an individual than to transactions between individuals.)

6. *Psychodrama Groups*. We expected these leaders to make very liberal use of psychodrama techniques—role playing, doubling, role reversal, etc. Psychodrama in encounter groups is not employed in its more classical, Moreno sense but is instead a technique to accelerate and deepen the emotional intensity of the group experience.

7. *Synanon*. We expected the Synanon group to function in a very distinct style: a total emphasis on verbal attack. The "game" is put on each member in turn, and the group attacks him with much vehemence, presumably in the belief that if one is attacked in his weakest areas long enough, he will grow strong in them. The Synanon group can be an un-

settling experience; imagine, if you will, the very worst event that could befall you in a meeting—your own personal group Armageddon; Synanon tries to make that come true for you every session! The leaders are not professionally trained; they come from the ranks of Synanon—the wisest (and most indestructible) of the Synanon game players. Although the group is very aggressive, it is formally framed (and thus a "game") in the program; the Synanon therapeutic milieu provides considerable support during the remainder of the day.

8. *Psychoanalytically Oriented Experiential Group.* We expected the leader to emphasize cognition more than experience, to focus on the dynamics of the individual from the perspective of his personal historical development, to strive toward intellectual mastery of group dynamics and of the inter- and intrapersonal forces operating in the group.

9. *Marathon Group.* We expected the leader to meet for long stretches of time, to strive for high intensity, involvement, and expressivity. We expected a high degree of confrontation and self-disclosure (similar to the personal growth Rogerian model but abetted by sheer physical fatigue).

10. *Encounter-tapes Groups.* Two groups would be led by the Bell and Howell "Encounter-tape" program (see Chapter 13). A different audiotape is played each meeting, and, through suggested structured exercises, lecturettes, examples from other groups, it attempts to construct a cohesive, support climate in which members may experiment with risk-taking, self-disclosure, giving and receiving feedback, and the exploration of inter- and intrapersonal dynamics.

Two expert leaders representing each of these styles were selected. They were all highly experienced, senior leaders, many with national reputations and possessing professional clinical degrees in social psychology, clinical psychology, or psychiatry (aside from the Synanon leaders, and the leader of the sensory awareness group; there were also, of course, no professional leaders in the encounter-tape groups). There were a total of eighteen groups (one psychoanalytically oriented group, one sensory awareness group, two each of the other eight types). Of the 210 subjects who started in the eighteen groups, forty dropped out before attending half the meetings and 170 finished the thirty-hour group experience.

WHAT DID WE MEASURE?

We were most interested in an intensive examination of outcome and the relationship between outcome, leader technique, and group process variables. To evaluate outcome, an extensive psychological battery of instruments was administered to each subject three times: before beginning the group, immediately after completing the group, and six months after completion.

These self-administered instruments attempted to measure any changes one might think encounter groups would effect: e.g., self-esteem, self-ideal discrepancy, interpersonal attitudes and behavior life values, defense mechanisms, emotional expressivity, values, friendship patterns, major life decisions, etc. (See *Encounter Groups: First Facts* [18] for details of the research instrumentation.) Much third-party outcome assessment was collected: evaluations by leaders, by other group members, and by a network of each subject's personal acquaintances. The assessment outcome was strikingly similar to that of a psychotherapy project but with one important difference: since the subjects were not patients but ostensibly healthy individuals seeking growth, no assessment of "target symptoms" or "chief complaints" was made.

Leader style was studied by teams of trained raters, who observed all meetings and coded all behaviors of the leader, by tape recordings and written transcripts of the meetings in which all leader statements were recorded and analyzed and by questionnaires filled out by participants.

Process data were collected by the observers and from questionnaires filled out by participants at the end of each meeting.

RESULTS—WHAT DID WE FIND?

First, the participants' testimony was very high. At the termination of the group, the 170 subjects who completed the groups considered them pleasant (65 percent), constructive (78 percent), a good learning experience (61 percent), and a "turned-on experience" (50 percent). Over 90 percent felt that encounter groups should be a regular part of the elective college curriculum. Six months later the enthusiasm had waned, but the overall evaluation was still positive. To put it another way, at the end of the group for every one participant who viewed the experience negatively, 4.7 participants perceived it as productive; six months later the ratio was still positive but had dropped to 2.3 to 1.

So much for testimony—these results mirror out everyday impression that encounter group participants are generally positively inclined toward the experience and believe it has been useful to them. What of the overall, more objective battery of assessment measures? Each participant's outcome (judged from all assessment measures) was rated and placed in one of six categories: high learner, moderate changer, unchanged, negative changer, casualty (significant, enduring, psychological decompensation which was due to being in the group), and dropout. The results for all 206 * experimental subjects and for the sixty-nine control subjects may be summarized in Table 1. ("Short post" is at termination of group and "long post" is at six-month follow-up.)

TABLE 1

	CASUALTIES	NEGATIVE CHANGER	DROP-OUTS	UN-CHANGED	MODERATE CHANGER	HIGH LEARNER	TOTAL
Short Post							
Participants	16 (08%)	17 (08%)	27 (13%)	78 (38%)	40 (20%)	28 (14%)	206
Controls		16 (23%)		41 (60%)	9 (13%)	3 (04%)	69
Long Post							
Participants	16 (10%)	13 (08%)	27 (17%)	52 (33%)	37 (23%)	15 (09%)	160
Controls		7 (15%)		32 (68%)	5 (11%)	3 (06%)	47

SOURCE: *Encounter Groups: First Facts*, by Morton A. Lieberman, Irvin D. Yalom, and Matthew B. Miles. New York: Basic Books, Inc., 1973.

Table 1 indicates that approximately one-third of the participants at the termination of the group and at the six months follow-up had undergone moderate or considerable positive change. (The control population, who were studied with the same instruments, showed much less change, i.e., more in "unchanged" slot, fewer negative or positive changers. The encounter group, thus, clearly influenced change, but for both better and worse.) Maintenance of change was high: of those who changed positively, 75 percent maintained their change for at least six months.

Put in a critical fashion, one might say Table 1 indicates that of all subjects who began a thirty-hour encounter group led by an acknowledged expert, approximately two-thirds found it an unrewarding experience (either dropout, casualty, negative change, or unchanged).

Viewing the results more generously, one might put it this way. "This is a college course. One does not expect that students who drop out will profit. Let us, therefore, eliminate the dropouts from the data. If that is done (see Table 2), then it appears that 39 percent of all students taking a one-quarter college course underwent some significant positive personal change which persisted for at least six months— not a bad batting average for a twelve-week, thirty-hour course!"

However, even if one considers the goblet one-third full rather than two-thirds empty, it is difficult to escape the conclusion that, in this project, encounter groups did not appear to be a highly potent agent of change. Furthermore, it must be noted that there was a very signifi-

* Four participants were judged from interview data to have left for "physical" reasons (i.e., schedule conflicts).

TABLE 2
Index of Change for Those Who Completed Group
(N = 179 Short Post, 133 Long Post)

	CASUALTIES	NEGATIVE CHANGER	UNCHANGED	MODERATE CHANGER	HIGH LEARNER
Short Post	09%	10%	44%	22%	16%
Long Post	12%	10%	39%	28%	11%

SOURCE: *Encounter Groups: First Facts*, by Morton A. Lieberman, Irvin D. Yalom, and Matthew B. Miles. New York: Basic Books, Inc., 1973.

cant risk factor involved: 16 (8 percent) of the 210 subjects suffered psychological injury which produced sequellae still present six months after the end of the group.

Still, much caution must be exercised in the interpretation of the results. It would do violence to the data to conclude that encounter groups per se are ineffective or even dangerous. First, it is difficult to gauge the degree to which we can generalize these findings to populations other than an undergraduate college student sample. But, even more important, we must take note that these are all massed results: the data are handled as though all subjects were in one encounter group. There was no standard encounter group experience; there were eighteen different groups, each with a distinct culture, each offering a different experience, and each with very different outcomes. In some groups almost every member underwent some positive change with no one suffering injury; in other groups not a single member benefited and one was fortunate to remain unchanged.

The next obvious question then is: Which type of leader had the best and which the worst results? The T-group leader, the gestalt, the T.A., the psychodrama leader, etc.? However, we soon learned that the question, posed in this form, was not meaningful. The behavior of the leaders when carefully chartered by observers varied greatly and did not conform to our pre-group expectations. *The ideological school to which the leader belonged told us little about the actual behavior of the leader.* We found that the behavior of the leader of one school, for example transactional analysis, resembled the behavior of the other T.A. leader no more closely than that of any of the other seventeen leaders. In other words, the behavior of the leader is not predictable from his membership in a particular ideological school. Yet the effectiveness of the group was, in large part, a function of the leader's behavior.

What is needed, then, to answer the question, "Which is the more effective leadership style?" is a more accurate, empirically derived leader taxonomy. A factor analysis of a large number of leader behavior variables (rated by observers) resulted in four basic leadership functions:

1. Emotional Stimulation (challenging, confronting, activity; intrusive modeling by personal risk-taking and high self-disclosure).
2. Caring (offering support, affection, praise, protection, warmth, acceptance, genuineness, concern).
3. Meaning Attribution (explaining, clarifying, interpreting, providing a cognitive framework for change; translating feelings and experiences into ideas).
4. Executive Function (setting limits, rules, norms, goals; managing time; pacing, stopping, interceding, suggesting procedures).

These four leadership functions have a clear and striking relationship to outcome. *Caring* and *Meaning Attribution* have a linear relationship to positive outcome. *The higher the caring and the higher the meaning attribution, the higher the positive outcome.* The other two functions, *Emotional Stimulation* and *Executive Function,* have a curvilinear relationship to outcome—the rule of the golden mean: *too much or too little of these leader behaviors results in lower positive outcome.* For example, too little leader emotional stimulation results in an unenergetic, devitalized group; too much stimulation (especially with insufficient meaning attribution) resulted in a highly emotionally charged climate with the leader pressing for more emotional interaction than the members could integrate. Too little executive function—a laissez-faire style—resulted in a bewildered, floundering group; too much executive function resulted in a highly structured, authoritarian arhythmic group, which failed to develop a sense of member autonomy or a freely flowing interactional sequence.

The most successful leader, then, was one moderate in amount of stimulation and in expression of executive function and high in caring and meaning attribution. Both caring and meaning attribution seemed critical, but neither, alone, was sufficient to insure success.

Using these four dimensions, several types of leader styles emerged from the data:

1. *Energizer* (high emotional stimulation, highly zealous, charismatic, high on executive function, highly supportive and attacking). These leaders were only moderately successful and produced large numbers of dropouts and the more severe casualties.
2. *Provider* (provision of two basic supplies: meaning and caring). These leaders were by far the most effective in producing high positive outcome with low risk.
3. *Social Engineers* (high meaning attribution, group process oriented, impersonal, moderately supportive). These leaders had a balanced outcome

picture of a moderate number of high learners balanced by a few dropouts and some casualties.

4. *Impersonal* (distant aggressive stimulators, low on caring and executive function, high on emotional stimulation). These leaders had a poor outcome with no high learners and high risk factors.

5. *Laissez-Faire* (low caring executive function and emotional stimulation, high meaning attribution). Poor outcome, high dropout rate, moderately high risk factor.

6. *Manager* (Only one leader in this type; he differed significantly from the other leaders because of his extremely high score on executive function. He employed a vast number of structured interventions.) Outcome was exceedingly poor; not one member benefited from the group experience. Risk factor was moderate.

7. *Encounter Tapes* Of course, these groups cannot be compared with others in terms of leader style. Their outcome was good with high positive change and extremely low risk factor.

It would seem that these findings from encounter groups strongly corroborate the functions of the group therapist as discussed in Chapter 5. Both emotional stimulation and cognitive structuring are essential. The Rogerian factors of empathy, genuineness, and unconditional positive regard thus seem incomplete; we must add the cognitive function of the leader. The research does not tell us what kind of meaning attribution is essential. (Both group process and interpersonal dynamic clarification seemed useful.) What seems important is the *process* of explanation which, in a number of ways, enabled the participant to integrate his experience, to generalize from it, and to transport it into other life situations.*

The Relationship Between the Encounter Group and the Therapy Group

I have already traced the development of the encounter group to a point where it began to approach the province of psychotherapy and

---

* The importance of meaning attribution received powerful support from another source. When members were asked to report (at the end of each session) the most significant event of the meeting and the reason for its significance, we found that those members who gained from the experience were far more prone to report incidents involving cognitive integration. (Even so revered an activity as self-disclosure bore little relationship to change unless it was accompanied by intellectual insight.) The pervasiveness and strength of this finding was impressive as well as unexpected (occurring in encounter groups with a fundamental anti-intellectual ethos).

shall now turn to the evolution of the therapy group to set the stage for the inevitable meeting (or collision) of the two disciplines.

EVOLUTION OF GROUP THERAPY

The history of group therapy has been too thoroughly described in other texts [19,20,21,22] to warrant repetition here. A rapid sweep will reveal the basic trends. Joseph Hershey Pratt, a Boston internist, is generally acknowledged to be the father of contemporary group therapy. Pratt undertook in 1905 the treatment of a large number of patients with far-advanced tuberculosis. Recognizing the relationship between psychological health and the physical course of tuberculosis, Pratt undertook to treat the person rather than the disease. He designed a treatment regimen which included home visits, diary keeping by patients, and weekly meetings of a tuberculosis class of approximately twenty-five patients. At these classes the diaries were inspected, weight gains were recorded publicly on the blackboard, and testimonials were given by successful patients. A degree of cohesiveness and mutual support developed which appeared helpful in combating the depression and isolation so common to tubercular patients.

During the 1920s and 1930s several psychiatrists experimented with group methods. Alder employed group methods in Europe because of his awareness of the social nature of man's problems and because of a desire to provide psychotherapeutic help to the working classes.[23] Lazell [24] in 1921 met with groups of schizophrenic patients in St. Elizabeth's Hospital in Washington, D.C., and delivered lectures on schizophrenia. Marsh,[25] a few years later, used groups for a wide range of clinical problems, including psychosis, psychoneurosis, psychophysiological disorders and stammering. He employed a variety of techniques, including such didactic methods as lectures and homework assignments as well as exercises designed to promote considerable interaction; for example, members were asked to "treat" one another, or all were asked to discuss such topics as one's earliest memory, ingredients of one's inferiority complex, night dreams, and daydreams. Wender [26] used analytic group methods with hospitalized nonpsychotic patients in the 1930s, while Burrows [27] and Schilder [28] applied these techniques to the treatment of psychoneurotic outpatients. Slavson,[29] who worked with groups of disturbed children and young adolescents, exerted considerable influence in the field through his teaching and writing at a time when group therapy was not yet considered by most workers as an effective therapeutic approach. Moreno,[30] who first used the term "group therapy," employed group methods before 1920 but has been primarily identified with psychodrama, which he introduced into America in 1925.

These tentative beginnings in the use of group therapy were vastly accelerated by World War II, when the large number of military psychiatric patients and the small number of trained psychiatric workers made individual therapy impractical and required that more economic modes of treatment be used.

During the 1950s the main thrust of the group therapy field was in a different direction: toward the application of group therapy in different clinical settings and for different types of clinical problems. Theoreticians—Freudian, Sullivanian, Horneyan, Rogerian—explored the application of their conceptual framework to group therapy theory and practice.

The T-group, as we have seen, derived from an educational tradition. Until the mid-sixties, NTL, the spokesman for the field, often emphasized that the T-group experience was an educational, not a therapeutic, one. For example, in 1967 Leland Bradford, director of the National Training Laboratories, wrote the following in a letter to the editor of the *New Yorker:*

Contrary to the report carried in your April 15, 1967, issue—"The Thursday Group," by Renata Adler—the National Training Laboratories does not conduct group therapy sessions in its various educational programs. We do conduct a variety of experience-based learning programs relating to group dynamics, but these programs are not designed for or intended as psychotherapy or as substitutes for psychotherapy. We feel that this clarification is important, since persons reading the article might be misled into seeking psychiatric assistance from our programs when they are neither designed for nor intended for that purpose.[31]

The T-group and the therapy group thus arose from different disciplines, and for many years the two disciplines, each generating its own store of theory and technique, continued as two parallel streams of knowledge, even though some leaders straddled both fields and, in different settings, led both T-groups and therapy groups. The T-group maintained a deep commitment to research and continued to identify with the fields of social psychology, education, organizational science, and industrial management. Indeed, many of the leading trainers held academic positions in graduate schools of business. The T-group literature consequently appeared in the journals of these disciplines and was relatively inaccessible to group therapy clinicians. Until the early

1960s, to the best of my knowledge, no clinical journal published material related to the practice or theory of T-groups.

THERAPY GROUP AND ENCOUNTER GROUP: FIRST INTERCHANGES

The evolution of the T-group into the modern encounter group tokened an entirely different concourse between the two fields. To speak of group therapy for normals and at the same time to suggest that, because of the stresses inherent in our culture, patienthood is ubiquitous can only lead to deep questioning about differences between the goals of encounter and therapy groups.

Considerable encounter group–therapy group traffic began to occur in the 1960s. Many mental health professionals participated in some form of encounter group during their training and subsequently led encounter groups and/or applied encounter techniques to their psychotherapeutic endeavors. Encounter group leaders, on the other hand, felt strongly that their group participants had had a therapeutic experience and that there was in reality no difference between personal growth and psychotherapy (between "mind expansion" and "head shrinking"). Furthermore, it became evident that there was much overlap between the population seeking psychotherapy and those seeking encounter experiences. Thus, many encounter group leaders concluded they were practicing psychotherapy—indeed a more rapid and effective type of psychotherapy—and advertised their services accordingly.

The response of the traditional mental health field to this perceived encroachment was one of great concern. Psychotherapists were alarmed at the recklessness of the new groups and at possible risks to participants. They were equally concerned about ethical issues: the lack of clinical training of the encounter group leaders; the advertising which suggested that months, even years of therapy could be condensed into a single, intensive weekend; the lack of responsibility of many of the leaders. Soon, increasing polarization occurred and in many areas the mental health professions launched campaigns urging their local governments to pass legislation to regulate encounter group practice and to hold leaders legally responsible for untoward effects.

In part, the vigorous response of the mental health profession was an irrational reaction to what was perceived as an invasion of territory. Practitioners felt threatened by a new and strange methodology and reacted by protecting their turf. There is, of course, a long tradition of territoriality in the profession. For decades the medically based psychiatric profession battled mightily to prevent social workers and psychologists from practicing psychotherapy. Such present-day euphemisms as "case work," "counseling," and "group work" attest to the tenacity of such efforts.

In part, however, the response was appropriate to certain excesses in some factions of the encounter field. These excesses issued from a crash-program mentality, successful in such ventures as space exploration and industrialization, but resulting in a *reductio ad absurdum* in human relations ventures. If something is good, more is better. If self-disclosure is good in groups, then total, immediate, indiscriminate disclosure in the nude must be better. If involvement is good, then prolonged, continuous, marathon involvement must be better. If expression of feeling is good, then hitting, touching, feeling, kissing, and fornicating must be better. If a group experience is good, then it is good for everyone—in all stages of the life cycle, in all life situations. These excesses are often offensive to the public taste and may be dangerous to some participants.

The issue of danger is respresentative of the polemic nature of the discourse. Many encounter group leaders and growth centers deny the existence of any risk; they claim that they have seen no untoward effects of the experiential group. A lengthy review of the literature in 1970 concludes that "there is little basis for the widespread concern among lay groups about the traumatic effects of group training." [32] Yet the Lieberman, Yalom, and Miles study demonstrated a significant risk factor.[18] Furthermore, our study revealed that the leaders were often unaware that some members had suffered negative consequences from the group experience. The reception to this aspect of the study is noteworthy. The article describing the casualties has been so widely reprinted that we decided to refuse further requests to include the article in new anthologies. The mass media cited the study widely (for example, *Readers Digest* published a review of it entitled "Encounter Groups—Dangerous for your Health"). Thousands of reprint requests were received, many, I believe, from workers who were glad to have their fears confirmed. (It is interesting to note that I also wrote a chapter on the "High Learner," [19] the highly successful encounter group member, and have yet to receive a single inquiry about this aspect of the study.) The casualty research findings have resonated with so many preconceptions that encounter groups per se are now, as a result of the study, described as more dangerous than I, the principle investigator of the casulty research, believe them to be. I believe that if the leader is well trained (both clinically and in group dynamics), is responsible, screens his members either before or during the group, provides sufficient information for applicants to de-select themselves, and permits members to proceed at their own pace, the group experience is quite likely to be a safe and rewarding one.

Excesses by some encounter group leaders have resulted in a rising wave of criticism directed indiscriminately against the entire encounter field. Several important industrial corporations have abandoned their human relations programs, school supervisors have campaigned and won elections largely on an anti-sensitivity training platform. I have seen some vitally needed, well thought-out human relations programs for recently integrated schools rejected for highly irrational reasons (e.g., some parents feared that students would be forced to reveal family secrets to their classes!). The *Congressional Record* has included a thirty thousand word blistering attack on sensitivity training, likening it to Bolshevistic brainwashing.[33]

It will be unfortunate if mental health professionals fail to differentiate between responsibly conducted experiental groups and those segments of the field with these excesses. Such a failure of discrimination would jeopardize the recent constructive interchange betweer the group therapy and sensitivity training fields. Clinical researchers have learned a great deal from the T-group research methodology; T-groups are commonly used now in the training of group therapists:[34,35,36] T-groups have been used in psychiatric hospitals in the treatment program of chronically hospitalized patients;[37] some clinicians refer their individual therapy patients to a T-group for "opening-up"; and finally, some T-group techniques have been adopted by clinicians, resulting in a gradual shift in the practice of group therapy. For example, the increased emphasis on the here-and-now, the concept of feedback, greater leader transparency, the use of group structured exercises, both verbal and nonverbal, and the time-extended meeting, have in part been the legacy of the T-group to group therapy.

So there is considerable confusion at present and the confusion is compounded by the fact that clinicians are on both sides of the controversy: many psychotherapists, as we have stated, participate in encounter groups, lead them, use them in training and consultation, and adapt encounter techniques in their psychotherapy.

Of course, scurrying in between these tumbling pillars is the confused would-be patient faced, on the one hand, with the mass media promulgation of the breakthrough effectiveness of encounter groups and, on the other hand, with mental health professionals' stern storm warnings, while they themselves offer at the same time a profusion of varying group formats, many indistinguishable from encounter group approaches.

THE THERAPY GROUP AND THE ENCOUNTER GROUP: SHARED PROPERTIES AND CONCERNS

Starting from their widely different point of origin, the recent courses of the encounter group and the therapy group have shown a convergence to the point where there is a considerable interface between the two fields. Indeed, so many similarities are present that many observers wonder whether there are any intrinsic differences between the two types of group work.

Development of the Individual's Positive Potential. The traditions from which each have derived have undergone considerable evolution, which has resulted in a major shift in group goals, theory, and technology. Human relations education, as we have indicated, has changed its emphasis from the acquisition of specific theory and interpersonal skills to the present encounter group goals of total enhancement of the individual. Human relations education now means that the individual becomes educated about his relationship to others as well as to his various internal selves. In the field of psychotherapy there has been a gradual evolution from a model of personality development based on the transmutations of the individual's libidinal and aggressive energies to the current emphasis on ego psychology. Many theorists have posited the existence of an additional positively valenced drive which must perforce be allowed to unfold rather than be inhibited or sublimated: thus Hendrick's "instinct to master," [38] Berlyne's "exploratory drive," [39] Horney's "self-realization," [40] White's "effectance motivation," [41] Hartmann's "neutralized energy," [42] Angyal's "self-determination," [43] and Goldstein's, Rogers', and Maslow's "self-actualization." [44] Thus, the development of the individual entails more than the inhibition or sublimation of potentially destructive instinctual forces: He must, in addition, fulfill his creative potential, and the efforts of the therapist are best directed toward this goal. Horney [40] states that the task of the therapist should be to help remove obstructions; given favorable circumstances, the individual will realize his own potential, "just as an acorn will develop into an oak." Similarly, Rogers refers to the therapist as a facilitator.

A closely related trend in psychotherapy, beginning with Fromm, Reichmann, Erickson, Lindemann, and Hamburg, has been the strategy of building on the patient's strengths. Psychotherapists have come to appreciate, for example, that individuals may encounter great discomfort at certain junctures in the life cycle, not because of poor ego strength but because there have been inadequate opportunities for the learning relevant to that life stage to occur; psychotherapy may be directed toward the facilitation of this learning. Hamburg, in particular, has explored adaptive methods of coping with severe life challenges and has suggested strategies of psychotherapy based on the facilitation of coping.[45] This shift in therapy orientation has brought the group therapist and the T-group leader closer together. The T-group leader has always espoused the goal of acquisition of competence; he has always believed that the reinforcement of strengths is no less vital than the correction of deficiencies.

Outcome Goals. Hoped-for changes occurring in the individual as a result of his T-group experience closely parallel (despite differences in language) the changes that group therapists wish to see in their patients. For example, one T-group outcome study [46] investigated the following fifteen variables: sending communication, receiving communication, relational facility, risk-taking, increased interdependence, functional flexibility, self-control, awareness of behavior, sensitivity to group process, sensitivity to others, acceptance of others, tolerance of new information, confidence, comfort, insight into self, and role. The Liebermann, Yalom, and Miles outcome criteria for their encounter group project [19] also closely resembled psychotherapy outcome criteria with the single obvious exception of target symptoms ("chief complaints").

Supra-Individual Focus. One important difference between T-groups and therapy groups present in their early phases but now diminished was that the T-group often had supra-individual goals, whereas the therapy group concerned itself solely with the personal goals of each individual member. For example, the first T-group described earlier had the goal of facilitating the operation of the Connecticut Fair Employment Practices Act. Other T-groups frequently have the supra-individual goal of increasing the effectiveness of the contracting agency. Group therapy, on the other hand, had no goals other than the relief of suffering of each of its members.

Both disciplines have altered their original positions. T-groups often consist of strangers, each of whom has highly personalized goals, whereas many of the supra-individual goals are split off from the T-group and assigned to other activities of the human relations laboratory. Psychotherapy, on the other hand, has gradually become more aware of the importance of supra-individual goals. Stanton and Schwartz [47] in 1954 first noted that in a large social system, the psychi-

atric hospital, the improvement or deterioration of the individual patient was a function of the structural properties of the large group. For
example, if the large group had evolved norms whoch prevented the
resolution of intrastaff conflict, patients were more likely to have psychotic exacerbations. Similar observations have been made in military, prison, and community settings. Gradually, an important principle of psychotherapeutic intervention has evolved: a supra-individual
focus—the cohesiveness and norms of the large group—can facilitate
the attainment of each member's individual goals. In fact, often there
is little choice; for example, the great majority of therapists would
agree that the individual treatment of the underprivileged adolescent
drug user without involvement of his social group is a futile endeavor.
The small therapy group analogue of this principle was fully described in Chapter 3 in the discussion of cohesiveness as a curative
factor in group psychotherapy.

Group Composition. Encounter group and therapy group composition have also grown more similar over the years. No longer do psychotherapists solely treat individuals with major mental health problems. An increasing number of fairly well-integrated individuals with
minor problems in living are seeking psychotherapy. A number of factors are responsible: increased public acceptance and understanding
of psychotherapy, curiosity-arousing mass media depictions of psychotherapy, and increased affluence and leisure time which have resulted in a shift upward on the hierarchy of needs. Conversely, many
patients have come to regard the encounter groups, especially the
weekend marathon variety, as crash psychotherapy programs. Lieberman and Gardner [3] studied participants of several growth centers and
report that 81 percent had had psychotherapy in the past or were currently in therapy. Moreover, using the criteria of amount of stress,
symptomatology, and reasons for seeking help, they found that 70 percent closely resembled new patients applying for help at psychiatric
outpatient clinics. Indeed, as Rogers [48] observed, a new clinical syndrome—the group addict—has recently arisen; these individuals
spend every weekend in some encounter group, searching them out
up and down the West Coast.

The Common Social Malady. Both encounter groups and therapy
groups highly value self-disclosure, and the content of what is disclosed is remarkably similar from group to group. Loneliness, confusion, and alienation haunt T-groups and therapy groups alike. The
great majority of individuals, both patients and nonpatients, share a
common malady, which is deeply imbedded in the character of modern Western society. In much of America the past two decades have

witnessed an inexorable decomposition of social institutions which ordinarily provide for human intimacy; the extended family living arrangement, the lifelong marriage (one out of two California marriages ends in divorce), the small, stable work group and home community are often part of the nostalgic past. Organized religion has become irrelevant to many of the young, often little more than a "Sunday morning tedium," [49] and the neighborhood merchant and the family doctor are rapidly disappearing.

Modern medical practice is a case in point. Spurred on by advances in medical technology, the doctor has become an efficient scientist. But at what a price! The president of the American Medical Association stated recently:

> In the future, the family doctor will be almost as extinct as a dodo. When you're hurt or sick, you'll go to the nearest hospital for emergency treatment, administered by physicians especially trained in these procedures.
>
> You may not even see the doctor on your initial visit. Your case history will be taken by assistants—even, eventually, by computers. Trained aides may do some of the preliminary examination.
>
> The kindly old gentleman with the bedside manner was wonderful in his day, but society can no longer afford him. The modern doctor is more efficient, more scientific, and less subject to error. Unfortunately, he is often more impersonal. But people are already beginning to accept this, as they are beginning to accept changes in all areas of personal service.
>
> It's part of a normal trend in society. In all forms of human service, there is less concern for the individual. We are no longer served as well as we used to be in stores and restaurants. The relationship between people and those who provide them with service is deteriorating, and there is no chance of its return. [50]

In short, the institutions which provide intimacy in our culture have atrophied and their replacements—the television set, the supermarket, dial-a-prayer, and drop-in rap centers—are the accoutrements of the lonely crowd. Yet the human need for closeness persists and intimacy-sponsoring endeavors like the encounter group have multiplied at a near astronomical rate in the past few years. As the future comes upon us, a periodic social immerson—a rehumanization station (God forbid)—may become a necessity if we are to survive the dehumanizing march of a socially blind scientific technology.

Modern man is personally as well as socially alienated; he is separated from his own self and gropes for some sense of personal identity. The modeling process by which children establish their personal and sexual identity has been disrupted. The broken homes, the confused role of the mother-homemaker-career woman, the father whose occupation is invisible or incomprehensible to the child, the television teaching machine, the absent extended kinship, all contribute to the identity confusion. The current generation is the first in the history of the world which has nothing to learn from grandparents; in fact, the pace of change is such that children can scarcely learn from peers five years older. One can, in passing, only muse about the effects on the unused identificatory figures. What does it mean to the father who is unable to extend himself into the future through his son? *

Increased literacy, education, mass media, leisure time have made modern man, patient and nonpatient alike, more aware of a discrepancy between his values and his behavior. Many enlightened individuals who consider their chief life values to be humanitarian, esthetic, egalitarian, or intellectual find that, under self-scrutiny, they pay only lip service to these and instead base their behavior on the values of aggrandizement: the "philistine triumvirate" [52] of material wealth, prestige, and power. The awareness of this discrepancy may result in a pervasive anxiety, self-abrogation, and sense of emptiness which often beget a harried attempt to avoid reflection by compulsive working and hobbying.

Another discrepancy is experienced between work and one's sense of creativity; the great majority of individuals rarely experience a sense of pride, completion, or effectiveness in their work. The gap between the worker and the finished product, originally a blight of the industrial revolution, continues to widen as the technological maelstrom whirls man into an anonymous automation. These developments result in a growing sense of personal inadequacy. Although the individual may obtain some sense of pride from the achievements of his megagroup, generally the individual's sense of personal worth is inversely proportional to the size and power of the megamachine, to use Mumford's term,[53] in which he is ensconced.

Although any of these concerns may be more important to one group member than another, each is likely to have some real meaning to all, be they labeled patient, student, delegate, trainer, or therapist. All

---

* Has the rapidity of change precluded the type of relationship that the Odysseus of Kazantzakis experienced with Telemacus?

> He who has borne a son dies not; the father turned,
> and his sea-battered vagrant heart swelled up with pride.
> Good seemed to him his young son's neck, his chest and sides,
> the swift articulation of his joints, his royal veins
> that from tall temples down to lithesome ankles throbbed.
> Like a horse-buyer, with swift glances he enclosed
> with joy his son's well-planted and keen-bladed form.
> "It's I who stand before my own discarded husk,
> my lips unshaven, my heart still covered with soft down,
> all my calamities still buds, my wars, carnations,
> and my far journeys still faint flutterings on my brow." [51]

these factors, then, indicate that there is an enormous overlap between encounter groups and therapy groups. Both types of groups have similar goals, similar views of man, rely on similar mechanisms of change or curative factors, have similar ground rules (here-and-now, inter- and intrapersonal honesty, feedback, admitting weaknesses and uncertainty, establishing mutual trust, understanding and analyzing behavior) and similar shared concerns. Obviously, groups with so many shared properties will and must go through comparable processes.

THERAPY GROUPS AND ENCOUNTER GROUPS: SIMILAR LEARNING ENVIRONMENTS

The Lieberman, Yalom, Miles encounter group project suggested that not only do encounter groups and therapy groups resemble each other in form but that similar rules of learning and change apply to both approaches. When the outcome (both on a group level and on an individual level) was correlated with the course of events during the life of the group, several conclusions emerged which have obvious relevance to the process of change in therapy group. For example, the study concluded that if encounter groups were to be effective vehicles of personal change, several basic encounter group maxims need to be reformulated in the following ways:

1. "Feelings not thought" should be altered to "feelings, only with thought."
2. "Let it all hang out" is best revised to "let more of it hang out than usual, if it feels right in the group, and if you can give some thought to what it means." Self-disclosure, emotional expressiveness (of either positive or negative feelings) was not in itself sufficient for change.
3. "Getting out the anger is essential" to "getting out the anger may be okay, but keeping it out there steadily isn't." High expression of anger was counterproductive: it was not associated with high learning and generally increased risk.
4. "Stay with the here-and-now" to "here-and-now is not enough, add the personal there-and-then." The more productive groups were those with more flexible boundaries. Though the here-and-now was essential, groups which were flexible and permitted other personal material (sexual concerns, dream material, feelings of pride, happiness, etc.) were more productive.
5. "There is no group, only persons" to "group processes make a difference in learning, whether or not the leader pays attention to them." Learning was heavily influenced by such group properties as cohesiveness, climate, norms, and the group role occupied by the individual member.

6. "High yield requires high risk" to "the risk in encounter groups is considerable and unrelated to positive gain." The high-risk groups, those that produced large numbers of casualties, did not at the same time produce high learners. The productive groups were safe ones. The high-yield–high-risk group is, according to our study, a myth.

7. "You may not know what you've learned now, but when you put it all together. . ." to "bloom now, don't count on later." It is often thought that individuals may be shaken up ("unfrozen") during the group experience but that later, after the group is over, they integrate their experience in the group and come out stronger than ever. In our projects individuals who had a negative outcome at the termination of the group *never* moved to the positive side of the ledger when studied six months later.

Similarities in Ideological Development. The therapy group and encounter group fields share another common feature: their recent baroque development—their burgeoning diversity of leader technologies and ideological schools. (Recall the list of workshop titles with which I began this chapter.) The Lieberman, Yalom, Miles encounter group study helps us understand this development by examining the methods by which leaders regulate and evaluate their behavior. Consider, for example, the use of structured exercises. Every leader in the project used some structured interventions, some to a very great extent. We found that the more exercises a leader used, the more his group members considered him competent, effective, and understanding. Furthermore, the members of the high exercise groups were active proselytizers; they urged others to join encounter groups. However, *the long-term outcome of the members of those groups was poor;* any change that occurred seemed to be transitory (probably because members did not experience what happened in the group as a product of their own activity). The leaders of these groups, however, had no way of knowing of the deterioration of their results; they were only aware of their members' enthusiasm about their procedures.

There is an obvious generalization to be made here about the basis of the leader's self-assessment. The group leader commonly makes the error of equating "potency" and "effectiveness." There is general consensus that the encounter group is "potent" in that it almost invariably provides an emotionally charged, intense experience. Members almost always are "touched"; they find an encounter group to be a moving experience. (In fact, this is such an inherent property of the experiential group that it requires a particularly inept or interfering leader to block its occurrence.) Yet, as we see from the results of this experiment, "potent" does not mean effective; the most "potent" (most intense, most emotional) groups were not necessarily potent agents of change.

So the encounter leader often feels his group is effective when it is not, and even when he is successful, he often attributes his success to the wrong factors. In general, encounter group leaders (both successful and unsuccessful) overvalue their direct contributions: their immediate impact on each of the members of the group, their specialized techniques, their ability to stimulate, to challenge, to offer insight, to help members become aware of their feelings, to express emotions, to get in touch with their bodies. Yet there are many important psychosocial factors which heavily influence outcome and often operate outside the leader's level of awareness. Effective leaders must, at some level, appreciate these forces and harness them in the service of therapy. For example, consider the role in the group occupied by the member. One role in which the member is highly active and influential and, in the eyes of the other members, exhibits behavior in harmony with the values of the group correlates highly with positive outcome. Another role, the deviant (as defined by sociometrics), correlates very highly with negative outcome: a member deemed by the others, even very early in the course of the group, to be "out" of the group has virtually no chance of benefiting from the group and a strong chance of suffering harm. The successful leader appraises himself of these factors and acts accordingly: he reinforces each member's activity and participation in norm construction, he searches for ways to escort the deviant back into the group, and he discourages the development of scapegoating and judgmentalism.

Group properties are equally relevant. The successful leader, whether he knows it or not, builds a group with high cohesiveness, harmonious climate, and a norm profile which favors positive yield (peer rather than leader control, flexible procedural boundaries, expressivity, nonjudgmentalism, etc.).[18]

But if leaders mistake potency for effectiveness or if they attribute their success to the wrong factors, it is not difficult to understand why encounter group leadership methods have passed so quickly into the baroque phase I described at the beginning of this chapter. Since there is a need for group leadership training, successful and gifted leaders often establish training institutes in which they, too often, teach those techniques which they value but which may only be their idiosyncratic behavioral characteristics and irrelevant to the change process. The successful leader may fail to transmit his intuitive appreciation and use of the potent psychosocial forces in the group. Thus, many technique-based ideological schools arise which stress their uniqueness and do not appreciate or emphasize the degree to which successful leaders use similar basic strategies in their work.

Although there is much overlap and many similarities between encounter and therapy groups, we must not make the mistake of equating the two. There are, I believe, some very fundamental differences between the therapy group and the encounter group.

Therapy Groups and Encounter Groups—Differences

I must make a few qualifications before discussing these differences. The nature of the encounter group or the therapy group depends upon the goals and techniques of the leader. Certain encounter leaders and therapists, particularly those who straddle both fields, may lead their groups in such similar fashion that differences between the two are blurred, whereas others operate so differently that even the unpracticed observer can readily enumerate fundamental differences. In other words, the differences *within* both the T-group field and the therapy group field may be greater than the differences *between* the two fields. Second, there are both extrinsic and intrinsic differences. Extrinsic or procedural differences are expendable and arise from the different customs, settings, and traditions of the two fields from which the two types of groups originated and are not valuable indicators in understanding underlying principles of the groups. Intrinsic differences, on the other hand, are core differences and arise from the vital differences in the goals and composition of the two types of groups. Even here, however, we must acknowledge the overlap; many encounter group leaders and group therapists will contest the distinctions which I shall make.

EXTRINSIC DIFFERENCES

Setting. The encounter group differs from the therapy group in size, duration, and physical setting. Generally, it consists of ten to sixteen members who may be total strangers or who may be associates at work. Not infrequently, the encounter group meets as part of a larger residential human relations laboratory lasting one to two weeks. The group, in this setting, usually meets in two- to three-hour sessions once or twice a day. The members usually spend the entire day with one another and the encounter group atmosphere spills over into other activities. Often, encounter groups meet, like therapy groups, in shorter sessions spaced over a longer period of time. Almost always, however, the encounter group's life spans a shorter period of time.

Unlike the therapy group, the encounter group's ethos is one of informality and pleasure. The physical surroundings are often resortlike, and more consideration is given to the pursuit of fun: laughter is heard more often in the encounter group; the leader may often tell jokes to explicate certain issues in the group, and some leaders state clearly that it is important to them that the group members have a good time. Not only does the group have more fun during the meetings, but it devotes more attention to the role fun occupies in the lives of each of the members. To the reasonably well-integrated encounter group member, the ability to play and to enjoy the leisure his affluence has brought him is an issue of considerable import. To the more survival-oriented psychiatric patient, fun occupies a less pressing, more distant position on his hierarchy of needs.

Role of the Leader. Generally, there is a far greater gap between the leader and the members in a therapy group than in an encounter group. This is a result both of the leader's behavior and the characteristics of the members. Although encounter group members may, as we have mentioned, overvalue the leader, generally they tend to see him more realistically than do psychiatric patients. Encounter group members, partially because of their greater self-esteem and also because of a greater opportunity to socialize between meetings with the leader, perceive the leader as similar to themselves, except insofar as he has superior skill and knowledge in a specialized area. Much of the prestige the leader enjoys in the group he earns as a result of his contributions. Eventually, he begins to participate in a similar manner to the other members and in time assumes full membership in the group, although his technical expertise continues to be employed and appreciated.

Part of the encounter group leader's task is to transmit not only his knowledge but also his skills; he expects his group members to learn methods of diagnosing and resolving interpersonal problems. Often, he explicitly behaves as a teacher; for example, he may, as an aside, explicate some point of theory and may introduce some group exercise, verbal or nonverbal, as an experiment for the group to study. It is not unusual for encounter group members to seek further human relations education and subsequently to become leaders themselves. (Occasionally, this has had some unfortunate repercussions resulting in excesses, since some members, without the necessary skills and background, have considered one or two experiences as a group member sufficient training for them to undertake new careers as group leaders.)

Group therapists are viewed far more unrealistically by their group members (see Chapter 6). In part, the therapist's deliberately enigmatic and mystifying behavior generates this distortion. He has entirely different roles of conduct from the other members in the group; he is rarely transparent or self-disclosing and too often reveals only his professional front. It is a rare therapist who socializes or even drinks coffee with his group members. In part, however, the distortion resides within the patients and springs from their hope for an omniscient figure who will intercede in their behalf. They do not view the therapist merely as an individual similar to themselves aside from his specialized professional skills; for better or for worse, they attribute to him the archetypal abilities and powers of the healer. Often the group members and the therapist conspire together to define his role: the leader often chooses, for technical reasons, to be perceived unrealistically, and the group members, for survival reasons, do not allow his real personage to emerge. Although, as the group proceeds, the therapist's role may change so that he behaves more like a member, he never becomes a full group member: he almost never presents his personal problems in living to the group; his statements and actions continue to be perceived as powerful and sagacious regardless of their content. Furthermore, the therapist is not concerned with teaching his skills to the group members; rarely does a therapy group member use his group experience to launch himself on a career as a group therapist.

INTRINSIC DIFFERENCES

Beyond the Common Social Malady. Most of the fundamental differences between encounter groups and therapy groups derive from the difference in composition. Although much overlapping may occur, the encounter group is generally composed of well-functioning individuals who seek greater competence and growth, whereas the therapy group has a population of individuals who often cannot cope with minor everyday stress without discomfort; they seek relief from anxiety, depression, or from a sterile and ungratifying intra- and interpersonal existence. Earlier in this chapter I described a common social malady that to a greater or lesser degree affects all individuals. However, and this is a point often overlooked by clinically untrained encounter group leaders, psychiatric patients have, in addition, a set of far more pressing concerns. The common social malady is woven into the fabric of their personality but is not synonymous with their psychopathology.

To illustrate, consider the concept of self-alienation—one of the common results of the "culture game" described above. Horney's formulations, to use one of several available personality constructs, also postulates an alienation from the self as a core problem of many individuals. (She defines neurosis as a "disturbance in one's relationship to self and to others.") [40] However, whereas the "culture game" concept describes self-alienation as a commonplace phenomenon emanating from the facade-wearing ritual of the adult world, Horney describes self-alienation as a defensive maneuver occurring early in the individual's life as a response to basic anxiety stemming from severe disharmonies in the parent-child relationship. The child is faced with the problem of dealing with parents too wrapped up in their own neurotic conflicts to conceive of him and treat him as a separate individual with his own needs and potential. As a survival mechanism, the child diverts his energies, which would ordinarily be devoted to the task of actualization of his real self, to the construction and realization of an idealized self—a self the individual feels he should and ought to become for the sake of survival. Horney then proceeds to delineate a complex development of the individual in terms of the relationship between his ideal self, his potential self, and his actual self (the person he perceives himself to be), but this need not concern us now. *The important point is that this split occurs early in life and profoundly influences all aspects of subsequent development.* The individual attempts, all his life, to shape himself in the form of the idealized (and unattainable) self, develops a far-reaching pride system based on idealized characteristics, blots out opposing trends in himself, experiences self-hatred when the discrepancy between the idealized and actual selves seems particularly great, and evolves a pervasive network of claims on the environment and restrictive demands on himself. In light of the far-reaching consequences of these developments on the neurotic person, it would seem that little benefit could accrue from a brief encounter group, such as a twelve-hour group (six two-hour meetings) advertised in the newspaper,[54] which was entitled "The Courage to be Real" and which planned to ". . . deal with such problems as telling the difference between phoniness and reality in one's self and in others. . . ."

To return to the central issue, the fact that patients and nonpatients alike share many common concerns should not obscure the point that patients have, by definition, an additional and far deeper basis for their alienation and dysphoria.

Orientation to Learning. One of the basic tasks of the encounter group—the acquisition of interpersonal competence—requires a degree of interpersonal skill which most psychiatric patients do not possess. Encounter group leaders ordinarily make certain assumptions about their group members: they must be able to send and receive communications about their own and other members' behavior with a minimum of distortion; they must, if they are to convey accurate information and be receptive to feedback, have a relatively high degree of self-awareness and self-acceptance. Furthermore, participants must desire interpersonal change. They must be well-intentioned and constructive in their relationship to the other members and must believe in a fundamental constructive attitude on the part of the others if a cohesive, mutually trusting group is to form. The members must be willing, after receiving feedback, to question previously cherished beliefs about themselves (unfreezing) and be willing to experiment with new attitudes and behavior, which may replace older, less successful modes of behavior.

The participants must then transfer these modes of behavior beyond the group situation to interpersonal situations in their "back-home" life. Generalized adjunctive learning is also necessary; for example, Argyris [55] notes:

. . . if the individual learns to express his feelings of anger or love more openly, he may also have to develop new competence in dealing with individuals who are threatened with such openness. It is important, therefore, for the individual to learn how to express these feelings in such a way that he minimizes the probability that his behavior will cause someone else to become defensive, thereby creating a potentially threatening environment.

These intra- and interpersonal prerequisities which most encounter group leaders take for granted in their group members are the very attributes sorely deficient in the typical psychiatric patient, who generally has lower levels of self-esteem and self-awareness. The stated group goals of increased interpersonal competence are often perceived as incompatible with their personal goals of relief from suffering. Their initial response to others is often based on distrust rather than trust, and, most important of all, their ability to question their belief system and to risk new forms of behavior is severely impaired. In fact, the inability to learn from new experience is central to the basic problem of the neurotic. To illustrate with a classic example, consider Anna Freud's study of Patrick, who during the London blitz in 1943 was separated from his parents and developed an obsessive-compulsive neurosis. In the evacuation center he stood alone in a corner and chanted continuously, "Mother will come and put on my overcoat and my leggings, she will zip my zipper, she will put on my pixie hat," etc.[56] Consequently, Patrick, unlike the other children, could not avail himself of the learning opportunities in the center. He remained isolated from the other adults and children and formed no other relationships which could have relieved his fear and permitted him to continue his growth and the development of his social skills. The frozen compulsive behavior did provide some solace for Patrick by preventing panic but so tied up his energy that he could not appraise the situation and take new, adaptive action.

Not only does the neurotic defense preclude testing and resolution of the core conflict, but it characteristically generalizes to include an ever-widening sphere of the individual's life space. Generalization may occur directly or indirectly. It may operate directly, as in traumatic or war neuroses in which the feared situation takes an increasingly broader definition. For example, a phobia once confined to a specific form of moving vehicle may generalize so as to apply to all forms of transportation. Indirectly the individual suffers since, as with little Patrick, the inhibition prevents him from exploring his physical and interpersonal environment and developing his potential. A vicious circle arises since maladaptive interpersonal techniques beget further stress and may preclude the formation of gratifying relationships.

The important point is that the individual with neurotic defenses is frozen into a closed position; he is not open for learning, and he is generally searching not for growth but for safety. Argyris[55] puts it nicely when he differentiates a "survival orientation" from a "competence orientation." The more an individual is competence-oriented, the more receptive and flexible he is. He becomes an "open system" and in the interpersonal area is able to use his experience to develop greater interpersonal competence. On the other hand, an individual may be more concerned with protecting himself in order to survive. Through the use of defence mechanisms he withdraws, distorts, or attacks the environment.

This, in turn, begins to make the individual more closed and less subject to influence. The more closed the individual becomes, the more his adaptive reactions will be controlled by his internal system. But since his internal system is composed of many defense mechanisms, the behavior will not tend to be functional or economical. The behavior may eventually become compulsive, repetitive, inwardly stimulated, and observably dysfunctional. The individual becomes more of a "closed" system.[55]

The survival-oriented individual does not give or accept accurate feedback; if left to his own devices he will generate those kinds of experiences which will strengthen his defensive position. He may, for example, be particularly attentive to feedback that confirms the rationality of his having to be closed. Similarly, the feedback he gives to others may be highly colored by his survival orientation: he may be far more concerned with engendering in others certain attitudes toward himself than with giving accurate feedback.

Individuals are neither all open or all closed; they may be closed in specific areas and open in others. Nor, as we have stated, are all therapy group members more closed than all encounter group members. Consider for a moment the vast scope and diversity of the group therapies; it is possible, for example, that the affluent members of an analytic group in Manhattan may be as integrated and congruent as the members of an average encounter group. The label of "patient" is often a purely arbitrary one which is a consequence of the request for help, not of the need for help. (It is possible that once the therapist has labeled an individual as a patient, he initiates a self-fulfilling prophecy: by expecting, and unwittingly reinforcing, patient-like behavior he elicits closed rather than open behavior.) Generally, however, the therapy group is composed of individuals with a survival rather a competence orientation and who therefore cannot readily take advantage of the interpersonal learning opportunities of the group. Therapy group members cannot easily follow the simple encounter group mandate to be open, honest, and trusting when they are experiencing profound feelings of suspicion, fear, distrust, anger, and self-hatred. A great deal of work must be done to overcome these maladaptive interpersonal stances so that patients can begin to participate constructively in the group. Jerome Frank came close to the heart of the matter when he said that "therapy groups are as much or more concerned with helping patients to unlearn old patterns as they are with helping them to learn new ones." [57] Accordingly, in therapy groups the task of interpersonal competence acquisition goes hand in hand with (and sometimes straggles far behind) the task of removing maladaptive defenses.

Differences Early and Late. Thus there are two intrinsic differences between T-groups and therapy groups, both emanating from the composition and goals of the group. First, therapy group members are in a greatly different state of readiness to learn. Second, although they share many aspects of a common social malady with encounter group members, they nevertheless have deep highly personalized splits within themselves explicable only on the basis of each one's developmental history. Each member must be helped to understand the form, the irrationality, and the maladaptive implications of his behavior. This type of exploration can only occur once a highly cohesive, mutually trusting group with highly therapeutic norms has been formed. In one sense, this work begins at a point where many encounter groups end. The improved interpersonal sensititivy and communication which may be the goal of the encounter group is a means to an end for the intensive therapy group. Frank, while acknowledging he was overstating the point for purposes of explication, noted, "The therapy group reaches maximal usefulness at the point where the T-group ceases to be useful." [57]

The therapy group, then, differs from the encounter group early and late. It differs early by beginning more painfully and laboriously. Encounter group members may begin a group with trepidation; they face an unknown situation in which they will be asked to expose themselves and to take risks. Nevertheless, they are generally backed up by a relatively high self-esteem level and a reservoir of professional and interpersonal success. Psychiatric patients, on the other hand, begin a therapy group with dread and suspicion. Self-disclosure is infinitely more threatening in the face of a belief in one's basic worthlessness and badness. The pace is slower; the group must deal with one vexing interpersonal problem after another. The encounter group, after all, does not often have to face the problem of an angry paranoid patient, or a suicidal depressive one, or a denying patient who attributes all his difficulties in living to his spouse, or a fragile borderline schizophrenic individual, or the easily discouraged members who constantly threaten to leave the group. The therapist, unlike the trainer, must constantly modulate the amount of confrontation, self-disclosure, and tension the group can tolerate.

The therapy group differs later by having a different termination point for each member. Unlike the encounter group, which invariably ends as a unit and generally at a predetermined time, the therapy group continues for each member until his goals have been reached. In fact, as Frank points out, one reason that the therapy group is so threatening is that its task, "broad personal modification," has scarcely any limit and furthermore there is no restriction as to what can, and perhaps must, be discussed.[57] Often in an encounter group it is enough for the group to recognize and to surmount a problem area; not so in the therapy group, in which problem areas must be explored in depth for each of the members involved.

For example, in a twelve-session encounter group of mental health professionals which I once led, the members (who were also my students) experienced great difficulty in their relationship to me. They felt frightened and inhibited by me, vied for my attention, addressed a preponderance of their comments to me, overvalued the wisdom of my remarks, and harbored unrealistic expectations of me. I responded to this issue by helping the group members recognize their behavior, their distortions, and unrealistic expectations. I then helped them appreciate the effects of their unrealistic and dependent attitudes toward me on the course of the group and called their attention to the implications of this phenomenon on their future role as group therapists. Next, we discussed some of the members' feelings toward the more dependent members of the group: for example, how it felt to have someone ostensibly talk to you but at the same time fix his gaze on the leader. Once these tasks were accomplished, I felt that it was important that the group move past this block and proceed to focus on other facets of the group experience, for it was abundantly clear that the group could spend all of its remaining sessions attempting to resolve fully its struggle with the issue of leadership and authority. I helped to turn the group's attention to other current but untouched group issues—for example, their feelings about three silent and seemingly uninvolved members, the hierarchy of dominance in the group, and the general issue of intermember competition and competence, always a specter looming large in encounter groups of mental health workers.

In a therapy group the leader would approach the same issue in a different fashion with different objectives in mind. He would encourage the patients especially conflicted in this area to discuss in depth their feelings and fantasies toward him. Rather than consider ways in which to help the group move on, he would help plunge them into the issue so that each member might understand his overt behavior toward him, as well as his avoided behavior and the fantasied calamitous effects of such behavior. Although he would, by a degree of transparency, assist the members in their reality testing, he would attempt to modulate the timing of this behavior so as to allow the formation and full exploration of their feelings toward him. (See Chapter 6 for a detailed discussion of this issue.) The goal of clarifying other facets of group dynamics is, of course, irrelevant for the therapy group; the only reason for changing the focus of the group is that the current issue is no longer the most fertile one for the therapeutic work: either the group has pursued the areas as far as possible at that time or some other more immediate issue has arisen in the group.

To summarize, the basic intrinsic difference between encounter groups and therapy groups arises from the differences in composition (and thereby the goals) of the groups. As a general rule, psychiatric patients have different goals, more deeply disrupted intra- and interpersonal relations, and a different (closed, survival-based) orientation to learning. These factors result in a number of process and procedural differences both in the early stages and in the late working-through stages of the group.

REFERENCES

1. Julian Silvermen, personal communication, 1975.
2. C. Rogers, "Interpersonal Relationships: Year 2000," *J. Appl. Behav. Sci., 4:* 265–280, 1968.
3. M. A. Lieberman and J. Gardner, "Institutional Alternatives to Psychotherapy: A Study of Growth Center Users," *Archives General Psychiatry,* in press.
4. H. Coffey, personal communication, 1967.
5. A. Bavelas, personal communication, 1967.
6. A. Marrow, "Events Leading to the Establishment of the National Training Laboratories," *J. Appl. Behav. Sci., 3:* 144–150, 1967.
7. L. P. Bradford, "Biography of an Institution," *J. Appl. Behav. Sci., 3:* 127–144, 1967.
8. K. Benne, "History of the T-Group in the Laboratory Setting," in Bradford, Gibb, and Benne, *op. cit.,* pp. 80–135.
9. K. Lewin, R. Lippit, and R. K. White, "Patterns of Aggressive Behavior in Experimentally Created Social Climates," *J. Soc. Psychol., 10:* 271–299, 1939.
10. K. Lewin, "Forces Behind Food Habits and Methods of Change," *Bull. Nat. Res. Council, 108:* 35–65, 1943.
11. D. Stock, "A Survey of Research on T-Groups," in Bradford, Gibb, and Benne, *op. cit.,* pp. 395–441.
12. R. R. Blake and J. S. Mouton, "Reactions to Intergroup Competition Under Win-Lose Conditions," *Management Science, 7:* 420–435, 1961.
13. Schein and Bennis, *op. cit.,* p. 41.
14. *Ibid.,* p. 43.
15. A. Camus, cited in *ibid.,* p. 46.
16. J. Luft, *Group Processes: An Introduction to Group Dynamics* (Palo Alto, Calif.: National Press, 1966).
17. I. R. Wechsler, F. Messarik, and R. Tannenbaum, "The Self in Process: A Sensitivity Training Emphasis," in I. R. Wechsler and E. H. Schein (eds.), *Issues in Training* (Washington, D.C.: National Education Association, National Training Laboratories, 1962), pp. 33–46.
18. M. A. Lieberman, I. Yalom, and M. Miles, *Encounter Groups: First Facts* (New York: Basic Books, 1973).
19. H. I. Kaplan and B. J. Sadock, *Comprehensive Group Psychotherapy* (Baltimore: Williams & Wilkins Co., 1971).
20. M. Rosenbaum and M. Berger (eds.), *Group Psychotherapy and Group Function* (New York: Basic Books, 1963).
21. A. L. Kadis, J. D. Krasner, and C. Winick, *A Practicum of Group Psychotherapy* (New York: Harper and Row, 1963).
22. H. Mullan and M. Rosenbaum, *Group Psychotherapy; Theory and Practice* (New York: Free Press of Glencoe, 1962).
23. Rosenbaum and Berger, *op. cit.,* p. 5.
24. E. W. Lazell, "The Group Treatment of Dementia Praecox," *Psychoanal. Rev., 8:* 168–179, 1921.

25. L. C. Marsh, "Group Therapy and the Psychiatric Clinic," *J. Nerv. Ment. Dis.*, *32*: 381–392, 1935.
26. L. Wender, "Current Trends in Group Psychotherapy," *Am. J. Psychother.*, *3*: 381–404, 1951.
27. T. Burrows, "The Group Method of Analysis," *Psychoanal. Rev.*, *19*: 268–280, 1927.
28. P. Schilder, "Results and Problems of Group Psychotherapy in Severe Neurosis," *Ment. Hyg.*, *23*: 87–98, 1939.
29. S. Slavson, "Group Therapy," *Ment. Hyg.*, *24*: 36–49, 1940.
30. J. L. Moreno, *Who Shall Survive?* (New York: Beacon House, 1953).
31. L. Bradford, in *Human Relations Training News*, Vol. *1*, No. 1 (May 1967).
32. J. Gibbs, "The Effects of Human Relations Training," in A. E. Bergin and S. Garfield (eds.), *Handbook of Psychotherapy and Behavior Change* (New York: John Wiley & Sons, 1974), pp. 829–862.
33. "Sensitivity Training," *Congressional Record—House*, June 10, 1969, pp. H4666–H4679.
34. L. Horwitz, "Training Groups for Psychiatric Residents," *Int. J. Group Psychother.*, *17*: 421–435, 1967.
35. L. Horwitz, "Transference in Training Groups and Therapy Groups," *Int. J. Group Psychother.*, *14*: 202–213, 1964.
36. S. Kaplan, "Therapy Groups and Training Groups: Similarities and Differences," *Int. J. Group Psychother.*, *17*: 473–504, 1967.
37. R. Morton, "The Patient Training Laboratory: An Adaptation of the Instrumented Training Laboratory," in Schein and Bennis, *op. cit.*, pp. 114–152.
38. I. Hendrick, "Instinct and the Ego During Infancy," *Psychoanal. Quart. 11*: 33–58, 1952.
39. D. E. Berlyne, "The Present Status of Research on Exploratory and Related Behavior," *J. Indiv. Psychol.*, *14*: 121–126, 1958.
40. K. Horney, *Neurosis and Human Growth: The Struggle Toward Self-Realization* (New York: W. W. Norton, 1950).
41. R. White, "Motivation Reconsidered," *Psychol. Rev.*, *66*: 297–333, 1959.
42. H. Hartmann, "Notes on the Psychoanalytic Theory of the Ego," *Psychoanal. Stud. Child*, *5*: 74–95, 1950.
43. A. Angyal, *Foundations for a Science of Personality* (New York: Commonwealth Fund, 1941).
44. K. Goldstein, *Human Nature in Light of Psychopathology* (Cambridge, Mass.: Harvard University Press, 1940).
45. G. V. Coelho, D. A. Hamburg and J. E. Adams (eds.), *Coping and Adaptation* (New York: Basic Books, 1974).
46. D. Bunker, "The Effect of Laboratory Education Upon Individual Behavior," in Schein and Bennis, *op. cit.*, pp. 257–267.
47. A. Stanton and M. S. Schwartz, *The Mental Hospital* (New York: Basic Books, 1954).
48. C. Rogers, personal communication, 1967.
49. J. D. Rockefeller, "In Praise of Young Revolutionaries," *Saturday Review of Literature*, *51*: 18–20, 1968.
50. D. Wilber, *Palo Alto Times*, October 24, 1968.
51. N. Kazantzakis, *The Odyssey: A Modern Sequel* (New York: Simon and Schuster, 1958), Book One, I. 135–145, p. 6. © 1958 by Simon & Schuster, Inc.
52. I. Sarnoff, *Society with Tears* (New York: Citadel Press, 1966), p. 17.
53. L. Mumford, *The Myth of the Machine: Techniques and Human Development* (New York: Harcourt, Brace and World, 1967).
54. *Palo Alto Times*, October 12, 1968.
55. C. Argyris, "Conditions for Competence Acquisition and Therapy," *J. Appl. Behav. Sci.*, *4*: 147–179, 1968.
56. A. Freud and D. Burlingham, *War and Children* (New York: Medical War Books, 1943), pp. 99–104.
57. J. Frank, "Training and Therapy," in L. P. Bradford, J. R. Gibb, and K. D. Benne, (eds.), *T-Group Theory and Laboratory Method; Innovation in Education* (New York: John Wiley and Sons, 1964).

15

THE TRAINING OF
THE GROUP THERAPIST

The training of the group therapist is an especially timely issue: not only has the increased practice of group therapy produced a sharply increased need for group clinicians, but as we have seen in Chapter 14, flux in the field has resulted in considerable unclarity about effective training procedures.

In this chapter I shall present my views about group therapy training, not only in specific recommendations for a training curriculum but also in the form of general considerations concerning an underlying philosophy of training. The approach to therapy described in this book is based both upon clinical experience and an appraisal of the best available research evidence. Similarly, in the educational process, a clinical and a research orientation are closely interrelated: the acquisition of a research or inquiring attitude to his own work and to the work of others is necessary in the development of the mature therapist.

Most training programs for mental health professionals are based on the individual therapy model and either do not provide group therapy training or offer it as an elective part of the program. In fact, it is not unusual for students to be given excellent intensive individual therapy supervision and then, early in their program, to be asked to lead therapy groups with no specialized guidance whatsoever. The program directors apparently expect that the student will be able, somehow, to translate his individual therapy training into group therapy skills.

Fortunately, many educators have recognized the folly of this approach, and mental health training programs are becoming increasingly appreciative of the need for well organized group training programs. Slowly, much too slowly, we have come to recognize that one-to-one psychotherapy cannot possibly suffice to meet the pressing mental health needs of the country. It is abundantly clear that, as time passes, we will rely on group approaches ever more heavily, and I believe that any psychotherapy training program which does not acknowledge this and does not fully expect students to become as proficient in group as in individual therapy is failing to meet its responsibilities to the field.

The following section is not intended as a complete blueprint for a group psychotherapy training program. But it does discuss the four major components which I consider essential to a comprehensive training program. I believe that student group therapists profit from (1) observing experienced group therapists at work; (2) close clinical supervision of their maiden groups; (3) a personal group experience; and (4) from personal psychotherapeutic (or self-exploratory) work.

Observation of Experienced Clinicians

Student therapists derive enormous benefit from watching an experienced group therapist at work. At first, clinicians often feel considerable dis-ease at the thought of being observed, but once they have taken the plunge, the process becomes not only comfortable, but rewarding for all parties—students, therapists and group members.

The format of observation depends, of course, on the physical facilities. I prefer using a two-way mirror, but if the students' schedules do not permit them to be present at the group, the meeting may be videotaped and replayed in a seminar with the therapist. This procedure, of course, requires a greater time investment for the therapist and some increased inconvenience for the members because of the presence of the TV camera. If there are only one or two observers, they may sit in the group room without unduly distracting the group, but I suggest they remain outside the group circle.

Regardless of the format employed, the group members should be fully informed about the presence of observers and the purpose of observation. I have always found the reflections and feedback of observers, regardless of their level of experience, to be personally helpful to me and thus to the functioning of the group. I inform the group members of these facts in the hope that they will regard the observation as beneficial to them, as well as to the unknown patients whom the student observers will treat in the future.

The total length of time students observe a group is, unfortunately, generally determined by service and training rotations. If there is sufficient program flexibility, I would suggest that observation continue at least four months, which generally provides a sufficient period of time for changes to occur in group development, in interactional patterns and in perceivable intrapersonal growth. A format that I have used to my satisfaction is to have my students observe a group which meets twice weekly. If their schedules preclude their attendance at more than one meeting a week, I dictate a detailed summary of each meeting and distribute it to the students prior to the next meeting. In this way they are able to follow a twice-weekly group, which has a greater likelihood of showing noticeable progression.

A post-meeting discussion is an absolute training necessity and there is no better time for the group leader to meet with his student observers than immediately following the group. I prefer to meet for approximately thirty minutes and use that time in a variety of ways: to obtain the student's observations, to answer questions about underlying reasons for my interventions, to share with them my feelings about the group. Though some basic didactic sessions are necessary, I find that much of the fundamental material presented in this book can be discussed with students around appropriate clinical material which arises over a several months' course of an observed group.

The relationship between observers and group therapist is important; there will be times when an inordinate amount of carping ("Why didn't you. . . . . ?") creates discomfort for the therapist and impairs his efficiency. Indeed, I have on occasion conducted post-group discussions which focused more upon the process of the observer group than upon the therapy group. Not infrequently, observers complain of boredom and therapists feel some strain to increase the group's entertainment quotient. My experience is that, in general, boredom is inversely related to experience; as students gain in experience and sophistication, they appreciate, to a much greater extent, the many subtle layers underlying every transaction.

Supervision

A supervised clinical experience is a *sine qua non* in the education of the group therapist. This book posits a general approach to therapy, delineates broad principles of technique, and, especially when discussing the opening and closing stages of therapy, suggests some specific tactics. But the laborious working-through process which comprises the bulk of therapy cannot be thoroughly depicted in a text; there are an infinite number of situations which arise, each of which may require a rich, imaginative approach. It is precisely at these points that the supervisor makes a valuable and unique contribution to the student therapist's education.

The neophyte therapist's first group is also a highly threatening experience; without an experienced clinician as guide, the student may be so anxious that he cannot remain open to learning, but instead grasps for the safety of a highly structured, clinical approach. My colleagues and I [1] once studied twelve nonprofessionals who led groups in a psychiatric hospital. Half of the leaders received ongoing supervision as well as an intensive training course in group leadership; the others received neither. Naïve observers rated the therapists at the beginning of their groups and six months later. The results indicated that not only did the trained therapists improve but the untrained therapists, at the end of six months, were less skilled than at the beginning. Sheer experience, apparently, is not enough; without ongoing supervision and evaluation, original errors may be reinforced by simple repetition.

In many ways group therapy supervision is more taxing than individual therapy supervision. For one thing, mastering the cast of characters is, in itself, a formidable task. Furthermore, there is such an abundance of data that the student and supervisor must often be highly selective in their focus. A few practical recommendations. One supervisory hour per one group therapy session is, in my experience, the optimal ratio. The supervisor does well to observe the group periodically not only to fix names with faces but also to savour the affective climate of the group. Video tapes may serve this purpose also; audio tapes, too, though far less satisfactorily. It is wise to hold the supervisory session soon after the group session, preferably the following day. One excellent format, if schedules permit, is to observe the last thirty minutes of each meeting and hold the supervisory session immediately thereafter. If much time elapses between the group and the supervisory session, the events of the meeting fade, and students are well advised to make post group notes to prod their memories. Therapists develop their own style of note taking. My preference is to record the major themes (generally one to three) of each session, the transition between themes, each member's contribution to the meeting, the therapist's interventions, and his feelings about the meeting as a whole and toward each of the members.

A ninety minute group session provides a wealth of material. If trainees present a narrative of the meeting, discuss each patient's verbal and nonverbal contribution as well as their own participation, and explore in depth their realistically based feelings and countertransference toward each of the members and toward their co-therapist, there should be more than enough important material to occupy the supervisory hour. If not, if the trainee runs quickly out of material and if the supervisor finds himself searching for ways to be useful, something is going seriously wrong in the supervisory process. The supervisor would do well at these times to turn his attention to the relationship between himself and his trainee(s). Are the students guarded? Distrustful? Fearful of exposing themselves to their supervisor? Cautious lest the supervisor censure them or control them by placing pressure on them to operate in the group in a manner which feels alien to them?

The supervisory session is no less a microcosm than the therapy group, and the supervisor should be able to obtain much information about the therapist's behavior in his therapy group by attending to his behavior in supervision. If students lead groups as co-therapy teams (and for reasons stated in Chapter 13, I recommend that format for neophyte therapists), a process focus in the supervisory hour is particularly rich. Are the co-therapists open and trusting with one another and with their supervisor? Who reports the events of the meeting? Who defers to whom? Does the supervisor feel bewildered by two very different views of the group? Is there much competition for his attention? Is there a sense of heightened tension in the supervisory session? The relationship between co-therapists is of crucial importance for the therapy group and, not infrequently, the supervisor may be maximally effective by focusing his attention on this relationship. For example, I recently supervised two residents whose personal relationship was strained. In the supervisory session, each vied for my attention, there was a dysrhythmic quality to the hour since neither pursued the other's lead but instead brought up different material, or the same material from an entirely different aspect. Supervision was a microcosm of the group since in the therapy sessions they competed

intensely with each other to make star interpretations and to enlist patients on their respective "teams." They never complemented each
other's work by pursuing the theme that one had brought up; instead,
each remained silent, waiting for an opportunity to introduce his own
different line of inquiry. The group, of course, paid the price for the
therapists' poor working relationship: no good work was done, absenteeism was high, and demoralization evident. Supervision in this instance focused almost entirely on the co-therapy relationship and took
on many of the characteristics of dyadic therapy. For example, one of
the leaders brought in this dream:

I organized a group of patients, but had a bad feeling of having selected
poorly. Jack and I were trying to lead the group but the patients were too out-
of-it to do anything but make a lot of noise with one another. Finally in frustration, I leaped into the center and shouted an interpretation at Jack which he
could not hear and I woke up feeling very frustrated.

Supervision worked on their competitive wish to impress the supervisor. One had just transferred from another residency and felt
strongly pressed to prove her competence. The other felt he had made
a great mistake in blindly accepting a co-therapist and felt trapped in
the relationship. Dissolution of the team was considered, but eventually they decided there was little chance of persuading patients to
work on their relationships while demonstrating that the therapists
themselves refused to do the same. If the co-therapy relationship is a
troubled one such a supervisory approach has much to recommend it.
Not only does the supervisor facilitate therapy by improving the inter-
leader relationship, but he also effectively models a process approach
to the resolution of problems in human relationships.

In the ongoing work of supervision it is obviously important for the
supervisor to focus on the student therapist's behavior in the group.
Are his verbal and nonverbal interventions congruent with his feelings and do they help to establish the types of group norms he considers useful to the group? At the same time the supervisor must avoid
making the student so self-conscious that his spontaneity is stunted.
Groups are not so fragile that a single statement markedly influences
their direction; it is the therapist's overall gestalt which counts. Every
supervisor will, at times, tell the supervisee what he would have said
at some particular juncture of the group. This is a useful and perhaps
essential part of the modeling process; however, many student therapists are inclined to ape the supervisor's comments at a not entirely
appropriate spot in the following group meeting. The next supervisory
session generally begins with, "I did what you said, but. . . ." Thus,

when, on occasion, I tell a student what I would have said, I preface my comments with a specific caveat: "Don't say this next meeting. . . ."

Many teachers have, with profit, expanded the supervisory hour into an ongoing seminar for a number of student therapists. The group leaders take turns presenting their group to the entire class. Since it takes time to assimilate data about all the members of the group, I prefer that one group be presented for four to six weeks before moving on to another. In this format three to four groups can be followed throughout the year.

A Group Experience for Trainees

A personal group experience has become widely accepted as an integral part of a training program; for example, the accreditation committee of the American Group Psychotherapy Association has recommended a minimum requirement of sixty hours as a participant in a group. Such an experience may offer many types of learning not elsewhere available. The student is able to learn at an emotional level what he may previously have known only intellectually: he experiences the power of the group, its power to wound or heal; he learns how important it is to be accepted by the group; he learns what self-disclosure really entails, how difficult it is to reveal one's secret world, one's fantasies, one's feelings of vulnerability, hostility, and tenderness; he appreciates his own strengths as well as his weaknesses; he learns about his own preferred role in the group; and perhaps most striking of all, he learns about the role of the leader as he becomes aware of his own dependency and his own unrealistic appraisal of the leader's power and knowledge.

WHAT KIND OF GROUP?

Some programs, for example the British Group Analytic Institute, require candidates to participate as a patient in an out-patient therapy group led by a senior clinician and composed, in addition to one or two trainees, of non-professionals seeking personal therapy. Other institutions, my own included, offer a T-group composed of all the trainees in the program. Some programs offer a short-term group lasting approximately a dozen sessions. My preference is to continue the group throughout the entire one to three year training program. Some programs combine these approaches and offer a short trainee T-group and, in addition, recommend that their students begin therapy in another group.

I have led groups of psychology interns and psychiatric residents since 1961 and, without exception, have found them to be a highly valuable teaching technique. Indeed, many students, when reviewing their training programs, have rated the T-group as the single most valuable experience in their curriculum. A group experience with one's peers has a great deal to recommend it; not only do the members reap the benefits of a group experience, but, if the group is led properly, it will so facilitate relationships and communication within the trainee class, that the entire training experience is enriched. Students always learn a great deal from their peers and any efforts which potentiate that process increase the value of the program.

Are there disadvantages as well as advantages to a group experience? In the past, one often heard storm warnings about the possible destructive effects of staff or trainee experiential groups. These were, I believe, based on irrational premises: for example, that enormous amounts of destructive hostility would ensue once the group unlocked suppressive floodgates or that the groups would constitute an enormous invasion of privacy as forced confessionals would be wrung one by one from each of the hapless trainees. We know now that responsibly led groups facilitate communication and constructive working relationships. Indeed, there is such powerful evidence that poor inter-staff relationships result in poor therapy outcome that the program director who continues to act as though open communication were destructive needs, in my opinion, to consider in great depth the sources of his conviction.

SHOULD GROUPS IN A TRAINING PROGRAM BE VOLUNTARY?

An experiential group is always more effective if the participants engage voluntarily and if the members view the group not only as a training exercise but as an opportunity for personal growth. Indeed, I prefer that trainees begin such a group with an explicit formulation of what they want to obtain from the experience personally as well as professionally. To this end it is important that the group be introduced and described to the trainees in such a way that they consider it to be consonant with their personal and professional goals. I prefer to frame the group within the students' training career by asking them to project themselves into the field of the future. It is, after all, highly probable that mental health practitioners will spend an increasingly greater amount of their time in groups—as leaders of therapy groups and as members and leaders of treatment teams; to be effective in his role, the clinician of the future will simply have to know his way around groups. He will have to learn how groups work and he will have to know, in the deepest possible sense, how he works in groups.

Once an experiential group is introduced as a regular part of the training program and once the faculty develops confidence in the group as a valuable training adjunct, there is little difficulty in "selling" it to incoming trainees. In fact, my experience in several training programs is that the trainees not only look forward to the group with much anticipation but experience strong disappointment, even indignation, if for some reason the opportunity for a group experience is withheld from them. If a student steadfastly refuses to enter the training group or any other type of experiential group, it is my opinion that some investigation of his resistance is warranted. Occasionally such a refusal stems from misconceptions about groups in general, or is a reflection of some respected senior faculty member's negative bias toward groups but, if not, if the refusal is based on a pervasive dread or distrust of group situations and if the student does not have the flexibility to work on this either in individual therapy or in a supportive group, I believe a serious question exists as to whether he is wise to pursue a career as a psychotherapist.

WHO SHOULD LEAD AN EXPERIENTIAL GROUP FOR STUDENT PSYCHOTHERAPISTS?

A caveat to directors of training programs: Select the leader with great care. For one thing, the group experience is an extraordinarily influential event in the students' training career; the leader will often serve as an important role model for the trainees. He should therefore have the highest possible professional standards with extensive clinical and group experience. The overriding criteria is, of course, the personal qualities and the skill of the leader: The professional degree (whether the leader be, for example, a psychiatric social worker, a psychiatrist or a clinical psychologist) is a very secondary consideration.

I believe also that the trainee's first group experience should not be one of a highly specialized format (for example, T.A. or gestalt). For one thing, as I discussed in Chapter 13, many such specialized approaches focus more on one-to-one work within the group and fail to provide the trainee with a basic foundation of interactional and group dynamics upon which he may then build to accommodate any of the specialized approaches. Furthermore, since the experiential group is an important and delicate enterprise, it may be unwise to burden it with unnecessary additional ideological freight. I have seen trainees fail to profit from an experiential group not because of a failure to accept the group approach but because of their rejection (or their supervisor's or role model's rejection) of the specialized approach.

Another reason that the leader should be selected with great care is that groups of mental health professionals who will continue to work together throughout their training are extremely difficult groups to lead. The pace is slow, intellectualization is common, and self-disclosure and risk-taking minimal. The neophyte therapist realizes that his chief professional instrument is his own person and, thus, feels that self-disclosure places him in double jeopardy: not only his personal competence but his professional competence is at stake.

SHOULD THE LEADER BE A STAFF OR FACULTY MEMBER OF THE TRAINING PROGRAM?

My experience is that a leader who wears two hats compounds the problem even further for the group members; they feel restricted by the presence of someone who may in the future play an evaluative role in their careers. Mere reassurance to the group that the leader will maintain strictest confidentiality or neutrality is insufficient to deal with this very real concern of the members.

I have on many occasions been placed in this double role and have approached the problem in various ways but with only limited success. One approach is to confront the problem very energetically with the group. I affirm the reality that I do have a dual role and though I shall attempt in every way to be merely a group leader, though I shall remove myself from any administrative evaluative duties, I may not be able to free myself from all unconscious vestiges of the second role. I thus address myself in an uncompromising fashion to the problem facing the group. But, as the group proceeds, I also address myself to the fact that each member faces the identical problem. Yet each may respond to it in a very different fashion: some may so distrust the leader that they choose to remain hidden in silence, some curry his favor, some trust him completely and participate with full abandon in the group, others persistently challenge him. All of these stances toward the leader reflect basic attitudes toward authority and are good grist for the mill, provided there is even a modicum of willingness to work. An additional approach which the dual-hatted leader may take is to be unusually self-disclosing—in effect to give the members more on him than he has on them. In so doing the leader models openness and demonstrates the universality of human problems and the unlikelihood of his adopting a judgmental stance toward them.

My experience has been that, even using the best techniques, the leader who is also an administrator is laboring under a severe handicap and his group is likely to be restricted and guarded. The group becomes a far more effective vehicle for personal growth and for training if led by a leader outside the institution who will play no role in student evaluation. Whatever his administrative position, it is important that the leader, at the onset of the group, make it very explicit that under no circumstances will he ever be willing to contribute letters of reference—either favorable or unfavorable—for them.

IS THE GROUP A THERAPY GROUP?

No other issue is so often used in the service of group resistance as the question of whether or not the group is a therapy group. It is wise for the leader to present a clear formulation of his position at the onset of the group. I begin by asking that the members make certain commitments to the group. Each member should be aware of the requirements for membership, i.e., a willingness to invest himself emotionally in the group, to disclose feelings toward himself and the other members and to explore areas in which he would like to make some personal changes. There is a useful distinction to be made between a therapy group and a therapeutic group. A training group, though it is not a therapy group, is a therapeutic group in that it offers the opportunity to do therapeutic work. Some members take advantage of that opportunity and have an excellent therapeutic experience. By no means, though, is each member expected to do extensive work on himself.

The basic contract of the group, in fact, its raison d'être, is training, not therapy. To a great extent these goals overlap: There is no better group therapy model that the leader can offer than that of an effective therapeutic group. Furthermore, every intensive group experience contains within it a great therapeutic potential; members cannot engage in an effective interactional group, cannot fully assume the role of a group member, without therapeutic spinoff. Yet that is different from a therapy group which assembles for the purpose of accomplishing extensive therapeutic change for each member. In a therapy group, the intensive group experience, the expression and integration of affect, the recognition of here-and-now process, are all essential but secondary considerations to the primary goal of individual therapeutic change. In a training group of mental health professionals, the reverse is true.

COMMON GROUP THEMES

The training group of mental health professionals confronts all the common themes which emerge in experiential groups but, because of its unusual composition, also has some unique characteristics. In no other type of group do concerns around the issue of competition and competence play such a pervasive role. The group members often experience one another as competitors—competitors for jobs in the future, competitors for professional standing or, even more commonly, they view one another as professional standards against which they measure themselves. Their competence is a function of their personal integration; consequently they fear that revelation of perceived weaknesses or flaws will result in negative professional judgment from their peers. And, in fact, it is true that some group members secretly make judgments as to whether they would refer a patient to another member who is rigid, or insensitive, or gay, or who feels panic when faced with an emergency, or who is more depressed, drug dependent, insomniac or anxious than his patients.

Try as they will, it is difficult for group members to escape competition issues. They may, for example, participate in other more academically oriented conferences where differences in intellectual ability are clearly evident; one of them may have to be chosen as chief resident; one may choose to transfer to another, more "high powered," program; some, because of superior performance, may be offered staff or faculty positions at the parent training institute.

Groups respond to this tension in several ways, the most common of which is a tacit or open pact of equality: the group denies any inter-member differences and often bands together against the evaluatory menace of the hostile outside world. There is often much shared resentment against tyrannical judging administrators or against certifying boards which evaluate candidates. In one training group, for example, one member was so severely disabled because of a severe depression that he missed several months of his training. The group unanimously condemned the administration for refusing to grant training credit for this period; none dared consider the obvious justification for the administration's action.

The group solution of equality has the effect of leveling or deskilling members. Even though all of the members may have had experience as group leaders or individual therapists, they do not feel able to exercise these skills in the group. Instead, the group even more than most patient groups, often becomes dependent upon the leader to make even the simplest, most natural inquiries.

Some other common themes of the training group include many shared concerns issuing from their professional experience: their confusion over the limits of their responsibility, their discouragement over their failures or, should it occur, their anguish over the suicide of one of their patients. One very important concern is that the members often feel drained by their patients; they experience their own strong craving for nurturance yet despair of finding either an opportunity to express it or a person to gratify it. As the end of training approaches, as the trainees prepare to cut their last comforting ties to institutionalized studenthood, the group often spends considerable time dealing with the emotions aroused by this final and true transition to adulthood. Feelings about being "grown-up," being looked up to, being one of the "big people," being on one's own, surface again and again.

LEADER TECHNIQUE

The leader of a training group of mental health professionals has a demanding task: not only does he provide a role model by shaping and conducting an effective group but he must also make certain modifications in technique to deal with the specific educational needs of his group members.

The basic approach, however, does not deviate from the guidelines outlined earlier in the book. For example, the leader is well advised to retain an interactional here-and-now focus. It is an error, in my opinion, to allow the group to move into a supervisory format where members describe problems they encounter in their therapeutic work with patients. That would be the province of the supervisory hour; whenever the group is engaged in discourse that could be held equally well in another formal setting, I believe it fails to use the unique properties and full potential of the group. Instead, members can discuss these work-related problems in more profitable group-relevant ways; for example, they might discuss how it would feel to them to be the patient of a particular member. The group is also an excellent place for two members who happen to work together in therapy groups, or in marital or family therapy to work on their relationship.

There are many ways for the leader to use his members' professional experience in the service of the group work. For example, I have often made statements to the training group in the following vein: "The group has been very slow moving today. When I inquired, you told me that you felt 'lazy' or that it was too soon after lunch to work. If you were the leader of a group and heard this, what would you make of it? What would you do?" or "Not only are John and Stewart refusing to work on their differences but others are lining up behind them. What are the options available to me as a leader today?", etc. In a training group I am inclined, much more than in a therapy group, to explicate group process. In therapy groups if there is no therapeutic advantage in clarifying group process, I see no reason to do so. In training groups there is always the superordinate goal of education. Often process commentary combined with a view from the leader's seat is particularly useful. For example: "Let me tell you what I felt today as a group leader. A half hour ago I felt uncomfortable with the massive encouragement and support everyone was giving Tom. This has happened before and though it was reassuring, I haven't felt it was really helpful to Tom. I was tempted to intervene by inquiring about Tom's tendency to pull this behavior from the group; but I chose not to, partly because I've gotten so much flak lately for being so non-supportive. So I remained silent. I think I made the right choice since it seems to me that the meeting developed into a very productive one with some of you getting deeply into your feelings of needing care and support. How do the rest of you see what's happened today?"

Because of the superordinate goal of education the training group leader has a large degree of freedom. To a much greater extent than the group therapist, he feels that, within certain broad limits, anything that happens in the group is okay as long as the members are able to learn from it. Thus, the leader may feel completely comfortable if the members want to experiment with the format by, for example, focusing each meeting on a single member or using structured exercises, provided that after a period of time the members evaluate the effects of these procedures upon the work of the group. I shall discuss shortly the desirability of inculcating in students a research (or "inquiring") orientation toward their own clinical work but shall anticipate myself by noting that the leader of the training group has a splendid opportunity to model such an attitude by consistently using the group as a source of data about the process and progress of the group. He may, for example, ask a troubled member how useful the meeting was to him, or which parts of the session and which lines of inquiry seemed helpful, and which seemed non-productive or even restrictive.

Personal Psychotherapy

The training group rarely suffices to provide all the personal therapy the student requires. Though we cannot set firm guidelines for so individualized a process, few would dispute that some extensive self-exploratory venture is necessary for the maturation of the group therapist. An inability to perceive countertransference responses, to recognize personal distortions and blind spots, to use his own feelings and fantasies in his work limits the effectiveness of any therapist. The therapist who lacks insight into his own motivations may, for example, avoid conflict in the group because of his proclivity to mute his feelings; or he may unduly encourage confrontation in a search for aliveness in himself. He may be overeager to prove himself or to make consistently brilliant interpretations and thereby emasculate the group; he may himself fear intimacy and prevent open expression of feelings by premature interpretations. He may do the opposite—overemphasize feelings, make too few connections, and so overstimulate his patients that they are left in agitated turmoil. He may so need acceptance that he is unable to challenge the group and, like the members, may be swept along by the prevailing group current; he may be so devastated by an attack on himself and so unclear as to his presentation of self that he is unable to distinguish the realistic from the transference aspects of the attack. A supervisor-observer, a co-therapist, or a video-recording playback may help to provide feedback for the student group therapist, which may assist him in discovering many of these blind spots; however, some type of guided self-exploration is usually necessary for fuller understanding and correction.

The training experiences I have thus far described—observation of an experienced clinician, group therapy supervision, experiential group participation, and personal therapy—constitute, in my view, the minimum essential components of a program to train group therapists.

(I assume that the trainee has previously had or is simultaneously being trained in general clinical areas: e.g., interviewing, psychopathology, personality theory, and other forms of psychotherapy.) The sequence of the group therapy training experiences may depend on the structural characteristics of the training institute. I prefer that the observation, personal therapy, and experiential group begin very early in the training program, to be followed in a few months by the formation of a group and ongoing supervision. I feel it is wise for trainees to have a clinical experience in which they deal with basic group and interactional dynamics in an open-ended group of non-psychotic, highly motivated patients before they begin to work with goal-limited groups of highly specialized patient populations or with one of the new specialized therapy approaches.

Training is, of course, a life long process. It is important that clinicians maintain contact with colleagues, either informally or through professional organizations. For growth to continue, continual new input is required. Many formats for continued education exist, including reading, working with different co-therapists, teaching, participation in professional workshops, and informal discussions with colleagues.

Beyond Technique

The group therapy training program not only has the task of teaching students how to do but also of teaching them how to learn. What we must not convey is a sense of certainty in either our techniques or in our underlying assumptions about therapeutic change: the field is far too primitive for disciples of unwavering faith. To this end I believe it is most important that we teach and model a basic research orientation to continuing education in the field. By research orientation I do not refer to a steel-spectacled Chi square efficiency but instead to an open, self-critical, inquiring attitude toward clinical and research evidence and conclusions—a posture toward experience which is consistent with a sensitive and humanistic clinical approach.

We need to help students evaluate their own work in a critical fashion and maintain sufficient flexibility (both technically and attitudinally) so that they can be responsive to their own observations. The mature therapist is an evolving therapist, a therapist who regards each patient, each group, indeed his whole career as a learning experience.

It is equally important to train students to evaluate systematic group therapy research and, if appropriate, adapt the research conclusions to their clinical work. The inclusion of readings and seminars in clinical research methodology is thus highly desirable. Although only a few clinicians will ever have the time, funding, and institutional backing to engage in large scale research, many clinicians can engage in intensive single patient or single group research and all clinicians must evaluate clinical research. If the group therapy field is to develop in a coherent fashion, it must respond to responsible, well executed, relevant, and credible research; otherwise, group therapy will continue its capricious, helter-skelter course, and research will become even more of a futile, effete exercise.

To illustrate, let us consider how the student may be introduced to a major research problem: outcome assessment. Seminars may be devoted to a consideration of the voluminous literature on the problems of outcome research. (There are several excellent recent reviews,[2,3,4] which may serve to anchor the discussions.) In addition to seminars, each may engage in a research practicum by interviewing patients who, for one reason or another, recently terminated group therapy. In fact, few training hours are more profitably spent. It is a very valuable exercise for the student to attempt to evaluate the degree of change, the nature of change, the mechanisms whereby the group experience effected that change, and the contributing role of other factors in the patient's environment. The exercise becomes richer yet if the student has available a tape of the initial interview to which he and the patient can listen.

Once he has engaged even to a limited extent in an assessment of change, the student becomes more sensitive and more critical toward research which involves outcome. (And it is outcome which remains the single greatest problem in group therapy research.) The problem, as the student grows to understand, is that conventional research approaches continue to perpetuate the error of extensive design, of failing to individualize outcome assessment. Clinicians fail to heed or even believe research in which outcome is measured by before-after changes in the MMPI or some other standardized instrument, and with good reason, for there is abundant clinical and research evidence to indicate that change means something different to each patient. Some patients need to experience less anxiety or hostility; for other patients improvement would be accompanied by greater anxiety or hostility.[5,6]

Even self-esteem changes need to be individualized. It has been demonstrated [7] that a high self-esteem score on traditional self-administered questionnaires could reflect *either* a genuinely healthy regard of self *or* a defensive posture in which the individual maintains a high self-esteem at the expense of self-awareness. These latter individuals would as a result of successful treatment have *lower* (but more accurate) self-esteem as measured by questionnaires.

In short, it is important for the clinician as well as the researcher to recognize the severe limitations of the traditional standardized (nomothetic) approach to outcome. I can think of no alternative except a laborious individualized (ideographic) approach to outcome. Shapiro,[8] Phillips,[9] and Kellam and Chassan [10] have demonstrated the feasibility of an individualized outcome scale for each patient. Malan [11] has proposed an outcome strategy in which each patient is interviewed pre-therapy and a judgment made by experienced clinicians as to what types of changes would occur if that patient were to improve in therapy. At the conclusion of therapy the patient is re-examined and each of the predictions is examined. My colleagues and I [12] have demonstrated the feasibility of such an individualized approach using videotaped interviews pre- and post-therapy.

Not only must the general strategy of outcome assessment be altered, but the criteria for outcome must also be reformulated. It may be an error to use, in group therapy research, criteria originally designed for individual therapy outcome. I suspect that, although group and individual therapies may be equivalent in overall effectiveness, each modality may affect different variables and have a different type of outcome. For example, group therapy graduates may become more interpersonally skilled, more inclined to be affiliative in times of stress, more capable of sustaining a number of meaningful relationships, or more empathic, whereas individual therapy patients may be more self-sufficient, introspective, and attuned to inner processes.

For years group therapists have considered therapy as a multidimensional laboratory for living, and it is time to acknowledge this in outcome research. As a result of therapy some patients alter their hierarchy of life values to decathect values of material wealth and power influence in order to stress humanistic or aesthetic ones; others may make major decisions which will influence the course of their lives; others may be more interpersonally sensitive and more able to communicate their feelings; still others may become less petty and more elevated in their life concerns; others may have a greater sense of commitment to other individuals or projects; others may experience a great flow of ideas and a greater energy level; others may come to terms in a meaningful manner with their own mortality; while others may find themselves more adventuresome, more receptive to new concepts and experiences.

A research orientation demands that the therapist throughout his career remain flexible and responsive to new evidence; it also requires that he live with a degree of uncertainty and that is no small request. Uncertainty which stems from the absence of a definitive treatment begets anxiety. Working with deeply troubled, anxious individuals also begets anxiety. Many practitioners seek solace by embracing the Loreleis of orthodox belief systems. They commit themselves to one of the many ideological schools of conviction which offer not only a comprehensive system of explanation but also screen out discrepant facts and discount new evidence. This commitment usually entails a lengthy apprenticeship and initiation. Once within the system the student finds it difficult to disengage himself: first, he has usually undergone such a lengthy apprenticeship that denouncement of the school is equivalent to denouncing a part of himself; secondly, it is extremely difficult to abandon a position of certainty for one of uncertainty. Clearly, however, such a position of certainty is antithetical to growth and particularly stunting to the development of the student therapist.

There are certain potential dangers in the abrogation of certainty. For example, there is some evidence that a therapist with a firm sense of conviction in his beliefs is more effective.[13] There is also a danger of therapeutic nihilism in the student who consequently may refuse to master any organized technique of therapy. The teacher, by his personal example, must offer an alternative model: that the best evidence available leads him to believe that a particular system is effective and that as new information becomes available he would expect to improve his approach. Furthermore, he takes pride in being part of a field which attempts to progress and is honest enough to know its own limitations.

Without a research orientation with which to evaluate new developments, the practitioner is in a difficult position. How is he, for example, to react to the myriad of recent innovations in the field? Unfortunately the current state of affairs is that the adoption of a new method is a function of the vigor, persuasiveness, or charisma of its proponent, and some new therapeutic approaches have been extraordinarily successful in rapidly obtaining both visibility and adherents. Many therapists without a consistent and critical approach to evidence have found themselves unreasonably unreceptive to all new approaches or, on the contrary, swept along with a current fad and then, dissatisfied with its limitations, they have gone on to yet another.

The critical problem facing the field, then, is one of balance. A traditional, conservative sector is less receptive to change than is optimal; an innovative, challenging sector is less receptive to stability than is optimal. The field is swayed by fashion, whereas it should be influenced by evidence. Psychotherapy is a science as well as an art and there is no place in science for uncritical orthodoxy or for innovation solely for its own sake. Orthodoxy offers safety for adherents but leads to stagnation; the field becomes insensitive to the *Zeitgeist* and is left behind as the public goes elsewhere. Innovation provides zest and a readily apparent creative outlet for proponents but, if unevaluated, results in a kaleidoscopic field without substance, a field "which rides off madly in all directions." [14]

REFERENCES

1. G. O. Ebersole, P. H. Leiderman, and I. D. Yalom, "Training the Nonprofessional Group Therapist," *J. Nerv. Ment. Dis.*, 149: 385, 1969.
2. A. Bergin, "The Evaluation of Therapeutic Outcomes" in A. Bergin, S. Garfield *Handbook of Psychotherapy and Behavior Change* (New York: John Wiley & Sons, 1971), pp. 217–271.
3. D. Malan, "The Outcome Problem in Psychotherapy Research" *Arch. Gen. Psychiatry* 29: 719–729, 1973.
4. L. Luborsky, et al, "Factors Influencing the Outcome of Therapy, A Review of Quantitative Research," *Psychological Bull.* 75: 145–185, 1971.
5. W. O. Jewell, cited by T. Volsky, T. M. Magoon, W. T. Norman, and D. P. Hoyt (eds.), *The Outcomes of Counseling and Psychotherapy: Theory and Research* (Minneapolis: University of Minnesota Press, 1965), p. 154.
6. J. B. Chassan, *Research Design in Clinical Psychology and Psychiatry* (New York: Appleton-Century Crofts, 1967), p. 254.
7. E. Silber and J. S. Tippet, "Self-Esteem: Clinical Assessment and Validation," *Psychol. Rep.* 16: 1017–1071, 1965.
8. M. B. Shapiro, "The Measurement of Clinically Relevant Variables," *J. Psychosom. Res.*, 8: 245–254, 1964.
9. J. P. N. Phillips, "Techniques for Scaling the Symptoms of an Individual Psychiatric Patient," *J. Psychosom. Res.*, 8: 255–271, 1964.
10. S. Kellam and J. B. Chassan "Social Context and Symptom Fluctuation," *Psychiatry*, 25: 370–381, 1962.
11. D. H. Malan, H. A. Bacal, E. S. Heath, and F. H. G. Balfour, "A Study of Psychodynamic Changes in Untreated Neurotic Patients. I. Improvements that are Questionable on Dynamic Criteria," *Brit. J. Psychiat.*, 114: 525–551, 1968.
12. I. Yalom, S. Bloch, B. Qualls, E. Zimmerman, Individualized Outcome Criteria; Clinical Assessment of Videotaped Interviews. In Preparation.
13. J. Frank, *Persuasion and Healing, A Comparative Study of Psychotherapy* (New York: Schocken Books, 1963).
14. S. Leacock, "Gertrude the Governess or Simple 17," in *A Treasury of the Best Works of Stephen Leacock* (New York: Dodd Mead, 1954).

NAME INDEX

SUBJECT INDEX